CODE OF VIRGINIA
1950

With Provisions for Subsequent Pocket Parts

ANNOTATED

Prepared under the Supervision of

The Virginia Code Commission

BY

The Editorial Staff of the Publishers

VOLUME 2B

2006 REPLACEMENT VOLUME

*Includes acts adopted at the 2006 Regular Session, Acts 2006, cc. 1 to 947,
of the General Assembly*

LexisNexis

R
348
.755
VI

4902212

ISBN 1-4224-3150-9

www.lexisnexis.com

Customer Service: 1-800-833-9844

(Pub.49005)

Scope of Annotations

To better serve our customers, by making our annotations more current, LexisNexis has changed the sources that are read to create annotations for this publication. Rather than waiting for cases to appear in printed reporters, we now read court decisions as they are released by the courts. A consequence of this more current reading of cases, as they are posted online on LEXIS, is that the most recent cases annotated may not yet have print reporter citations. These will be provided, as they become available, through later publications.

This publication contains annotations taken from decisions of the Virginia Supreme Court posted on LEXIS as of April 1, 2006, decisions of the Virginia Court of Appeals posted as of April 1, 2006, and decisions of the appropriate federal courts posted as of April 1, 2006. These cases will be printed in the following reports:

South Eastern Reporter, Second Series.
Supreme Court Reporter.
Federal Reporter, Third Series.
Federal Supplement, Second Series.
Federal Rules Decisions.
Bankruptcy Reporter.

Additionally, annotations have been taken from the following sources:

Virginia Law Review, through Volume 91, p. 1739.
Washington and Lee Law Review, through Volume 62, p. 830.
William and Mary Law Review, through Volume 46, p. 2213.
University of Richmond Law Review, through Volume 39, p. 989.
George Mason University Law Review, through Volume 13, p. 250.
Circuit Court Opinions, 1999 Va. Cir. LEXIS 727 (6/25/99) through 2006 Va. Cir. LEXIS 10 (3/8/06).
Opinions of the Attorney General through January 2005.

Unpublished Opinions of Court of Appeals

Some of the annotations contained in this supplement are derived from unpublished opinions of the Court of Appeals of Virginia. These opinions will not appear in the Court of Appeals Reports or any other court reporter. The unpublished opinions can be identified by their citation, which gives the parties' names, a case number, "Ct. of Appeals," and a date.

The Court of Appeals has placed the following footnote on all unpublished opinions: "Pursuant to Code § 17.1-413, recodifying § 17-116.010, this opinion is not designated for publication."

"Although an unpublished opinion of the Court has no precedential value, a court or commission does not err by considering the rationale and adopting it to the extent it is persuasive." Fairfax County School Board v. Rose, 29 Va. App. 32, 509 S.E.2d 525 (Va. App. 1999).

A copy of the full text of any unpublished opinion can be obtained by contacting: Court of Appeals of Virginia, Attention: Clerk's Assistant (Opinions), 109 North Eighth Street, Richmond, Virginia 23219.

User's Guide

In order to assist both the legal profession and the layman in obtaining the maximum benefit from the Code of Virginia, a User's Guide has been included iv

in Volume 1. This guide contains comments and information on the many features found within the Code of Virginia intended to increase the usefulness of this set of laws to the user. See Volume 1 of this set for the complete User's Guide.

Suggestions, comments, or questions about the Code of Virginia or this Cumulative Supplement are welcome. You may call us toll free at (800) 446-3410, fax us toll free at (800) 643-1280, email us at Customer.Support@LexisNexis.com, or write Code of Virginia Editor, LexisNexis, P.O. Box 7587, Charlottesville, Virginia 22906-7587.

For an online bookstore, technical and customer support, and other company information, visit LexisNexis' Internet home page at **http://www.lexisnexis.com.**

Table of Titles

In addition, this publication contains

Table of Contents

VOLUME 2B

TITLE 9.

COMMISSIONS, BOARDS AND INSTITUTIONS GENERALLY.

[Repealed.]

TITLE 9.1.

COMMONWEALTH PUBLIC SAFETY.

TITLE 10.

CONSERVATION GENERALLY.

[Repealed.]

TITLE 10.1.

CONSERVATION.

Subtitle I.
Activities Administered by the Department of
Conservation and Recreation.

Subtitle II.
Activities Administered by Other Entities.

Subtitle III.
Activities Administered by the Department of Historic Resources.

CODE OF VIRGINIA

Title 9.
Commissions, Boards and Institutions Generally.

[Repealed.]

§§ 9-1 through 9-410: Repealed by Acts 2001, c. 844, cl. 12, effective October 1, 2001.

Cross references. — For note regarding the recodification of former Titles 2.1 and 9 as new Titles 2.2 and 9.1, and accompanying revisions of other material, see Editor's note under § 9.1-100.

Title 9.1.

Commonwealth Public Safety.

CHAPTER 1.

DEPARTMENT OF CRIMINAL JUSTICE SERVICES.

Article 1.

General Provisions.

3

ARTICLE 1.

General Provisions.

§ 9.1-100. Department of Criminal Justice Services. — A. There is created a Department of Criminal Justice Services (the "Department") that shall be headed by a Director appointed by the Governor, subject to confirmation by the General Assembly. The Director shall serve at the pleasure of the Governor.

B. The Director of the Department shall, under the direction and control of the Governor, exercise the powers and perform the duties conferred or imposed upon him by law and perform such other duties required by the Governor or the Criminal Justice Services Board. (1981, c. 632, §§ 9-174, 9-175, 9-176; 1984, c. 720; 2001, c. 844.)

Editor's note. — In accordance with § 9-77.10 (now § 30-149), the Virginia Code Commission, in 1998, undertook a three-year recodification of Titles 2.1 and 9. Title 2.1 had last been recodified in 1965 and Title 9 had never been recodified. The Commission's draft of this revision, which was published as House Document 51 of the 2001 Session, was sent to the Governor and General Assembly in January, 2001. The revision, as amended by the General Assembly, became Acts 2001, c. 844, effective October 1, 2001.

Title 2.1 was rewritten primarily as new Title 2.2, with certain material now incorporated into Titles 6.1, 9.1, 17.1, 30, 37.1 and 51.1, and Title 9 was rewritten primarily as new Title 9.1, with certain material now incorporated into Titles 3.1, 2.2, and 30. In addition, the Virginia Public Procurement Act, §§ 11-35 to 11-80, was rewritten as § 2.2-4300 et seq. [see now § 2.2-4300 et seq.], and §§ 53.1-180 to 53.1-185.3, the Comprehensive Community Corrections Act for Local-Responsible Offenders, was rewritten as § 9.1-173 to 9.1-183.

In addition to revision by Acts 2001, c. 844, Titles 2.1 and 9, § 11-35 et seq. [see now § 2.2-4300 et seq.] and § 53.1-183 [see now § 9.1-178] were also amended by other acts passed at the 2001 Session. As required by § 30-152, the Code Commission has incorporated the majority of these amendments into the new sections.

Where appropriate, the historical citations to former sections have been added to corresponding new sections.

The case notes appearing under new sections were decided under corresponding former sections or under prior law.

For tables of corresponding former and new sections, see the tables in Volume 10.

Acts 2001, c. 844, cl. 2, effective October 1, 2001, provides: "That whenever any of the conditions, requirements, provisions or contents of any section or chapter of Title 2.1 or Title 9 or any other title of the Code of Virginia as such titles existed prior to October 1, 2001, are transferred in the same or modified form to a new section or chapter of Title 2.2 or Title 9.1 or any other title of the Code and whenever any such former section or chapter is given a new number in Title 2.2 or Title 9.1 or any other title, all references to any such former section or chapter of Title 2.1 or Title 9 or other title appearing in this Code shall be construed to apply to the new or renumbered section or chapter containing such conditions, requirements, provisions, contents or portions thereof."

Acts 2001, c. 844, cl. 3, effective October 1, 2001, provides: "That the regulations of any department or agency affected by the revision of Title 2.1, Title 9 or such other titles in effect on the effective date of this act shall continue in effect to the extent that they are not in conflict with this act and shall be deemed to be regulations adopted under this act."

Acts 2001, c. 844, cl. 4, effective October 1, 2001, provides: "That this title revision of Title 2.1 as Title 2.2 and Title 9 as Title 9.1 and the repeal of Chapter 7 (§ 11-35 et seq.) of Title 11 shall not be construed to require the reappointment of any officer or any member of a board, council, committee or other appointed body referred to in Title 2.2 or Title 9.1 and each such officer and member shall continue to serve for the term for which appointed pursuant to the provisions of Title 2.1, Title 9, or Chapter 7 (§ 11-35 et seq.) of Title 11. The revision of Title 2.1 as Title 2.2 and Title 9 as Title 9.1 in this act shall not affect the classification or assignment of any state agency, institution, board, commission, council or other collegial body within the executive branch currently in effect pursuant to Title 2.1 or Title 9; such classifications and assignments within the executive branch which existed prior to the effective date of this act shall continue unless reclassified or reassigned by a later enactment of the General Assembly and signed by the Governor."

Acts 2001, c. 844, cl. 5, effective October 1, 2001, provides: "That this title revision of Title 2.1 as Title 2.2 or Title 9 as Title 9.1 shall not be construed to affect the term of office of any elected officeholder holding office on October 1, 2001."

Acts 2001, c. 844, cl. 6, effective October 1, 2001, provides: "That the provisions of § 30-152, formerly § 9-77.11, of the Code of Virginia shall apply to the codification of Title 2.2 and Title 9.1 so as to give effect to other laws enacted by the 2001 Session of the General Assembly notwithstanding the delay in the effective date of this act."

Acts 2001, c. 844, cl. 7, effective October 1, 2001, provides: "That the repeal of Title 2.1, Title 9, and Chapter 7 (§ 11-35 et seq.) of Title 11 effective as of October 1, 2001, shall not affect any act or offense done or committed, or any penalty incurred, or any right established, accrued or accruing on or before such date, or any proceeding, prosecution, suit or action pending on that day. Except as otherwise provided in this act, neither the repeal of Title 2.1, Title 9 or Chapter 7 (§ 11-35 et seq.) of Title 11 nor the enactment of Title 2.2 or the enactment

of Title 9.1, shall apply to offenses committed prior to October 1, 2001, and prosecution for such offenses shall be governed by the prior law, which is continued in effect for that purpose. For the purpose of this enactment, an offense was committed prior to October 1, 2001, if any of essential elements of the offense occurred prior thereto."

Acts 2001, c. 844, cl. 8, effective October 1, 2001, provides: "That any notice given, recognizance taken, or process or writ issued before October 1, 2001, shall be valid although given, taken or to be returned to a day after such date, in like manner as if Title 2.2 and Title 9.1 had been effective before the same was given, taken or issued."

Acts 2001, c. 844, cl. 9, contains a severability clause.

Acts 2001, c. 844, cl. 14, effective October 1, 2001, provides: "That the provisions of this act shall become effective on October 1, 2001."

Effective date. — This title became effective October 1, 2001.

§ 9.1-101. Definitions. — As used in this chapter or in Chapter 23 (§ 19.2-387 et seq.) of Title 19.2, unless the context requires a different meaning:

"Administration of criminal justice" means performance of any activity directly involving the detection, apprehension, detention, pretrial release, post-trial release, prosecution, adjudication, correctional supervision, or rehabilitation of accused persons or criminal offenders or the collection, storage, and dissemination of criminal history record information.

"Board" means the Criminal Justice Services Board.

"Conviction data" means information in the custody of any criminal justice agency relating to a judgment of conviction, and the consequences arising therefrom, in any court.

"Correctional status information" means records and data concerning each condition of a convicted person's custodial status, including probation, confinement, work release, study release, escape, or termination of custody through expiration of sentence, parole, pardon, or court decision.

"Criminal history record information" means records and data collected by criminal justice agencies on adult individuals consisting of identifiable descriptions and notations of arrests, detentions, indictments, informations, or other formal charges, and any disposition arising therefrom. The term shall not include juvenile record information which is controlled by Chapter 11 (§ 16.1-226 et seq.) of Title 16.1, criminal justice intelligence information, criminal justice investigative information, or correctional status information.

"Criminal justice agency" means (i) a court or any other governmental agency or subunit thereof which as its principal function performs the administration of criminal justice and any other agency or subunit thereof which performs criminal justice activities, but only to the extent that it does so; (ii) for the purposes of Chapter 23 (§ 19.2-387 et seq.) of Title 19.2, any private corporation or agency which, within the context of its criminal justice activities employs officers appointed under § 15.2-1737, or special conservators of the peace or special policemen appointed under Chapter 2 (§ 19.2-12 et seq.) of Title 19.2, provided that (a) such private corporation or agency requires its officers, special conservators or special policemen to meet compulsory training standards established by the Criminal Justice Services Board and submits reports of compliance with the training standards and (b) the private corpo-

ration or agency complies with the provisions of Article 3 (§ 9.1-126 et seq.) of this chapter, but only to the extent that the private corporation or agency so designated as a criminal justice agency performs criminal justice activities; and (iii) the Office of the Attorney General, for all criminal justice activities otherwise permitted under subdivision (i) and for the purpose of performing duties required by the Civil Commitment of Sexually Violent Predators Act (§ 37.2-900 et seq.).

"Criminal justice agency" includes the Virginia State Crime Commission.

"Criminal justice agency" includes any program certified by the Commission on VASAP pursuant to § 18.2-271.2.

"Criminal justice information system" means a system including the equipment, facilities, procedures, agreements, and organizations thereof, for the collection, processing, preservation, or dissemination of criminal history record information. The operations of the system may be performed manually or by using electronic computers or other automated data processing equipment.

"Department" means the Department of Criminal Justice Services.

"Dissemination" means any transfer of information, whether orally, in writing, or by electronic means. The term shall not include access to the information by officers or employees of a criminal justice agency maintaining the information who have both a need and right to know the information.

"Law-enforcement officer" means any full-time or part-time employee of a police department or sheriff's office which is a part of or administered by the Commonwealth or any political subdivision thereof, and who is responsible for the prevention and detection of crime and the enforcement of the penal, traffic or highway laws of the Commonwealth, and shall include any (i) special agent of the Department of Alcoholic Beverage Control; (ii) police agent appointed under the provisions of § 56-353; (iii) officer of the Virginia Marine Police; (iv) game warden who is a full-time sworn member of the enforcement division of the Department of Game and Inland Fisheries; (v) investigator who is a full-time sworn member of the security division of the State Lottery Department; or (vi) conservation officer of the Department of Conservation and Recreation commissioned pursuant to § 10.1-115. Part-time employees are those compensated officers who are not full-time employees as defined by the employing police department or sheriff's office. Full-time sworn members of the enforcement division of the Department of Motor Vehicles meeting the Department of Criminal Justice Services qualifications shall be deemed to be "law-enforcement officers" when fulfilling their duties pursuant to § 46.2-217.

"School resource officer" means a certified law-enforcement officer hired by the local law-enforcement agency to provide law-enforcement and security services to Virginia public elementary and secondary schools.

"School security officer" means an individual who is employed by the local school board for the singular purpose of maintaining order and discipline, preventing crime, investigating violations of school board policies, and detaining students violating the law or school board policies on school property or at school-sponsored events and who is responsible solely for ensuring the safety, security, and welfare of all students, faculty, staff, and visitors in the assigned school. (1981, c. 632, § 9-169; 1982, c. 419; 1983, c. 357; 1984, c. 543; 1989, c. 233; 1991, c. 338; 1992, cc. 422, 569; 1993, cc. 533, 622, 866; 2000, c. 426; 2001, c. 844; 2002, cc. 789, 836, 868; 2003, cc. 744, 934, 937; 2004, c. 30; 2005, c. 914.)

Cross references. — As to special conservators of the peace, see § 9.1-150.1 et seq., § 19.2-13. For provision voiding appointments of special conservators of the peace granted to school security officers as defined in § 9.1-101 prior to July 1, 2002, see § 19.2-13 E. As to availability of court ordered psychiatric reports of criminal defendants, see § 19.2-301. As to deeming of local social services department fraud prevention and investigation units to be criminal justice agencies as defined in § 9.1-101, see § 63.2-526.

The 2005 amendments. — The 2005 amendment by c. 914, effective April 6, 2005, added clause (iii) of the paragraph defining "Criminal justice agency" and made related changes.

Michie's Jurisprudence. — For related discussion, see 11B M.J. Jury, § 17.

CASE NOTES

Editor's note. — The cases below were decided under former corresponding provisions.

Law enforcement officer. — A police department employee responsible for monitoring the status of individuals subject to house arrest was not a "law enforcement officer" under this section; although the employee was expected to report observed violations to a law enforcement officer, she carried no badge, had only a civilian identification card, had no arrest authority and could not enforce the law. Jones v. Commonwealth, 32 Va. App. 30, 526 S.E.2d 281 (2000).

Commonwealth's Attorney constitutes criminal justice agency. — Because the administration of criminal justice, by definition, includes "the prosecution . . . of accused persons or criminal offenders," the Office of the Commonwealth's Attorney constitutes a "criminal justice agency" within the meaning of this section; thus, § 19.2-389 A 1 authorizes the Commonwealth's Attorney to review the criminal background records of prospective jurors. Salmon v. Commonwealth, 32 Va. App. 586, 529 S.E.2d 815, 2000 Va. App. LEXIS 428 (2000).

OPINIONS OF THE ATTORNEY GENERAL

A commissioner of accounts is not permitted access to criminal history records of delinquent fiduciaries through the Virginia Criminal Information Network, unless such records are released pursuant to a circuit court order or rule. See opinion of Attorney General to The Honorable Thomas D. Horne, Judge, Twentieth Judicial Circuit, 00-011 (4/8/02).

State Police may provide mental health information to FBI to determine a person's eligibility to possess, purchase, or transfer a firearm. — The Department of State Police has the authority to provide certain mental health information maintained in the Central Criminal Records Exchange to the Federal Bureau of Investigation, so long as it is (i) kept confidential; and (ii) used only to determine a person's eligibility to possess, purchase or transfer a firearm. See opinion of Attorney General to Colonel W. Gerald Massengill, Superintendent, Department of State Police, 01-062 (4/4/02).

§ 9.1-102. Powers and duties of the Board and the Department. —

The Department, under the direction of the Board, which shall be the policy-making body for carrying out the duties and powers hereunder, shall have the power and duty to:

1. Adopt regulations, pursuant to the Administrative Process Act (§ 2.2-4000 et seq.), for the administration of this chapter including the authority to require the submission of reports and information by law-enforcement officers within the Commonwealth. Any proposed regulations concerning the privacy, confidentiality, and security of criminal justice information shall be submitted for review and comment to any board, commission, or committee or other body which may be established by the General Assembly to regulate the privacy, confidentiality, and security of information collected and maintained by the Commonwealth or any political subdivision thereof;

2. Establish compulsory minimum training standards subsequent to employment as a law-enforcement officer in (i) permanent positions, and (ii) temporary or probationary status, and establish the time required for completion of such training;

3. Establish minimum training standards and qualifications for certification and recertification for law-enforcement officers serving as field training officers;

4. Establish compulsory minimum curriculum requirements for in-service and advanced courses and programs for schools, whether located in or outside the Commonwealth, which are operated for the specific purpose of training law-enforcement officers;

5. Establish (i) compulsory minimum training standards for law-enforcement officers who utilize radar or an electrical or microcomputer device to measure the speed of motor vehicles as provided in § 46.2-882 and establish the time required for completion of the training and (ii) compulsory minimum qualifications for certification and recertification of instructors who provide such training;

6. Establish compulsory training courses for law-enforcement officers in laws and procedures relating to entrapment, search and seizure, evidence, and techniques of report writing, which training shall be completed by law-enforcement officers who have not completed the compulsory training standards set out in subdivision 2, prior to assignment of any such officers to undercover investigation work. Failure to complete the training shall not, for that reason, constitute grounds to exclude otherwise properly admissible testimony or other evidence from such officer resulting from any undercover investigation;

7. Establish compulsory minimum entry-level, in-service and advanced training standards for those persons designated to provide courthouse and courtroom security pursuant to the provisions of § 53.1-120, and to establish the time required for completion of such training;

8. Establish compulsory minimum entry-level, in-service and advanced training standards for deputy sheriffs designated to serve process pursuant to the provisions of § 8.01-293, and establish the time required for the completion of such training;

9. Establish compulsory minimum entry-level, in-service, and advanced training standards for persons employed as deputy sheriffs and jail officers by local criminal justice agencies and for correctional officers employed by the Department of Corrections under the provisions of Title 53.1, and establish the time required for completion of such training;

10. Establish compulsory minimum training standards for all dispatchers employed by or in any local or state government agency, whose duties include the dispatching of law-enforcement personnel. Such training standards shall apply only to dispatchers hired on or after July 1, 1988;

11. Consult and cooperate with counties, municipalities, agencies of the Commonwealth, other state and federal governmental agencies, and with universities, colleges, community colleges, and other institutions, whether located in or outside the Commonwealth, concerning the development of police training schools and programs or courses of instruction;

12. Approve institutions, curricula and facilities, whether located in or outside the Commonwealth, for school operation for the specific purpose of training law-enforcement officers; but this shall not prevent the holding of any such school whether approved or not;

13. Establish and maintain police training programs through such agencies and institutions as the Board deems appropriate;

14. Establish compulsory minimum qualifications of certification and recertification for instructors in criminal justice training schools approved by the Department;

15. Conduct and stimulate research by public and private agencies which shall be designed to improve police administration and law enforcement;

16. Make recommendations concerning any matter within its purview pursuant to this chapter;

17. Coordinate its activities with those of any interstate system for the exchange of criminal history record information, nominate one or more of its members to serve upon the council or committee of any such system, and participate when and as deemed appropriate in any such system's activities and programs;

18. Conduct inquiries and investigations it deems appropriate to carry out its functions under this chapter and, in conducting such inquiries and

investigations, may require any criminal justice agency to submit information, reports, and statistical data with respect to its policy and operation of information systems or with respect to its collection, storage, dissemination, and usage of criminal history record information and correctional status information, and such criminal justice agencies shall submit such information, reports, and data as are reasonably required;

19. Conduct audits as required by § 9.1-131;

20. Conduct a continuing study and review of questions of individual privacy and confidentiality of criminal history record information and correctional status information;

21. Advise criminal justice agencies and initiate educational programs for such agencies with respect to matters of privacy, confidentiality, and security as they pertain to criminal history record information and correctional status information;

22. Maintain a liaison with any board, commission, committee, or other body which may be established by law, executive order, or resolution to regulate the privacy and security of information collected by the Commonwealth or any political subdivision thereof;

23. Adopt regulations establishing guidelines and standards for the collection, storage, and dissemination of criminal history record information and correctional status information, and the privacy, confidentiality, and security thereof necessary to implement state and federal statutes, regulations, and court orders;

24. Operate a statewide criminal justice research center, which shall maintain an integrated criminal justice information system, produce reports, provide technical assistance to state and local criminal justice data system users, and provide analysis and interpretation of criminal justice statistical information;

25. Develop a comprehensive, statewide, long-range plan for strengthening and improving law enforcement and the administration of criminal justice throughout the Commonwealth, and periodically update that plan;

26. Cooperate with, and advise and assist, all agencies, departments, boards and institutions of the Commonwealth, and units of general local government, or combinations thereof, including planning district commissions, in planning, developing, and administering programs, projects, comprehensive plans, and other activities for improving law enforcement and the administration of criminal justice throughout the Commonwealth, including allocating and subgranting funds for these purposes;

27. Define, develop, organize, encourage, conduct, coordinate, and administer programs, projects and activities for the Commonwealth and units of general local government, or combinations thereof, in the Commonwealth, designed to strengthen and improve law enforcement and the administration of criminal justice at every level throughout the Commonwealth;

28. Review and evaluate programs, projects, and activities, and recommend, where necessary, revisions or alterations to such programs, projects, and activities for the purpose of improving law enforcement and the administration of criminal justice;

29. Coordinate the activities and projects of the state departments, agencies, and boards of the Commonwealth and of the units of general local government, or combination thereof, including planning district commissions, relating to the preparation, adoption, administration, and implementation of comprehensive plans to strengthen and improve law enforcement and the administration of criminal justice;

30. Do all things necessary on behalf of the Commonwealth and its units of general local government, to determine and secure benefits available under the Omnibus Crime Control and Safe Streets Act of 1968 (P.L. 90-351, 82 Stat.

197), as amended, and under any other federal acts and programs for strengthening and improving law enforcement, the administration of criminal justice, and delinquency prevention and control;

31. Receive, administer, and expend all funds and other assistance available to the Board and the Department for carrying out the purposes of this chapter and the Omnibus Crime Control and Safe Streets Act of 1968, as amended;

32. Apply for and accept grants from the United States government or any other source in carrying out the purposes of this chapter and accept any and all donations both real and personal, and grants of money from any governmental unit or public agency, or from any institution, person, firm or corporation, and may receive, utilize and dispose of the same. Any arrangements pursuant to this section shall be detailed in the annual report of the Board. Such report shall include the identity of the donor, the nature of the transaction, and the conditions, if any. Any moneys received pursuant to this section shall be deposited in the state treasury to the account of the Department. To these ends, the Board shall have the power to comply with conditions and execute such agreements as may be necessary;

33. Make and enter into all contracts and agreements necessary or incidental to the performance of its duties and execution of its powers under this chapter, including but not limited to, contracts with the United States, units of general local government or combinations thereof, in Virginia or other states, and with agencies and departments of the Commonwealth;

34. Adopt and administer reasonable regulations for the planning and implementation of programs and activities and for the allocation, expenditure and subgranting of funds available to the Commonwealth and to units of general local government, and for carrying out the purposes of this chapter and the powers and duties set forth herein;

35. Certify and decertify law-enforcement officers in accordance with §§ 15.2-1706 and 15.2-1707;

36. Establish training standards and publish a model policy for law-enforcement personnel in the handling of family abuse, domestic violence, sexual assault and stalking cases, including standards for determining the predominant physical aggressor in accordance with § 19.2-81.3;

37. Establish training standards and publish a model policy for law-enforcement personnel in communicating with and facilitating the safe return of individuals diagnosed with Alzheimer's disease;

38. Establish compulsory training standards for basic training and the recertification of law-enforcement officers to ensure sensitivity to and awareness of cultural diversity and the potential for biased policing;

39. Review and evaluate community-policing programs in the Commonwealth, and recommend where necessary statewide operating procedures, guidelines, and standards which strengthen and improve such programs, including sensitivity to and awareness of cultural diversity and the potential for biased policing;

40. Publish and disseminate a model policy or guideline that may be used by state and local agencies to ensure that law-enforcement personnel are sensitive to and aware of cultural diversity and the potential for biased policing;

41. [Expired.]

42. Establish a Virginia Law-Enforcement Accreditation Center. The Center shall, in cooperation with Virginia law-enforcement agencies, provide technical assistance and administrative support, including staffing, for the establishment of voluntary state law-enforcement accreditation standards. The Center may provide accreditation assistance and training, resource material, and research into methods and procedures that will assist the Virginia law-enforcement community efforts to obtain Virginia accreditation status;

43. Promote community policing philosophy and practice throughout the Commonwealth by providing community policing training and technical assis-

tance statewide to all law-enforcement agencies, community groups, public and private organizations and citizens; developing and distributing innovative policing curricula and training tools on general community policing philosophy and practice and contemporary critical issues facing Virginia communities; serving as a consultant to Virginia organizations with specific community policing needs; facilitating continued development and implementation of community policing programs statewide through discussion forums for community policing leaders, development of law-enforcement instructors; promoting a statewide community policing initiative; and serving as a statewide information source on the subject of community policing including, but not limited to periodic newsletters, a website and an accessible lending library;

44. Establish, in consultation with the Department of Education and the Virginia State Crime Commission, compulsory minimum standards for employment and job-entry and in-service training curricula and certification requirements for school security officers, which training and certification shall be administered by the Virginia Center for School Safety pursuant to § 9.1-184. Such training standards shall include, but shall not be limited to, the role and responsibility of school security officers, relevant state and federal laws, school and personal liability issues, security awareness in the school environment, mediation and conflict resolution, disaster and emergency response, and student behavioral dynamics. The Department shall establish an advisory committee consisting of local school board representatives, principals, superintendents, and school security personnel to assist in the development of these standards and certification requirements;

45. Establish training standards and publish a model policy and protocols for local and regional sexual assault response teams;

46. License and regulate property bail bondsmen and surety bail bondsmen in accordance with Article 11 (§ 9.1-185 et seq.) of this chapter;

47. License and regulate bail enforcement agents in accordance with Article 12 (§ 9.1-186 et seq.) of this chapter;

48. **(Effective July 1, 2007)** Establish minimum standards for (i) employment, (ii) job-entry and in-service training curricula, and (iii) certification requirements for campus security officers. Such training standards shall include, but not be limited to, the role and responsibility of campus security officers, relevant state and federal laws, school and personal liability issues, security awareness in the campus environment, and disaster and emergency response. The Department shall provide technical support and assistance to campus police departments and campus security departments on the establishment and implementation of policies and procedures, including but not limited to: the management of such departments, investigatory procedures, judicial referrals, the establishment and management of databases for campus safety and security information sharing, and development of uniform record keeping for disciplinary records and statistics, such as campus crime logs, judicial referrals and Clery Act statistics. The Department shall establish an advisory committee consisting of college administrators, college police chiefs, college security department chiefs, and local law-enforcement officials to assist in the development of the standards and certification requirements and training pursuant to this subdivision;

49. In conjunction with the Virginia State Police and the State Compensation Board, advise criminal justice agencies regarding the investigation, registration, and dissemination of information requirements as they pertain to the Sex Offender and Crimes Against Minors Registry Act (§ 9.1-900 et seq.); and

50. Perform such other acts as may be necessary or convenient for the effective performance of its duties. (1981, c. 632, § 9-170; 1982, c. 473; 1984, cc. 515; 779; 1986, c. 128; 1988, cc. 46, 560; 1990, c. 632; 1991, c. 345; 1994, cc. 850,

905; 1996, cc. 154, 866, 952; 1998, cc. 31, 471, 523; 1999, cc. 307, 495; 2000, c. 561; 2001, cc. 162, 210, 434, 458, 844; 2002, cc. 490, 810, 818, 836, 868; 2004, cc. 397, 460, 972, 980, 1016; 2005, cc. 868, 881; 2006, cc. 203, 233, 857, 914.)

Cross references. — As to disability and line of duty death benefits training for law-enforcement or public safety officers, see § 9.1-407.

Editor's note. — Acts 2000, c. 561, cl. 2 provided that the provisions of c. 561, which added former subdivision 41, would expire on July 1, 2005.

Acts 2001, cc. 162, 210, 434 and 458 amended former § 9-170, from which this section is derived. Pursuant to § 30-152, Acts 2001, cc. 162, 210, 434 and 458 have been given effect in this section as set out above.

Acts 2002, cc. 810 and 818, cl. 2, provide: "That the Supreme Court shall establish reasonable judicial training regarding domestic violence and the resources available for victims in the Commonwealth of Virginia."

Acts 2002, cc. 810 and 818, cl. 3, provide: "That the Commonwealth Attorney's Services Council shall provide training to attorneys for the Commonwealth regarding the prosecution of domestic violence cases."

Acts 2002, cc. 836 and 868, cl. 2, as amended by Acts 2003, c. 617, cls. 1 and 2, provide: "That, with such funds as may be appropriated for such purpose, the training and employment standards required by § 9.1-184 shall be applicable to persons employed as school security officers on and after September 15, 2004."

Acts 2004, c. 397, which added subdivision 47, in cl. 2 provides: "That the provisions of this act, except for § 9.1-186.14, shall become effective on October 1, 2005."

Acts 2004, c. 397, cl. 3, provides: "That the Board shall promulgate regulations to implement the provisions of this act to be effective within 280 days of its enactment."

Acts 2004, c. 460, cl. 2, provides: "That the State Corporation Commission shall forward all surety bail bondsman licensing records in its custody to the Department of Criminal Justice Services by June 30, 2005."

Acts 2004, c. 460, cl. 3, provides: "That the Department of Criminal Justice Services shall promulgate regulations to implement the provisions of this act to be effective within 280 days of its enactment."

Acts 2004, c. 460, which added subdivision 46, in cl. 5 provides: "That the provisions of this act, except for § 16.1-77, shall become effective on July 1, 2005."

Acts 2004, cc. 972 and 980, cl. 3, provide: "That in establishing training standards and model policies regarding sexual assault for use by law-enforcement personnel pursuant to subdivision 37 [see now subdivision 36] of § 9.1-102 of the Code of Virginia, the Department of

Criminal Justice Services shall include information on the impact of sexual assault on its victims, investigative techniques, the use of polygraph examinations in sexual assault cases, and the availability of forensic examinations in any instance where there is an allegation of sexual assault."

Acts 2004, cc. 972 and 980, cl. 4, provide: "That a model policy for law-enforcement personnel in the handling of family abuse and domestic violence cases established pursuant to subdivision 37 [see now subdivision 36] of § 9.1-102 of the Code of Virginia shall include information on repeat offenders of family abuse or domestic violence."

Acts 2004, cc. 972 and 980, cl. 5, provide: "That the Department of Criminal Justice Services shall promote the use of local and regional sexual assault response team policy and protocol, established pursuant to subdivision 46 [see now subdivision 45] of § 9.1-102 of the Code of Virginia, as an integral part of an effective coordinated community response to sexual assaults."

Acts 2004, cc. 972 and 980, cl. 6, provide: "That the Office of the Executive Secretary of the Supreme Court shall determine appropriate standards for the approval of education and treatment programs for persons accused of assault and battery against a family or household member pursuant to § 18.2-57.3 and arrange for such programs to be approved by an appropriate entity."

Acts 2006, cc. 203 and 233, which added subdivision 48, in cl. 2 provide: "That the provisions of this act shall be effective July 1, 2007."

Acts 2006, c. 857, cl. 4, provides: "That the provisions of this act may result in a net increase in periods of imprisonment or commitment. Pursuant to § 30-19.1:4, the estimated amount of the necessary appropriation is $2,419,496 for periods of imprisonment in state adult correctional facilities and is $0 for periods of commitment to the custody of the Department of Juvenile Justice."

Acts 2006, c. 914, cl. 5, provides: "That the provisions of this act may result in a net increase in periods of imprisonment or commitment. Pursuant to § 30-19.1:4, the estimated amount of the necessary appropriation is at least $2,419,496 for periods of imprisonment in state adult correctional facilities and is $0 for periods of commitment to the custody of the Department of Juvenile Justice."

The 2004 amendments. — The 2004 amendment by c. 397, effective October 1, 2005, deleted "and" at the end of subdivision 45;

inserted subdivision 48; and made related changes.

The 2004 amendment by c. 460, effective July 1, 2005, deleted "and" at the end of subdivision 45; inserted subdivision 47; and made related changes.

The 2004 amendments by cc. 972 and 980 are identical, and in subdivision 37, deleted "and" preceding "domestic violence" and inserted "sexual assault and stalking" near the end; inserted subdivision 46; and made related changes.

The 2004 amendment by c. 1016 added the language beginning "including standards for determining" at the end of subdivision 37.

The 2005 amendments. — The 2005 amendments by cc. 868 and 881 are identical, and rewrote the first sentence in subdivision 1; deleted former subdivision 36 which read: "Provide forensic laboratory services as detailed in Article 2 (§ 9.1-117 et seq.) of this chapter"; and redesignated former subdivisions 37 through 49 as subdivisions 36 through 48.

The 2006 amendments. — The 2006 amendments by cc. 203 and 233, effective July 1, 2007, are identical, and added subdivision 48; and made a related change.

The 2006 amendments by cc. 857 and 914 are identical, and added subdivision 49; redesignated former subdivision 48 as subdivision 50; and made a related change.

§ 9.1-103. Direct operational responsibilities in law enforcement not authorized. — Nothing in this chapter shall be construed as authorizing the Department to undertake direct operational responsibilities in law enforcement or the administration of criminal justice. (1981, c. 632, § 9-183; 2001, c. 844.)

§ 9.1-104. Establishment of victim and witness assistance programs; purpose; guidelines. — A. The Department shall adopt guidelines, the purpose of which shall be to make funds available to local governments for establishing, operating and maintaining victim and witness assistance programs which provide services to the victims of crime and witnesses in the criminal justice system.

B. The Department shall establish a grant procedure to govern funds awarded for this purpose. (1984, c. 561, § 9-173.3; 2001, c. 844.)

§ 9.1-105. Intensified Drug Enforcement Jurisdictions Fund. — There is created a special nonreverting fund to be administered by the Department, known as the Intensified Drug Enforcement Jurisdictions Fund. This Fund shall be established on the books of the Comptroller and any funds remaining in such Fund at the end of the biennium shall not revert to the general fund but shall remain in the Fund. Interest earned on the Fund shall be credited to the Fund. (1990, c. 971, § 14.1-133.3; 1998, c. 872, § 9-178.1; 2001, c. 844.)

§ 9.1-106. Regional Criminal Justice Academy Training Fund; local fee. — There is created a special nonreverting fund to be administered by the Department, known as the Regional Criminal Justice Academy Training Fund. This Fund shall be established on the books of the Comptroller and any funds remaining in such Fund at the end of the biennium shall not revert to the general fund, but shall remain in the Fund. Interest earned on the Fund shall be credited to the Fund. The Fund shall consist of moneys forwarded to the State Treasurer for deposit in the Fund as provided in §§ 16.1-69.48:1, 17.1-275.1, 17.1-275.2, 17.1-275.3, 17.1-275.4, 17.1-275.7, 17.1-275.8, and 17.1-275.9, which sums shall be deposited in the state treasury to the credit of the Fund. Money in the Fund shall be used to provide financial support for regional criminal justice training academies, and shall be distributed as directed by the Department.

Notwithstanding any other provision of law, nothing in this section shall prohibit a locality from charging a similar fee if the locality does not participate in a regional criminal justice training academy and if the locality was operating a certified independent criminal justice academy as of January 1, 2003. Any and all funds from such local fee shall support the local academy.

Existing funds for the regional criminal justice training academies shall not be reduced by either state or local entities as a result of the enactment of Chapter 215 of the Acts of Assembly of 1997. (1997, c. 215, § 14.1-133.4; 1998, c. 872, § 9-178.2; 1999, c. 546; 2001, c. 844; 2003, cc. 993, 1028.)

§ 9.1-107. Powers and duties of Director. — A. The Director shall be charged with executive and administrative responsibility to (i) carry out the specific duties imposed on the Department under § 9.1-102 and (ii) maintain appropriate liaison with federal, state and local agencies and units of government, or combinations thereof, in order that all programs, projects and activities for strengthening and improving law enforcement and the administration of criminal justice may function effectively at all levels of government.

B. In addition, the Director shall have the power and duty to:

1. Accept grants from the United States government and agencies and instrumentalities thereof, and any other source. To these ends, the Department shall have the power to comply with such conditions and execute such agreements as may be necessary, convenient or desirable.

2. In accordance with the standards of classification of the Personnel Act (§ 2.2-2900 et seq.), employ and fix the salaries of Department personnel and enter into contracts for services necessary in the performance of the Department's functions.

3. Do all acts necessary or convenient to carry out the purpose of this chapter and to assist the Board in carrying out its responsibilities under § 9.1-102.

C. The Director shall be the Executive Director of the Board, but shall not be a member of the Board. (1981, c. 632, §§ 9-176, 9-177; 1984, c. 720; 2001, c. 844.)

§ 9.1-108. Criminal Justice Services Board membership; terms; vacancies; members not disqualified from holding other offices; designation of chairmen; meetings; compensation. — A. The Criminal Justice Services Board is established as a policy board within the meaning of § 2.2-2100, in the executive branch of state government. The Board shall consist of 29 members as follows: the Chief Justice of the Supreme Court of Virginia, or his designee; the Attorney General or his designee; the Superintendent of the Department of State Police; the Director of the Department of Corrections; the Director of the Department of Juvenile Justice; the Superintendent of the Department of Correctional Education; the Chairman of the Parole Board; the Executive Director of the Virginia Indigent Defense Commission or his designee; and the Executive Secretary of the Supreme Court of Virginia. In those instances in which the Executive Secretary of the Supreme Court of Virginia, the Superintendent of the Department of State Police, the Director of the Department of Corrections, the Director of the Department of Juvenile Justice, the Superintendent of the Department of Correctional Education, or the Chairman of the Parole Board will be absent from a Board meeting, he may appoint a member of his staff to represent him at the meeting.

Sixteen members shall be appointed by the Governor from among citizens of the Commonwealth. At least one shall be a representative of a crime victims' organization or a victim of crime as defined in subsection B of § 19.2-11.01. The remainder shall be representative of the broad categories of state and local governments, criminal justice systems, and law-enforcement agencies, including but not limited to, police officials, sheriffs, attorneys for the Commonwealth, defense counsel, the judiciary, correctional and rehabilitative activities, and other locally elected and appointed administrative and legislative officials. Among these members there shall be two sheriffs representing the Virginia Sheriffs Association selected from among names submitted by the Association; one member who is an active duty law-enforcement officer appointed after consideration of the names, if any, submitted by police or fraternal associations that have memberships of at least 1,000; two representatives of the Chiefs of Police Association appointed after consideration of the names submitted by the Association, if any; one attorney for the Commonwealth appointed after consideration of the names submitted by the Association for Commonwealth's Attorneys, if any; one person who is a mayor, city or town manager, or member of a city or town council representing the Virginia Municipal League appointed after consideration of the names submitted by the League, if any; one person who is a county executive, manager, or member of a county board of supervisors representing the Virginia Association of Counties appointed after consideration of the names submitted by the Association, if any; one member representing the Virginia Crime Prevention Association appointed after consideration of the names submitted by the Association, if any; one member of the Private Security Services Advisory Board; and one representative of the Virginia Association of Regional Jail Superintendents appointed after consideration of the names submitted by the Association, if any.

Four members of the Board shall be members of the General Assembly appointed as follows: one member of the House Committee on Appropriations appointed by the Speaker of House of Delegates after consideration of the recommendation by the committee's chairman; one member of the House Committee for Courts of Justice appointed by the Speaker of the House of Delegates after consideration of the recommendation by the committee's chairman; one member of the Senate Committee on Finance appointed by the Senate Committee on Rules after consideration of the recommendation of the chairman of the Senate Committee on Finance; and one member of the Senate Committee for Courts of Justice appointed by the Senate Committee on Rules after consideration of the recommendation of the chairman of the Senate Committee for Courts of Justice. The legislative members shall serve for terms coincident with their terms of office and shall serve as ex officio, nonvoting members. Legislative members may be reappointed for successive terms.

B. The members of the Board appointed by the Governor shall serve for terms of four years, provided that no member shall serve beyond the time when he holds the office or employment by reason of which he was initially eligible for appointment. Gubernatorial appointed members of the Board shall not be eligible to serve for more than two consecutive full terms. Three or more years within a four-year period shall be deemed a full term. Any vacancy on the Board shall be filled in the same manner as the original appointment, but for the unexpired term.

C. The Governor shall appoint a chairman of the Board, and the Board shall designate one or more vice-chairmen from among its members, who shall serve at the pleasure of the Board.

D. Notwithstanding any provision of any statute, ordinance, local law, or charter provision to the contrary, membership on the Board shall not disqualify any member from holding any other public office or employment, or cause the forfeiture thereof.

E. The Board shall hold no less than four regular meetings a year. Subject to the requirements of this subsection, the chairman shall fix the times and places of meetings, either on his own motion or upon written request of any five members of the Board.

F. The Board may adopt bylaws for its operation.

G. Legislative members of the Board shall receive such compensation as provided in § 30-19.12 and nonlegislative citizen members shall receive such compensation as provided in § 2.2-2813 for the performance of their duties. All members shall be reimbursed for all reasonable and necessary expenses incurred in the performance of their duties as provided in §§ 2.2-2813 and 2.2-2825. Funding for the costs of compensation and expenses of the members shall be provided by the Department of Criminal Justice Services. (1981, c. 632, § 9-168; 1984, cc. 30, 515, 538, 734; 1986, c. 519; 1987, c. 144; 1989, c. 733; 1990, c. 98; 1991, cc. 59, 685; 1993, c. 415; 1994, cc. 20, 226; 1997, cc. 32, 795, 883; 1999, c. 495; 2001, c. 844; 2004, c. 1000; 2005, cc. 594, 672.)

Editor's note. — Acts 2004, c. 1000, cl. 5, provides: "That this act shall not be construed to affect existing appointments for which the terms have not expired. However, any new appointments or appointments to fill vacancies made after the effective date of this act shall be made in accordance with the provisions of this act."

The 2005 amendments. — The 2005 amendment by c. 594 substituted "28 members" for "27 members" and inserted "the Executive Director of the Virginia Indigent Defense Commission or his designee" in subsection A.

The 2005 amendment by c. 672, in subsection A, substituted "28 members" for "27 members" in the first paragraph and in the second paragraph of subsection A, substituted "Sixteen members" for "Fifteen members" and inserted "one member who is an active duty law-enforcement officer appointed after consideration of the names, if any, submitted by police or fraternal associations that have memberships of at least 1,000."

The first paragraph of subsection A is set out in the form above at the direction of the Virginia Code Commission.

§ 9.1-109. Administration of federal programs. — The Board is designated as the supervisory board and the Department is designated as the planning and coordinating agency responsible for the implementation and administration of any federal programs for strengthening and improving law enforcement, the administration of criminal justice, and delinquency prevention and control throughout the Commonwealth. (1981, c. 632, § 9-171; 2001, c. 844.)

§ 9.1-110. School Resource Officer Grants Program and Fund. — A. From the funds appropriated for such purpose and from the gifts, donations, grants, bequests, and other funds received on its behalf, there is established (i) the School Resource Officer Grants Program, to be administered by the Board, in consultation with the Board of Education, and (ii) a special nonreverting fund within the state treasury known as the School Resource Officer Incentive Grants Fund, hereinafter known as the "Fund." The Fund shall be established on the books of the Comptroller, and any moneys remaining in the Fund at the end of the biennium shall not revert to the general fund but shall remain in the Fund. Interest earned on such funds shall remain in the Fund and be credited to it.

Subject to the authority of the Board to provide for its disbursement, the Fund shall be disbursed to award matching grants to local law-enforcement agencies and local school boards that have established a collaborative agreement to employ uniformed school resource officers, as defined in § 9.1-101, in middle and high schools within the relevant school division. The Board may disburse annually up to five percent of the Fund for the training of the school resource officers. School resource officers shall be certified law-enforcement officers and shall be employed to help ensure safety, to prevent truancy and violence in schools, and to enforce school board rules and codes of student conduct.

B. The Board shall establish criteria for making grants from the Fund, including procedures for determining the amount of a grant and the required local match. Any grant of general funds shall be matched by the locality on the basis of the composite index of local ability to pay. The Board may adopt guidelines governing the Program and the employment and duties of the school resource officers as it deems necessary and appropriate. (1999, c. 512, § 9-171.1; 2000, c. 785; 2001, cc. 33, 844; 2002, cc. 836, 868.)

Editor's note. — Acts 2001, c. 33 amended former § 9-171.1, from which this section is derived. Pursuant to § 30-152, Acts 2001, c. 33 has been given effect in this section as set out above. The 2001 amendment by c. 33 added the second sentence in the second paragraph of subsection A.

§ 9.1-111. Advisory Committee on Juvenile Justice; membership; terms; quorum; compensation and expenses; duties. — A. The Advisory Committee on Juvenile Justice (the Advisory Committee) is established as an advisory committee in the executive branch of state government. The Advisory Committee shall have the responsibility for advising and assisting the Board, the Department, all agencies, departments, boards and institutions of the Commonwealth, and units of local government, or combinations thereof, on matters related to the prevention and treatment of juvenile delinquency and the administration of juvenile justice in the Commonwealth.

The membership of the Advisory Committee shall comply with the membership requirements contained in the Juvenile Justice and Delinquency Prevention Act pursuant to 42 U.S.C. § 5633, as amended, and shall consist of: the Commissioner of the Department of Mental Health, Mental Retardation and Substance Abuse Services; the Commissioner of the Department of Social Services; the Director of the Department of Juvenile Justice; the Superintendent of Public Instruction; one member of the Senate Committee for Courts of Justice appointed by the Senate Committee on Rules after consideration of the recommendation of the Chairman of the Senate Committee for Courts of Justice; one member of the House Committee on Health, Welfare and Institutions appointed by the Speaker of the House of Delegates after consideration of the recommendation of the Chairman of the House Committee on Health, Welfare and Institutions; and such number of nonlegislative citizen members appointed by the Governor to comply with the membership range established by such federal act.

Legislative members, the Superintendent of Public Instruction, and the agency directors shall serve terms coincident with their terms of office. All other members shall be citizens of the Commonwealth and be appointed by the Governor for a term of four years. However, no member shall serve beyond the time when he holds the office or employment by reason of which he was initially eligible for appointment.

The Advisory Committee shall elect its chairman and vice-chairman from among its members.

B. Gubernatorial appointed members of the Advisory Committee shall not be eligible to serve for more than two consecutive full terms. Three or more years within a four-year period shall be deemed a full term. Any vacancy on the Advisory Committee shall be filled in the same manner as the original appointment, but for the unexpired term.

C. The majority of the members of the Advisory Committee shall constitute a quorum. The Advisory Committee shall hold no less than four regular meetings a year. Subject to the requirements of this subsection, the chairman shall fix the times and places of meetings, either on his own motion or upon written request of any five members of the Advisory Committee.

D. The Advisory Committee may adopt bylaws for its operation.

E. Members of the Advisory Committee shall not receive compensation, but shall be reimbursed for all reasonable and necessary expenses incurred in the performance of their duties as provided in §§ 2.2-2813 and 2.2-2825. Funding for the costs of the expenses shall be provided from federal funds received for such purposes by the Department of Criminal Justice Services.

F. The Advisory Committee shall have the following duties and responsibilities to:

1. Review the operation of the juvenile justice system in the Commonwealth, including facilities and programs, and prepare appropriate reports;

2. Review statewide plans, conduct studies, and make recommendations on needs and priorities for the development and improvement of the juvenile justice system in the Commonwealth; and

3. Advise on all matters related to the federal Juvenile Justice and Delinquency Prevention Act of 1974 (P. L. 93-415, as amended), and recommend such actions on behalf of the Commonwealth as may seem desirable to secure benefits of that or other federal programs for delinquency prevention of the administration of juvenile justice.

G. The Department of Criminal Justice Services shall provide staff support to the Advisory Committee. Upon request, each administrative entity or collegial body within the executive branch of the state government shall cooperate with the Advisory Committee as it carries out its responsibilities. (1981, c. 632, § 9-168; 1984, cc. 30, 515, 538, 734; 1986, c. 519; 1987, c. 144; 1989, c. 733; 1990, c. 98; 1991, cc. 59, 685; 1993, c. 415; 1994, cc. 20, 226; 1997, cc. 32, 795, 883; 1999, c. 495; 2001, c. 844; 2004, c. 1000.)

Editor's note. — For the federal Juvenile Justice and Delinquency Prevention Act of 1974 (P.L. 93-415, as amended) generally, see 42 U.S.C.S. § 5601 et seq.

Acts 2004, c. 1000, cl. 5, provides: "That this act shall not be construed to affect existing appointments for which the terms have not expired. However, any new appointments or appointments to fill vacancies made after the effective date of this act shall be made in accordance with the provisions of this act."

§ 9.1-112. Committee on Training; membership.

— There is created a permanent Committee on Training under the Board that shall be the policy-making body responsible to the Board for effecting the provisions of subdivisions 2 through 16 of § 9.1-102. The Committee on Training shall be composed of thirteen members of the Board as follows: the Superintendent of the Department of State Police; the Director of the Department of Corrections; a member of the Private Security Services Advisory Board; the Executive Secretary of the Supreme Court of Virginia; two sheriffs representing the Virginia State Sheriffs Association; two representatives of the Chiefs of Police Association; the attorney for the Commonwealth representing the Association for Attorneys for the Commonwealth; a representative of the Virginia Municipal League; a representative of the Virginia Association of Counties; a regional jail superintendent representing the Virginia Association of Regional Jails; and one member designated by the chairman of the Board from among the other appointments made by the Governor.

The Committee on Training shall annually elect its chairman from among its members. (1981, c. 632, § 9-168; 1984, cc. 30, 515, 538, 734; 1986, c. 519; 1987, c. 144; 1989, c. 733; 1990, c. 98; 1991, cc. 59, 685; 1993, c. 415; 1994, cc. 20, 226; 1997, cc. 32, 795, 883; 1999, c. 495; 2001, c. 844.)

§ 9.1-113. Compliance with minimum training standards by certain officers; exceptions.

— The provisions of this chapter shall not be construed to require (i) law-enforcement officers serving under permanent appointment on July 1, 1971, (ii) officers serving under permanent appointment under the provisions of § 56-353 appointed prior to July 1, 1982, or (iii) officers serving under permanent appointment under the provisions of § 10.1-115 appointed prior to July 1, 2003; to meet the compulsory minimum training standards provided for in subdivision 2 of § 9.1-102. Nor shall failure of any such officer to meet such standards make him ineligible for any promotional examination for which he is otherwise eligible. However, any law-enforcement officer designated under the provisions of § 53.1-120 to provide courthouse and courtroom security shall be required to meet the standards provided under subdivision 7 of § 9.1-102. Any full-time deputy sheriff who is a law-enforcement officer and who is exempted from the compulsory minimum training standards under this section shall be eligible for the minimum salary established pursuant to Article 3 (§ 15.2-1609 et seq.) of Chapter 16 of Title 15.2. (1981, c. 632, § 9-179; 1982, c. 419; 1984, c. 779; 1999, c. 495; 2001, c. 844; 2003, c. 744.)

§ 9.1-114. Compliance with minimum training standards by officers employed after July 1, 1971, by officers appointed under § 56-353 after July 1, 1982, and by part-time officers. — Every full-time law-enforcement officer employed after July 1, 1971, officers appointed under the provisions of § 56-353 after July 1, 1982, and every part-time law-enforcement officer employed after July 1, 1989, shall comply with the compulsory minimum training standards established by the Board within a period of time fixed by the Board in accordance with the Administrative Process Act (§ 2.2-4000 et seq.). However, any part-time law-enforcement officer employed for eighty, or fewer, compensated hours in a calendar year, or any noncompensated auxiliary deputy sheriff, or noncompensated auxiliary police officer who carries a firearm in the course of his employment shall be required to have completed basic firearms training and received ongoing in-service firearms training, as defined by the Board. The Board may require law-enforcement agencies of the Commonwealth and its political subdivisions to submit rosters of their personnel and pertinent data with regard to the training status of such personnel. (1981, c. 632, § 9-180; 1982, c. 419; 1989, c. 233; 2001, c. 844.)

§ 9.1-115. Forfeiture of office for failing to meet training standards; termination of salary and benefits; extension of term. — A. Every person required to comply with the training standards adopted by the Board, excluding private security services business personnel, who fails to comply with the standards within the time limits established by the regulations adopted by the Board shall forfeit his office, upon receipt of notice, as provided in subsection B. Such forfeiture shall create a vacancy in the office and all pay and allowances shall cease.

B. Notice shall be by certified mail, in a form approved by the Board, to the officer failing to comply and the chief administrative officer of the agency employing the officer. Notice shall be mailed to the State Compensation Board, if approval of that Board of the necessity of his office or compensation is required by law.

C. If the necessity for the officer or compensation of the officer is required by law to be approved by the State Compensation Board, that Board, upon receipt of notice as provided in subsection B, shall notify the Comptroller, who shall cause payment of his compensation to cease as of the date of receipt of the notice by the State Compensation Board of the notice.

D. It shall be the duty of the chief administrative officer of any agency employing a person who fails to meet the training standards to enforce the provisions of § 9.1-114 and this section. Willful failure to do so shall constitute misfeasance in office, and, in addition, upon conviction, shall constitute a Class 3 misdemeanor. (1981, c. 632, § 9-181; 2001, c. 844.)

Cross references. — As to punishment for Class 3 misdemeanors, see § 18.2-11.

§ 9.1-116. Exemptions of certain persons from certain training requirements. — The Director of the Department, with the approval of the

Board, may exempt a chief of police or any law-enforcement officer or any courthouse and courtroom security officer, jail officer, dispatcher, process server, or custodial officer or corrections officer of the Commonwealth or any political subdivision who has demonstrated sensitivity to cultural diversity issues and had previous experience and training as a law-enforcement officer, courthouse and courtroom security officer, jail officer, dispatcher, process server or custodial officer or corrections officer with any law-enforcement or custodial agency, from the mandatory attendance of any or all courses which are required for the successful completion of the compulsory minimum training standards established by the Board.

The exemption authorized by this section shall be available to all law-enforcement officers, courthouse and courtroom security officers, jail officer, dispatchers, process servers and custodial officers, and corrections officers, regardless of any officer's date of initial employment, and shall entitle the officer when exempted from mandatory attendance to be deemed in compliance with the compulsory minimum training standards and eligible for the minimum salary established pursuant to Article 3 (§ 15.2-1609 et seq.) of Chapter 16 of Title 15.2, provided that the officer is otherwise qualified. (1981, c. 632, § 9-173; 1984, c. 515; 1988, c. 138; 2001, cc. 162, 844.)

Editor's note. — Acts 2001, c. 162 amended former § 9-173, from which this section is derived. Pursuant to § 30-152, Acts 2001, c. 162 has been given effect in this section as set out above. The 2001 amendment by c. 162 inserted "demonstrated sensitivity to cultural diversity issues and" in the first sentence.

§ 9.1-116.1. Virginia Sexual and Domestic Violence Victim Fund; purpose; guidelines.

— A. There is created the Virginia Sexual and Domestic Violence Victim Fund as a special nonreverting fund to be administered by the Department of Criminal Justice Services to support the prosecution of domestic violence cases and victim services.

B. The Department shall adopt guidelines, the purpose of which shall be to make funds available to (i) local attorneys for the Commonwealth for the purpose of funding the cost of additional attorneys or to further dedicate existing resources to prosecute felonies and misdemeanors involving domestic violence, sexual violence, sexual abuse, stalking and family abuse, and (ii) law-enforcement authorities or appropriate programs, including civil legal assistance, to assist in protecting and providing necessary services to victims of and children affected by domestic violence, sexual abuse, stalking and family abuse.

C. A portion of the sum collected pursuant to § 16.1-69.48:1 as specified in that section shall be deposited into the state treasury to the credit of this Fund in addition to any other monies appropriated, allocated or received specifically for such purpose. The Fund shall be distributed according to grant procedures adopted pursuant to this section and shall be established on the books of the Comptroller. Any funds remaining in such Fund at the end of the biennium shall not revert to the general fund but shall remain in the Fund. Interest earned on the Fund shall be credited to the Fund.

D. The Department shall establish a grant procedure to govern funds awarded for this purpose. (2004, c. 375; 2006, c. 288.)

Editor's note. — Acts 2004, c. 375, cl. 2, provides: "The Department of Criminal Justice Services, in cooperation with the Statewide Facilitator for Victims of Domestic Violence within the Office of the Attorney General, shall make all reasonable efforts to secure federal funds or other grant monies that may be made available for programs consistent with the purposes delineated in § 9.1-116.1."

The 2006 amendments. — The 2006

amendment by c. 288 inserted "Sexual and" in
the section heading and in subsection A; and
inserted "sexual violence" in subsection B.

ARTICLE 2.

Division of Forensic Science.

§§ 9.1-117 through 9.1-125: Repealed by Acts 2005, cc. 868 and 881, cl. 2.

Cross references. — As to the Department
of Forensic Science, see § 9.1-1100 et seq.
Editor's note. — Acts 2005, cc. 868 and 881,
cl. 3, provide: "That as of July 1, 2005, the
Department of Forensic Science shall be
deemed successor in interest to the Division of
Forensic Science of the Department of Criminal
Justice Services to the extent that this act
transfers powers and duties. All right, title and
interest in and to any real or tangible personal
property vested in the Division of Forensic
Science of the Department of Criminal Justice
Services shall be transferred to and taken as
standing in the name of the Department of
Forensic Science."

ARTICLE 3.

Criminal Justice Information System.

§ 9.1-126. Application and construction of article. — A. This article
shall apply to original or copied criminal history record information, maintained by a criminal justice agency of (i) the Commonwealth or its political
subdivisions and (ii) the United States or another state or its political
subdivisions which exchange such information with an agency covered in
clause (i), but only to the extent of that exchange.

B. The provisions of this article shall not apply to original or copied (i)
records of entry, such as police blotters, maintained by a criminal justice
agency on a chronological basis and permitted to be made public, if such
records are not indexed or accessible by name, (ii) court records of public
criminal proceedings, including opinions and published compilations thereof,
(iii) records of traffic offenses disseminated to or maintained by the Department of Motor Vehicles for the purpose of regulating the issuance, suspension,
revocation, or renewal of drivers' or other operators' licenses, (iv) statistical or
analytical records or reports in which individuals are not identified and from
which their identities cannot be ascertained, (v) announcements of executive
clemency, pardons, or removals of political disabilities, (vi) posters, announcements, or lists for identifying or apprehending fugitives or wanted persons,
(vii) criminal justice intelligence information, or (viii) criminal justice investigative information.

C. Nothing contained in this article shall be construed as prohibiting a
criminal justice agency from disclosing to the public factual information
concerning the status of an investigation, the apprehension, arrest, release, or
prosecution of an individual, the adjudication of charges, or the correctional
status of an individual, which is related to the offense for which the individual
is currently within the criminal justice system. (1981, c. 632, § 9-184; 2001, c.
844.)

Cross references. — As to personal information systems which are exempt from the
Government Data Collection and Dissemination Practices Act, see § 2.2-3802.

**§ 9.1-127. Establishment of statewide criminal justice information
system; duties of Board generally; assistance of other agencies; relationship to Department of State Police.** — A. The Board shall provide for

the coordination of the operation of a statewide comprehensive criminal justice information system for the exchange of criminal history record information among the criminal justice agencies of the Commonwealth and its political subdivisions. The Board shall develop standards and goals for such system, define the requirements of such system, define system objectives, recommend development priorities and plans, review development efforts, coordinate the needs and interests of the criminal justice community, outline agency responsibilities, appoint ad hoc advisory committees, and provide for the participation of the statewide comprehensive criminal justice information system in interstate criminal justice systems.

B. The Board may request technical assistance of any state agency, board, or other body and such state entities shall render such assistance as is reasonably required.

C. The Department of State Police shall be the control terminal agency for the Commonwealth and perform all functions required of a control terminal agency by the regulations of the National Crime Information Center. Notwithstanding any other provision to the contrary in this chapter, the Central Criminal Records Exchange and the Department of State Police shall remain the central repository for criminal history record information in the Commonwealth, and the Department shall continue to be responsible for the management and operation of such exchange. (1981, c. 632, §§ 9-170, 9-185; 1982, c. 473; 1984, cc. 515; 779; 1986, c. 128; 1988, cc. 46, 560; 1990, c. 632; 1991, c. 345; 1994, cc. 850, 905; 1996, cc. 154, 866, 952; 1998, cc. 31, 471, 523; 1999, cc. 307, 495; 2000, c. 561; 2001, c. 844.)

§ 9.1-128. Dissemination of criminal history record information; Board to adopt regulations and procedures. — A. Criminal history record information shall be disseminated, whether directly or through an intermediary, only in accordance with § 19.2-389.

B. The Board shall adopt regulations and procedures for the interstate dissemination of criminal history record information by which criminal justice agencies of the Commonwealth shall ensure that the limitations on dissemination of criminal history record information set forth in § 19.2-389 are accepted by recipients and will remain operative in the event of further dissemination.

C. The Board shall adopt regulations and procedures for the validation of an interstate recipient's right to obtain criminal history record information from criminal justice agencies of the Commonwealth. (1981, c. 632, §§ 9-187, 9-188; 2001, c. 844.)

§ 9.1-129. Participation of state and local agencies in interstate system; access to system limited. — A. The Board shall regulate participation of state and local agencies in any interstate system for the exchange of criminal history record information and shall be responsible for ensuring the consistency of such participation with the terms and purposes of this article. The Board shall have no authority to compel any agency to participate in any such interstate system.

B. Direct access to any such system shall be limited to the criminal justice agencies expressly designated for that purpose by the Board. (1981, c. 632, § 9-189; 2001, c. 844.)

§ 9.1-130. Procedures to be adopted by agencies maintaining criminal justice information systems. — Each criminal justice agency maintaining and operating a criminal justice information system shall adopt procedures reasonably designed to ensure:

1. The physical security of the system and the prevention of unauthorized disclosure of the information in the system;

2. The timeliness and accuracy of information in the system;

3. That all criminal justice agencies to which criminal offender record information is disseminated or from which it is collected are currently and accurately informed of any correction, deletion, or revision of such information;

4. Prompt purging or sealing of criminal offender record information when required by state or federal statute, regulation, or court order;

5. Use or dissemination of criminal offender record information by criminal justice agency personnel only after it has been determined to be the most accurate and complete information available to the criminal justice agency. (1981, c. 632, § 9-191; 2001, c. 844.)

§ 9.1-131. Annual audits. — The Board shall ensure that annual audits are conducted of a representative sample of state and local criminal justice agencies to ensure compliance with this article and Board regulations. The Board shall adopt such regulations as may be necessary for the conduct of audits, the retention of records to facilitate such audits, the determination of necessary corrective actions, and the reporting of corrective actions taken. (1981, c. 632, § 9-186; 1984, cc. 30, 734; 2001, c. 844.)

§ 9.1-132. Individual's right of access to and review and correction of information. — A. Any individual who believes that criminal history record information is being maintained about him by the Central Criminal Records Exchange (the "Exchange"), or by the arresting law-enforcement agency in the case of offenses not required to be reported to the Exchange, shall have the right to inspect a copy of his criminal history record information at the Exchange or the arresting law-enforcement agency, respectively, for the purpose of ascertaining the completeness and accuracy of the information. The individual's right to access and review shall not extend to any information or data other than that defined in § 9.1-101.

B. The Board shall adopt regulations with respect to an individual's right to access and review criminal history record information about himself reported to the Exchange or, if not reported to the Exchange, maintained by the arresting law-enforcement agency. The regulations shall provide for (i) public notice of the right of access; (ii) access to criminal history record information by an individual or an attorney-at-law acting for an individual; (iii) the submission of identification; (iv) the places and times for review; (v) review of Virginia records by individuals located in other states; (vi) assistance in understanding the record; (vii) obtaining a copy for purposes of initiating a challenge to the record; (viii) procedures for investigation of alleged incompleteness or inaccuracy; (ix) completion or correction of records if indicated; and (x) notification of the individuals and agencies to whom an inaccurate or incomplete record has been disseminated.

C. If an individual believes information maintained about him is inaccurate or incomplete, he may request the agency having custody or control of the records to purge, modify, or supplement them. Should the agency decline to so act, or should the individual believe the agency's decision to be otherwise unsatisfactory, the individual may make written request for review by the Board. The Board or its designee shall, in each case in which it finds prima facie basis for a complaint, conduct a hearing at which the individual may appear with counsel, present evidence, and examine and cross-examine witnesses. The Board shall issue written findings and conclusions. Should the record in question be found to be inaccurate or incomplete, the criminal justice agency maintaining the information shall purge, modify, or supplement it in accordance with the findings and conclusions of the Board. Notification of purging, modification, or supplementation of criminal history record information shall be promptly made by the criminal justice agency maintaining the previously inaccurate information to any individuals or agencies to which the information in question was communicated, as well as to the individual who is the subject of the records.

D. Criminal justice agencies shall maintain records of all agencies to whom criminal history record information has been disseminated, the date upon which the information was disseminated, and such other record matter for the number of years required by regulations of the Board.

E. Any individual or agency aggrieved by any order or decision of the Board may appeal the order or decision in accordance with the Administrative Process Act (§ 2.2-4000 et seq.). (1981, c. 632, § 9-192; 1986, c. 615; 2001, c. 844.)

§ 9.1-133. Certain information not subject to review or correction. — A. Background checks for security clearances and investigative information not connected with a criminal prosecution or litigation including investigations of rule infractions in correctional institutions shall not be subject to review or correction by data subjects.

B. Correctional information about an offender including counselor reports, diagnostic summaries and other sensitive information not explicitly classified as criminal history record information shall not be subject to review or correction by data subjects. (1981, c. 632, § 9-193; 2001, c. 844.)

§ 9.1-134. Sealing of criminal history record information. — The Board shall adopt procedures reasonably designed to (i) ensure prompt sealing or purging of criminal history record information when required by state or federal law, regulation or court order, and (ii) permit opening of sealed information under conditions authorized by law. (1981, c. 632, § 9-190; 2001, c. 844.)

§ 9.1-135. Civil remedies for violation of this chapter or Chapter 23 of Title 19.2. — A. Any person may institute a civil action in the circuit court of the jurisdiction in which the Board has its administrative headquarters, or in the jurisdiction in which any violation is alleged to have occurred:

1. For actual damages resulting from violation of this article or to restrain any such violation, or both.

2. To obtain appropriate equitable relief against any person who has engaged, is engaged, or is about to engage in any acts or practices in violation of Chapter 23 (§ 19.2-387 et seq.) of Title 19.2, this chapter or rules or regulations of the Board.

B. This section shall not be construed as a waiver of the defense of sovereign immunity. (1981, c. 632, § 9-194; 2001, c. 844.)

§ 9.1-136. Criminal penalty for violation. — Any person who willfully and intentionally requests, obtains, or seeks to obtain criminal history record information under false pretenses, or who willfully and intentionally disseminates or seeks to disseminate criminal history record information to any agency or person in violation of this article or Chapter 23 (§ 19.2-387 et seq.) of Title 19.2, shall be guilty of a Class 2 misdemeanor. (1981, c. 632, § 9-195; 2001, c. 844.)

Cross references. — As to punishment for Class 2 misdemeanors, see § 18.2-11.

§ 9.1-137. Article to control over other laws; exceptions. — A. In the event any provisions of this article conflict with other provisions of law, the provision of this article shall control, except as provided in subsection B.

B. Notwithstanding the provisions of subsection A, this article shall not alter, amend, or supersede any provisions of the Code of Virginia relating to the collection, storage, dissemination, or use of juvenile records. (1981, c. 632, § 9-196; 2001, c. 844.)

ARTICLE 4.

Private Security Services Businesses.

§ 9.1-138. Definitions. — In addition to the definitions set forth in § 9.1-101, as used in this article, unless the context requires a different meaning:

"Alarm respondent" means an individual who responds to the signal of an alarm for the purpose of detecting an intrusion of the home, business or property of the end user.

"Armed" means a private security registrant who carries or has immediate access to a firearm in the performance of his duties.

"Armed security officer" means a natural person employed to (i) safeguard and protect persons and property or (ii) deter theft, loss, or concealment of any tangible or intangible personal property on the premises he is contracted to protect, and who carries or has access to a firearm in the performance of his duties.

"Armored car personnel" means persons who transport or offer to transport under armed security from one place to another, money, negotiable instruments or other valuables in a specially equipped motor vehicle with a high degree of security and certainty of delivery.

"Business advertising material" means display advertisements in telephone directories, letterhead, business cards, local newspaper advertising and contracts.

"Central station dispatcher" means an individual who monitors burglar alarm signal devices, burglar alarms or any other electrical, mechanical or electronic device used (i) to prevent or detect burglary, theft, shoplifting, pilferage or similar losses; (ii) to prevent or detect intrusion; or (iii) primarily to summon aid for other emergencies.

"Certification" means the method of regulation indicating that qualified persons have met the minimum requirements as private security services training schools, private security services instructors, compliance agents, or certified detector canine handler examiners.

"Compliance agent" means an individual who owns or is employed by a licensed private security services business to ensure the compliance of the private security services business with this title.

"Courier" means any armed person who transports or offers to transport from one place to another documents or other papers, negotiable or nonnegotiable instruments, or other small items of value that require expeditious services.

"Detector canine" means any dog that detects drugs or explosives or both drugs and explosives.

"Detector canine handler" means any individual who uses a detector canine in the performance of private security duties.

"Detector canine handler examiner" means any individual who examines the proficiency and reliability of detector canines and detector canine handlers in the detection of drugs or explosives or both drugs and explosives.

"Detector canine team" means the detector canine handler and his detector canine performing private security duties.

"Electronic security business" means any person who engages in the business of or undertakes to (i) install, service, maintain, design or consult in the design of any electronic security equipment to an end user; (ii) respond to or cause a response to electronic security equipment for an end user; or (iii) have access to confidential information concerning the design, extent, status, password, contact list, or location of an end user's electronic security equipment.

"Electronic security employee" means an individual who is employed by an electronic security business in any capacity which may give him access to information concerning the design, extent, status, password, contact list, or location of an end user's electronic security equipment.

"Electronic security equipment" means (i) electronic or mechanical alarm signaling devices including burglar alarms or holdup alarms used to safeguard and protect persons and property; or (ii) cameras used to detect intrusions, concealment or theft, to safeguard and protect persons and property. This shall not include tags, labels, and other devices that are attached or affixed to items offered for sale, library books, and other protected articles as part of an electronic article surveillance and theft detection and deterrence system.

"Electronic security sales representative" means an individual who sells electronic security equipment on behalf of an electronic security business to the end user.

"Electronic security technician" means an individual who installs, services, maintains or repairs electronic security equipment.

"Electronic security technician's assistant" means an individual who works as a laborer under the supervision of the electronic security technician in the course of his normal duties, but who may not make connections to any electronic security equipment.

"Employed" means to be in an employer/employee relationship where the employee is providing work in exchange for compensation and the employer directly controls the employee's conduct and pays some taxes on behalf of the employee. The term "employed" shall not be construed to include independent contractors.

"End user" means any person who purchases or leases electronic security equipment for use in that person's home or business.

"Firearms training verification" means the verification of successful completion of either initial or retraining requirements for handgun or shotgun training, or both.

"General public" means individuals who have access to areas open to all and not restricted to any particular class of the community.

"License number" means the official number issued to a private security services business licensed by the Department.

"Natural person" means an individual person.

"Personal protection specialist" means any individual who engages in the duties of providing close protection from bodily harm to any person.

"Private investigator" means any individual who engages in the business of, or accepts employment to make, investigations to obtain information on (i) crimes or civil wrongs; (ii) the location, disposition, or recovery of stolen property; (iii) the cause of accidents, fires, damages, or injuries to persons or to property; or (iv) evidence to be used before any court, board, officer, or investigative committee.

"Private security services business" means any person engaged in the business of providing, or who undertakes to provide, armored car personnel, security officers, personal protection specialists, private investigators, couriers, security canine handlers, security canine teams, detector canine handlers, detector canine teams, alarm respondents, central station dispatchers, electronic security employees, electronic security sales representatives or electronic security technicians and their assistants to another person under contract, express or implied.

"Private security services instructor" means any individual certified by the Department to provide mandated instruction in private security subjects for a certified private security services training school.

"Private security services registrant" means any qualified individual who has met the requirements under this article to perform the duties of alarm respondent, armored car personnel, central station dispatcher, courier, electronic security sales representative, electronic security technician, electronic security technician's assistant, personal protection specialist, private investigator, security canine handler, detector canine handler, unarmed security officer or armed security officer.

"Private security services training school" means any person certified by the Department to provide instruction in private security subjects for the training of private security services business personnel in accordance with this article.

"Registration" means a method of regulation whereby certain personnel employed by a private security services business are required to register with the Department pursuant to this article.

"Registration category" means any one of the following categories: (i) unarmed security officer and armed security officer/courier, (ii) security canine handler, (iii) armored car personnel, (iv) private investigator, (v) personal protection specialist, (vi) alarm respondent, (vii) central station dispatcher, (viii) electronic security sales representative, (ix) electronic security technician, (x) electronic technician's assistant, or (xi) detector canine handler.

"Security canine" means a dog that has attended, completed, and been certified as a security canine by a certified security canine handler instructor in accordance with approved Department procedures and certification guidelines. "Security canines" shall not include detector dogs.

"Security canine handler" means any individual who utilizes his security canine in the performance of private security duties.

"Security canine team" means the security canine handler and his security canine performing private security duties.

"Supervisor" means any individual who directly or indirectly supervises registered or certified private security services business personnel.

"Unarmed security officer" means a natural person who performs the functions of observation, detection, reporting, or notification of appropriate authorities or designated agents regarding persons or property on the premises he is contracted to protect, and who does not carry or have access to a firearm in the performance of his duties. (1976, c. 737, § 54-729.27; 1977, c. 376, § 54.1-1900; 1980, c. 425, cc. 57, 779; 1988, c. 765; 1992, c. 578, § 9-183.1; 1994, cc. 45, 335, 810; 1995, c. 79; 1996, c. 541; 1997, c. 80; 1998, cc. 122, 807; 1999, c. 33; 2001, cc. 821, 844; 2003, c. 124; 2004, c. 470; 2005, c. 365.)

Cross references. — As to exclusions for persons licensed under this Article as a private security services business from certain licensing requirements of Chapter 11, § 54.1-1100 et seq., see § 54.1-1103.

Editor's note. — Acts 2001, c. 821 amended former § 9-183.1, from which this section is derived. Pursuant to § 30-152, Acts 2001, c. 821 has been given effect in this section as set out above. The 2001 amendment by c. 821 inserted paragraphs defining the terms "Employed," "General Public," and "Natural Person."

The 2005 amendments. — The 2005 amendment by c. 365, in the first sentence of the definition of "Electronic security equipment," inserted the clause (i) and (ii) designations and "used to safeguard and protect persons and property" and made a related change.

§ 9.1-139. Licensing, certification, and registration required; qualifications; temporary licenses. — A. No person shall engage in the private security services business or solicit private security business in the Commonwealth without having obtained a license from the Department. No person shall be issued a private security services business license until a compliance agent is designated in writing on forms provided by the Department. The compliance agent shall ensure the compliance of the private security services business with this article and shall meet the qualifications and perform the duties required by the regulations adopted by the Board. A compliance agent shall have either a minimum of (i) three years of managerial or supervisory experience in a private security services business; with a federal, state or local law-enforcement agency; or in a related field or (ii) five years of experience in a private security services business; with a federal, state or local law-enforcement agency; or in a related field.

B. No person shall act as private security services training school or solicit students for private security training in the Commonwealth without being certified by the Department. No person shall be issued a private security services training school certification until a school director is designated in writing on forms provided by the Department. The school director shall ensure the compliance of the school with the provisions of this article and shall meet the qualifications and perform the duties required by the regulations adopted by the Board.

C. No person shall be employed by a licensed private security services business in the Commonwealth as armored car personnel, courier, armed security officer, detector canine handler, unarmed security officer, security canine handler, private investigator, personal protection specialist, alarm respondent, central station dispatcher, electronic security sales representative, electronic security technician's assistant, or electronic security technician without possessing a valid registration issued by the Department, except as provided in this article.

D. A temporary license may be issued in accordance with Board regulations for the purpose of awaiting the results of the state and national fingerprint search. However, no person shall be issued a temporary license until (i) he has designated a compliance agent who has complied with the compulsory minimum training standards established by the Board pursuant to subsection A of § 9.1-141 for compliance agents, (ii) each principal of the business has submitted his fingerprints for a National Criminal Records search and a Virginia Criminal History Records search, and (iii) he has met all other requirements of this article and Board regulations.

E. No person shall be employed by a licensed private security services business in the Commonwealth unless such person is certified or registered in accordance with this chapter.

F. A temporary registration may be issued in accordance with Board regulations for the purpose of awaiting the results of the state and national fingerprint search. However, no person shall be issued a temporary registration until he has (i) complied with, or been exempted from the compulsory minimum training standards established by the Board, pursuant to subsection A of § 9.1-141, for armored car personnel, couriers, armed security officers, detector canine handlers, unarmed security officers, security canine handlers, private investigators, personal protection specialists, alarm respondents, central station dispatchers, electronic security sales representatives, electronic security technician's assistants, or electronic security technicians, (ii) submitted his fingerprints to be used for the conduct of a National Criminal Records search and a Virginia Criminal History Records search, and (iii) met all other requirements of this article and Board regulations.

G. A temporary certification as a private security instructor or private security training school may be issued in accordance with Board regulations for the purpose of awaiting the results of the state and national fingerprint search. However, no person shall be issued a temporary certification as a private security services instructor until he has (i) met the education, training and experience requirements established by the Board and (ii) submitted his fingerprints to be used for the conduct of a National Criminal Records search and a Virginia Criminal History Records search. No person shall be issued a temporary certification as a private security services training school until (a) he has designated a training director, (b) each principal of the training school has submitted his fingerprints to be used for the conduct of a National Criminal Records search and a Virginia Criminal History Records search, and (c) he has met all other requirements of this article and Board regulations.

H. A licensed private security services business in the Commonwealth shall not employ as an unarmed security officer, electronic security technician's assistant, unarmed alarm respondent, central station dispatcher, electronic security sales representative, or electronic security technician, any person who has not complied with, or been exempted from, the compulsory minimum training standards established by the Board, pursuant to subsection A of § 9.1-141, except that such person may be so employed for not more than 90 days while completing compulsory minimum training standards.

I. No person shall be employed as an electronic security employee, electronic security technician's assistant, unarmed alarm respondent, central station dispatcher, electronic security sales representative, electronic security technician or supervisor until he has submitted his fingerprints to the Department to be used for the conduct of a National Criminal Records search and a Virginia Criminal History Records search. The provisions of this subsection shall not apply to an out-of-state central station dispatcher meeting the requirements of subdivision 19 of § 9.1-140.

J. The compliance agent of each licensed private security services business in the Commonwealth shall maintain documentary evidence that each private security registrant and certified employee employed by his private security services business has complied with, or been exempted from, the compulsory minimum training standards required by the Board. Before January 1, 2003, the compliance agent shall ensure that an investigation to determine suitability of each unarmed security officer employee has been conducted, except that any such unarmed security officer, upon initiating a request for such investigation under the provisions of subdivision 11 of subsection A of § 19.2-389, may be employed for up to 30 days pending completion of such investigation. After January 1, 2003, no person shall be employed as an unarmed security officer until he has submitted his fingerprints to the Department for the conduct of a National Criminal Records search and a Virginia Criminal History Records search. Any person who was employed as an unarmed security officer prior to January 1, 2003, shall submit his fingerprints to the Department in accordance with subsection B of § 9.1-145.

K. No person with a criminal conviction for a misdemeanor involving (i) moral turpitude, (ii) assault and battery, (iii) damage to real or personal property, (iv) controlled substances or imitation controlled substances as defined in Article 1 (§ 18.2-247 et seq.) of Chapter 7 of Title 18.2, (v) prohibited sexual behavior as described in Article 7 (§ 18.2-61 et seq.) of Chapter 4 of Title 18.2, or (vi) firearms, or any felony shall be (a) employed as a registered or certified employee by a private security services business or training school, or (b) issued a private security services registration, certification as an unarmed security officer, electronic security employee or technician's assistant, a private security services training school or instructor certification, compliance agent certification, or a private security services business license, except that, upon written request, the Director of the Department may waive such prohibition.

L. The Department may grant a temporary exemption from the requirement for licensure, certification, or registration for a period of not more than 30 days in a situation deemed an emergency by the Department.

M. All private security services businesses and private security services training schools in the Commonwealth shall include their license or certification number on all business advertising materials.

N. A licensed private security services business in the Commonwealth shall not employ as armored car personnel any person who has not complied with, or been exempted from, the compulsory minimum training standards established by the Board pursuant to subsection A of § 9.1-141, except such person may serve as a driver of an armored car for not more than 90 days while completing compulsory minimum training standards, provided such person does not possess or have access to a firearm while serving as a driver. (1976, c. 737, § 54-729.29; 1977, c. 376, § 54.1-1902; 1978, cc. 28, 428; 1984, cc. 57, 779; 1988, cc. 48, 765; 1991, c. 589; 1992, c. 578, § 9-183.3; 1994, cc. 45, 47, 810; 1995, c. 79; 1996, c. 541; 1998, cc. 53, 122, 807; 2000, c. 26; 2001, cc. 821, 844; 2002, cc. 578, 597; 2003, c. 124; 2004, c. 470.)

Editor's note. — Acts 2001, c. 821 amended former § 9-183.3, from which this section is derived. Pursuant to § 30-152, Acts 2001, c. 821 has been given effect in this section as set out above. The 2001 amendment by c. 821, in subsection J, substituted "conviction for" for "record of," inserted "(i)" before "moral turpitude," inserted "(ii) assault and battery, (iii) damage to real or personal property, (iv) controlled substances or imitation controlled substances as defined in Article 1 (§ 18.2-247 et seq.) of Chapter 7 of Title 18.2, (v) prohibited sexual behavior as described in Article 7 (§ 18.2-61 et seq.) of Chapter 4 of Title 18.2, or (vi) firearms," following "moral turpitude" and substituted "(a)" and "(b)" for "(i)" and "(ii)."

§ 9.1-140. Exceptions from article; training requirements for out-of-state central station dispatchers. — The provisions of this article shall not apply to:

1. An officer or employee of the United States, the Commonwealth, or a political subdivision of either, while the officer or employee is performing his official duties.

2. A person, except a private investigator as defined in § 9.1-138, engaged exclusively in the business of obtaining and furnishing information regarding an individual's financial rating or a person engaged in the business of a consumer reporting agency as defined by the Federal Fair Credit Reporting Act.

3. An attorney or certified public accountant licensed to practice in Virginia or his employees.

4. The legal owner of personal property which has been sold under any security agreement while performing acts relating to the repossession of such property.

5. A person receiving compensation for private employment as a security officer, or receiving compensation under the terms of a contract, express or implied, as a security officer, who is also a law-enforcement officer as defined by § 9.1-101 and employed by the Commonwealth or any of its political subdivisions.

6. Any person appointed under § 46.2-2003 or § 56-353 while engaged in the employment contemplated thereunder, unless they have successfully completed training mandated by the Department.

7. Persons who conduct investigations as a part of the services being provided as a claims adjuster, by a claims adjuster who maintains an ongoing claims adjusting business, and any natural person employed by the claims adjuster to conduct investigations for the claims adjuster as a part of the services being provided as a claims adjuster.

8. Any natural person otherwise required to be registered pursuant to § 9.1-139 who is employed by a business that is not a private security services business for the performance of his duties for his employer. Any such employee, however, who carries a firearm and is in direct contact with the general public in the performance of his duties shall possess a valid registration with the Department as required by this article.

9. Persons, sometimes known as "shoppers," employed to purchase goods or services solely for the purpose of determining or assessing the efficiency, loyalty, courtesy, or honesty of the employees of a business establishment.

10. Licensed or registered private investigators from other states entering Virginia during an investigation originating in their state of licensure or registration when the other state offers similar reciprocity to private investigators licensed and registered by the Commonwealth.

11. Unarmed regular employees of telephone public service companies where the regular duties of such employees consist of protecting the property of their employers and investigating the usage of telephone services and equipment furnished by their employers, their employers' affiliates, and other communications common carriers.

12. An end user.

13. A material supplier who renders advice concerning the use of products sold by an electronics security business and who does not provide installation, monitoring, repair or maintenance services for electronic security equipment.

14. Members of the security forces who are directly employed by electric public service companies.

15. Any professional engineer or architect licensed in accordance with Chapter 4 (§ 54.1-400 et seq.) of Title 54.1 to practice in the Commonwealth, or his employees.

16. Any person who only performs telemarketing or schedules appointments without access to information concerning the electronic security equipment purchased by an end user.

17. Any certified forensic scientist employed as an expert witness for the purpose of possibly testifying as an expert witness.

18. Members of the security forces who are directly employed by shipyards engaged in the construction, design, overhaul or repair of nuclear vessels for the United States Navy.

19. An out-of-state central station dispatcher employed by a private security services business licensed by the Department provided he (i) possesses and maintains a valid license, registration, or certification as a central station dispatcher issued by the regulatory authority of the state in which he performs the monitoring duties and (ii) has submitted his fingerprints to the regulatory authority for the conduct of a national criminal history records search.

20. Any person, or independent contractor or employee of any person, who (i) exclusively contracts directly with an agency of the federal government to conduct background investigations and (ii) possesses credentials issued by such agency authorizing such person, subcontractor or employee to conduct background investigations.

21. Any person whose occupation is limited to the technical reconstruction of the cause of accidents involving motor vehicles as defined in § 46.2-100, regardless of whether the information resulting from the investigation is to be used before a court, board, officer, or investigative committee, and who is not otherwise a private investigator as defined in § 9.1-138. (1976, c. 737, § 54-729.28; 1977, c. 376, § 54.1-1901; 1981, c. 538; 1983, c. 569; 1984, c. 375; 1988, c. 765; 1992, c. 578, § 9-183.2; 1994, cc. 45, 810; 1995, c. 79; 1996, cc. 541, 543, 576; 1997, cc. 80, 204; 2000, c. 26; 2001, cc. 388, 650, 821, 844; 2002, cc. 578, 597; 2003, c. 136.)

Editor's note. — Acts 2001, cc. 388, 650 and 821 amended former § 9-183.2, from which this section is derived. Pursuant to § 30-152, Acts 2001, cc. 388, 650 and 821 have been given effect in this section as set out above.

Section 46.2-2003, referred to in subdivision 6, was repealed effective July 1, 2002, by Acts 2001, c. 596.

§ 9.1-141. Powers of Board relating to private security services business. — A. The Board may adopt regulations in accordance with the Administrative Process Act (§ 2.2-4000 et seq.), establishing compulsory minimum, entry-level, in-service, and advanced training standards for persons employed by private security services businesses in classifications defined in § 9.1-138. The regulations may include provisions delegating to the Board's staff the right to inspect the facilities and programs of persons conducting training to ensure compliance with the law and Board regulations. In establishing compulsory training standards for each of the classifications defined in § 9.1-138, the Board shall be guided by the policy of this section to secure the public safety and welfare against incompetent or unqualified persons engaging in the activities regulated by this section and Article 4 (§ 9.1-138 et seq.) of this chapter. The regulations may provide for exemption from such training for persons having previous employment as law-enforcement officers for a state or the federal government. However, no such exemption shall be granted to persons having less than five continuous years of such employment, nor shall an exemption be provided for any person whose employment as a law-enforcement officer was terminated because of his misconduct or incompetence. The regulations may include provisions for partial exemption from compulsory training for persons having previous training that meets or exceeds the minimum training standards and has been approved by the Department, or for persons employed in classifications defined in § 9.1-138. However, no exemption shall be granted to persons having less than five continuous years of such employment, nor shall an exemption be provided for any person whose employment as a private security services business employee was terminated because of his misconduct or incompetence.

B. The Board may enter into an agreement with other states for reciprocity or recognition of private security services businesses and their employees, duly licensed by such states. The agreements shall allow those businesses and their employees to provide and perform private security services within the Commonwealth to secure the public safety and welfare against incompetent, unqualified, unscrupulous, or unfit persons engaging in the activities of private security services businesses.

C. The Board may adopt regulations in accordance with the Administrative Process Act (§ 2.2-4000 et seq.) to secure the public safety and welfare against incompetent, unqualified, unscrupulous, or unfit persons engaging in the activities of private security services businesses that:

1. Establish the qualifications of applicants for registration, certification, or licensure under Article 4 (§ 9.1-138) of this chapter;

2. Examine, or cause to be examined, the qualifications of each applicant for registration, certification, or licensure, including when necessary the preparation, administration and grading of examinations;

3. Certify qualified applicants for private security training schools and instructors or license qualified applicants as practitioners of private security services businesses;

4. Levy and collect fees for registration, certification, or licensure and renewal that are sufficient to cover all expenses for administration and operation of a program of registration, certification, and licensure for private security services businesses and training schools;

5. Are necessary to ensure continued competency, and to prevent deceptive or misleading practices by practitioners and effectively administer the regulatory system adopted by the Board;

6. Receive complaints concerning the conduct of any person whose activities are regulated by the Board, to conduct investigations, and to take appropriate disciplinary action if warranted; and

7. Revoke, suspend or fail to renew a registration, certification, or license for just cause as enumerated in Board regulations.

D. In adopting its regulations under subsections A and C, the Board shall seek the advice of the Private Security Services Advisory Board established pursuant to § 9.1-143. (1981, c. 632, § 9-182; 1990, c. 354; 1992, c. 578; 1994, cc. 45, 335, 810; 1995, c. 79; 1998, cc. 122, 807; 2001, c. 844.)

CASE NOTES

Editor's note. — The case below was decided under former corresponding provisions.

Applicability. — Virginia's licensing and registration requirements are inapplicable to private investigators working solely for the Federal Bureau of Investigation because the state regulations interfere with federal objectives. United States v. Commonwealth, 139 F.3d 984 (4th Cir. 1998).

§ 9.1-142. Powers of Department relating to private security services businesses. — A. In addition to the powers otherwise conferred upon it by law, the Department may:

1. Charge each applicant for licensure, certification or registration a nonrefundable fee as established by the Board to cover the costs of the Department for processing an application for a registration, certification or license, and enforcement of these regulations, and other costs associated with the maintenance of this program of regulation.

2. Charge nonrefundable fees for private security services training as established by the Board for processing school certifications and enforcement of training standards.

3. Conduct investigations to determine the suitability of applicants for registration, licensure, or certification of compliance agents, training schools, and instructors. For purposes of this investigation, the Department shall have access to criminal history record information maintained by the Central Criminal Records Exchange of the Department of State Police and shall conduct a background investigation, to include a National Criminal Records search and a Virginia Criminal History Records search.

4. Issue subpoenas. The Director or a designated subordinate may make an ex parte application to the circuit court for the city or county wherein evidence sought is kept or wherein a licensee does business, for the issuance of a subpoena duces tecum in furtherance of the investigation of a sworn complaint within the jurisdiction of the Department or the Board to request production of any relevant records, documents and physical or other evidence of any person, partnership, association or corporation licensed or regulated by the Department pursuant to this article. The court may issue and compel compliance with such a subpoena upon a showing of reasonable cause. Upon determining that reasonable cause exists to believe that evidence may be destroyed or altered, the court may issue a subpoena duces tecum requiring the immediate production of evidence.

5. Recover costs of the investigation and adjudication of violations of this article or Board regulations. Such costs may be recovered from the respondent when a sanction is imposed to fine or place on probation, suspend, revoke, or deny the issuance of any license, certification, or registration. Such costs shall be in addition to any monetary penalty which may be imposed. All costs recovered shall be deposited into the state treasury to the credit of the Private Security Services Regulatory Fund.

6. Institute proceedings to enjoin any person from engaging in any lawful act enumerated in § 9.1-147. Such proceedings shall be brought in the name of the Commonwealth by the Department in circuit court of the city or county in which the unlawful act occurred or in which the defendant resides.

B. The Director, or agents appointed by him, shall be vested with the authority to administer oaths or affirmations for the purpose of receiving complaints and conducting investigations of violations of this article, or any Board regulation promulgated pursuant to authority given by this article. Information concerning alleged criminal violations shall be turned over to law-enforcement officers in appropriate jurisdictions. Agents shall be vested with authority to serve such paper or process issued by the Department or the Board under regulations approved by the Board. (1976, c. 737, § 54-729.30; 1977, c. 376, § 54.1-1903; 1984, cc. 57, 779; 1985, c. 448; 1988, c. 765; 1991, c. 589; 1992, c. 578, § 9-183.4; 1994, c. 46; 1998, cc. 122, 807; 2001, c. 844.)

§ 9.1-143. Private Security Services Advisory Board; membership.
— The Private Security Services Advisory Board is established as an advisory board within the meaning of § 2.2-2100, in the executive branch of state government. The Private Security Services Advisory Board shall consist of 13 members as follows: two members shall be private investigators; two shall be representatives of electronic security businesses; three shall be representatives of private security services businesses providing security officers, armed couriers or guard dog handlers; one shall be a representative of a private security services business providing armored car personnel; one shall be a representative of a private security services business involving personal protection specialists; one shall be a certified private security services instructor; one shall be a special conservator of the peace appointed pursuant to § 19.2-13; one shall be a licensed bail bondsman and one shall be a representative of law enforcement. The Private Security Services Advisory Board shall be appointed by the Criminal Justice Services Board and shall advise the Criminal Justice Services Board on all issues relating to regulation of private security services businesses. (1976, c. 737, § 54-729.30; 1977, c. 376, § 54.1-1904; 1984, cc. 57, 779; 1985, c. 448; 1988, c. 765; 1992, c. 578, § 9-183.5; 1994, c. 810; 1997, c. 79; 2001, c. 844; 2003, c. 922; 2004, c. 460.)

Editor's note. — Acts 2004, c. 460, cl. 5, provides: "That the provisions of this act, except for § 16.1-77, shall become effective on July 1, 2005."

Acts 2004, c. 460, cl. 2, provides: "That the State Corporation Commission shall forward all surety bail bondsman licensing records in its custody to the Department of Criminal Justice Services by June 30, 2005."

Acts 2004, c. 460, cl. 3, provides: "That the Department of Criminal Justice Services shall promulgate regulations to implement the provisions of this act to be effective within 280 days of its enactment."

Acts 2004, c. 460, cl. 6, provides: "That the provisions of this act may result in a net increase in periods of imprisonment or commitment. Pursuant to § 30-19.1:4, the estimated amount of the necessary appropriation cannot be determined for periods of imprisonment in state adult correctional facilities and is $0 for periods of commitment to the custody of the Department of Juvenile Justice."

The 2004 amendments. — The 2004 amendment by c. 460, effective July 1, 2005, in the next-to-last sentence, substituted "13" for "12" and inserted "one shall be a licensed bail bondsman" near the end.

§ 9.1-144. Bond or insurance required; actions against bond. —
A. Every person licensed as a private security services business under subsection A of § 9.1-139 or certified as a private security services training school under subsection B of § 9.1-139 shall, at the time of receiving the license or certification and before the license or certification shall be operative, file with the Department (i) a cash bond or evidence that the licensee or certificate holder is covered by a surety bond, executed by a surety company authorized to do business in the Commonwealth, in a reasonable amount to be fixed by the Department, conditioned upon the faithful and honest conduct of his business or employment; or (ii) evidence of a policy of liability insurance in an amount and with coverage as fixed by the Department. The bond or liability insurance shall be maintained for so long as the licensee or certificate holder is licensed or certified by the Department.

B. If any person aggrieved by the misconduct of any person licensed or certified under subsection A or B of § 9.1-139 recovers judgment against the licensee or certificate holder, which judgment is unsatisfied in whole or in part, such person may bring an action in his own name on the bond of the licensee or certificate holder. (1976, c. 737, § 54-729.31; 1988, c. 765, § 54.1-1905; 1992, c. 578, § 9-183.6; 1998, cc. 122, 807; 2001, c. 844.)

§ **9.1-145. Fingerprints required; penalty.** — A. Each applicant for initial registration, licensure or certification as a compliance agent, private security services training school or instructor or unarmed security officer under the provisions of this article and every person employed as an electronic security employee or electronic security technician's assistant shall submit his fingerprints to the Department on a form provided by the Department. The Department shall use the applicant's fingerprints and personal descriptive information for the conduct of a National Criminal Records search and a Virginia Criminal History Records search.

B. Each currently certified unarmed security officer applying for renewal between January 1, 2003, and December 31, 2004, shall submit his fingerprints to the Department on a form provided by the Department. The Department shall use the applicant's fingerprints and personal descriptive information for the conduct of a National Criminal Records search and a Virginia Criminal History Records search.

C. The Department may suspend the registration, license or certification of any applicant who is subsequently convicted of a misdemeanor involving (i) moral turpitude, (ii) assault and battery, (iii) damage to real or personal property, (iv) controlled substances or imitation controlled substances as defined in Article 1 (§ 18.2-247 et seq.) of Chapter 7 of Title 18.2, (v) prohibited sexual behavior as described in Article 7 (§ 18.2-61 et seq.) of Chapter 4 of Title 18.2, or (vi) firearms or any felony.

D. Any person willfully and intentionally making a false statement in the personal descriptive information required on the fingerprint card is guilty of a Class 5 felony. (1976, c. 737, § 54-729.32; 1988, c. 765, § 54.1-1906; 1992, c. 578, § 9-183.7; 1994, c. 810; 1995, c. 79; 1998, cc. 122, 807; 2001, c. 844; 2002, cc. 578, 597.)

Cross references. — As to punishment for Class 5 felonies, see § 18.2-10.

Editor's note. — Acts 2002, cc. 578 and 597, cl. 2, provide: "That the provisions of this act may result in a net increase in periods of imprisonment or commitment. Pursuant to § 30-19.1:4, the estimated amount of the necessary appropriation is $0 for periods of imprisonment in state adult correctional facilities and is $0 for periods of commitment to the custody of the Department of Juvenile Justice."

§ **9.1-146. Limitation on powers of registered armed security officers.** — Compliance with the provisions of this article shall not itself authorize any person to carry a concealed weapon or exercise any powers of a conservator of the peace. A registered armed security officer of a private security services business while at a location which the business is contracted to protect shall have the power to effect an arrest for an offense occurring (i) in his presence on such premises or (ii) in the presence of a merchant, agent, or employee of the merchant the private security business has contracted to protect, if the merchant, agent, or employee had probable cause to believe that the person arrested had shoplifted or committed willful concealment of goods as contemplated by § 18.2-106. For the purposes of § 19.2-74, a registered armed security officer of a private security services business shall be considered an arresting officer. (1976, c. 737, § 54-729.33; 1978, c. 560, § 54.1-1907; 1980, c. 425; 1988, cc. 48, 765; 1992, c. 578, § 9-183.8; 1994, c. 45; 2001, c. 844.)

CASE NOTES

Editor's note. — The case below was decided under former corresponding provisions.

Registered security guard not "conservator of the peace." — In accordance with the express language in this section, a registered, armed security guard was not a "conservator of the peace" so as to be exempt from the prohibition on carrying weapons on school grounds for conservators of the peace. Frias v. Commonwealth, 34 Va. App. 193, 538 S.E.2d 374, 2000 Va. App. LEXIS 838 (2000).

§ 9.1-147. Unlawful conduct generally; penalty. — A. It shall be unlawful for any person to:

1. Practice any trade or profession licensed, certified or registered under this article without obtaining the necessary license, certification or registration required by statute or regulation;

2. Materially misrepresent facts in an application for licensure, certification or registration;

3. Willfully refuse to furnish the Department information or records required or requested pursuant to statute or regulation; and

4. Violate any statute or regulation governing the practice of the private security services businesses or training schools regulated by this article.

B. Any person who is convicted of willful violation of subsection A shall be guilty of a Class 1 misdemeanor. Any person convicted of a third or subsequent offense under this section during a thirty-six-month period shall be guilty of a Class 6 felony. (1992, c. 578, § 9-183.11; 1998, cc. 122, 807; 2001, c. 844.)

Cross references. — As to punishment for Class 6 felonies, see § 18.2-10. As to punishment for Class 1 misdemeanors, see § 18.2-11.

§ 9.1-148. Unlawful procurement of a license; penalty. — A. It shall be unlawful for any person to:

1. Procure, or assist another to procure, through theft, fraud or other illegal means, a registration or license, by giving to, or receiving from, any person any information, oral, written or printed, during the administration of the examination, which is intended to, or will, assist any person taking the examination in passing the examination and obtaining the required registration or license;

2. Attempt to procure, through theft, fraud or other illegal means, any questions intended to be used by the Department conducting the examination, or the answers to the questions;

3. Promise or offer any valuable or other consideration to a person having access to the questions or answers as an inducement to procure for delivery to the promisor, or any other person, a copy of any questions or answers.

B. No person, other than a designee of the Department, shall procure or have in his possession prior to the beginning of an examination, without written authority of the Department, any question intended to be used by the Department, or receive or furnish to any person taking the examination, prior to or during the examination, any written or printed material purporting to be answers to, or aid in answering such questions;

C. If an examination is divided into separate parts, each of the parts shall be deemed an examination for the purposes of this section.

D. Any person convicted of a violation of subsections A or B shall be guilty of a Class 2 misdemeanor. (1992, c. 578, § 9-183.10; 2001, c. 844.)

Cross references. — As to punishment for Class 2 misdemeanors, see § 18.2-11.

§ 9.1-149. Unlicensed activity prohibited; penalty. — A. No person:

1. Required to possess a registration under subsection C of § 9.1-139 shall be employed by a private security services business, except as provided in this article, as armored car personnel, courier, armed security officer, security canine handler, personal protection specialist, private investigator, alarm respondent, central station dispatcher, electronic security sales representative or electronic security technician without possessing a valid registration.

2. Licensed or required to be licensed under subsection A of § 9.1-139 shall employ or otherwise utilize, except as provided in this article, as armored car personnel, courier, armed security officer, security canine handler, personal protection specialist, private investigator, alarm respondent, central station dispatcher, electronic security sales representative or electronic security technician, any person not possessing a valid registration.

3. Required to possess an instructor certification under subsection D of § 9.1-139 shall provide mandated instruction, except as provided in § 9.1-141 and Board regulations, without possessing a valid private security instructor certification.

4. Certified or required to be certified as a private security services training school under subsection B of § 9.1-139 shall employ or otherwise utilize, except as provided in § 9.1-141 and Board regulations, as a private security instructor, any person not possessing a valid instructor certification.

B. No compliance agent employed or otherwise utilized by a person licensed or required to be licensed under subsection A of § 9.1-139 shall:

1. Employ or otherwise utilize as an unarmed security officer, except as provided in this article, any individual for whom the compliance agent does not possess documentary evidence of compliance with, or exemption from, the compulsory minimum training standards established by the Board for unarmed security officers and before January 1, 2003, maintain documentary evidence that an investigation to determine suitability has been conducted.

2. Employ or otherwise utilize as an electronic security technician's assistant, except as provided in this article, any individual for whom the compliance agent does not possess documentary evidence of compliance with, or exemption from, the compulsory minimum training standards established by the Board for electronic security technician's assistants.

C. Any person convicted of a violation of subsections A or B shall be guilty of a Class 1 misdemeanor. (1976, c. 737, § 54-729.34; 1980, c. 425, § 54.1-1908; 1988, cc. 48, 765; 1992, c. 578, § 9-183.9; 1994, cc. 45, 810; 1995, c. 79; 1998, cc. 122, 807; 2001, c. 844; 2002, cc. 578, 597.)

Cross references. — As to punishment for
Class 1 misdemeanors, see § 18.2-11.

§ 9.1-150. Monetary penalty. — Any person licensed, certified or registered by the Board pursuant to this article who violates any statute or Board regulation who is not criminally prosecuted shall be subject to the monetary penalty provided in this section. If the Board determines that a respondent is guilty of the violation complained of, the Board shall determine the amount of the monetary penalty for the violation, which shall not exceed $2,500 for each violation. The penalty may be sued for and recovered in the name of the Commonwealth. The monetary penalty shall be paid into the state treasury to the credit of the Literary Fund in accordance with § 19.2-353. (1992, c. 578, § 9-183.12; 1994, c. 810; 1998, cc. 122, 807; 2001, c. 844.)

ARTICLE 4.1.

Special Conservators of the Peace.

§ 9.1-150.1. Definitions. — In addition to the definitions set forth in § 9.1-101, as used in this article, unless the context requires a different meaning:

"Special conservator of the peace" means any individual appointed pursuant to § 19.2-13 on or after September 15, 2004. (2003, c. 922.)

§ 9.1-150.2. Powers of Criminal Justice Services Board relating to special conservators of the peace appointed pursuant to § 19.2-13. — The Board may adopt regulations establishing compulsory minimum, entry-level, in-service, and advanced training standards for special conservators of the peace. The regulations may include provisions delegating to the Board's staff the right to inspect the facilities and programs of persons conducting training to ensure compliance with the law and its regulations. In establishing compulsory training standards for special conservators of the peace, the Board shall ensure the public safety and welfare against incompetent or unqualified persons engaging in the activities regulated by this section. The regulations may provide for exemption from training of persons having previous employment as law-enforcement officers for a state or the federal government. However, no such exemption shall be granted to persons having less than five continuous years of such employment, nor shall an exemption be provided for any person whose employment as a law-enforcement officer was terminated because of his misconduct or incompetence. The regulations may include provisions for partial exemption from such training for persons having previous training that meets or exceeds the minimum training standards and has been approved by the Department. The Board may also adopt regulations that (i) establish the qualifications of applicants for registration; (ii) cause to be examined the qualifications of each applicant for registration; (iii) provide for collection of fees for registration and renewal that are sufficient to cover all expenses for administration and operation of a program of registration; (iv) ensure continued competency and prevent deceptive or misleading practices by practitioners; (v) effectively administer the regulatory system promulgated by the Board; (vi) provide for receipt of complaints concerning the conduct of any person whose activities are regulated by the Board; (vii) provide for investigations, and appropriate disciplinary action if warranted; and (viii) allow the Board to revoke, suspend or refuse to renew a registration, certification, or license for just cause as enumerated in regulations of the Board. The Board shall not adopt compulsory, minimum, entry-level training standards in excess of 24 hours for unarmed special conservators of the peace or in excess of 40 hours for armed special conservators of the peace. In adopting its regulations, the Board shall seek the advice of the Private Security Services Advisory Board established pursuant to § 9.1-143. (2003, c. 922.)

§ 9.1-150.3. Powers of Department of Criminal Justice Services relating to special conservators of the peace appointed pursuant to § 19.2-13. — A. In addition to the powers otherwise conferred upon it by law, the Department may (i) charge each applicant for registration a nonrefundable fee as established by the Board to cover the costs of the Department for processing an application for registration, and enforcement of the regulations, and other costs associated with the maintenance of the program of regulation; (ii) charge nonrefundable fees for private security services training as established by the Board for processing school certifications and enforcement of training standards; and (iii) conduct investigations to determine the suitability of applicants for registration, including a drug and alcohol screening. For purposes of this investigation, the Department shall require the applicant to provide personal descriptive information to be forwarded, along with the applicant's fingerprints, to the Central Criminal Records Exchange for the purpose of conducting a Virginia criminal history records search. The Central Criminal Records Exchange shall forward the fingerprints and personal description to the Federal Bureau of Investigation for the purpose of obtaining a national criminal record check.

B. The Director or his designee may make an ex parte application to the circuit court for the city or county wherein evidence sought is kept or wherein a licensee does business for the issuance of a subpoena duces tecum in furtherance of the investigation of a sworn complaint within the jurisdiction of the Department or the Board to request production of any relevant records, documents and physical or other evidence of any person, partnership, association or corporation licensed or regulated by the Department pursuant to this article. The court may issue and compel compliance with such a subpoena upon a showing of reasonable cause. Upon determining that reasonable cause exists to believe that evidence may be destroyed or altered, the court may issue a subpoena duces tecum requiring the immediate production of evidence. Costs of the investigation and adjudication of violations of this article or Board regulations may be recovered. All costs recovered shall be deposited into the state treasury to the credit of the Conservators of the Peace Regulatory Fund. Such proceedings shall be brought in the name of the Commonwealth by the Department in the circuit court of the city or county in which the unlawful act occurred or in which the defendant resides. The Director, or agents appointed by him, shall have the authority to administer oaths or affirmations for the purpose of receiving complaints and conducting investigations of violations of this article, or any regulation promulgated hereunder and to serve process issued by the Department or the Board. (2003, c. 922.)

§ **9.1-150.4. Unlawful conduct; penalties.** — A. It shall be unlawful for any person to (i) misrepresent facts in an application for registration; (ii) willfully refuse to furnish the Department information or records required or requested pursuant to statute or regulation; or (iii) violate any statute or regulation governing the practice of special conservators of the peace regulated by this article or § 19.2-13.

B. Any person registered by the Department pursuant to § 19.2-13 who the Department or the Board determines has violated any statute or Board regulation and who is not criminally prosecuted shall be subject to a monetary penalty not to exceed $2,500 for each violation. The penalty may be sued for and recovered in the name of the Commonwealth and shall be paid into the state treasury to the credit of the Literary Fund in accordance with § 19.2-353.

C. Any person who is convicted of a willful violation of the provisions of this article or § 19.2-13 is guilty of a Class 1 misdemeanor. Any person convicted of a third or subsequent offense under this article or § 19.2-13 during a 36-month period is guilty of a Class 6 felony. (2003, c. 922.)

Cross references. — As to penalty for Class 6 felonies, see § 18.2-10. As to penalty for Class 1 misdemeanors, see § 18.2-11.

ARTICLE 5.

Court-Appointed Special Advocate Program.

§ 9.1-151. Court-Appointed Special Advocate Program; appointment of advisory committee.

— A. There is established a Court-Appointed Special Advocate Program (the "Program") that shall be administered by the Department. The Program shall provide services in accordance with this article to children who are subjects of judicial proceedings involving allegations that the child is abused, neglected, in need of services or in need of supervision, and for whom the juvenile and domestic relations district court judge determines such services are appropriate. The Department shall adopt regulations necessary and appropriate for the administration of the Program.

B. The Board shall appoint an Advisory Committee to the Court-Appointed Special Advocate Program, consisting of fifteen members, knowledgeable of court matters, child welfare and juvenile justice issues and representative of both state and local interests. The duties of the Advisory Committee shall be to advise the Board on all matters relating to the Program and the needs of the clients served by the Program, and to make such recommendations as it may deem desirable. (1990, c. 752, § 9-173.6; 1994, c. 24; 2001, c. 844.)

Cross references. — As to the Attorney General representing Staff members or volunteers participating in a court-appointed special advocate program pursuant to this section, see § 2.2-507. For requirement that persons who are designated court-appointed special advocates pursuant to § 9.1-151 et seq. report the matter when they have reason to suspect that a child is abused or neglected, see § 63.2-1509.

§ 9.1-152. Local court-appointed special advocate programs; powers and duties.

— A. The Department shall provide a portion of any funding appropriated for this purpose to applicants seeking to establish and operate a local court-appointed special advocate program in their respective judicial districts. Only local programs operated in accordance with this article shall be eligible to receive state funds.

B. Local programs may be established and operated by local boards created for this purpose. Local boards shall ensure conformance to regulations adopted by the Board and may:

1. Solicit and accept financial support from public and private sources.

2. Oversee the financial and program management of the local court-appointed special advocate program.

3. Employ and supervise a director who shall serve as a professional liaison to personnel of the court and agencies serving children.

4. Employ such staff as is necessary to the operation of the program. (1990, c. 752, § 9-173.7; 1991, c. 421; 2001, c. 844.)

§ 9.1-153. Volunteer court-appointed special advocates; powers and duties; assignment; qualifications; training.

— A. Services in each local court-appointed special advocate program shall be provided by volunteer court-appointed special advocates, hereinafter referred to as advocates. The advocate's duties shall include:

1. Investigating the case to which he is assigned to provide independent factual information to the court.

2. Submitting to the court of a written report of his investigation in compliance with the provisions of § 16.1-274. The report may, upon request of the court, include recommendations as to the child's welfare.

3. Monitoring the case to which he is assigned to ensure compliance with the court's orders.

4. Assisting any appointed guardian ad litem to represent the child in providing effective representation of the child's needs and best interests.

5. Reporting a suspected abused or neglected child pursuant to § 63.2-1509.

B. The advocate is not a party to the case to which he is assigned and shall not call witnesses or examine witnesses. The advocate shall not, with respect to the case to which he is assigned, provide legal counsel or advice to any person, appear as counsel in court or in proceedings which are part of the judicial process, or engage in the unauthorized practice of law. The advocate may testify if called as a witness.

C. The program director shall assign an advocate to a child when requested to do so by the judge of the juvenile and domestic relations district court having jurisdiction over the proceedings. The advocate shall continue his association with each case to which he is assigned until relieved of his duties by the court or by the program director.

D. The Department shall adopt regulations governing the qualifications of advocates who for purposes of administering this subsection shall be deemed to be criminal justice employees. The regulations shall require that an advocate be at least twenty-one years of age and that the program director shall obtain with the approval of the court (i) a copy of his criminal history record or certification that no conviction data are maintained on him and (ii) a copy of information from the central registry maintained pursuant to § 63.2-1515 on any investigation of child abuse or neglect undertaken on him or certification that no such record is maintained on him. Advocates selected prior to the adoption of regulations governing qualifications shall meet the minimum requirements set forth in this article.

E. An advocate shall have no associations which create a conflict of interests or the appearance of such a conflict with his duties as an advocate. No advocate shall be assigned to a case of a child whose family has a professional or personal relationship with the advocate. Questions concerning conflicts of interests shall be determined in accordance with regulations adopted by the Department.

F. No applicant shall be assigned as an advocate until successful completion of a program of training required by regulations. The Department shall set standards for both basic and ongoing training. (1990, c. 752, § 9-173.8; 1994, cc. 700, 830; 1997, c. 606; 1999, c. 606; 2001, c. 844.)

Cross references. — For provision that no charge be made for checking the central registry of founded complaints of child abuse and neglect for persons who have volunteered with a court-appointed special advocate program pursuant to § 9.1-153, see § 63.2-1515.

CASE NOTES

Testimony regarding whether child should be returned to parent. — In a proceeding to terminate parental rights, it was not error to allow a former court appointed special advocate to testify whether she believed the child should be returned to the mother since such testimony did not intrude on the trial court's obligation to decide whether to terminate the mother's parental rights. Padilla v. Norfolk Division of Social Services, No. 1388-98-1 (Ct. of Appeals Jan. 26, 1999) (decided under prior law).

Trial court did not err in permitting the testimony of a court-appointed special advocate (CASA) for the children, regarding her opinion as to the children's best interests, as the CASA worker was not required to be reappointed by the circuit court after having been appointed by the juvenile court. Nelson v. Petersburg Dep't of Soc. Servs., No. 1343-04-2, 2005 Va. App. LEXIS 72 (Ct. of Appeals Feb. 22, 2005).

Evidence regarding whether child should be returned to parent. — Trial court did not err in admitting, as evidence in a termination of parental rights proceeding, the court-appointed special advocate's reports and their attachments, which discussed what was best for the son's welfare, as statutory law permitted the court-appointed special advocate to submit such a report and permitted the trial court in considering it in determining whether the father's parental rights should be terminated; accordingly, the father's objection that the reports and attachment violated the hearsay rule had to be rejected. Holley v. Amherst County Dep't of Soc. Servs., No. 3397-02-3, 2003 Va. App. LEXIS 330 (Ct. of Appeals June 10, 2003).

§ 9.1-154. Immunity. — No staff of or volunteers participating in a program, whether or not compensated, shall be subject to personal liability while acting within the scope of their duties, except for gross negligence or intentional misconduct. (1990, c. 752, § 9-173.10; 2001, c. 844.)

§ 9.1-155. Notice of hearings and proceedings. — The provision of § 16.1-264 regarding notice to parties shall apply to ensure that an advocate is notified of hearings and other proceedings concerning the case to which he is assigned. (1990, c. 752, § 9-173.9; 2001, c. 844.)

§ 9.1-156. Inspection and copying of records by advocate; confidentiality of records. — A. Upon presentation by the advocate of the order of his appointment and upon specific court order, any state or local agency, department, authority, or institution, and any hospital, school, physician, or other health or mental health care provider shall permit the advocate to inspect and copy, without the consent of the child or his parents, any records relating to the child involved in the case. Upon the advocate presenting to the mental health provider the order of the advocate's appointment and, upon specific court order, in lieu of the advocate inspecting and copying any related records of the child involved, the mental health care provider shall be available within seventy-two hours to conduct for the advocate a review and an interpretation of the child's treatment records which are specifically related to the investigation.

B. An advocate shall not disclose the contents of any document or record to which he becomes privy, which is otherwise confidential pursuant to the provisions of this Code, except upon order of a court of competent jurisdiction. (1990, c. 752, §§ 9-173.11, 9-173.12; 1995, c. 490; 2001, c. 844.)

§ 9.1-157. Cooperation of state and local entities. — All state and local departments, agencies, authorities, and institutions shall cooperate with the Department and with each local court-appointed special advocate program to facilitate its implementation of the Program. (1990, c. 752, § 9-173.13; 2001, c. 844.)

ARTICLE 6.

Crime Prevention Programs.

§ 9.1-158. Crime Prevention Center; purpose. — The Department shall establish a Crime Prevention Center for the purpose of providing crime prevention assistance and training, resource material, and research into methods and procedures to reduce the opportunity for crime. (1994, cc. 60, 868, § 9-173.16; 2001, c. 844.)

§ 9.1-159. Creation of McGruff House Program; duties of Department. — The symbol of "McGruff" with the phrase "McGruff House" shall be the symbol used to designate a house in the Commonwealth where a child who is abused, neglected or otherwise emotionally or physically in danger may seek refuge and assistance.

The Department shall adopt a standard symbol to be used throughout the Commonwealth which is the same as or substantially similar to the McGruff House symbol in use in other states. The Department shall establish by regulation appropriate procedures governing (i) qualifications and criteria for designation as a McGruff House and participants' duties and responsibilities, including the reporting of incidents to the local law-enforcement agency and department of social services' child-protective services program, (ii) programs to publicize the McGruff House Program, (iii) dissemination of the McGruff House symbol to day-care centers, schools, and law-enforcement agencies, (iv) designation and registration of McGruff Houses with, and monitoring and periodic review of such houses by, local law-enforcement agencies, and (v) coordination of the program with the child-protective services component of the local department of social services.

Nothing in this section shall prohibit the use of a symbol other than "McGruff" by a locality which currently has some other safe house program in existence and operation. (1994, cc. 60, 868, § 9-173.17; 2001, c. 844.)

§ 9.1-160. Designation of McGruff House; application; penalty. — All persons displaying the McGruff House symbol so that it is visible from the outside of their house shall first apply for designation as a McGruff House with a local law-enforcement agency. Upon receipt of an application for designation, the local law-enforcement agency shall conduct a background check of the applicant in accordance with Chapter 23 (§ 19.2-387 et seq.) of Title 19.2 and Department regulations at no charge to the applicant. Any background checks of applicants for this program conducted by the Department of Social Services through the Child Abuse Registry shall be done at no charge. Upon finding that the applicant meets the criteria established by the Department for maintaining a McGruff House and receipt of a signed statement by the applicant agreeing to the terms and conditions of the McGruff House Program, the law-enforcement agency shall provide the applicant with the McGruff House symbol.

The McGruff House symbol shall remain the property of the local law-enforcement agency. Upon a determination by the issuing law-enforcement agency that a house no longer meets the established criteria for a McGruff House, the symbol shall promptly be returned to the issuing law-enforcement agency.

Failure to return the symbol promptly after receipt of a written request to do so, which shall state the reason for the request, shall be subject to a civil penalty of up to $100. Persons not designated pursuant to this section to display the McGruff House symbol shall be subject to a civil penalty of up to $100. (1994, cc. 60, 868, § 9-173.18; 2001, c. 844.)

§ 9.1-161. Crime prevention specialists; duties. — The Board shall adopt regulations establishing minimum standards for certification of crime prevention specialists. Such regulations shall require that the chief law-enforcement officer of the locality or the campus police departments of institutions of higher education established by Chapter 17 (§ 23-232 et seq.) of Title 23 wherein the person serves shall approve the certification before a candidate for certification may serve as a crime prevention specialist. A crime prevention specialist shall have the duty to:

1. Provide citizens living within his jurisdiction information concerning personal safety and the security of property, and other matters relating to the reduction of criminal opportunity;

2. Provide business establishments within his jurisdiction information concerning business and employee security, and other matters relating to reduction of criminal activity;

3. Provide citizens and businesses within his jurisdiction assistance in forming and maintaining neighborhood and business watch groups and other community-based crime prevention programs;

4. Provide assistance to other units of government within his jurisdiction in developing plans and procedures related to the reduction of criminal activity within government and the community; and

5. Promote the reduction and prevention of crime within his jurisdiction and the Commonwealth. (1994, cc. 60, 868, § 9-173.19; 2001, c. 844; 2004, c. 466.)

§ 9.1-162. Eligibility for crime prevention specialists. — Any employee of a local, state or federal government agency who serves in a law-enforcement, crime prevention or criminal justice capacity is eligible to be trained and certified as a crime prevention specialist.

The chief executive of any local, state or federal government agency may designate one or more employees in his department or office, who serves in a law-enforcement, crime prevention or criminal justice capacity, to be trained and certified as a crime prevention specialist.

No person who is a candidate for certification shall serve as a crime prevention specialist unless his certification is approved by the chief law-enforcement officer of the locality wherein the person serves. (1994, cc. 60, 868, § 9-173.20; 2001, c. 844; 2002, c. 209; 2004, c. 466.)

ARTICLE 7.

Detoxification Programs.

§ 9.1-163. Definitions. — As used in this article, unless the context requires a different meaning:

"Detoxification center program" means any facility program or procedure for the placement of public inebriates as an alternative to arresting and jailing such persons, for the purpose of monitoring the withdrawal from excessive use of alcohol.

"Public inebriate" means any person who is drunk in a public place and would be subject to arrest for drunkenness under § 18.2-388 or local ordinance established for the same offense. (1982, c. 666, § 9-173.2; 2001, c. 844.)

§ 9.1-164. Establishment of programs; purpose; regulations; judicial approval of facilities. — A. It is the purpose of this article to enable any city, county, or combination thereof, to develop, establish, operate, maintain, or to contract with any qualified public or private agency for local or regional detoxification center programs, services, or facilities.

B. The Department shall adopt regulations for the implementation of such programs.

C. Detoxification center programs established or operated pursuant to this section shall be governed solely by the regulations adopted by the Department. The Department shall award funds as may be appropriated for such purposes to local units of government.

D. The chief judge of the general district court in the jurisdiction that will be served by the facility shall approve the facility for the diversion of public inebriates from arrest and jail pursuant to § 18.2-388. (1982, c. 666, § 9-173.1; 2001, c. 844.)

ARTICLE 8.

Law-Enforcement Expenditures.

§ 9.1-165. Definitions. — As used in this article, unless the context requires a different meaning:

"Adjusted crime index" means the potential crime rate for a locality multiplied by the base year population of the locality as estimated by the Center for Public Service.

"Average crime rate" for a city or eligible county means the annual average number of violent and property index crimes per 100,000 persons, as reported by the Superintendent of State Police, for the base year and the fiscal year immediately preceding, and the fiscal year immediately following, the base year. If the data are not available for the fiscal year immediately following the base year, the average shall be based on the base year and the two immediately preceding fiscal years.

"Base year" means the most recent fiscal year for which comparable data are available for: (i) population estimates by the Center for Public Service or the United States Bureau of the Census, adjusted for annexation as determined by the Department, (ii) actual state expenditures for salaries and expenses of sheriffs as reported by the Compensation Board, (iii) number of persons eligible for Temporary Assistance to Needy Families as defined in § 63.2-100, (iv) number of persons in foster care, as defined in § 63.2-100, and (v) the number of persons receiving maintenance payments in a general relief program as defined in § 63.2-100.

"Distribution formula" means that linear equation derived biennially by the Department, using standard statistical procedures, which best predicts average crime rates in all cities and eligible counties in the Commonwealth on the basis of the following factors in their simplest form:

1. The total base year number of (i) persons enrolled in Temporary Assistance to Needy Families, (ii) persons in foster care, and (iii) persons receiving maintenance payments in a general relief program, per 100,000 base year population; and

2. The local population density, based on the base year population estimates of the Center for Public Service, adjusted for annexation as determined by the Department, and the land area in square miles of the city or eligible county as reported by the United States Census Bureau, adjusted for annexation as determined by the Department.

"Eligible county" means any county which operates a police department.

"Police department" means that organization established by ordinance by a local governing body that is responsible for the prevention and detection of crime, the apprehension of criminals, the safeguard of life and property, the preservation of peace and the enforcement of state and local laws, regulations, and ordinances. Such department shall have a chief of police, which in the case of counties may be the sheriff, and such officers, privates, and other personnel as may be provided for in the ordinance, one sworn member of which shall be a full-time employee. All law-enforcement officers serving as members of such police department, whether full-time or part-time, and whether permanently or temporarily employed, shall meet the minimum training standards established pursuant to §§ 9.1-102 and 9.1-114, unless such personnel are exempt from the minimum training standards as provided in §§ 9.1-113 and 9.1-116. Any police department established subsequent to July 1, 1981, shall also have, at a minimum, one officer on duty at all times for the purposes set forth above.

However, notwithstanding any contrary provision of this definition,

1. Any locality receiving funds under this article during the 1980-82 biennium shall be considered to have a valid police department eligible for funds as long as such police department continues in operation;

2. Any town receiving funds under this article during the 1986-1988 biennium shall be considered to have a valid police department eligible for funds even though police services for such town may thereafter be provided by the sheriff of the county in which the town is located by agreement made pursuant to § 15.2-1726. Eligibility for funds under this subdivision shall last

as long as such agreement remains in effect. Police services for the town furnished by the sheriff shall be equal to or greater than the police services last furnished by the town's police department.

"Population served by police departments" means the total base year population of the Commonwealth less the population served by sheriffs only.

"Population served by sheriffs only" means the total base year population of those counties without a police department, less the latest available estimate from the United States Bureau of the Census of the total population of towns, or portions of towns, having police departments, located in such counties.

"Potential crime rate" means the number of crimes per 100,000 persons in the base year population for each city or eligible county, as derived from the distribution formula.

"State aid to localities with police" means that amount which bears the same relationship to the population served by police departments as state aid to sheriff-only localities bears to the population served by sheriffs only.

"State aid to sheriff-only localities" means the estimated total amount for salaries and expenses to be paid by the Commonwealth, pursuant to Article 3 (§ 15.2-1609 et seq.) of Chapter 16 of Title 15.2, to sheriffs' offices in those counties without a police department, based on the actual percentage of total state expenditures in the base year distributed to those counties without police departments. (1979, c. 83, § 14.1-84.2; 1981, c. 485; 1982, c. 600; 1984, c. 779; 1985, c. 140; 1989, cc. 84, 292; 1998, c. 872, § 9-183.14; 2001, c. 844.)

§ 9.1-166. Local governments to receive state funds for law enforcement. — The Department of the Treasury shall disburse funds to cities, towns and counties, to aid in the law-enforcement expenditures of those local governments, pursuant to the terms of this article. (1979, c. 83, § 14.1-84.1; 1981, c. 485; 1998, c. 872, § 9-183.13; 2001, c. 844.)

§ 9.1-167. Calculation of adjusted crime index; use. — By January 1 of each even-numbered year, the Department, using the relevant base year data, shall calculate the adjusted crime index for each city and each eligible county. Such calculation shall be used for the succeeding fiscal biennium adjusted for annexation as determined by the Department. (1979, c. 83, § 14.1-84.3; 1981, c. 485; 1989, c. 84; 1998, c. 872, § 9-183.15; 2001, c. 844.)

§ 9.1-168. Eligibility for funds. — A. Any city, county, or town establishing a police department shall provide the Department written notice of its intent to seek state funds in accordance with the provisions of this article. Such city, county, or town shall become eligible to receive funds at the beginning of the next fiscal year which commences not sooner than twelve months after the filing of this notice.

B. No city, county, or town shall receive any funds in accordance with the terms of this article unless it notifies the Department prior to July 1 each year that its law-enforcement personnel, whether full-time or part-time and whether permanently or temporarily employed, have complied with the minimum training standards as provided in §§ 9.1-102 and 9.1-114, unless such personnel are exempt from the minimum training standards as provided in §§ 9.1-113 and 9.1-116 or that an effort will be made to have its law-enforcement personnel comply with such minimum training standards during the ensuing fiscal year. Any city, county, or town failing to make an effort to comply with the minimum training standards may be declared ineligible for funding in the succeeding fiscal year by the Department.

C. A change in the form of government from city to tier-city shall not preclude the successor tier-city which continues to provide a police department from eligibility for funds.

D. Any county consolidated under the provisions of Chapter 35 (§ 15.2-3500 et seq.) of Title 15.2 shall be eligible to receive financial assistance for law-enforcement expenditures subject to the provisions of this article. The consolidated county shall be eligible to receive, on behalf of the formerly incorporated towns that became shires, boroughs or special service tax districts within the consolidated county, law-enforcement assistance under the provisions of this article, provided that the consolidation agreement approved pursuant to Chapter 35 (§ 15.2-3500 et seq.) of Title 15.2 provides for the additional law-enforcement governmental services previously provided by the police department of such incorporated towns. (1981, c. 485, § 14.1-84.6:1; 1982, c. 600; 1983, c. 4, § 14.1-84.6:2; 1984, cc. 695, 779; 1998, c. 872, §§ 9-183.19, 9-183.20; 2001, c. 844.)

§ 9.1-169. Total amount and method of distribution of funds to counties and cities. — A. The total amount of funds to be distributed as determined by the Department shall be equal to the amount of state aid to localities with police, as defined in § 9.1-165, minus (i) the salaries and expenses of sheriffs' offices in such cities and counties as estimated pursuant to Article 3 (§ 15.2-1609 et seq.) of Chapter 16 of Title 15.2 and (ii) five percent of the remainder, which shall be placed in a discretionary fund to be administered as specified in § 9.1-171. However, the percentage change in the total amount of funds to be distributed for any fiscal year from the preceding fiscal year shall be equal to the anticipated percentage change in total general fund revenue collections for the same time period as stated in the appropriation act.

B. Each city and eligible county shall receive a percentage of such total amount to be distributed equal to the percentage of the total adjusted crime index attributable to such city or county. Payments to the cities and eligible counties shall be made in equal quarterly installments by the State Treasurer on warrants issued by the Comptroller. Notwithstanding the foregoing provisions, the General Assembly, through the appropriation act, may appropriate specific dollar amounts to provide financial assistance to localities with police departments. (1979, c. 83, § 14.1-84.4; 1981, c. 485; 1986, c. 235; 1998, c. 872, § 9-183.16; 2001, c. 844.)

§ 9.1-170. Distribution of funds to towns. — A. Towns located in eligible counties and which have police departments shall receive a percentage of the funds distributed to the county in accordance with § 9.1-169, such percentage to be equal to the ratio of the town's population as determined by the Department to the total population of the county.

B. Towns located in noneligible counties shall be assigned an adjusted crime index based on their population and the average of the three lowest predicted crime rates for cities. Such towns shall receive funds based on such adjusted crime index in the same manner as cities and eligible counties as provided in § 9.1-169. (1979, c. 83, § 14.1-84.5; 1981, c. 485; 1998, c. 872, § 9-183.17; 2001, c. 844.)

§ 9.1-171. Distribution of discretionary fund. — In the case of a city with a population of more than 200,000 receiving per capita aid for law enforcement in accordance with § 9.1-169 of less than sixty-five percent of the average per capita aid to law enforcement received by all other cities with a population of more than 200,000 under such provisions, exclusive of amounts payable by reason of this section, the discretionary fund established by § 9.1-169 shall first be used to pay such city an aggregate sum so as to make its per capita receipts for law enforcement under § 9.1-169 equal to sixty-five percent of the average per capita aid for law enforcement disbursed to all other cities with a population of more than 200,000. The remainder, if any, shall be distributed per capita among (i) cities with populations under 200,000, (ii) eligible counties, and (iii) towns having police departments. (1979, c. 83, § 14.1-84.6; 1981, c. 485; 1998, c. 872, § 9-183.18; 2001, c. 844.)

§ **9.1-172. Periodic determination of weights and constants.** — Prior to the convening of the General Assembly in each even-numbered year, the Department shall determine whether the variables incorporated in the equation used in the distribution formula are statistically acceptable for such computation, and to determine whether any other variables would be better predictors of crime. If, as a result of this research, the Department determines that the variables used in the equation should be changed, it shall recommend to the General Assembly appropriate legislation to accomplish this change. (1979, c. 83, § 14.1-84.7; 1981, c. 485; 1998, c. 872, § 9-183.21; 2001, c. 844.)

ARTICLE 9.

Comprehensive Community Corrections Act for Local-Responsible Offenders.

§ **9.1-173. Purpose.** — It is the purpose of this article to enable any city, county or combination thereof to develop, establish and maintain local community-based probation programs to provide the judicial system with sentencing alternatives for certain misdemeanants or persons convicted of felonies that are not felony acts of violence, as defined in § 19.2-297.1 and sentenced pursuant to § 19.2-303.3, for whom the court imposes a sentence of twelve months or less and who may require less than institutional custody.

The article shall be interpreted and construed so as to:

1. Allow individual cities, counties, or combinations thereof greater flexibility and involvement in responding to the problem of crime in their communities;

2. Provide more effective protection of society and to promote efficiency and economy in the delivery of correctional services;

3. Provide increased opportunities for offenders to make restitution to victims of crimes through financial reimbursement or community service;

4. Permit cities, counties or combinations thereof to operate and utilize local community-based probation programs and services specifically designed to meet the rehabilitative needs of selected offenders; and

5. Provide appropriate post-sentencing alternatives in localities for certain offenders with the goal of reducing the incidence of repeat offenders. (1980 c. 300, § 53.1-180; 1982, c. 636; 1983, c. 344; 1990, c. 578; 1992, c. 196; 1994, 2nd Sp. Sess., cc. 1, 2; 1995, cc. 502, 574; 1996, c. 568; 2000, c. 1040; 2001, c. 844; 2002, c. 491.)

Cross references. — As to the confidentiality of court records, see § 16.1-305. As to dissemination of juvenile record information, see § 19.2-389.1.

§ **9.1-174. Establishment of program.** — To facilitate local involvement and flexibility in responding to the problem of crime in their communities and to permit locally designed probation programs that will fit its needs, any city, county or combination thereof may, and any city, county or combination thereof that is required by § 53.1-82.1 to file a community-based corrections plan shall establish a system of community-based services pursuant to this article. This system is to provide alternative programs for (i) offenders who are convicted and sentenced pursuant to § 19.2-303.3 and who are considered suitable candidates for programs that require less than incarceration in a local correctional facility and (ii) defendants who are provided a deferred proceeding and placed on probation. Such programs and services may be provided by qualified public agencies or by qualified private agencies pursuant to appropriate contracts. (Code 1950, § 53-128.17; 1980, c. 300; 1982, c. 636, § 53.1-181; 1983, c. 344; 1992, c. 196; 1994, 2nd Sp. Sess., cc. 1, 2; 1995, cc. 502, 574; 1999, c. 372; 2000, c. 1040; 2001, c. 844; 2006, c. 883.)

The 2006 amendments. — The 2006 amendment by c. 883, in the first sentence, inserted "probation" and substituted "that" for "which" twice, in the second sentence, deleted "defendents and" preceding clause (i), added the clause (i) designation, in clause (i), inserted "are convicted or sentenced" and deleted "are convicted, sentenced and placed on probation services through a court" following "§ 19.2-303.3," added clause (ii), and inserted "by qualified" in the last sentence.

§ 9.1-175. Board to prescribe standards; biennial plan. — The Board shall approve standards as prescribed by the Department for the development, implementation, operation and evaluation of local community-based probation programs, services and facilities authorized by this article. Any city, county or combination thereof which establishes programs and provides services pursuant to this article shall submit a biennial criminal justice plan to the Department for review and approval. (Code 1950, § 53-128.18; 1980, c. 300; 1982, c. 636, § 53.1-182; 1994, 2nd Sp. Sess., cc. 1, 2; 1999, c. 372; 2000, c. 1040; 2001, c. 844; 2002, c. 491.)

§ 9.1-176. Mandated services; optional programs. — Any city, county or combination thereof that elects or is required to establish a local community-based probation program pursuant to this article shall provide to the judicial system the following programs and services as components of local probation supervision: community service; home incarceration with or without electronic monitoring; electronic monitoring; and substance abuse screening, assessment, testing and treatment. Additional programs and services, including, but not limited to, local day reporting center programs and services, local halfway house programs and services for the temporary care of adults placed on probation, and law-enforcement diversion into detoxification center programs, as defined in § 9.1-163, may be established by the city, county or combination thereof. (1994, 2nd Sp. Sess., cc. 1, 2, § 53.1-182.1; 1996, c. 569; 1997, c. 339; 1999, c. 372; 2000, c. 1040; 2001, c. 844; 2002, c. 491.)

§ 9.1-176.1. Duties and responsibilities of local probation officers. — A. Each local probation officer, for the localities served, shall:

1. Supervise and assist all local-responsible adult offenders, residing within the localities served and placed on local probation by any judge of any court within the localities served;

2. Ensure offender compliance with all orders of the court, including the requirement to perform community service;

3. Conduct, when ordered by a court, substance abuse screenings, or conduct or facilitate the preparation of assessments pursuant to state approved protocols;

4. Conduct, at his discretion, random drug and alcohol tests on any offender whom the officer has reason to believe is engaged in the illegal use of controlled substances or marijuana, or the abuse of alcohol or prescribed medication;

5. Facilitate placement of offenders in substance abuse education or treatment programs or other education or treatment programs based on the needs of the offender;

6. Seek a capias from any judicial officer in the event of failure to comply with conditions of probation or supervision on the part of any offender provided that noncompliance resulting from intractable behavior presents a risk of flight, or a risk to public safety or to the offender;

7. Seek a motion to show cause for offenders requiring a subsequent hearing before the court;

8. Provide information to assist any law-enforcement officer with the return to custody of defendants placed on supervision for which a capias has been sought; and

9. Keep such records and make such reports as required by the Department of Criminal Justice Services.

B. Each local probation officer may provide the following optional services, as appropriate and when available resources permit:

1. Supervise local-responsible adult offenders placed on home incarceration with or without home electronic monitoring as a condition of probation;

2. Investigate and report on any local-responsible adult offender and prepare or facilitate the preparation of any other screening, assessment, evaluation, testing or treatment required as a condition of probation;

3. Monitor placements of local-responsible adults who are required to perform court-ordered community service at approved work sites;

4. Assist the courts, when requested, by monitoring the collection of court costs, fines and restitution to the victims of crime for offenders placed on local probation; and

5. Collect supervision and intervention fees pursuant to § 9.1-182 subject to local approval and the approval of the Department of Criminal Justice Services. (2003, c. 142.)

§ 9.1-177. Form of oath of office for local probation officers. — Every local probation officer who is an employee of a local community-based probation agency, established by any city, county or combination thereof, or operated pursuant to this article, that provides probation and related services pursuant to the requirements of this article, shall take an oath of office as prescribed in § 49-1 before entering the duties of his office. The oath of office shall be taken before any general district or circuit court judge in any city or county that has established services for the judicial system pursuant to this article. (2000, c. 1040, § 53.1-182.1:1; 2001, c. 844.)

§ 9.1-177.1. Confidentiality of records of and reports on adult persons under investigation by or placed on probation supervision with a local community-based probation program. — A. Any investigation report, including a presentencing investigation report, prepared by a local probation officer is confidential and is exempt from the Virginia Freedom of Information Act (§ 2.2-3700 et seq.). Such reports shall be filed as a part of the case record. Such reports shall be made available only by court order and shall be sealed upon final order by the court; except that such reports shall be available upon request to (i) any criminal justice agency, as defined in § 9.1-101, of this or any other state or of the United States; (ii) any agency where the accused is referred for assessment or treatment; or (iii) counsel for the person who is the subject of the report.

B. Any report on the progress of an offender under the supervision or of a local community-based probation agency and any information relative to the identity of or inferring personal characteristics of an accused, including demographic information, diagnostic summaries, records of office visits, medical, substance abuse, psychiatric or psychological records or information, substance abuse screening, assessment and testing information, and other sensitive information not explicitly classified as criminal history record information, is exempt from the Virginia Freedom of Information Act (§ 2.2-3700 et seq.). However, such information may be disseminated to criminal justice agencies as defined in § 9.1-101 in the discretion of the custodian of these records. (2002, c. 769; 2003, c. 146; 2006, c. 289.)

The **2006 amendments.** — The 2006
amendment by c. 289 inserted "including a
presentencing investigation report" in the first
sentence of subsection A.

§ 9.1-178. Community criminal justice boards. — A. Each county or
city or combination thereof developing and establishing a local pretrial
services or a community-based probation program pursuant to this article
shall establish a community criminal justice board. Each county and city
participating in a local pretrial services or a community-based probation
program shall be represented on the community criminal justice board. In the
event that one county or city appropriates funds to the program as part of a
multijurisdictional effort, any other participating county or city shall be
considered to be participating in a program if such locality appropriates funds
to the program. Appointments to the board shall be made by each local
governing body. In cases of multijurisdictional participation, unless otherwise
agreed upon, each participating city or county shall have an equal number of
appointments. Boards shall be composed of the number of members established by a resolution or ordinance of each participating jurisdiction.

B. Each board shall include, at a minimum, the following members: a
person appointed by each governing body to represent the governing body; a
judge of the general district court; a circuit court judge; a juvenile and domestic
relations district court judge; one chief magistrate; one chief of police or the
sheriff in a jurisdiction not served by a police department to represent law
enforcement; an attorney for the Commonwealth; a public defender or an
attorney who is experienced in the defense of criminal matters; a sheriff or the
regional jail administrator responsible for jails serving those jurisdictions
involved in the local pretrial services and community-based probation program; a local educator; and a community services board administrator. Any
officer of the court appointed to a community criminal justice board pursuant
to this subsection may designate a member of his staff approved by the
governing body to represent him at meetings of the board. (Code 1950,
§ 53-128.19; 1980, c. 300; 1982, c. 636, § 53.1-183; 1983, c. 344; 1988, c. 557;
1994, 2nd Sp. Sess., cc. 1, 2; 1995, cc. 502, 574, 768; 1996, c. 342; 1997, c. 339;
2000, c. 1040; 2001, c. 593; 2001, c. 844; 2002, c. 491; 2004, c. 395.)

§ 9.1-179. Withdrawal from program. — Any participating city or county
may, at the beginning of any calendar quarter, by ordinance or resolution of its
governing body, notify the Director of the Department and, in the case of
multijurisdictional programs, the other member jurisdictions, of its intention
to withdraw from the local community-based probation program. Withdrawal
shall be effective as of the last day of the quarter in which the notice is given.
(Code 1950, § 53-128.20; 1980, c. 300; 1982, c. 636, § 53.1-184; 1994, 2nd Sp.
Sess., cc. 1, 2; 1995, cc. 502, 574; 2000, c. 1040; 2001, c. 844; 2002, c. 491.)

§ 9.1-180. Responsibilities of community criminal justice boards. —
On behalf of the counties, cities, or combinations thereof which they represent,
the community criminal justice boards shall have the responsibility to:

1. Advise on the development and operation of local pretrial services and
community-based probation programs and services pursuant to §§ 19.2-152.2
and 9.1-176 for use by the courts in diverting offenders from local correctional
facility placements;

2. Assist community agencies and organizations in establishing and modifying programs and services for offenders on the basis of an objective assessment of the community's needs and resources;

3. Evaluate and monitor community programs, services and facilities to
determine their impact on offenders;

4. Develop and amend the criminal justice plan in accordance with guidelines and standards set forth by the Department and oversee the development

and amendment of the community-based corrections plan as required by § 53.1-82.1 for approval by participating local governing bodies;

5. Review the submission of all criminal justice grants regardless of the source of funding;

6. Facilitate local involvement and flexibility in responding to the problem of crime in their communities; and

7. Do all things necessary or convenient to carry out the responsibilities expressly given in this article. (Code 1950, § 53-128.21; 1980, c. 300; 1982, c. 636, § 53.1-185; 1983, c. 344; 1991, c. 43; 1992, c. 740; 1994, 2nd Sp. Sess., cc. 1, 2; 1995, cc. 502, 574; 2000, c. 1040; 2001, c. 844; 2002, c. 491.)

§ 9.1-181. Eligibility to participate. — A. Any city, county, or combination thereof, which elects to, or is required to establish programs shall participate in a local community-based probation program by ordinance or resolution of its governing authority. In cases of multijurisdictional participation, each ordinance or resolution shall identify the chosen administrator and fiscal agent as set forth in § 9.1-183. Such ordinances or resolutions shall be provided to the Director of the Department, regardless of funding source for the established programs.

B. Any local community-based probation program established pursuant to this article shall be available as a sentencing alternative for persons sentenced to incarceration in a local correctional facility or who otherwise would be sentenced to incarceration and who would have served their sentence in a local or regional correctional facility. (1992, c. 196, § 53.1-185.1; 1994, 2nd Sp. Sess., cc. 1, 2; 2000, c. 1040; 2001, c. 844.)

§ 9.1-182. Funding; failure to comply; prohibited use of funds. — A. Counties and cities shall be required to establish a local community-based probation program under this article only to the extent funded by the Commonwealth through the general appropriation act.

B. The Department shall periodically review each program established under this article to determine compliance with the submitted plan and operating standards. If the Department determines that a program is not in substantial compliance with the submitted plan or standards, the Department may suspend all or any portion of financial aid made available to the locality for purposes of this article until there is compliance.

C. Funding shall be used for the provision of services and operation of programs and facilities but shall not be used for capital expenditures.

D. The Department, in conjunction with local boards, shall establish a statewide system of supervision and intervention fees to be paid by offenders participating in programs established under this article for reimbursement towards the costs of their supervision.

E. Any supervision or intervention fees collected by local programs established under this article shall be retained by the locality serving as fiscal agent and shall be utilized solely for program expansion and program development, or to supplant local costs of the program operation. Any program collecting such fees shall keep records of the collected fees, report the amounts to the locality serving as fiscal agent and make all records available to the community criminal justice board. Such fees shall be in addition to any other imposed on a defendant or offender as a condition of a deferred proceeding, conviction or sentencing by a court as required by general law. (1994, 2nd Sp. Sess., cc. 1, 2, § 53.1-185.2; 1995, cc. 502, 574, 768; 2000, c. 1040; 2001, c. 844.)

§ 9.1-183. City or county to act as administrator and fiscal agent. — Any single participating city or county shall act as the administrator and fiscal agent for the funds awarded for purposes of implementing a local pretrial services or community-based probation program. In cases of multijurisdictional participation, the governing authorities of the participating localities shall select one of the participating cities or counties, with its consent, to act as administrator and fiscal agent for the funds awarded for purposes of implementing the local pretrial services or community-based probation program on behalf of the participating jurisdictions.

The participating city or county acting as administrator and fiscal agent pursuant to this section may be reimbursed for the actual costs associated with the implementation of the local pretrial services or community-based probation program, including fiscal administration, accounting, payroll services, financial reporting, and auditing. Any costs must be approved by the community criminal justice board and reimbursed from those funds received for the operation of the local community-based probation program, and may not exceed one percent of those funds received in any single fiscal year. (1994, 2nd Sp. Sess., cc. 1, 2, § 53.1-185.3; 1995, cc. 502, 574; 1996, c. 969; 2000, c. 1040; 2001, c. 844.)

Cross references. — As to eligibility to participate in a program governed by the Comprehensive Community Corrections Act for Local-Responsible Offenders, see § 9.1-181.

CASE NOTES

Effect of good time credits on life sentence. — If an inmate is serving a life sentence, good time credits count only towards hastening his parole eligibility date, not his release date, since he has no release date and, once the inmate has become eligible for parole, additional good time credits have no further effect. Jennings v. Parole Bd., 61 F. Supp. 2d 462 (E.D. Va. 1999) (decided under former § 53.1-185.3).

ARTICLE 10.

Virginia Center for School Safety.

§ 9.1-184. Virginia Center for School Safety created; duties. — A. From such funds as may be appropriated, the Virginia Center for School Safety (the "Center") is hereby established within the Department. The Center shall:

1. Provide training for Virginia public school personnel in school safety and the effective identification of students who may be at risk for violent behavior and in need of special services or assistance;

2. Serve as a resource and referral center for Virginia school divisions by conducting research, sponsoring workshops, and providing information regarding current school safety concerns, such as conflict management and peer mediation, school facility design and technology, current state and federal statutory and regulatory school safety requirements, and legal and constitutional issues regarding school safety and individual rights;

3. Maintain and disseminate information to local school divisions on effective school safety initiatives in Virginia and across the nation;

4. Collect, analyze, and disseminate various Virginia school safety data, including school safety audit information submitted to it pursuant to § 22.1-279.8, collected by the Department;

5. Encourage the development of partnerships between the public and private sectors to promote school safety in Virginia;

6. Provide technical assistance to Virginia school divisions in the development and implementation of initiatives promoting school safety;

7. Develop a memorandum of understanding between the Commissioner of the Department of Criminal Justice Services and the Superintendent of Public Instruction to ensure collaboration and coordination of roles and responsibil-

ities in areas of mutual concern, such as school safety audits and crime prevention; and

8. Provide training for and certification of school security officers, as defined in § 9.1-101 and consistent with § 9.1-110.

B. All agencies of the Commonwealth shall cooperate with the Center and, upon request, assist the Center in the performance of its duties and responsibilities. (2000, c. 519, § 9-173.21; 2001, cc. 436, 440, 844; 2002, cc. 836, 868.)

Editor's note. — Acts 2000, c. 519, cl. 2, provided: "That the provisions of this act shall not become effective unless an appropriation effectuating the purposes of this act is included in the 2000 Appropriation Act, passed during the 2000 Session of the General Assembly and signed into law by the Governor." An appropriation was made in the 2000-2002 budget.

Acts 2001, cc. 436 and 440 amended former § 9-173.21, from which this section is derived. Pursuant to § 30-152, Acts 2001, cc. 436 and 440 have been given effect in this section as set out above. The 2001 amendments by cc. 436 and 440 are identical, and inserted "submitted to it pursuant to § 22.1-278.1 [now § 22.1-279.8]" in subdivision A 4, and inserted "development and" in subdivision A 6.

Acts 2002, cc. 836 and 868, cl. 2, as amended by Acts 2003, c. 617, cls. 1 and 2, provide: "That, with such funds as may be appropriated for such purpose, the training and employment standards required by § 9.1-184 shall be applicable to persons employed as school security officers on and after September 15, 2004."

ARTICLE 11.

Bail Bondsmen.

§ 9.1-185. Definitions. — As used in this article, unless the context requires a different meaning:

"Bail bondsman" means any person who is licensed by the Department who engages in the business of bail bonding and is thereby authorized to conduct business in all courts of the Commonwealth.

"Board" means the Criminal Justice Services Board.

"Certificate" means a certificate issued by a judge on or before June 30, 2005, pursuant to former § 19.2-152.1.

"Department" means the Department of Criminal Justice Services.

"Property bail bondsman" means a person licensed pursuant to this article who, for compensation, enters into a bond or bonds for others, whether as a principal or surety, or otherwise pledges real property, cash or certificates of deposit issued by a federally insured institution, or any combination thereof as security for a bond as defined in § 19.2-119 that has been posted to assure performance of terms and conditions specified by order of an appropriate judicial officer as a condition of bail.

"Surety bail bondsman" means a person licensed pursuant to this article who is also licensed by the State Corporation Commission as a property and casualty insurance agent, and who sells, solicits, or negotiates surety insurance as defined in § 38.2-121 on behalf of insurers licensed in the Commonwealth, pursuant to which the insurer becomes surety on or guarantees a bond, as defined in § 19.2-119, that has been posted to assure performance of terms and conditions specified by order of an appropriate judicial officer as a condition of bail. (2004, c. 460.)

The numbers for the sections contained in this article, §§ 9.1-185 to 9.1-185.18, were assigned by the Virginia Code Commission, the numbers in the 2004 act having been §§ 9.1-185 to 9.1-199.4.

Editor's note. — Acts 2004, c. 460, cl. 2, provides: "That the State Corporation Commission shall forward all surety bail bondsman licensing records in its custody to the Department of Criminal Justice Services by June 30, 2005."

Acts 2004, c. 460, cl. 3, provides: "That the Department of Criminal Justice Services shall promulgate regulations to implement the provisions of this act to be effective within 280 days of its enactment."

Acts 2004, c. 460, cl. 5, provides: "That the provisions of this act, except for § 16.1-77, shall become effective on July 1, 2005."

Acts 2004, c. 460, cl. 6, provides: "That the provisions of this act may result in a net increase in periods of imprisonment or commitment. Pursuant to § 30-19.1:4, the estimated amount of the necessary appropriation cannot be determined for periods of imprisonment in state adult correctional facilities and is $0 for periods of commitment to the custody of the Department of Juvenile Justice."

Effective date. — This article became effective July 1, 2005.

§ 9.1-185.1. Inapplicability of this article. — This article shall not apply to a person who does not receive profit or consideration for his services. (2004, c. 460.)

§ 9.1-185.2. Powers of the Criminal Justice Services Board relating to bail bondsmen. — The Board shall have full regulatory authority and oversight of property and surety bail bondsmen.

The Board shall adopt regulations that are necessary to ensure respectable, responsible, safe and effective bail bonding within the Commonwealth. The Board's regulations shall include but not be limited to regulations that (i) establish the qualifications of applicants for licensure and renewal under this article; (ii) examine, or cause to be examined, the qualifications of each applicant for licensure, including when necessary the preparation, administration, and grading of examinations; (iii) levy and collect nonrefundable fees for licensure and renewal that are sufficient to cover all expenses for administration and operation of a program of licensure; (iv) ensure continued competency and prevent deceptive or misleading practices by practitioners; (v) administer the regulatory system; (vi) provide for receipt of complaints concerning the conduct of any person whose activities are regulated by the Board; (vii) provide for investigations and appropriate disciplinary action if warranted; (viii) establish standards for professional conduct, solicitation, collateral received in the course of business, firearms training and usage, uniforms and identification, documentation and recordkeeping requirements, reporting requirements, and methods of capture for the recovery of bailees; and (ix) allow the Board to suspend, revoke or refuse to issue, reissue or renew a license for just cause. The Board shall not adopt compulsory, minimum, firearms training standards in excess of 24 hours per year for bail bondsmen. In adopting its regulations, the Board shall seek the advice of the Private Security Services Advisory Board established pursuant to § 9.1-143. (2004, c. 460.)

§ 9.1-185.3. Powers of Department of Criminal Justice Services relating to bail bondsmen. — A. In addition to the powers otherwise conferred upon it by law, the Department may (i) charge each applicant for licensure a nonrefundable fee as established by the Board to cover the costs of processing an application for licensure, enforcement of the regulations, and other costs associated with the maintenance of the program of regulation; (ii) charge nonrefundable fees for training, processing school certifications and enforcement of training standards; (iii) conduct investigations to determine the suitability of applicants for licensure; and (iv) conduct investigations to determine if any disciplinary actions against a licensed bondsman are warranted. For purposes of determining eligibility for licensure, the Department shall require the applicant to provide personal descriptive information to be forwarded, along with the applicant's fingerprints, to the Central Criminal Records Exchange for the purpose of conducting a Virginia criminal history records search. The Central Criminal Records Exchange shall forward the fingerprints and personal description to the Federal Bureau of Investigation for the purpose of obtaining a national criminal record check.

B. The Director or his designee may make an ex parte application to the circuit court for the city or county wherein evidence sought is kept or wherein a licensee does business for the issuance of a subpoena duces tecum in furtherance of the investigation of a sworn complaint within the jurisdiction of the Department or the Board to request production of any relevant records, documents and physical or other evidence of any person, partnership, association or corporation licensed or regulated by the Department pursuant to this article. The court may issue and compel compliance with such a subpoena upon a showing of reasonable cause. Upon determining that reasonable cause exists to believe that evidence may be destroyed or altered, the court may issue a subpoena duces tecum requiring the immediate production of evidence. Costs of the investigation and adjudication of violations of this article or Board regulations may be recovered. All costs recovered shall be deposited into the state treasury to the credit of the Bail Bondsman Regulatory Fund. Such proceedings shall be brought in the name of the Commonwealth by the Department in the circuit court of the city or county in which the unlawful act occurred or in which the defendant resides. The Director, or agents appointed by him, shall have the authority to administer oaths or affirmations for the purpose of receiving complaints and conducting investigations of violations of this article, or any regulation promulgated hereunder and to serve process issued by the Department or the Board. (2004, c. 460.)

§ **9.1-185.4. Limitations on licensure.** — A. In order to be licensed as a bail bondsman a person shall (i) be 18 years of age or older, (ii) have received a high school diploma or GED, and (iii) have successfully completed the bail bondsman exam required by the Board or successfully completed prior to July 1, 2005, a surety bail bondsman exam required by the State Corporation Commission under former § 38.2-1865.7.

B. The following persons are not eligible for licensure as bail bondsmen and may not be employed nor serve as the agent of a bail bondsman:

1. Persons who have been convicted of a felony within the Commonwealth, any other state, or the United States, who have not been pardoned, or whose civil rights have not been restored;

2. Employees of a local or regional jail;

3. Employees of a sheriff's office;

4. Employees of a state or local police department;

5. Persons appointed as conservators of the peace pursuant to Article 4.1 (§ 9.1-150.1 et seq.) of this chapter;

6. Employees of an office of an attorney for the Commonwealth;

7. Employees of the Department of Corrections, Department of Criminal Justice Services, or a local community corrections agency; and

8. Spouses of or any persons residing in the same household as persons referred to in subdivisions 2 through 7 of this section.

C. The exclusions in subsection B shall not be construed to limit the ability of a licensed bail bondsman to employ or contract with a licensed bail enforcement agent authorized to do business in the Commonwealth. (2004, c. 460.)

§ **9.1-185.5. Bail bondsman licensure requirements.** — A. An applicant for a bail bondsman license shall apply for such license in a form and manner prescribed by the Board, and containing any information the Board requires.

B. Prior to the issuance of any bail bondsman license, each bondsman applicant shall:

1. File with the Department an application for such license on the form and in the manner prescribed by the Board.

2. Pass the bail bondsman exam as prescribed by the Board pursuant to this article or have successfully completed a surety bail bondsman exam as required by the State Corporation Commission under former § 38.2-1865.7. Any applicant who improperly uses notes or other reference materials, or otherwise cheats on the exam, shall be ineligible to become a licensed bail bondsman.

3. Submit to fingerprinting by a local or state law-enforcement agency and provide personal descriptive information to be forwarded, along with the applicant's fingerprints, to the Department of State Police Central Criminal Records Exchange. The Central Criminal Records Exchange shall forward the applicant's fingerprints and personal descriptive information to the Federal Bureau of Investigation for the purpose of obtaining national criminal history record information regarding such applicant. The applicant shall pay for the cost of such fingerprinting and criminal records check. The Department of State Police shall forward to the Director of the Department, or his designee, who shall be a governmental entity, the results of the records search from the Central Criminal Records Exchange and the Federal Bureau of Investigation. The Director of the Department, or his designee, who shall be a governmental entity, shall review the record and if the report indicates a prior felony conviction, the individual shall be prohibited from pursuing the application process for issuance of a bail bondsman license unless the individual submits proof that his civil rights have been restored by the Governor or other appropriate authority.

4. Submit the appropriate nonrefundable application processing fee to the Department.

C. Additionally, prior to the issuance of a property bail bondsman license, each property bail bondsman applicant shall provide proof of collateral of $200,000 on his bonds and proof of collateral of $200,000 on the bonds of each of his agents. Any collateral that is not in the form of real estate, cash, or certificates of deposit issued by a FDIC-insured financial institution shall be specifically approved by the Department before it may be used as collateral.

1. If the property used as collateral is real estate, such real estate shall be located in the Commonwealth. In addition, the property bail bondsman applicant shall submit to the Department:

a. A true copy of the current real estate tax assessment thereof, certified by the appropriate assessing officer of the locality wherein such property is located or, at the option of the property bail bondsman, an appraisal of the fair market value of the real estate, which appraisal shall have been prepared by a licensed real estate appraiser, within one year of its submission.

b. A new appraisal, if, at its discretion, the Department so orders for good cause shown prior to certification. At the discretion of the Department, after the original submission of any property appraisal or tax assessment, further appraisals or tax assessments for that property may not be required more than once every five years.

c. An affidavit by the property bail bondsman applicant that states, to the best of such person's knowledge, the amount of equity in the real estate, and the amounts due under any obligations secured by liens or similar encumbrances against the real estate, including any delinquent taxes, as of the date of the submission. At its discretion, the Department may require additional documentation to verify these amounts.

2. If the property used as collateral consists of cash or certificates of deposit, the property bail bondsman applicant shall submit to the Department verification of the amounts, and the names of the financial institution in which they are held.

3. Any property bail bondsman issued a certificate by a judge pursuant to former § 19.2-152.1, prior to July 1, 1989, who has continuously maintained

his certification and who has never provided to a court collateral of $200,000 or more, shall continue to be exempt from the $200,000 collateral requirements specified above. Those property bail bondsmen who are exempted from this provision shall satisfy all of the other requirements in this article for bail bondsmen, and shall provide to the Department the collateral amount to which they may bond and provide proof of his prior certification by obtaining a certified copy of: (i) the certificate issued pursuant to former § 19.2-152.1 and (ii) the documents held by the originating court that stated the collateral amount for which they were able to bond.

4. Each property bail bondsman, if so directed by the Department, shall place a deed of trust on the real estate that he is using for the limit of his expected bonded indebtedness to secure the Commonwealth and shall name the attorney for the Commonwealth of the affected locality as trustee under the deed of trust, and furnish the Department an acceptable appraisal and title certificate of the real estate subject to any such deed of trust.

D. Prior to the issuance of a surety bail bondsman license, each surety bail bondsman applicant shall:

1. Submit proof of current licensing as a property and casualty insurance agent validated by the State Corporation Commission.

2. Submit copies of each qualifying power of attorney that will be used to provide surety. All qualifying powers of attorney filed with the Department shall contain the name and contact information for both the surety agent and the registered agent of the issuing company. In the event an applicant for a surety bail bondsman license is unable to obtain a qualifying power of attorney prior to the issuance of his license, he may be granted his license, on the condition that each qualifying power of attorney obtained after his licensure be filed with the Department within 30 days after its receipt. A surety bail bondsman shall not be permitted to write bail bonds for any insurance company without first filing the company qualifying power of attorney with the Department.

3. All surety bail bondsman licenses in effect with the State Corporation Commission shall become void after June 30, 2005. Applicants for licensure for bail bondsmen may submit an application to the Department on or after May 1, 2005.

4. Any surety bail bondsman license issued pursuant to this article shall terminate immediately upon the termination of the licensee's property and casualty insurance agent license, and may not be applied for again until the individual has been issued a new property and casualty insurance agent license. Upon notification from the State Corporation Commission of a license suspension, the Department shall immediately suspend a surety bondsman's license, pending the results of an investigation conducted pursuant to this article. In the event a surety bail bondsman is under investigation by the State Corporation Commission for allegations regarding his activities as a licensed property and casualty agent, the Commission shall notify the Department of such investigation and the Department and the Commission may conduct a joint investigation of the individual. All powers granted to the Department and the Commission regarding investigation and disciplinary proceedings shall be permitted to be applied to any such joint investigation, and both the Department and the Commission shall be permitted to utilize their own rules and internal procedures in determining appropriate disciplinary proceedings, if any. (2004, c. 460.)

§ **9.1-185.6. Licenses; renewal.** — A. A license granted to a bondsman by the Department shall authorize such person to enter into bonds, as defined in § 19.2-119, in any county or city in the Commonwealth.

B. Every bail bondsman license issued pursuant to this article shall be for a term of two years.

C. A bail bondsman license may be renewed for an ensuing two-year period, upon the filing of an application in the form prescribed by the Department and payment of the nonrefundable renewal application processing fee prescribed by the Department. In addition, applicants for renewal of a bail bondsman license shall undergo a criminal history background check as set out in subdivision B 3 of § 9.1-185.5 and shall provide all other documentation listed in subsections C and D of § 9.1-185.5 as the Department deems appropriate.

D. On or before the first day of the month prior to the month his license is due to expire, the licensee shall make application for license renewal and shall at that time pay the renewal application fee.

E. Any license not renewed by its expiration date shall terminate on such date. (2004, c. 460.)

§ **9.1-185.7. Licensure of nonresidents.** — A. All nonresident transfers and applicants for a bail bondsman license shall satisfy all licensing requirements for residents of the Commonwealth.

B. For the purposes of this article, any individual whose physical place of residence and physical place of business are in a county or city located partly within the Commonwealth and partly within another state may be considered as meeting the requirements as a resident of the Commonwealth, provided the other state has established by law or regulation similar requirements as to residence of such individuals. (2004, c. 460.)

§ **9.1-185.8. Professional conduct standards; grounds for disciplinary actions.** — A. Any violations of the restrictions or standards under this statute shall be grounds for placing on probation, refusal to issue or renew, sanctioning, suspension or revocation of the bail bondsman's license. A licensed bail bondsman is responsible for ensuring that his employees, partners and individuals contracted to perform services for or on behalf of the bonding business comply with all of these provisions, and do not violate any of the restrictions that apply to bail bondsmen. Violations by a bondsman's employee, partner, or agent may be grounds for disciplinary action against the bondsman, including probation, suspension or revocation of license.

B. A licensed bail bondsman shall not:

1. Knowingly commit, or be a party to, any material fraud, misrepresentation, concealment, conspiracy, collusion, forgery, scheme or device whereby any other person lawfully relies upon the word, representation, or conduct of the bail bondsman.

2. Solicit sexual favors or extort additional consideration as a condition of obtaining, maintaining, or exonerating bail bond, regardless of the identity of the person who performs the favors.

3. Conduct a bail bond transaction that demonstrates bad faith, dishonesty, coercion, incompetence, extortion or untrustworthiness.

4. Coerce, suggest, aid and abet, offer promise of favor, or threaten any person on whose bond he is surety or offers to become surety, to induce that person to commit any crime.

5. Give or receive, directly or indirectly, any gift of any kind to any nonelected public official or any employee of a governmental agency involved with the administration of justice, including but not limited to law-enforcement personnel, magistrates, judges, and jail employees, as well as attorneys. De minimis gifts, not to exceed $50 per year per recipient, are acceptable, provided the purpose of the gift is not to directly solicit business, or would otherwise be a violation of Board regulations or the laws of the Commonwealth.

6. Fail to comply with any of the statutory or regulatory requirements governing licensed bail bondsmen.

7. Fail to cooperate with any investigation by the Department.

8. Fail to comply with any subpoena issued by the Department.

9. Provide materially incorrect, misleading, incomplete or untrue information in a license application, renewal application, or any other document filed with the Department.

10. Provide bail for any person if he is also an attorney representing that person.

11. Provide bail for any person if the bondsman was initially involved in the arrest of that person.

C. A licensed bail bondsman shall ensure that each recognizance on all bonds for which he signs shall contain the name and contact information for both the surety agent and the registered agent of the issuing company.

D. An administrative fee may be charged by a bail bondsman, not to exceed reasonable costs. Reasonable costs may include, but are not limited to, travel, court time, recovery fees, phone expenses, administrative overhead and postage.

E. A property bail bondsman shall not enter into any bond if the aggregate of the penalty of such bond and all other bonds, on which he has not been released from liability, is in excess of the true market value of the equity in his real estate, cash or certificates of deposit issued by a federally insured institution, or any combination thereof.

F. A property bail bondsman or his agent shall not refuse to cover any forfeiture of bond against him or refuse to pay such forfeiture after notice and final order of the court.

G. A surety bail bondsman shall not write bail bonds on any qualifying power of attorney for which a copy has not been filed with the Department.

H. A surety bail bondsman shall not violate any of the statutes or regulations that govern insurance agents. (2004, c. 460.)

§ 9.1-185.9. Solicitation of business; standards; restrictions and requirements.

§ 9.1-185.9. Solicitation of business; standards; restrictions and requirements. — A. Only licensed bail bondsmen shall be authorized to solicit bail bond business in the Commonwealth.

B. A licensed bail bondsman shall not:

1. Solicit bail bond business by directly initiating contact with any person in any court, jail, lock-up, or surrounding government property.

2. Loiter by any jail or magistrate's office unless there on legitimate business.

3. Refer a client or a principal for whom he has posted bond to an attorney for financial profit or other consideration.

C. The Board shall adopt regulations as to what constitutes impermissible solicitations by bondsmen, their employees and agents. (2004, c. 460.)

§ 9.1-185.10. Collateral received in the course of business; standards and requirements.

§ 9.1-185.10. Collateral received in the course of business; standards and requirements. — A. A licensed bail bondsman shall be permitted to accept collateral security or other indemnity from the principal, which shall be returned upon final termination of liability on the bond, including the conclusion of all appeals or appeal periods. Such collateral security or other indemnity required by the bail bondsman shall be reasonable in relation to the amount of the bond.

B. When a bondsman accepts collateral, he shall give a written receipt to the depositor. The receipt shall provide a full description of the collateral received and the terms of redemption or forfeiture. The receipt shall also include the depositor's name and contact information.

C. Any bail bondsman who receives collateral in connection with a bail transaction shall receive such collateral in a fiduciary capacity, and prior to any forfeiture of bail shall keep it separate and apart from any other funds or assets of such bail bondsman. In the event a bondsman receives collateral in the nature of a tangible good, it shall be a per se violation of the bail bondsman's fiduciary duty to make personal use of any such collateral unless there is a proper forfeiture of bail.

D. Any collateral received shall be returned with all due diligence to the person who deposited it with the bail bondsman or any assignee other than the bail bondsman as soon as the obligation is discharged and all fees owed to the bail bondsman have been paid. In any event, after a specific request for the return of the collateral by the depositor, the collateral shall be returned within 15 days after all fees owed have been paid. (2004, c. 460.)

§ 9.1-185.11. Firearms, training and usage; standards and requirements. — A. If a bail bondsman chooses to carry a firearm in the course of his duties, he shall be required to:

1. First complete basic firearms training, as defined by the Board; and
2. Receive ongoing in-service firearms training, as defined by the Board.

B. In the event a bail bondsman discharges a firearm during the course of his duties, he shall report it to the Department within 24 business hours. (2004, c. 460.)

§ 9.1-185.12. Uniforms and identification; standards and restrictions. — A. A bail bondsman shall not wear, carry, or display any uniform, badge, shield, or other insignia or emblem that implies he is an agent of state, local, or federal government.

B. A bail bondsman shall wear or display only identification issued by, or whose design has been approved by, the Department. (2004, c. 460.)

§ 9.1-185.13. Documentation and recordkeeping standards and requirements. — A. The bail bondsman shall retain, for a minimum of the three calendar years from the date of the termination of the liability:

1. Copies of all written representations made to any court or to any public official for the purpose of avoiding a forfeiture of bail, setting aside a forfeiture, or causing a defendant to be released on his own recognizance.
2. Copies of all affidavits and receipts made in connection with collateral received in the course of business.
3. Evidence of the return of any security or collateral received in the course of business, including a copy of the receipt showing when and to whom the collateral was returned.

B. Upon request of the Department, a bail bondsman shall provide any documents required to be kept pursuant to this section. (2004, c. 460.)

§ 9.1-185.14. Reporting standards and requirements. — A. Each licensed bail bondsman shall report within 30 calendar days to the Department any change in his residence, name, business name or business address, and ensure that the Department has the names and all fictitious names of all companies under which he carries out his bail bonding business.

B. Each licensed bail bondsman convicted of a felony shall report within 30 calendar days to the Department the facts and circumstances regarding the criminal conviction.

C. Each licensed bail bondsman shall report to the Department within 30 calendar days of the final disposition of the matter any administrative action taken against him by another governmental agency in the Commonwealth or in another jurisdiction. Such report shall include a copy of the order, consent to order or other relevant legal documents.

D. Each licensed property bail bondsman shall submit to the Department, on a prescribed form, not later than the fifth day of each month, a list of all outstanding bonds on which he was obligated as of the last day of the preceding month, together with the amount of the penalty of each such bond.

E. Each licensed property bail bondsman shall report to the Department any change in the number of agents in his employ within seven days of such change and concurrently provide proof of collateral of $200,000 for each new agent, in accordance with subsection C of § 9.1-185.5.

F. Each licensed surety bail bondsman shall report to the Department within 30 days any change in his employment or agency status with a licensed insurance company. If the surety bail bondsman receives a new qualifying power of attorney from an insurance company, he shall forward a copy thereof within 30 days to the Department, in accordance with subdivision D 2 of § 9.1-185.5.

G. Each licensed property bail bondsman shall report to the Department within five business days if any new lien, encumbrance, or deed of trust is placed on any real estate that is being used as collateral on his or his agents' bonds as well as the amount it is securing. The reporting requirement deadline is deemed to begin as soon as the licensed property bail bondsman learns of the new lien, encumbrance, or deed of trust, or should have reasonably known that such a lien, encumbrance, or deed of trust had been recorded. (2004, c. 460.)

§ 9.1-185.15. Recovery of bailees; methods of capture; standards and requirements; limitations. — A. During the recovery of a bailee, a bail bondsman shall have a copy of the relevant recognizance for the bailee. In the event a bail bondsman is recovering the bailee of another bondsman, he shall also have written authorization from the bailee's bondsman, obtained prior to effecting the capture. The Department shall develop the written authorization form to be used in such circumstances.

B. A bail bondsmen shall not enter a residential structure without first verbally notifying the occupants who are present at the time of the entry.

C. Absent exigent circumstances, a bail bondsman shall give prior notification of at least 24 hours to local law enforcement or state police of the intent to apprehend a bailee. In all cases, a bail bondsman shall inform local law enforcement within 30 minutes of capturing a bailee.

D. A bail bondsman shall not break any laws of the Commonwealth in the act of apprehending a bailee. (2004, c. 460.)

§ 9.1-185.16. Department submission to the State Corporation Commission. — A. The Department shall provide to the State Corporation Commission a list of all newly licensed surety bondsmen each month.

B. When the Department terminates a surety bail bondsman's license, the Department shall immediately notify the State Corporation Commission of the surety bail bondsman's termination and the reason for such termination. (2004, c. 460.)

§ 9.1-185.17. Department submissions to local and regional correctional facilities. — Once a year, the Department shall provide to each local and regional correctional facility a list of all licensed bail bondsmen in the Commonwealth. The list shall consist of each bondsman's individual name, the name of the bondsman's business and the address where the bondsman's office is physically located. The Department shall update the list monthly and have the list available on its website. (2004, c. 460.)

§ 9.1-185.18. Penalties. — It shall be a Class 1 misdemeanor to engage in bail bonding for profit or other consideration without a valid license issued by the Department in this Commonwealth. A third conviction shall be a Class 6 felony.

Any person licensed by the Board pursuant to this article who violates any statute or Board regulation who is not criminally prosecuted shall be subject to the monetary penalty provided in this section. If the Board determines that a respondent has committed the violation complained of, the Board shall determine the amount of the monetary penalty for the violation, which shall not exceed $2,500 for each violation. The penalty may be sued for and recovered in the name of the Commonwealth. (2004, c. 460.)

Cross references. — As to punishment for Class 6 felonies, see § 18.2-10. As to punishment for Class 1 misdemeanors, see § 18.2-11.

ARTICLE 12.

Bail Enforcement Agents.

The number of this article was assigned by the Virginia Code Commission, the number in the 2004 act having been Article 11.

§ 9.1-186. Definitions. — As used in this chapter, unless the context requires a different meaning:

"Bail enforcement agent," also known as *"bounty hunter,"* means any individual engaged in bail recovery.

"Bail recovery" means an act whereby a person arrests a bailee with the object of surrendering the bailee to the appropriate court, jail, or police department, for the purpose of discharging the bailee's surety from liability on his bond. "Bail recovery" shall include investigating, surveilling or locating a bailee in preparation for an imminent arrest, with such object and for such purpose.

"Bailee" means a person who has been released on bail, and who is or has been subject to a bond, as defined in § 19.2-119.

"Board" means the Criminal Justice Services Board.

"Department" means the Department of Criminal Justice Services. (2004, c. 397.)

The numbers for the sections contained in this article, §§ 9.1-186 to 9.1-186.14, were assigned by the Virginia Code Commission, the numbers in the 2004 act having been §§ 9.1-185 to 9.1-199.

Editor's note. — Acts 2004, c. 397, cl. 2, provides: "That the provisions of this act, except for § 9.1-186.14, shall become effective on October 1, 2005."

Acts 2004, c. 397, cl. 3, provides: "That the Board shall promulgate regulations to implement the provisions of this act to be effective within 280 days of its enactment."

Acts 2004, c. 397, cl. 4, provides: "That the provisions of this act may result in a net increase in periods of imprisonment or commitment. Pursuant to § 30-19.1:4, the estimated amount of the necessary appropriation cannot be determined for periods of imprisonment in state adult correctional facilities and is $0 for periods of commitment to the custody of the Department of Juvenile Justice."

Effective date. — This article became effective October 1, 2005.

§ 9.1-186.1. Inapplicability of article. — The provisions of this article shall not apply to licensed bail bondsmen nor to law-enforcement officers. (2004, c. 397.)

§ 9.1-186.2. Powers of Department and Board relating to bail enforcement agents. — A. The Board shall have full regulatory authority and oversight of bail enforcement agents.

B. The Board shall adopt regulations establishing compulsory minimum, entry-level and in-service training and education for bail enforcement agents. The regulations may include provisions allowing the Department to inspect the facilities and programs of persons conducting training to ensure compliance with the law and regulations. In establishing compulsory training standards for bail enforcement agents, the Board shall ensure the public safety and welfare against incompetent or unqualified persons engaging in the activities regulated by this article. The regulations may provide for exemption from training of persons having previous employment as law-enforcement officers for a local, state or the federal government. However, no such exemption shall be granted for any person whose employment as a law-enforcement officer was terminated because of his misconduct or incompetence. The regulations may include provisions for partial exemption from such training for persons having previous training that meets or exceeds the minimum training standards and has been approved by the Department.

C. The Board shall adopt regulations that are necessary to ensure respectable, responsible, safe and effective bail enforcement within the Commonwealth and shall include but not be limited to regulations that: (i) establish qualifications of applicants for licensure and renewal under this article; (ii) examine, or cause to be examined, the qualifications of each applicant for licensure, including when necessary the preparation, administration, and grading of examinations; (iii) levy and collect nonrefundable fees for licensure and renewal that are sufficient to cover all expenses for administration and operation of a program of licensure; (iv) ensure continued competency and prevent deceptive or misleading practices by practitioners; (v) administer the regulatory system; (vi) provide for receipt of complaints concerning the conduct of any person whose activities are regulated by the Board; (vii) provide for investigations, and appropriate disciplinary action if warranted; (viii) establish professional conduct standards, firearms training and usage standards, uniform and identification standards, reporting standards, and standards for the recovery and capture of bailees; (ix) allow the Board to revoke, suspend or refuse to renew a license for just cause; and (x) establish an introductory training curriculum which includes search, seizure and arrest procedure, pursuit, arrest, detainment and transportation of a bailee, specific duties and responsibilities regarding entering an occupied structure, the laws and rules relating to the bail bond business, the rights of the accused, ethics and Virginia law and regulation. The Board shall adopt annual compulsory, minimum, firearms training standards for bail enforcement agents. In adopting its regulations, the Board shall seek the advice of the Private Security Services Advisory Board established pursuant to § 9.1-143. (2004, c. 397.)

§ 9.1-186.3. Powers of Department relating to bail enforcement agents. — A. In addition to the powers otherwise conferred upon it by law, the Department may charge each applicant for licensure or licensee a nonrefundable fee as established by the Board to (i) cover the costs of processing an application for licensure, enforcement of the regulations, and other costs associated with the maintenance of the program of regulation; (ii) cover the costs of bail recovery training, processing school certifications and enforcement of training standards; (iii) conduct investigations to determine the suitability of applicants for licensure and (iv) conduct investigations to determine if any disciplinary actions against a licensed bail enforcement agent are warranted. For purposes of determining eligibility for licensure, the Department shall require the applicant to provide personal descriptive information to be forwarded, along with the applicant's fingerprints, to the Central Criminal Records Exchange for the purpose of conducting a Virginia criminal history records search. The Central Criminal Records Exchange shall forward the fingerprints and personal description to the Federal Bureau of Investigation for the purpose of obtaining a national criminal record check.

B. The Director or his designee may make an ex parte application to the circuit court for the city or county wherein evidence sought is kept or wherein a licensee does business for the issuance of a subpoena duces tecum in furtherance of the investigation of a sworn complaint within the jurisdiction of the Department or the Board to request production of any relevant records, documents and physical or other evidence of any person, partnership, association or corporation licensed or regulated by the Department pursuant to this article. The court may issue and compel compliance with such a subpoena upon a showing of reasonable cause. Upon determining that reasonable cause exists to believe that evidence may be destroyed or altered, the court may issue a subpoena duces tecum requiring the immediate production of evidence. Costs of the investigation and adjudication of violations of this article or Board regulations may be recovered. All costs recovered shall be deposited into the state treasury to the credit of the Bail Enforcement Agent Regulatory Fund. Such proceedings shall be brought in the name of the Commonwealth by the Department in the circuit court of the city or county in which the unlawful act occurred or in which the defendant resides. The Director, or agents appointed by him, shall have the authority to administer oaths or affirmations for the purpose of receiving complaints and conducting investigations of violations of this article, or any regulation promulgated hereunder and to serve process issued by the Department or the Board. (2004, c. 397.)

§ **9.1-186.4. Limitations on licensure.** — A. In order to be licensed as a bail enforcement agent a person shall (i) be 21 years of age or older, (ii) have received a high school diploma or GED, and (iii) have satisfactorily completed a basic certification course in training for bail enforcement agents offered by the Department. Partial exemptions to the training requirements may be approved by the Department if the individual has received prior training.

B. The following persons are not eligible for licensure as a bail enforcement agent and may not be employed nor serve as agents for a bail enforcement agent:

1. Persons who have been convicted of a felony within the Commonwealth, any other state, or the United States, who have not been pardoned, or whose civil rights have not been restored.

2. Persons who have been convicted of any misdemeanor within the Commonwealth, any other state, or the United States within the preceding five years. This prohibition may be waived by the Department, for good cause shown, so long as the conviction was not for one of the following or a substantially similar misdemeanor: carrying a concealed weapon, assault and battery, sexual battery, a drug offense, driving under the influence, discharging a firearm, a sex offense, or larceny.

3. Persons who have been convicted of any misdemeanor within the Commonwealth, any other state, or the United States, that is substantially similar to the following: brandishing a firearm or stalking. The Department may not waive the prohibitions under this subdivision 3.

4. Persons currently the subject of a protective order within the Commonwealth or another state.

5. Employees of a local or regional jail.

6. Employees of a sheriff's office, or a state or local police department.

7. Commonwealth's Attorneys, and any employees of their offices.

8. Employees of the Department of Corrections, Department of Criminal Justice Services, or a local community corrections agency.

C. The exclusions in subsection B shall not be construed to prohibit law enforcement from accompanying a bail enforcement agent when he engages in bail recovery. (2004, c. 397.)

§ 9.1-186.5. Bail enforcement agent license; criminal history records check.

— A. An applicant for a bail enforcement license shall apply for such license in a form and manner prescribed by the Board, and containing any information the Board requires.

B. Prior to the issuance of any bail enforcement agent license, each applicant shall:

1. File with the Department an application for such license on the form and in the manner prescribed by the Board.

2. Complete the basic certification courses in training for bail enforcement agents required by the Department. Any applicant who improperly uses notes or other reference materials, or otherwise cheats in any course, shall be ineligible to become a licensed bail enforcement agent.

3. Submit the appropriate nonrefundable application processing fee to the Department.

4. Submit to fingerprinting by a local or state law-enforcement agency and provide personal descriptive information to be forwarded, along with the applicant's fingerprints, to the Department of State Police Central Criminal Records Exchange. The Central Criminal Records Exchange shall forward the applicant's fingerprints and personal descriptive information to the Federal Bureau of Investigation for the purpose of obtaining national criminal history record information regarding such applicant. The applicant shall pay for the cost of such fingerprinting and criminal records check. The Department of State Police shall forward it to the Director of the Department, or his designee, who shall be a governmental entity, who shall review the record, and if the report indicates a prior conviction listed in subsection B of § 9.1-186.4, the individual shall be prohibited from pursuing the application process for issuance of a bail enforcement agent license unless the individual submits proof that his civil rights have been restored by the Governor or other appropriate authority. (2004, c. 397.)

§ 9.1-186.6. Licenses; renewal.

— A. A license granted to a bail enforcement agent by the Department shall authorize such person to engage in the business of bail recovery.

B. Every bail enforcement agent license issued pursuant to this article shall be for a term of two years.

C. A bail enforcement agent license may be renewed for an ensuing two-year period, upon the filing of an application in the form prescribed by the Department and payment of the nonrefundable renewal application processing fee prescribed by the Department. In addition, applicants for renewal of a bail enforcement agent's license shall provide all other documentation as the Department deems appropriate, including but not limited to, a criminal history background check.

D. On or before the first day of the month prior to the month his license is due to expire, the licensee shall make application for license renewal and shall at that time pay the renewal application fee.

E. Any license not renewed by its expiration date shall terminate on such date.

F. Prior to license renewal, bail enforcement agents shall be required to complete eight hours of continuing education approved by the Department. (2004, c. 397.)

§ 9.1-186.7. Licensure of nonresidents.

— A. All nonresident transfers and applicants for a bail enforcement agent license shall satisfy all licensing requirements for residents of the Commonwealth.

B. For the purposes of this article, any individual whose physical place of residence and physical place of business are in a county or city located partly within the Commonwealth and partly within another state may be considered as meeting the requirements as a resident of the Commonwealth, provided the other state has established by law or regulation similar requirements as to residence of such individuals. (2004, c. 397.)

§ 9.1-186.8. Professional conduct standards; grounds for disciplinary actions. — A. Any violations of the restrictions or standards under subsection B shall be grounds for placing on probation, refusal to issue or renew, sanctioning, suspension or revocation of the bail enforcement agent's license. A licensed bail enforcement agent is responsible for ensuring that his employees, partners and individuals contracted to perform services for or on his behalf comply with all of these provisions, and do not violate any of the restrictions that apply to bail enforcement agents. Violations by a bail enforcement agent's employee, partner or agent may be grounds for disciplinary action against the bail enforcement agent, including probation, suspension, or revocation of license.

B. A licensed bail enforcement agent shall not:

1. Engage in any fraud or willful misrepresentation, or provide materially incorrect, misleading, incomplete or untrue information in applying for an original license, or renewal of an existing license, or in submitting any documents to the Department.

2. Use any letterhead, advertising, or other printed matter in any manner representing that he is an agent, employee, or instrumentality of the federal government, a state, or any political subdivision of a state.

3. Impersonate, permit or aid and abet any employee to impersonate, a law-enforcement officer or employee of the United States, any state, or a political subdivision of a state.

4. Use a name different from that under which he is currently licensed for any advertising, solicitation, or contract to secure business unless the name is an authorized fictitious name.

5. Coerce, suggest, aid and abet, offer promise of favor, or threaten any person to induce that person to commit any crime.

6. Give or receive, directly or indirectly, any gift of any kind to any nonelected public official or any employee of a governmental agency involved with the administration of justice, including but not limited to law-enforcement personnel, magistrates, judges, jail employees, and attorneys. De minimis gifts, not to exceed $50 per year per recipient, are acceptable, provided the purpose of the gift is not to directly solicit business, or would otherwise be a violation of Department regulations or the laws of the Commonwealth.

7. Knowingly violate, advise, encourage, or assist in the violation of any statute, court order, or injunction in the course of conducting activities regulated under this chapter.

8. Solicit business for an attorney in return for compensation.

9. Willfully neglect to render to a client services or a report as agreed between the parties and for which compensation has been paid or tendered in accordance with the agreement of the parties, but if the bail enforcement agent chooses to withdraw from the case and returns the funds for work not yet done, no violation of this section exists.

10. Fail to comply with any of the statutory or regulatory requirements governing licensed bail enforcement agents.

11. Fail or refuse to cooperate with any investigation by the Department.

12. Fail to comply with any subpoena issued by the Department.

13. Employ or contract with any unlicensed or improperly licensed person or agency to conduct activities regulated under this article, if the licensure status was known or could have been ascertained by reasonable inquiry.

14. Solicit or receive a bribe or other consideration in exchange for failing to recover or detain a bailee.

C. The Department shall have the authority to place on probation, suspend or revoke a bail enforcement agent's license if an agent is arrested or issued a summons for a criminal offense, or becomes the subject of a protective order. (2004, c. 397.)

§ 9.1-186.9. Firearms, training and usage; standards and requirements. — A. If a bail enforcement agent chooses to carry a firearm, either concealed or visible, in the course of his duties, he shall be required to:

1. First complete basic firearms training, as defined by the Board; and

2. Receive ongoing in-service firearms training, as defined by the Board.

B. In the event a bail enforcement agent discharges a firearm during the course of his duties, he shall report it to the Department within 24 business hours. (2004, c. 397.)

§ 9.1-186.10. Uniforms and identification; standards and restrictions. — A. A bail enforcement agent shall not wear, carry, or display any uniform, badge, shield, or other insignia or emblem that implies he is an agent of state, local, or federal government.

B. A bail enforcement agent shall wear or display only identification issued by, or whose design has been approved by, the Department. (2004, c. 397.)

§ 9.1-186.11. Reporting standards and requirements. — A. Each licensed bail enforcement agent shall report within 30 calendar days to the Department any change in his residence, name, or business name or business address, and ensure that the Department has the names and fictitious names of all companies under which he carries out his bail recovery business.

B. Each licensed bail enforcement agent arrested or issued a summons for any crime shall report such fact within 30 calendar days to the Department, and shall report to the Department within 30 days the facts and circumstances regarding the final disposition of his case.

C. Each licensed bail enforcement agent shall report to the Department within 30 calendar days of the final disposition any administrative action taken against him by another governmental agency in this Commonwealth or in another jurisdiction. Such report shall include a copy of the order, consent to order or other relevant legal documents. (2004, c. 397.)

§ 9.1-186.12. Recovery of bailees; methods of capture; standards and requirements; limitations. — A. During the recovery of a bailee, a bail enforcement agent shall have a copy of the relevant recognizance for the bailee. He shall also have written authorization from the bailee's bondsman, obtained prior to effecting the capture. The Department shall develop the written authorization form to be used in such circumstances.

B. A bail enforcement agent shall not enter the residence of another without first verbally notifying the occupants who are present at the time of entry.

C. Absent exigent circumstances, a bail enforcement agent shall give prior notification of at least 24 hours to local law enforcement or state police of the intent to apprehend a bailee. In all cases, a bail enforcement agent shall inform local law enforcement within 60 minutes of capturing a bailee.

D. A bail enforcement agent shall not break any laws of the Commonwealth in the act of apprehending a bailee. (2004, c. 397.)

§ 9.1-186.13. Penalties, criminal and monetary. — Any person who engages in bail recovery in the Commonwealth without a valid license issued by the Department is guilty of a Class 1 misdemeanor. A third conviction under this section is a Class 6 felony.

Any person who violates any statute or Board regulation who is not criminally prosecuted shall be subject to the monetary penalty provided in this section. If the Board determines that a respondent is guilty of the violation complained of, the Board shall determine the amount of the monetary penalty for the violation, which shall not exceed $2,500 for each violation. The penalty may be sued for and recovered in the name of the Commonwealth. (2004, c. 397.)

Cross references. — As to punishment for Class 6 felonies, see § 18.2-10. As to punishment for Class 1 misdemeanors, see § 18.2-11.

§ 9.1-186.14: Expired.

Editor's note. — Acts 2004, c. 397, cl. 2, provides: "That the provisions of this act, except for § 9.1-186.14, shall become effective on October 1, 2005."

CHAPTER 2.

DEPARTMENT OF FIRE PROGRAMS.

§ **9.1-200. Department of Fire Programs.** — There is created a Department of Fire Programs that shall be headed by a Director who shall be appointed by the Governor to serve at his pleasure. The Department shall be the designated state agency to receive and disburse any funds available to the Commonwealth under the Federal Fire Prevention and Control Act (P. L. 93-498). (1978, c. 606, § 9-153; 1980, c. 728; 1981, c. 154; 1984, c. 720; 2001, c. 844.)

Cross references. — As to compensation and expenses of boards, commissions and similar bodies, see §§ 2.2-2104, 2.2-2813.

Editor's note. — Acts 1981, c. 154, cl. 4, provides: "That all rules and regulations adopted by the Virginia State Fire Services Commission and the Office of Fire Service Training which are in effect as of the effective date of this act [July 1, 1982] and which pertain to the subject of this act, shall remain in full force and effect until altered, amended, or rescinded by the Department of Fire Programs."

The Federal Fire Prevention and Control Act (P.L. 93-498), referred to in this section, may be found in 15 U.S.C. §§ 278f and 2201 through 2223, and 42 U.S.C. § 290a.

§ **9.1-201. Powers of Executive Director.** — The Executive Director shall have the following powers to:
1. Supervise the administration of the Department;
2. Prepare, approve, and submit all requests for appropriations and be responsible for all expenditures pursuant to appropriations;
3. Employ such staff as is necessary to carry out the powers and duties of this chapter, within the limits of available appropriations;
4. Accept on behalf of the Department grants from the United States government and agencies and instrumentalities thereof and any other sources.

To these ends, the Executive Director shall have the power to execute such agreements in accordance with the policies of the Virginia Fire Services Board;

5. Do all acts necessary or convenient to carry out the purpose of this chapter and to assist the Board in carrying out its responsibilities and duties;

6. Make and enter into all contracts and agreements necessary or incidental to the performance of its duties and the execution of its powers under this chapter, including, but not limited to, contracts with the United States, other states, and agencies and governmental subdivisions of the Commonwealth;

7. Appoint a director of fire services training;

8. Receive funds as appropriated by the General Assembly collected pursuant to § 38.2-401, on an annual basis to be used as provided in subsection C of § 38.2-401; and

9. Administer the Thermal Imaging Camera Grant Funds established pursuant to § 9.1-205. (1978, c. 606, § 9-154; 1981, c. 154; 1985, cc. 397, 545; 2001, c. 844; 2002, c. 721.)

Editor's note. — Acts 2001, cc. 864 and 871, cl. 1 amended former § 9-154, from which this section was derived, by adding a subdivision 9, relating to a Thermal Imaging Camera Grant Fund. However, cl. 2 of cc. 864 and 871 provided: "That the provisions of this act shall not become effective unless an appropriation of general funds effectuating the purposes of this act is included in the 2001 Appropriation Act, passed during the 2001 Session of the General Assembly and signed into law by the Governor."

The appropriation was not made. Hence, the amendment by cc. 864 and 871 did not take effect.

Acts 2002, c. 721, cl. 2, provides: "That the provisions of this act shall not become effective unless an appropriation effectuating the purposes of this act is included in the 2002 Appropriation Act passed during the 2002 Session of the General Assembly and signed into law by the Governor." Money for this project was appropriated by Acts 2002, c. 899, Item 438.

§ 9.1-202. Virginia Fire Services Board; membership; terms; compensation. — A. The Virginia Fire Services Board (the Board) is established as a policy board within the meaning of § 2.2-2100 in the executive branch of state government. The Board shall consist of 15 members to be appointed by the Governor as follows: a representative of the insurance industry; two members of the general public with no connection to the fire services, one of whom shall be a representative of those industries affected by SARA Title III and OSHA training requirements; and one member each from the Virginia Fire Chief's Association, the Virginia Firemen's Association, the Virginia Association of Professional Firefighters, the Virginia Fire Service Council, the Virginia Fire Prevention Association, the State Chapter of the International Association of Arson Investigators, the Virginia Municipal League, and the Virginia Association of Counties, and a member of the Virginia Chapter of the International Society of Fire Service Instructors who is a faculty member who teaches fire science at a public institution of higher education. Of these appointees, at least one shall be a volunteer firefighter. The State Fire Marshal, the State Forester and a member of the Board of Housing and Community Development, appointed by the chairman of that Board shall also serve as members of the Board.

Each of the organizations represented shall submit names for the Governor's consideration in making these appointments.

B. Members of the Board appointed by the Governor shall serve for terms of four years. An appointment to fill a vacancy shall be for the unexpired term. No appointee shall serve more than two successive four-year terms but neither shall any person serve beyond the time he holds the office or organizational membership by reason of which he was initially eligible for appointment.

C. The Board annually shall elect its chairman and vice-chairman from among its membership and shall adopt rules of procedure.

D. Members of the Board shall receive such compensation for the performance of their duties as provided in § 2.2-2813. All members shall be reimbursed for all reasonable and necessary expenses incurred in the perfor- mance of their duties as provided in § 2.2-2825. Funding for the compensation and costs of expenses of the members shall be provided from the Fire Programs Fund established pursuant to § 38.2-401. (1981, c. 154, § 9-153.1; 1985, c. 448; 1986, c. 60; 1989, c. 258; 1992, c. 213; 2001, c. 844; 2002, c. 211; 2003, c. 836; 2006, c. 58.)

The **2006 amendments.** — The 2006 amendment by c. 58, in subsection D, substi- tuted "receive such compensation for the per- formance of their duties as provided in § 2.2- 2813" for "not be entitled to compensation but shall be reimbursed for all reasonable and necessary expenses incurred in the discharge of their duties as provided in § 2.2-2825" in the first sentence and added the last two sentences.

§ 9.1-203. Powers and duties of Virginia Fire Services Board; limi- tation. — A. The Board shall have the responsibility for promoting the coordination of the efforts of fire service organizations at the state and local levels. To these ends, it shall have the following powers and duties to:

1. Establish a process, involving state and local agencies, public and private, for setting priorities for implementing the Virginia Fire Prevention and Control Plan and coordinating the activities of state and local agencies, public and private, in implementing the Plan;

2. Develop a five-year statewide plan for fire education and training;

3. Establish criteria for the disbursement of any grant funds received from the federal government and any agencies thereof and any other source and to disburse such funds in accordance therewith;

4. Provide technical assistance and advice to local fire departments, other fire services organizations, and local governments;

5. Develop and recommend personnel standards for fire services personnel;

6. Develop and implement a statewide plan for the collection, analysis and reporting of data relating to fires in the Commonwealth, utilizing appropriate resources of other state agencies when deemed proper by the Board;

7. Make recommendations to the Governor and General Assembly concern- ing legislation affecting fire prevention and protection and fire services organizations in Virginia;

8. Evaluate all state programs or functions which have a bearing on fire prevention and protection and to make to the appropriate government officials any recommendations deemed necessary to improve the level of fire prevention and protection in the Commonwealth;

9. Provide training and information to localities relative to the Statewide Fire Prevention Code;

10. Study and develop alternative means of providing financial support for volunteer fire departments and to make appropriate recommendations regard- ing the implementation of such alternatives;

11. Conduct training schools for fire service personnel in various areas of the Commonwealth; and

12. Render assistance to local fire departments and volunteer fire compa- nies in training firefighters.

B. Except for those policies established in § 38.2-401, compliance with the provisions of § 9.1-201 and this section and any policies or guidelines enacted pursuant thereto shall be optional with, and at the full discretion of, any local governing body and any volunteer fire department or volunteer fire depart- ments operating under the same corporate charters. (1978, c. 606, § 9-155; 1981, c. 154; 1984, c. 734; 1986, c. 60; 1988, c. 133; 1997, c. 791; 2001, c. 844.)

§ 9.1-204. Fire service training facilities; allocation of funds there- for. — A. At the beginning of each fiscal year, the Board may allocate available funds to counties, cities, and towns within the Commonwealth for the purpose of assisting such counties, cities, towns and volunteer fire companies in the construction, improvement or expansion of fire service training facilities.

B. Available funds shall be allocated at the discretion of the Board, based upon the following:

1. The total amount of funds available for distribution;

2. Financial participation by counties, cities, towns and volunteer fire companies, any such participation being optional on the part of the locality or the particular volunteer fire company;

3. Anticipated use of such facilities by the Commonwealth, its subdivisions or volunteer fire companies.

C. Such funds shall be distributed to the counties, cities, and towns pursuant to contracts prepared by the office of Attorney General.

D. Allocations of such funds to volunteer fire companies shall not be contingent upon or conditioned in any way upon compliance with the provisions of § 9.1-201 or with any rules, regulations, or guidelines enacted pursuant to the provisions of § 9.1-201. (1981, c. 154, § 9-155.1; 2001, c. 844.)

Editor's note. — Acts 2001, cc. 864 and 871, cl. 1 added a § 9-155.3 relating to a Thermal Imaging Camera Grant Fund. However, cl. 2 of cc. 864 and 871 provided: "That the provisions of this act shall not become effective unless an appropriation of general funds effectuating the purposes of this act is included in the 2001 Appropriation Act, passed during the 2001 Session of the General Assembly and signed into law by the Governor." The appropriation was not made. Hence, the section added by cc. 864 and 871 will not take effect. But see now § 9.1-205, enacted by Acts 2002, c. 721.

§ 9.1-205. Thermal Imaging Camera Grant Fund established. — A. From only such funds as are appropriated from the general fund by the General Assembly for this purpose and from such gifts, donations, grants, bequests and other funds as may be received on its behalf, there is hereby created in the state treasury a special nonreverting fund to be known as the Virginia Thermal Imaging Camera Grant Fund, hereinafter referred to as the "VTIC Fund." No moneys from the Fire Programs Fund established pursuant to § 38.2-401 may be used or expended for the VTIC Fund. The VTIC Fund is established to assist the localities of the Commonwealth providing fire service operations in purchasing thermal imaging cameras and equipment associated with the use of thermal imaging cameras. The VTIC Fund shall be administered by the Department of Fire Programs and established on the books of the Comptroller. Any moneys remaining in the VTIC Fund at the end of each fiscal year shall not revert to the general fund but shall remain in the VTIC Fund. Moneys in the VTIC Fund shall not be diverted or expended for any purpose not authorized by this section. Notwithstanding any other provision of law to the contrary, policies established by the Virginia Fire Services Board, and any grants provided from the VTIC Fund, that are not inconsistent with the purposes set out in this section shall be binding upon any locality that accepts such funds or related grants. Expenditures for administration of and disbursements from the VTIC Fund shall be made by the State Treasurer on warrants issued by the Comptroller upon written request signed by the Executive Director of the Department of Fire Programs or his designee.

B. When, and only if, funds are available in the VTIC Fund, a Virginia Thermal Imaging Camera Advisory Panel (the Panel) shall be convened to make recommendations to the Department of Fire Programs for the use of the VTIC Fund. The Panel shall consist of eleven members as follows: three members from the State Fire Chief's Association, three members from the Virginia Professional Firefighters Association and three members from the Virginia State Firefighters Association, appointed by the Fire Services Board from a list of names submitted by each such organization. At least two members shall be appointed from each of the fire program areas established by the Department of Fire Programs. The Panel shall be selected annually only if moneys are available in the VTIC Fund and shall report directly to the Executive Director of the Department of Fire Programs. The Panel shall not have any responsibility or authority over any other matters not specified in this section. Members of the Panel shall not receive compensation, but shall be reimbursed for their reasonable and necessary expenses in the discharge of their duties. (2002, c. 721.)

Editor's note. — Acts 2002, c. 721, cl. 2, provides: "That the provisions of this act shall not become effective unless an appropriation effectuating the purposes of this act is included in the 2002 Appropriation Act passed during the 2002 Session of the General Assembly and signed into law by the Governor." Money for this project was appropriated by Acts 2002, c. 899, Item 438. See note at § 9.1-204.

CHAPTER 3.

FIREFIGHTERS AND EMERGENCY MEDICAL TECHNICIANS PROCEDURAL GUARANTEE ACT.

§ 9.1-300. Definitions. — As used in this chapter, unless the context requires a different meaning:

"Emergency medical technician" means any person who is employed solely within the fire department or public safety department of an employing agency as a full-time emergency medical technician whose primary responsibility is the provision of emergency care to the sick and injured, using either basic or advanced techniques. Emergency medical technicians may also provide fire protection services and assist in the enforcement of the fire prevention code.

"Employing agency" means any municipality of the Commonwealth or any political subdivision thereof, including authorities and special districts, which employs firefighters and emergency medical technicians.

"Firefighter" means any person who is employed solely within the fire department or public safety department of an employing agency as a full-time firefighter whose primary responsibility is the prevention and extinguishment of fires, the protection of life and property, and the enforcement of local and state fire prevention codes and laws pertaining to the prevention and control of fires.

"Interrogation" means any questioning of a formal nature as used in Chapter 4 (§ 9.1-500 et seq.) of this title that could lead to dismissal, demotion, or suspension for punitive reasons of a firefighter or emergency medical technician. (1987, c. 509, § 2.1-116.9:1; 2001, c. 844.)

§ 9.1-301. Conduct of interrogation. — The provisions of this section shall apply whenever a firefighter or emergency medical technician is subjected to an interrogation which could lead to dismissal, demotion or suspension for punitive reasons:

1. The interrogation shall take place at the facility where the investigating officer is assigned, or at the facility which has jurisdiction over the place where the incident under investigation allegedly occurred, as designated by the investigating officer.

2. No firefighter or emergency medical technician shall be subjected to interrogation without first receiving written notice of sufficient detail of the

investigation in order to reasonably apprise the firefighter or emergency medical technician of the nature of the investigation.

3. All interrogations shall be conducted at a reasonable time of day, preferably when the firefighter or emergency medical technician is on duty, unless the matters being investigated are of such a nature that immediate action is required.

4. The firefighter or emergency medical technician under investigation shall be informed of the name, rank, and unit or command of the officer in charge of the investigation, the interrogators, and all persons present during any interrogation.

5. Interrogation sessions shall be of reasonable duration and the firefighter or emergency medical technician shall be permitted reasonable periods for rest and personal necessities.

6. The firefighter or emergency medical technician being interrogated shall not be subjected to offensive language or offered any incentive as an inducement to answer any questions.

7. If a recording of any interrogation is made, and if a transcript of the interrogation is made, the firefighter or emergency medical technician under investigation shall be entitled to a copy without charge. Such record may be electronically recorded.

8. No firefighter or emergency medical technician shall be discharged, disciplined, demoted, denied promotion or seniority, or otherwise disciplined or discriminated against in regard to his employment, or be threatened with any such treatment as retaliation for his exercise of any of the rights granted or protected by this chapter. (1987, c. 509, § 2.1-116.9:2; 2001, c. 844.)

§ **9.1-302. Breach of procedures.** — Any breach of the procedures required by this chapter shall not exclude any evidence from being presented in any case against a firefighter or emergency medical technician and shall not cause any charge to be dismissed unless the firefighter or emergency medical technician demonstrates that the breach prejudiced his case. (1987, c. 509, § 2.1-116.9:5; 2001, c. 844.)

§ **9.1-303. Informal counseling not prohibited.** — Nothing in this chapter shall be construed to prohibit the informal counseling of a firefighter or emergency medical technician by a supervisor in reference to a minor infraction of policy or procedure which does not result in disciplinary action being taken against the firefighter or emergency medical technician. (1987, c. 509, § 2.1-116.9:3; 2001, c. 844.)

§ **9.1-304. Rights nonexclusive.** — The rights of firefighters and emergency medical technicians as set forth in this chapter shall not be construed to diminish the rights and privileges of firefighters or emergency medical technicians that are guaranteed to all citizens by the Constitution and laws of the United States and the Commonwealth or limit the granting of broader rights by other law, ordinance or rule.

This section shall not abridge or expand the rights of firefighters or emergency medical technicians to bring civil suits for injuries suffered in the course of their employment as recognized by the courts, nor is it designed to abrogate any common law or statutory limitation on the rights of recovery. (1987, c. 509, § 2.1-116.9:4; 2001, c. 844.)

CHAPTER 4.

LINE OF DUTY ACT.

§ **9.1-400. Title of chapter; definitions.** — A. This chapter shall be known and designated as the Line of Duty Act.

B. As used in this chapter, unless the context requires a different meaning:

"Beneficiary" means the spouse of a deceased person and such persons as are entitled to take under the will of a deceased person if testate, or as his heirs at law if intestate.

"Deceased person" means any individual whose death occurs on or after April 8, 1972, as the direct or proximate result of the performance of his duty, including the presumptions under §§ 27-40.1, 27-40.2, 51.1-813, and 65.2-402, as a law-enforcement officer of the Commonwealth or any of its political subdivisions; a correctional officer as defined in § 53.1-1; a jail officer; a regional jail or jail farm superintendent; a sheriff, deputy sheriff, or city sergeant or deputy city sergeant of the City of Richmond; a police chaplain; a member of any fire company or department or rescue squad that has been recognized by an ordinance or a resolution of the governing body of any county, city or town of the Commonwealth as an integral part of the official safety program of such county, city or town; a member of the Virginia National Guard or the Virginia State Defense Force while such member is serving in the Virginia National Guard or the Virginia State Defense Force on official state duty or federal duty under Title 32 of the United States Code; any special agent of the Virginia Alcoholic Beverage Control Board; any regular or special game warden who receives compensation from a county, city or town or from the Commonwealth appointed pursuant to the provisions of § 29.1-200; any commissioned forest warden appointed under the provisions of § 10.1-1135; any member or employee of the Virginia Marine Resources Commission granted the power of arrest pursuant to § 28.2-900; any Department of Emergency Management hazardous materials officer; any other employee of the Department of Emergency Management who is performing official duties of the agency, when those duties are related to a major disaster or emergency, as defined in § 44-146.16, that has been or is later declared to exist under the authority of the Governor in accordance with § 44-146.28; any employee of any county, city, or town performing official emergency management or emergency services duties in cooperation with the Department of Emergency Management, when those duties are related to a major disaster or emergency, as defined in § 44-146.16, that has been or is later declared to exist under the authority of the Governor in accordance with § 44-146.28 or a local emergency, as defined in § 44-146.16, declared by a local governing body; any nonfirefighter regional hazardous materials emergency response team member; or any conservation officer of the Department of Conservation and Recreation commissioned pursuant to § 10.1-115.

"Disabled person" means any individual who, as the direct or proximate result of the performance of his duty in any position listed in the definition of deceased person in this section, has become mentally or physically incapaci-

tated so as to prevent the further performance of duty where such incapacity is likely to be permanent. The term shall also include any state employee included in the definition of a deceased person who was disabled on or after January 1, 1966.

"Line of duty" means any action the deceased or disabled person was obligated or authorized to perform by rule, regulation, condition of employment or service, or law. (1995, cc. 112, 156, 597, §§ 2.1-133.5, 2.1-133.6; 1996, cc. 66, 174; 1998, c. 712; 2001, cc. 678, 844; 2003, cc. 37, 41, 1005; 2004, c. 30; 2005, cc. 907, 910; 2006, c. 824.)

Editor's note. — Acts 2001, c. 678 amended former § 2.1-133.6, from which this section is derived. Pursuant to § 30-152, Acts 2001, c. 678 has been given effect in this section as set out above. The 2001 amendment by c. 678, in the paragraph defining "Deceased person," substituted "the Commonwealth" for "this Commonwealth" in two places, and inserted "a police chaplain in the City of Virginia Beach."

Acts 2005, cc. 907 and 910, cl. 2 provides: "That any person eligible for benefits solely by virtue of the provisions of § 9.1-400 of this act shall be entitled to such benefits only on a prospective basis upon approval of a claim pursuant to §§ 9.1-403 and 9.1-404 that is made on or after July 1, 2005."

Acts 2006, c. 824, cl. 2, provides: "That any person eligible for benefits solely by virtue of the provisions of § 9.1-400 of this act shall be entitled to such benefits only on a prospective basis upon approval of a claim pursuant to §§ 9.1-403 and 9.1-404 that is made on or after July 1, 2006."

The 2005 amendments. — The 2005 amendments by cc. 907 and 910 are identical, and added the last sentence of the paragraph defining "Disabled person."

The 2006 amendments. — The 2006 amendment by c. 824 substituted "January 1, 1966" for "January 1, 1972" in the last sentence in the definition of "Disabled person" in subsection B.

§ 9.1-401. Continued health insurance coverage for disabled persons, their spouses and dependents, and for the surviving spouse and dependents of certain deceased law-enforcement officers, firefighters, etc. — A. The surviving spouse and any dependents of a deceased person shall be afforded continued health insurance coverage, the cost of which shall be paid in full out of the general fund of the state treasury.

B. If the disabled person's disability (i) occurred while in the line of duty as the direct or proximate result of the performance of his duty or (ii) was subject to the provisions of §§ 27-40.1, 27-40.2, 51.1-813 or § 65.2-402, and arose out of and in the course of his employment, the disabled person, his surviving spouse and any dependents shall be afforded continued health insurance coverage. The cost of such health insurance coverage shall be paid in full out of the general fund of the state treasury.

C. The continued health insurance coverage provided by this section shall be the same plan of benefits which the deceased or disabled person was entitled to on the last day of his active duty or comparable benefits established as a result of a replacement plan.

D. For any spouse, continued health insurance provided by this section shall terminate upon such spouse's death or coverage by alternate health insurance.

E. For dependents, continued health insurance provided by this section shall terminate upon such dependent's death, marriage, coverage by alternate health insurance or twenty-first birthday. Continued health care insurance shall be provided beyond the dependent's twenty-first birthday if the dependent is a full-time college student and shall continue until such time as the dependent ceases to be a full-time student or reaches his twenty-fifth birthday, whichever occurs first. Continued health care insurance shall also be provided beyond the dependent's twenty-first birthday if the dependent is mentally or physically disabled, and such coverage shall continue until three months following the cessation of the disability.

F. For any disabled person, continued health insurance provided by this section shall automatically terminate upon the disabled person's death, recovery or return to full duty in any position listed in the definition of deceased person in § 9.1-400. (1998, c. 712, § 2.1-133.7:1; 2000, c. 616; 2001, c. 844.)

OPINIONS OF THE ATTORNEY GENERAL

Payments through the state health benefits program. — Certain individuals entitled to health benefits under the Line of Duty Act may receive those benefits through the state health benefits program. See opinion of Attorney General to Ms. Sara Redding Wilson, Director, Department of Human Resource Management, 03-090 (12/18/03).

§ 9.1-402. Payments to beneficiaries of certain deceased law-enforcement officers, firefighters, etc., and retirees. — A. The beneficiary of a deceased person whose death occurred on or before December 31, 2005, while in the line of duty as the direct or proximate result of the performance of his duty shall be entitled to receive the sum of $75,000, which shall be payable out of the general fund of the state treasury, in gratitude for and in recognition of his sacrifice on behalf of the people of the Commonwealth.

B. The beneficiary of a deceased person whose death occurred on or after January 1, 2006, while in the line of duty as the direct or proximate result of the performance of his duty shall be entitled to receive the sum of $100,000, which shall be payable out of the general fund of the state treasury, in gratitude for and in recognition of his sacrifice on behalf of the people of the Commonwealth.

C. Subject to the provisions of §§ 27-40.1, 27-40.2, 51.1-813, or § 65.2-402, if the deceased person's death (i) arose out of and in the course of his employment or (ii) was within five years from his date of retirement, his beneficiary shall be entitled to receive the sum of $25,000, which shall be payable out of the general fund of the state treasury. (1995, cc. 156, 597, § 2.1-133.7; 2000, c. 314; 2001, c. 844; 2006, c. 878.)

The 2006 amendments. — The 2006 amendment by c. 878 inserted "on or before December 31, 2005" in subsection A; inserted subsection B; and redesignated former subsection B as subsection C.

§ 9.1-403. Claim for payment; costs. — Every beneficiary, disabled person or his spouse, or dependent of a deceased or disabled person shall present his claim to the chief officer, or his designee, of the appropriate division or department that last employed the deceased or disabled person on forms to be provided by the State Comptroller's office. The chief officer or his designee shall submit a request to the Superintendent of the Department of the State Police, who shall investigate and report upon the circumstances surrounding the deceased or disabled person, calling upon the additional information and services of any other appropriate agents or agencies of the Commonwealth. The Superintendent, or his designee, shall report his findings to the Comptroller within ten business days after completion of the investigation. The Department of State Police shall take action to conduct the investigation as expeditiously as possible. The Department shall be reimbursed for the cost of investigations conducted pursuant to this section from the appropriate employer that last employed the deceased or disabled employee. (1995, c. 156, § 2.1-133.8; 1998, c. 712; 2001, cc. 427, 844.)

Editor's note. — Acts 2001, c. 427 amended former § 2.1-133.8, from which this section is derived. Pursuant to § 30-152, Acts 2001, c. 427 has been given effect in this section as set out above. The 2001 amendment by c. 427, in the third sentence, substituted "Superintendent" for "chief officer," and substituted "ten business days after completion of the investigation" for "forty-five days of receipt of a claim," and added the last two sentences.

§ 9.1-404. Order of Comptroller. — A. If it appears to the Comptroller that the requirements of either subsection A or B of § 9.1-402 have been satisfied, he shall issue his warrant in the appropriate amount for payment out of the general fund of the state treasury to the surviving spouse or to such persons and subject to such conditions as may be proper in his administrative discretion, and in the event there is no beneficiary, the Comptroller shall issue the payment to the estate of the deceased person. The Comptroller shall issue a decision, and payment, if appropriate, shall be made no later than forty-five days following receipt of the report required under § 9.1-403.

B. If it appears to the Comptroller that the requirements of either subsection A or B of § 9.1-401 have been satisfied, he shall issue his warrants in the appropriate amounts for payment from the general fund of the state treasury to ensure continued health care coverage for the persons designated under § 9.1-401. The Comptroller shall issue a decision, and payments, if appropriate, shall commence no later than forty-five days following receipt of the report required under § 9.1-403. The payments shall be retroactive to the first date that the disability existed. (1995, cc. 156, 597, § 2.1-133.9; 1998, c. 712; 2001, c. 844.)

§ 9.1-405. Appeal from decision of Comptroller. — Any beneficiary, disabled person or his spouse or dependent of a deceased or disabled person aggrieved by the decision of the Comptroller shall present a petition to the court in which the will of the deceased person is probated or in which the personal representative of the deceased person is qualified or might qualify or in the jurisdiction in which the disabled person resides.

The Commonwealth shall be represented in such proceeding by the Attorney General or his designee. The court shall proceed as chancellor without a jury. If it appears to the court that the requirements of this chapter have been satisfied, the judge shall enter an order to that effect. The order shall also direct the Comptroller to issue his warrant in the appropriate amount for the payment out of the general fund of the state treasury to such persons and subject to such conditions as may be proper. If, in the case of a deceased person, there is no beneficiary, the judge shall direct such payment as is due under § 9.1-402 to the estate of the deceased person. (1995, cc. 156, 597, § 2.1-133.10; 1998, c. 712; 2001, c. 844.)

§ 9.1-406. Appeals. — Appeals from judgments entered pursuant to this chapter shall be allowed as in civil actions generally. (1995, c. 156, § 2.1-133.11; 2001, c. 844; 2005, c. 681.)

The 2005 amendments. — The 2005 amendment by c. 681, effective January 1, 2006, substituted "civil actions" for "chancery matters."

§ 9.1-407. Training. — Any law-enforcement or public safety officer entitled to benefits under this Chapter shall receive training concerning the benefits available to himself or his beneficiary in case of disability or death in the line of duty. The Secretary of Public Safety shall develop training information to be distributed to agencies and localities with employees subject to this Chapter. The agency or locality shall be responsible for providing the training. Such training shall not count towards in-service training requirements for law-enforcement officers pursuant to § 9.1-102. (2006, c. 535.)

CHAPTER 5.

LAW-ENFORCEMENT OFFICERS PROCEDURAL GUARANTEE ACT.

§ 9.1-500. Definitions. — As used in this chapter, unless the context requires a different meaning:

"Agency" means the Department of State Police, the Division of Capitol Police, the Virginia Marine Resources Commission, the Virginia Port Authority, the Department of Game and Inland Fisheries, the Department of Alcoholic Beverage Control, or the Department of Motor Vehicles; or the political subdivision or the campus police department of any public institution of higher education of the Commonwealth employing the law-enforcement officer.

"Law-enforcement officer" means any person, other than a Chief of Police or the Superintendent of the Department of State Police, who, in his official capacity, is (i) authorized by law to make arrests and (ii) a nonprobationary officer of one of the following agencies:

a. The Department of State Police, the Division of Capitol Police, the Virginia Marine Resources Commission, the Virginia Port Authority, the Department of Game and Inland Fisheries, the Department of Alcoholic Beverage Control, or the Department of Motor Vehicles;

b. The police department, bureau or force of any political subdivision or the campus police department of any public institution of higher education of the Commonwealth where such department, bureau or force has ten or more law-enforcement officers; or

c. Any game warden as defined in § 9.1-101.

For the purposes of this chapter, "law-enforcement officer" shall not include the sheriff's department of any city or county. (1978, c. 19, § 2.1-116.1; 1979, c. 592; 1983, c. 357; 1995, c. 730; 2001, c. 844.)

Cross references. — As to exemptions from the provisions of the State Grievance Procedure, see § 2.2-3002.

CASE NOTES

Editor's note. — The cases below were decided under former corresponding provisions.

Violation of guarantees does not necessarily compel finding of due process violation. — Police department's violation of the Law-Enforcement Officers' Procedural Guarantees does not necessarily compel a finding of a due process violation. Riccio v. County of Fairfax, 907 F.2d 1459 (4th Cir. 1990).

Statutory procedures exceed requirements of due process. — While this state law provides those to whom it applies with a property interest in employment, it also provides for more process than what the constitution would otherwise require and, for this reason, the specific procedures it establishes need not be complied with fully to satisfy federal due process. Mansoor v. County of Albemarle, 124 F. Supp. 2d 367, 2000 U.S. Dist. LEXIS 18612 (W.D. Va. 2000).

§ 9.1-501. Conduct of investigation. — The provisions of this section shall apply whenever an investigation by an agency focuses on matters which could lead to the dismissal, demotion, suspension or transfer for punitive reasons of a law-enforcement officer:

1. Any questioning of the officer shall take place at a reasonable time and place as designated by the investigating officer, preferably when the officer under investigation is on duty and at the office of the command of the investigating officer or at the office of the local precinct or police unit of the officer being investigated, unless matters being investigated are of such a nature that immediate action is required.

2. Prior to the officer being questioned, he shall be informed of (i) the name and rank of the investigating officer and of any individual to be present during the questioning and (ii) the nature of the investigation.

3. When a blood or urine specimen is taken from a law-enforcement officer for the purpose of determining whether the officer has used drugs or alcohol, the specimen shall be divided and placed into two separate containers. One specimen shall be tested while the other is held in a proper manner to preserve the specimen by the facility collecting or testing the specimen. Should the first specimen test positive, the law-enforcement officer shall have the right to require the second specimen be sent to a laboratory of his choice for independent testing in accordance generally with the procedures set forth in §§ 18.2-268.1 through 18.2-268.12. The officer shall notify the chief of his agency in writing of his request within 10 days of being notified of positive specimen results. The laboratory chosen by the officer shall be accredited or certified by one or more of the following bodies: the American Society of Crime Laboratory Directors/Laboratory Accreditation Board (ASCLD/LAB), the College of American Pathologists (CAP), the United States Department of Health and Human Services Substance Abuse and Mental Health Services Administration (SAMHSA), or the American Board of Forensic Toxicology (ABFT). (1978, c. 19, § 2.1-116.2; 1992, c. 221; 1993, c. 229; 2001, c. 844; 2005, cc. 868, 881.)

The 2005 amendments. — The 2005 amendments by cc. 868 and 881 are identical, and in subdivision 3, substituted "10" for "ten," and "accredited or certified by one or more of the following bodies: the American Society of Crime Laboratory Directors/Laboratory Accreditation Board (ASCLD/LAB), the College of American Pathologists (CAP), the United States Department of Health and Human Services Substance Abuse and Mental Health Services Administration (SAMHSA), or the American Board of Forensic Toxicology (ABFT)" for "on the approved list of the Division of Forensic Science."

§ 9.1-502. Notice of charges; response; election to proceed under grievance procedure of local governing body.

— A. Before any dismissal, demotion, suspension without pay or transfer for punitive reasons may be imposed, the following rights shall be afforded:

1. The law-enforcement officer shall be notified in writing of all charges, the basis therefor, and the action which may be taken;

2. The law-enforcement officer shall be given an opportunity, within a reasonable time limit after the date of the written notice provided for above, to respond orally and in writing to the charges. The time limit shall be determined by the agency, but in no event shall it be less than five calendar days unless agreed to by the law-enforcement officer;

3. In making his response, the law-enforcement officer may be assisted by counsel at his own expense; and

4. The law-enforcement officer shall be given written notification of his right to initiate a grievance under the grievance procedure established by the local governing body pursuant to §§ 15.2-1506 and 15.2-1507. A copy of the local governing body's grievance procedure shall be provided to the law-enforcement officer upon his request.

B. A law-enforcement officer may proceed under either the local governing body's grievance procedure or the law-enforcement officer's procedural guarantees, but not both. (1978, c. 19, § 2.1-116.4; 1987, c. 461; 2001, c. 844.)

CASE NOTES

Investigation after giving of notice did not deny due process. — Where plaintiff was given notice at the outset of the investigation, which could not in and of itself result in adverse action, and where a grievance procedure was provided for in the event the investigation would lead to collateral action such as dismissal, defendants could not be found to have violated due process in conducting the investigation. Morrell v. Stone, 638 F. Supp. 163 (W.D. Va. 1986) (decided under prior law).

Due process not denied where basis for dismissal existed and plaintiff voluntarily resigned. — Where plaintiff's threatened termination was made in good faith, as there was a for cause basis to substantiate his proposed

dismissal, and where rather than resigning, plaintiff could have chosen to challenge through the grievance procedure made available to him under former § 2.1-116.5 (see now § 9.1-504) of the "Law-Enforcement Officers' Procedural Guarantees" any adverse disciplinary action taken against him by the defendants, and where plaintiff admitted that he talked with his attorney before making the decision to submit his resignation, plaintiff's resignation was voluntary as a matter of law, and having voluntarily resigned, plaintiff could not claim he was denied procedural protections that he waived. Morrell v. Stone, 638 F. Supp. 163 (W.D. Va. 1986) (decided under prior law).

CIRCUIT COURT OPINIONS

No notice of disciplinary sanction. — County manager's decision holding that a police officer's 80-hour suspension was non-grievable was reversed, where at the time the police officer submitted his resignation, he had not been informed that he was to receive a

disciplinary sanction and the county's action of waiting until the eleventh hour to advise the officer of the sanction effectively deprived him of his right to participate in the grievance process. In re Williams, 62 Va. Cir. 383, 2003 Va. Cir. LEXIS 314 (Arlington County 2003).

§ 9.1-503. Personal assets of officers. — No law-enforcement officer shall be required or requested to disclose any item of his property, income, assets, source of income, debts, or personal or domestic expenditures, including those of any member of his family or household, unless (i) such information is necessary in investigating a possible conflict of interest with respect to the performance of his official duties(ii) such disclosure is required by law, or (iii) such information is related to an investigation. Nothing in this section shall preclude an agency from requiring the law-enforcement officer to disclose any place of off-duty employment and where he may be contacted. (1978, c. 19, § 2.1-116.3; 2001, c. 844.)

§ 9.1-504. Hearing; hearing panel recommendations. — A. Whenever a law-enforcement officer is dismissed, demoted, suspended or transferred for punitive reasons, he may, within a reasonable amount of time following such action, as set by the agency, request a hearing. If such request is timely made, a hearing shall be held within a reasonable amount of time set by the agency. However, the hearing shall not be set later than fourteen calendar days following the date of request unless a later date is agreed to by the law-enforcement officer. At the hearing, the law-enforcement officer and his agency shall be afforded the opportunity to present evidence, examine and cross-examine witnesses. The law-enforcement officer shall also be given the opportunity to be represented by counsel at the hearing unless the officer and agency are afforded, by regulation, the right to counsel in a subsequent de novo hearing.

B. The hearing shall be conducted by a panel consisting of one member from within the agency selected by the grievant, one member from within the agency of equal rank of the grievant but no more than two ranks above appointed by the agency head, and a third member from within the agency to be selected by the other two members. In the event that such two members cannot agree upon their selection, the chief judge of the judicial circuit wherein the duty station of the grievant lies shall choose such third member. The hearing panel may, and on the request of either the law-enforcement officer or his agency shall, issue subpoenas requiring the testimony of witnesses who have refused or failed to appear at the hearing. The hearing panel shall rule on the admissibility of the evidence. A record shall be made of the hearing.

C. At the option of the agency, it may, in lieu of complying with the provisions of § 9.1-502, give the law-enforcement officer a statement, in writing, of the charges, the basis therefor, the action which may be taken, and provide a hearing as provided for in this section prior to dismissing, demoting, suspending or transferring for punitive reasons the law-enforcement officer.

D. The recommendations of the hearing panel, and the reasons therefor, shall be in writing and transmitted promptly to the law-enforcement officer or his attorney and to the chief executive officer of the law-enforcement agency. Such recommendations shall be advisory only, but shall be accorded significant weight. (1978, c. 19, §§ 2.1-116.5, 2.1-116.7; 1980, c. 191; 2001, c. 844.)

CASE NOTES

Editor's note. — The cases below were decided under former corresponding provisions.

No automatic right to pretermination hearing. — Failure to afford police officers a hearing prior to discharge did not violate due process, because there is no automatic right to a preterminaton hearing under subdivision 3 of former § 2.1-116.5 (see now subsection C of § 9.1-504). Kersey v. Shipley, 673 F.2d 730 (4th Cir.), cert. denied, 459 U.S. 836, 103 S. Ct. 80, 74 L. Ed. 2d 77 (1982).

Property interest in continued employment. — A law-enforcement officer's procedural guarantees as set out in this section provide the police officer with a property interest in his continued employment, and the due process clause of the Fourteenth Amendment becomes implicated if, as a factual matter, the officer is deprived of the benefits conferred by this chapter. Himmelbrand v. Harrison, 484 F. Supp. 803 (W.D. Va. 1980). But see Mandel v. Allen, 889 F. Supp. 857 (E.D. Va. 1995), aff'd, 81 F.3d 478 (4th Cir. 1996).

Investigation after giving of notice did not deny due process. — Where plaintiff was given notice at the outset of the investigation, which could not in and of itself result in adverse action, and where a grievance procedure was provided for in the event the investigation would lead to collateral action such as dismissal, defendants could not be found to have violated due process in conducting the investigation. Morrell v. Stone, 638 F. Supp. 163 (W.D. Va. 1986).

Due process not denied where basis for dismissal existed and plaintiff voluntarily resigned. — Where plaintiff's threatened termination was made in good faith, as there was a for cause basis to substantiate his proposed dismissal, and where rather than resigning, plaintiff could have chosen to challenge through the grievance procedure made available to him under this section of the "Law-Enforcement Officers' Procedural Guarantees" any adverse disciplinary action taken against him by the defendants, and where plaintiff admitted that he talked with his attorney before making the decision to submit his resignation, plaintiff's resignation was voluntary as a matter of law, and having voluntarily resigned, plaintiff could not claim he was denied procedural protections that he waived. Morrell v. Stone, 638 F. Supp. 163 (W.D. Va. 1986).

Immediate suspension. — Although former § 2.1-116.6 (see now § 9.1-505) does in certain specified circumstances permit "immediate suspension," even in such cases of "immediate suspension" the extensive post-termination procedures prescribed in this section must be complied with. Himmelbrand v. Harrison, 484 F. Supp. 803 (W.D. Va. 1980). But see Mandel v. Allen, 889 F. Supp. 857 (E.D. Va. 1995), aff'd, 81 F.3d 478 (4th Cir. 1996).

§ 9.1-505. Immediate suspension. — Nothing in this chapter shall prevent the immediate suspension without pay of any law-enforcement officer whose continued presence on the job is deemed to be a substantial and immediate threat to the welfare of his agency or the public, nor shall anything in this chapter prevent the suspension of a law-enforcement officer for refusing to obey a direct order issued in conformance with the agency's written and disseminated regulations. In such a case, the law-enforcement officer shall, upon request, be afforded the rights provided for under this chapter within a reasonable amount of time set by the agency. (1978, c. 19, § 2.1-116.6; 2001, c. 844.)

CASE NOTES

Editor's note. — The case below was decided under former corresponding provisions.

Immediate suspension. — Although this section does in certain specified circumstances permit "immediate suspension," even in such cases of "immediate suspension" the extensive post-termination procedures prescribed in former § 2.1-116.5 (see now § 9.1-504) must be complied with. Himmelbrand v. Harrison, 484 F. Supp. 803 (W.D. Va. 1980). But see Mandel v. Allen, 889 F. Supp. 857 (E.D. Va. 1995), aff'd, 81 F.3d 478 (4th Cir. 1996).

§ 9.1-506. Informal counseling not prohibited. — Nothing in this chapter shall be construed to prohibit the informal counseling of a law-enforcement officer by a supervisor in reference to a minor infraction of policy or procedure which does not result in disciplinary action being taken against the law-enforcement officer. (1978, c. 19, § 2.1-116.8; 2001, c. 844.)

§ 9.1-507. Chapter accords minimum rights. — The rights accorded law-enforcement officers in this chapter are minimum rights and all agencies shall adopt grievance procedures that are consistent with this chapter. However, an agency may provide for additional rights of law-enforcement officers in its grievance procedure. (1978, c. 19, § 2.1-116.9; 2001, c. 844.)

CHAPTER 6.

CIVILIAN PROTECTION IN CASES OF POLICE MISCONDUCT.

Sec.
9.1-600. Civilian protection in cases of police
            misconduct; minimum standards.

§ 9.1-600. Civilian protection in cases of police misconduct; minimum standards. — A. State, local, and other public law-enforcement agencies, which have ten or more law-enforcement officers, shall have procedures as established in subsection B, allowing citizen submission of complaints regarding the conduct of the law-enforcement agency, law-enforcement officers in the agency, or employees of the agency.

B. Law-enforcement agencies shall ensure, at a minimum, that in the case of all written complaints:

1. The general public has access to the required forms and information concerning the submission of complaints;

2. The law-enforcement agency assists individuals in filing complaints; and

3. Adequate records are maintained of the nature and disposition of such cases. (1993, c. 722, § 2.1-116.9:6; 2001, cc. 153, 844.)

Editor's note. — Acts 2001, c. 153 amended former § 2.1-116.9:6, from which this section is derived. Pursuant to § 30-152, Acts 2001, c. 153 has been given effect in this section as set out above. The 2001 amendment by c. 153 deleted subsection C, which had read: "The provisions of this chapter shall not apply to constitutional officers."

CHAPTER 7.

OVERTIME COMPENSATION FOR LAW-ENFORCEMENT EMPLOYEES AND FIREFIGHTERS, EMERGENCY MEDICAL TECHNICIANS, AND OTHER FIRE PROTECTION EMPLOYEES.

§ 9.1-700. Definitions. — As used in this chapter, unless the context requires a different meaning:

"Employer" means any political subdivision of the Commonwealth, including any county, city, town, authority, or special district that employs fire protection employees except any locality with five or fewer paid firefighters that is exempt from overtime rules by 29 U.S.C. § 207 (k).

"Fire protection employee" means any person, other than an employee who is exempt from the overtime provisions of the Fair Labor Standards Act, who is employed by an employer as a paid firefighter, paramedic, emergency medical technician, rescue worker, ambulance personnel, or hazardous materials worker who is (i) trained in fire suppression and has the legal authority and responsibility to engage in fire suppression, and is employed by a fire department of an employer; and (ii) engaged in the prevention, control, and extinguishment of fires or response to emergency situations where life, property, or the environment is at risk.

"Law-enforcement employee" means any person who is responsible for the prevention and detection of crime and the enforcement of the penal, traffic or highway laws of the Commonwealth, other than an employee who is exempt from the overtime provisions of the Fair Labor Standards Act, and who is a full-time employee of either (i) a police department or (ii) a sheriff's office that is part of or administered by the Commonwealth or any political subdivision thereof.

"Regularly scheduled work hours" means those hours that are recurring and fixed within the work period and for which an employee receives a salary or hourly compensation. "Regularly scheduled work hours" does not include on-call, extra duty assignments or any other nonrecurring and nonfixed hours. (2001, c. 768, § 2.1-116.9:7; 2005, c. 732.)

Editor's note. — Acts 2001, c. 768 enacted a new Chapter 10.1:3 of Title 2.1, consisting of §§ 2.1-116.9:7 through 2.1-116.9:13 (repealed October 1, 2001), from which this Chapter 7 (§§ 9.1-700 through 9.1-706) was derived. Pursuant to § 30-152, Acts 2001, c. 768 has been given effect as this Chapter 7 of Title 9.1.

The 2005 amendments. — The 2005 amendment by c. 732 inserted "Law-Enforcement Employees and" preceding "Firefighters" in the chapter heading; inserted the definition of "Law-enforcement employee" and made minor stylistic changes.

§ 9.1-701. Overtime compensation rate. — A. Employers shall pay fire protection or law-enforcement employees overtime compensation or leave, as under the Fair Labor Standards Act, 29 U.S.C. § 207 (o), at a rate of not less than one and one-half times the employee's regular rate of pay for all hours of work between the statutory maximum permitted under 29 U.S.C. § 207 (k) and the hours for which an employee receives his salary, or if paid on an hourly basis, the hours for which the employee receives hourly compensation. A fire protection or law-enforcement employee who is paid on an hourly basis shall have paid leave counted as hours of work in an amount no greater than the numbers of hours counted for other fire protection or law-enforcement employees working the same schedule who are paid on a salaried basis in that jurisdiction.

B. Nothing in this chapter shall be construed to affect the right of any employer to provide overtime compensation to fire protection or law-enforcement employees in an amount that exceeds the amounts required by this section.

C. The provisions of this section pertaining to law-enforcement employees shall only apply to employers of 100 or more law-enforcement employees. (2001, c. 768, § 2.1-116.9:8; 2005, c. 732.)

Editor's note. — Acts 2001, c. 768 enacted former § 2.1-116.9:8 from which this section is derived. Pursuant to § 30-152, Acts 2001, c. 768 has been given effect in this section as set out above.

The 2005 amendments. — The 2005 amendment by c. 732 inserted "or law-enforcement" three times in subsection A and once in subsection B; and added subsection C.

§ 9.1-702. Work period.

— Employers may adopt any work period to compute overtime compensation for fire protection or law-enforcement employees between seven and 28 days provided that the work period is recurring and fixed, and is not changed for purposes of denying overtime compensation to such employees to which they may be entitled under subsection A of § 9.1-701. The provisions of this section pertaining to law-enforcement employees shall only apply to employers of 100 or more law-enforcement employees. (2001, c. 768, § 2.1-116.9:9; 2005, c. 732.)

Editor's note. — Acts 2001, c. 768 enacted former § 2.1-116.9:9 from which this section is derived. Pursuant to § 30-152, Acts 2001, c. 768 has been given effect in this section as set out above.

The 2005 amendments. — The 2005 amendment by c. 732 inserted "or law-enforcement" preceding "employees," substituted "28" for "twenty-eight," and added the last sentence.

§ 9.1-703. Hours of work.

— For purposes of computing fire protection or law-enforcement employees' entitlement to overtime compensation, all hours that an employee works or is in a paid status during his regularly scheduled work hours shall be counted as hours of work. The provisions of this section pertaining to law-enforcement employees shall only apply to such employees of an employer of 100 or more law-enforcement employees. (2001, c. 768, § 2.1-116.9:10; 2005, c. 732.)

Editor's note. — Acts 2001, c. 768 enacted former § 2.1-116.9:10 from which this section is derived. Pursuant to § 30-152, Acts 2001, c. 768 has been given effect in this section as set out above.

The 2005 amendments. — The 2005 amendment by c. 732 inserted "or law-enforcement" preceding "employees" and added the last sentence.

§ 9.1-704. Employee's remedies; award of attorneys' fees and costs.

— A. In an action brought under this chapter, an employer who violates the provisions of this chapter shall be liable to the fire protection or law-enforcement employee affected in an amount of double the amount of the unpaid compensation due such employee. However, if the employer can prove that his violation was in good faith, he shall be liable only for the amount of the unpaid compensation plus interest at the rate of eight percent per year, commencing on the date the compensation was due to the employee.

B. Where the fire protection or law-enforcement employee prevails, the court shall award him attorneys' fees and costs to be paid by the employer.

C. The provisions of this section pertaining to law-enforcement employees shall only apply in instances where the employer employs 100 or more law-enforcement employees. (2001, c. 768, § 2.1-116.9:11; 2005, c. 732.)

Editor's note. — Acts 2001, c. 768 enacted former § 2.1-116.9:11 from which this section is derived. Pursuant to § 30-152, Acts 2001, c. 768 has been given effect in this section as set out above.

The 2005 amendments. — The 2005 amendment by c. 732 inserted "or law-enforcement" preceding "employee" in subsections A and B; and added subsection C.

§ 9.1-705. Limitation of actions. — Actions brought under this chapter shall be commenced within two years of the date the unpaid compensation was due, or if the violation is willful, within three years of the date the unpaid compensation was due. (2001, c. 768, § 2.1-116.9:12.)

Editor's note. — Acts 2001, c. 768 enacted former § 2.1-116.9:12 from which this section is derived. Pursuant to § 30-152, Acts 2001, c. 768 has been given effect in this section as set out above.

§ 9.1-706. Sovereign immunity. — The immunity of the Commonwealth and of any "agency" as defined in § 8.01-195.2 is hereby preserved. (2001, c. 768, § 2.1-116.9:13.)

Editor's note. — Acts 2001, c. 768 enacted former § 2.1-116.9:13 from which this section is derived. Pursuant to § 30-152, Acts 2001, c. 768 has been given effect in this section as set out above.

CHAPTER 8.

COMMONWEALTH PUBLIC SAFETY MEDAL OF VALOR ACT.

§ 9.1-800. Commonwealth Public Safety Medal of Valor. — There is hereby established the Commonwealth Public Safety Medal of Valor. The Governor may award and present the Commonwealth Public Safety Medal of Valor, of appropriate design with ribbons and appurtenances, to a Virginia public safety officer for performance above and beyond the call of duty involving extraordinary valor in the face of grave danger, at great personal risk. The public safety officer shall have exhibited uncommon valor, which clearly distinguishes the officer as performing above and beyond normal job requirements. The Commonwealth Public Safety Medal of Valor shall be the highest award for valor by a public safety officer conferred by the Commonwealth. The Governor may select no more than three recipients for the Commonwealth Public Safety Medal of Valor award each year, unless the Governor determines that extraordinary circumstances warrant the selection of additional recipients. (2002, c. 150.)

§ 9.1-801. Public safety officer defined. — As used in this chapter, the term *"public safety officer"* includes a law-enforcement officer of this Commonwealth or any of its political subdivisions; a correctional officer as defined in § 53.1-1; a correctional officer employed at a juvenile correctional facility as the term is defined in § 66-25.3; a jail officer; a regional jail or jail farm superintendent; a member of any fire company or department or rescue squad that has been recognized by an ordinance or resolution of the governing body of any county, city or town of this Commonwealth as an integral part of the official safety program of such county, city or town; an arson investigator; a member of the Virginia National Guard or the Virginia State Defense Force while such a member is serving in the Virginia National Guard or the Virginia State Defense Force on official state duty or federal duty under Title 32 of the United States Code; any special agent of the Virginia Alcoholic Beverage Control Board; any police agent appointed under the provisions of § 56-353; any regular or special game warden who receives compensation from a county, city or town or from the Commonwealth appointed pursuant to § 29.1-200; any commissioned forest warden appointed pursuant to § 10.1-1135; any member or employee of the Virginia Marine Resources Commission granted the power to arrest pursuant to § 28.2-900; any Department of Emergency Management hazardous materials officer; any nonfirefighter regional hazardous materials emergency response team member; any investigator who is a full-time sworn member of the security division of the State Lottery Department; any full-time sworn member of the enforcement division of the Department of Motor Vehicles meeting the Department of Criminal Justice Services qualifications, when fulfilling duties pursuant to § 46.2-217; any campus police officer appointed under the provisions of Chapter 17 (§ 23-232 et seq.) of Title 23; and any conservation officer of the Department of Conservation and Recreation commissioned pursuant to § 10.1-115. (2002, c. 150.)

§ 9.1-802. Medal of Valor Review Board. — The Medal of Valor Review Board is established as an advisory board, within the meaning of § 2.2-2100, in the executive branch of state government. The Board shall be composed of seven members appointed by the Governor as follows: one police officer, one deputy sheriff, one paid firefighter, one volunteer firefighter, one corrections officer, one volunteer rescue squad member and one citizen member. The Virginia Public Safety Foundation may nominate persons to serve as Board members. The police officer, paid firefighter, corrections officer and citizen member shall serve four-year terms, and the remainder shall serve three-year terms. All terms shall commence July 1, 2002. No member shall serve more than two successive terms. A vacancy occurring other than by expiration of term shall be filled for the unexpired term.

Each year, the Board shall elect a chairman and a vice-chairman from among its members. A majority of the members of the Board shall constitute a quorum. (2002, c. 150.)

§ 9.1-803. Powers and duties of the Board. — The Board shall have the power and duty to:

1. Recommend to the Governor any public safety officers to receive the Commonwealth Public Safety Medal of Valor and any lesser awards established pursuant to this chapter;

2. Recommend to the Governor the establishment of public safety officer awards lesser than the Commonwealth Public Safety Medal of Valor Award;

3. Apply for, accept and expend gifts, grants, or donations from public or private sources to enable it to carry out its objectives;

4. Establish criteria for the nomination and selection of public safety officers to receive awards pursuant to this chapter; and

5. Do all things necessary and convenient to carry out the purposes of this chapter. (2002, c. 150.)

CHAPTER 9.

Sex Offender and Crimes Against Minors Registry Act.

§ 9.1-900. Purpose of the Sex Offender and Crimes Against Minors Registry.

— The purpose of the Sex Offender and Crimes Against Minors Registry (Registry) shall be to assist the efforts of law-enforcement agencies and others to protect their communities and families from repeat sex offenders and to protect children from becoming victims of criminal offenders by helping to prevent such individuals from being allowed to work directly with children. (2003, c. 584.)

Law Review. — For article, "Legal Issues Involving Children," see 35 U. Rich. L. Rev. 741 (2001). For comment, "Sex Offender Registration and Community Notification Laws: Will These Laws Survive?," see 37 U. Rich. L. Rev. 1245 (2003). For annual survey article on legal issues involving children, see 38 U. Rich. L. Rev. 161 (2003).

CASE NOTES

Constitutionality. — Where defendant was convicted of rape and malicious wounding, and as part of defendant's sentence, defendant was requested to register with local law enforcement officers as a sex offender pursuant to former § 19.2-298.1, and where former § 19.2-298.1 was enacted after the offenses occurred, the trial court did not violate defendant's federal and state constitutional rights against the imposition of an ex post facto law. Kitze v. Commonwealth, 23 Va. App. 213, 475 S.E.2d 830 (1996), cert. denied, 522 U.S. 817, 118 S. Ct. 66, 139 L. Ed. 2d 28 (1997) (decided under former § 19.2-298.1).

Inmate's challenge to the Virginia Sex Offender and Crimes Against Minors Registry Act (Sex Offender Act), § 9.1-900 et seq., was dismissed because the Sex Offender Act was civil in nature and did not violate the Ex Post Facto law and the protections against Double Jeopardy; the inmate's due process rights were not violated because the only issue that could be asserted at a hearing would be a challenge to the conviction, which was not contested, and the inmate did not have a protected liberty interest in precluding truthful information about his conviction being disseminated over the internet. Ballard v. Chief of FBI, — F. Supp. 2d —, 2004 U.S. Dist. LEXIS 1095 (W.D. Va. Jan. 20, 2004).

Purpose. — Sex offender registration requirement is not penal, and the General Assembly intended to facilitate law enforcement and protection of children. Kitze v. Commonwealth, 23 Va. App. 213, 475 S.E.2d 830 (1996), cert. denied, 522 U.S. 817, 118 S. Ct. 66, 139 L. Ed. 2d 28 (1997) (decided under former § 19.2-298.1).

§ 9.1-901. Persons for whom registration required. — A. Every person convicted on or after July 1, 1994, including a juvenile tried and convicted in the circuit court pursuant to § 16.1-269.1, whether sentenced as an adult or juvenile, of an offense set forth in § 9.1-902 and every juvenile found delinquent of an offense for which registration is required under subsection C of § 9.1-902 shall register and reregister as required by this chapter. Every person serving a sentence of confinement on or after July 1, 1994, for a conviction of an offense set forth in § 9.1-902 shall register and reregister as required by this chapter. Every person under community supervision as defined by § 53.1-1 or any similar form of supervision under the laws of the United States or any political subdivision thereof, on or after July 1, 1994, resulting from a conviction of an offense set forth in § 9.1-902 shall register and reregister as required by this chapter.

B. All provisions of the Sex Offender and Crimes Against Minors Registry Act shall apply retroactively except as provided under subsection C of § 9.1-902. This subsection is declaratory of existing law. (2003, c. 584; 2005, c. 586.)

Editor's note. — Acts 2005, c. 586, cl. 2, provides: "That the provisions of this act may result in a net increase in periods of imprisonment or commitment. Pursuant to § 30-19.1:4, the estimated amount of the necessary appropriation cannot be determined for periods of imprisonment in state adult correctional facilities and is $0 for periods of commitment to the custody of the Department of Juvenile Justice."

The 2005 amendments. — The 2005 amendment by c. 586 rewrote subsection A; and added subsection B.

CASE NOTES

Constitutionality. — Inmate's challenge to the Virginia Sex Offender and Crimes Against Minors Registry Act (Sex Offender Act), § 9.1-900 et seq., was dismissed because the Sex Offender Act was civil in nature and did not violate the Ex Post Facto law and the protections against Double Jeopardy; the inmate's due process rights were not violated because the only issue that could be asserted at a hearing would be a challenge to the conviction, which was not contested, and the inmate did not have a protected liberty interest in precluding truthful information about his conviction being disseminated over the internet. Ballard v. Chief of FBI, — F. Supp. 2d —, 2004 U.S. Dist. LEXIS 1095 (W.D. Va. Jan. 20, 2004).

§ 9.1-902. Offenses requiring registration. — A. For purposes of this chapter:

"Offense for which registration is required" means:

1. A violation or attempted violation of § 18.2-63, 18.2-64.1, former § 18.2-67.2:1, § 18.2-90 with the intent to commit rape, § 18.2-374.1 or subsection D of § 18.2-374.1:1; or a third or subsequent conviction of (i) § 18.2-67.4, (ii) subsection C of § 18.2-67.5 or (iii) § 18.2-386.1;

If the offense was committed on or after July 1, 2006, (i) a violation or attempted violation of § 18.2-91 with the intent to commit any felony offense listed in this section; (ii) a violation or attempted violation of subsection A of § 18.2-374.1:1; or (iii) a felony violation under § 18.2-67.5:1.

2. Clause (iv) of subsection B of § 18.2-374.3 or where the victim is a minor or is physically helpless or mentally incapacitated as defined in § 18.2-67.10, a violation or attempted violation of subsection A of § 18.2-47, clause (i) or (iii) of § 18.2-48, § 18.2-67.4, subsection C of § 18.2-67.5, § 18.2-361 or 18.2-366;

3. A violation of Chapter 117 (18 U.S.C. § 2421 et seq.) of Title 18 of the United States Code;

4. A "sexually violent offense";

5. "Murder"; or

6. Criminal homicide in conjunction with a violation of clause (i) of § 18.2-371 or § 18.2-371.1, when the offenses arise out of the same incident.

90

"Murder" means a violation of § 18.2-31 or 18.2-32 where the victim is (i) under 15 years of age or (ii) where the victim is at least 15 years of age but under 18 years of age and the murder is related to an offense listed in this section.

"Sexually violent offense" means a violation or attempted violation of:

1. Clause (ii) of § 18.2-48, § 18.2-61, 18.2-67.1, 18.2-67.2, 18.2-67.3, § 18.2-67.4 where the perpetrator is 18 years of age or older and the victim is under the age of six, subsections A and B of § 18.2-67.5, § 18.2-370, or 18.2-370.1;

2. Sections 18.2-63, 18.2-64.1, former § 18.2-67.2:1, § 18.2-90 with the intent to commit rape or, where the victim is a minor or is physically helpless or mentally incapacitated as defined in § 18.2-67.10, a violation or attempted violation of subsection A of § 18.2-47, § 18.2-67.4, subsection C of § 18.2-67.5, clause (i) or (iii) of § 18.2-48, § 18.2-361, 18.2-366, or 18.2-374.1. An offense listed under this subdivision shall be deemed a sexually violent offense only if the person has been convicted or adjudicated delinquent of any two or more such offenses, provided that person had been at liberty between such convictions or adjudications; or

3. If the offense was committed on or after July 1, 2006, a violation or attempted violation of § 18.2-91 with the intent to commit any felony offense listed in this section. An offense listed under this subdivision shall be deemed a sexually violent offense only if the person has been convicted or adjudicated delinquent of any two or more such offenses, provided that person had been at liberty between such convictions or adjudications.

B. *"Offense for which registration is required"* and *"sexually violent offense"* shall also include any similar offense under the laws of (i) any foreign country or any political subdivision thereof, (ii) the United States or any political subdivision thereof and any offense for which registration in a sex offender and crimes against minors registry is required under the laws of the jurisdiction where the offender was convicted.

C. Juveniles adjudicated delinquent shall not be required to register; however, where the offender is a juvenile over the age of 13 at the time of the offense who is tried as a juvenile and is adjudicated delinquent of any offense enumerated in subdivisions A 1 through A 4 on or after July 1, 2005, the court may, in its discretion and upon motion of the attorney for the Commonwealth, find that the circumstances of the offense require offender registration. In making its determination, the court shall consider all of the following factors that are relevant to the case: (i) the degree to which the delinquent act was committed with the use of force, threat or intimidation, (ii) the age and maturity of the complaining witness, (iii) the age and maturity of the offender, (iv) the difference in the ages of the complaining witness and the offender, (v) the nature of the relationship between the complaining witness and the offender, (vi) the offender's prior criminal history, and (vii) any other aggravating or mitigating factors relevant to the case. (2003, cc. 584, 732; 2004, cc. 414, 444; 2005, cc. 586, 603, 631; 2006, cc. 857, 875, 914, 931.)

Cross references. — As to prohibition on adoption by violent sex offenders, see § 63.2-1205.1.

Editor's note. — Acts 2003, c. 732 amended § 19.2-298.1, which was repealed by Acts 2003, c. 584, cl. 2. At the direction of the Virginia Code Commission, effect has been given in this section, as set out above, to Acts 2003, c. 732. In accordance with c. 732, the amendment, in subdivision A 1, added clause designations (i) and (ii), deleted "or a third or subsequent conviction of" preceding "subsection C of § 18.2-67.5," and added clause (iii).

Acts 2005, cc. 586 and 603, cl. 2 provide: "That the provisions of this act may result in a net increase in periods of imprisonment or commitment. Pursuant to § 30-19.1:4, the estimated amount of the necessary appropriation cannot be determined for periods of imprisonment in state adult correctional facilities and is $0 for periods of commitment to the custody of the Department of Juvenile Justice."

Acts 2005, c. 631, cl. 3 provides: "That the provisions of this act may result in a net increase in periods of imprisonment or commitment. Pursuant to § 30-19.1:4, the estimated amount of the necessary appropriation is $43,177 for periods of imprisonment in state adult correctional facilities and is $0 for periods of commitment to the custody of the Department of Juvenile Justice.

Acts 2006, c. 857, cl. 4, provides: "That the provisions of this act may result in a net increase in periods of imprisonment or commitment. Pursuant to § 30-19.1:4, the estimated amount of the necessary appropriation is $2,419,496 for periods of imprisonment in state adult correctional facilities and is $0 for periods of commitment to the custody of the Department of Juvenile Justice."

Acts 2006, c. 875, cl. 2, provides: "That the provisions of this act may result in a net increase in periods of imprisonment or commitment. Pursuant to § 30-19.1:4, the estimated amount of the necessary appropriation is $207,814 for periods of imprisonment in state adult correctional facilities and is $0 for periods of commitment to the custody of the Department of Juvenile Justice."

Acts 2006, c. 914, cl. 5, provides: "That the provisions of this act may result in a net increase in periods of imprisonment or commitment. Pursuant to § 30-19.1:4, the estimated amount of the necessary appropriation is at least $2,419,496 for periods of imprisonment in state adult correctional facilities and is $0 for periods of commitment to the custody of the Department of Juvenile Justice."

Acts 2006, c. 931, cl. 2, provides: "That the provisions of this act may result in a net increase in periods of imprisonment or commitment. Pursuant to § 30-19.1:4, the estimated amount of the necessary appropriation is $616,909 for periods of imprisonment in state adult correctional facilities and is $0 for periods of commitment to the custody of the Department of Juvenile Justice."

The 2005 amendments. — The 2005 amendment by c. 586, in subsection A, subdivision 2 of the definition of "Sexually violent offense," substituted "An offense" for "Conviction of an offense," inserted "or adjudicated delinquent" and "or adjudications"; added subsection C; and made minor stylistic changes.

The 2005 amendment by c. 603 added subdivision A 5 in the definition of "Offense for which registration is required"; inserted "§ 18.2-67.4 where the perpetrator is 18 years of age or older and the victim is under the age of six" in the definition of "Sexually violent offense" in subsection A; and inserted "and any offense for which registration in a sex offender and crimes against minors registry is required under the laws of the political subdivision where the offender was convicted" in subsection B; and made stylistic changes.

The 2005 amendment by c. 631, under the definition of "Sexually violent offense," inserted "former" preceding "§ 18.2-67.2:1" in subdivision 1 under the definition of "Offense for which registration is required" and subdivision b under the definition of "Sexually violent offense"; and made minor stylistic changes.

The 2006 amendments. — The 2006 amendments by cc. 857, 914 and 931 are identical, and in subsection A, in the definition of "Offense for which registration is required," added the last paragraph of subdivision A 1, in subdivision A 2, inserted "Clause (iv) of subsection B of § 18.2-374.3 or" at the beginning and deleted "or clause (iv) of subsection B of § 18.2-374.3" at the end, deleted "pursuant to § 18.2-31 or 18.2-32 where the victim is a minor" at the end of subdivision A 5, added subdivision A 6 and made related changes, added the definition of "Murder," added subdivision A 3 in the definition of "sexually violent offense" and made related changes; and in subsection B, inserted "(i) any foreign country or any political subdivision thereof, (ii)" and substituted "jurisdiction" for "political subdivision."

The 2006 amendment by c. 875 added "or a felony violation under § 18.2-67.5:1 committed on or after July 1, 2006" in subdivision 1 of the paragraph defining "Offense for which registration is required" in subsection A.

Subdivision A 1 in the definition of "Offense for which registration is required" is set out in the form above at the direction of the Virginia Code Commission.

CASE NOTES

Constitutionality. — Where defendant was convicted of rape and malicious wounding, and as part of defendant's sentence, defendant was requested to register with local law enforcement officers as a sex offender pursuant to this section, and where this section was enacted after the offenses occurred, the trial court did not violate his federal and state constitutional rights against the imposition of an ex post facto law. Kitze v. Commonwealth, 23 Va. App. 213, 475 S.E.2d 830 (1996), cert. denied, 522 U.S. 817, 118 S. Ct. 66, 139 L. Ed. 2d 28 (1997) (decided under former § 19.2-298.1).

Purpose. — Sex offender registration requirement is not penal, and the General Assembly intended to facilitate law enforcement and protection of children. Kitze v. Commonwealth, 23 Va. App. 213, 475 S.E.2d 830 (1996), cert. denied, 522 U.S. 817, 118 S. Ct. 66, 139 L. Ed. 2d 28 (1997) (decided under former § 19.2-298.1).

Registration requirement proper. — Trial court did not err in requiring defendant to register as a sex offender based on defendant's conviction of computer solicitation for sex with a minor based on defendant's actions in using his computer to solicit sex from someone he thought was a 13-year-old girl, but who was, in fact, a police officer posing as a 13-year-old girl. Colbert v. Commonwealth, 47 Va. App. 390, 624 S.E.2d 108, 2006 Va. App. LEXIS 7 (2006).

§ 9.1-903. Registration procedures. — A. Every person convicted, including juveniles tried and convicted in the circuit courts pursuant to § 16.1-269.1, whether sentenced as an adult or juvenile, of an offense for which registration is required and every juvenile found delinquent of an offense for which registration is required under subsection C of § 9.1-902 shall be required upon conviction to register and reregister with the Department of State Police. The court shall order the person to provide to the local law-enforcement agency of the county or city where he physically resides all information required by the State Police for inclusion in the Registry. The court shall immediately remand the person to the custody of the local law-enforcement agency for the purpose of obtaining the person's fingerprints and photographs of a type and kind specified by the State Police for inclusion in the Registry. Upon conviction, the local law-enforcement agency shall forthwith forward to the State Police all the necessary registration information.

B. Every person required to register shall register in person within three days of his release from confinement in a state, local or juvenile correctional facility, in a state civil commitment program for sexually violent predators or, if a sentence of confinement is not imposed, within three days of suspension of the sentence or in the case of a juvenile of disposition. A person required to register shall register, submit to be photographed as part of the registration, and submit to have a sample of his blood, saliva, or tissue taken for DNA (deoxyribonucleic acid) analysis to determine identification characteristics specific to the person, and provide information regarding place of employment. The local law-enforcement agency shall obtain from the person who presents himself for registration or reregistration one set of fingerprints, place of employment information, proof of residency and a photograph of a type and kind specified by the State Police for inclusion in the Registry and advise the person of his duties regarding reregistration. The local law-enforcement agency shall obtain from the person who presents himself for registration a sample of his blood, saliva or tissue taken for DNA (deoxyribonucleic acid) analysis to determine identification characteristics specific to the person. If a sample has been previously taken from the person, as indicated by the Local Inmate Data System (LIDS), no additional sample shall be taken. The local law-enforcement agency shall forthwith forward to the State Police all necessary registration information.

C. To establish proof of residence in Virginia, a person shall present one photo-identification form issued by a governmental agency of the Commonwealth which contains the person's complete name, gender, date of birth and complete physical address.

D. Any person required to register shall also reregister in person with the local law-enforcement agency following any change of residence, whether within or without the Commonwealth. If his new residence is within the Commonwealth, the person shall register in person with the local law-enforcement agency where his new residence is located within three days following his change in residence. If the new residence is located outside of the Commonwealth, the person shall register in person with the local law-enforcement agency where he previously registered within 10 days prior to his change of residence. If a probation or parole officer becomes aware of a change of residence for any of his probationers or parolees required to register, the probation or parole officer shall notify the State Police forthwith of learning of the change of residence. Whenever a person subject to registration changes residence to another state, the State Police shall notify the designated law-enforcement agency of that state.

E. Any person required to register shall reregister in person with the local law-enforcement agency where his residence is located within three days following any change of the place of employment, whether within or without the Commonwealth. If a probation or parole officer becomes aware of a change of the place of employment for any of his probationers or parolees required to register, the probation or parole officer shall notify the State Police forthwith upon learning of the change of the person's place of employment. Whenever a person subject to registration changes his place of employment to another state, the State Police shall notify the designated law-enforcement agency of that state.

F. The registration shall be maintained in the Registry and shall include the person's name, all aliases that he has used or under which he may have been known, the date and locality of the conviction for which registration is required, his fingerprints and a photograph of a type and kind specified by the State Police, his date of birth, social security number, current physical and mailing address and a description of the offense or offenses for which he was convicted. The registration shall also include the locality of the conviction and a description of the offense or offenses for previous convictions for the offenses set forth in § 9.1-902.

G. The local law-enforcement agency shall forthwith forward to the State Police all necessary registration or reregistration information received by it. Upon receipt of registration or reregistration information the State Police shall forthwith notify the chief law-enforcement officer of the locality listed as the person's address on the registration and reregistration. (2003, c. 584; 2004, c. 834; 2005, c. 586; 2006, cc. 857, 914.)

Editor's note. — Acts 2005, c. 586, cl. 2, provides: "That the provisions of this act may result in a net increase in periods of imprisonment or commitment. Pursuant to § 30-19.1:4, the estimated amount of the necessary appropriation cannot be determined for periods of imprisonment in state adult correctional facilities and is $0 for periods of commitment to the custody of the Department of Juvenile Justice."

Acts 2006, c. 857, cl. 4, provides: "That the provisions of this act may result in a net increase in periods of imprisonment or commitment. Pursuant to § 30-19.1:4, the estimated amount of the necessary appropriation is $2,419,496 for periods of imprisonment in state adult correctional facilities and is $0 for periods of commitment to the custody of the Department of Juvenile Justice."

Acts 2006, c. 914, cl. 5, provides: "That the provisions of this act may result in a net increase in periods of imprisonment or commitment. Pursuant to § 30-19.1:4, the estimated amount of the necessary appropriation is at least $2,419,496 for periods of imprisonment in state adult correctional facilities and is $0 for periods of commitment to the custody of the Department of Juvenile Justice."

The 2005 amendments. — The 2005 amendment by c. 586 inserted "and every juvenile found delinquent of an offense for which registration is required under subsection C of § 9.1-902" in the first sentence of subsection A.

The 2006 amendments. — The 2006 amendments by cc. 857 and 914 are identical, and in subsection A, inserted "immediately" in the third sentence and, in the last sentence, inserted "Upon conviction" and "forthwith" and deleted "within seven days of the date of sentencing" at the end; in subsection B, substituted "three days" for "10 days" twice in the first sentence, added the second sentence, in the third sentence, substituted "one set" for "two sets," inserted "place of employment information" and substituted "one photograph" for "two photographs," added the fourth and fifth sentences, and substituted "forthwith" for "promptly" in the last sentence; inserted "physical" in subsection C; in subsection D, substituted "three days" for "10 days" in the second sentence and "forthwith" for "within 10 days" in the fourth sentence; added subsection E; redesignated former subsections E and F as subsections F and G; and substituted "forthwith" for "promptly" in the first sentence of subsection G.

§ **9.1-904. Reregistration.** — A. Every person required to register, other than a person convicted of a sexually violent offense or murder, shall reregister with the State Police on an annual basis from the date of the initial registration. Every person convicted of a sexually violent offense or murder shall reregister with the State Police every 90 days from the date of initial registration. Reregistration means that the person has notified the State Police, confirmed his current physical and mailing address and provided such other information, including identifying information, which the State Police may require. Upon registration and as may be necessary thereafter, the State Police shall provide the person with an address verification form to be used for reregistration. The form shall contain in bold print a statement indicating that failure to comply with the registration required is punishable as provided in § 18.2-472.1.

B. Any person convicted of a violation of § 18.2-472.1, other than a person convicted of a sexually violent offense or murder, shall reregister with the State Police every 180 days from the date of such conviction. Any person convicted of a violation of § 18.2-472.1, in which such person was included on the Registry for a conviction of a sexually violent offense or murder, shall reregister with the State Police every 30 days from the date of conviction. Reregistration means the person has notified the State Police, confirmed his current physical and mailing address and provided such other information, including identifying information, which the State Police may require. Upon registration and as may be necessary thereafter, the State Police shall provide the person with an address verification form to be used for reregistration. The form shall state the registration requirements and contain in bold print a statement indicating that failure to comply with the registration requirements is punishable as provided in § 18.2-472.1.

C. Every person required to register pursuant to this chapter shall submit to be photographed by a local law-enforcement agency every two years commencing with the date of initial registration. Photographs shall be in color, be taken with the registrant facing the camera, and clearly show the registrant's face and shoulders only. No person other than the registrant may appear in the photograph submitted. The photograph shall indicate the registrant's full name, date of birth and the date the photograph was taken. The local law-enforcement agency shall forthwith forward the photograph and the registration form to the State Police. Where practical, the local law-enforcement agency may electronically transfer a digital photograph containing the required information to the Sex Offender and Crimes Against Minors Registry within the State Police. (2003, c. 584; 2006, cc. 857, 914.)

Editor's note. — Acts 2006, c. 857, cl. 4, provides: "That the provisions of this act may result in a net increase in periods of imprisonment or commitment. Pursuant to § 30-19.1:4, the estimated amount of the necessary appropriation is $2,419,496 for periods of imprisonment in state adult correctional facilities and is $0 for periods of commitment to the custody of the Department of Juvenile Justice."

Acts 2006, c. 914, cl. 5, provides: "That the provisions of this act may result in a net increase in periods of imprisonment or commitment. Pursuant to § 30-19.1:4, the estimated amount of the necessary appropriation is at least $2,419,496 for periods of imprisonment in state adult correctional facilities and is $0 for periods of commitment to the custody of the Department of Juvenile Justice."

The 2006 amendments. — The 2006 amendments by cc. 857 and 914 are identical, and inserted the subsection A designation at the beginning of the first paragraph; in subsection A, inserted "or murder" in the first and second sentences and deleted "a Class 1 misdemeanor or a Class 6 felony as" following "punishable as" in the last sentence; and added subsections B and C.

§ 9.1-905. New residents and nonresident offenders; registration required.

§ 9.1-905. New residents and nonresident offenders; registration required. — A. All persons required to register shall register within three days of establishing a residence in the Commonwealth.

B. Nonresident offenders entering the Commonwealth for an extended visit, for employment, to carry on a vocation, or as a student attending school who are required to register in their state of residence or who would be required to register if a resident of the Commonwealth shall, within three days of entering the Commonwealth for an extended visit, accepting employment or enrolling in school in the Commonwealth, be required to register and reregister in person with the local law-enforcement agency.

C. To document employment or school attendance in Virginia a person shall present proof of enrollment as a student or suitable proof of temporary employment in the Commonwealth and one photo-identification form issued by a governmental agency of the person's state of residence which contains the person's complete name, gender, date of birth and complete address.

D. For purposes of this section:

"Employment" and *"carry on a vocation"* include employment that is full-time or part-time for a period of time exceeding 14 days or for an aggregate period of time exceeding 30 days during any calendar year, whether financially compensated, volunteered, or for the purpose of government or educational benefit.

"Extended visit" means a period of visitation for any purpose in the Commonwealth of 30 days or more.

"Student" means a person who is enrolled on a full-time or part-time basis, in any public or private educational institution, including any secondary school, trade or professional institution, or institution of higher education. (2003, c. 584; 2005, c. 603; 2006, cc. 857, 914.)

Editor's note. — Acts 2005, c. 603, cl. 2, provides: "That the provisions of this act may result in a net increase in periods of imprisonment or commitment. Pursuant to § 30-19.1:4, the estimated amount of the necessary appropriation cannot be determined for periods of imprisonment in state adult correctional facilities and is $0 for periods of commitment to the custody of the Department of Juvenile Justice."

Acts 2006, c. 857, cl. 4, provides: "That the provisions of this act may result in a net increase in periods of imprisonment or commitment. Pursuant to § 30-19.1:4, the estimated amount of the necessary appropriation is $2,419,496 for periods of imprisonment in state adult correctional facilities and is $0 for periods of commitment to the custody of the Department of Juvenile Justice."

Acts 2006, c. 914, cl. 5, provides: "That the provisions of this act may result in a net increase in periods of imprisonment or commitment. Pursuant to § 30-19.1:4, the estimated amount of the necessary appropriation is at least $2,419,496 for periods of imprisonment in state adult correctional facilities and is $0 for periods of commitment to the custody of the Department of Juvenile Justice."

The 2005 amendments. — The 2005 amendment by c. 603, in subsection B, inserted "an extended visit, for" preceding "employment, to carry" and "entering the Commonwealth for an extended visit" preceding "accepting employment"; and added the definition of "Extended visit" in subsection D.

The 2006 amendments. — The 2006 amendments by cc. 857 and 914 are identical, and substituted "three days" for "10 days" in subsections A and B.

§ 9.1-906. Enrollment or employment at institution of higher learning; information required. — A. Persons required to register or reregister who are enrolled in or employed at institutions of higher learning shall, in addition to other registration requirements, indicate on their registration and reregistration form the name and location of the institution attended by or employing the registrant whether such institution is within or without the Commonwealth. In addition, persons required to register or reregister shall notify the local law-enforcement agency in person within three days of any change in their enrollment or employment status with an institution of higher learning. The local law-enforcement agency shall forthwith forward to the State Police all necessary registration or reregistration information received by it.

B. Upon receipt of a registration or reregistration indicating enrollment or employment with an institute of higher learning or notification of a change in status, the State Police shall notify the chief law-enforcement officer of the institution's law-enforcement agency or, if there is no institutional law-enforcement agency, the local law-enforcement agency serving that institution, of the registration, reregistration, or change in status. The law-enforcement agency receiving notification under this section shall make such information available upon request.

C. For purposes of this section:

"Employment" includes full- or part-time, temporary or permanent or contractual employment at an institution of higher learning either with or without compensation.

"Enrollment" includes both full- and part-time.

"Institution of higher learning" means any post-secondary school, trade or professional institution, or institution of higher education. (2003, c. 584; 2006, cc. 857, 914.)

Editor's note. — Acts 2006, c. 857, cl. 4, provides: "That the provisions of this act may result in a net increase in periods of imprisonment or commitment. Pursuant to § 30-19.1:4, the estimated amount of the necessary appropriation is $2,419,496 for periods of imprisonment in state adult correctional facilities and is $0 for periods of commitment to the custody of the Department of Juvenile Justice."

Acts 2006, c. 914, cl. 5, provides: "That the provisions of this act may result in a net increase in periods of imprisonment or commit-

ment. Pursuant to § 30-19.1:4, the estimated amount of the necessary appropriation is at least $2,419,496 for periods of imprisonment in state adult correctional facilities and is $0 for periods of commitment to the custody of the Department of Juvenile Justice."

The 2006 amendments. — The 2006 amendments by cc. 857 and 914 are identical, and in subsection A, substituted "three days" for "10 days" in the second sentence and "forthwith" for "promptly" in the last sentence.

§ 9.1-907. Procedures upon a failure to register or reregister. — A. Whenever it appears from the records of the State Police that a person has failed to comply with the duty to register or reregister, the State Police shall promptly investigate and, if there is probable cause to believe a violation has occurred, obtain a warrant or assist in obtaining an indictment charging a violation of § 18.2-472.1 in the jurisdiction in which the person last registered or reregistered or, if the person failed to comply with the duty to register, in the jurisdiction in which the person was last convicted of an offense for which registration or reregistration is required or if the person was convicted of an offense requiring registration outside the Commonwealth, in the jurisdiction in which the person resides. The State Police shall forward to the jurisdiction an affidavit signed by the custodian of the records that such person failed to comply with the duty to register or reregister. Such affidavit shall be admitted into evidence as prima facie evidence of the failure to comply with the duty to register or reregister in any trial for the violation of § 18.2-472.1. The State Police shall also promptly notify the local law-enforcement agency of the jurisdiction of the person's last known residence as shown in the records of the State Police.

B. Nothing in this section shall prohibit a law-enforcement officer employed by a sheriff's office or police department of a locality from enforcing the provisions of this chapter, including obtaining a warrant, or assisting in obtaining an indictment for a violation of § 18.2-472.1. The local law-enforcement agency shall notify the State Police forthwith of such actions taken pursuant to this chapter or under the authority granted pursuant to this section.

C. The State Police shall physically verify or cause to be physically verified the registration information within 30 days of the initial registration and semiannually each year thereafter and within 30 days of a change of address of those persons who are not under the control of the Department of Corrections or Community Supervision as defined by § 53.1-1, who are required to register pursuant to this chapter. Whenever it appears that a person has provided false registration information, the State Police shall promptly investigate and, if there is probable cause to believe that a violation has occurred, obtain a warrant or assist in obtaining an indictment charging a violation of § 18.2-472.1 in the jurisdiction in which the person last registered or reregistered. The State Police shall forward to the jurisdiction an affidavit signed by the custodian of the records that such person failed to comply with the provisions of this chapter. Such affidavit shall be admitted into evidence as prima facie evidence of the failure to comply with the provisions of this chapter in any trial for the violation of § 18.2-472.1. The State Police shall also promptly notify the local law-enforcement agency of the jurisdiction of the person's last known residence as shown in the records of the State Police.

D. The Department of Corrections shall physically verify the registration information within 30 days of the original registration and semiannually each year thereafter and within 30 days of a change of address of all persons who are under the control of the Department of Corrections or Community Supervision as defined by § 53.1-1, who are required to register pursuant to this chapter. The Department of Corrections, upon request, shall provide the State Police the verification information, in an electronic format approved by the State Police, regarding persons under their control who are required to register pursuant to the chapter. Whenever it appears that a person has provided false registration information, the Department of Corrections shall promptly notify the State Police, who shall investigate and, if there is probable cause to believe that a violation has occurred, obtain a warrant or assist in obtaining an indictment charging a violation of § 18.2-472.1 in the jurisdiction in which the person last registered or reregistered. The State Police shall forward to the jurisdiction an affidavit signed by the custodian of the records that such person failed to comply with the provisions of this chapter. Such affidavit shall be admitted into evidence as prima facie evidence of the failure to comply with the provisions of this chapter in any trial for the violation of § 18.2-472.1. The State Police shall also promptly notify the local law-enforcement agency of the jurisdiction of the person's last known residence as shown in the records of the State Police. (2003, c. 584; 2005, c. 603; 2006, cc. 857, 914.)

Editor's note. — Acts 2005, c. 603, cl. 2, provides: "That the provisions of this act may result in a net increase in periods of imprisonment or commitment. Pursuant to § 30-19.1:4, the estimated amount of the necessary appropriation cannot be determined for periods of imprisonment in state adult correctional facilities and is $0 for periods of commitment to the custody of the Department of Juvenile Justice."

Acts 2006, c. 857, cl. 4, provides: "That the provisions of this act may result in a net increase in periods of imprisonment or commitment. Pursuant to § 30-19.1:4, the estimated amount of the necessary appropriation is $2,419,496 for periods of imprisonment in state adult correctional facilities and is $0 for periods of commitment to the custody of the Department of Juvenile Justice."

Acts 2006, c. 914, cl. 5, provides: "That the provisions of this act may result in a net in-crease in periods of imprisonment or commitment. Pursuant to § 30-19.1:4, the estimated amount of the necessary appropriation is at least $2,419,496 for periods of imprisonment in state adult correctional facilities and is $0 for periods of commitment to the custody of the Department of Juvenile Justice."

The 2005 amendments. — The 2005 amendment by c. 603 deleted "together with the warrant" preceding "an affidavit signed" in subsection A; and added subsection B.

The 2006 amendments. — The 2006 amendments by cc. 857 and 914 are identical, and in subsection A, in the first sentence, inserted "or assist in obtaining an indictment" and added the language beginning "or if the person was convicted" at the end; in subsection B, added the language beginning "including obtaining a warrant" at the end of the first sentence and added the last sentence; and added subsections C and D.

§ 9.1-908. Duration of registration requirement. — Any person required to register or reregister shall be required to register for a period of 10

years from the date of initial registration or for a period of 10 years from the date of his last conviction for a violation of § 18.2-472.1, whichever is longer, except that any person who has been convicted of (i) any sexually violent offense, (ii) murder or (iii) former § 18.2-67.2:1 shall have a continuing duty to reregister for life.

Any period of confinement in a federal, state or local correctional facility, hospital or any other institution or facility during the otherwise applicable 10-year period shall toll the registration period and the duty to reregister shall be extended. Persons confined in a federal, state, or local correctional facility shall not be required to reregister until released from custody. (2003, c. 584; 2005, c. 631; 2006, cc. 857, 914.)

Editor's note. — Acts 2005, c. 631, cl. 3, provides: "That the provisions of this act may result in a net increase in periods of imprisonment or commitment. Pursuant to § 30-19.1:4, the estimated amount of the necessary appropriation is $43,177 for periods of imprisonment in state adult correctional facilities and is $0 for periods of commitment to the custody of the Department of Juvenile Justice."

Acts 2006, c. 857, cl. 4, provides: "That the provisions of this act may result in a net increase in periods of imprisonment or commitment. Pursuant to § 30-19.1:4, the estimated amount of the necessary appropriation is $2,419,496 for periods of imprisonment in state adult correctional facilities and is $0 for periods of commitment to the custody of the Department of Juvenile Justice."

Acts 2006, c. 914, cl. 5, provides: "That the provisions of this act may result in a net increase in periods of imprisonment or commitment. Pursuant to § 30-19.1:4, the estimated amount of the necessary appropriation is at least $2,419,496 for periods of imprisonment in state adult correctional facilities and is $0 for periods of commitment to the custody of the Department of Juvenile Justice."

The 2005 amendments. — The 2005 amendment by c. 631 inserted "former" preceding "§ 18.2-67.2:1" in the first paragraph.

The 2006 amendments. — The 2006 amendments by cc. 857 and 914 are identical, and in the first paragraph, inserted "or for a period of 10 years from the date of his last conviction for a violation of § 18.2-472.1, whichever is longer" and "murder or (iii)" and made a related change.

CASE NOTES

Adoption. — As § 9.1-908 did not operate to preclude a convicted sex offender who was required to register annually for ten years and who had not yet registered from adopting a child, and nothing in § 63.2-1205 automati-cally precluded adoption in such a case, a birth father's challenge to his child's adoption by withholding his consent was denied. Gray v. Bourne, 46 Va. App. 11, 614 S.E.2d 661, 2005 Va. App. LEXIS 237 (2005).

§ 9.1-909. Relief from registration or reregistration. — A. Upon expiration of three years from the date upon which the duty to register as a sexually violent offender or murderer is imposed, the person required to register may petition the court in which he was convicted or, if the conviction occurred outside of the Commonwealth, the circuit court in the jurisdiction where he currently resides, for relief from the requirement to reregister every 90 days. After five years from the date of his last conviction for a violation of § 18.2-472.1, a sexually violent offender or murderer may petition for relief from the requirement to reregister monthly. A person who is required to register may similarly petition the circuit court for relief from the requirement to reregister every 180 days after five years from the date of his last conviction for a violation of § 18.2-472.1. The court shall hold a hearing on the petition, on notice to the attorney for the Commonwealth, to determine whether the person suffers from a mental abnormality or a personality disorder that makes the person a menace to the health and safety of others or significantly impairs his ability to control his sexual behavior. Prior to the hearing the court shall order a comprehensive assessment of the applicant by a panel of three certified sex offender treatment providers as defined in § 54.1-3600. A report of the assessment shall be filed with the court prior to the hearing. The costs of the assessment shall be taxed as costs of the proceeding.

If, after consideration of the report and such other evidence as may be presented at the hearing, the court finds by clear and convincing evidence that the person does not suffer from a mental abnormality or a personality disorder that makes the person a menace to the health and safety of others or significantly impairs his ability to control his sexual behavior, the petition shall be granted and the duty to reregister more frequently than once a year shall be terminated. The court shall promptly notify the State Police upon entry of an order granting the petition. The person shall, however, be under a continuing duty to register annually for life. If the petition is denied, the duty to reregister with the same frequency as before shall continue. An appeal from the denial of a petition shall lie to the Supreme Court.

A petition for relief pursuant to this subsection may not be filed within three years from the date on which any previous petition for such relief was denied.

B. The duly appointed guardian of a person convicted of an offense requiring registration or reregistration as either a sex offender, sexually violent offender or murderer, who due to a physical condition is incapable of (i) reoffending and (ii) reregistering, may petition the court in which the person was convicted for relief from the requirement to reregister. The court shall hold a hearing on the petition, on notice to the attorney for the Commonwealth, to determine whether the person suffers from a physical condition that makes the person (i) no longer a menace to the health and safety of others and (ii) incapable of reregistering. Prior to the hearing the court shall order a comprehensive assessment of the applicant by at least two licensed physicians other than the person's primary care physician. A report of the assessment shall be filed with the court prior to the hearing. The costs of the assessment shall be taxed as costs of the proceeding.

If, after consideration of the report and such other evidence as may be presented at the hearing, the court finds by clear and convincing evidence that due to his physical condition the person (i) no longer poses a menace to the health and safety of others and (ii) is incapable of reregistering, the petition shall be granted and the duty to reregister shall be terminated. However, for a person whose duty to reregister was terminated under this subsection, the Department of State Police shall, annually for sex offenders and quarterly for persons convicted of sexually violent offenses and murder, verify and report to the attorney for the Commonwealth in the jurisdiction in which the person resides that the person continues to suffer from the physical condition that resulted in such termination.

The court shall promptly notify the State Police upon entry of an order granting the petition to terminate the duty to reregister.

If the petition is denied, the duty to reregister shall continue. An appeal from the denial of a petition shall be to the Virginia Supreme Court.

A petition for relief pursuant to this subsection may not be filed within three years from the date on which any previous petition for such relief was denied.

If, at any time, the person's physical condition changes so that he is capable of reoffending or reregistering, the attorney for the Commonwealth shall file a petition with the circuit court in the jurisdiction where the person resides and the court shall hold a hearing on the petition, with notice to the person and his guardian, to determine whether the person still suffers from a physical condition that makes the person (i) no longer a menace to the health and safety of others and (ii) incapable of reregistering. If the petition is granted, the duty to reregister shall commence from the date of the court's order. An appeal from the denial or granting of a petition shall be to the Virginia Supreme Court. Prior to the hearing the court shall order a comprehensive assessment of the applicant by at least two licensed physicians other than the person's primary care physician. A report of the assessment shall be filed with the court prior to the hearing. The costs of the assessment shall be taxed as costs of the proceeding. (2003, c. 584; 2006, cc. 857, 914.)

Editor's note. — Acts 2006, c. 857, cl. 4, provides: "That the provisions of this act may result in a net increase in periods of imprisonment or commitment. Pursuant to § 30-19.1:4, the estimated amount of the necessary appropriation is $2,419,496 for periods of imprisonment in state adult correctional facilities and is $0 for periods of commitment to the custody of the Department of Juvenile Justice."

Acts 2006, c. 914, cl. 5, provides: "That the provisions of this act may result in a net increase in periods of imprisonment or commitment. Pursuant to § 30-19.1:4, the estimated amount of the necessary appropriation is at least $2,419,496 for periods of imprisonment in state adult correctional facilities and is $0 for periods of commitment to the custody of the Department of Juvenile Justice."

The 2006 amendments. — The 2006 amendments by cc. 857 and 914 are identical, and in subsection A, in the first pararaph,

inserted "or murderer" and "or, if the conviction occurred outside the Commonwealth, the circuit court in the jurisdiction where he currently resides" in the first sentence, and added the second and third sentences; in the second paragraph, substituted "more frequently than once a year" for "every 90 days" in the first sentence, deleted "and the State Police shall remove Registry information on the offender from the Internet system" at the end of the second sentence, and substituted "with the same frequency as before" for "every 90 days" in the third sentence; in subsection B, inserted "or murderer" in the first sentence of the first paragraph and made a related change, in the last sentence of the second paragraph, inserted "persons convicted of" and substituted "offenses and murder" for "offenders," and at the end of the third paragraph, deleted "and the State Police shall remove any Registry information on the offender from the Internet system."

§ 9.1-910. Removal of name and information from Registry. —

A. Any person required to register, other than a person who has been convicted of any (i) sexually violent offense, (ii) two or more offenses for which registration is required, (iii) a violation of former § 18.2-67.2:1, or (iv) murder, may petition the circuit court in which he was convicted or the circuit court in the jurisdiction where he then resides for removal of his name and all identifying information from the Registry. A petition may not be filed earlier than 10 years after the date of initial registration nor earlier than 10 years from the date of his last conviction for a violation of § 18.2-472.1. The court shall hold a hearing on the petition at which the applicant and any interested persons may present witnesses and other evidence. If, after such hearing, the court is satisfied that such person no longer poses a risk to public safety, the court shall grant the petition. In the event the petition is not granted, the person shall wait at least 24 months from the date of the denial to file a new petition for removal from the Registry.

B. The State Police shall remove from the Registry the name of any person and all identifying information upon receipt of an order granting a petition pursuant to subsection A or at the end of the period for which the person is required to register under § 9.1-908. (2003, c. 584; 2005, c. 631; 2006, cc. 857, 914.)

Editor's note. — Acts 2005, c. 631, cl. 3, provides: "That the provisions of this act may result in a net increase in periods of imprisonment or commitment. Pursuant to § 30-19.1:4, the estimated amount of the necessary appropriation is $43,177 for periods of imprisonment in state adult correctional facilities and is $0 for periods of commitment to the custody of the Department of Juvenile Justice."

Acts 2006, c. 857, cl. 4, provides: "That the provisions of this act may result in a net increase in periods of imprisonment or commit-

ment. Pursuant to § 30-19.1:4, the estimated amount of the necessary appropriation is $2,419,496 for periods of imprisonment in state adult correctional facilities and is $0 for periods of commitment to the custody of the Department of Juvenile Justice."

Acts 2006, c. 914, cl. 5, provides: "That the provisions of this act may result in a net increase in periods of imprisonment or commitment. Pursuant to § 30-19.1:4, the estimated amount of the necessary appropriation is at least $2,419,496 for periods of imprisonment in state adult correctional facilities and is $0 for periods of commitment to the custody of the Department of Juvenile Justice."

The 2005 amendments. — The 2005 amendment by c. 631 inserted "former" preceding "§ 18.2-67.2:1" in subsection A.

The 2006 amendments. — The 2006 amendments by cc. 857 and 914 are identical, and in subsection A, deleted "or" preceding (iii) and inserted "or (iv) murder" in the first sentence, and inserted "nor earlier than 10 years from the date of his last conviction for a violation of § 18.2-472.1" at the end of the second sentence.

§ 9.1-911. Registry maintenance. — The Registry shall include conviction data received from the courts, including the disposition records for juveniles tried and convicted in the circuit courts pursuant to § 16.1-269.1, on convictions for offenses for which registration is required and registrations and reregistrations received from persons required to do so. The Registry shall also include a separate indication that a person has been convicted of a sexually violent offense. The State Police shall forthwith transmit the appropriate information as required by the Federal Bureau of Investigation for inclusion in the National Sex Offender Registry. (2003, c. 584.)

§ 9.1-912. Registry access and dissemination; fees. — A. Except as provided in § 9.1-913 and subsection B of this section, Registry information shall be disseminated upon request made directly to the State Police or to the State Police through a local law-enforcement agency. Such information may be disclosed to any person requesting information on a specific individual in accordance with subsection B. The State Police shall make Registry information available, upon request, to criminal justice agencies including local law-enforcement agencies through the Virginia Criminal Information Network (VCIN). Registry information provided under this section shall be used for the purposes of the administration of criminal justice, for the screening of current or prospective employees or volunteers or otherwise for the protection of the public in general and children in particular. The Superintendent of State Police may by regulation establish a fee not to exceed $15 for responding to requests for information from the Registry. Any fees collected shall be deposited in a special account to be used to offset the costs of administering the Registry.

B. Information regarding a specific person shall be disseminated upon receipt of an official request form that may be submitted directly to the State Police or to the State Police through a local law-enforcement agency. The official request form shall include a statement of the reason for the request; the name and address of the person requesting the information; the name, address and, if known, the social security number of the person about whom information is sought; and such other information as the State Police may require to ensure reliable identification. (2003, c. 584.)

§ 9.1-913. Public dissemination by means of the Internet. — The State Police shall develop and maintain a system for making certain Registry information on persons convicted of an offense for which registration is required publicly available by means of the Internet. The information to be made available shall include the offender's name; all aliases that he has used or under which he may have been known; the date and locality of the conviction and a brief description of the offense; his age, current address and photograph; and such other information as the State Police may from time to time determine is necessary to preserve public safety including but not limited to the fact that an individual is wanted for failing to register or reregister. The system shall be secure and not capable of being altered except by the State Police. The system shall be updated each business day with newly received registrations and reregistrations. The State Police shall remove all information that it knows to be inaccurate from the Internet system. (2003, c. 584; 2005, c. 603; 2006, cc. 857, 914.)

Editor's note. — Acts 2005, c. 603, cl. 2, provides: "That the provisions of this act may result in a net increase in periods of imprisonment or commitment. Pursuant to § 30-19.1:4, the estimated amount of the necessary appropriation cannot be determined for periods of imprisonment in state adult correctional facilities and is $0 for periods of commitment to the custody of the Department of Juvenile Justice."

Acts 2006, c. 857, cl. 4, provides: "That the provisions of this act may result in a net increase in periods of imprisonment or commitment. Pursuant to § 30-19.1:4, the estimated amount of the necessary appropriation is $2,419,496 for periods of imprisonment in state adult correctional facilities and is $0 for periods of commitment to the custody of the Department of Juvenile Justice."

Acts 2006, c. 914, cl. 5, provides: "That the provisions of this act may result in a net increase in periods of imprisonment or commitment. Pursuant to § 30-19.1:4, the estimated amount of the necessary appropriation is at least $2,419,496 for periods of imprisonment in state adult correctional facilities and is $0 for periods of commitment to the custody of the Department of Juvenile Justice."

The 2005 amendments. — The 2005 amendment by c. 603 inserted "persons convicted of murder of a minor and" in the first sentence.

The 2006 amendments. — The 2006 amendments by cc. 857 and 914 are identical, and substituted "an offense for which registration is required" for "murder of a minor and violent sex ofenders" in the first sentence.

CASE NOTES

Constitutionality. — Inmate's challenge to the Virginia Sex Offender and Crimes Against Minors Registry Act (Sex Offender Act), § 9.1-900 et seq., was dismissed because the Sex Offender Act was civil in nature and did not violate the Ex Post Facto law and the protections against Double Jeopardy; the inmate's due process rights were not violated because the only issue that could be asserted at a hearing would be a challenge to the conviction, which was not contested, and the inmate did not have a protected liberty interest in precluding truthful information about his conviction being disseminated over the internet. Ballard v. Chief of FBI, — F. Supp. 2d —, 2004 U.S. Dist. LEXIS 1095 (W.D. Va. Jan. 20, 2004).

§ 9.1-914. Automatic notification of registration to certain entities; electronic notification to requesting persons. — Any school, day-care service and child-minding service, and any state-regulated or state-licensed child day center, child day program, children's residential facility, family day home or foster home as defined in § 63.2-100, nursing home or certified nursing facility as defined in § 32.1-123, and any institution of higher education may request from the State Police and, upon compliance with the requirements therefor established by the State Police, shall be eligible to receive from the State Police electronic notice of the registration or reregistration of any sex offender and if such entities do not have the capability of receiving such electronic notice, the entity may register with the State Police to receive written notification of sex offender registration or reregistration. Within three business days of receipt by the State Police of registration or reregistration, the State Police shall electronically or in writing notify an entity listed above that has requested such notification, has complied with the requirements established by the State Police and is located in the same or a contiguous zip code area as the address of the offender as shown on the registration.

The Virginia Council for Private Education shall annually provide the State Police, in an electronic format approved by the State Police, with the location of every private school in the Commonwealth that is accredited through one of the approved accrediting agencies of the Council, and an electronic mail address for each school if available, for purposes of receiving notice under this section.

Any person may request from the State Police and, upon compliance with the requirements therefor established by the State Police, shall be eligible to receive from the State Police electronic notice of the registration or reregistration of any sex offender. Within three business days of receipt by the State Police of registration or reregistration, the State Police shall electronically notify a person who has requested such notification, has complied with the requirements established by the State Police and is located in the same or a contiguous zip code area as the address of the offender as shown on the registration.

The State Police shall establish reasonable guidelines governing the automatic dissemination of Registry information, which may include the payment of a fee, whether a one-time fee or a regular assessment, to maintain the electronic access. The fee, if any, shall defray the costs of establishing and maintaining the electronic notification system and notice by mail.

For the purposes of this section:

"Child-minding service" means provision of temporary custodial care or supervisory services for the minor child of another;

"Day-care service" means provision of supplementary care and protection during a part of the day for the minor child of another; and

"School" means any public, religious or private educational institution, including any preschool, elementary school, secondary school, post-secondary school, trade or professional institution, or institution of higher education. (2003, c. 584; 2005, c. 928; 2006, cc. 857, 914.)

Editor's note. — Acts 2006, c. 857, cl. 4, provides: "That the provisions of this act may result in a net increase in periods of imprisonment or commitment. Pursuant to § 30-19.1:4, the estimated amount of the necessary appropriation is $2,419,496 for periods of imprisonment in state adult correctional facilities and is $0 for periods of commitment to the custody of the Department of Juvenile Justice."

Acts 2006, c. 914, cl. 5, provides: "That the provisions of this act may result in a net increase in periods of imprisonment or commitment. Pursuant to § 30-19.1:4, the estimated amount of the necessary appropriation is at least $2,419,496 for periods of imprisonment in state adult correctional facilities and is $0 for periods of commitment to the custody of the Department of Juvenile Justice."

The 2005 amendments. — The 2005 amendment by c. 928 substituted "religious" for "parochial, denominational" in the last paragraph.

The 2006 amendments. — The 2006 amendments by cc. 857 and 914 are identical, and in the first paragraph, inserted "nursing home or certified nursing facility as defined in § 32.1-123, and any institution of higher education" and substituted "and if such entities" for "Entities that request and are entitled to this notification, and that" in the first sentence, and inserted "listed above" in the last sentence; added the second and third paragraphs; and made stylistic changes.

§ 9.1-915. Regulations. — The Superintendent of State Police shall promulgate regulations and develop forms to implement and enforce this chapter; including the operation and maintenance of the Registry and the removal of records on persons who are deceased, whose convictions have been reversed or who have been pardoned, and those for whom an order of removal or relief from frequent registration has been entered. Such regulations and forms shall not be subject to the provisions of Article 2 (§ 2.2-4006 et seq.) of the Administrative Process Act. (2003, c. 584.)

§ 9.1-916. Requests for Registry data by Virginia Criminal Sentencing Commission; confidentiality. — Upon request of the Virginia Criminal Sentencing Commission, the Department of State Police shall provide the Commission with Registry data in an electronic format. The Commission may use the data for research, evaluative or statistical purposes only and shall ensure the confidentiality and security of the data. (2003, c. 391.)

The number of this section was assigned by the Virginia Code Commission, the section having been added as subsection E of § 19.2-390.1, by Acts 2003, c. 391.

§ 9.1-917. Limitation on liability. — No liability shall be imposed upon any law-enforcement official who disseminates information or fails to disseminate information in good faith compliance with the requirements of this chapter, but this provision shall not be construed to grant immunity for gross negligence or willful misconduct. (2003, c. 584.)

The number of this section The number of this section was assigned by the Virginia Code Commission, the number in the 2003 act having been 9.1-916.

§ 9.1-918. Misuse of registry information; penalty. — Use of registry information for purposes not authorized by this chapter is prohibited, the unlawful use of the information contained in or derived from the Registry for purposes of intimidating or harassing another is prohibited, and a willful violation of this chapter is a Class 1 misdemeanor. For purposes of this section, absent other aggravating circumstances, the mere republication or reasonable distribution of material contained on or derived from the publicly available Internet sex offender database shall not be deemed intimidation or harassment. (2003, c. 584; 2006, cc. 857, 914.)

The number of this section was assigned by the Virginia Code Commission, the number in the 2003 act having been 9.1-917.

Cross references. — As to penalty for Class 1 misdemeanors, see § 18.2-11.

Editor's note. — Acts 2006, c. 857, cl. 4, provides: "That the provisions of this act may result in a net increase in periods of imprisonment or commitment. Pursuant to § 30-19.1:4, the estimated amount of the necessary appropriation is $2,419,496 for periods of imprisonment in state adult correctional facilities and is $0 for periods of commitment to the custody of the Department of Juvenile Justice."

Acts 2006, c. 914, cl. 5, provides: "That the provisions of this act may result in a net increase in periods of imprisonment or commitment. Pursuant to § 30-19.1:4, the estimated amount of the necessary appropriation is at least $2,419,496 for periods of imprisonment in state adult correctional facilities and is $0 for periods of commitment to the custody of the Department of Juvenile Justice."

The 2006 amendments. — The 2006 amendments by cc. 857 and 914 are identical, and added the last sentence.

§ 9.1-919. Notice of penalty on forms and documents. — The Virginia Criminal Information Network and any form or document used by the Department of State Police to disseminate information from the Registry shall provide notice that any unauthorized use of the information with the intent to harass or intimidate another is a crime punishable as a Class 1 misdemeanor. (2003, c. 391.)

The number of this section was assigned by the Virginia Code Commission, the section having been added as subsection H of § 19.2-390.1, by Acts 2003, c. 391.

Cross references. — As to penalty for Class 1 misdemeanor, see § 18.2-11.

§ 9.1-920. Severability; liberal construction. — The provisions of this chapter are severable, and if any of its provisions shall be declared unconstitutional or invalid by any court of competent jurisdiction, the decision of such court shall not affect or impair any of the other provisions of this chapter. This chapter, being necessary for the welfare of the Commonwealth and its inhabitants, shall be liberally construed to effect the purposes hereof. (2003, c. 584.)

The number of this section was assigned by the Virginia Code Commission, the number in the 2003 act having been 9.1-918.

§ 9.1-921. Exemption of information systems from provisions related to the Virginia Information Technologies Agency.

— The provisions of Chapter 20.1 (§ 2.2-2005 et seq.) of Title 2.2 shall not apply to the Sex Offender and Crimes Against Minors Registry pursuant to Chapter 9 (§ 9.1-900 et seq.) of Title 9.1, operated by the Department of State Police or to information technology as defined in § 2.2-2006 operated by the Department of Juvenile Justice, Department of Corrections or the Virginia Compensation Board that interact, furnish, update, contain or exchange information with the Sex Offender and Crimes Against Minors Registry. (2006, cc. 857, 914.)

Editor's note. — Acts 2006, c. 857, cl. 4, provides: "That the provisions of this act may result in a net increase in periods of imprisonment or commitment. Pursuant to § 30-19.1:4, the estimated amount of the necessary appropriation is $2,419,496 for periods of imprisonment in state adult correctional facilities and is $0 for periods of commitment to the custody of the Department of Juvenile Justice."

Acts 2006, c. 914, cl. 5, provides: "That the provisions of this act may result in a net increase in periods of imprisonment or commitment. Pursuant to § 30-19.1:4, the estimated amount of the necessary appropriation is at least $2,419,496 for periods of imprisonment in state adult correctional facilities and is $0 for periods of commitment to the custody of the Department of Juvenile Justice."

CHAPTER 10.

RETIRED LAW ENFORCEMENT IDENTIFICATION.

§ 9.1-1000. Retired law-enforcement officers; photo identification cards.

— Upon the retirement of a law-enforcement officer, as defined in § 9.1-101, the employing department or agency shall, upon request of the retiree, issue the individual a photo identification card indicating that such individual is a retired law-enforcement officer of that department or agency. Upon request, such a card shall also be issued to any law-enforcement officer who retired before July 1, 2004. (2004, c. 419.)

CHAPTER 11.

DEPARTMENT OF FORENSIC SCIENCE.

ARTICLE 1.

General Provisions.

§ **9.1-1100. Department of Forensic Science created; Director.** — There is hereby created in the executive branch of state government, a Department of Forensic Science (the Department), which formerly existed as a division within the Department of Criminal Justice Services. The Department shall be headed by a Director appointed by the Governor, subject to confirmation by the General Assembly if in session when such appointment is made, and if not in session, then at its next succeeding session. In making his appointment, the Governor shall choose a candidate meeting the qualifications recommended by the Forensic Science Board created pursuant to § 9.1-1109. The Director shall serve for a term of six years, or until his successor shall be appointed and qualified. Any vacancy shall be filled for the unexpired term in the same manner as the original appointment.

The Director, under the direction and control of the Governor, shall exercise the powers and perform the duties conferred or imposed upon him by law and perform such other duties required by the Governor or requested by the Forensic Science Board created pursuant to § 9.1-1109. (2005, cc. 868, 881.)

Editor's note. — Acts 2005, cc. 868 and 881, cl. 3 provides: "That as of July 1, 2005, the Department of Forensic Science shall be deemed successor in interest to the Division of Forensic Science of the Department of Criminal Justice Services to the extent that this act transfers powers and duties. All right, title and interest in and to any real or tangible personal property vested in the Division of Forensic Science of the Department of Criminal Justice Services shall be transferred to and taken as standing in the name of the Department of Forensic Science."

Acts 2005, cc. 868 and 881, cl. 4 provides: "That the Governor may transfer an appropriation or any portion thereof within a state agency established, abolished, or otherwise affected by the provisions of this act, or from one such agency to another, to support the changes in organization or responsibility resulting from or required by the provisions of this act."

Acts 2005, cc. 868 and 881, cl. 5 provides: "That any general fund and nongeneral fund positions at the Division of Forensic Science of the Department of Criminal Justice Services on July 1, 2005, shall be transferred to the Department of Forensic Science to support the changes in organization or responsibility resulting from or required by the provisions of this act."

Acts 2005, cc. 868 and 881, cl. 6 provides: "That all rules and regulations adopted by the Department of Criminal Justice Services which are in effect as of July 1, 2005, and which pertain to the subject of this act, shall remain in full force and effect until altered, amended, or rescinded by the Board of Forensic Science."

Acts 2005, cc. 868 and 881, cl. 7 provides: "That on and after July 1, 2005, any reference in the Code of Virginia or in the Acts of Assembly to the Division of Forensic Science shall be construed to mean the Department of Forensic Science."

Acts 2005, cc. 868 and 881, cl. 8 provides: "That the Department of Criminal Justice Services shall continue to provide administrative support services to the Department of Forensic Science."

Acts 2005, cc. 868 and 881, cl. 9 provides: "That the Department of Criminal Justice Services and the Division of Forensic Science shall complete a Memorandum of Understanding detailing the activities related to the Division of Forensic Science becoming an independent agency. The Memorandum of Understanding shall include, but not be limited to, the transfer of existing equipment and personnel and such administrative services to be provided by the Department of Criminal Justice Services."

§ **9.1-1101. Powers and duties of the Department.** — A. It shall be the responsibility of the Department to provide forensic laboratory services upon request of the Superintendent of State Police; the Chief Medical Examiner, the

Assistant Chief Medical Examiners, and local medical examiners; any attorney for the Commonwealth; any chief of police, sheriff, or sergeant responsible for law enforcement in the jurisdiction served by him; any local fire department; or any state agency in any criminal matter. The Department shall provide such services to any federal investigatory agency within available resources.

B. The Department shall:

1. Provide forensic laboratory services to all law-enforcement agencies throughout the Commonwealth and provide laboratory services, research, and scientific investigations for agencies of the Commonwealth as needed; and

2. Establish and maintain a DNA testing program in accordance with Article 1.1 (§ 19.2-310.2 et seq.) of Chapter 18 of Title 19.2 to determine identification characteristics specific to an individual.

C. The Department shall have the power and duty to:

1. Receive, administer, and expend all funds and other assistance available for carrying out the purposes of this chapter;

2. Make and enter into all contracts and agreements necessary or incidental to the performance of its duties and execution of its powers under this chapter including, but not limited to, contracts with the United States, units of general local government or combinations thereof in Virginia or other states, and with agencies and departments of the Commonwealth; and

3. Perform such other acts as may be necessary or convenient for the effective performance of its duties.

D. The Director may appoint and employ a deputy director and such other personnel as are needed to carry out the duties and responsibilities conferred by this chapter. (2005, cc. 868, 881; 2006, cc. 327, 551.)

The 2006 amendments. — The 2006 amendments by cc. 327 and 551 are identical, and added subsection C; and redesignated former subsection C as subsection D.

§ 9.1-1102. Department to be isolated; security and protection of evidence. — A. The Department and its facilities shall be located so as to ensure the protection of evidence.

B. The Department shall provide for security and protection of evidence, official samples, and all other samples submitted to the Department for analysis or examination.

C. The Department shall ensure that its services are performed by skilled professionals who are qualified to testify in court regarding such services. (2005, cc. 868, 881.)

§ 9.1-1103. Forensic Science Academy. — The Forensic Science Academy, formerly within the Division of Forensic Science, shall be transferred to the Department, and shall provide advanced training to law-enforcement agencies in the location, collection, and preservation of evidence. (2005, cc. 868, 881.)

§ 9.1-1104. Rights of accused person or his attorney to results of investigation or to investigation. — Upon the request of any person accused of a crime or upon the request of an accused person's attorney, the Department or the Division of Consolidated Laboratory Services shall furnish to the accused or his attorney the results of any investigation that has been conducted by it and that is related in any way to a crime for which the person is accused. In any case in which an attorney of record for a person accused of violation of any criminal law of the Commonwealth, or the accused, may desire a scientific investigation, he shall, by motion filed before the court in which the charge is pending, certify that in good faith he believes that a scientific investigation may be relevant to the criminal charge. The motion shall be

heard ex parte as soon as practicable, and the court shall, after a hearing upon the motion and being satisfied as to the correctness of the certification, order that the same be performed by the Department or the Division of Consolidated Laboratory Services and shall prescribe in its order the method of custody, transfer, and return of evidence submitted for scientific investigation. Upon the request of the attorney for the Commonwealth of the jurisdiction in which the charge is pending, he shall be furnished the results of the scientific investigation. (2005, cc. 868, 881.)

§ 9.1-1105. Reexamination by independent experts. — Independent experts employed by (i) an attorney of record for a person accused of violation of any criminal law of the Commonwealth or (ii) the accused, for the purpose of reexamination of materials previously examined in any laboratory of the Department, shall conduct their analyses or examinations independently of the facilities, equipment, or supplies of the Department. (2005, cc. 868, 881.)

§ 9.1-1106. Disposal of certain hazardous materials. — Any material that is seized in any criminal investigation and that is deemed to be hazardous to health and safety, may be disposed of upon written application of the Department to the attorney for the Commonwealth in the city or county where the material is seized or where any criminal prosecution in which the material is proposed to be evidence is pending. Upon receipt thereof, the attorney for the Commonwealth shall file the application in the circuit court of such county or city. A sworn analysis report signed by a person designated by the Director of the Department shall accompany the application for disposal and shall clearly identify and designate the material to be disposed of. The application shall state the nature of the hazardous materials, the quantity thereof, the location where seized, the person from whom the materials were seized, and the manner whereby the materials shall be destroyed.

When the ownership of the hazardous material is known, notice shall be given to the owner at least three days prior to any hearing relating to the destruction, and, if any criminal charge is pending in any court as a result of the seizure, the notice shall be given to the accused if other than the owner.

Upon receipt of the analysis report and the application, the court may order the destruction of all, or a part of, the material. However, a sufficient and representative quantity of the material shall be retained to permit an independent analysis when a criminal prosecution may result from the seizure. A return under oath, reporting the time, place, and manner of destruction, shall be made to the courts. Copies of the analysis report, application, order, and return shall be made a part of the record of any criminal prosecution. The sworn analysis report shall be admissible as evidence to the same extent as the disposed-of material would have been admissible. (2005, cc. 868, 881.)

§ 9.1-1107. Disposal of certain other property after analysis. — Personal property, including drugs, not disposed of under § 9.1-1106, that has been submitted to the Department for analysis or examination and that has not been reclaimed by the agency submitting the property for analysis or examination, may be disposed of by the Department in accordance with this section if, after the expiration of 120 days after the receipt by the Department of the property, the Director notifies the circuit court of the county or city from which the property was taken, in writing, that the analysis or examination has been completed, and a report submitted to the agency that the property has not been reclaimed by the agency submitting it and that the Department proposes to dispose of the property. The notice shall state the nature of the property, the quantity thereof, the location where seized, the name of the accused, if known, and the proposed method of disposing of the property.

When the ownership of the property is known, a copy of the notice shall be sent simultaneously with the notice to the court to the owner, or, if any criminal charge is pending in any court relating to the property, the copy shall be sent to the accused at his last known address. Notice shall be by certified mail. The court, within 30 days after receipt of the notice, may direct that the property be disposed of by the Department, by an alternative method designed to preserve the property, at the expense of the agency submitting the property to the Department. If the court does not so direct within the 30-day period, then the Department may dispose of the property by the method set out in the notice. Copies of the analysis report and notice shall be made a part of the record of any criminal prosecution. The report, if sworn to, shall be admissible as evidence to the same extent as the disposed-of property would have been admissible. (2005, cc. 868, 881.)

§ 9.1-1108. Disposal of property held by Department for more than 15 years. — Notwithstanding the provisions of §§ 9.1-1106 and 9.1-1107, the Department may file an application in the Circuit Court of the City of Richmond seeking an order authorizing the disposal of all personal property, including drugs, received by the Department more than 15 years prior to the filing of the application. The application, under oath, shall list each item of property, the date of submission to the Department, the agency or individual submitting the property, any previous court orders entered regarding the storage of the property, and the proposed method of disposal. The application shall also state that written notice by first-class mail was given to each agency or individual submitting property listed at least 30 days prior to the application, and that no agency or individual objected to the disposal. A return, under oath, reporting the time, place, and manner of disposal, shall be made to the court. (2005, cc. 868, 881.)

ARTICLE 2.

Forensic Science Board.

§ 9.1-1109. Forensic Science Board; membership. — A. The Forensic Science Board (the Board) is established as a policy board within the meaning of § 2.2-2100, in the executive branch of state government. The Board shall consist of 13 members as follows:

1. The Superintendent of the State Police or his designee;
2. The Director of the Department of Criminal Justice Services or his designee;
3. The Chief Medical Examiner or his designee;
4. The Executive Director of the Virginia Board of Pharmacy or his designee;
5. The Attorney General, or his designee;
6. The Executive Secretary of the Supreme Court of Virginia or his designee;
7. The Chairman of the Virginia State Crime Commission or his designee;
8. The Chairman of the Board of the Virginia Institute of Forensic Science and Medicine or his designee;
9. Two members of the Scientific Advisory Committee, chosen by the chairman of that committee; and
10. Three members, appointed by the Governor, from among the citizens of the Commonwealth as follows:
   a. A member of law enforcement;
   b. A member of the Virginia Commonwealth's Attorneys Association; and
   c. A member who is a criminal defense attorney having specialized knowledge in the area of forensic sciences.

B. The legislative members shall serve for terms coincident with their terms of office. The members appointed by the Governor shall serve for terms of four years, provided that no member shall serve beyond the time when he holds the office or employment by reason of which he was initially eligible for appointment. Any vacancy on the Board shall be filled in the same manner as the original appointment, but for the unexpired term.

C. Notwithstanding any provision of any statute, ordinance, local law, or charter provision to the contrary, membership on the Board shall not disqualify any member from holding any other public office or employment, or cause the forfeiture thereof.

D. The Board shall elect its chairman and vice-chairman. A majority of the members shall constitute a quorum. Members shall be paid reasonable and necessary expenses incurred in the performance of their duties. Legislative members shall receive compensation as provided in § 30-19.12 and nonlegislative citizen members shall receive compensation for their services as provided in §§ 2.2-2813 and 2.2-2825.

E. The Board shall hold no less than four regular meetings a year. Subject to the requirements of this subsection, the chairman of the Board shall fix the times and places of meetings, either on his own motion or upon written request of any five members of the Board. (2005, cc. 868, 881.)

§ **9.1-1110. Functions of Forensic Science Board.** — A. The Board shall have the power and duty to:

1. Adopt regulations, pursuant to the Administrative Process Act (§ 2.2-4000 et seq.), for the administration of (i) this chapter or (ii) §§ 18.2-268.6, 18.2-268.9, 19.2-188.1, and 19.2-310.5 and for any provisions of the Code as they relate to the responsibilities of the Department. Any proposed regulations concerning the privacy, confidentiality, and security of criminal justice information or DNA identification shall be submitted for review and comment to any board, commission, or committee or other body that may be established by the General Assembly to regulate the privacy, confidentiality, and security of information collected and maintained by the Commonwealth or any political subdivision thereof;

2. Develop and establish program and fiscal standards and goals governing the operations of the Department;

3. Ensure the development of long-range programs and plans for the incorporation of new technologies as they become available;

4. Review and comment on all budgets and requests for appropriations for the Department prior to their submission to the Governor and on all applications for federal funds;

5. Monitor the activities of the Department and its effectiveness in implementing the standards and goals of the Board;

6. Advise the Governor, Director, and General Assembly on matters relating to the Department and forensic science in general;

7. Review, amend, and approve recommendations of the Scientific Advisory Committee;

8. Monitor the receipt, administration, and expenditure of all funds and other assistance available for carrying out the purposes of this chapter;

9. Approve Department applications for grants from the United States government or any other source in carrying out the purposes of this chapter and approve of acceptance of any and all donations both real and personal, and grants of money from any governmental unit or public agency, or from any institution, person, firm or corporation, and may receive, utilize and dispose of the same. With regard to any grants of money from a governmental or public agency, the Board may delegate or assign the duties under this subdivision to the chairman of the Board who may, with the concurrence of the vice-chairman

and in consultation with the Director, make such determinations. Any grants or donations received pursuant to this section shall be detailed in the annual report of the Board. The report shall include the identity of the donor, the nature of the transaction, and the conditions, if any. Any moneys received pursuant to this section shall be deposited in the state treasury to the account of the Department;

10. Monitor all contracts and agreements necessary or incidental to the performance of the duties of the Department and execution of its powers under this chapter, including but not limited to, contracts with the United States, units of general local government or combinations thereof, in Virginia or other states, and with agencies and departments of the Commonwealth; and

11. Recommend actions to foster and promote coordination and cooperation between the Department and the user programs that are served.

B. By November 1 of each year, the Board shall review and make recommendations to the Chairmen of the House Committee on Appropriations, the Senate Committee on Finance, and the Crime Commission concerning:

1. New major programs and plans for the activities of the Department and elimination of programs no longer needed;

2. Policy and priorities in response to agency needs;

3. General fiscal year operational budget and any major changes in appropriated funds;

4. Actions to foster and promote coordination and cooperation between the Department and the user programs which are served;

5. Rules and regulations necessary to carry out the purposes and intent of this chapter; and

6. Any recommendations submitted to the Board or the Director by the Scientific Advisory Committee. (2005, cc. 868, 881; 2006, cc. 327, 551.)

The 2006 amendments. — The 2006 amendments by cc. 327 and 551 are identical, and substituted "Monitor the receipt, administration, and expenditure of" for "Receive, administer, and expand" in subdivision A 8; in subdivision A 9, inserted the second sentence, substituted "grants or donations received" for "arrangements" near the beginning of the third sentence, and deleted the former last sentence, which read: "To these ends, the Board shall have the power to comply with conditions and execute such agreements as may be necessary"; and substituted "the duties of the Department" for "its duties" in subdivision A 10.

§ 9.1-1111. Scientific Advisory Committee; membership. — The Scientific Advisory Committee is hereby established as an advisory board within the meaning of § 2.2-2100, in the executive branch of state government. The Scientific Advisory Committee (the Committee) shall consist of 13 members, consisting of the Director of the Department, and 12 members appointed by the Governor as follows: a director of a private or federal forensic laboratory located in the Commonwealth; a forensic scientist or any other person, with an advanced degree, who has received substantial education, training, or experience in the subject of laboratory standards or quality assurance regulation and monitoring; a forensic scientist with an advanced degree who has received substantial education, training, or experience in the discipline of molecular biology; a forensic scientist with an advanced degree and having experience in the discipline of population genetics; a scientist with an advanced degree and having experience in the discipline of forensic chemistry; a scientist with an advanced degree and having experience in the discipline of forensic biology; a forensic scientist or any other person, with an advanced degree who has received substantial education, training, or experience in the discipline of trace evidence; a scientist with a doctoral degree and having experience in the discipline of forensic toxicology, who is certified by the American Board of Forensic Toxicologists; a member of the Board of the International Association for Identification; a member of the Board of the Association of Firearms and

Toolmark Examiners; a member of the International Association of Chemical Testing; and a member of the American Society of Crime Laboratory Directors.

Members of the Committee initially appointed shall serve the following terms: four members shall serve a term of one year, four members shall serve a term of two years, and four members shall serve a term of four years. Thereafter, all appointments shall be for a term of four years. A vacancy other than by expiration of term shall be filled by the Governor for the unexpired term.

Members of the Committee shall be paid reasonable and necessary expenses incurred in the performance of their duties, and shall receive compensation for their services as provided in §§ 2.2-2813 and 2.2-2825. (2005, cc. 868, 881.)

§ **9.1-1112. Meetings and chairman.** — The Committee shall meet twice a year in the City of Richmond and at such other times and places as it determines or as directed by the Governor or the Forensic Science Board. A chairman shall be elected from among the members appointed by the Governor. Staff to the Committee shall be provided by the Department of Forensic Science. (2005, cc. 868, 881.)

§ **9.1-1113. Functions of the Scientific Advisory Committee.** — A. The Committee may review laboratory operations of the Department and make recommendations concerning the quality and timeliness of services furnished to user agencies.

B. The Committee shall review and make recommendations as necessary to the Director of the Department and the Forensic Science Board concerning:

1. New scientific programs, protocols, and methods of testing;

2. Plans for the implementation of new programs, sustaining existing programs and improving upon them where possible, and the elimination of programs no longer needed;

3. Protocols for testing and examination methods, and guidelines for the presentation of results in court; and

4. Qualification standards for the various scientists of the Department, including the Director.

C. Upon request of the Director of the Department, the Forensic Science Board, or the Governor, the Committee shall review analytical work, reports, and conclusions of scientists employed by the Department. The Committee shall recommend to the Forensic Science Board a review process for the Department to use in instances where there has been an allegation of misidentification or other testing error made by the Department during its examination of evidence. (2005, cc. 868, 881.)

CHAPTER 12.

STATEWIDE COMMUNICATIONS INTEROPERABILITY.

The number of this chapter was assigned by the Virginia Code Commission, the number in the 2005 act having been 11.

§ 9.1-1200. Review of strategic plan; state and local compliance. —
The office of the Governor shall ensure that the annual review and update of
the statewide interoperability strategic plan is accomplished and implemented
to achieve effective and efficient communication between state, local, and
federal communication systems.

All state agencies and localities shall achieve consistency with and support
the goals of the statewide interoperability strategic plan by July 1, 2015, in
order to remain eligible to receive state or federal funds for communications
programs and systems. (2005, c. 221.)

The number of this section was assigned
by the Virginia Code Commission, the number
in the 2005 act having been § 9.1-1100.

Title 10.

Conservation Generally.

[Repealed.]

§§ 10-1 through 10-312: Repealed by Acts 1988, c. 891.

Cross references. — As to conservation, see now Title 10.1 (§ 10.1-100 et seq.).

Title 10.1.

Conservation.

Subtitle I.

Activities Administered by the Department of Conservation and Recreation.

Subtitle II.

Activities Administered by Other Entities.

Subtitle III.

Activities Administered by the Department of Historic Resources.

SUBTITLE I.

ACTIVITIES ADMINISTERED BY THE DEPARTMENT OF CONSERVATION AND RECREATION.

CHAPTER 1.

GENERAL PROVISIONS.

Michie's Jurisprudence. — For related discussion, see 7A M.J. Eminent Domain, § 2.

ARTICLE 1.

Department of Conservation and Recreation.

§ 10.1-100. Definitions. — As used in this subtitle, unless the context requires a different meaning:

"Department" means the Department of Conservation and Recreation.

"Director" means the Director of the Department of Conservation and Recreation. (1988, c. 891; 1989, c. 656.)

Editor's note. — Acts 1988, c. 891, cl. 2, 4 and 5 provide: "2. That whenever any of the conditions, requirements, provisions or contents of any section, article or chapter of Title 10 or any other title of this Code as such titles existed prior to July 1, 1988, are transferred in the same or modified form to a new section, article or chapter of this title or any other title of this Code and whenever any such former section, article or chapter is given a new number in this or any other title, all references to any such former section, article or chapter of Title 10 or other title appearing in this Code shall be construed to apply to the new or renumbered section, article or chapter containing such conditions, requirements, provisions, contents or portions thereof.

"4. That this recodification of Title 10 as Title 10.1 shall not be construed to require the reappointment of any officer or any member of a board, council, committee or other appointed body referred to in Title 10.1 and each such officer and member shall continue to serve the term for which appointed pursuant to the provisions of Title 10.

"5. That this act shall be deemed to have been enacted prior to any other act enacted in the 1988 regular session of the General Assembly, and any act purporting to amend and reenact any law contained in Title 10 or Title 10.1 of the Code of Virginia is deemed to be added to, amendatory of, or a repealer of, as the case may be, any corresponding law contained in this act; provided, that effect shall be given to such other or subsequent act only to the extent of any apparent changes in the law as it existed prior to the commencement of such session."

Law Review. — For article addressing significant developments in Virginia law pertaining to air quality, water quality and solid and hazardous waste, between 1990 and 1992, see "Environmental Law," 26 U. Rich. L. Rev. 729 (1992). For an article, "The Rhetoric and Reality of Nature Protection: Toward a New Discourse," see 57 Wash. & Lee L. Rev. 11 (2000).

Research References. — Berz and Spracker, Environmental Law in Real Estate and Business Transactions (Matthew Bender).

Cooke and Davis, The Law of Hazardous Waste: Management, Cleanup, Liability, and Litigation (Matthew Bender).

Frank P. Grad, Treatise on Environmental Law (Matthew Bender).

Michael B. Gerard, Environmental Law Practice Guide: State and Federal Law (Matthew Bender).

§ 10.1-101. Department continued; appointment of Director. — The Department of Conservation and Historic Resources is continued as the Department of Conservation and Recreation. The Department shall be headed by a Director appointed by the Governor to serve at his pleasure for a term coincident with his own. (1984, c. 750, § 10-252; 1988, c. 891; 1989, c. 656.)

§ 10.1-102. Powers and duties of Director. — The Director, under the direction and control of the Governor, shall exercise the powers and perform the duties that are conferred upon him by law and he shall perform such other duties as may be required of him by the Governor or the appropriate citizen boards. (1984, c. 750, § 10-252.1; 1988, c. 891.)

§ 10.1-103. Organization of the Department. — The Director shall establish divisions through which the functions of the Department and the corresponding powers and duties may be exercised and discharged. The Director shall appoint competent persons to direct the various functions and programs of the Department, and may delegate any of the powers and duties conferred or imposed by law upon him. (1984, c. 750, § 10-253; 1986, c. 567; 1987, c. 234; 1988, c. 891; 1989, c. 656.)

§ 10.1-104. Powers of the Department. — A. The Department shall have the following powers, which may be delegated by the Director:

1. To employ such personnel as may be required to carry out those duties conferred by law;

2. To make and enter into all contracts and agreements necessary or incidental to the performance of its duties and the execution of its powers, including but not limited to contracts with private nonprofit organizations, the United States, other state agencies and political subdivisions of the Commonwealth;

3. To accept bequests and gifts of real and personal property as well as endowments, funds, and grants from the United States government, its agencies and instrumentalities, and any other source. To these ends, the Department shall have the power to comply with such conditions and execute such agreements as may be necessary, convenient or desirable;

4. To prescribe rules and regulations necessary or incidental to the performance of duties or execution of powers conferred by law;

5. To perform acts necessary or convenient to carry out the duties conferred by law; and

6. To assess civil penalties for violations of § 10.1-200.3.

B. Pursuant to the Administrative Process Act (§ 2.2-4000 et seq.), the Department may promulgate regulations necessary to carry out the purposes and provisions of this subtitle. A violation of any regulation shall constitute a Class 1 misdemeanor, unless a different penalty is prescribed by the Code of Virginia. (1984, c. 739, §§ 10-21.3:4, 10-21.3:5; 1984, c. 750, § 10-254; 1985, c. 448; 1988, c. 891; 2001, c. 370.)

Cross references. — As to punishment for Class 1 misdemeanors, see § 18.2-11.

Editor's note. — Acts 2001, c. 247, cls. 1 to 3, provide: "§ 1. That, in accordance with and as evidence of General Assembly approval pursuant to § 10.1-104 of the Code of Virginia, the Department of Conservation and Recreation is hereby authorized to acquire, with the approval of the Governor and in a form approved by the Attorney General, that certain parcel of real property and appurtenances thereto, consisting of 154 acres, plus or minus, known as the Mary B. Stratton Estate property fronting on State Route 643, in Chesterfield County.

"§ 2. Further, in accordance with and as evidence of General Assembly approval pursuant to § 10.1-109 of the Code of Virginia, the Department of Conservation and Recreation is hereby authorized to lease to Chesterfield County upon terms and conditions the Department deems proper, with approval of the Governor, the above described property. The lease shall require that the property be maintained and open to public recreational use. If this condition is not met, the lease shall terminate and control shall revert to the Department of Conservation and Recreation.

"§ 3. Notwithstanding the lease term limits under § 10.1-109, the initial term of this lease shall be for a term of thirty years and may be renewed for three additional periods of similar length. All lease renewals shall require approval of the Governor."

Acts 2002, c. 436, cl. 1, effective April 2, 2002,

provides: "§ 1. That in accordance with and as evidence of General Assembly approval pursuant to § 10.1-104 of the Code of Virginia, the Department of Conservation and Recreation is hereby authorized to accept on behalf of the Commonwealth, upon terms and conditions the Department deems proper, with the approval of the Governor and by deed in a form approved by the Attorney General, a conveyance from The Trust for Public Land of a parcel of unimproved real property, known as the Taskinas Creek tract, in James City County of 45.38 acres, more or less, which is adjacent to York River State Park."

"§ 2. Such real property when conveyed shall be included as a parcel within York River State Park."

Acts 2002, c. 809, cls. 1-6, as amended by Acts 2004, c. 825 and Acts 2006, c. 39, provide:

"§ 1. That, in accordance with and as evidence of General Assembly approval pursuant to §§ 10.1-104 and 10.1-109 of the Code of Virginia, the Department of Conservation and Recreation is hereby authorized to amend on behalf of the Commonwealth, upon terms and conditions the Department deems proper, with approval of the Governor and in a form approved by the Attorney General, a certain lease by and between the Secretary of the Army and the Commonwealth of Virginia. Department of Conservation and Recreation, and to enter into a sublease on behalf of the Commonwealth, upon terms and conditions that the Department deems proper, with approval of the Governor and in a form approved by the Attorney General, with any public entity for a portion of the Occoneechee State Park in Mecklenburg County.

"§ 2. The purpose of the amendment is to allow certain property currently owned by the federal government and leased by the Commonwealth within Occoneechee State Park, if approved by the federal government, to be used for a recreational facility not operated under the purview of the Department of Conservation and Recreation, if approved by the federal government.

"§ 3. The amendment to the lease shall be subject to (i) the public participation guidelines of the Administrative Process Act (§ 2.2-4000 et seq.) and (ii) inclusion in the master plan for the park.

"§ 4. The sublease shall require approval by the Secretary of the Army.

"§ 5. Any further subletting of the property by the public entity shall be to another public entity and shall be subject to review and approval by the Department, with approval of the Governor and in a form approved by the Attorney General. Upon expiration of the sublease,

or when the sublessee no longer wishes to have the property operated under the terms of the sublease, the sublessee shall return the property to the Department in the condition specified by the sublease.

"§ 6. The provisions of this act shall expire on July 1, 2008, unless the amendment has been incorporated into the lease agreement by July 1, 2008."

Acts 2004, c. 290, cl. 1, provides: "§ 1. That, in accordance with and as evidence of General Assembly approval pursuant to § 10.1-104 of the Code of Virginia, the Department of Conservation and Recreation is hereby authorized to accept from the Norfolk Southern Corporation, upon terms and conditions the Department deems proper, with the approval of the Governor, a parcel of real estate comprising abandoned railroad right-of-way from Burkesville to Pamplin City between milepost north 133.4 and north 169.06, a distance of approximately 35.66 miles, partially located in the Counties of Appomattox, Cumberland, Nottoway and Prince Edward.

"§ 2. Any deed of conveyance shall be in a form approved by the Attorney General."

OPINIONS OF THE ATTORNEY GENERAL

Carrying concealed handguns in state parks. — The Department of Conservation and Recreation does not have the authority to issue regulations prohibiting, within state parks, the carrying of concealed handguns by valid permit holders. See opinion of Attorney General to The Honorable Richard H. Black, Member, House of Delegates, 02-074 (9/9/02).

§ 10.1-104.1. Department to be lead agency for nonpoint source pollution program. — A. The Department, with the advice of the Board of Conservation and Recreation and the Virginia Soil and Water Conservation Board and in cooperation with other agencies, organizations, and the public as appropriate, shall have the lead responsibility for the Commonwealth's nonpoint source pollution management program. This responsibility includes coordination of the nonpoint source control elements of programs developed pursuant to certain state and federal laws including § 319 of the Clean Water Act and § 6217 of the Coastal Zone Management Act. Further responsibilities include, but are not limited to, the distribution of assigned funds, the identification and establishment of priorities of nonpoint source related water quality problems, and the administration of the Statewide Nonpoint Source Advisory Committee.

B. The Department shall be assisted in performing its nonpoint source pollution management responsibilities by Virginia's soil and water conservation districts. Assistance by the soil and water conservation districts in the delivery of local programs and services may include (i) the provision of technical assistance to advance adoption of conservation management services, (ii) delivery of educational initiatives targeted at youth and adult groups to further awareness and understanding of water quality issues and solutions, and (iii) promotion of incentives to encourage voluntary actions by landowners and land managers in order to minimize nonpoint source pollution contributions to state waters.

The provisions of this section shall not limit the powers and duties of other state agencies. (1993, cc. 19, 830; 2004, c. 474.)

Editor's note. — For § 319 of the Clean Water Act, referred to in subsection A above, see now 33 U.S.C.S. § 1329. For § 6217 of the Coastal Zone Management Act, referred to in subsection A above, see 16 U.S.C.S. § 1455b.

§ 10.1-104.2. Voluntary nutrient management training and certification program.

— A. The Department shall operate a voluntary nutrient management training and certification program to certify the competence of persons preparing nutrient management plans for the purpose of assisting land owners and operators in the management of land application of fertilizers, municipal sewage sludges, animal manures, and other nutrient sources for agronomic benefits and for the protection of the Commonwealth's ground and surface waters. The Department shall promulgate regulations:

1. Specifying qualifications and standards for individuals to be deemed competent in nutrient management plan preparation, and providing for the issuance of documentation of certification to such individuals;

2. Specifying conditions under which a certificate issued to an individual may be suspended or revoked;

3. Providing for criteria relating to the development of nutrient management plans for various agricultural and urban agronomic practices;

4. Establishing fees to be paid by individuals enrolling in the training and certification programs;

5. Providing for the performance of other duties and the exercise of other powers by the Director as may be necessary to provide for the training and certification of individuals preparing nutrient management plans; and

6. Giving due consideration to relevant existing agricultural certification programs.

B. There is hereby established a special, nonreverting fund in the state treasury to be known as the Nutrient Management Training and Certification Fund. The fund shall consist of all fees collected by the Department pursuant to subsection A. No part of the fund, either principal or interest, shall revert to the general fund. The fund shall be administered by the Director, and shall be used solely for the payment of expenses of operating the nutrient management training and certification program. (1994, c. 159.)

§ 10.1-104.3. Clean Water Farm Award Program.

— The Director shall establish the Clean Water Farm Award Program to recognize farms in the Commonwealth which utilize practices designed to protect water quality and soil resources. A farm shall be eligible for recognition upon application from the farmer or the local soil and water conservation district, if the district concurs that the farmer is fully implementing a nutrient management plan. The Director may establish guidelines for limiting the quantity of annual recipients, receiving and ranking applications, ensuring geographical representation of awards from the major watersheds of the Commonwealth including the Chesapeake Bay watershed, providing local farm recognition through the local soil and water conservation districts, and providing special statewide recognition to select farms, to be known as the Bay-Friendly Farm Awards, within the Chesapeake Bay watershed, and as the Clean Water Farm Awards in all other areas of the Commonwealth. The Department shall report to the General Assembly annually by December 1, the names, addresses and location of signs posted at recipient farms. Recognition under this program shall not be a requirement under any other state program. (1998, c. 93.)

§ 10.1-104.4. Nutrient management plans required for state lands; review of plans.

— A. On or before July 1, 2006, all state agencies, state colleges and universities, and other state governmental entities that own land upon which fertilizer, manure, sewage sludge or other compounds containing nitrogen or phosphorous are applied to support agricultural, turf, plant growth, or other uses shall develop and implement a nutrient management

121

plan for such land. The plan shall be in conformance with the following nutrient management requirements:

1. For all state-owned agricultural and forestal lands where nutrient applications occur, state agencies, state colleges and universities, and other state governmental entities shall submit site-specific individual nutrient management plans prepared by a certified nutrient management planner pursuant to § 10.1-104.2 and regulations promulgated thereunder. However, where state agencies are conducting research involving nutrient application rate and timing on state-owned agricultural and forestal lands, such lands shall be exempt from the application rate and timing provisions contained in the regulations developed pursuant to § 10.1-104.2.

2. For all state-owned lands other than agricultural and forestal lands where nutrient applications occur, state agencies, state colleges and universities, and other state governmental entities shall submit nutrient management plans prepared by a certified nutrient management planner pursuant to § 10.1-104.2 and regulations promulgated thereunder or planning standards and specifications acceptable to the Department.

B. Plans or planning standards and specifications submitted under subdivisions A 1 and A 2 shall be reviewed and approved by the Department. Such approved plans and planning standards and specifications shall be in effect for a maximum of three years, and shall be revised and submitted for approval to the Department at least once every three years thereafter.

C. State agencies, state colleges and universities, and other state governmental entities shall maintain and properly implement any such nutrient management plan or planning standards or specifications on all areas where nutrients are applied.

D. The Department may (i) provide technical assistance and training on the development and implementation of a nutrient management plan, (ii) conduct periodic reviews as part of its responsibilities authorized under this section, and (iii) assess an administrative charge to cover a portion of the costs for services associated with its responsibilities authorized under this section.

E. The Department shall develop written procedures for the development, submission, and the implementation of a nutrient management plan or planning standards and specifications that shall be provided to all state agencies, state colleges and universities, and other state governmental entities that own land upon which nutrients are applied. (2005, c. 65.)

ARTICLE 2.

Board of Conservation and Recreation.

§ **10.1-105. Board of Conservation and Recreation.** — The Board of Conservation and Recreation shall be reorganized and is established as a policy board in the executive branch in accordance with § 2.2-2100 and shall consist of 12 members to be appointed by the Governor. The Board shall be the successor to the Board on Conservation and Development of Public Beaches and the Virginia State Parks Foundation. The members of the Board shall initially be appointed for terms of office as follows: three for a one-year term, three for a two-year term, three for a three-year term, and three for a four-year term. The Governor shall designate the term to be served by each appointee at the time of appointment. Appointments thereafter shall be made for four-year terms. No person shall serve more than two consecutive full terms. Any vacancy shall be filled by the Governor for the unexpired term. All terms shall begin July 1. Board members shall serve at the pleasure of the Governor. In making appointments, the Governor shall endeavor to select persons suitably qualified to consider and act upon the various special interests and problems related to the programs of the Department. The Board may appoint subcommittees of not less than three to consider and deal with special interests and problems related to programs of the Department. (Code 1950, § 10-3; 1954, c. 487; 1958, c. 427; 1966, cc. 477, 510; 1984, c. 750; 1988, c. 891; 1989, c. 656; 1991, c. 84; 2003, cc. 79, 89.)

Editor's note. — Acts 2003, cc. 79 and 89, cl. 3, provide: "That all rules and regulations adopted by the Board on Conservation and Development of Public Beaches that are in effect as of the effective date of this act shall remain in full force and effect until amended or rescinded by the Board of Conservation and Recreation. The Board of Conservation and Recreation shall promulgate as soon as practicable any necessary changes to the regulations to complete the consolidation of the Boards."

Acts 2003, cc. 79 and 89, cl. 4, provide: "That of the members currently serving on the Board of Conservation and Recreation, the Virginia State Parks Foundation, and the Board on Conservation and Development of Public Beaches, a minimum of two members of each shall be appointed by the Governor to new first-term appointments to the reconstituted Board of Conservation and Recreation."

§ 10.1-106. Officers; meetings; quorum. — The Board shall elect one of its members chairman, and another as vice-chairman. The Director or his designee shall serve as executive secretary to the Board.

The Board shall meet at least three times a year on the call of the chairman or the Director. The vice-chairman shall fill the position of chairman in the event the chairman is not available. A majority of the members of the Board shall constitute a quorum of the Board. (Code 1950, §§ 10-4, 10-5; 1958, c. 427; 1968, c. 126; 1988, c. 891; 1991, c. 84; 2003, cc. 79, 89.)

§ 10.1-107. General powers and duties of the Board. — A. The Board shall advise the Governor and the Director on activities of the Department. Upon the request of the Governor, or the Director, the Board shall institute investigations and make recommendations.

The Board shall formulate recommendations to the Director concerning:

1. Requests for grants or loans pertaining to outdoor recreation.

2. Designation of recreational sites eligible for recreational access road funds.

3. Designations proposed for scenic rivers, scenic highways, and Virginia byways.

4. Acquisition of real property by fee simple or other interests in property for the Department including, but not limited to, state parks, state recreational areas, state trails, greenways, natural areas and natural area preserves, and other lands of biological, environmental, historical, recreational or scientific interest.

5. Acquisition of bequests, devises and gifts of real and personal property, and the interest and income derived therefrom.

6. Stage one and stage two plans, master plans, and substantial acquisition or improvement amendments to master plans as provided in § 10.1-200.1.

B. The Board shall have the authority to promulgate regulations necessary for the execution of the Public Beach Conservation and Development Act, Article 2 (§ 10.1-705 et seq.) of Chapter 7 of this title.

C. The Board shall assist the Department in the duties and responsibilities described in Subtitle I (§ 10.1-100 et seq.) of Title 10.1.

D. The Board is authorized to conduct fund-raising activities as deemed appropriate and will deposit such revenue into the State Parks Projects Fund pursuant to subsection D of § 10.1-202. (Code 1950, § 10-12; 1958, c. 427; 1962, c. 355; 1984, c. 750; 1988, c. 891; 1991, c. 84; 1998, c. 780; 2003, cc. 79, 89; 2005, cc. 25, 102.)

Editor's note. — Acts 2005, c. 102, cl. 2, provides: "That the Governor shall make new appointments for each of the three at-large members of the Board in accordance with the provisions of this act on July 1, 2005. The new appointments of the at-large members of the

Board shall go into effect upon the expiration of the current members' terms in January 2006, and the terms shall be staggered as follows: one member for a term of two years; one member for a term of three years; and one member for a term of four years. The Governor shall designate the term to be served by each appointee at the time of appointment and may reappoint the existing at-large members of the Board."

Acts 2005, c. 102, cl. 3, provides: "That the Director of the Department of Conservation and Recreation shall amend the Stormwater Management Regulations by removing the out-of-date Best Management Practices (BMP) nu-trient removal efficiency information and adding it into the Virginia Stormwater Management Handbook guidance document where it shall be more effectively updated for public use."

The 2005 amendments. — The 2005 amendment by c. 25 deleted "and historical" following "recreational" in subdivision A 2.

The 2005 amendment by c. 102 deleted "Virginia Stormwater Management Act, Article 1.1 § 10.1-603.1 et seq.) of Chapter 6 of this title and for the execution of the" preceding "Public Beach" in B.

ARTICLE 3.

Disposition of Department Lands.

§ 10.1-108. Definitions. — As used in this article, unless the context requires a different meaning:

"Environment" means the natural, scenic, scientific and historic attributes of the Commonwealth.

"Exploration" means the examination and investigation of land for the purpose of locating and determining the extent of minerals, by excavating, drilling, boring, sinking shafts, sinking wells, driving tunnels, or other means.

"Mineral" means petroleum, natural gas, coal, ore, rock and any other solid chemical element or compound which results from the inorganic process of nature. For the purposes of this article, the word mineral shall not include timber. (1978, c. 835, § 10-17.113; 1988, c. 891.)

§ 10.1-109. Conveyance or lease of lands and other properties. — A. The Director is authorized, subject to the consent and approval of the Governor and the General Assembly, following review as to form and content by the Attorney General and the provisions of this article, to convey, lease or demise to any person for consideration, by proper deed or other appropriate instrument signed and executed by the Director, in the name of the Commonwealth: (i) any lands or other properties held for general recreational or other public purposes by the Department, for the Commonwealth; (ii) any lands over which the Department has supervision and control, or any part of such lands; or (iii) any right, interest or privilege with respect to such lands. The Director, subject to the consent and approval of the Governor, may renew any such lease, contract or agreement without the consent and approval of the General Assembly. Whenever land is acquired by purchase or otherwise for public recreation and conservation purposes under the administration of the Department, the Director is authorized to lease the land or any portion of it to the owner from whom the land is acquired upon terms and conditions in the public interest. No lease granted under this section shall be for an initial term longer than ten years, but any such lease may contain provisions for lease renewals, either contingent or automatic at the discretion of the Director, for a like period upon the same terms and conditions as originally granted. If written notice of termination is received by the Director from the lessee or if use of the lease is in fact abandoned by the lessee at any time prior to the end of the initial term or any renewal, the Director may immediately terminate the lease.

B. The Director is authorized to lease state-owned housing under the control of the Department to state employees. Such leases shall be approved as to form and content by the Attorney General and the Department of General Services. The leasing of Department-controlled housing to state employees shall be for the purposes of providing security to property of the Department and shall not cause the property to be considered surplus to the agency's need.

(1978, c. 835, § 10-17.114; 1980, c. 451; 1984, c. 739; 1987, c. 453; 1988, c. 891; 1991, c. 461.)

Editor's note. — Acts 1987, c. 52, cl. 1 and 2, provided: that the Director of the Department of Conservation and Historic Resources (now Department of Conservation and Recreation) could execute the appropriate instruments necessary to convey real estate in the Appalachian Trail held in the name of the Commonwealth to the United States of America, Department of the Interior, National Park Service in exchange for real estate in the Appalachian Trail held in the name of the United States of America, and that any such instruments were subject to former § 10-17.114 (now §§ 10.1-109 through 10.1-112), including review and approval by the Board of Conservation and Historic Resources (Board of Conservation and Recreation), approval by the Governor and approval of the Attorney General as to form and content. Instruments were executed in October, 1987, from the United States to Virginia and from Virginia to the United States making such conveyances.

Acts 1998, c. 248, cl. 1, provides: "That notwithstanding the provisions of § 10.1-109 of the Code of Virginia, the Department of Conservation and Recreation is hereby authorized to lease to the Chesapeake Bay Foundation, Inc., upon terms as the Department deems proper, with the approval of the Governor and the Attorney General, that parcel of land known as the Jammes property, containing 8.8781 acres, more or less, as shown on a boundary survey recorded in the Office of the Clerk of the Circuit Court of Fairfax County, Virginia, in Deed Book 9501, page 985, together with a parcel adjoining the northwest corner of the Jammes property and providing access to Occoquan Bay, both parcels being a portion of Mason Neck State Park in Fairfax County. The terms of the lease shall require the lessee to make substantial renovations to the existing improvements on the Jammes property, and shall provide that the parcels shall be used as the situs of environmental education programs and such other uses as the Department and the lessee determine are consistent with the purposes for which the parcels were acquired by the Commonwealth. The initial term of this lease shall be for thirty years, and the lease shall be renewable at the option of the lessee for like periods upon the same terms and conditions as the initial lease term. Prior to execution, the lease shall be submitted to the chairmen of the Senate Finance Committee, the Senate Committee for Courts of Justice, the House Committee on Conservation and Natural Resources and the House Appropriations Committee for review."

Acts 1998, c. 282, cls. 1 and 2, provide: "§ 1.

That notwithstanding the lease term limits under § 10.1-109, the initial term of this lease shall be for a term of thirty years and may be renewed for three additional periods of similar length. All lease renewals shall require the approval of the Governor and the Attorney General."

"2. Notwithstanding the lease term limits under § 10.1-109, the initial term of this lease shall be for a term of thirty years and may be renewed for three additional periods of similar length. All lease renewals shall require the approval of the Governor and the Attorney General."

Acts 2000, c. 263, cls. 1 and 2, provide: "§ 1. That in accordance with and as evidence of General Assembly approval pursuant to § 10.1-109 of the Code of Virginia, the Department of Conservation and Recreation is hereby authorized to lease to Franklin County, upon terms and conditions the Department deems proper, with the approval of the Governor and the Attorney General, a certain parcel of land located on Smith Mountain Lake in Franklin County containing thirty-seven acres, more or less. The lease shall require that the property be developed, maintained, and kept open for public recreational use; if this condition is not satisfied, the lease shall terminate and control of the property shall revert to the Department of Conservation and Recreation.

"§ 2. Notwithstanding the lease term limits under § 10.1-109, the initial term of this lease shall be for a term of thirty years and may be renewed for three additional periods of similar length. All lease renewals shall require the approval of the Governor and the Attorney General."

Acts 2000, c. 371, cls. 1 to 3, provide: "§ 1. That in accordance with and as evidence of General Assembly approval pursuant to § 10.1-109 of the Code of Virginia, the Department of Conservation and Recreation is hereby authorized to convey to Woodland Pond, upon such terms as the Department deems proper with the approval of the National Park Service, Governor and Attorney General, a certain parcel of real property containing approximately one acre on the southeast boundary of Pocahontas State Park in Chesterfield County.

"§ 2. In consideration for such conveyance, the Department is authorized to accept on behalf of the boundary of approximately equal acreage and of equal or greater economic and recreational value.

"§ 3. The exchange of real property shall be for due consideration as determined by the Department and Woodland Pond.

"The deeds of conveyance shall be in the form

approved by the Attorney General."

Acts 2001, c. 247, cls. 1 to 3, provide: "§ 1. That, in accordance with and as evidence of General Assembly approval pursuant to § 10.1-104 of the Code of Virginia, the Department of Conservation and Recreation is hereby authorized to acquire, with the approval of the Governor and in a form approved by the Attorney General, that certain parcel of real property and appurtenances thereto, consisting of 154 acres, plus or minus, known as the Mary B. Stratton Estate property fronting on State Route 643, in Chesterfield County.

"§ 2. Further, in accordance with and as evidence of General Assembly approval pursuant to § 10.1-109 of the Code of Virginia, the Department of Conservation and Recreation is hereby authorized to lease to Chesterfield County upon terms and conditions the Department deems proper, with approval of the Governor, the above described property. The lease shall require that the property be maintained and open to public recreational use. If this condition is not met, the lease shall terminate and control shall revert to the Department of Conservation and Recreation.

"§ 3. Notwithstanding the lease term limits under § 10.1-109, the initial term of this lease shall be for a term of thirty years and may be renewed for three additional periods of similar length. All lease renewals shall require approval of the Governor."

Acts 2002, c. 809, cls. 1-6, as amended by Acts 2004, c. 825 and Acts 2006, c. 39, provide:

"§ 1. That, in accordance with and as evidence of General Assembly approval pursuant to §§ 10.1-104 and 10.1-109 of the Code of Virginia, the Department of Conservation and Recreation is hereby authorized to amend on behalf of the Commonwealth, upon terms and conditions the Department deems proper, with approval of the Governor and in a form approved by the Attorney General, a certain lease by and between the Secretary of the Army and the Commonwealth of Virginia. Department of Conservation and Recreation, and to enter into a sublease on behalf of the Commonwealth, upon terms and conditions that the Department deems proper, with approval of the Governor and in a form approved by the Attorney General, with any public entity for a portion of

the Occoneechee State Park in Mecklenburg County.

"§ 2. The purpose of the amendment is to allow certain property currently owned by the federal government and leased by the Commonwealth within Occoneechee State Park, if approved by the federal government, to be used for a recreational facility not operated under the purview of the Department of Conservation and Recreation, if approved by the federal government.

"§ 3. The amendment to the lease shall be subject to (i) the public participation guidelines of the Administrative Process Act (§ 2.2-4000 et seq.) and (ii) inclusion in the master plan for the park.

"§ 4. The sublease shall require approval by the Secretary of the Army.

"§ 5. Any further subletting of the property by the public entity shall be to another public entity and shall be subject to review and approval by the Department, with approval of the Governor and in a form approved by the Attorney General. Upon expiration of the sublease, or when the subleasee no longer wishes to have the property operated under the terms of the sublease, the subleasee shall return the property to the Department in the condition specified by the sublease.

"§ 6. The provisions of this act shall expire on July 1, 2008, unless the amendment has been incorporated into the lease agreement by July 1, 2008."

Acts 2003, c. 100, cls. 1 and 2, provide: "§ 1. That in accordance with and as evidence of General Assembly approval pursuant to § 10.1-109 of the Code of Virginia, the Department of Conservation and Recreation is hereby authorized to convey to the Mount Vernon Ladies' Association of the Union, upon terms as the Department deems proper, with the approval of the Governor, and the Attorney General as to form of the instrument of conveyance, certain parcels of real property containing 15.4 acres more or less, located in Fairfax County adjacent to George Washington's grist mill.

"§ 2. If such property is conveyed to the Mount Vernon Ladies' Association of the Union, the deed shall require that the property be maintained for and open to public use. If this condition is not met, the property shall revert to the Department of Conservation and Recreation."

CASE NOTES

Editor's note. — The case cited in the notes below was decided under former § 10-21.1.

Racial discrimination forbidden. — The state is required to operate a state park on a nondiscriminatory basis, or, if the park is leased, to see that it is operated by the lessee without racial discrimination. Tate v. Depart-

ment of Conservation & Dev., 133 F. Supp. 53 (E.D. Va. 1955), aff'd, 231 F.2d 615 (4th Cir.), cert. denied, 352 U.S. 838, 77 S. Ct. 58, 1 L. Ed. 2d 56 (1956).

The "separate but equal" doctrine as applied to the enjoyment of public beaches and bathhouses maintained by public authorities was abolished by Dawson v. Mayor & City Council, 220 F.2d 386 (4th Cir. 1955). It follows that state parks, even where "separate but equal" facilities exist, are governed by the same general principles. Tate v. Department of Conservation & Dev., 133 F. Supp. 53 (E.D. Va. 1955), aff'd, 231 F.2d 615 (4th Cir.), cert. denied, 352 U.S. 838, 77 S. Ct. 58, 1 L. Ed. 2d 56 (1956).

Closing of state park not matter for court determination. — If, in the wisdom of the leaders of this Commonwealth, it is deter-

mined to close a state park, this is not a matter for determination by the court. Tate v. Department of Conservation & Dev., 133 F. Supp. 53 (E.D. Va. 1955), aff'd, 231 F.2d 615 (4th Cir.), cert. denied, 352 U.S. 838, 77 S. Ct. 58, 1 L. Ed. 2d 56 (1956), wherein the court said: "Nor is this court passing upon the right to sell or lease this facility in absolute good faith by giving due notice of its intentions in such a manner that interested parties, regardless of race, may avail themselves of the equal opportunity afforded to submit bids with respect to same."

§ 10.1-110. Easements to governmental agencies and public service corporations.

§ 10.1-110. Easements to governmental agencies and public service corporations. — A. The Director is authorized, subject to the consent and approval of the Governor following review as to form and content by the Attorney General, to grant to any governmental agency, political subdivision, public utility company, public service corporation, public service company or authority for consideration by proper deed or other appropriate instrument signed and executed by the Director in the name of the Commonwealth, any easement over, upon and across any lands or other properties held by the Commonwealth or over which it has supervision and control, provided that the easement is consistent with and not in derogation of the general purpose for which the land or other property is held. No easement shall be granted for an initial term longer than ten years, but may contain provisions for renewals either contingent or automatic at the discretion of the Director, for a like period on the same terms and conditions as originally granted. If written notice of termination is received by the Director from the grantee or if use of the easement is in fact abandoned by the grantee at any time prior to the end of the initial term or any renewal, the Director may immediately terminate the easement. If the Department amends its master site plan to include buildings, structures or improvements on or in the vicinity of any easement granted under this section, the Director reserves the right to require, upon written notice given 180 days in advance, the relocation of the easement at the expense of the grantee of the easement.

B. The relocation requirement of subsection A shall not apply to any easement granted by the Director to the Virginia Department of Transportation. (1978, c. 835, § 10-17.114; 1980, c. 451; 1984, c. 739; 1987, c. 453; 1988, c. 891; 1991, c. 360.)

§ 10.1-111. Removal of minerals.

§ 10.1-111. **Removal of minerals.** — The Director, with the approval of the Governor, is authorized to make and execute leases, contracts or deeds in the name of the Commonwealth, for the removal or mining of minerals that may be found in Departmental lands whenever it appears to the Director that it would be in the best interest of the Commonwealth to dispose of these minerals. Before any deed, contract or lease is made or executed, it shall be approved as to form by the Attorney General, and bids therefor shall be received after notice by publication once each week for four successive weeks in two newspapers of general circulation. The Director shall have the right to reject any or all bids and to readvertise for bids. The accepted bidder shall give bond with good and sufficient surety to the satisfaction of the Director, and in any amount that the Director may fix for the faithful performance of all the conditions and covenants of the lease, contract or deed. The proceeds arising from any contract, deed, or lease shall be deposited into the state treasury to the credit of the State Park Conservation Resources Fund established in subsection A of § 10.1-202. (1978, c. 835, § 10-17.114; 1980, c. 451; 1984, c. 739; 1987, c. 453; 1988, c. 891; 2003, cc. 79, 89.)

§ 10.1-112. Capital improvement projects. — The Director is authorized to make and execute leases and contracts in the name of the Commonwealth for the development and operation of revenue-producing capital improvement projects in Virginia state parks upon the written approval of the Governor. Prior to approval, the Governor shall consider the written recommendation of the Director of the Department of General Services and the Attorney General shall review such leases and contracts as to form.

Any contract or lease for the development and operation of the capital improvement project shall be in accordance with the provisions of the Virginia Public Procurement Act (§ 2.2-4300 et seq.). The accepted bidder shall give a performance bond for the construction, operation and maintenance of the project with good and sufficient surety in an amount fixed by the Director for the faithful performance of the conditions and covenants of such lease or contract.

Such lease or contract, with an initial term not exceeding 30 years, shall be subject to terms, conditions, and limitations as the Director may prescribe and may be renewed with the approval of the Director. The proceeds arising from a contract or lease executed pursuant to this section shall be paid into the State Park Conservation Resources Fund established in subsection A of § 10.1-202. (1987, c. 835, § 10-17.114; 1980, c. 451; 1984, c. 739; 1987, c. 453; 1988, c. 891; 1998, c. 168; 2003, cc. 79, 89.)

§ 10.1-113. Sale of trees. — For the purpose of maintaining the production of forest products in Departmental lands, the Director, upon the recommendation of the State Forester, may designate and appraise trees to be cut under the principles of scientific forest management, and may sell them for not less than their appraised value. When the appraised value of the trees to be sold is more than $10,000, the Director, before selling them, shall receive bids, after notice by publication once a week for two weeks in two newspapers of general circulation; but the Director shall have the right to reject any and all bids and to readvertise for bids. The proceeds arising from the sale of the timber and trees shall be paid into the State Park Conservation Resources Fund established in subsection A of § 10.1-202. (1988, c. 891; 2003, cc. 79, 89.)

§ 10.1-114. Commemorative facilities and historic sites management; duties of Director. — In order to further public understanding and appreciation of the persons, places and events that contributed substantially to the development and enhancement of our Commonwealth's and nation's democratic and social values and ideals and in order to encourage, stimulate and support the identification, protection, preservation and rehabilitation of the Department's significant historic, architectural and archaeological sites, the Director has the following duties:

1. To ensure that Departmental historical and cultural facilities are suitable for public, patriotic, educational and recreational assemblies and events;

2. To plan, establish, construct, operate, maintain and manage historic museums, commemorative memorials and other facilities as directed by acts of the General Assembly;

3. To acquire lands, property and structures deemed necessary to the purposes of this chapter by purchase, lease, gift, devise or condemnation proceedings. The title to land and property acquired shall be in the name of the Commonwealth. In the exercise of the power of eminent domain granted under this section, the Director may proceed in the manner provided in Chapter 3 (§ 25.1-300 et seq.) of Title 25.1; and

4. To lease acquired property to any person, association, firm or corporation for terms and conditions determined by the Director with the Governor's consent. (1989, c. 656; 2003, c. 940.)

ARTICLE 4.

Conservation Officers.

§ 10.1-115. Appointment of conservation officers; qualifications; oath. — A. The Director of the Department, when he deems it necessary, may request the Governor to commission individuals designated by the Director to act as conservation officers of the Commonwealth. Upon concurring with the Director's request, the Governor shall direct the Secretary of the Commonwealth to issue a conservation officer commission to the designated individual. The Secretary of the Commonwealth shall deliver a copy of the commission to the Director. Any individual so commissioned shall hold his commission during his term of employment with the Department, subject to the provisions of § 10.1-118.

B. To be qualified to receive a conservation officer commission, a person shall (i) be at least twenty-one years of age and (ii) have graduated from high school or obtained an equivalent diploma.

C. Each conservation officer shall qualify before the clerk of the circuit court of the city or county in which he resides, or in which he first is assigned duty, by taking the oaths prescribed by law.

D. The Director may designate certain conservation officers to be special conservation officers. Special conservation officers shall have the same authority and power as sheriffs throughout the Commonwealth to enforce the laws of the Commonwealth. (1994, c. 205.)

Cross references. — As to exception for conservation officers from minimum training standards, see § 9.1-113. As to the Line of Duty Act, see § 9.1-400.

Editor's note. — Acts 1994, c. 205, cl. 2 provides that all commissions or appointments of conservators of the peace pursuant to § 19.2-16 shall be null and void except for appointment of persons currently employed by the Department of Conservation and Recreation. Any Commission or appointment issued pursuant to § 19.2-16 to persons currently employed by the Department of Conservation and Recreation shall continue in full force and effect until it is replaced by a conservation officer commission issued pursuant to § 10.1-115 or until the individual ceases to be employed by the Department.

§ 10.1-116. Jurisdiction of conservation officers. — Conservation officers shall have jurisdiction throughout the Commonwealth on all Department lands and waters and upon lands and waters under the management or control of the Department; on property of the United States government or a department or agency thereof on which the Commonwealth has concurrent jurisdiction and is contiguous with land of the Department or on which the Department has a management interest; on a property of another state agency or department whose property is contiguous with land of the Department; and in those local jurisdictions in which mutual aid agreements have been established pursuant to § 15.2-1736.

Special conservation officers appointed pursuant to § 10.1-115 shall have jurisdiction throughout the Commonwealth. (1994, c. 205; 2005, c. 87.)

The 2005 amendments. — The 2005 amendment by c. 87 added "on a property ... pursuant to § 15.2-1736" to the end of the present first paragraph and added the second paragraph.

§ 10.1-117. Powers and duties of conservation officers. — A. It shall be the duty of all conservation officers to uphold and enforce the laws of the Commonwealth and the regulations of the Department.

B. Commissioned conservation officers shall be law-enforcement officers and shall have the power to enforce the laws of the Commonwealth and the regulations of the Department and the collegial bodies under administrative support of the Department. If requested by the chief law-enforcement officer of the locality, conservation officers shall coordinate the investigation of felonies with the local law-enforcement agency. (1994, c. 205; 2005, c. 88.)

The 2005 amendments. — The 2005 amendment by c. 88 deleted the former last sentence of subsection A; and, in subsection B, deleted "and conservators of the peace" following "law-enforcement officers," and substituted "the power to enforce" for "all of the powers of a conservator of the peace as provided in Article 2 (§ 19.2-18 et seq.) of Chapter 2 of Title 19.2 to enforce" in the first sentence, and rewrote the last sentence.

§ 10.1-118. Decommissioning of conservation officers. — Upon separation from the Department, incapacity, death, or other good cause, the Director may recommend in writing the decommissioning of any conservation officer to the Governor. Upon concurring with the Director's request, the Governor shall direct the Secretary of the Commonwealth to issue a certificate of decommissioning to the conservation officer. The Secretary of the Commonwealth shall deliver a copy of the certificate to the Director. Upon receipt of the decommissioning certificate, the Director shall ensure that the certificate is recorded at the office of the clerk of the circuit court of any city or county in which the individual took his oath of office. (1994, c. 205.)

CHAPTER 2.

PARKS AND RECREATION.

ARTICLE 1.

State Parks.

§ 10.1-200. Duties related to parks and outdoor recreation; additional powers. — To facilitate and encourage the public use of parks and recreational areas, to further take advantage of the positive economic impact of outdoor recreational facilities to localities and the Commonwealth, to foster the upkeep and maintenance of such resources, and to provide additional means by which the Governor and the General Assembly may determine necessary general fund appropriations and the need for other funding measures, the Department shall establish and implement a long-range plan for acquisition, maintenance, improvement, protection and conservation for public use of those areas of the Commonwealth best adapted to the development of a comprehensive system of outdoor recreational facilities in all fields, including, but not limited to: parks, forests, camping grounds, fishing and hunting grounds, scenic areas, waters and highways, boat landings, beaches and other areas of public access to navigable waters. The Department shall have the power and duty to:

1. Administer all funds available to the Department for carrying out the purposes of this chapter, and to disburse funds to any department, commission, board, agency, officer or institution of the Commonwealth, or any political subdivision thereof or any park authority.

2. Study and appraise on a continuing basis the outdoor recreational needs of the Commonwealth; assemble and disseminate information on outdoor recreation; and prepare, maintain and keep up-to-date a comprehensive plan for the development of outdoor recreational facilities of the Commonwealth.

3. Establish and promote standards for outdoor recreational facilities; encourage and assist in the coordination of federal, state, and local recreational planning; aid and advise various state institutions in the use of existing state parks and similar recreational facilities; work with the appropriate state agencies to develop areas for multiple recreational use, including, but not limited to, traditional uses such as hunting, fishing, hiking, swimming, and boating.

4. Study and develop plans and, upon request, provide assistance regarding the establishment and implementation of recreational programs for state institutions, agencies, commissions, boards, officers, political subdivisions, and park authorities.

5. Assist upon request any department, commission, board, agency, officer or institution of the Commonwealth or any political subdivision thereof or any park authority in planning outdoor recreational facilities in conformity with its respective powers and duties and encourage and assist in the coordination of federal, state and local recreational planning.

6. Apply to any appropriate agency or officer of the United States for participation in or receipt of aid from any federal program respecting outdoor recreation, and in respect thereto, enter into contracts and agreements with the United States or any appropriate agency thereof; keep financial and other records relating to contracts and agreements with the United States or any appropriate agency thereof, and furnish appropriate officials and agencies of the United States reports and information necessary to enable the officials and agencies to perform their duties under federal programs respecting outdoor recreation.

7. Act either independently or jointly with any department, commission, board, agency, officer or institution of the Commonwealth or any political subdivision thereof or any park authority to carry out the Department's powers and duties; and coordinate its activities with and represent the interests of the

above entities having interests in the planning, maintenance, improvement, protection and conservation of outdoor recreation facilities.

8. Develop a standard against which the public can determine the extent to which the Commonwealth is meeting park and recreational needs. The standard shall be based on park usage, population trends and densities, and outdoor recreational facility demands. The standard shall be expressed in terms of acres and facilities needed on a regional and a statewide level to serve existing and projected needs and conservation goals. In the comprehensive plan cited in subsection 2 of this section, the Department shall report on (i) the development of the standard; (ii) where the Commonwealth's park system falls short of, meets or exceeds the standard; and (iii) the methodology used for determining clause (ii). (1984, c. 739, §§ 10-21.3:3, 10-21.3:5; 1988, c. 891; 1998, c. 780; 2004, c. 58.)

Law Review. — For article, "Legal Issues Affecting Local Governments in Implementing the Chesapeake Bay Preservation Act," see 24 U. Rich. L. Rev. 1 (1989).

OPINIONS OF THE ATTORNEY GENERAL

Carrying concealed handguns in state parks. — The Department of Conservation and Recreation does not have the authority to issue regulations prohibiting, within state parks, the carrying of concealed handguns by valid permit holders. See opinion of Attorney General to The Honorable Richard H. Black, Member, House of Delegates, 02-074 (9/9/02).

§ 10.1-200.1. State park master planning. — A. The Department shall undertake a master planning process (i) for all existing state parks, (ii) following the substantial acquisition of land for a new state park, and (iii) prior to undertaking substantial improvements to state parks. A master plan shall be considered a guide for the development, utilization and management of a park and its natural, cultural and historic resources and shall be adhered to closely. Each plan shall be developed in stages allowing for public input.

Stage one of the plan shall include the development of a characterization map indicating, at a minimum, boundaries, inholdings, adjacent property holdings, and other features such as slopes, water resources, soil conditions and types, natural resources, and cultural and historic resources. The stage one plan shall include a characterization of the potential types of uses for different portions of the parks and shall provide a narrative description of the natural, physical, cultural and historic attributes of the park. The stage one plan shall include the specific purposes for the park and goals and objectives to support those purposes.

Upon completion of a stage one plan, a stage two plan shall be developed by the Department which shall include the potential size, types and locations of facilities and the associated infrastructure including roads and utilities, as applicable. Proposed development of any type shall be in keeping with the character of existing improvements, if appropriate, and the natural, cultural and historic heritage and attributes of the park. The stage two plan shall include a proposed plan for phased development of the potential facilities and infrastructure. The Department shall project the development costs and the operational, maintenance, staffing and financial needs necessary for each of the various phases of park development. Projections shall also be made for the park's resource management needs and related costs. The projections shall be made part of the stage two plan.

Upon completion of the stage two plan, the stage one and stage two plans along with supporting documents shall be combined to form a master plan for the park. Development of a park shall not begin until the master plan has been reviewed by the Board and adopted by the Director.

B. All members of the General Assembly shall be given notice of public meetings and, prior to their adoption, the availability for review of stage one, stage two and master plans and proposed amendments for substantial improvements.

C. The master planning process shall not be considered an impediment to the acquisition of inholdings or adjacent properties. Such properties, when acquired, shall be incorporated into the master plan and their uses shall be amended into the master plan.

D. Stage one and stage two plans shall be considered complete following review and adoption by the Director. Stage one and stage two plans may only be adopted by the Director following public notice and a public meeting. The Director may make nonsubstantial amendments to master plans following public notice. A master plan or a substantial amendment to a master plan may only be adopted by the Director after considering the recommendations of the Board following public notice and a public meeting.

E. The Department shall solicit and consider public comment in the development of the stage one and two plans as well as the master plan and any amendments thereto.

F. Master plans shall be reviewed and updated by the Department and the Board no less frequently than once every five years and shall be referenced in the Virginia Outdoors Plan.

G. Materials, documents and public testimony and input produced or taken for purposes of park planning prior to January 1, 1999, may be utilized in lieu of the process established in this section provided that it conforms with the requirements of this section and that a master plan shall be developed that conforms with this section which shall not be deemed complete until reviewed and approved in accordance with subsection D.

H. The planning process contained in this section satisfies the Department of General Services master planning requirements for lands owned or managed by the Department of Conservation and Recreation. The Department of Conservation and Recreation's Facility Development Plans shall continue to meet the Department of General Service's requirements.

I. For purposes of this section, unless the context requires a different meaning:

"Development of a park" means any substantial physical alterations within the park boundaries other than those necessary for the repair or maintenance of existing resources or necessary for the development of the master plan.

"Substantial acquisition" means the purchase of land valued at $500,000 or more or the acquisition of the major portion of land for a new state park whichever is less.

"Substantial improvement" means physical improvements and structures valued at $500,000 or more. (1998, c. 780.)

§ **10.1-200.2. Littering in state parks; civil penalty.** — No person shall improperly dispose of litter, as defined in § 10.1-1414, within a Virginia state park. In addition to any penalties that may be assessed under § 10.1-104 or § 33.1-346, any person in violation of this section may be assessed a civil penalty not to exceed $250. All civil penalties imposed under this section shall be deposited in the Conservation Resources Fund. (2001, c. 172.)

§ **10.1-200.3. Admittance and parking in state parks; prohibitions; civil penalty.** — A. No person shall make use of, gain admittance to, or attempt to use or gain admittance to the facilities in any state park for the use of which a charge is assessed by the Department, unless the person pays the charge or price established by the Department.

B. No owner or driver shall cause or permit a vehicle to stand:

1. Anywhere in a state park outside of designated parking spaces, except for a reasonable time in order to receive or discharge passengers; or

2. In any space in a state park designated for use by the handicapped unless the vehicle displays a license plate or decal issued by the Commissioner of the Department of Motor Vehicles, or a similar identification issued by a similar authority of another state or the District of Columbia, which authorizes parking in a handicap space.

C. Any person violating any provision of this section may, in lieu of any criminal penalty, be assessed a civil penalty of twenty-five dollars by the Department. Civil penalties assessed under this section shall be paid into the Conservation Resources Fund. (2001, c. 370.)

The number of this section was assigned by the Virginia Code Commission, the number in the 2001 act having been 10.1-200.2.

§ **10.1-201. Acquisition of lands of scenic beauty, recreational utility or historical interest.** — A. The Director is authorized to acquire by gift or purchase or by the exercise of the power of eminent domain, areas, properties, lands or any estate or interest therein, of scenic beauty, recreational utility, historical interest, biological significance or any other unusual features which in his judgment should be acquired, preserved and maintained for the use, observation, education, health and pleasure of the people of Virginia. Any acquisition shall be within the limits of any appropriation made by the General Assembly for the purchase of such properties, or of voluntary gifts or contributions placed at the disposal of the Department for such purposes.

B. The Director is authorized to institute and prosecute any proceedings in the exercise of the power of eminent domain for the acquisition of such properties for public use in accordance with Chapter 2 (§ 25.1-200 et seq.) of Title 25.1.

C. Before any property is purchased or acquired by condemnation, the Director may request the Attorney General to examine and report upon the title of the property, and it shall be the duty of the Attorney General to make such examination and report.

D. When any property is acquired by the Director under the provisions of this section without the aid of any appropriation made by the General Assembly and exclusively with the aid of gifts or contributions placed at the disposal of the Department for that purpose, he may place the property in the custody of the person or association making such gifts or contributions, or lease the property to such person or association, for a period not to exceed 99 years, upon terms and conditions approved by the Governor, which will best preserve and maintain such property for the use, observation, education, health or pleasure of the people of Virginia. (Code 1950, § 10-21; 1950, p. 394; 1984, c. 750; 1988, c. 891; 2003, c. 940.)

Cross references. — For constitutional authority, see Va. Const., Art. X, § 10.

Law Review. — For note, "Planning for Preservation in Virginia," see 51 Va. L. Rev. 1214 (1965).

§ **10.1-202. Gifts, funds, and fees designated for state parks; establishment of funds.** — A. The State Park Conservation Resources Fund shall consist of all entrance fees, fees from contractor-operated concessions, civil penalties assessed pursuant to § 10.1-200.2 and under § 10.1-200.3, and all funds accruing from, on account of, or to the use of state parks acquired or held by the Department. This special fund shall be noninterest bearing. The fund shall be under the direction and control of the Director and may be expended for the conservation, development, maintenance, and operations of state parks acquired or held by the Department, but the amount to be expended shall be annually approved by the Secretary of Natural Resources and shall be reported on a quarterly basis to the Chairmen of the House Committee on Appropriations and Senate Committee on Finance. Unexpended portions of the fund shall not revert to the state treasury at the close of any fiscal year unless specified by an act of the General Assembly.

B. The State Park Operated Concessions Fund shall consist of revenues generated from state park concessions operated by the Department. This special fund shall be noninterest bearing. The fund shall be under the direction and control of the Director for use in operating such concessions. Unexpended portions of the fund shall not revert to the state treasury at the close of any fiscal year unless specified by an act of the General Assembly.

C. The State Park Acquisition and Development Fund shall consist of the proceeds from the sale of surplus property. This special fund shall be noninterest bearing. The fund shall be under the direction and control of the Director and shall be used exclusively for the acquisition and development of state parks. Unexpended portions of the fund shall not revert to the state treasury at the close of any fiscal year unless specified by an act of the General Assembly.

D. The State Park Projects Fund shall consist of all income, including grants from any source, gifts and bequests of money, securities and other property, and gifts and devises of real property or interests therein given or bequeathed to the Department for the conservation, development, maintenance, or operations of state parks. This special fund shall be interest bearing and any income earned from these gifts, bequests, securities or other property shall be deposited to the credit of the fund. This fund shall be under the control of the Director and may be expended with advice from the Board for the conservation, development, maintenance, or operations of state parks. Unexpended portions of the fund shall not revert to the state treasury at the close of any fiscal year unless specified by an act of the General Assembly.

E. The Director is authorized to receive and to sell, exchange, or otherwise dispose of or invest as he deems proper the moneys, securities, or other real or personal property or any interest therein given or bequeathed to the Department for any of the funds established under this section, unless such action is restricted by the terms of a gift or bequest. The Director may enter into contracts and agreements, as approved by the Attorney General, to accomplish the purposes of these funds. The Director may do any and all lawful acts necessary or appropriate to carry out the purposes for which the above funds were established.

F. These funds shall not include any gifts of money to the Virginia Land Conservation Foundation or other funds deposited in the Virginia Land Conservation Fund. (Code 1950, § 10-21.2; 1988, c. 891; 1992, c. 426; 1994, c. 391; 1996, cc. 677, 686; 1999, cc. 900, 906; 2001, cc. 172, 370; 2003, cc. 79, 89.)

Editor's note. — Acts 1996, cc. 677 and 686, cls. 2, provide: "[t]hat the provision of this act which requires that expenditures from the Conservation Resources Fund for operation of state parks not exceed, in any fiscal year, an amount equal to forty-five percent of the revenues deposited into the Conservation Resources Fund from fees and charges paid by visitors to state parks shall expire on July 1, 1997, and thereafter, expenditures for this purpose from the Conservation Resources Fund shall not exceed, in any fiscal year, an amount equal to twenty-five percent."

Acts 2003, cc. 79 and 89, cl. 5, provide: "That all assets remaining in the Virginia State Parks Foundation Fund, established pursuant to former § 10.1-221, shall be deposited in the State Park Projects Fund established pursuant to subsection D of § 10.1-202."

§ 10.1-202.1. Golden Passport established; free entry into state parks.

— The Department of Conservation and Recreation shall establish a Golden Passport card that authorizes persons receiving social security disability payments to enter Virginia's state parks without having to pay an admittance or parking fee. Persons seeking such a card shall, upon the presentation of proof of receiving such disability payments, be issued a card by the Division of State Parks. The card shall remain valid during the time a person is receiving such payments. (1998, c. 778.)

§ 10.1-203. Establishment, protection and maintenance of Appalachian Trail.

— A. The Appalachian Trail shall be developed and administered primarily as a footpath, consonant with the provisions of the National Trails Systems Act applicable to the Appalachian Trail as part of the National Scenic Trails System, and its natural scenic beauty shall be preserved insofar as is practicable. The use of motorized vehicles by the general public along the trail is prohibited, and violation of this prohibition shall constitute a Class 1 misdemeanor. However, the owner of private land over which the trail passes may use or authorize use of motorized vehicles on or across the trail for purposes incident to ownership and management of the land and the Department may authorize use of the trail by motorized emergency vehicles. The Department may permit other uses of the trail and land acquired hereunder, by the owner of adjoining land or others, in a manner and for purposes that will not substantially interfere with the primary use of the trail. Furthermore, the Department may grant temporary or permanent rights-of-way across lands acquired under this section, under terms and conditions deemed advisable. Nothing in this section shall limit the right of the public to pass over existing public roads which are part of the trail, or prevent the Department from performing work necessary for forest fire prevention and control, insect, pest and disease control, and the removal of damage caused by natural disaster. The Department may enter into cooperative agreements with agencies of the federal government or with private organizations to provide for the maintenance of the trail. A person who has granted a right-of-way for the trail across his land, or his successor in title, shall not be liable to any user of the trail for injuries suffered on that portion of the trail unless the injuries are caused by his willful or wanton misconduct.

B. The Department is authorized to (i) enter into written cooperative agreements with landowners, private organizations and individuals and (ii) acquire by agreement, gift or purchase land, rights-of-way and easements for the purpose of establishing, protecting and maintaining a walking trail right-of-way across the Commonwealth, under such terms and conditions, including payment by the Department of property taxes on trail lands or property so acquired or subject to such use, as shall protect the interests of the actual or adjacent landowners or land users and as shall further the purposes of this section. Any department or agency of the Commonwealth, or any political subdivision, may transfer to the Department land or rights in land for these purposes, on terms and conditions as agreed upon, or may enter into an agreement with the Department providing for the establishment and protection of the trail. (1971, Ex. Sess., c. 136, § 10-21.3:1; 1972, c. 413; 1984, cc. 739, 750; 1988, c. 891.)

Cross references. — As to punishment for Class 1 misdemeanors, see § 18.2-11.

§ 10.1-204. Statewide system of trails.

— A. The Department is authorized to enter into such agreements and to acquire interests as may be necessary to establish, maintain, protect and regulate a statewide system of trails in order to provide for the ever-increasing outdoor recreational needs of an expanding population, and in order to promote public access to, travel within, and enjoyment and appreciation of the outdoor, natural and remote areas of the Commonwealth. Notwithstanding any other provision of law, the Department shall not develop, establish, or extend any system of trails, including linear parks or greenways, in any county having the county manager form of government, unless it has submitted to the appropriate local agency, commission, or board, a plan of development, where such plan is required by local ordinance, for the proposed system of trails.

B. The statewide system of trails shall be composed of:

1. Scenic trails so located as to provide maximum potential for the appreciation of natural areas and for the conservation and enjoyment of the significant scenic, historic, natural, ecological, geological or cultural qualities of the areas through which such trails may pass;

2. Recreation trails to provide a variety of outdoor recreation uses in or reasonably accessible to urban areas; and

3. Connecting trails or side trails to provide additional points of public access to recreation trails or scenic trails, or to provide connections between such trails, or to provide access from urban areas to major outdoor recreation sites.

Each trail shall be limited to foot, horse or nonmotorized bicycle use, or a combination thereof, as deemed appropriate by the Department. The use of motorized vehicles by the public shall be prohibited along any of the scenic, recreation or connecting trails. This statewide system of trails may contain, at the discretion of the Department, camping sites, shelters, and related public-use and management facilities, which will not substantially interfere with the nature and purposes of the trails. (1971, Ex. Sess., c. 136, § 10-21.3:1; 1972, c. 413; 1984, cc. 739, 750; 1988, c. 891; 1993, c. 755.)

§ 10.1-205. Management of False Cape State Park. — A. The Director shall adopt measures to safeguard the environment of False Cape State Park. These shall include, but not be limited to, the following:

1. Provisions to ensure that adequate drinking water and environmentally sound sewage disposal are provided for visitors to the Park;

2. Adequate measures to protect the dunes, wildlife, and sensitive areas of the Park;

3. Adequate measures to protect, wherever practicable, nesting areas of sea turtles, beach nesting birds, peregrine falcons, and other endangered species.

B. The Director shall be responsible for providing that law-enforcement, fire and rescue services are available for the Park.

C. The Director shall consider limiting visitors into the Park to less than 2,000 per day if such a lower limit is necessary to preserve the Park environment.

D. The Director shall consider further limiting visitors into the Park during certain portions of the year if such a limitation is necessary to preserve the environment of the Park and of the Back Bay National Wildlife Refuge.

E. No motor powered vehicle of any kind shall be permitted upon the land of False Cape State Park except as follows:

1. A public transportation system operated by the Department, or its licensee or designee, to transport not more than 2,000 persons per day into and out of the Park;

2. Official vehicles of the Commonwealth and of the City of Virginia Beach;

3. Vehicles engaged in the construction and maintenance of improvements within the Park authorized by the Commonwealth;

4. Police and emergency vehicles;

5. Vehicles for which the operators thereof have been issued permits (i) by the Department of Interior, prior to July 1, 1984, pursuant to Public Law

96-315 to travel through the Back Bay National Wildlife Refuge and (ii) by the Department to travel through the Park. (1984, c. 706, § 10-21.3:2; 1988, c. 891.)

Editor's note. — Acts 1984, c. 706, cl. 2 provides that the Division of Parks and Recreation of the Department of Conservation and Economic Development is authorized to enter into an agreement with the U.S. Department of the Interior pertaining to rights of ingress and egress through Back Bay National Wildlife Refuge to False Cape State Park. Clause 2 also sets forth the terms of the agreement.

Acts 1984, c. 706, cl. 4 and 5 provide:

"4. That the provisions of this act shall be effective upon concurrent execution of this agreement by the Governor on behalf of the Commonwealth and the United States Secretary of the Interior on behalf of the United States Department of the Interior.

"5. That the instrument granting and conveying the right or license of ingress and egress along an access corridor shall be signed and executed in a manner and form approved by the Attorney General."

This section became effective November 7, 1996, following the completion of a Memorandum of Understanding between the U.S. Department of Interior, Fish and Wildlife Service and the Commonwealth of Virginia.

ARTICLE 2.

Outdoor Recreation.

§ 10.1-206: Repealed by Acts 1991, c. 84.

§ 10.1-207. Cooperation of other departments, etc. — All departments, commissions, boards, agencies, officers, and institutions of the Commonwealth, or any political subdivision thereof and park authorities shall cooperate with the Department in the preparation, revision and implementation of a comprehensive plan for the development of outdoor recreational facilities, and such local and detailed plans as may be adopted pursuant thereto. (1984, c. 739, § 10-21.3:6; 1988, c. 891.)

§ 10.1-208. Acquisition of property; making property available for agricultural and timbering uses, outdoor and recreational uses. — A. The Director is authorized to acquire by gift or purchase (i) unrestricted fee simple title to tracts, (ii) fee simple title to such land subject to reservation of farming rights or timber rights or (iii) easements in gross or other interests in real estate as are designed to maintain the character of the land as open-space land. Whenever practicable in the judgment of the Director, real property acquired pursuant to this chapter shall be made available for agricultural and timbering uses which are compatible with the purposes of this chapter.

B. The Director is authorized to acquire, in the name of the Commonwealth, by gift or purchase, any real property or any interest therein, as the Director deems necessary for obtaining, maintaining, improving, protecting and conserving outdoor areas suitable for the development of a system of outdoor recreational facilities, and to transfer such property to other state agencies as provided in § 2.2-1150. (1984, c. 739, § 10-21.3:7; 1988, c. 891.)

ARTICLE 3.

Virginia Natural Area Preserves Act.

§ 10.1-209. Definitions. — Whenever used or referred to in this article, unless a different meaning clearly appears from the text:

"Fund" means the Natural Area Preservation Fund.

"Dedication" means the transfer to the Commonwealth of an estate, interest, or right in a natural area by any manner authorized in § 10.1-213.

"Instrument of dedication" means any written document by which an estate, interest, or right in a natural area conveys formal dedication as a natural area preserve pursuant to the provisions of § 10.1-213.

"Natural area" means any area of land, water, or both land and water, whether publicly or privately owned, that retains or has reestablished its natural character, though it need not be completely natural and undisturbed; or which is important in preserving rare or vanishing flora, fauna, native ecological systems, geological, natural historical, scenic or similar features of scientific or educational value benefiting the citizens of the Commonwealth.

"Natural area preserve" means a natural area that has been dedicated pursuant to § 10.1-213.

"Natural heritage resources" means the habitat of rare, threatened, or endangered plant and animal species, rare or state significant natural communities or geologic sites, and similar features of scientific interest benefiting the welfare of the citizens of the Commonwealth.

"Program" means the Virginia Natural Heritage Program.

"Owner" means any individual, corporation, partnership, trust or association, and all governmental units except the state, its department, agencies or institutions.

"Registry" means an agreement between the Director and the owner of a natural area to protect and manage the natural area for its specified natural heritage resource values.

"System" means the state system of natural area preserves established under § 10.1-214. (1989, c. 553.)

Law Review. — For an article, "The Rhetoric and Reality of Nature Protection: Toward a New Discourse," see 57 Wash. & Lee L. Rev. 11 (2000).

§ 10.1-210. Additional powers of the Department. — In addition to other powers conferred by law and subject to the provisions of this article, the Department shall have the power, which may be delegated by the Director:

1. To establish criteria for the selection, registration and dedication of natural areas and natural area preserves.

2. To purchase, lease or otherwise acquire in the name of the Commonwealth, using moneys from the Natural Area Preservation Fund, lands suitable for natural area preserves.

3. To acquire by gift, devise, purchase, or otherwise, absolutely or in trust, and to hold and, unless otherwise restricted by the terms of a gift or devise, to encumber, convey or otherwise dispose of, any real property, any estate or interests therein, or products on or derived from such real property, as may be necessary and proper in carrying into effect the provisions of this article.

4. To accept, hold and administer gifts and bequests of money, securities, or other property, absolutely or in trust, made for purposes of this article. Unless otherwise restricted by the terms of the gift or bequest, the Department may sell, exchange or otherwise dispose of such money, securities or other property given or bequeathed to the Department. The principal of such funds, together with the income and all revenues derived therefrom, shall be placed in the Natural Area Preservation Fund. (1989, c. 553.)

§ 10.1-211. Additional duties of the Department. — In addition to other duties conferred by law, the Department shall, subject to the provisions of this article:

1. Preserve the natural diversity of biological resources of the Commonwealth.

2. Maintain a Natural Heritage Program to select and nominate areas containing natural heritage resources for registration, acquisition, and dedication of natural areas and natural area preserves.

3. Develop and implement a Natural Heritage Plan that shall govern the Natural Heritage Program in the creation of a system of registered and dedicated natural area preserves.

4. Publish and disseminate information pertaining to natural areas and natural area preserves.

5. Grant permits to qualified persons for the conduct of scientific research and investigations within natural area preserves.

6. Provide recommendations to the Commissioner of the Department of Agriculture and Consumer Services and to the Board of Agriculture and Consumer Services on species for listing under the Virginia Endangered Plant and Insect Act, prior to the adoption of regulations therefor.

7. Provide recommendations to the Executive Director of the Department of Game and Inland Fisheries and to the Board of Game and Inland Fisheries on species for listing under the Virginia Endangered Species Act, prior to the adoption of regulations therefor.

8. Cooperate with other local, state and federal agencies in developing management plans for real property under their stewardship that will identify, maintain and preserve the natural diversity of biological resources of the Commonwealth.

9. Provide for management, development and utilization of any lands purchased, leased or otherwise acquired and enforce the provisions of this article governing natural area preserves, the stewardship thereof, the prevention of trespassing thereon, or other actions deemed necessary to carry out the provisions of this article. (1989, c. 553.)

§ **10.1-212. Virginia Natural Heritage Program.** — A. The Virginia Natural Heritage Program is hereby established and shall be administered by the Department.

B. For purposes of this Program the Department shall:

1. Produce an inventory of the Commonwealth's natural heritage resources, including their location and ecological status.

2. Maintain a natural heritage data bank of inventory data and other relevant information for ecologically significant sites supporting natural heritage resources. Information from this data bank will be made available to public agencies and may be made available to private institutions or individuals for environmental assessment and land management purposes.

3. Develop a Natural Heritage Plan which establishes priorities for the protection, acquisition and management of registered and dedicated natural areas and natural area preserves.

C. The Program shall include other functions as may be assigned by the Director for the registration, dedication, protection and stewardship of natural areas and natural area preserves. (1989, c. 553.)

§ **10.1-213. Dedication of natural area preserves.** — A. The Director may, in the name of the Department, accept the dedication of natural areas on lands deemed by the Director to qualify as natural area preserves under the provisions of this article. Natural area preserves may be dedicated by voluntary act of the owner. The owner of a qualified natural area may transfer fee simple title or other interest in land to the Commonwealth. Natural area preserves may be acquired by gift, grant, or purchase.

B. Dedication of a natural preserve shall become effective only upon acceptance of the instrument of dedication by the Director.

C. The instrument of dedication may:

1. Contain restrictions and other provisions relating to management, use, development, transfer, and public access, and may contain any other restrictions and provisions as may be necessary or advisable to further the purposes of this article;

2. Define, consistently with the purposes of this article, the respective rights and duties of the owner and of the Commonwealth and provide procedures to be followed in case of violations of the restrictions;

3. Recognize and create reversionary rights, transfers upon conditions or with limitations, and gifts over; and

4. Vary in provisions from one natural area preserve to another in accordance with differences in the characteristics and conditions of the several areas.

D. Public departments, commissions, boards, counties, municipalities, corporations, colleges, universities and all other agencies and instrumentalities of the Commonwealth and its political subdivisions are empowered to dedicate suitable areas within their jurisdiction as natural area preserves.

E. Subject to the approval of the Governor, the Commonwealth may enter into amendments to the instrument of dedication upon finding that the amendment will not permit an impairment, disturbance, use, or development of the area inconsistent with the provisions of this article. If the fee simple estate in the natural area preserve is not held by the Department under this article, no amendment may be made without the written consent of the owner of the other interests therein. (1989, c. 553.)

§ 10.1-214. Virginia natural area preserves system established. — A state system of natural area preserves is hereby established and shall be called the Virginia Natural Area Preserves System. The system shall consist of natural area preserves dedicated as provided in § 10.1-213. Once dedicated, a natural area preserve shall be managed in a manner consistent with continued preservation of the natural heritage resources it supports. (1989, c. 553.)

§ 10.1-215. Natural Area Preservation Fund established. — A. A fund consisting of general fund appropriations, gifts, bequests, devises, fees, lease proceeds, and funds accruing from, or attributable to, the use or management of state natural area preserves acquired or held by the Department known as the Natural Area Preservation Fund is hereby established.

B. Any funds remaining in such fund at the end of the biennium, including all appropriations, gifts, bequests, devises, fees, lease proceeds, and funds accruing from, or attributable to, the use or management of state natural area preserves acquired or held by the Department, and interest accruing thereon, shall not revert to the general fund but shall remain in the Natural Area Preservation Fund. (1989, c. 553; 2005, c. 94.)

The 2005 amendments. — The 2005 amendment by c. 94 substituted "devises, fees, lease … by the Department" for "and devises" in subsections A and B, and made minor stylistic changes.

§ 10.1-216. Natural area registry. — A. The Department shall maintain a state registry of voluntarily protected natural areas to be called the Virginia Registry of Natural Areas. Registration of natural areas shall be accomplished through voluntary agreement between the owner of the natural area and the Director. State-owned lands may be registered by agreement with the agency to which the land is allocated. Registry agreements may be terminated by either party at any time, and upon such termination the area shall be removed from the registry.

B. A natural area shall be registered when an agreement to protect and manage the natural area for its specified natural heritage resource has been signed by the owner and the Director. The owner of a registered natural area shall be given a certificate signifying the inclusion of the area in the registry. (1989, c. 553.)

§ 10.1-217. Gifts, devises and bequests. — Gifts, devises or bequests, whether personal or real property, and the income derived therefrom, accepted by the Director, shall be deemed as gifts to the Commonwealth, which shall be exempt from all state and local taxes, and shall be regarded as the property of the Commonwealth for the purposes of all tax laws. (1989, c. 553.)

CHAPTER 2.1.

Virginia State Parks Foundation.

§§ 10.1-218 through 10.1-225: Repealed by Acts 2003, cc. 79 and 89.

Cross references. — For funds designated for state parks, see § 10.1-202. For Board of Conservation and Recreation, see § 10.1-105 et seq.

CHAPTER 3.

State Park Development Revenue Bond Act.

Michie's Jurisprudence. — For related discussion, see 14A M.J. Parks, Public Squares and Playgrounds, § 2.

§ 10.1-300. Definitions. — As used in this chapter, unless the context requires a different meaning:

"Camping and recreational facilities" means camp sites, cabins, lodges, halls, tent camps, trailer camps, public and park lands, as well as equipment, structures and roads which are appurtenant to and useful in connection with state parks including, but not limited to sanitary and utility services, restaurants, cafeterias, stables, horses and riding equipment, bathing beaches, boathouses, boats, conference facilities, sightseeing facilities, sports facilities, bridges, access highways, and all incidental rights, easements, equipment and structures now under the control of the Department or acquired, constructed, enlarged or improved under the provisions of this chapter.

"Cost of camping and recreational facilities" means the purchase price, the cost of construction, the cost of all lands, properties, rights, easements and franchises acquired for construction, enlargements or improvements, reserve funds for the payment of principal or interest on the bonds, interest during

construction of the enlargements or improvements, engineering and legal expenses, cost of plans, specifications, surveys, estimates of cost and of revenues, expenses for determining the feasibility or practicability of the enterprise, administrative expense, and other expenses necessary or incident to the financing and operation of any authorized project. (Code 1950, § 10-100; 1966, c. 41; 1970, c. 651; 1984, c. 750; 1986, c. 498; 1988, c. 891.)

§ 10.1-301. General powers of Director. — In addition to other powers conferred by law, the Director may, subject to the provisions of this chapter:

1. Acquire, construct, enlarge, improve, operate and maintain camping and recreational facilities in any of the state parks under the control of the Department;

2. Issue revenue bonds of the Commonwealth to pay the cost of camping and recreational facilities and to pledge to the payment of the principal of and the interest on such revenue bonds all or any portion of the revenues to be derived from camping and recreational facilities to be acquired or constructed from the proceeds of such revenue bonds, after obtaining the consent of the Governor;

3. Establish and collect fees and charges for the use of camping and recreational facilities;

4. Receive and accept from any agency or instrumentality of the United States or other public or private body, contributions of either money or property or other things of value, to be held, used and applied for the purposes of this chapter;

5. Make and enter into all contracts or agreements necessary or incidental to the execution of his powers under this chapter;

6. Enter into or obtain contracts or policies of insurance, letters of credit or other agreements to secure payment of the bonds authorized to be issued pursuant to this chapter. (Code 1950, § 10-101; 1966, c. 41; 1984, c. 750; 1986, c. 498; 1988, c. 891.)

§ 10.1-302. Payment of cost of camping and recreational facilities. — The cost of camping and recreational facilities financed under this chapter shall be paid solely from the proceeds of revenue bonds issued under the provisions of this chapter, or from proceeds from any grant or contribution which may be made pursuant to the provisions of this chapter. (Code 1950, § 10-102; 1988, c. 891.)

§ 10.1-303. Revenue bonds; form and requirements. — A. The Director is authorized to provide for the issuance of revenue bonds of the Commonwealth for the purpose of paying all or any part of the cost of camping and recreational facilities. The principal and interest of the bonds shall be payable solely from the special fund provided in this chapter for such payment. All bonds shall be issued and sold through the Treasury Board whose approval of each of the determinations and designations specified in subsection B of this section shall be required.

B. The revenue bonds shall be dated, shall bear interest rates and be payable at times determined by the Director. The bonds shall mature no longer than thirty years from their date and may be made redeemable before maturity, at a price and under terms and conditions established by the Director prior to the issuance of the bonds. The principal and interest of bonds may be made payable in any lawful medium.

C. The Director shall determine the form of the bonds, including any attached interest coupons, and shall fix the denominations of the bonds and the places of payment of principal and interest, which may be at any bank or trust company. The bonds shall be signed by the Director and the State Treasurer and shall bear the lesser seal of the Commonwealth or a facsimile thereof, and any attached coupons shall bear the facsimile signature of the Director. The bonds may be executed with the facsimile signature of the Director and the State Treasurer, in which case the bonds shall be authenticated by a corporate trustee or other authenticating agent approved by the Director. If any officer whose signature appears on the bonds or coupons ceases to be such officer before delivery of the bonds, the signature shall nevertheless be valid and sufficient for all purposes.

D. All revenue bonds issued under the provisions of this chapter shall have all the qualities and incidents of negotiable instruments under the negotiable instruments law of the Commonwealth. Such bonds and the income therefrom shall be exempt from all taxation within the Commonwealth.

E. The bonds may be issued in coupon or in registered form, or both, as the Director may determine, and provision may be made for the registration of any coupon bond as to both principal and interest, and for the reconversion of any bonds registered as to both principal and interest into coupon bonds. (Code 1950, § 10-103; 1958, c. 484; 1986, c. 498; 1988, c. 891.)

§ 10.1-304. Sale and proceeds of revenue bonds; additional or temporary bonds. — A. The Treasury Board as agent for the Director may sell revenue bonds at private or public sale for such price and in the manner it determines to be in the best interests of the Commonwealth.

B. The proceeds of the bonds shall be used solely for the payment of the cost of camping and recreational facilities for which they are issued, and shall be disbursed by the Director.

C. If the proceeds of the bonds of any issue are less than the cost of the camping and recreational facilities for which the bonds were issued, additional bonds may be issued to provide the amount of the deficit. Unless otherwise provided in the resolution authorizing the issuance of the bonds or in the trust indenture described in this chapter, the additional bonds shall be deemed to be of the same issue and shall be entitled to payment from the same fund without preference or priority of the bonds first issued for the facilities.

D. If the proceeds of any bonds issued to pay the cost of camping and recreational facilities exceed the facilities cost, the surplus shall be paid into the fund provided for the payment of principal and interest of the bonds.

E. Prior to the preparation of definitive bonds, temporary bonds may be issued, under similar restrictions, with or without coupons, exchangeable for subsequently issued definitive bonds.

F. The Director may replace any bond which is mutilated, destroyed or lost.

G. The revenue bonds may be issued in accordance with the specific proceedings and conditions required by this chapter. (Code 1950, § 10-103; 1958, c. 484; 1986, c. 498; 1988, c. 891.)

§ 10.1-305. Bonds not to constitute debt of Commonwealth. — Revenue bonds issued under the provisions of this chapter shall not constitute a debt of the Commonwealth or a pledge of the faith and credit of the Commonwealth, but such bonds shall be payable solely from the funds provided from fees and charges. The bonds shall state on their face that the Commonwealth is not obligated to pay the bonds or the interest on them except from the special fund provided from fees and charges under this chapter, and that the faith and credit of the Commonwealth are not pledged to the payment of the principal or interest of the bonds. The issuance of revenue bonds under the provisions of this chapter shall not obligate the Commonwealth to levy or to pledge any form of taxation for the bonds or to make any appropriation for their payment, other than to appropriate available funds derived as revenue from fees and charges collected under this chapter. (Code 1950, § 10-104; 1988, c. 891.)

§ 10.1-306. Trust indenture; provisions applicable to bond resolution.

— Any issue of revenue bonds may be secured by a trust indenture by and between the Director, in the name of the Commonwealth, and a corporate trustee, which may be any trust company or bank having the powers of a trust company. The trust indenture may pledge fees and charges to be received from the use of and for the services rendered by any camp and recreational facilities to be acquired or constructed from the proceeds of such revenue bonds, but no trust indenture shall convey or mortgage any camping or recreational facilities or any part thereof.

Either the resolution providing for the issuance of revenue bonds or the trust indenture may contain provisions for protecting and enforcing the rights and remedies of the bondholders as may be reasonable and proper and not in violation of law, including covenants setting forth the duties of the Director in relation to the acquisition, construction, improvement, maintenance, operation, repair and insurance of such facilities, and the custody, safeguarding and application of all moneys. The trust indenture may also provide that camping and recreational facilities shall be acquired, constructed, enlarged or improved, and paid for under the supervision and approval of consulting engineers employed or designated by the Director, in the name of the Commonwealth, and satisfactory to the original purchasers of the bonds issued. The trust indenture may further require that the security given by contractors and by any depository of the proceeds of the bonds or revenues of the camping and recreational facilities or other moneys pertaining to the facilities be satisfactory to the purchasers. It shall be lawful for any bank or trust company incorporated under the laws of this Commonwealth to act as depository and to furnish indemnifying bonds or to pledge securities required by the Director. Such indenture may set forth the rights and remedies of the bondholders and of the trustee, and may restrict the individual right of action of bondholders as is customary in trust indentures securing bonds and debentures of corporations.

In addition, the indenture may contain other provisions that the Director deems reasonable and proper for the security of the bondholders. (Code 1950, § 10-105; 1986, c. 498; 1988, c. 891.)

§ 10.1-307. Fees and charges.

— The Director shall establish and collect fees and charges for the use of camping and recreational facilities. These revenues shall be pledged to pay the principal of and the interest on revenue bonds issued under the provisions of this chapter. The fees and charges shall be established and adjusted in respect of the aggregate fees and charges for the camping and recreational facilities the revenues of which shall have been pledged to provide a fund sufficient to pay (i) the cost of maintaining, repairing and operating the facilities unless such cost is otherwise provided for, (ii) the bonds and the interest thereon as the bonds become due and (iii) reasonable reserves for such purposes. Such fees and charges shall not be subject to supervision or regulation by any other state commission, board, bureau or agency. (Code 1950, § 10-106; 1966, c. 41; 1986, c. 498; 1988, c. 891.)

§ 10.1-308. Sinking fund.

— The fees, charges and revenues derived from any camping and recreational facilities subject to revenue bonds issued under the provisions of this chapter, except charges required to pay the cost of maintaining, repairing and operating such facilities and to provide fund reserves, shall be set aside in a sinking fund. The sinking fund is pledged to and charged with the payment of (i) the interest upon the bonds as it becomes due, (ii) the principal of the bonds as it becomes due, (iii) the necessary charges of paying agents for paying the interest and principal, and (iv) any premium upon bonds retired by call or purchase as provided in this chapter. The use and disposition of the sinking fund shall be subject to regulations provided in the resolution or the trust indenture. Unless otherwise provided in the resolution or trust indenture, the sinking fund shall be a fund for all such bonds without distinction or priority of one bond over another. Any moneys in the sinking fund in excess of an amount equal to one year's interest on all bonds then outstanding may be applied to the purchase or redemption of bonds. (Code 1950, § 10-107; 1966, c. 41; 1988, c. 891.)

§ 10.1-309. Remedies of bondholders and trustee. — Any holder of revenue bonds or attached coupons issued under the provisions of this chapter and any trustee under the trust indenture may protect and enforce all rights granted under the laws of the Commonwealth or under the resolution or trust indenture, and may enforce all duties required by this chapter, or by the resolution or trust indenture, to be performed by the Director, including the establishing, charging and collecting of fees and charges for the use of camping and recreational facilities. (Code 1950, § 10-108; 1986, c. 498; 1988, c. 891.)

§ 10.1-310. All moneys received to be trust funds; disbursements. — All moneys received pursuant to the authority of this chapter, whether as proceeds from the sale of revenue bonds, as grants or other contributions, or as tolls and revenues, shall be held and applied solely as provided in this chapter. The Director shall, in the resolution or the trust indenture, provide for the payment of the proceeds of the sale of the bonds and the tolls and revenues to be received into the state treasury and carried on the books of the Comptroller in a special account. The Director may provide for the turning over, transfer or paying over of such funds from the state treasury to any officer, agency, bank or trust company, who shall act as trustee of the funds, and hold and apply the fees for the purposes of this chapter subject to such regulation as this chapter and the resolution or trust indenture may provide.

All moneys paid into the state treasury pursuant to the provisions of this chapter are hereby appropriated to the Department for the purpose of carrying out the provisions of this chapter. Disbursements and payments of moneys so paid into the state treasury shall be made by the State Treasurer upon warrants of the State Comptroller which he shall issue upon vouchers signed by the Director or his designee. (Code 1950, § 10-109; 1986, c. 498; 1988, c. 891.)

§ 10.1-311. Revenue refunding bonds. — The Director is authorized to provide for the issuance of revenue refunding bonds of the Commonwealth, subject to the applicable provisions of this chapter, for the purpose of refunding any revenue bonds issued under the provisions of this chapter and then outstanding, including the redemption premium on the bonds after first obtaining the consent of the Governor. (Code 1950, § 10-110; 1986, c. 498; 1988, c. 891.)

§ 10.1-312. Bonds declared legal and authorized investments. — The bonds issued pursuant to this chapter shall be legal and authorized investments for banks, savings institutions, trust companies, building and loan associations, insurance companies, fiduciaries, trustees, guardians and for all public funds of the Commonwealth or other political subdivisions of the Commonwealth. Such bonds shall be eligible to secure the deposit of public funds of the Commonwealth and public funds of counties, cities, towns, school districts or other political subdivisions of the Commonwealth. In addition, the bonds shall be lawful and sufficient security for deposits to the extent of their value when accompanied by all unmatured coupons. (1986, c. 498, § 10-112.1; 1988, c. 891; 1996, c. 77.)

CHAPTER 4.

Scenic Rivers Act.

Michie's Jurisprudence. — For related discussion, see 20 M.J. Waters and Watercourses, § 3.

---

§ **10.1-400. Definitions.** — As used in this chapter, unless the context requires a different meaning:

"Board" means the Virginia Scenic River Board.

"Department" means the Department of Conservation and Recreation.

"Director" means the Director of the Department of Conservation and Recreation.

"River" means a flowing body of water, or a section or portion thereof.

"Scenic river" means a river or section or portion of a river that has been designated a "scenic river" by an act of the General Assembly and that possesses superior natural and scenic beauty, fish and wildlife, and historic, recreational, geologic, cultural, and other assets.

"Virginia Scenic Rivers System" means those rivers or sections of rivers designated as a scenic river by an act of the General Assembly. (1970, c. 468, § 10-168; 1984, c. 739; 1985, c. 346; 1988, c. 891; 1989, c. 656; 2003, c. 240.)

Law Review. — For 2003/2004 survey of environmental law, see 39 U. Rich. L. Rev. 203 (2004).

§ **10.1-401. Powers and duties of Director; acquisition of property.** — A. The Director shall have the duty to:

1. Identify rivers or sections of rivers, including their shores and natural environs, which should be considered for designation because of their scenic, recreational and historic attributes and natural beauty.

2. Conduct studies of rivers or sections of rivers to be considered for designation as wild, scenic or recreational rivers in cooperation with appropriate agencies of the Commonwealth and the United States.

3. Recommend to the Governor and to the General Assembly rivers or sections thereof to be considered for designation as scenic rivers.

4. Appoint Scenic River Advisory Committees or other local or regional committees of not less than three members to consider and manage scenic river interests and issues. The committees shall assist and advise the Director and the local governing body with the protection or management of the scenic river segment in their jurisdiction. The committees may consider and comment to the Director on any federal, state, or local governmental plans to approve, license, fund, or construct facilities that would alter any of the assets that qualified the river for scenic designation.

B. The Director is authorized to acquire in the name of the Commonwealth, either by gift or purchase, any real property or interest therein which the Director considers necessary or desirable for the protection of any scenic river, and may retain title to or transfer the property to other state agencies. The Director may not exercise the right of eminent domain in acquiring any such property or interest. (1970, c. 468, §§ 10-167, 10-169, 10-170, 10-175; 1984, c. 739; 1985, c. 346; 1988, c. 891; 2003, c. 240.)

Law Review. — For note, "Public Regulation of Water Quality in Virginia," see 13 Wm. & Mary L. Rev. 424 (1971). For article assessing the adequacy of Virginia's water policy, see 14 Wm. & Mary L. Rev. 312 (1972). For article on stream flow maintenance in Virginia, see 18 U. Rich. L. Rev. 485 (1984).

§ 10.1-402. Development of water and related resources and evaluation as scenic resource.

— The Department may review and make recommendations regarding all planning for the use and development of water and related land resources including the construction of impoundments, diversions, roadways, crossings, channels, locks, canals, or other uses that change the character of a stream or waterway or destroy its scenic assets, so that full consideration and evaluation of the river as a scenic resource will be given before alternative plans for use and development are approved. To effectuate the purposes of this section, all state and local agencies shall consider the recommendations of the Department. (1970, c. 468, § 10-167; 1988, c. 891; 2003, c. 240.)

§ 10.1-403. Hearing.

— Prior to submitting recommendations to the Governor and the General Assembly, the Director shall upon request of any interested state agency or political subdivision, or upon his own motion, hold a public hearing on a proposal to designate a scenic river. (1970, c. 468, § 10-172; 1984, c. 739; 1985, c. 346; 1988, c. 891.)

§ 10.1-404. Recommendation that a river be designated a scenic river.

— A recommendation to the Governor and General Assembly that a river or section thereof be designated a scenic river shall be submitted with:

1. The views and recommendations of the State Water Control Board and other affected agencies; and

2. A report showing the proposed area and classification, the characteristics which qualify the river or section of river for designation, the general ownership and land use in the area, and the estimated costs of acquisition and administration in the Scenic Rivers System. (1970, c. 468, § 10-171; 1984, cc. 739, 750; 1988, c. 891.)

§ 10.1-405. Duties and powers of the Department; eminent domain prohibited. — A. The Department shall:

1. Administer the Virginia Scenic Rivers System to preserve and protect its natural beauty and to assure its use and enjoyment for its scenic, recreational, geologic, fish and wildlife, historic, cultural or other assets and to encourage the continuance of existing agricultural, horticultural, forestry and open space land and water uses.

2. Periodically survey each scenic river and its immediate environs and monitor all existing and proposed uses of each scenic river and its related land resources.

3. Assist local governments in solving problems associated with the Virginia Scenic Rivers System, in consultation with the Director, the Board, and the advisory committees.

B. The Department shall not exercise the right of eminent domain to acquire any real property or interest therein for the purpose of providing additional access to any scenic river. Nothing in this subsection shall limit or modify any powers granted otherwise to any locality.

C. The Department may seek assistance and advice related to the scenic river program from the Department of Game and Inland Fisheries, the Department of Forestry, the Department of Historic Resources, the Virginia Marine Resources Commission, the United States Forest Service, other state and federal agencies and instrumentalities, and affected local governing bodies.

D. The Department shall have the following powers, which may be delegated by the Director:

1. To make and enter into all contracts and agreements necessary or incidental to the performance of its scenic river duties and the execution of its scenic river powers, including but not limited to contracts with private nonprofit organizations, the United States, other state agencies and political subdivisions of the Commonwealth;

2. To accept bequests and gifts of real and personal property as well as endowments, funds, and grants from the United States government, its agencies and instrumentalities, and any other source. To these ends, the Department shall have the power to comply with such conditions and execute such agreements as may be necessary, convenient, or desirable; and

3. To conduct fund-raising activities as deemed appropriate related to scenic river issues. (1970, c. 468, §§ 10-167, 10-173; 1988, c. 891; 2003, c. 240.)

Editor's note. — Acts 2003, c. 240, cl. 3, provides: "That the Department of Conservation and Recreation shall submit a report to the Governor and the General Assembly in 2009, no later than November 1, that evaluates the effectiveness of the Virginia Scenic River Board. The Department shall examine the activities of the Board, determine whether the Board should be continued, abolished, or modified, and recommend other improvements for the administration of the Virginia Scenic Rivers System. The report shall be submitted as provided in the procedures of the Division of Legislative Automated Systems for the processing of legislative documents and reports."

§ 10.1-406. Virginia Scenic River Board. — A. The Virginia Scenic River Board (the Board) is established as an advisory board, within the meaning of § 2.2-2100, in the executive branch of state government. The Board, which shall have a broad geographical representation, shall be composed of 16 voting members as follows: the Director and 15 members-at-large appointed by the Governor. The 15 members-at-large shall initially be appointed for terms of office as follows: three for a one-year term, four for a two-year term, four for a three-year term, and four for a four-year term. The Governor shall designate the term to be served by each appointee at the time of appointment. Appointments thereafter shall be made for four-year terms. No person shall serve more than two consecutive full terms. Any vacancy shall be filled by the Governor for the unexpired term. All terms shall begin July 1. In making appointments, the Governor shall select persons suitably qualified to consider and act upon the various special interests and problems related to scenic river issues. The Advisory Board shall elect a chairman and a vice-chairman from among its members-at-large. Members of the Board shall serve at the pleasure of the Governor and receive no compensation.

The Director, or his designee, shall serve as executive secretary to the Board.

The Board shall meet at least two times a year with additional meetings at the call of the chairman or the Director. The vice-chairman shall fill the position of chairman in the event that the chairman is not available. A majority of the members of the Board shall constitute a quorum of the Board.

The Board shall have no regulatory authority.

B. The Board shall advise the Governor and the Director concerning the protection or management of the Virginia Scenic Rivers System. Upon the request of the Governor, or the Director, the Board shall institute investigations and make recommendations. The Board shall have general powers and duties to (i) advise the Director on the appointment of Scenic River Advisory Committees or other local or regional committees pursuant to § 10.1-401; (ii) formulate recommendations concerning designations for proposed scenic rivers or extensions of existing scenic rivers; (iii) consider and comment to the Director on any federal, state or local governmental plans to approve, license, fund or construct facilities that would alter any of the assets that qualified the river for scenic designation; (iv) assist the Director in reviewing and making recommendations regarding all planning for the use and development of water and related land resources including the construction of impoundments, diversions, roadways, crossings, channels, locks, canals, or other uses that change the character of a stream or waterway or destroy its scenic assets, so that full consideration and evaluation of the river as a scenic resource will be given before alternative plans for use and development are approved; (v) assist the Director in preserving and protecting the natural beauty of the scenic rivers, assuring the use and enjoyment of scenic rivers for fish and wildlife, scenic, recreational, geologic, historic, cultural or other assets, and encouraging the continuance of existing agricultural, horticultural, forestal and open space land and water uses; (vi) advise the Director and the affected local jurisdiction on the impacts of proposed uses of each scenic river and its related land resources; and (vii) assist local governments in solving problems associated with the Virginia Scenic Rivers System, in consultation with the Director. (1970, c. 468, § 10-170; 1984, c. 739; 1985, c. 346; 1988, c. 891; 2003, c. 240.)

Editor's note. — Acts 2003, c. 240, cl. 3, provides: "That the Department of Conservation and Recreation shall submit a report to the Governor and the General Assembly in 2009, no later than November 1, that evaluates the effectiveness of the Virginia Scenic River Board. The Department shall examine the activities of the Board, determine whether the Board should be continued, abolished, or modified, and recommend other improvements for the administration of the Virginia Scenic Rivers System. The report shall be submitted as provided in the procedures of the Division of Legislative Automated Systems for the processing of legislative documents and reports."

§ 10.1-406.1. Powers of local governments. — In consultation with the Director, local governments shall have the authority, where a committee has not been established pursuant to subdivision A 4 of § 10.1-401, to appoint a local scenic river advisory committee to advise the local government and the Director in administering that section of designated scenic river within the local government's jurisdiction. The committees shall assist and advise the Director and the local governing body on the protection or management of the scenic river segment in their jurisdiction. The committees may consider and comment to the Director on any federal, state or local governmental plans to approve, license, fund or construct facilities that would alter any of the assets that qualified the river for scenic designation. (2003, c. 240.)

§ **10.1-407. Act of General Assembly required to construct, etc., dam or other structure.** — After designation of any river or section of river as a scenic river by the General Assembly, no dam or other structure impeding the natural flow thereof shall be constructed, operated, or maintained in such river or section of river unless specifically authorized by an act of the General Assembly. (1970, c. 468, § 10-174; 1988, c. 891.)

Law Review. — For article on siting electric power facilities, see 58 Va. L. Rev. 257 (1972).

§ **10.1-408. Riparian uses.** — Except as provided in § 10.1-407, all riparian land and water uses along or in the designated section of a river which are permitted by law shall not be restricted by this chapter. (1988, c. 891.)

§ **10.1-409. Appomattox State Scenic River.** — The Appomattox River 100 feet from the base of the Lake Chesdin Dam, to the Route 36 bridge crossing in the City of Petersburg, a distance of approximately 6.2 miles, is hereby designated a component of the Virginia Scenic Rivers System. (1984, c. 739, § 10-173.4; 1985, cc. 346, 448; 1988, c. 891; 1998, cc. 82, 167; 2003, c. 240.)

§ **10.1-410. Catoctin Creek State Scenic River.** — A. The Catoctin Creek from bank to bank in Loudoun County from the Town of Waterford to its junction with the Potomac River, a distance of approximately 16 river miles, is hereby designated a component of the Virginia Scenic Rivers System.
B. No dam or other structure that impedes the natural flow of Catoctin Creek shall be constructed, operated, or maintained within the section of Catoctin Creek designated as a scenic river by this legislation unless specifically authorized by an act of the General Assembly.
As used in this section, the words *"dam or other structure"* mean any structure extending from bank to bank of Catoctin Creek that will interfere with the normal movement of waterborne traffic, interfere with the normal movement of fish or wildlife, raise the water level on the upstream side of the structure or lower the water level on the downstream side of the structure. (1984, c. 739, § 10-173.3; 1985, cc. 346, 448; 1988, c. 891; 2003, c. 240.)

§ **10.1-410.1. Chickahominy State Scenic River.** — A. The main channel of the Chickahominy River from the Mechanicsville Turnpike (Route 360) eastward until the terminus of the Henrico County/Hanover County border, is hereby designated a component of the Virginia Scenic Rivers System.
B. Nothing in this chapter shall preclude the construction or reconstruction of any road or bridge by the Commonwealth or by any county, city or town.
C. Nothing in this chapter shall preclude the construction, operation, repair, maintenance, or replacement of a natural gas pipeline for which the State Corporation Commission has issued a certificate of public convenience and necessity or any connections with such pipeline owned by the Richmond Gas Utility and connected to such pipeline. (1990, c. 173; 2003, c. 240.)

§ **10.1-410.2. Clinch State Scenic River.** — A. The Clinch River in Russell County from its confluence with the Little River to the Nash Ford Bridge at mile 279.5, a distance of approximately 20 miles and including its tributary, Big Cedar Creek from the confluence to mile 5.8 near Lebanon, is hereby designated a component of the Virginia Scenic Rivers System.

B. This designation shall not be used:

1. To designate the lands along the river and its tributaries as unsuitable for mining pursuant to § 45.1-252 or regulations promulgated with respect to such section; however, the Department shall still be permitted to exercise the powers granted under § 10.1-402; or

2. To be a criterion for purposes of imposing water quality standards under the federal Clean Water Act. (1992, c. 308; 1994, c. 329; 2003, c. 240.)

§ **10.1-411. Goose Creek State Scenic River.** — A. Goose Creek, from bank to bank in Loudoun County from the Loudoun-Fauquier County line to its junction with the Potomac River, a distance of approximately 28 river miles, is hereby designated a component of the Virginia Scenic Rivers System.

B. The Northern Virginia Regional Park Authority is authorized to acquire, either by gift or purchase, any real property or interests therein that the Northern Virginia Regional Park Authority considers necessary or desirable to provide public use areas as identified in the Goose Creek Scenic River Report published in 1975.

C. No new dam or other structure or enlargement of an existing dam or other structure that impedes the natural flow of Goose Creek shall be constructed, operated or maintained within the section of Goose Creek designated as a Scenic River by this legislation unless specifically authorized by an act of the General Assembly.

As used in this section, the words *"dam or other structure"* mean any structure extending from bank to bank of Goose Creek that will interfere with the normal movement of waterborne traffic, interfere with the normal movement of fish or wildlife, or raise the water level on the upstream side of the structure or lower the water level on the downstream side of the structure.

D. Nothing in this chapter shall preclude the continued use, operation, and maintenance of the existing Fairfax City water impoundment, or the installation of new water intake facilities in the existing reservoir located within the designated section of Goose Creek. (1984, c. 739, § 10-173.2; 1985, cc. 346, 448; 1988, c. 891; 2003, c. 240.)

§ **10.1-411.1. Clinch-Guest State Scenic River.** — A. The Clinch River from the Route 58 bridge in St. Paul to the junction with the Guest River, a distance of approximately 9.2 miles, and a segment of the Guest River in Wise County, from a point 100 feet downstream from the Route 72 bridge to its confluence with the Clinch River, a distance of approximately 6.5 miles, are hereby designated a component of the Virginia Scenic Rivers System; however, this description shall not be construed as making the lands along such river unsuitable for underground mining pursuant to § 45.1-252 or regulations promulgated thereunder.

B. Nothing in this chapter shall be construed to prevent the construction, use, operation and maintenance of a natural gas pipeline on or beneath the two existing railroad trestles, one located just south of the Swede Tunnel and the other located just north of the confluence of the Guest River with the Clinch River, or to prevent the use, operation and maintenance of such railroad trestles in furtherance of the construction, operation, use and maintenance of such pipeline. Nothing in this chapter shall be construed to prevent the construction, use, operation and maintenance of a natural gas pipeline traversing the river at, or at any point north of, the existing power line that is located approximately 200 feet north of the northern entrance to the Swede Tunnel.

C. Nothing in this chapter shall preclude the federal government, Commonwealth or a local jurisdiction from constructing or reconstructing any road or bridge. (1990, c. 397; 1991, c. 487; 2002, c. 251; 2003, c. 240.)

§ 10.1-412. Historic Falls of the James State Scenic River. — A. The Historic Falls of the James from Orleans Street extended in the City of Richmond westward to the 1970 corporate limits of the city is hereby designated a component of the Virginia Scenic Rivers System.

B. The City of Richmond shall be allowed to reconstruct, operate and maintain existing facilities at the Byrd Park and Hollywood Hydroelectric Power Stations at current capacity.

C. Nothing in this chapter shall be construed to prevent the Commonwealth, the City of Richmond or any common carrier railroad from constructing or reconstructing floodwalls or public common carrier facilities that may traverse the river, such as road or railroad bridges, raw water intake structures, or water or sewer lines that would be constructed below water level. (1972, c. 404, § 10-176; 1984, cc. 176, 739; 1985, c. 346; 1988, c. 891; 2003, c. 240.)

§ 10.1-413. James River State Scenic River. — A. That portion of the James River in Botetourt County, from a point two miles southeast of the point where Route 43 (old Route 220) crosses the James River at Eagle Rock running approximately 14 miles southeastward to the point where Route 630 crosses the James River at Springwood is hereby designated a component of the Virginia Scenic Rivers System.

B. No dam or other structure that impedes the natural flow of the James River in Botetourt County shall be constructed, operated or maintained within the section of the James River designated as a scenic river by this statute unless specifically authorized by an act of the General Assembly. (1985, c. 501, § 10-173.9; 1988, c. 891; 2003, c. 240.)

§ 10.1-413.1. Moormans State Scenic River. — A. The Moormans River in Albemarle County, from the Charlottesville Reservoir to its junction with the Mechums River, is hereby designated a component of the Virginia Scenic Rivers System.

B. No dam or other structure impeding the natural flow of the river shall be constructed, operated, or maintained unless specifically authorized by an act of the General Assembly. (1988, cc. 21, 300, 891; 2003, c. 240.)

§ 10.1-413.2. North Landing and Tributaries State Scenic River. — A. The North Landing from the North Carolina line to the bridge at Route 165, the Pocaty River from its junction with the North Landing River to the Blackwater Road bridge, West Neck Creek from the junction with the North Landing River to Indian River Road bridge, and Blackwater Creek from the junction with the North Landing River to the confluence, approximately 4.2 miles, of an unnamed tributary approximately 1.75 miles, more or less, west of Blackwater Road, are hereby designated as components of the Virginia Scenic Rivers System.

B. No dam or other structure impeding the natural flow of the river shall be constructed, operated, or maintained unless specifically authorized by an act of the General Assembly. (1988, cc. 490, 891; 1989, c. 656; 2003, c. 240.)

§ 10.1-414. Nottoway State Scenic River. — The Nottoway River in Sussex County and Southampton County, from the Route 40 bridge at Stony Creek to the Careys Bridge at Route 653, a distance of approximately 39 ½ miles, is hereby designated a component of the Virginia Scenic Rivers System. (1984, c. 739, § 10-173.6; 1985, cc. 346, 448; 1988, c. 891; 1992, c. 183; 2003, c. 240.)

§ 10.1-415. Rappahannock State Scenic River. — A. The mainstem of the Rappahannock River in Rappahannock, Culpeper, Fauquier, Stafford, and

Spotsylvania Counties and the City of Fredericksburg from its headwaters near Chester Gap to the Ferry Farm-Mayfield Bridge, a distance of approximately 86 river miles, is hereby designated a component of the Virginia Scenic Rivers System.

B. Nothing in this chapter shall preclude the continued operation and maintenance of existing dams in the designated section.

C. Nothing in this chapter shall preclude the continued operation, maintenance, alteration, expansion, or destruction of the Embrey Dam or its appurtenances by the City of Fredericksburg, including the old VEPCO canal and the existing City Reservoir behind the Embrey Dam, or any other part of the City's waterworks.

D. Nothing in this chapter shall preclude the Commonwealth, the City of Fredericksburg, or the Counties of Stafford, Spotsylvania, or Culpeper from constructing or reconstructing any road or bridge or from constructing any new raw water intake structures or devices, including pipes and reservoirs but not dams, or laying water or sewer lines below water level.

E. Nothing in this chapter shall preclude the construction, operation, repair, maintenance, or replacement of the natural gas pipeline, case number PUE 860065, for which the State Corporation Commission has issued a certificate of public convenience and necessity. (1985, c. 124, § 10-173.8; 1988, c. 891; 1990, c. 225; 2003, c. 240.)

§ 10.1-415.1. Rockfish State Scenic River. — A. The Rockfish River in Albemarle and Nelson Counties from the Route 693 bridge in Schuyler to its confluence with the James River, a distance of approximately 9.75 miles, is hereby designated a component of the Virginia Scenic Rivers System.

B. Nothing in this chapter shall preclude the Commonwealth or local governing body from constructing or reconstructing any road or bridge. (1990, cc. 381, 422; 2003, c. 240.)

§ 10.1-416. Rivanna State Scenic River. — A. The river, stream or waterway known as the Rivanna from the base of the dam of the woolen mills in the City of Charlottesville to the junction of the Rivanna with the James River, a distance of approximately 37 miles, is hereby designated the Rivanna Scenic River, a component of the Virginia Scenic Rivers System.

B. No dam or other structure impeding the natural flow of the river shall be constructed, operated, or maintained unless specifically authorized by an act of the General Assembly. (1984, c. 739, § 10-173.1; 1988, cc. 20, 299, 891; 2003, c. 240.)

§ 10.1-417. Shenandoah State Scenic River. — A. The Shenandoah River in Clarke County from the Warren-Clarke County line to the Virginia line, a distance of approximately 21.6 miles, is hereby designated a component of the Virginia Scenic Rivers System.

B. No dam or other structure that impedes the natural flow of the Shenandoah River shall be constructed, operated, or maintained within the section of the Shenandoah River designated as a scenic river by this legislation unless specifically authorized by an act of the General Assembly.

As used in this section, the words *"dam or other structure"* mean any structure extending from bank to bank of the Shenandoah River that will interfere with the normal movement of fish or wildlife, raise the water level on the upstream side of the structure or lower the water level on the downstream side of the structure. (1984, c. 739, § 10-173.7; 1985, cc. 346, 448; 1988, c. 891; 1992, c. 341; 2003, c. 240.)

§ 10.1-418. Staunton State Scenic River. — The river, stream or waterway known as the Staunton or the Roanoke from State Route 360 to State

Route 761 at the Long Island Bridge, a distance of approximately 51.3 river miles, is hereby designated the Staunton State Scenic River, a component of the Virginia Scenic Rivers System. (1984, c. 739, § 10-173.5; 1988, c. 891; 2001, c. 58; 2003, cc. 240, 687.)

§ 10.1-418.1. North Meherrin State Scenic River. — The North Meherrin River in Lunenburg County from the Route 712 Bridge to the junction with the South Meherrin River, a distance of approximately 7.5 miles, is hereby designated a component of the Virginia Scenic Rivers System. (1997, cc. 45, 505; 2003, c. 240.)

§ 10.1-418.2. St. Mary's State Scenic River. — A. As the authority of the federal government over the St. Mary's River prevents the Commonwealth from legally including the river as a component of the Virginia Scenic Rivers System, the segment of the St. Mary's River from its headwaters to the border of the George Washington National Forest, all on national forest property, is hereby recognized as one of Virginia's Scenic River resources and is worthy of designation as such.

B. All land and water uses along this portion of the St. Mary's River that are permitted by law shall not be restricted.

C. The Department shall consult with the Augusta County Board of Supervisors and the Supervisor of the George Washington National Forest on matters related to this Scenic River. (2003, c. 240.)

§ 10.1-418.3. Meherrin River State Scenic River. — The Meherrin River within Brunswick County, a distance of approximately 37 miles, is hereby designated a component of the Virginia Scenic Rivers System. (2006, cc. 4, 44.)

The number of this section was assigned by the Virginia Code Commission, the number in Acts 2006, cc. 4 and 44, having been § 10.1-418.2.

CHAPTER 4.1.

HISTORIC LOWER JAMES RIVER.

§ 10.1-419. Declared a state historic river; planning for use and development; advisory committee established. — A. In keeping with the public policy of the Commonwealth of Virginia to conserve the portions of certain rivers possessing superior natural beauty, thereby assuring their use and enjoyment for their historic, scenic, recreational, geologic, fish and wildlife, cultural and other values, that portion of the Lower James River in Charles City, James City and Surry Counties, from an unnamed tributary to the James River approximately 1.2 miles east of Trees Point in Charles City County (northside) and Upper Chippokes Creek (southside) to Grices Run (northside) and Lawnes Creek (southside), is hereby declared to be an historic river with noteworthy scenic and ecological qualities.

B. In all planning for the use and development of water and related land resources which changes the character of a stream or waterway or destroys its historic, scenic or ecological values, full consideration and evaluation of the river as an historic, scenic and ecological resource should be given before such work is undertaken. Alternative solutions should also be considered before such work is undertaken.

C. The Counties of Charles City, James City and Surry and the Governor shall appoint a seven-member advisory committee of area residents and other qualified persons. The governing bodies of the Counties of James City and Surry shall each appoint two persons to the Lower James River Advisory Committee. The governing body of Charles City County shall appoint one person to the Advisory Committee. The Governor shall appoint two persons to the Advisory Committee. Committee members will serve four-year terms, without compensation.

The Advisory Committee shall assist and advise the Department of Conservation and Recreation, the political subdivisions through which the Lower James River passes, and other public bodies concerning the protection and management of this portion of the River. The Advisory Committee shall have no regulatory authority.

D. The General Assembly hereby designates the Department of Conservation and Recreation as the agency of the Commonwealth responsible for assuring that the purposes of this chapter are achieved. Nothing in this designation shall impair the powers and duties of the local jurisdictions listed above or the Virginia Department of Transportation. (1988, cc. 721, 891; 1989, c. 656.)

CHAPTER 5.

SOIL AND WATER CONSERVATION.

Michie's Jurisprudence. — For related discussion, see 20 M.J. Waters and Watercourses, § 3.

ARTICLE 1.

General Provisions.

§ 10.1-500. Definitions. — As used in this chapter, unless the context requires a different meaning:

"Board" means the Virginia Soil and Water Conservation Board.

"County" includes towns.

"City" includes all cities chartered under the Commonwealth.

"District" or *"soil and water conservation district"* means a political subdivision of this Commonwealth organized in accordance with the provisions of this chapter.

"District director" means a member of the governing body of a district authorized to serve as a director.

"Due notice" means notice published at least twice, with an interval of at least seven days between the two publication dates, in a newspaper or other publication of general circulation within the appropriate area, or if no such publication of general circulation is available, by posting at a reasonable number of conspicuous places within the appropriate area. Such posting shall include, where possible, posting at public places where it is customary to post notices concerning county or municipal affairs. Hearings held pursuant to such notice, at the time and place designated in the notice, may be adjourned from time to time without renewing the notice for the adjourned dates.

"Governing body of a city or county" means the entire governing body regardless of whether all or part of that city or county is included or to be included within a district.

"Government" or *"governmental"* includes the government of this Commonwealth, the government of the United States, and any of their subdivisions, agencies or instrumentalities.

"Land occupier" or *"occupier of land"* includes any person, firm or corporation who holds title to, or is in possession of, any lands lying within a district organized, or proposed to be organized, under the provisions of this chapter, in the capacity of owner, lessee, renter, tenant, or cropper. The terms "land occupier" and "occupier of land" shall not include an ordinary employee or hired hand who is furnished a dwelling, garden, utilities, supplies, or the like, as part payment, or payment in full, for his labor.

"Locality" means a county, city or town. (Code 1950, § 21-3; 1950, p. 76; 1954, c. 670; 1964, c. 512; 1970, c. 480; 1985, c. 448; 1988, c. 891.)

§ 10.1-501. Duty of the attorney for the Commonwealth. — The attorney for the Commonwealth of the county or city in which the suits or actions under this chapter may arise shall represent the district directors or districts in such suits or actions unless the Attorney General provides legal services pursuant to § 2.2-507. (Code 1950, § 21-89; 1964, c. 512; 1970, c. 480; 1988, c. 891; 2005, c. 236.)

The 2005 amendments. — The 2005 amendment by c. 236 added "unless the Attorney General provides legal services pursuant to § 2.2-507" at the end of the section.

§ 10.1-501.1. Defense of claims. — The Attorney General shall provide the legal defense against any claim made against any soil and water conservation district, director, officer, agent or employee thereof (i) arising out of the ownership, maintenance or use of buildings, grounds or properties owned, leased or maintained by any soil and water conservation district or used by district employees or other authorized persons in the course of their employment, or (ii) arising out of acts or omissions of any nature while acting in an authorized governmental or proprietary capacity and in the course and scope of employment or authorization. (1988, cc. 763, 780, 891.)

ARTICLE 2.

Virginia Soil and Water Conservation Board.

§ 10.1-502. Soil and Water Conservation Board; composition. — The Virginia Soil and Water Conservation Board is continued and shall perform the functions conferred upon it in this chapter. The Board shall consist of 10 voting members. The Director of the Department of Conservation and Recreation, or his designee, shall be a member of the Board. Three at-large members of the Board shall be appointed by the Governor. After the initial staggering of terms, nonlegislative citizen members shall be appointed for a term of four years. At least two of the three at-large members should have a demonstrated interest in natural resource conservation with a background or knowledge in dam safety, soil conservation, water quality protection, or urban point or nonpoint source pollution control. Additionally, four members shall be farmers and two members shall be farmers or district directors, appointed by the Governor from a list of two qualified nominees for each vacancy submitted by the Board of Directors of the Virginia Association of Soil and Water Conservation Districts and the Soil and Water Conservation Board in joint session, each for a term of four years. All appointed members shall not serve more than two consecutive full terms. Appointments to fill vacancies shall be made in the same manner as described above, except that such appointments shall be for the unexpired terms only. The Board may invite the Virginia State Conservationist, Natural Resources Conservation Service, to serve as an advisory nonvoting member. The Board shall keep a record of its official actions, shall adopt a seal and may perform acts, hold public hearings, and promulgate regulations necessary for the execution of its functions under this chapter. (Code 1950, § 21-6; 1950, p. 77; 1954, c. 670; 1956, c. 654; 1960, c. 208; 1964, c. 512; 1968, c. 149; 1970, c. 480; 1984, c. 750; 1985, c. 448; 1988, c. 891; 1989, c. 656; 1991, c. 188; 1992, c. 121; 2003, c. 128; 2005, c. 102.)

Editor's note. — Acts 2005, c. 102, cl. 2, provides: "That the Governor shall make new appointments for each of the three at-large members of the Board in accordance with the provisions of this act on July 1, 2005. The new appointments of the at-large members of the Board shall go into effect upon the expiration of the current members' terms in January 2006, and the terms shall be staggered as follows: one member for a term of two years; one member for a term of three years; and one member for a term of four years. The Governor shall designate the term to be served by each appointee at the time of appointment and may reappoint the existing at-large members of the Board."

Acts 2005, c. 102, cl. 3, provides: "That the Director of the Department of Conservation and Recreation shall amend the Stormwater Management Regulations by removing the out-of-date Best Management Practices (BMP) nutrient removal efficiency information and adding it into the Virginia Stormwater Management Handbook guidance document where it shall be more effectively updated for public use."

The 2005 amendments. — The 2005 amendment by c. 102 deleted "to serve at the pleasure of the Governor, for a term coincident with that of the appointing Governor; vacancies in the office of such appointed members shall be filled by the Governor" following "Governor" in the fourth sentence, inserted the present fifth sentence, substituted "Additionally, four members" for "Four members" in the seventh sentence and substituted "All appointed" for "Appointed" in the eighth sentence.

Law Review. — For 2003/2004 survey of environmental law, see 39 U. Rich. L. Rev. 203 (2004).

§ 10.1-503. Administrative officer and other employees; executive committee. — The Director shall provide technical experts and other agents and employees, permanent and temporary, necessary for the execution of the functions of the Board. The Board may create an executive committee and delegate to the chairman of the Board, or to the committee or to the Director, such powers and duties as it deems proper. Upon request of the Board, for the purpose of carrying out any of its functions, the supervising officer of any state agency or of any state institution of learning shall, insofar as possible under available appropriations, and having due regard for the needs of the agency to which the request is directed, assign or detail to the Board, members of the staff or personnel of the agency or institution, and make special reports, surveys, or studies requested by the Board. (Code 1950, § 21-7; 1964, c. 512; 1984, cc. 444, 750; 1988, c. 891; 2003, c. 128.)

§ 10.1-504. Chairman; quorum. — The Board shall designate its chairman and may, from time to time, change such designation. Six members of the Board shall constitute a quorum, and the concurrence of a majority of those present and voting shall be required for all determinations. (Code 1950, § 21-8; 1964, c. 512; 1988, c. 891.)

§ 10.1-505. Duties of Board. — In addition to other duties and powers conferred upon the Board, it shall have the following duties and powers:

1. To give or loan appropriate financial and other assistance to district directors in carrying out any of their powers and programs.

2. To keep district directors informed of the activities and experience of all other districts, and to facilitate an interchange of advice and experience between the districts.

3. To coordinate the programs of the districts so far as this may be done by advice and consultation.

4. To secure the cooperation and assistance of the United States and any of its agencies, and of agencies of the Commonwealth, in the work of the districts.

5. To disseminate information throughout the Commonwealth concerning the activities and programs of the districts, and to encourage the formation of such districts in areas where their organization is desirable.

6. To assist persons, associations, and corporations engaged in furthering the programs of the districts; to encourage and assist in the establishment and operation of such associations and corporations, and to authorize financial assistance to the officers and members of such associations and corporations in the discharge of their duties.

7. To receive, review, approve or disapprove applications for assistance in planning and carrying out works of improvement under the Watershed Protection and Flood Prevention Act (Public Law 566 — 83rd Congress, as amended), and to receive, review and approve or disapprove applications for any other similar soil and water conservation programs provided in federal laws which by their terms or by related executive orders require such action by a state agency.

8. To advise and recommend to the Governor approval or disapproval of all work plans developed under Public Law 83-566 and Public Law 78-535 and to advise and recommend to the Governor approval or disapproval of other similar soil and water conservation programs provided in federal laws which by their terms or by related executive orders require approval or comment by the Governor.

9. To provide for the conservation of soil and water resources, control and prevention of soil erosion, flood water and sediment damages thereby preserving the natural resources of the Commonwealth. (Code 1950, § 21-10; 1956, c. 654; 1958, c. 410; 1962, c. 213; 1964, c. 512; 1970, c. 480; 1972, c. 557; 1988, c. 891.)

Editor's note. — For the Watershed Protection and Flood Prevention Act, referred to above, see generally 16 U.S.C.S. § 1001.

ARTICLE 3.

Soil and Water Conservation Districts.

§ 10.1-506. Power to create new districts and to relocate or define district boundaries; composition of districts. — A. The Board shall have the power to (i) create a new district from territory not previously within an existing district, (ii) merge or divide existing districts, (iii) transfer territory from an existing district to another district, (iv) modify or create a district by a combination of the above and (v) relocate or define the boundaries of soil and water conservation districts in the manner hereinafter prescribed.

B. An incorporated town within any county having a soil and water conservation district shall be a part of that district. If a town lies within the boundaries of more than one county, it shall be considered to be wholly within the county in which the larger portion of the town lies. (Code 1950, § 21-2; 1956, c. 654; 1970, c. 480, § 21-12.1; 1988, c. 891.)

§ 10.1-507. Petitions filed with the Board. — Petitions to modify or create districts, or relocate or define boundaries of existing districts, shall be initiated and filed with the Board for its approval or disapproval by any of the following methods:

1. By petition of a majority of the directors of any or each district or by petition from a majority of the governing body of any or each county or city.

2. By petition of a majority of the governing body of a county or city not within an existing district, requesting to be included in an existing district and concurred in by the district directors.

3. By petition of a majority of the governing body of a county or city or parts thereof not included within an existing district, requesting that a new district be created.

4. By petition, signed by a number of registered voters equal to twenty-five percent of the vote cast in the last general election, who are residents of a county or city not included within an existing district, requesting that a new district be created, or requesting to be included within an existing district. If the petition bears the signatures of the requisite number of registered voters of a county or city, or two or more cities, then the petition shall be deemed to be the joint petition of the particular combination of political subdivisions named in the petition. If the petition deals in whole or in part with a portion or portions of a political subdivision or subdivisions, then the number of signatures necessary for each portion of a political subdivision shall be the same as if the whole political subdivision were involved in the petition, and may come from the political subdivision at large. (1970, c. 480, § 21-12.2; 1988, c. 891.)

§ 10.1-508. Contents and form of petition. — The petition shall set forth:

1. The proposed name of the district;

2. That there is need, in the interest of the public health, safety, and welfare, for the proposed district to function in the territory described in the petition, and a brief statement of the grounds upon which this conclusion is based;

3. A description of the territory proposed to be organized as a district, which description shall not be required to be given by metes and bounds or by legal subdivision, but shall be deemed sufficient if generally accurate;

4. A request that the Board define the boundaries for such district; that a hearing be held within the territory so defined on the question of the creation of a district in such territory; and that the Board determine that such a district be created.

Where more than one petition is filed covering parts of the same territory, the Board may consolidate the petitions.

The Board shall prescribe the petition form. (Code 1950, § 21-13; 1964, c. 512; 1970, c. 480; 1988, c. 891.)

§ 10.1-509. Disapproval of petition. — If the Board disapproves the petition, its determination shall be recorded, and if the petitioners are the governing body of a district, county or city or a part of a county or city, the governing body shall be notified in writing. If the petitioners are the requisite number of registered voters prescribed by subdivision 4 of § 10.1-507, notification shall be by a notice printed once in a newspaper of general circulation within the area designated in the petition. (1970, c. 480, § 21-13.1; 1988, c. 891.)

§ 10.1-510. Petition approved; Board to give notice of hearing. — If the Board approves the petition, within sixty days after such determination, the Board shall provide due notice of the approval in a newspaper of general circulation in each county or city involved. The notice shall include notice of a hearing upon the question of the desirability and necessity, in the interest of the public health, safety, and welfare, of the action proposed by the petition upon (i) the question of the appropriate boundaries to be assigned to such district, (ii) the propriety of the petition and other proceedings taken under this chapter, and (iii) all questions relevant to such inquiries. (Code 1950, § 21-14; 1964, c. 512; 1970, c. 480; 1988, c. 891.)

§ 10.1-511. Adjournment of hearing when additional territory appears desirable. — If it appears upon the hearing that it may be desirable to include within the proposed district territory outside of the area within which due notice of the hearing has been given, the hearing shall be adjourned and due notice of a further hearing shall be given throughout the entire area considered for inclusion in the district. (Code 1950, § 21-16; 1988, c. 891.)

§ 10.1-512. Determination of need for district. — After a public hearing, if the Board determines that there is need, in the interest of the public health, safety, and welfare, for the proposed district to function in the territory considered at the hearing, it shall record its determination, and shall define, by metes and bounds or by legal subdivisions the boundaries of the district. In so doing, the Board shall consider (i) the topography of the area considered and of the Commonwealth, (ii) the composition of soils in the area, (iii) the distribution of erosion, (iv) the prevailing land-use practices, (v) the desirability and necessity of including within the boundaries the particular lands under consideration and the benefits the lands may receive from being included within such boundaries, (vi) the relation of the proposed area to existing watersheds and to other soil and water conservation districts already organized or proposed for organization, (vii) the existing political subdivisions, and (viii) other relevant physical, geographical, economic, and funding factors. The territory to be included within such boundaries need not be contiguous. (Code 1950, § 21-17; 1964, c. 512; 1970, c. 480; 1988, c. 891; 2002, c. 192.)

§ 10.1-513. Determination that district not needed. — If the Board determines after the hearing, and after due consideration of the relevant facts, that there is no need for a soil and water conservation district to function in the territory considered at the hearing, it shall record its determination and deny the petition. (Code 1950, § 21-18; 1964, c. 512; 1988, c. 891.)

§ 10.1-514. Determination of feasibility of operation. — After the Board has made and recorded a determination that there is need for the organization of the proposed district in a particular territory, and has defined the boundaries, it shall consider whether the operation of a district within such boundaries is administratively practicable and feasible. In making its determination, the Board shall consider the attitudes of the occupiers of lands lying within the defined boundaries, the probable expense of the operation of such district, the effect upon the programs of any existing districts, and other relevant economic and social factors. If the Board determines that the operation of a district is administratively practicable and feasible, it shall record its determination and proceed with the organization of the district. If the Board determines that the operation of a district is not administratively practicable and feasible, it shall record its determination and deny the petition. If the petition is denied, the Board shall notify the petitioner in the manner provided in this chapter. (Code 1950, § 21-20; 1964, c. 512; 1970, c. 480; 1988, c. 891.)

§ 10.1-515. Composition of governing body. — If the Board determines that the operation of the proposed district within the defined boundaries is administratively practicable and feasible, and the proposed district is created, then its governing body shall be a board of district directors appointed or elected in the number and manner specified as follows:

1. If the district embraces one county or city, or less than one county or city, the board of district directors shall consist of five members, three to be elected by the registered voters of the district and two appointed by the Board.

2. If the district embraces more than one county or city, or parts thereof, the board of district directors shall consist of two members elected by the registered voters from each county or city, or parts thereof embraced by the district. Two members-at-large shall be appointed by the Board. (Code 1950, § 21-27; 1964, c. 512; 1970, c. 480; 1978, c. 763; 1988, c. 891; 2002, cc. 143, 236.)

§ 10.1-516. Status of district directors in event of transfer, merger, or division of districts. — In the event of the transfer, merger, or division of districts, the status of the district directors involved shall be affected as follows:

1. The composition of an existing district board of a district to which territory is transferred shall remain in effect until the terms of office of the present elected members expire. Upon the transfer of a county or city, or parts thereof, from one district to another district, (i) elected district directors residing within the territory transferred shall be appointed as directors of the district to which the territory is transferred for a term of office to coincide with that of the elected directors of the district to which the territory is transferred; and (ii) appointed district directors residing within the territory transferred shall be appointed as directors of the district to which the territory is transferred for a term of office to coincide with that of the appointed directors, either as an extension agent appointee or an at-large appointee of the district to which the territory is transferred. At the option of the petitioners, a petition may request that a proposed transfer be treated as a merger or division for the purpose of this section, and the Board at its discretion may grant or refuse such request.

2. Upon the merger of existing districts, or upon the separation from two or more existing districts of a county or city, or parts thereof, which merge to

create a new district, all district directors residing within the territory merged shall be appointed as directors of the new district. Following the merger, (i) elected district directors residing within the territory of the new district shall be appointed as directors of the new district for a term of office to coincide with that of elected directors as provided in § 10.1-529; and (ii) appointed district directors residing within the new district shall be appointed as directors of the new district for a term of office to coincide with that of the appointed directors, either as an extension agent appointee or an at-large appointee of the district as provided in § 10.1-529.

3. Upon the division of an existing district, to create a new district, all elected or appointed district directors residing within the territory to be divided from the existing district shall be appointed as directors of the new district. Following the division, (i) elected district directors residing within the territory of the new district shall be appointed as directors of the new district for a term of office to coincide with that of elected directors as provided in § 10.1-529; and (ii) appointed district directors residing within the territory of the new district shall be appointed as directors of the new district for a term of office to coincide with that of the appointed directors, either as an extension agent appointee or an at-large appointee of the district as provided in § 10.1-529.

This section shall not be construed as broadening or limiting the size of a governing body of a district as prescribed by § 10.1-515. If the operation of this section results in a governing body larger or smaller than the appropriate size permitted by § 10.1-515, then such a variation, if not otherwise corrected by operation of this section, shall be cured by appropriate appointments by the Board and with the next general election after the transfer, merger, or division in which all those elected directors prescribed by § 10.1-515 may be elected. (1970, c. 480, § 21-27.2; 1988, c. 891; 2002, cc. 143, 236.)

§ 10.1-517. Application and statement to the Secretary of the Commonwealth. — Upon the creation of a district by any means authorized by this chapter, two district directors appointed by the Board and authorized by the Board to do so, shall present to the Secretary of the Commonwealth an application signed by them, which shall set forth: (i) that a petition for the creation of the district was filed with the Board pursuant to the provisions of this chapter, and that the proceedings specified in this chapter were conducted; (ii) that the application is being filed in order to complete the organization of the district as a political subdivision under this chapter; (iii) that the Board has appointed them as district directors; (iv) the name and official residence of each of the district directors together with a certified copy of the appointments evidencing their right to office; (v) the term of office of each of the district directors; (vi) the proposed name of the district; and (vii) the location of the principal office of the district directors. The application shall be subscribed and sworn to by the two district directors authorized by the Board to make such application before an officer authorized by the laws of the Commonwealth to take and certify oaths. The application shall be accompanied by a certified statement by the Board that the district was created as required by law. The statement shall set forth the boundaries of the district as they have been defined by the Board.

If the creation of a district necessitates the dissolution of an existing district, an application shall be submitted to the Secretary of the Commonwealth, with the application for the district to be created, by the directors of the district to be dissolved, for the discontinuance of such district, contingent upon the creation of the new district. The application for discontinuance, duly verified, shall simply state that the lands encompassed in the district to be dissolved shall be included within the territory of the district created. The application for discontinuance of such district shall be accompanied by a certified statement by the Board that the discontinued district was dissolved as required by law and the new district was created as required by law. The statement shall contain a description of the boundaries of each district dissolved and shall set forth the boundaries of the district created as defined by the Board. The Secretary of the Commonwealth shall issue to the directors of each district a certificate of dissolution and shall record the certificate in an appropriate book of record in his office.

When the boundaries of districts are changed pursuant to the provisions of this chapter, the various affected district boards shall each present to the Secretary of the Commonwealth an application, signed by them, for a new certificate of organization evidencing the change of boundaries. The application shall be filed with the Secretary of the Commonwealth accompanied by a certified statement by the Board that the boundaries have been changed in accordance with the provisions of this chapter. The statement by the Board shall define the new boundary line in a manner adequate to describe the boundary changes of districts. When the application and statement have been filed with the Secretary of the Commonwealth, the change of boundary shall become effective and the Secretary of the Commonwealth shall issue to the directors of each of the districts a certificate of organization evidencing the change of boundaries. (Code 1950, § 21-28; 1964, c. 512; 1970, c. 480; 1988, c. 891.)

§ **10.1-518. Action of Secretary on the application and statement; change of name of district.** — The Secretary of the Commonwealth shall examine the application and statement and, if he finds that the name proposed for the district is not identical to that of any other soil and water conservation district shall receive and file them and shall record the application in an appropriate book of record in his office. If the Secretary of the Commonwealth finds that the name proposed for the district is identical to that of any other soil and water conservation district, or so nearly similar as to lead to confusion and uncertainty, he shall certify such fact to the Board, which shall submit to the Secretary of the Commonwealth a new name for the district. Upon receipt of the new name, the Secretary of the Commonwealth shall record the application, with the name so modified, in an appropriate book of record in his office. When the application and statement have been made, filed and recorded, as herein provided, the district shall constitute a political subdivision of the Commonwealth. The Secretary of the Commonwealth shall make and issue to the directors a certificate, under the lesser seal of the Commonwealth, of the due organization of the district and shall record the certificate with the application and statement. The boundaries of the district shall include the territory as determined by the Board, but shall not include any area included within the boundaries of another district, except in those cases otherwise provided for in this article. The name of any district may be changed if a petition for such change is subscribed by twenty-five or more landowners from each county or city comprising the district and adopted by resolution of the district directors at any regular meeting. The district directors shall submit a copy of the resolution to the Board and, if the Board concurs, it shall present the resolution, together with a certified statement that it concurs, to the Secretary of the Commonwealth who shall file the resolution and issue a new or amended certificate of organization. (Code 1950, § 21-29; 1954, c. 670; 1958, c. 409; 1960, c. 208; 1962, c. 212; 1964, c. 512; 1970, c. 480; 1988, c. 891.)

§ **10.1-518.1. Secretary to send copies of certificates to State Board of Elections.** — Whenever the Secretary issues a certificate creating, dissolving, or changing the name or composition of a district, the Secretary shall promptly send a certified copy of such certificate to the State Board of Elections. (2001, c. 53.)

§ 10.1-519. Renewal of petition after disapproval or denial. — After six months have expired from the date of the disapproval or denial of any petition for a soil and water conservation district, subsequent petitions covering the same or substantially the same territory may be filed with the Board as provided in this chapter. (Code 1950, § 21-30; 1964, c. 512; 1970, c. 480; 1988, c. 891.)

§ 10.1-520. Contracts to remain in force; succession to rights and obligations. — Upon consummation of any transfer, merger, or division, or any combination thereof, using territory within a previously existing district to form a new district or to add to an existing district, all contracts in effect at the time of the consummation, affecting or relating to the territory transferred, merged, or divided, to which the governing body of the district from which such territory was acquired is a party shall remain in force for the period provided in the contracts. Rights and obligations acquired or assumed by the district from which the territory was acquired shall succeed to the district to which the territory is transferred. (1970, c. 480, § 21-31.2; 1988, c. 891.)

§ 10.1-521. Determination of status of district boundaries upon annexation or consolidation. — Notwithstanding the provisions of § 10.1-507, the Board may, in its discretion, relocate or redefine district boundaries on its own motion pending or subsequent to any annexation or consolidation.

If the Board determines on its own motion to relocate or redefine district boundaries, the Board shall serve written notice of its determination, containing the full terms of the proposed relocation or redefinition, on the governing body of each district, county, city and town affected by the relocation or redefinition of boundaries. If within forty-five days from the date of service of such notice each governing body affected approves the Board's action by resolution of a majority of the members, the Board may then proceed to act on its motion without a public hearing. (1970, c. 480, § 21-31.3; 1988, c. 891.)

§ 10.1-522. Certificate of Secretary of Commonwealth as evidence. — In any suit, action, or proceeding involving the validity or enforcement of, or relating to, any contract, proceeding, or action of the district, the district shall be deemed to have been established, reorganized, or renamed, in accordance with the provisions of this chapter upon proof of the issuance of the certificate by the Secretary of the Commonwealth. A copy of such certificate shall be admissible in evidence in any such suit, action, or proceeding and shall be proof of the issuance and contents thereof. (Code 1950, § 21-32; 1954, c. 670; 1988, c. 891.)

§ 10.1-523. Nominating petitions; notice of election for district directors. — A. Beginning thirty days after the date of issuance by the Secretary of the Commonwealth of a certificate of organization of a district, but not later than the filing date specified in § 24.2-507 for the November 2003 general election and each fourth year thereafter, nominating petitions, statements of qualifications, and declarations of candidacy shall be filed with the general registrar of the county or city where the candidate resides, pursuant to §§ 24.2-501, 24.2-503, 24.2-505, 24.2-506, and 24.2-507, to nominate candidates for elected directors of such districts. Nominating petitions, statements of qualifications, and declarations of candidacy for elected directors of existing districts shall be filed with the general registrar of the county or city where the candidate resides, pursuant to §§ 24.2-501, 24.2-503, 24.2-505, 24.2-506, and 24.2-507. Notice of the date for filing such petitions and the time of the election shall be published in a newspaper of general circulation within the district at least thirty days before the filing date.

B. Registered voters may sign more than one nominating petition to nominate more than one candidate for district director.

C. The Virginia Soil and Water Conservation Board shall give due notice of an election to be held for the election of district directors.

D. Beginning in the year 2003, elections shall be held only at the November general election in 2003 and at the November general election in each fourth year thereafter. (Code 1950, §§ 21-33 to 21-36; 1964, c. 512; 1970, c. 480; 1988, c. 891; 2001, c. 53; 2002, cc. 143, 236.)

§ 10.1-524. Names of nominees furnished electoral board; how ballots printed, etc. — The names of all nominees shall be furnished to the secretary of the electoral board of the respective county or city and shall be printed upon ballots. The ballots shall be printed, voted, counted and canvassed in conformity with the provisions of general law relating to elections, except as herein otherwise provided. (Code 1950, § 21-37; 1960, c. 208; 1970, c. 480; 1988, c. 891.)

§ 10.1-525. Canvassing returns. — The result of the election shall be canvassed and certified by the electoral board for the county or city in which the candidate resides pursuant to §§ 24.2-671 through 24.2-678. The State Board of Elections shall, promptly after the meeting required by § 24.2-679, certify to the Director of the Department of Conservation and Recreation a list of the candidates elected and certified as Directors of Soil and Water Conservation Districts, as reported pursuant to § 24.2-675. (Code 1950, § 21-38; 1960, c. 208; 1964, c. 512; 1988, c. 891; 2001, c. 53; 2002, cc. 143, 236.)

§ 10.1-526. Persons eligible to vote. — All registered voters residing within each county or city or part thereof shall be eligible to vote in the election for their respective nominees. (Code 1950, § 21-39; 1970, c. 480; 1988, c. 891.)

§ 10.1-527. Determination of candidates elected. — If the district embraces one county or city, or less than one county or city, the three candidates who receive the largest number of the votes cast in the election shall be elected directors for the district.

If the district embraces more than one county or city, or parts thereof, the two candidates from each county or city, or part thereof, receiving the largest number of the votes cast in the election shall be the elected directors for the district. (Code 1950, § 21-40; 1970, c. 480; 1988, c. 891.)

§ 10.1-528. Expenses and publication of results. — The expenses of such elections shall be paid by the counties or cities concerned. The State Board of Elections shall publish, or have published within the district, the results of the election. (Code 1950, § 21-41; 1960, c. 208; 1964, c. 512; 1988, c. 891; 2002, cc. 143, 236.)

§ 10.1-529. District directors constitute governing body; qualifications. — The governing body of the district shall consist of five or more district directors, elected and appointed as provided in this article.

The two district directors appointed by the Board shall be persons who are by training and experience qualified to perform the specialized skilled services which will be required of them in the performance of their duties. One of the appointed district directors shall be the extension agent of the county or city, or one of the counties or cities constituting the district, or a part thereof. Other appointed and elected district directors shall reside within the boundaries of the district. (Code 1950, §§ 21-42, 21-43; 1954, c. 670; 1964, c. 512; 1970, c. 480; 1988, c. 891.)

§ **10.1-529.1. Duties of district directors.** — In addition to other duties and powers, district directors shall:

1. Identify soil and water issues and opportunities within the district or related to the district and establish priorities for addressing these issues;

2. Seek a comprehensive understanding of the complex issues that impact soil and water, and assist in resolving the identified issues at the watershed, local, regional, state, and national levels;

3. Engage in actions that will improve soil and water stewardship by use of locally led programs;

4. Increase understanding among community leaders, including elected officials and others, of their role in soil and water quality protection and improvement;

5. Foster discussion and advancement within the community of positions and programs by their district;

6. Actively participate in the activities of the district and ensure district resources are used effectively and managed wisely; and

7. Support and promote the advancement of districts and their capabilities. (2005, c. 73.)

§ **10.1-530. Designation of chairman; terms of office; filling vacancies.** — A. The district directors shall designate a chairman from the elected members, or from the Board-appointed members, of the district board and may change such designation.

B. The term of office of each district director shall be four years. A district director shall hold office until his successor has been elected or appointed and has qualified. The selection of successors to fill a full term shall be made in accordance with the provisions of this article. Beginning in the year 2003, the election of district directors shall be held at the November 2003 general election and each fourth year thereafter. The terms of office of elected district directors shall begin on January 1 following the November general election. The term of office of any district director elected in November 1999 shall be extended to the January 1 following the November 2003 general election. The term of office of any district director elected in November 2000 shall expire on the January 1 following the November 2003 general election. The term of office of any district director elected in November 2001 or 2002 shall be extended to expire on the January 1 following the November general election in 2007. Appointments made by the Board to the at-large position held by an extension agent shall be made to commence January 1, 2005, and each fourth year thereafter. Appointments made by the Board to the other at-large position shall be made to commence January 1, 2007, and each fourth year thereafter. Any appointment made by the Board prior to January 1, 2005, to an at-large position held by an extension agent shall be made to expire January 1, 2005; and any appointment made by the Board prior to January 1, 2007, to the other at-large position shall be made to expire January 1, 2007.

C. A vacancy shall exist in the event of the death, resignation or removal of residence from the district of any director or the elimination or detachment from the district of the territory in which a director resides, or by the removal of a director from office by the Board. Any vacancy in an elected or appointed director's position shall be filled by an appointment made by the Board for the unexpired term. In the event of the creation of a new district, the transfer of territory from an existing district to an existing district, or the addition of territory not previously within an existing district to an existing district, the Board may appoint directors to fill the vacancies of elected directors prescribed by § 10.1-515 in the newly created district or in the territory added to an existing district. Such appointed directors shall serve in office until the elected directors prescribed by § 10.1-515 take office after the next general election at which directors for the entire district are selected. (Code 1950, §§ 21-44, 21-45; 1954, c. 670; 1956, c. 654; 1964, c. 512; 1970, c. 480; 1988, c. 891; 2001, c. 54; 2002, cc. 143, 236.)

§ 10.1-531. Quorum and expenses. — A majority of the district directors currently in office shall constitute a quorum and the concurrence of a majority of those present and voting shall be required for all determinations. A district director shall receive no compensation for his services, but shall be entitled to expenses, including traveling expenses, necessarily incurred in the discharge of his duties. (Code 1950, § 21-46; 1970, c. 480; 1988, c. 891; 2003, c. 616.)

§ 10.1-532. Employment of officers, agents and employees. — The district directors may employ a secretary-treasurer, whose qualifications shall be approved by the Board, technical experts, and such other officers, agents and employees, permanent and temporary, as they may require, and shall determine their qualifications, duties and compensation. (Code 1950, § 21-47; 1964, c. 512; 1970, c. 480; 1988, c. 891.)

§ 10.1-533. Delegation of powers. — The district directors may delegate to their chairman or to one or more district directors, agents or employees such powers and duties as they may deem proper. (Code 1950, § 21-48; 1970, c. 480; 1988, c. 891.)

§ 10.1-534. Information furnished Board. — The district directors shall furnish to the Board or Department, upon request, copies of ordinances, rules, regulations, orders, contracts, forms, and other documents that they adopt or employ, and other information concerning their activities as the Board or Department may require in the performance of its duties under this chapter. (Code 1950, § 21-49; 1964, c. 512; 1970, c. 480; 1988, c. 891.)

§ 10.1-535. Bonds of officers and employees; records and accounts. — The district directors shall (i) provide for the execution of surety bonds for all employees and officers who shall be entrusted with funds or property; (ii) provide for the keeping of a full and accurate record of all proceedings and of all resolutions, regulations, and orders issued or adopted; and (iii) provide for an annual audit of the accounts of receipts and disbursements by the Auditor of Public Accounts or a certified public accountant approved by him. (Code 1950, § 21-50; 1970, c. 480; 1988, c. 891.)

§ 10.1-536. Removal from office. — Any district director may be removed by the Board for neglect of duty or malfeasance in office, or may be removed in accordance with the provisions of general law. Upon receipt of a sworn complaint against a director filed by a majority of the directors of that same district, the Board shall (i) notify the district director that a complaint has been filed against him and (ii) hold a hearing to determine whether the district director's conduct constitutes neglect of duty or malfeasance in office. (Code 1950, § 21-51; 1964, c. 512; 1970, c. 480; 1988, c. 891; 1996, c. 493.)

§ 10.1-537. Representatives of governing bodies to be invited to consult with directors. — The district directors shall invite the legislative body of any locality located near the territory comprised within the district to designate a representative to advise and consult with the directors of the district on all questions of program and policy which may affect the property, water supply, or other interests of such locality. (Code 1950, § 21-52; 1970, c. 480; 1988, c. 891.)

§ **10.1-538. District is political subdivision.** — A soil and water conservation district organized under the provisions of this article shall constitute a political subdivision of this Commonwealth. (Code 1950, § 21-53; 1964, c. 512; 1970, c. 480; 1988, c. 891.)

§ **10.1-539. Surveys and dissemination of information.** — Districts are authorized to (i) conduct surveys, investigations, and research relating to soil erosion and floodwater and sediment damages, and to agricultural and nonagricultural phases of the conservation, development, utilization, and disposal of water, and the preventive and control measures and works of improvement needed; (ii) publish the results of such surveys, investigations, or research; and (iii) disseminate information concerning preventive and control measures and works of improvement. However, in order to avoid duplication of research activities, no district shall initiate any research program except in cooperation with the government of the Commonwealth or the United States. (Code 1950, § 21-54; 1956, c. 654; 1970, c. 480; 1988, c. 891.)

§ **10.1-540. Demonstrational projects.** — Districts are authorized to conduct demonstrational projects within the district on lands owned or controlled by the Commonwealth or any of its agencies, with the consent and cooperation of the agency administering and having jurisdiction thereof, and on any other lands within the district upon obtaining the consent of the owner and occupier of such lands or the necessary rights or interests in such lands. The purpose of such projects is to demonstrate by example the means, methods, and measures by which soil and water resources may be conserved, and soil erosion in the form of soil washing may be prevented and controlled, and works of improvement for flood prevention or agricultural and nonagricultural phases of the conservation, development, utilization, and disposal of water may be carried out. (Code 1950, § 21-55; 1956, c. 654; 1970, c. 480; 1988, c. 891.)

§ **10.1-541. Preventive and control measures.** — Districts are authorized to carry out preventive and control measures and works of improvement for flood prevention or agricultural and nonagricultural phases of the conservation, development, utilization, and disposal of water within the district including, but not limited to, engineering operations, methods of cultivation, the growing of vegetation and changes in use of land on lands owned or controlled by the Commonwealth or any of its agencies, with the consent and cooperation of the agency administering and having jurisdiction thereof, and on any other lands within the district upon obtaining the consent of the owner and occupier of such lands or the necessary rights or interests in such lands. (Code 1950, § 21-56; 1956, c. 654; 1970, c. 480; 1988, c. 891.)

§ **10.1-542. Financial aid to agencies and occupiers.** — Districts are authorized to enter into agreements, within the limits of available appropriations, to give, lend or otherwise furnish financial or other aid to any governmental or other agency, or any occupier of lands within the district, to provide erosion-control and prevention operations and works of improvement for flood prevention or agricultural and nonagricultural phases of the conservation, development, utilization, and disposal of water within the district. Agreements shall be subject to such conditions as the directors may deem necessary to advance the purposes of this chapter. (Code 1950, § 21-57; 1956, c. 654; 1970, c. 480; 1988, c. 891.)

§ 10.1-543. Acquisition, improvement and disposition of property. — Districts are authorized to (i) obtain options upon and to acquire, by purchase, exchange, lease, gift, grant, bequest, devise, or otherwise, any property, real or personal, or rights or interests therein; (ii) maintain, administer, and improve any properties acquired, to receive income from such properties and to expend such income in carrying out the purposes and provisions of this article; and (iii) sell, lease, or otherwise dispose of any of their property or interests therein in furtherance of the provisions of this chapter. (Code 1950, § 21-58; 1988, c. 891.)

§ 10.1-544. Making material and equipment available. — Districts are authorized to make available, on terms they prescribe, to land occupiers within the district, agricultural and engineering machinery and equipment, fertilizer, seeds and seedlings and other material or equipment that will assist land occupiers to conserve soil resources, to prevent and control soil erosion and to prevent floods or to carry out the agricultural and nonagricultural phases of the conservation, development, utilization, and disposal of water. (Code 1950, § 21-59; 1956, c. 654; 1970, c. 480; 1988, c. 891.)

§ 10.1-545. Construction, improvement, operation and maintenance of structures. — Districts are authorized to construct, improve, operate and maintain such structures as may be necessary or convenient for the performance of any of the operations authorized in this chapter. (Code 1950, § 21-60; 1956, c. 654; 1988, c. 891.)

§ 10.1-546. Development of programs and plans. — Districts are authorized to develop comprehensive programs and plans for the conservation of soil resources, for the control and prevention of soil erosion, for flood prevention or for agricultural and nonagricultural phases of the conservation, development, utilization, and disposal of water within the district. Such programs and plans shall specify the acts, procedures, performances, and avoidances which are necessary or desirable to effect such programs and plans, including the specification of engineering operations, methods of cultivation, the growing of vegetation, cropping programs, tillage practices, and changes in use of land. After such programs and plans have been approved by the Board, districts are authorized to publish such programs and plans, and information, and bring them to the attention of occupiers of lands within the district. (Code 1950, § 21-61; 1956, c. 654; 1964, c. 512; 1970, c. 480; 1988, c. 891.)

§ 10.1-546.1. Delivery of Agricultural Best Management Practices Cost-Share Assistance Program. — Districts shall locally deliver the Commonwealth's Agricultural Best Management Practices Cost-Share Assistance Program, under the direction of the Department, as a means of promoting voluntary adoption of conservation management practices by farmers and land managers in support of the Department's nonpoint source pollution management program. (2004, c. 474.)

§ 10.1-547. Acquisition and administration of projects; acting as agent for United States, etc.; acceptance of gifts. — Districts shall have the following additional authority:

1. To acquire by purchase, lease, or other similar means, and to administer, any soil conservation, flood prevention, drainage, irrigation, agricultural and

nonagricultural water management, erosion control, or erosion prevention project, or combinations thereof, located within its boundaries undertaken by the United States or any of its agencies, or by the Commonwealth or any of its agencies;

2. To manage, as agent of the United States or any of its agencies, or of the Commonwealth or any of its agencies, any soil conservation, flood prevention, drainage, irrigation, agricultural and nonagricultural water management, erosion control or erosion prevention project, or combinations thereof, within its boundaries;

3. To act as agent for the United States or any of its agencies, or for the Commonwealth or any of its agencies, in connection with the acquisition, construction, maintenance, operation, or administration of any soil conservation, flood prevention, drainage, irrigation, agricultural and nonagricultural water management, erosion control, or erosion prevention project, or combinations thereof, within its boundaries;

4. To accept donations, gifts, and contributions in money, services, materials, or otherwise, from the United States or any of its agencies, or from the Commonwealth or any of its agencies or from any other source, and to use or expend such moneys, services, materials, or other contributions in carrying on its operations. (Code 1950, § 21-62; 1956, c. 654; 1970, c. 480; 1988, c. 891.)

§ **10.1-548. Contracts; rules.** — Districts are authorized to have a seal; to have perpetual succession unless terminated as hereinafter provided; to make and execute contracts and other instruments necessary or convenient to the exercise of their powers; to make, amend and repeal regulations not inconsistent with this chapter, to effect their purposes and powers. (Code 1950, § 21-63; 1988, c. 891.)

§ **10.1-549. Cooperation between districts.** — The directors of any two or more districts may cooperate in the exercise of any or all powers conferred in this chapter. (Code 1950, § 21-4; 1970, c. 480; 1988, c. 891.)

§ **10.1-549.1. Virginia Envirothon.** — Districts in partnership with other districts, agencies, organizations, and associations are authorized to coordinate and implement the Virginia Envirothon Program, administered by the Virginia Association of Soil and Water Conservation Districts, which enables learning experiences for high school students through competitive events focusing on natural resource conservation. (2003, c. 402.)

§ **10.1-550. State agencies to cooperate.** — Agencies of the Commonwealth which have jurisdiction over or administer any state-owned lands, and agencies of any political subdivision of the Commonwealth which have jurisdiction over or administer any publicly owned lands lying within the boundaries of any district, shall cooperate to the fullest extent with the district directors in the effectuation of programs and operations undertaken pursuant to this chapter. The district directors shall be given free access to enter and perform work upon such public-owned lands. (Code 1950, § 21-5; 1970, c. 480; 1988, c. 891.)

§ **10.1-551. Conditions for extension of benefits.** — As a condition to the extending of any benefits under this chapter to, or the performance of work upon, any lands not owned or controlled by the Commonwealth or any of its agencies, the district directors may require contributions in money, services, materials, or otherwise to any operations conferring such benefits, and may require land occupiers to enter into and perform such agreements or covenants as to the permanent use of such lands that will tend to prevent or control erosion and prevent floodwaters and sediment damages thereon. (Code 1950, § 21-64; 1956, c. 654; 1970, c. 480; 1988, c. 891.)

§ 10.1-552. Renting machinery and equipment. — Districts are authorized to rent the machinery and other equipment made available to them by the Department to governing bodies and, individuals, or groups of individuals to be used by them for the purpose of soil and water conservation upon such terms as the district directors deem proper. (Code 1950, § 21-65; 1954, c. 670; 1964, c. 512; 1970, c. 480; 1988, c. 891.)

§ 10.1-553. Petition by landowners. — Any time after two years after the organization of a district, any twenty-five owners of land lying within the boundaries of the district may file a petition with the Board requesting that the operations of the district be terminated and the existence of the district discontinued. (Code 1950, § 21-106; 1964, c. 512; 1988, c. 891.)

§ 10.1-554. Hearings. — The Board may conduct public meetings and public hearings upon the termination petition to assist it in the considerations thereof. (Code 1950, § 21-107; 1964, c. 512; 1988, c. 891.)

§ 10.1-555. Referendum. — Within sixty days after a termination petition has been received by the Board it shall give due notice of the holding of a referendum and shall supervise the referendum, and issue appropriate regulations governing the conduct thereof. The ballot shall contain the following question: "Shall the existence of the (name of the soil and water conservation district) be terminated?
☐ Yes
☐ No"
All registered voters residing within the boundaries of the district shall be eligible to vote in the referendum. No informalities in the conduct of the referendum or in any related matters shall invalidate the referendum or the result if proper notice has been given and if the referendum has been fairly conducted. (Code 1950, § 21-108; 1964, c. 512; 1988, c. 891.)

§ 10.1-556. Determination of Board. — The Board shall publish the result of the referendum and shall thereafter consider and determine whether the continued operation of the district within the defined boundaries is administratively practicable and feasible. If the Board determines that the continued operation of the district is administratively practicable and feasible, it shall record the determination and deny the petition. If the Board determines that the continued operation of the district is not administratively practicable and feasible, it shall record its determination and certify the determination to the district directors. In making its determination the Board shall consider the proportion of the votes cast in favor of the discontinuance of the district to the total number of votes cast, the probable expense of carrying on erosion control operations within the district, and other relevant economic and social factors. However, the Board shall not have authority to determine that the continued operation of the district is administratively practicable and feasible unless at least a majority of the votes cast in the referendum have been cast in favor of the continuance of such district. (Code 1950, § 21-109; 1964, c. 512; 1970, c. 480; 1988, c. 891.)

§ 10.1-557. Duty of directors after certification of Board. — Upon receiving from the Board certification that the Board has determined that the continued operation of the district is not administratively practicable and feasible, the district directors shall proceed to determine the affairs of the district. The district directors shall dispose of all property belonging to the district at public auction and shall pay the proceeds of the sale into the state treasury. The district directors shall then file an application, duly verified, with the Secretary of the Commonwealth, for the discontinuance of the district, and shall transmit with the application the certificate of the Board setting forth the determination of the Board that the continued operation of the district is not administratively practicable and feasible. The application shall recite that the property of the district has been disposed of and the proceeds paid over as provided by law, and shall set forth a full accounting of such properties and proceeds of the sale. The Secretary of the Commonwealth shall issue to the district directors a certificate of dissolution and shall record the certificate in an appropriate book of record in his office. (Code 1950, § 21-110; 1964, c. 512; 1970, c. 480; 1988, c. 891.)

§ 10.1-558. Effect of issuance of certificate of dissolution. — Upon issuance of a certificate of dissolution, all ordinances and regulations previously adopted and in force within such district shall be of no further force. All contracts entered into, to which the district or district directors are parties, shall remain in force for the period provided in the contracts. The Board shall be substituted for the district or district directors as party to the contracts. The Board shall be entitled to all benefits and subject to all liabilities under the contracts and shall have the same right and liability to perform, to require performance, to sue and be sued thereon, and to modify or terminate such contracts by mutual consent or otherwise, as the district directors would have had. (Code 1950, § 21-111; 1964, c. 512; 1970, c. 480; 1988, c. 891.)

§ 10.1-559. Petitions limited to once in five years. — The Board shall not entertain petitions for the discontinuance of any district, conduct elections upon such petitions or make determinations pursuant to such petitions more often than once in five years. (Code 1950, § 21-112; 1964, c. 512; 1988, c. 891.)

ARTICLE 3.1.

Agricultural Stewardship Act.

§ 10.1-559.1. Definitions. — As used in this article, unless the context requires a different meaning:

"Agricultural activity" means any activity used in the production of food and fiber, including, but not limited to, farming, feedlots, grazing livestock, poultry raising, dairy farming, and aquaculture activities.

"Agricultural stewardship plan" or *"plan"* means a site-specific plan for an agricultural activity to manage, through use of stewardship measures, one or more of the following: soil, water, plants, plant nutrients, pest controls, wastes, and animals.

"Commissioner" means the Commissioner of Agriculture and Consumer Services.

"Complaint" means an allegation made by any person to the Commissioner that an owner's or operator's agricultural activity is creating or, if not changed, will create pollution and that states the location and nature of such agricultural activity.

"Informal fact-finding conference" means an informal fact-finding conference conducted in accordance with § 2.2-4019.

"Operator" means any person who exercises managerial control over any agricultural activity.

"Owner" means any person who owns land on which an agricultural activity occurs.

"Person" means an individual, a partnership, an association, a corporation or any government or unit of government.

"Pollution" means any alteration of the physical, chemical or biological properties of any state waters resulting from sedimentation, nutrients, or toxins.

"State waters" means all water, on the surface or in the ground, wholly or partially within or bordering the Commonwealth or within its jurisdiction.

"Stewardship measures" or *"measures"* means measures for controlling the addition of pollutants from existing and new categories and classes of nonpoint sources of pollution which reflect the pollutant reduction achievable through the application of the best available nonpoint pollution control methods, technologies, processes, siting criteria, operating methods or other alternatives. "Stewardship measures" or "measures" includes (i) agricultural water quality protection management measures described in the Virginia Agricultural Best Management Practices Manual and (ii) agricultural water quality protection management measures contained in the United States Department of Agriculture's Natural Resources Conservation Service Field Office Technical Guide. (1996, c. 773; 2000, c. 973.)

Research References. — Neil E. Harl, Agricultural Law (Matthew Bender).

§ **10.1-559.2. Exclusions from article.** — This article shall not apply to any agricultural activity to which (i) Article 12 (§ 10.1-1181.1 et seq.) of Chapter 11 of this title or (ii) a permit issued by the State Water Control Board, applies. (1996, c. 773.)

§ **10.1-559.3. Complaint; investigation; agricultural stewardship plan.** — A. After April 1, 1997, upon receiving a complaint, unless the complaint was made anonymously, the Commissioner shall request that the directors of the district in which the land lies determine the validity of the information within twenty-one days. The Commissioner may investigate or ask the directors of the district to investigate an anonymous complaint.

B. The district chairman may, on behalf of the district, act upon or reject the Commissioner's request. If the district declines to act, it shall within five days so advise the Commissioner, who shall determine the validity of the complaint.

C. If, after investigating a complaint, the Commissioner determines that substantial evidence exists to prove that an agricultural activity is creating or will create pollution, the Commissioner shall notify the owner or operator by registered mail, return receipt requested. If, after investigation, the Commissioner determines that the pollution is a direct result of unusual weather events or other exceptional circumstances which could not have been reasonably anticipated, or determines that the pollution is not a threat to human health, animal health, or aquatic life, water quality or recreational or other beneficial uses, the Commissioner may forego any additional action. Copies of the notice shall be sent to the district in which the agricultural activity is located. The notice shall state that, within sixty days of the receipt of the notice, the owner or operator shall submit to the Commissioner and district an agricultural stewardship plan which includes stewardship measures needed to prevent or cease the pollution. The district shall review the plan and, if the plan includes such measures, the Commissioner shall approve the plan within thirty days after he receives it. Upon approving the owner's or operator's plan, the Commissioner shall inform the owner or operator and the complainant that a plan has been approved. The owner or operator shall begin implementing the approved agricultural stewardship plan within six months of the date on which the owner or operator received the notice that the agricultural activity is creating or will create pollution.

D. The plan shall include an implementation schedule, and implementation of the plan shall be completed within a period specified by the Commissioner, based upon the seasons and other temporal considerations so that the period is that during which the possibility of success in establishment or construction of the measures required in the plan is the greatest, which shall not exceed eighteen months from receipt of notice. However, the Commissioner may grant an extension of up to 180 days if (i) a hardship exists and (ii) the request for an extension was made not later than sixty days before the scheduled completion date. The Commissioner shall, within thirty days of receiving the request, inform the owner or operator whether or not an extension has been granted.

E. After implementing the approved plan according to the provisions of the chapter, the owner or operator shall maintain the stewardship measures established pursuant to the plan. The owner or operator may change the agricultural activity so long as the Commissioner is notified.

F. If the Commissioner determines that substantial evidence does not exist to prove that an agricultural activity is creating or will create pollution or that any pollution was caused by unusual weather events or other exceptional circumstances or that the pollution is not a threat to human health, animal health or aquatic life or recreational or other beneficial uses, he shall inform the complainant and the owner or operator of his determination. Upon approving the owner's or operator's agricultural stewardship plan, the Commissioner shall inform the owner or operator and the complainant that a plan has been approved. (1996, c. 773; 2000, c. 973.)

§ **10.1-559.4. Issuance of corrective orders.** — A. If any owner or operator who has been issued a notice under § 10.1-559.3 fails to submit an agricultural stewardship plan, begin actively implementing the plan, complete implementation of the plan, or maintain the stewardship measures as provided in § 10.1-559.3, the Commissioner shall issue a corrective order to such owner or operator. The order shall require that such activity be accomplished within a stated period of time.

B. A corrective order issued pursuant to subsection A shall be issued only after an informal fact-finding conference, with reasonable notice being given to the owner or operator, or both, of the time, place and purpose thereof, and shall become effective not less than five days after date of delivery to the last known address as provided in subsection C. The corrective order shall be suspended pending appeal by the recipient made within five days after delivery of such order to the last known address of the owner or operator.

C. The Commissioner shall mail a copy of the corrective order by certified mail, return receipt requested, sent to the last known address of the owner or operator, or by personal delivery by an agent of the Commonwealth.

D. Notwithstanding other provisions of this article, if the Commissioner determines that a recurring polluting condition which is the subject of an approved plan is occurring or that an emergency condition exists due to runoff from an agricultural activity which is causing or is likely to cause an imminent or substantial danger to (i) the public health, safety or welfare or to the health of animals, fish or aquatic life; (ii) a public water supply; or (iii) recreational, commercial, industrial, agricultural, or other beneficial uses, the Commissioner may issue, without advance notice, informal fact-finding conference or hearing, an emergency corrective order. Such order may direct the owner or operator of the agricultural activity, or both, to cease immediately all or part of the agricultural activity, and to implement specified stewardship measures or any necessary emergency measures within a stated period of time. Following the issuance of an emergency corrective order, the Commissioner shall provide the opportunity for a hearing or an informal fact-finding conference, after reasonable notice as to the time and place thereof, to the owner or operator, for the purpose of affirming, modifying, amending or canceling the emergency corrective order.

E. The Commissioner shall not issue a corrective order to any land owner or operator if the person is:

1. Actively implementing the agricultural stewardship plan which has been reviewed by the district in which the agricultural activity is located and approved by the Commissioner, or

2. Actively implementing stewardship measures that have failed to prevent pollution, if the Commissioner determines that the pollution is a direct result of unusual weather events or other exceptional circumstances which could not have been reasonably anticipated. (1996, c. 773; 2000, c. 973.)

§ 10.1-559.5. Right of entry; court enforcement. — A. The district or the Commissioner or his designee may enter land which is the subject of a complaint, after notice to the owner or operator, to determine whether the agricultural activity is causing or will cause pollution of state waters.

B. Upon failure of any owner or operator to allow the Commissioner or his designee entry in accordance with subsection A, to implement stewardship measures in the time specified in a corrective order, or to maintain stewardship measures in accordance with subsection E of § 10.1-559.3, the Commissioner may present to the circuit court of the county or city in which the land is located, a petition asking the court to require the owner or operator to allow the Commissioner or his designee entry or to carry out such measures within a specified time. If the owner or operator fails to implement the stewardship measures specified in the court order, the Commissioner or his representative may enter the land involved and implement the measures. The Commissioner shall have the authority to recover the costs of implementing the stewardship measures from the owner or operator. (1996, c. 773; 2000, c. 973.)

§ 10.1-559.6. Appeal. — Decisions of the Commissioner may be appealed by persons aggrieved to the Virginia Soil and Water Conservation Board and thereafter to the circuit court in accordance with the Administrative Process Act (§ 2.2-4000 et seq.). The imposition of any civil penalty shall be suspended pending such appeals. (1996, c. 773.)

§ 10.1-559.7. Penalties; injunctions; enforcement actions. — A. Any person violating § 10.1-559.4 or § 10.1-559.5 shall be subject to a civil penalty not to exceed $5,000 for every violation assessed by the Commissioner or Board. Each day the violation continues shall constitute a separate offense. Payments to satisfy such penalties shall be deposited in a nonreverting, special fund to be used by the Department of Conservation and Recreation to provide financial assistance to persons implementing measures specified in the Virginia Agricultural Best Management Practices Manual. No person who has been assessed a civil penalty under this section shall be eligible for such financial assistance until the violation has been corrected and the penalty paid.

B. In determining the amount of any penalty, factors to be considered shall include but not be limited to the willfulness of the violation, any history of noncompliance, the actions of the owner or operator in notifying, containing and cleaning up any discharge, the damage or injury to state waters or the impairment of its uses, and the nature and degree of injury to or interference with general health, welfare and property.

C. The Attorney General shall, upon request, bring an action for an injunction or other appropriate legal action on behalf of the Commissioner or Board to enforce the provisions of this article. (1996, c. 773.)

§ **10.1-559.8. Liens.** — If a person who is required to pay a civil penalty under this chapter fails to do so, the Commissioner may transmit a true copy of the order assessing such penalty to the clerk of the circuit court of any county or city wherein it is ascertained that the person owing such penalty has any estate; and the clerk to whom such copy is transmitted shall record it, as a judgment is required by law to be recorded, and shall index it in the name of the Commonwealth as well as in the name of the person owing the civil penalty, and thereupon there shall be a lien in favor of the Commonwealth on the property within such locality of the person owing the civil penalty in the amount of the civil penalty. The Commissioner and Board may collect civil penalties which are owed in the same manner as provided by law in respect to judgment of a court of record. (1996, c. 773.)

§ **10.1-559.9. Guidelines to be published by Commissioner; report.** — A. In consultation with the districts, the Department and interested persons, the Commissioner shall develop guidelines for the implementation of this article. These guidelines shall address, among other things, the conduct of investigations, sources of assistance for owners and operators, and intergovernmental cooperation. Within ninety days of the effective date of this section, the Commissioner shall submit the proposed guidelines to the Registrar of Regulations for publication in the Virginia Register of Regulations. At least thirty days shall be provided for public comment after the publication of the proposed guidelines. After the close of the public comment period, the Commissioner shall consider the comments that he has received and may incorporate any changes into the guidelines that he deems appropriate. He shall develop a written summary and analysis of the comments, which shall be made available to the public upon request. Thereafter, the Commissioner shall submit final guidelines for publication in the Register. The guidelines shall become effective on April 1, 1997. The Commissioner may alter the guidelines periodically after his proposed changes have been published in the Register and a public comment period has been provided.

B. The Commissioner shall compile a report by August 31 annually listing the number of complaints received, the nature of each complaint, the actions taken in resolution of each complaint, and any penalties which may have been assessed. The Commissioner shall have the discretion to exclude and keep confidential specific information regarding ongoing investigations. The Commissioner shall (i) provide the report to the Board, the Department and to every district, (ii) publish notice in the Virginia Register that the report is available, and (iii) make the report available to the public upon request. (1996, c. 773.)

§ **10.1-559.10. Local ordinances.** — A. Any county, city or town may adopt an ordinance creating a complaint, investigation and agricultural stewardship plan development program. Ordinances adopted pursuant to this section may contain only provisions which parallel §§ 10.1-559.2 and 10.1-559.3. No such ordinance shall provide for the imposition of civil or criminal sanctions against an operator or owner who fails to implement a plan. If an owner or operator fails to implement a plan, the local governing body shall submit a complaint to the Commissioner as provided in § 10.1-559.3.

B. This section shall not apply to any ordinance (i) in existence on July 1, 1996, or (ii) adopted pursuant to the Chesapeake Bay Preservation Act (§ 10.1-2100 et seq.). (1996, c. 773.)

§ 10.1-559.11. Construction of article. — Nothing in this article shall be construed as duplicative of regulations governing agricultural practices under the Chesapeake Bay Preservation Act. (1996, c. 773.)

ARTICLE 4.

Erosion and Sediment Control Law.

§ 10.1-560. Definitions. — As used in this article, unless the context requires a different meaning:

"Agreement in lieu of a plan" means a contract between the plan-approving authority and the owner that specifies conservation measures that must be implemented in the construction of a single-family residence; this contract may be executed by the plan-approving authority in lieu of a formal site plan.

"Applicant" means any person submitting an erosion and sediment control plan for approval or requesting the issuance of a permit, when required, authorizing land-disturbing activities to commence.

"Certified inspector" means an employee or agent of a program authority who (i) holds a certificate of competence from the Board in the area of project inspection or (ii) is enrolled in the Board's training program for project inspection and successfully completes such program within one year after enrollment.

"Certified plan reviewer" means an employee or agent of a program authority who (i) holds a certificate of competence from the Board in the area of plan review, (ii) is enrolled in the Board's training program for plan review and successfully completes such program within one year after enrollment, or (iii) is licensed as a professional engineer, architect, certified landscape architect or land surveyor pursuant to Article 1 (§ 54.1-400 et seq.) of Chapter 4 of Title 54.1.

"Certified program administrator" means an employee or agent of a program authority who (i) holds a certificate of competence from the Board in the area of program administration or (ii) is enrolled in the Board's training program for program administration and successfully completes such program within one year after enrollment.

"Conservation plan," "erosion and sediment control plan," or *"plan"* means a document containing material for the conservation of soil and water resources of a unit or group of units of land. It may include appropriate maps, an appropriate soil and water plan inventory and management information with needed interpretations, and a record of decisions contributing to conservation treatment. The plan shall contain all major conservation decisions to assure that the entire unit or units of land will be so treated to achieve the conservation objectives.

"District" or *"soil and water conservation district"* means a political subdivision of the Commonwealth organized in accordance with the provisions of Article 3 (§ 10.1-506 et seq.) of this chapter.

"Erosion impact area" means an area of land not associated with current land-disturbing activity but subject to persistent soil erosion resulting in the delivery of sediment onto neighboring properties or into state waters. This definition shall not apply to any lot or parcel of land of 10,000 square feet or less used for residential purposes or to shorelines where the erosion results from wave action or other coastal processes.

"Land-disturbing activity" means any land change that may result in soil erosion from water or wind and the movement of sediments into state waters or onto lands in the Commonwealth, including, but not limited to, clearing, grading, excavating, transporting and filling of land, except that the term shall not include:

1. Minor land-disturbing activities such as home gardens and individual home landscaping, repairs and maintenance work;

2. Individual service connections;

3. Installation, maintenance, or repair of any underground public utility lines when such activity occurs on an existing hard surfaced road, street or sidewalk provided the land-disturbing activity is confined to the area of the road, street or sidewalk that is hard surfaced;

4. Septic tank lines or drainage fields unless included in an overall plan for land-disturbing activity relating to construction of the building to be served by the septic tank system;

5. Surface or deep mining activities authorized under a permit issued by the Department of Mines, Minerals and Energy;

6. Exploration or drilling for oil and gas including the well site, roads, feeder lines and off-site disposal areas;

7. Tilling, planting, or harvesting of agricultural, horticultural, or forest crops, or livestock feedlot operations; including engineering operations as follows: construction of terraces, terrace outlets, check dams, desilting basins, dikes, ponds, ditches, strip cropping, lister furrowing, contour cultivating, contour furrowing, land drainage and land irrigation; however, this exception shall not apply to harvesting of forest crops unless the area on which harvesting occurs is reforested artificially or naturally in accordance with the provisions of Chapter 11 (§ 10.1-1100 et seq.) of this title or is converted to bona fide agricultural or improved pasture use as described in subsection B of § 10.1-1163;

8. Repair or rebuilding of the tracks, right-of-way, bridges, communication facilities and other related structures and facilities of a railroad company;

9. Agricultural engineering operations including but not limited to the construction of terraces, terrace outlets, check dams, desilting basins, dikes, ponds not required to comply with the provisions of the Dam Safety Act, Article 2 (§ 10.1-604 et seq.) of Chapter 6 of this title, ditches, strip cropping, lister furrowing, contour cultivating, contour furrowing, land drainage and land irrigation;

10. Disturbed land areas of less than 10,000 square feet in size; however, the governing body of the program authority may reduce this exception to a smaller area of disturbed land or qualify the conditions under which this exception shall apply;

11. Installation of fence and sign posts or telephone and electric poles and other kinds of posts or poles;

12. Shoreline erosion control projects on tidal waters when all of the land disturbing activities are within the regulatory authority of and approved by local wetlands boards, the Marine Resources Commission or the United States Army Corps of Engineers; however, any associated land that is disturbed outside of this exempted area shall remain subject to this article and the regulations adopted pursuant thereto; and

13. Emergency work to protect life, limb or property, and emergency repairs; however, if the land-disturbing activity would have required an approved erosion and sediment control plan, if the activity were not an emergency, then the land area disturbed shall be shaped and stabilized in accordance with the requirements of the plan-approving authority.

"*Local erosion and sediment control program*" or "*local control program*" means an outline of the various methods employed by a program authority to regulate land-disturbing activities and thereby minimize erosion and sedimentation in compliance with the state program and may include such items as local ordinances, policies and guidelines, technical materials, inspection, enforcement and evaluation.

"*Natural channel design concepts*" means the utilization of engineering analysis and fluvial geomorphic processes to create, rehabilitate, restore, or stabilize an open conveyance system for the purpose of creating or recreating a stream that conveys its bankfull storm event within its banks and allows larger flows to access its bankfull bench and its floodplain.

"*Owner*" means the owner or owners of the freehold of the premises or lesser estate therein, a mortgagee or vendee in possession, assignee of rents, receiver, executor, trustee, lessee or other person, firm or corporation in control of a property.

"*Peak flow rate*" means the maximum instantaneous flow from a given storm condition at a particular location.

"*Permittee*" means the person to whom the permit authorizing land-disturbing activities is issued or the person who certifies that the approved erosion and sediment control plan will be followed.

"*Person*" means any individual, partnership, firm, association, joint venture, public or private corporation, trust, estate, commission, board, public or private institution, utility, cooperative, county, city, town, or other political subdivision of the Commonwealth, any interstate body, or any other legal entity.

"*Plan-approving authority*" means the Board, the program authority, or a department of a program authority, responsible for determining the adequacy of a conservation plan submitted for land-disturbing activities on a unit or units of lands and for approving plans.

"*Program authority*" means a district, county, city, or town that has adopted a soil erosion and sediment control program that has been approved by the Board.

"*Runoff volume*" means the volume of water that runs off the land development project from a prescribed storm event.

"*State erosion and sediment control program*" or "*state program*" means the program administered by the Board pursuant to this article, including regulations designed to minimize erosion and sedimentation.

"*State waters*" means all waters on the surface and under the ground wholly or partially within or bordering the Commonwealth or within its jurisdiction.

"*Town*" means an incorporated town.

"*Water quality volume*" means the volume equal to the first one-half inch of runoff multiplied by the impervious surface of the land development project. (1973, c. 486, § 21-89.3; 1974, c. 265; 1977, c. 149; 1980, c. 305; 1988, cc. 690, 732, 891; 1990, c. 491; 1991, c. 469; 1992, c. 184; 1993, c. 925; 1994, c. 703; 2003, c. 423; 2004, c. 476; 2005, c. 107; 2006, c. 21.)

Cross references. — As to development of regulations pertaining to stormwater management programs, see § 10.1-603.4.

The 2005 amendments. — The 2005 amendment by c. 107 added the definition of "Natural channel design concepts."

The 2006 amendments. — The 2006 amendment by c. 21 added the paragraphs defining "Peak flow rate," "Runoff volume," and "Water quality volume."

Law Review. — For 2003/2004 survey of environmental law, see 39 U. Rich. L. Rev. 203 (2004).

§ 10.1-561. State erosion and sediment control program. — A. The Board shall develop a program and promulgate regulations for the effective control of soil erosion, sediment deposition, and nonagricultural runoff that must be met in any control program to prevent the unreasonable degradation of properties, stream channels, waters and other natural resources in accordance with the Administrative Process Act (§ 2.2-4000 et seq.). Stream restoration and relocation projects that incorporate natural channel design concepts are not man-made channels and shall be exempt from any flow rate capacity and velocity requirements for natural or man-made channels as defined in any regulations promulgated pursuant to this section, § 10.1-562, or 10.1-570. Any land-disturbing activity that provides for stormwater management intended to address any flow rate capacity and velocity requirements for natural or manmade channels shall satisfy the flow rate capacity and velocity requirements for natural or manmade channels if the practices are designed to (i) detain the water quality volume and to release it over 48 hours; (ii) detain and release over a 24-hour period the expected rainfall resulting from the one year, 24-hour storm; and (iii) reduce the allowable peak flow rate resulting from the 1.5, 2, and 10-year, 24-hour storms to a level that is less than or equal to the peak flow rate from the site assuming it was in a good forested condition, achieved through multiplication of the forested peak flow rate by a reduction factor that is equal to the runoff volume from the site when it was in a good forested condition divided by the runoff volume from the site in its proposed condition, and shall be exempt from any flow rate capacity and velocity requirements for natural or manmade channels as defined in any regulations promulgated pursuant to § 10.1-562 or 10.1-570.

The regulations shall:

1. Be based upon relevant physical and developmental information concerning the watersheds and drainage basins of the Commonwealth, including, but not limited to, data relating to land use, soils, hydrology, geology, size of land area being disturbed, proximate water bodies and their characteristics, transportation, and public facilities and services;

2. Include such survey of lands and waters as may be deemed appropriate by the Board or required by any applicable law to identify areas, including multijurisdictional and watershed areas, with critical erosion and sediment problems; and

3. Contain conservation standards for various types of soils and land uses, which shall include criteria, techniques, and methods for the control of erosion and sediment resulting from land-disturbing activities.

B. The Board shall provide technical assistance and advice to, and conduct and supervise educational programs for, districts and localities that have adopted local control programs.

C. The program and regulations shall be available for public inspection at the Department.

D. The Board shall promulgate regulations establishing minimum standards of effectiveness of erosion and sediment control programs, and criteria and procedures for reviewing and evaluating the effectiveness of erosion and sediment control programs. In developing minimum standards for program effectiveness, the Board shall consider information and standards on which the regulations promulgated pursuant to subsection A of this section are based.

E. The Board shall periodically conduct a comprehensive review and evaluation to ensure that all erosion and sediment control programs operating under the jurisdiction of this article meet minimum standards of effectiveness in controlling soil erosion, sediment deposition and nonagricultural runoff. The Board shall develop a schedule for conducting periodic reviews and evaluations of the effectiveness of erosion and sediment control programs.

F. The Board shall issue certificates of competence concerning the content, application and intent of specified subject areas of this chapter and accompanying regulations, including program administration, plan review, and project inspection, to personnel of program authorities and to any other persons who have completed training programs or in other ways demonstrated adequate knowledge. The Department shall administer education and training programs for specified subject areas of this chapter and accompanying regulations, and is authorized to charge persons attending such programs reasonable fees to cover the costs of administering the programs.

G. As of December 31, 2004, any Department personnel conducting inspections pursuant to this chapter shall hold a certificate of competence as provided in subsection F. (1973, c. 486, § 21-89.4; 1988, cc. 732, 891; 1993, c. 925; 2004, c. 431; 2005, c. 107; 2006, c. 21.)

The 2005 amendments. — The 2005 amendment by c. 107 added the second sentence in subsection A.

The 2006 amendments. — The 2006 amendment by c. 21 added the last sentence in the first paragraph of subsection A.

§ 10.1-561.1. Certification of local program personnel. — A.

The minimum standards of local program effectiveness established by the Board pursuant to subsection D of § 10.1-561 shall provide that within one year following the adoption of amendments to the local program adding the provisions of this section, (i) a conservation plan shall not be approved until it is reviewed by a certified plan reviewer; (ii) inspections of land-disturbing activities are conducted by a certified inspector; and (iii) a local program shall contain a certified program administrator, a certified plan reviewer, and a certified project inspector, who may be the same person.

B. Any person who holds a certificate of competence from the Board in the areas of plan review, project inspection, or program administration which was attained prior to the adoption of the mandatory certification provisions of subsection A of this section shall be deemed to satisfy the requirements of that area of certification. (1993, c. 925.)

§ 10.1-562. Local erosion and sediment control programs. — A.

Each district in the Commonwealth shall adopt and administer an erosion and sediment control program for any area within the district for which a county, city, or town does not have an approved erosion and sediment control program.

To carry out its program the district shall adopt regulations consistent with the state program. The regulations may be revised from time to time as necessary. Before adopting or revising regulations, the district shall give due notice and conduct a public hearing on the proposed or revised regulations except that a public hearing shall not be required when the district is amending its program to conform to revisions in the state program. However, a public hearing shall be held if a district proposes or revises regulations that are more stringent than the state program. The program and regulations shall be available for public inspection at the principal office of the district.

B. In areas where there is no district, a county, city, or town shall adopt and administer an erosion and sediment control program.

C. Any county, city, or town within a district may adopt and administer an erosion and sediment control program.

Any town, lying within a county which has adopted its own erosion and sediment control program, may adopt its own program or become subject to the county program. If a town lies within the boundaries of more than one county, the town shall be considered for the purposes of this article to be wholly within the county in which the larger portion of the town lies. Any county, city, or town with an erosion and sediment control program may designate its department of public works or a similar local government department as the plan-approving authority or may designate the district as the plan-approving authority for all or some of the conservation plans.

D. Any erosion and sediment control program adopted by a district, county, city, or town shall be approved by the Board if it is consistent with the state program and regulations for erosion and sediment control.

E. If a comprehensive review conducted by the Board of a local control program indicates that the program authority has not administered, enforced or conducted its program in a manner that satisfies the minimum standards of effectiveness established pursuant to subsection D of § 10.1-561, the Board shall notify the program authority in writing, which notice shall identify corrective action required to attain the minimum standard of effectiveness and shall include an offer to provide technical assistance to implement the corrective action. If the program authority has not implemented the corrective action identified by the Board within 30 days following receipt of the notice, or such additional period as is necessary to complete the implementation of the corrective action, then the Board shall have the authority to (i) issue a special order to any locality that has failed to enter into a corrective action agreement or, where such corrective action agreement exists, has failed to initiate or has not made substantial and consistent progress towards implementing an approved corrective action agreement within the deadline established by the Board to pay a civil penalty not to exceed $5,000 per day with the maximum amount not to exceed $20,000 per violation for noncompliance with the state program, to be paid into the state treasury and deposited in the Virginia Stormwater Management Fund established by § 10.1-603.4:1 or (ii) revoke its approval of the program. Prior to issuing a special order or revoking its approval of any local control program, the Board shall conduct a formal hearing pursuant to § 2.2-4020 of the Administrative Process Act. Judicial review of any order of the Board issuing a civil penalty pursuant to this section or revoking its approval of a local control program shall be made in accordance with Article 5 (§ 2.2-4025 et seq.) of the Administrative Process Act.

F. If the Board revokes its approval of a local control program of a county, city, or town, and the locality is in a district, the district shall adopt and administer an erosion and sediment control program for the locality.

G. If the Board (i) revokes its approval of a local control program of a district, or of a county, city, or town not in a district, or (ii) finds that a local program consistent with the state program and regulations has not been adopted by a district or a county, city, or town which is required to adopt and administer a local program, the Board shall, after such hearings or consultations as it deems appropriate with the various local interests involved, develop, adopt, and administer an appropriate program to be carried out within such district, county, city, or town, as applicable, by the Board.

H. If the Board has revoked its approval of any local control program, the program authority may request that the Board approve a replacement program, and the Board shall approve the replacement program if it finds that (i) the program authority is capable of administering the program in accordance with the minimum standards of effectiveness and (ii) the replacement program otherwise meets the requirements of the state program and regulations. The Board shall conduct a formal hearing pursuant to § 2.2-4020 of the Administrative Process Act on any request for approval of a replacement program.

I. Any program authority which administers an erosion and sediment control program may charge applicants a reasonable fee to defray the cost of program administration. A program authority shall hold a public hearing prior to enacting an ordinance establishing a schedule of fees. The fee shall not exceed an amount commensurate with the services rendered, taking into consideration the time, skill and administrators' expense involved.

J. The governing body of any county, city or town which (i) is in a district which has adopted a local control program, (ii) has adopted its own local control program, (iii) is subject to a local control program adopted by the Board, or (iv) administers a local control program, may adopt an ordinance providing that violations of any regulation or order of the Board, any provision of its program, any condition of a permit, or any provision of this article shall be subject to a civil penalty. The civil penalty for any one violation shall be $100, except that the civil penalty for commencement of land-disturbing activities without an approved plan as provided in § 10.1-563 shall be $1,000. Each day during which the violation is found to have existed shall constitute a separate offense. In no event shall a series of specified violations arising from the same operative set of facts result in civil penalties which exceed a total of $3,000, except that a series of violations arising from the commencement of land-disturbing activities without an approved plan for any site shall not result in civil penalties which exceed a total of $10,000. Adoption of such an ordinance providing that violations are subject to a civil penalty shall be in lieu of criminal sanctions and shall preclude the prosecution of such violation as a misdemeanor under subsection A of § 10.1-569. (1973, c. 486, § 21-89.5; 1976, c. 653; 1978, c. 450; 1980, c. 35; 1983, c. 189; 1988, cc. 732, 891; 1992, c. 298; 1993, c. 925; 2005, c. 129.)

The 2005 amendments. — The 2005 amendments by c. 129, in subsection E, inserted "comprehensive" in the first sentence, substituted "30" for "thirty," inserted "have the authority to," inserted clause (i) and the clause (ii) designation in the second sentence, inserted "issuing a special order or" in the third sentence and inserted "issuing a civil penalty pursuant to this section or" in the fourth sentence.

§ 10.1-563. Regulated land-disturbing activities; submission and approval of control plan.

— A. Except as provided in § 10.1-564, no person may engage in any land-disturbing activity until he has submitted to the district or locality an erosion and sediment control plan for the land-disturbing activity and the plan has been reviewed and approved by the plan-approving authority. Where land-disturbing activities involve lands under the jurisdiction of more than one local control program an erosion and sediment control plan may, at the option of the applicant, be submitted to the Board for review and approval rather than to each jurisdiction concerned. Where the land-disturbing activity results from the construction of a single-family residence, an agreement in lieu of a plan may be substituted for an erosion and sediment control plan if executed by the plan-approving authority.

B. The plan-approving authority shall review conservation plans submitted to it and grant written approval within 45 days of the receipt of the plan if it determines that the plan meets the requirements of the Board's regulations and if the person responsible for carrying out the plan certifies that he will properly perform the conservation measures included in the plan and will conform to the provisions of this article. In addition, as a prerequisite to engaging in the land-disturbing activities shown on the approved plan, the person responsible for carrying out the plan shall provide the name of an individual holding a certificate of competence to the program authority, as provided by § 10.1-561, who will be in charge of and responsible for carrying out the land-disturbing activity. However, any plan-approving authority may waive the certificate of competence requirement for an agreement in lieu of a plan for construction of a single family residence. If a violation occurs during the land-disturbing activity, then the person responsible for carrying out the agreement in lieu of a plan shall correct the violation and provide the name of an individual holding a certificate of competence, as provided by § 10.1-561. Failure to provide the name of an individual holding a certificate of competence prior to engaging in land-disturbing activities may result in revocation of the approval of the plan and the person responsible for carrying out the plan shall be subject to the penalties provided in this article.

When a plan is determined to be inadequate, written notice of disapproval stating the specific reasons for disapproval shall be communicated to the applicant within 45 days. The notice shall specify the modifications, terms and conditions that will permit approval of the plan. If no action is taken by the plan-approving authority within the time specified above, the plan shall be deemed approved and the person authorized to proceed with the proposed activity.

C. An approved plan may be changed by the authority that approved the plan in the following cases:

1. Where inspection has revealed that the plan is inadequate to satisfy applicable regulations; or

2. Where the person responsible for carrying out the approved plan finds that because of changed circumstances or for other reasons the approved plan cannot be effectively carried out, and proposed amendments to the plan, consistent with the requirements of this article, are agreed to by the plan-approving authority and the person responsible for carrying out the plan.

D. Electric, natural gas and telephone utility companies, interstate and intrastate natural gas pipeline companies and railroad companies shall file general erosion and sediment control specifications annually with the Board for review and approval. The specifications shall apply to:

1. Construction, installation or maintenance of electric transmission, natural gas and telephone utility lines and pipelines; and

2. Construction of the tracks, rights-of-way, bridges, communication facilities and other related structures and facilities of the railroad company.

The Board shall have 60 days in which to approve the specifications. If no action is taken by the Board within 60 days, the specifications shall be deemed approved. Individual approval of separate projects within subdivisions 1 and 2 of this subsection is not necessary when approved specifications are followed. Projects not included in subdivisions 1 and 2 of this subsection shall comply with the requirements of the appropriate local erosion and sediment control program. The Board shall have the authority to enforce approved specifications.

E. **(Contingent on 2006 Appropriation Act)** Any person engaging in the creation and operation of wetland mitigation banks in multiple jurisdictions, which have been approved and are operated in accordance with applicable federal and state guidance, laws, or regulations for the establishment, use, and operation of mitigation banks, pursuant to a permit issued by the Department of Environmental Quality, the Marine Resources Commission, or the U.S. Army Corps of Engineers, may, at the option of that person, file general erosion and sediment control specifications for wetland mitigation banks annually with the Board for review and approval consistent with guidelines established by the Board.

The Board shall have 60 days in which to approve the specifications. If no action is taken by the Board within 60 days, the specifications shall be deemed approved. Individual approval of separate projects under this subsection is not necessary when approved specifications are implemented through a project-specific erosion and sediment control plan. Projects not included in this subsection shall comply with the requirements of the appropriate local erosion and sediment control program. The Board shall have the authority to enforce approved specifications. Approval of general erosion and sediment control specifications by the Board does not relieve the owner or operator from compliance with any other local ordinances and regulations including requirements to submit plans and obtain permits as may be required by such ordinances and regulations.

F. In order to prevent further erosion a local program may require approval of a conservation plan for any land identified in the local program as an erosion impact area.

G. For the purposes of subsections A and B of this section, when land-disturbing activity will be required of a contractor performing construction work pursuant to a construction contract, the preparation, submission and approval of an erosion and sediment control plan shall be the responsibility of the owner. (1973, c. 486, § 21-89.6; 1979, c. 432; 1988, cc. 732, 891; 1993, c. 925; 1999, c. 555; 2001, c. 490; 2003, cc. 827, 966; 2006, c. 466.)

Subsection E contingent on 2006 General Appropriation Act. — Acts 2006, c. 466, which added subsection E, in cl. 2, provides: "That this act, for which general fund dollars are required, shall not take effect unless a specific appropriation has been included to support the provisions of this act within a general appropriation act taking effect July 1, 2006, that has been approved by the General Assembly and signed by the Governor."

The 2006 amendments. — The 2006 amendment by c. 466 added subsection E; and redesignated former subsections E and F as subsections F and G. For contingent effective date, see Editor's note.

§ **10.1-564. State agency projects.** — A. A state agency shall not undertake a project involving a land-disturbing activity unless (i) the state agency has submitted annual specifications for its conduct of land-disturbing activities which have been reviewed and approved by the Department as being consistent with the state program or (ii) the state agency has submitted a conservation plan for the project which has been reviewed and approved by the Department.

B. The Department shall not approve a conservation plan submitted by a federal or state agency for a project involving a land-disturbing activity (i) in any locality which has not adopted a local program with more stringent regulations than those of the state program or (ii) in multiple jurisdictions with separate local programs, unless the conservation plan is consistent with the requirements of the state program.

C. The Department shall not approve a conservation plan submitted by a federal or state agency for a project involving a land-disturbing activity in one locality with a local program with more stringent regulations than those of the state program unless the conservation plan is consistent with the requirements of the local program. If a locality has not submitted a copy of its local program regulations to the Department, the provisions of subsection B of this section shall apply.

D. The Department shall have sixty days in which to comment on any specifications or conservation plan submitted to it for review, and its comments shall be binding on the state agency and any private business hired by the state agency.

E. As on-site changes occur, the state agency shall submit changes in a conservation plan to the Department.

F. The state agency responsible for the land-disturbing activity shall ensure compliance with the approved plan or specifications. (1973, c. 486, § 21-89.6; 1979, c. 432; 1988, c. 891; 1993, c. 925.)

§ **10.1-565. Approved plan required for issuance of grading, building, or other permits; security for performance.** — Agencies authorized under any other law to issue grading, building, or other permits for activities involving land-disturbing activities may not issue any such permit unless the applicant submits with his application an approved erosion and sediment control plan and certification that the plan will be followed. Prior to issuance of any permit, the agency may also require an applicant to submit a reasonable performance bond with surety, cash escrow, letter of credit, any combination thereof, or such other legal arrangement acceptable to the agency, to ensure that measures could be taken by the agency at the applicant's expense should he fail, after proper notice, within the time specified to initiate or maintain appropriate conservation action which may be required of him by the approved plan as a result of his land-disturbing activity. The amount of the bond or other security for performance shall not exceed the total of the estimated cost to initiate and maintain appropriate conservation action based on unit price for new public or private sector construction in the locality and a reasonable allowance for estimated administrative costs and inflation which shall not exceed twenty-five percent of the estimated cost of the conservation action. If the agency takes such conservation action upon such failure by the permittee, the agency may collect from the permittee for the difference should the amount of the reasonable cost of such action exceed the amount of the security held.

Within sixty days of the achievement of adequate stabilization of the land-disturbing activity in any project or section thereof, the bond, cash escrow, letter of credit or other legal arrangement, or the unexpended or unobligated portion thereof, shall be refunded to the applicant or terminated based upon the percentage of stabilization accomplished in the project or section thereof. These requirements are in addition to all other provisions of law relating to the issuance of such permits and are not intended to otherwise affect the requirements for such permits. (1973, c. 486, § 21-89.7; 1980, c. 35; 1988, cc. 694, 891; 1996, c. 275.)

§ **10.1-566. Monitoring, reports and inspections.** — A. The plan-approving authority or, if a permit is issued in connection with land-disturbing activities that involve the issuance of a grading, building, or other permit, the permit-issuing authority (i) shall provide for periodic inspections of the land-disturbing activity and require that an individual holding a certificate of competence, as provided by § 10.1-561, who will be in charge of and responsible for carrying out the land-disturbing activity and (ii) may require monitoring and reports from the person responsible for carrying out the plan, to ensure compliance with the approved plan and to determine whether the measures required in the plan are effective in controlling erosion and sediment. However, any plan-approving authority may waive the certificate of competence requirement for an agreement in lieu of a plan for construction of a single family residence. The owner, permittee, or person responsible for carrying out the plan shall be given notice of the inspection. If the permit-issuing authority or plan-approving authority determines that there is a failure to comply with the plan, notice shall be served upon the permittee or person responsible for carrying out the plan by registered or certified mail to the address specified in the permit application or in the plan certification, or by delivery at the site of the land-disturbing activities to the agent or employee supervising such activities. Where the plan-approving authority serves notice, a copy of the notice shall also be sent to the issuer of the permit. The notice shall specify the measures needed to comply with the plan and shall specify the time within which such measures shall be completed. Upon failure to comply within the time specified, the permit may be revoked and the permittee or person responsible for carrying out the plan shall be deemed to be in violation of this article and shall be subject to the penalties provided by § 10.1-569.

B. Notwithstanding the above provisions of this section the following may be applied:

1. Where a county, city, or town administers the local control program and the permit-issuing authority and the plan-approving authority are not within the same local government department, the locality may designate one department to inspect, monitor, report and ensure compliance. In the event a district has been designated as the plan-approving authority for all or some of the conservation plans, the enforcement of the program shall be with the local government department; however, the district may inspect, monitor and make reports for the local government department.

2. Where a district adopts the local control program and permit-issuing authorities have been established by a locality, the district by joint resolution with the appropriate locality may exercise the responsibilities of the permit-issuing authorities with respect to monitoring, reports, inspections and enforcement.

3. Where a permit-issuing authority has been established, and such authority is not vested in an employee or officer of local government but in the commissioner of revenue or some other person, the locality shall exercise the responsibilities of the permit-issuing authority with respect to monitoring, reports, inspections and enforcement unless such responsibilities are transferred as provided for in this section.

C. Upon receipt of a sworn complaint of a violation of this section, § 10.1-563 or § 10.1-564 from the representative of the program authority or the Board responsible for ensuring program compliance, the chief administrative officer, or his designee, of the program authority or the Board may, in conjunction with or subsequent to a notice to comply as specified in subsection A above, issue an order requiring that all or part of the land-disturbing activities permitted on the site be stopped until the specified corrective measures have been taken or, if land-disturbing activities have commenced without an approved plan as provided in § 10.1-563, requiring that all of the land-disturbing activities be stopped until an approved plan or any required permits are obtained. Where the alleged noncompliance is causing or is in imminent danger of causing harmful erosion of lands or sediment deposition in waters within the watersheds of the Commonwealth, or where the land-disturbing activities have commenced without an approved plan or any required permits, such an order may be issued whether or not the alleged violator has been issued a notice to comply as specified in subsection A above. Otherwise, such an order may be issued only after the alleged violator has failed to comply with a notice to comply. The order shall be served in the same manner as a notice to comply, and shall remain in effect for seven days from the date of service pending application by the enforcing authority or alleged violator for appropriate relief to the circuit court of the jurisdiction wherein the violation was alleged to have occurred. If the alleged violator has not obtained an approved plan or any required permits within seven days from the date of service of the order, the chief administrative officer or his designee may issue an order to the owner requiring that all construction and other work on the site, other than corrective measures, be stopped until an approved plan and any required permits have been obtained. Such an order shall be served upon the owner by registered or certified mail to the address specified in the permit application or the land records of the locality in which the site is located. The owner may appeal the issuance of an order to the circuit court of the jurisdiction wherein the violation was alleged to have occurred. Any person violating or failing, neglecting or refusing to obey an order issued by the chief administrative officer or his designee may be compelled in a proceeding instituted in the circuit court of the jurisdiction wherein the violation was alleged to have occurred to obey same and to comply therewith by injunction, mandamus or other appropriate remedy. Upon completion and approval of corrective action or obtaining an approved plan or any required permits, the order shall immediately be lifted. Nothing in this section shall prevent the chief administrative officer or his designee from taking any other action specified in § 10.1-569. (1973, c. 486, § 21-89.8; 1986, c. 328; 1988, cc. 694, 891; 1992, c. 298; 1993, c. 925; 2001, c. 490; 2003, c. 827.)

§ **10.1-566.1. Reporting.** — Each locality's plan-approving authority shall report to the Department, in a method and on a time schedule established by the Department, a listing of each land-disturbing activity in the locality for which a plan has been approved under this article. (2005, c. 102.)

Editor's note. — Acts 2005, c. 102, cl. 2, provides: "That the Governor shall make new appointments for each of the three at-large members of the Board in accordance with the provisions of this act on July 1, 2005. The new appointments of the at-large members of the Board shall go into effect upon the expiration of the current members' terms in January 2006, and the terms shall be staggered as follows: one member for a term of two years; one member for a term of three years; and one member for a term of four years. The Governor shall designate the term to be served by each appointee at the time of appointment and may reappoint the existing at-large members of the Board."

Acts 2005, c. 102, cl. 3, provides: "That the Director of the Department of Conservation and Recreation shall amend the Stormwater Management Regulations by removing the out-of-date Best Management Practices (BMP) nutrient removal efficiency information and adding it into the Virginia Stormwater Management Handbook guidance document where it shall be more effectively updated for public use."

§ 10.1-567. Cooperation with federal and state agencies.

— The districts and localities operating their own programs, and the Board are authorized to cooperate and enter into agreements with any federal or state agency in connection with plans for erosion and sediment control with respect to land-disturbing activities. (1973, c. 486, § 21-89.9; 1988, c. 891.)

§ 10.1-568. Appeals.

— A. Final decisions of counties, cities or towns under this article shall be subject to review by the court of record of the county or city, provided that an appeal is filed within thirty days from the date of any written decision adversely affecting the rights, duties or privileges of the person engaging in or proposing to engage in land-disturbing activities.

B. Final decisions of the districts shall be subject to an administrative review by the Board, provided that an appeal is filed within thirty days from the date of the written decision.

C. Final decisions of the Board either upon its own action or upon the review of the action of a district shall be subject to judicial review in accordance with the provisions of the Administrative Process Act (§ 2.2-4000 et seq.). (1973, c. 486, § 21-89.10; 1986, c. 615; 1988, c. 891.)

§ 10.1-569. Penalties, injunctions and other legal actions.

— A. Violators of §§ 10.1-563, 10.1-564 or § 10.1-566 shall be guilty of a Class 1 misdemeanor.

B. If a locality has adopted an ordinance establishing a uniform schedule of civil penalties as permitted by subsection J of § 10.1-562, any person who violates any regulation or order of the Board, any condition of a permit, any provision of its program, or any provision of this article shall, upon a finding of an appropriate general district court, be assessed a civil penalty in accordance with the schedule. The erosion and sediment control administrator, his deputy or a certified inspector for the locality wherein the land lies may issue a summons for collection of the civil penalty and the action may be prosecuted by the locality wherein the land lies. In any trial for a scheduled violation, it shall be the burden of the locality to show the liability of the violator by a preponderance of the evidence. An admission or finding of liability shall not be a criminal conviction for any purpose. Any civil penalties assessed by a court shall be paid into the treasury of the locality wherein the land lies, except that where the violator is the locality itself, or its agent, the court shall direct the penalty to be paid into the state treasury.

C. The appropriate permit-issuing authority, the program authority, the Board, or the owner of property which has sustained damage or which is in imminent danger of being damaged, may apply to the circuit court in any jurisdiction wherein the land lies to enjoin a violation or a threatened violation under §§ 10.1-563, 10.1-564 or § 10.1-566 without the necessity of showing that an adequate remedy at law does not exist; however, an owner of property shall not apply for injunctive relief unless (i) he has notified in writing the person who has violated the local program, and the program authority, that a violation of the local program has caused, or creates a probability of causing, damage to his property, and (ii) neither the person who has violated the local program nor the program authority has taken corrective action within fifteen days to eliminate the conditions which have caused, or create the probability of causing, damage to his property.

D. In addition to any criminal or civil penalties provided under this chapter, any person who violates any provision of this chapter may be liable to the program authority, or the Board, as appropriate, in a civil action for damages.

E. Without limiting the remedies which may be obtained in this section, any person violating or failing, neglecting or refusing to obey any injunction, mandamus or other remedy obtained pursuant to this section shall be subject, in the discretion of the court, to a civil penalty not to exceed $2,000 for each violation. A civil action for such violation or failure may be brought by the locality wherein the land lies. Any civil penalties assessed by a court shall be paid into the treasury of the locality wherein the land lies, except that where the violator is the locality itself, or its agent, the court shall direct the penalty to be paid into the state treasury.

F. With the consent of any person who has violated or failed, neglected or refused to obey any regulation or order of the Board, or any condition of a permit or any provision of this article, the Board, the Director, or plan-approving or permit-issuing authority may provide, in an order issued by the Board or plan-approving or permit-issuing authority against such person, for the payment of civil charges for violations in specific sums, not to exceed the limit specified in subsection E of this section. Such civil charges shall be instead of any appropriate civil penalty which could be imposed under subsection B or E.

G. Upon request of a program authority, or the permit-issuing authority, the attorney for the Commonwealth shall take legal action to enforce the provisions of this article. Upon request of the Board, the Attorney General shall take appropriate legal action on behalf of the Board to enforce the provisions of this article.

H. Compliance with the provisions of this article shall be prima facie evidence in any legal or equitable proceeding for damages caused by erosion or sedimentation that all requirements of law have been met and the complaining party must show negligence in order to recover any damages. (1973, c. 486, § 21-89.11; 1988, cc. 694, 891; 1992, c. 298; 1993, c. 925; 1995, c. 832; 1996, c. 518.)

Cross references. — As to punishment for Class 1 misdemeanors, see § 18.2-11.

§ 10.1-569.1. Stop work orders by Board; civil penalties. — A. An aggrieved owner of property sustaining pecuniary damage resulting from a violation of an approved plan or required permit, or from the conduct of land-disturbing activities commenced without an approved plan or required permit, may give written notice of the alleged violation to the program authority and to the Director.

B. Upon receipt of the notice from the aggrieved owner and notification to the program authority, the Director shall conduct an investigation of the aggrieved owner's complaint.

C. If the program authority has not responded to the alleged violation in a manner which causes the violation to cease and abates the damage to the aggrieved owner's property within thirty days following receipt of the notice from the aggrieved owner, the aggrieved owner may request that the Director require the violator to stop the violation and abate the damage to his property.

D. If (i) the Director's investigation of the complaint indicates that the program authority has not responded to the alleged violation as required by the local program, (ii) the program authority has not responded to the alleged violation within thirty days from the date of the notice given pursuant to subsection A of this section, and (iii) the Director is requested by the aggrieved owner to require the violator to cease the violation, then the Director shall give written notice to the program authority that the Director will request the Board to issue an order pursuant to subsection E of this section.

E. If the program authority has not instituted action to stop the violation and abate the damage to the aggrieved owner's property within ten days following receipt of the notice from the Director, the Board is authorized to issue an order requiring the owner, permittee, person responsible for carrying out an approved plan, or person conducting the land-disturbing activities without an approved plan or required permit to cease all land-disturbing activities until the violation of the plan or permit has ceased, or an approved plan and required permits are obtained, as appropriate, and specified corrective measures have been completed.

F. Such orders are to be issued only after a hearing with reasonable notice to the affected person of the time, place and purpose thereof, and they shall become effective upon service on the person by certified mail, return receipt requested, sent to his address specified in the land records of the locality, or by personal delivery by an agent of the Director. However, if the Board finds that any such violation is grossly affecting or presents an imminent and substantial danger of causing harmful erosion of lands or sediment deposition in waters within the watersheds of the Commonwealth, it may issue, without advance notice or hearing, an emergency order directing such person to cease all land-disturbing activities on the site immediately and shall provide an opportunity for a hearing, after reasonable notice as to the time and place thereof, to such person, to affirm, modify, amend or cancel such emergency order.

G. If a person who has been issued an order or emergency order is not complying with the terms thereof, the Board may institute a proceeding in the appropriate circuit court for an injunction, mandamus, or other appropriate remedy compelling the person to comply with such order.

H. Any person violating or failing, neglecting or refusing to obey any injunction, mandamus or other remedy obtained pursuant to subsection G of this section shall be subject, in the discretion of the court, to a civil penalty not to exceed $2,000 for each violation. Any civil penalties assessed by a court shall be paid into the state treasury. (1993, c. 925.)

§ **10.1-570. Authorization for more stringent regulations.** — A district or locality is authorized to adopt more stringent soil erosion and sediment control regulations than those necessary to ensure compliance with the Board's regulations. However, this section shall not be construed to authorize any district or locality to impose any more stringent regulations for plan approval or permit issuance than those specified in §§ 10.1-563 and 10.1-565. (1973, c. 486, § 21-89.12; 1988, c. 891.)

§ **10.1-571. No limitation on authority of Water Control Board or Department of Mines, Minerals and Energy.** — The provisions of this article shall not limit the powers or duties presently exercised by the State Water Control Board under Chapter 3.1 (§ 62.1-44.2 et seq.) of Title 62.1, or the powers or duties of the Department of Mines, Minerals and Energy as they relate to strip mine reclamation under Chapters 16 (§ 45.1-180 et seq.), 17 (§ 45.1-198 et seq.) and 19 (§ 45.1-226 et seq.) of Title 45.1 or oil or gas exploration under the Virginia Oil and Gas Act (§ 45.1-361.1 et seq.). (1973, c. 486, § 21-89.13; 1988, c. 891; 1996, c. 688.)

ARTICLE 5.

Soil Survey.

§ **10.1-572. Duty of Department to complete Virginia portion of National Cooperative Soil Survey.** — In addition to other duties the Department shall be responsible for accelerating the Virginia portion of the National Cooperative Soil Survey and for coordinating efforts to complete the inventory of Virginia's soil resources by 2006, contingent upon the availability of federal and state mapping resources. (1972, c. 557, § 21-5.2; 1984, c. 177; 1988, c. 891; 1994, c. 465; 1999, c. 155.)

§ 10.1-573. Immunity from prosecution for trespass. — No criminal action for trespass shall lie against the Board, any agent or employee of the Department, or any agent or employee of the United States Department of Agriculture or Virginia Polytechnic Institute and State University, because of the mere entry upon the lands of any person for the purpose of performing duties in conjunction with the conduct and completion of the Virginia portion of the National Cooperative Soil Survey, provided that the agent or employee made a reasonable effort to obtain the consent of the owner of the land prior to his entry. (1975, c. 485, § 21-5.3; 1988, c. 891.)

CHAPTER 6.
FLOOD PROTECTION AND DAM SAFETY.

ARTICLE 1.

Flood Damage Reduction Act.

§ 10.1-600. Definitions. — As used in this article, unless the context requires a different meaning:

"Emergency flood insurance program" or *"emergency program"* means the Emergency Program of the Federal Insurance Administration which provides subsidized flood insurance for potential flood victims, applicable to both new and existing structures, pending completion of applicable actuarial rates which is a prerequisite for eligibility to participate in the regular program.

"Flood hazard area" means those areas susceptible to flooding.

"Flood plain" or *"flood-prone areas"* means those areas adjoining a river, stream, water course, ocean, bay or lake which are likely to be covered by floodwaters.

"Flood plain management regulations" means zoning ordinances, subdivision regulations, the building code, health regulations, special purpose ordinances such as flood plain ordinances, grading ordinances or erosion control ordinances, and other rules, regulations and ordinances which may affect flood plain uses. The term describes such legally enforceable regulations, in any combination thereof, which provide standards for the control of the use and occupancy of flood-prone areas.

"Hundred year flood" means a flood of that level which on the average will have a one percent chance of being equaled or exceeded in any given year at designated locations.

"Locality" means a county, city, or town.

"National flood insurance program" means the program established by the United States Congress under provisions of the National Flood Insurance Act of 1968, as amended, and as expanded in the Flood Disaster Protection Act of 1973, designed to provide flood insurance at rates made affordable through federal subsidy.

"Nonfederal cost" means the flood protection project costs provided by sources other than the federal government.

"Regular flood insurance program" means a program of insurance under the national flood insurance program, for which the Federal Insurance Administrator has issued a flood insurance rate map and applicable actuarial rates, and under which new construction will not be eligible for flood insurance except at the applicable actuarial rates. (1977, c. 310, § 62.1-44.110; 1987, c. 163; 1988, c. 891; 1989, cc. 468, 497.)

§ 10.1-601: Repealed by Acts 1989, cc. 468, 497.

Cross references. — As to powers and duties of the Department relating to flood protection, see § 10.1-602. As to comprehensive flood control program, see § 10.1-658 et seq.

§ 10.1-602. Powers and duties of Department. — The Department shall:

1. Develop a flood protection plan for the Commonwealth. This plan shall include:

 a. An inventory of flood-prone areas;

 b. An inventory of flood protection studies;

 c. A record of flood damages;

 d. Strategies to prevent or mitigate flood damage; and

 e. The collection and distribution of information relating to flooding and flood plain management.

2. Serve as the coordinator of all flood protection programs and activities in the Commonwealth, including the coordination of federal flood protection programs administered by the United States Army Corps of Engineers, the United States Department of Agriculture, the Federal Emergency Management Agency, the United States Geological Survey, the Tennessee Valley Authority, other federal agencies and local governments.

3. Make available flood and flood damage reduction data to localities for planning purposes, in order to assure necessary local participation in the planning process and in the selection of desirable alternatives which will fulfill the intent of this article. This shall include the development of a data base to include (i) all flood protection projects implemented by federal agencies and (ii) the estimated value of property damaged by major floods.

4. Assist localities in their management of flood plain activities in cooperation with the Department of Housing and Community Development.

5. Carry out the provisions of this article in a manner which will ensure that the management of flood plains will preserve the capacity of the flood plain to carry and discharge a hundred year flood.

6. Make, in cooperation with localities, periodic inspections to determine the effectiveness of local flood plain management programs, including an evaluation of the enforcement of and compliance with local flood plain management ordinances, rules and regulations.

7. Coordinate with the United States Federal Emergency Management Agency to ensure current knowledge of the identification of flood-prone communities and of the status of applications made by localities to participate in the National Flood Insurance Program.

8. Establish guidelines which will meet minimum requirements of the National Flood Insurance Program in furtherance of the policy of the Commonwealth to assure that all citizens living in flood-prone areas may have the opportunity to indemnify themselves from flood losses through the purchase of flood insurance under the regular flood insurance program of the National Flood Insurance Act of 1968 as amended.

9. Subject to the provisions of the Appropriations Act, provide financial and technical assistance to localities in an amount not to exceed fifty percent of the nonfederal costs of flood protection projects. (1977, c. 310, § 62.1-44.112; 1981, c. 315; 1987, c. 163; 1988, c. 891; 1989, cc. 468, 497.)

§ 10.1-603. State agency compliance. — All agencies and departments of the Commonwealth shall comply with the flood plain regulations established pursuant to this article when planning for facilities in flood plains. (1977, c. 310, § 62.1-44.108; 1988, c. 891; 1989, cc. 468, 497.)

ARTICLE 1.1.

Stormwater Management.

§ 10.1-603.1: Not set out.

Editor's note. — This section, pertaining to the reasons for establishing stormwater management programs, was enacted by Acts 1989, cc. 467, 499. In furtherance of the general policy of the Virginia Code Commission to include in the Code only provisions having general and permanent application, this section, which is limited in its purpose and scope, is not set out here, but attention is called to it by this reference.

Acts 1991, c. 84, cl. 3 provides: "That existing regulations promulgated by the Department of Conservation and Recreation under the stormwater management program (§ 10.1-603.1 et seq.) are transferred to the Board of Conservation and Recreation and shall remain in full force and effect until any such regulation is amended, modified, or repealed by the Board of Conservation and Recreation."

§ 10.1-603.2. Definitions. — As used in this article, unless the context requires a different meaning:

"Board" means the Virginia Soil and Water Conservation Board.

"CWA" means the federal Clean Water Act (33 USC § 1251 et seq.), formerly referred to as the Federal Water Pollution Control Act or Federal Water Pollution Control Act Amendments of 1972, Public Law 92-500, as amended by Public Law 95-217, Public Law 95-576, Public Law 96-483, and Public Law 97-117, or any subsequent revisions thereto.

"Department" means the Department of Conservation and Recreation.

"Director" means the Director of the Department of Conservation and Recreation.

"Flooding" means a volume of water that is too great to be confined within the banks or walls of the stream, water body, or conveyance system and that overflows onto adjacent lands, thereby causing or threatening damage.

"Land disturbance" or *"land disturbing activity"* means a manmade change to the land surface that potentially changes its runoff characteristics including any clearing, grading, or excavation associated with a construction activity regulated pursuant to the federal Clean Water Act.

"Linear development project" means a land development project that is linear in nature such as, but not limited to, (i) the construction of electric and telephone utility lines, and natural gas pipelines; (ii) construction of tracks, rights-of-way, bridges, communication facilities and other related structures of a railroad company; and (iii) highway construction projects.

"Local stormwater management program" or *"local program"* means the various methods employed by a locality to manage the quality and quantity of runoff resulting from land disturbing activities and shall include such items as local ordinances, permit requirements, policies and guidelines, technical materials, inspection, enforcement, and evaluation consistent with this article.

"Municipal separate storm sewer" means a conveyance or system of conveyances otherwise known as a municipal separate storm sewer system or "MS4," including roads with drainage systems, municipal streets, catch basins, curbs, gutters, ditches, manmade channels, or storm drains:

1. Owned or operated by a federal, state, city, town, county, district, association, or other public body, created by or pursuant to state law, having jurisdiction or delegated authority for erosion and sediment control and

stormwater management, or a designated and approved management agency under § 208 of the CWA that discharges to surface waters;

2. Designed or used for collecting or conveying stormwater;

3. That is not a combined sewer; and

4. That is not part of a publicly owned treatment works.

"Municipal Separate Storm Sewer System Management Program" means a management program covering the duration of a permit for a municipal separate storm sewer system that includes a comprehensive planning process that involves public participation and intergovernmental coordination, to reduce the discharge of pollutants to the maximum extent practicable, using management practices, control techniques, and system, design and engineering methods, and such other provisions that are appropriate.

"Nonpoint source pollution" means pollution whose sources cannot be pinpointed but rather is washed from the land surface in a diffuse manner by stormwater runoff.

"Peak flow rate" means the maximum instantaneous flow from a given storm condition at a particular location.

"Permit" means an approval issued by the permit issuing authority for the initiation of a land-disturbing activity, or for stormwater discharges from an MS4.

"Permit issuing authority" means the Board, the Department, or a locality that is delegated authority by the Board to issue, deny, revoke, terminate, or amend stormwater permits under the provisions of this article.

"Permittee" means the person or locality to which the permit is issued.

"Person" means an individual, corporation, partnership, association, state, municipality, commission, or political subdivision of a state, governmental body, any interstate body, or any other legal entity.

"Runoff volume" means the volume of water that runs off the land development project from a prescribed storm event.

"Stormwater" means precipitation that is discharged across the land surface or through conveyances to one or more waterways and that may include storm water runoff, snow melt runoff, and surface runoff and drainage.

"Stormwater management program" means a program established by a locality that is consistent with the requirements of this article and associated regulations and guidance documents.

"Subdivision" means the same as defined in § 15.2-2201.

"Virginia Stormwater Management Program (VSMP)" means the Virginia program for issuing, modifying, revoking and reissuing, terminating, monitoring and enforcing permits, and imposing and enforcing requirements pursuant to the federal Clean Water Act and this article.

"Water quality volume" means the volume equal to the first one-half inch of runoff multiplied by the impervious surface of the land development project.

"Watershed" means a defined land area drained by a river or stream or system of connecting rivers or streams such that all surface water within the area flows through a single outlet. (1989, cc. 467, 499; 1991, c. 84; 1994, cc. 605, 898; 2004, c. 372; 2006, cc. 21, 171.)

Editor's note. — Acts 2004, c. 372, cl. 3, provides: "That the provisions of the first enactment clause including the provisions that transfer the responsibility for administering the issuance of national pollutant discharge elimination system permits for the control of stormwater discharges from MS4 and construction activities shall become effective on January 1, 2005, or upon the U.S. Environmental Protection Agency's authorization for delega-tion of program authority to the Virginia Soil and Water Conservation Board, whichever is the latter." The U.S. Environmental Protection Agency approved the transfer of program authority to the Virginia Soil and Water Conservation Board in a letter dated December 30, 2004.

Acts 2004, c. 372, cl. 4, provides: "That the Department of Conservation and Recreation shall on or after July 1, 2004, seek authorization for delegation of program authority for the Virginia Soil and Water Conservation Board for the issuance of national pollutant discharge elimination system permits for the control of stormwater discharges from MS4 and construction activities from the U.S. Environmental Protection Agency under the federal Clean Water Act. Such permits issued by the State Water Control Board that have not expired or been revoked or terminated before or on the program transfer date shall continue to remain in effect until their specified expiration dates."

Acts 2004, c. 372, cl. 5, provides: "That the Virginia Stormwater Management Act regulations (4 VAC 3-20 et. seq.) shall be transferred from the Board of Conservation and Recreation to the Virginia Soil and Water Conservation Board on July 1, 2004 and the Virginia Soil and Water Conservation Board may amend, modify, or delete provisions in the these regulations in order to implement this Act. Such regulations that are in effect shall remain in full force and effect until altered, amended, or rescinded by the Virginia Soil and Water Conservation Board."

Acts 2004, c. 372, cl. 6, provides: "That the Virginia Pollutant Discharge Elimination System (VPDES) General Permit Regulation For Discharges of Storm Water From Construction Activities, 9 VAC 25-180-10 et seq., and the General Virginia Pollutant Discharge Elimination System (VPDES) Permit Regulation For Discharges Of Storm Water From Small Municipal Separate Storm Sewer Systems, 9 VAC 25-750-10 et seq., are hereby transferred from the State Water Control Board to the Virginia Soil and Water Conservation Board as set forth in the third enactment clause and shall remain in full force and effect until amended, modified, or repealed by the Virginia Soil and Water Conservation Board. Those amendments to the regulations necessitated by this act shall be exempt from Article 2 (§ 2.2-4006 et seq.) of the Administrative Process Act. Any future amendments shall be adopted in accordance with the provisions of the Administrative Process Act."

Acts 2004, c. 372, cl. 7, provides: "That the relevant provisions of Fees For Permits And Certificates Regulations, 9 VAC 25-20-10 et seq., and the Virginia Pollutant Discharge Elimination System (VPDES) Permit Regulations, 9 VAC 25-31-10 et seq., and other necessary regulations pertaining to the administration and implementation of an NPDES permit program associated with MS4 or construction activity stormwater discharge programs as adopted by the State Water Control Board shall be vested with and remain in full force and

effect for the State Water Control Board and also shall be hereby transferred to and be in full force and effect for the Virginia Soil and Water Conservation Board on the effective date as set forth in the third enactment clause, as identical regulations until amended, modified, or repealed by the individual actions of the Virginia Water Control Board or the Virginia Soil and Water Conservation Board to reflect each board's authorities as authorized by this act. Those amendments necessitated by this act shall be exempt from Article 2 (§ 2.2-4006 et seq.) of the Administrative Process Act."

Acts 2004, c. 372, cl. 8, provides: "That the Virginia Soil and Water Conservation Board, on or after July 1, 2004, shall have authority to transfer relevant provisions in the existing regulations of the State Water Control Board and program administration provisions that may be required by the U.S. Environmental Protection Agency into the Virginia Stormwater Management Act regulations (4 VAC 3-20 et. seq.). These actions shall be exempt from Article 2 (§ 2.2-4006 et seq.) of the Administrative Process Act. Such amendments shall be effective no earlier than the effective date as set forth in the third enactment clause."

Acts 2004, c. 372, cl. 9, provides: "That on or after July 1, 2004, the Virginia Soil and Water Conservation Board may amend, modify, or delete provisions in the existing Virginia Stormwater Management Act regulations (4 VAC 3-20 et. seq.) including but not limited to those pertaining to the standards and procedures for delegating authority for administering a stormwater management program to localities. Such amendments shall be effective no earlier than the effective date as set forth in the third enactment clause."

Acts 2005, c. 41, cl. 5, provides: "That the Chesapeake Bay Local Assistance Board shall have the authority to amend, modify, or delete provisions in the Chesapeake Bay Preservation Area Designation and Management Regulations (9-VAC 10-20 et seq.) in order to implement Chapter 372 of the Acts of Assembly of 2004 and the provisions of this act. Those amendments to the regulations necessitated by these acts shall be exempt from Article 2 (§ 2.2-4006 et seq.) of the Administrative Process Act."

The 2004 amendments. — The 2004 amendment by c. 372 rewrote the section. For effective date, see Editor's note.

The 2006 amendments. — The 2006 amendment by c. 21 added the paragraphs defining "Peak flow rate," "Runoff volume," and "Water quality volume."

The 2006 amendment by c. 171 added the paragraph defining "Person."

§ 10.1-603.2:1. Powers and duties of the Virginia Soil and Water Conservation Board. — In addition to other powers and duties conferred

upon the Board, it shall permit, regulate, and control stormwater runoff in the Commonwealth. In accordance with the VSMP, the Board may issue, deny, revoke, terminate, or amend stormwater permits; adopt regulations; approve and periodically review local stormwater management programs and management programs developed in conjunction with a municipal separate storm sewer permit; enforce the provisions of this article; and otherwise act to ensure the general health, safety and welfare of the citizens of the Commonwealth as well as protect the quality and quantity of state waters from the potential harm of unmanaged stormwater. The Board may:

1. Issue, deny, amend, revoke, terminate, and enforce permits for the control of stormwater discharges from Municipal Separate Storm Sewer Systems and land disturbing activities.

2. Delegate to the Department or to an approved locality any of the powers and duties vested in it by this article except the adoption and promulgation of regulations. Delegation shall not remove from the Board authority to enforce the provisions of this article.

3. Take administrative and legal actions to ensure compliance by permittees, any person subject to permit requirements under this article, and those localities with an approved local stormwater management program and management programs developed in conjunction with a municipal separate storm sewer system permit with the provisions of this article including the proper enforcement and implementation of, and continual compliance with, this article.

4. After notice and opportunity for a hearing by the Board, amend or revoke any permit issued by the permit issuing authority under this article on the following grounds or for good cause as may be provided by the regulations of the Board:

a. The permittee or any person subject to permit requirements under this article has violated any order or regulation of the Board, any condition of a permit, any provision of this article, any order of a court, or any order of the permit issuing authority, where such violation results in the unreasonable degradation of properties, water quality, stream channels, and other natural resources, or the violation is representative of a pattern of serious or repeated violations including the disregard for or inability to comply with applicable laws, regulations, permit conditions, orders, rules, or requirements;

b. The permittee or any person subject to permit requirements under this article has failed to disclose fully all relevant material facts or has misrepresented a material fact in applying for a permit, or in any other report or document required under this law or under the regulations of the Board;

c. The activity for which the permit was issued causes unreasonable degradation of properties, water quality, stream channels, and other natural resources; or

d. There exists a material change in the basis on which the permit was issued that requires either a temporary or a permanent reduction or elimination of any discharge or land disturbing activity controlled by the permit necessary to prevent unreasonable degradation of properties, water quality, stream channels, and other natural resources.

5. Cause investigations and inspections, or delegate authority to do so, to ensure compliance with any permits, conditions, policies, rules, regulations, rulings and orders which it may adopt, issue or establish and to furnish advice, recommendations, or instructions for the purpose of obtaining such compliance.

6. Adopt rules governing the procedure of the permit issuing authority with respect to: (i) hearings; (ii) the filing of reports; (iii) the issuance of permits and special orders; and (iv) all other matters relating to procedure; and to amend or cancel any rule adopted. Public notice of every rule adopted under this

section shall be by such means as the permit issuing authority may prescribe but must be consistent with the Administrative Process Act (§ 2.2-4000 et seq.).

7. Issue special orders to a permittee or any person subject to permit requirements under this article (i) who is permitting or causing the unreasonable degradation of properties, water quality, stream channels, and other natural resources to cease and desist from such activities, (ii) who has failed to construct facilities in accordance with final approved plans and specifications to construct such facilities, (iii) who has violated the terms and provisions of a permit issued by the permit issuing authority; to comply with the provisions of the permit, this article and any decision of the permit issuing authority, the Department, or the Board, or (iv) who has violated the terms of an order issued by the court, the permit issuing authority, the Department, or the Board: to comply with the terms of such order, and also to issue orders to require any permittee or any person subject to permit requirements under this article to comply with the provisions of this article and any decision of the Board.

Such special orders are to be issued only after a hearing with at least 30 days' notice to the affected permittee or any person subject to permit requirements under this article, of the time, place, and purpose thereof, and they shall become effective not less than 15 days after the date of mailing by certified mail of the notice to the last known address of the permittee or any person subject to permit requirements under this article; provided that if the Board finds that any such permittee or any person subject to permit requirements under this article is grossly affecting or presents an imminent and substantial danger to (i) the public health, safety or welfare, or the health of animals, fish or aquatic life; (ii) a public water supply; or (iii) recreational, commercial, industrial, agricultural or other reasonable uses, it may issue, without advance notice or hearing, an emergency special order directing the permittee or any person subject to permit requirements under this article to cease such pollution or discharge immediately, and shall provide an opportunity for a hearing, after reasonable notice as to the time and place thereof to the permittee or any person subject to permit requirements under this article, to affirm, modify, amend, or cancel such emergency special order. If the permittee or any person subject to permit requirements under this article who has been issued such a special order or an emergency special order is not complying with the terms thereof, the Board may proceed in accordance with § 10.1-603.14, and where the order is based on a finding of an imminent and substantial danger, the court shall issue an injunction compelling compliance with the emergency special order pending a hearing by the Board. If an emergency special order requires cessation of a discharge, the Board shall provide an opportunity for a hearing within 48 hours of the issuance of the injunction.

The provisions of this section notwithstanding, the Board may proceed directly under § 10.1-603.14 for any past violation or violations of any provision of this article or any regulation duly adopted hereunder.

With the consent of any permittee or any person subject to permit requirements under this article who has violated or failed, neglected, or refused to obey any regulation or order of the Board, any condition of a permit or any provision of this article, the Board may provide, in an order issued by the Board against such person, for the payment of civil charges for violations in specific sums not to exceed the limit specified in subsection A of § 10.1-603.14. Such civil charges shall be collected in lieu of any appropriate civil penalty that could be imposed pursuant to subsection A of § 10.1-603.14 and shall not be subject to the provisions of § 2.2-514. Such civil charges shall be paid into the state treasury and deposited by the State Treasurer into the Virginia Stormwater Management Fund established pursuant to § 10.1-603.4:1. (2004, c. 372; 2006, c. 171.)

Cross references. — For provisions of Acts 2004, c. 372, cls. 4 through 9, relating to the transfer of authority over stormwater discharge regulation to the Virginia Soil and Water Conservation Board, see the Editor's notes following § 10.1-603.2.

Editor's note. — Acts 2004, c. 372, cl. 3, provides: "That the provisions of the first enactment clause including the provisions that transfer the responsibility for administering the issuance of national pollutant discharge elimination system permits for the control of stormwater discharges from MS4 and construction activities shall become effective on January 1, 2005, or upon the U.S. Environmental Protection Agency's authorization for delegation of program authority to the Virginia Soil and Water Conservation Board, whichever is the latter." The U.S. Environmental Protection Agency approved the transfer of program authority to the Virginia Soil and Water Conservation Board in a letter dated December 30, 2004.

The 2006 amendments. — The 2006 amendment by c. 171 inserted "any person subject to permit requirements under this article" in subdivision 3; inserted "or any person subject to permit requirements under this article" in subdivisions 4 a, 4 b and throughout subdivision 7; and substituted "permittee or any person subject to permit requirements under this article" for "order" in clause (iv) of the first paragraph in subdivision 7.

§ **10.1-603.2:2. Permits.** — A. It shall be unlawful to cause a stormwater discharge from an MS4 or a land disturbing activity except in compliance with a permit issued by a permit issuing authority.

B. All permits issued by the permit issuing authority under this article shall have fixed terms. The term of a permit shall be based upon the projected duration of the project, the length of any required monitoring, or other project operations or permit conditions; however, the term shall not exceed five years. The term of a permit issued by the permit issuing authority shall not be extended by modification beyond the maximum duration and the permit shall expire at the end of the term unless an application for a new permit has been filed in a timely manner as required by the regulations of the Board, and the permit issuing authority is unable, through no fault of the permittee, to issue a new permit before the expiration date of the previous permit. (2004, c. 372; 2006, c. 171.)

Cross references. — For provisions of Acts 2004, c. 372, cls. 4 through 9, relating to the transfer of authority over stormwater discharge regulation to the Virginia Soil and Water Conservation Board, see the Editor's notes following § 10.1-603.2.

Editor's note. — Acts 2004, c. 372, cl. 3, provides: "That the provisions of the first enactment clause including the provisions that transfer the responsibility for administering the issuance of national pollutant discharge elimination system permits for the control of stormwater discharges from MS4 and construction activities shall become effective on January 1, 2005, or upon the U.S. Environmental Protection Agency's authorization for delegation of program authority to the Virginia Soil and Water Conservation Board, whichever is the latter." The U.S. Environmental Protection Agency approved the transfer of program authority to the Virginia Soil and Water Conservation Board in a letter dated December 30, 2004.

The 2006 amendments. — The 2006 amendment by c. 171 substituted "except in compliance with a permit issued by" for "without a permit from" in subsection A.

§ **10.1-603.3. Establishment of stormwater management programs by localities.** — A. Any locality located within Tidewater Virginia as defined by the Chesapeake Bay Preservation Act (§ 10.1-2100 et seq.), or any locality that is partially or wholly designated as an MS4 under the provisions of the federal Clean Water Act, shall be required to adopt a local stormwater management program for land disturbing activities consistent with the provisions of this article according to a schedule set by the Board but no sooner than 12 months and not more than 18 months following the effective date of the regulation that establishes local program criteria and delegation procedures.

B. Any locality not specified in subsection A may elect to adopt and administer a local stormwater management program for land disturbing activities pursuant to this article. Such localities shall inform the Board and the Department of their initial intention to seek delegation for the stormwater management program for land disturbing permits within six months following the effective date of the regulation that establishes local program criteria and delegation procedures. Thereafter, the Department shall provide an annual schedule by which localities can submit applications for delegation.

C. In the absence of the delegation of a stormwater management program to a locality, the Department will administer the responsibilities of this article within the given jurisdiction.

D. The Department shall develop a model ordinance for establishing a local stormwater management program consistent with this article.

E. Each locality that is required to or that elects to adopt and administer an approved local stormwater management program shall, by ordinance, establish a local stormwater management program that may be administered in conjunction with a local MS4 program and a local erosion and sediment control program, which shall include, but is not limited to, the following:

1. Consistency with regulations adopted in accordance with provisions of this article;

2. Provisions for long-term responsibility for and maintenance of stormwater management control devices and other techniques specified to manage the quality and quantity of runoff; and

3. Provisions for the integration of locally adopted stormwater management programs with local erosion and sediment control, flood insurance, flood plain management, and other programs requiring compliance prior to authorizing construction in order to make the submission and approval of plans, issuance of permits, payment of fees, and coordination of inspection and enforcement activities more convenient and efficient both for the local governments and those responsible for compliance with the programs.

F. The Board shall delegate a local stormwater management program to a locality when it deems a program consistent with this article.

G. Delegated localities may enter into agreements with soil and water conservation districts, adjacent localities, or other entities to carry out the responsibilities of this article.

H. Localities that adopt a local stormwater management program shall have the authority to issue a consolidated stormwater management and erosion and sediment control permit that is consistent with the provisions of the Erosion and Sediment Control Law (§ 10.1-560 et seq.).

I. Any local stormwater management program adopted pursuant to and consistent with this article shall be considered to meet the stormwater management requirements under the Chesapeake Bay Preservation Act (§ 10.1-2100 et seq.) and attendant regulations. (1989, cc. 467, 499; 2004, c. 372; 2006, c. 171.)

Cross references. — For provisions of Acts 2004, c. 372, cls. 4 through 9, relating to the transfer of authority over stormwater discharge regulation to the Virginia Soil and Water Conservation Board, see the Editor's notes following § 10.1-603.2.

Editor's note. — Acts 2004, c. 372, cl. 3, provides: "That the provisions of the first enactment clause including the provisions that transfer the responsibility for administering the issuance of national pollutant discharge elimination system permits for the control of stormwater discharges from MS4 and construction activities shall become effective on January 1, 2005, or upon the U.S. Environmental Protection Agency's authorization for delega-

tion of program authority to the Virginia Soil and Water Conservation Board, whichever is the latter." The U.S. Environmental Protection Agency approved the transfer of program authority to the Virginia Soil and Water Conservation Board in a letter dated December 30, 2004.

The 2004 amendments. — The 2004 amendment by c. 372 rewrote the section. For effective date, see Editor's note.

The 2006 amendments. — The 2006 amendment by c. 171 substituted "according to a schedule set by the Board but no sooner than 12 months and not more than 18 months following the effective date of the regulation that establishes local program criteria and delegation procedures" for "by July 1, 2006" in subsection A; and substituted "within six months following the effective date of the regulation that establishes local program criteria and delegation procedures" for "no later than July 1, 2005" in the second sentence of subsection B.

§ 10.1-603.4. Development of regulations. — The Board is authorized to adopt regulations that specify minimum technical criteria and administrative procedures for stormwater management programs in Virginia. The regulations shall:

1. Establish standards and procedures for delegating the authority for administering a stormwater management program to localities;

2. Establish minimum design criteria for measures to control nonpoint source pollution and localized flooding, and incorporate the stormwater management regulations adopted pursuant to the Virginia Erosion and Sediment Control Law (§ 10.1-560 et seq.), as they relate to the prevention of stream channel erosion. These criteria shall be periodically modified as required in order to reflect current engineering methods;

3. Require the provision of long-term responsibility for and maintenance of stormwater management control devices and other techniques specified to manage the quality and quantity of runoff;

4. Require as a minimum the inclusion in local programs of certain administrative procedures which include, but are not limited to, specifying the time period within which a local government that has adopted a stormwater management program must grant permit approval, the conditions under which approval shall be granted, the procedures for communicating disapproval, the conditions under which an approved permit may be changed and requirements for inspection of approved projects;

5. Establish, with the concurrence of the Director, a statewide permit fee schedule for stormwater management related to land disturbing activities of one acre or greater. The fee schedule shall also include a provision for a reduced fee for land disturbing activities between 2,500 square feet and up to 1 acre in Chesapeake Bay Preservation Act (§ 10.1-2100 et seq.) localities. The regulations shall be governed by the following:

a. The revenue generated from the statewide stormwater permit fee shall be collected and remitted to the State Treasurer for deposit in the Virginia Stormwater Management Fund established pursuant to § 10.1-603.4:1. However, whenever the Board has delegated a stormwater management program to a locality or is required to do so under this article, no more than 30 percent of the total revenue generated by the statewide stormwater permit fees collected within the locality shall be remitted to the State Treasurer, for deposit in the Virginia Stormwater Management Fund.

b. Fees collected pursuant to this section shall be in addition to any general fund appropriation made to the Department; however, the fees shall be set at a level sufficient for the Department to carry out its responsibilities under this article;

6. Establish statewide standards for stormwater management from land disturbing activities of one acre or greater, except as specified otherwise within this article, and allow for the consolidation in the permit of a comprehensive approach to addressing stormwater management and erosion and sediment control, consistent with the provisions of the Erosion and Sediment Control Law (§ 10.1-560 et seq.) and this article. However, such standards shall also apply to land disturbing activity exceeding an area of 2500 square feet in all areas of the jurisdictions designated as subject to the Chesapeake Bay Preservation Area Designation and Management Regulations (9 VAC 10-20 et seq.) adopted pursuant to the Chesapeake Bay Preservation Act (§ 10.1-2100 et seq.);

7. Require that stormwater management programs maintain after-development runoff rate of flow and characteristics that replicate, as nearly as

practicable, the existing predevelopment runoff characteristics and site hydrology, or improve upon the contributing share of the existing predevelopment runoff characteristics and site hydrology if stream channel erosion or localized flooding is an existing predevelopment condition. Any land-disturbing activity that provides for stormwater management shall satisfy the conditions of this subsection if the practices are designed to (i) detain the water quality volume and to release it over 48 hours; (ii) detain and release over a 24-hour period the expected rainfall resulting from the one year, 24-hour storm; and (iii) reduce the allowable peak flow rate resulting from the 1.5, 2, and 10-year, 24-hour storms to a level that is less than or equal to the peak flow rate from the site assuming it was in a good forested condition, achieved through multiplication of the forested peak flow rate by a reduction factor that is equal to the runoff volume from the site when it was in a good forested condition divided by the runoff volume from the site in its proposed condition, and shall be exempt from any flow rate capacity and velocity requirements for natural or manmade channels as defined in any regulations promulgated pursuant to this section, or any ordinances adopted pursuant to § 10.1-603.3 or 10.1-603.7;

8. Encourage low impact development designs, regional and watershed approaches, and nonstructural means for controlling stormwater; and

9. Establish, with the concurrence of the Director, a statewide permit fee schedule for stormwater management related to municipal separate storm sewer system permits. (1989, cc. 467, 499; 1991, c. 84; 2004, c. 372; 2005, c. 102; 2006, c. 21.)

Cross references. — For provisions of Acts 2004, c. 372, cls. 4 through 9, relating to the transfer of authority over stormwater discharge regulation to the Virginia Soil and Water Conservation Board, see the Editor's notes following § 10.1-603.2.

Editor's note. — Acts 2004, c. 372, cl. 3, provides: "That the provisions of the first enactment clause including the provisions that transfer the responsibility for administering the issuance of national pollutant discharge elimination system permits for the control of stormwater discharges from MS4 and construction activities shall become effective on January 1, 2005, or upon the U.S. Environmental Protection Agency's authorization for delegation of program authority to the Virginia Soil and Water Conservation Board, whichever is the latter." The U.S. Environmental Protection Agency approved the transfer of program authority to the Virginia Soil and Water Conservation Board in a letter dated December 30, 2004.

Acts 2005, c. 102, cl. 2, provides: "That the Governor shall make new appointments for each of the three at-large members of the Board in accordance with the provisions of this act on July 1, 2005. The new appointments of the at-large members of the Board shall go into effect upon the expiration of the current members' terms in January 2006, and the terms shall be staggered as follows: one member for a term of two years; one member for a term of three years; and one member for a term of four years. The Governor shall designate the term to

be served by each appointee at the time of appointment and may reappoint the existing at-large members of the Board."

Acts 2005, c. 102, cl. 3, provides: "That the Director of the Department of Conservation and Recreation shall amend the Stormwater Management Regulations by removing the out-of-date Best Management Practices (BMP) nutrient removal efficiency information and adding it into the Virginia Stormwater Management Handbook guidance document where it shall be more effectively updated for public use."

The 2004 amendments. — The 2004 amendment by c. 372, in the introductory paragraph, substituted "adopt" for "promulgate" and "The" for "In order to inhibit the deterioration of existing waters and waterways, the"; rewrote subdivision 1; in subdivision 2, in the first sentence, substituted "adopted" for "promulgated" and deleted "Article" following "Sediment Control Law" and "of Chapter 5 of this title" following "(§ 10.1-560 et seq.)"; in subdivision 4, substituted "permit" for "written," deleted "of a plan" following the first occurrence of "approval," and substituted "permit" for "plan"; added subdivisions 5 through 8; and made minor stylistic changes. For effective date, see Editor's note.

The 2005 amendments. — The 2005 amendment by c. 102 substituted "schedule shall" for "schedule may" in subdivision 5.

The 2006 amendments. — The 2006 amendment by c. 21 added the last sentence in subdivision 7.

§ 10.1-603.4:1. Virginia Stormwater Management Fund established.
— There is hereby created in the state treasury a special nonreverting fund to
be known as the Virginia Stormwater Management Fund, hereafter referred to
as "the Fund." The Fund shall be established on the books of the Comptroller.
All moneys collected pursuant to § 10.1-603.4 shall be paid into the state
treasury and credited to the Fund. Interest earned on moneys in the Fund
shall remain in the Fund and be credited to it. Any moneys remaining in the
Fund, including interest thereon, at the end of each fiscal year shall not revert
to the general fund but shall remain in the Fund. Moneys in the Fund shall be
used solely for the purposes of carrying out the Department's responsibilities
under this article. Expenditures and disbursements from the Fund shall be
made by the State Treasurer on warrants issued by the Comptroller upon
written request signed by the Director.

An accounting of moneys received by and distributed from the Fund shall be
kept by the State Comptroller. (2004, c. 372.)

Cross references. — For provisions of Acts
2004, c. 372, cls. 4 through 9, relating to the
transfer of authority over stormwater discharge regulation to the Virginia Soil and Water Conservation Board, see the Editor's notes
following § 10.1-603.2.

Editor's note. — Acts 2004, c. 372, cl. 3,
provides: "That the provisions of the first enactment clause including the provisions that
transfer the responsibility for administering
the issuance of national pollutant discharge
elimination system permits for the control of

stormwater discharges from MS4 and construction activities shall become effective on January 1, 2005, or upon the U.S. Environmental
Protection Agency's authorization for delegation of program authority to the Virginia Soil
and Water Conservation Board, whichever is
the latter." The U.S. Environmental Protection
Agency approved the transfer of program authority to the Virginia Soil and Water Conservation Board in a letter dated December 30,
2004.

§ 10.1-603.5. State agency projects. — A. A state agency may not undertake any land clearing, soil movement, or construction activity involving soil
movement or land disturbance unless the agency has submitted a permit
application for the land-disturbing activity and the application has been
reviewed and approved and a stormwater permit issued by the Department.
State agencies may submit a single permit application containing stormwater
management standards and specifications for all land disturbing activities
conducted under the requirements of this article. State agency stormwater
management standards and specifications shall include, but are not limited to:

1. Technical criteria to meet the requirements of this article and regulations
developed under this article;

2. Provisions for the long-term responsibility and maintenance of
stormwater management control devices and other techniques specified to
manage the quantity and quality of runoff;

3. Provisions for erosion and sediment control and stormwater management
program administration, plan design, review and approval, and construction
inspection and enforcement;

4. Provisions for ensuring that responsible personnel and contractors obtain
certifications or qualifications for erosion and sediment control and
stormwater management comparable to those required for local government;

5. Implementation of a project tracking and notification system to the
Department of all land disturbing activities covered under this article; and

6. Requirements for documenting on-site changes as they occur to ensure
compliance with the requirements of the article.

B. All state agencies shall comply with the provisions of this article and the
stormwater management provisions of the Erosion and Sediment Control Law
(§ 10.1-560 et seq.), and related regulations. The state agency responsible for
the land-disturbing activity shall ensure compliance with the issued permit,
permit conditions, and plan specifications. The Department shall perform

random site inspections to assure compliance with this article, the Erosion and Sediment Control Law and regulations adopted thereunder.

C. The Department shall have 30 days in which to review the permit application and to issue its permit decision, which shall be binding on the state agency or the private business hired by the state agency.

As on-site changes occur, the state agency shall submit changes in the permit application to the Department.

D. The Department may assess an administrative charge to cover a portion of the costs of services rendered associated with its responsibilities pursuant to this section. (1989, cc. 467, 499; 2004, c. 372.)

Cross references. — For provisions of Acts 2004, c. 372, cls. 4 through 9, relating to the transfer of authority over stormwater discharge regulation to the Virginia Soil and Water Conservation Board, see the Editor's notes following § 10.1-603.2.

Editor's note. — Acts 2004, c. 372, cl. 3, provides: "That the provisions of the first enactment clause including the provisions that transfer the responsibility for administering the issuance of national pollutant discharge elimination system permits for the control of stormwater discharges from MS4 and construction activities shall become effective on January 1, 2005, or upon the U.S. Environmental Protection Agency's authorization for delegation of program authority to the Virginia Soil and Water Conservation Board, whichever is the latter." The U.S. Environmental Protection Agency approved the transfer of program authority to the Virginia Soil and Water Conservation Board in a letter dated December 30, 2004.

The 2004 amendments. — The 2004 amendment by c. 372 rewrote the section. For effective date, see Editor's note.

§ 10.1-603.6. Duties of the Department.

§ **10.1-603.6. Duties of the Department.** — A. The Department shall provide technical assistance, training, research, and coordination in stormwater management technology to the local governments consistent with the purposes of this article.

B. The Department is authorized to review the permit application for any project with real or potential interjurisdictional impacts upon the request of one of the involved localities to determine that the plan is consistent with the provisions of this article. Any such review shall be completed and a report submitted to each locality involved within 90 days of such request being accepted.

C. The Department shall be responsible for the implementation of this article. (1989, cc. 467, 499; 2004, c. 372.)

Cross references. — For provisions of Acts 2004, c. 372, cls. 4 through 9, relating to the transfer of authority over stormwater discharge regulation to the Virginia Soil and Water Conservation Board, see the Editor's notes following § 10.1-603.2.

Editor's note. — Acts 2004, c. 372, cl. 3, provides: "That the provisions of the first enactment clause including the provisions that transfer the responsibility for administering the issuance of national pollutant discharge elimination system permits for the control of stormwater discharges from MS4 and construction activities shall become effective on January 1, 2005, or upon the U.S. Environmental Protection Agency's authorization for delegation of program authority to the Virginia Soil and Water Conservation Board, whichever is the latter." The U.S. Environmental Protection Agency approved the transfer of program authority to the Virginia Soil and Water Conservation Board in a letter dated December 30, 2004.

The 2004 amendments. — The 2004 amendment by c. 372, in subsection B, substituted "permit application" for "plan" in the first sentence and substituted "90" for "ninety" and inserted "being accepted" at the end in the last sentence; and added subsection C. For effective date, see Editor's note.

§ 10.1-603.7. Authorization for more stringent ordinances.

§ **10.1-603.7. Authorization for more stringent ordinances.** — A. Localities are authorized to adopt more stringent stormwater management ordinances than those necessary to ensure compliance with the Board's minimum regulations, provided that the more stringent ordinances are based upon factual findings of local or regional comprehensive watershed management studies or findings developed through the implementation of a MS4 permit or a locally adopted watershed management study and are determined by the locality to be necessary to prevent any further degradation to water resources or to address specific existing water pollution including nutrient and sediment loadings, stream channel erosion, depleted groundwater resources, or excessive localized flooding within the watershed and that prior to adopting more stringent ordinances a public hearing is held after giving due notice.

B. Any local stormwater management program in existence before January 1, 2005 that contains more stringent provisions than this article shall be exempt from the requirements of subsection A. (1989, cc. 467, 499; 1991, c. 84; 2004, c. 372.)

Cross references. — For provisions of Acts 2004, c. 372, cls. 4 through 9, relating to the transfer of authority over stormwater discharge regulation to the Virginia Soil and Water Conservation Board, see the Editor's notes following § 10.1-603.2.

Editor's note. — Acts 2004, c. 372, cl. 3, provides: "That the provisions of the first enactment clause including the provisions that transfer the responsibility for administering the issuance of national pollutant discharge elimination system permits for the control of stormwater discharges from MS4 and construction activities shall become effective on January 1, 2005, or upon the U.S. Environmental Protection Agency's authorization for delegation of program authority to the Virginia Soil and Water Conservation Board, whichever is the latter." The U.S. Environmental Protection Agency approved the transfer of program authority to the Virginia Soil and Water Conservation Board in a letter dated December 30, 2004.

The 2004 amendments. — The 2004 amendment by c. 372 rewrote the section. For effective date, see Editor's note.

§ 10.1-603.8. Regulated activities; submission and approval of a permit application; security for performance; exemptions. — A. A person shall not develop any land for residential, commercial, industrial, or institutional use until he has submitted a permit application to the permit issuing authority and has obtained a permit. The permit issuing authority shall act on any permit application within 60 days after it has been determined by the permit issuing authority to be a complete application. The permit issuing authority may either issue the permit or deny the permit and shall provide written rationale for the denial. The permit issuing authority shall act on any permit application that has been previously disapproved within 45 days after the application has been revised, resubmitted for approval, and deemed complete. Prior to issuance of any permit, the permit issuing authority may also require an applicant, excluding those regulated under § 10.1-603.5, to submit a reasonable performance bond with surety, cash escrow, letter of credit, any combination thereof, or such other legal arrangement acceptable to the permit issuing authority, to ensure that measures could be taken by the permit issuing authority at the applicant's expense should he fail, after proper notice, within the time specified to initiate or maintain appropriate actions which may be required of him by the permit conditions as a result of his land disturbing activity. If the permit issuing authority takes such action upon such failure by the applicant, the permit issuing authority may collect from the applicant for the difference should the amount of the reasonable cost of such action exceed the amount of the security held. Within 60 days of the completion of the requirements of the permit conditions, such bond, cash escrow, letter of credit or other legal arrangement, or the unexpended or unobligated portion thereof, shall be refunded to the applicant or terminated. These requirements are in addition to all other provisions of law relating to the issuance of permits and are not intended to otherwise affect the requirements for such permits.

B. Notwithstanding any other provisions of this article, the following activities are exempt:

1. Permitted surface or deep mining operations and projects, or oil and gas operations and projects conducted under the provisions of Title 45.1;

2. Clearing of lands specifically for agricultural purposes and the management, tilling, planting or harvesting of agricultural, horticultural, or forest crops;

3. Single-family residences separately built and disturbing less than one acre and not part of a larger common plan of development or sale, including additions or modifications to existing single-family detached residential structures. However, localities subject to the Chesapeake Bay Preservation Act (§ 10.1-2100 et seq.) may regulate these single family residences where land disturbance exceeds 2,500 square feet;

4. Land disturbing activities that disturb less than one acre of land area except for land disturbing activity exceeding an area of 2,500 square feet in all areas of the jurisdictions designated as subject to the Chesapeake Bay Preservation Area Designation and Management Regulations (9 VAC 10-20 et seq.) adopted pursuant to the Chesapeake Bay Preservation Act (§ 10.1-2100 et seq.) or activities that are part of a larger common plan of development or sale that is one acre or greater of disturbance; however, the governing body of a locality which has adopted a stormwater management program may reduce this exception to a smaller area of disturbed land or qualify the conditions under which this exception shall apply;

5. Linear development projects, provided that (i) less than one acre of land will be disturbed per outfall or watershed, (ii) there will be insignificant increases in peak flow rates, and (iii) there are no existing or anticipated flooding or erosion problems downstream of the discharge point;

6. Discharges to a sanitary sewer or a combined sewer system;

7. Activities under a State or federal reclamation program to return an abandoned property to an agricultural or open land use; and

8. Routine maintenance that is performed to maintain the original line and grade, hydraulic capacity, or original construction of the project and that disturbs less than five acres of land.

C. Electric, natural gas, and communication utility companies, interstate and intrastate natural gas pipeline companies, and railroad companies may not undertake any land clearing, soil movement, or construction activity involving soil movement or land disturbance one acre or greater unless the company has submitted a permit application for the land-disturbing activity and the application has been reviewed and approved and a stormwater permit issued by the Board. Companies may submit a single permit application containing stormwater management standards and specifications for all land disturbing activities conducted under the requirements of this article. (1989, cc. 467, 499; 1994, cc. 605, 898; 2004, c. 372.)

Cross references. — For provisions of Acts 2004, c. 372, cls. 4 through 9, relating to the transfer of authority over stormwater discharge regulation to the Virginia Soil and Water Conservation Board, see the Editor's notes following § 10.1-603.2.

Editor's note. — Acts 2004, c. 372, cl. 3, provides: "That the provisions of the first enactment clause including the provisions that transfer the responsibility for administering the issuance of national pollutant discharge elimination system permits for the control of stormwater discharges from MS4 and construc-

tion activities shall become effective on January 1, 2005, or upon the U.S. Environmental Protection Agency's authorization for delegation of program authority to the Virginia Soil and Water Conservation Board, whichever is the latter." The U.S. Environmental Protection Agency approved the transfer of program authority to the Virginia Soil and Water Conservation Board in a letter dated December 30, 2004.

The 2004 amendments. — The 2004 amendment by c. 372 rewrote the section. For effective date, see Editor's note.

§ 10.1-603.9. Permit application required for issuance of grading, building, or other permits.

§ 10.1-603.9. **Permit application required for issuance of grading, building, or other permits.** — Upon the adoption of a local ordinance no grading, building or other permit shall be issued for a property unless a stormwater permit application has been approved that is consistent with the stormwater program and this article and unless the applicant has certified that all land clearing, construction, disturbance, land development and drainage will be done according to the approved permit conditions. (1989, cc. 467, 499; 2004, c. 372.)

Cross references. — For provisions of Acts 2004, c. 372, cls. 4 through 9, relating to the transfer of authority over stormwater discharge regulation to the Virginia Soil and Water Conservation Board, see the Editor's notes following § 10.1-603.2.

Editor's note. — Acts 2004, c. 372, cl. 3, provides: "That the provisions of the first enactment clause including the provisions that transfer the responsibility for administering the issuance of national pollutant discharge elimination system permits for the control of stormwater discharges from MS4 and construction activities shall become effective on January 1, 2005, or upon the U.S. Environmental Protection Agency's authorization for delegation of program authority to the Virginia Soil and Water Conservation Board, whichever is the latter." The U.S. Environmental Protection Agency approved the transfer of program authority to the Virginia Soil and Water Conservation Board in a letter dated December 30, 2004.

The 2004 amendments. — The 2004 amendment by c. 372 substituted "permit application" for "management plan" and "stormwater" for "local," inserted "disturbance," and substituted "permit conditions" for "plan." For effective date, see Editor's note.

§ 10.1-603.10. (For contingent repeal, see Editor's note) Recovery of administrative costs.

§ 10.1-603.10. **(For contingent repeal, see Editor's note) Recovery of administrative costs.** — Any locality which administers a stormwater management program may charge applicants a reasonable fee to defray the cost of program administration, including costs associated with plan review, issuance of permits, periodic inspection for compliance with approved plans, and necessary enforcement, provided that charges for such costs are not made under any other law, ordinance or program. The fee shall not exceed an amount commensurate with the services rendered and expenses incurred or $1,000, whichever is less. (1989, cc. 467, 499.)

Section contingently repealed. — This section is contingently repealed by Acts 2004, c. 372. See Editor's note.

Editor's note. — Acts 2004, c. 372, cl. 2, provides: "That § 10.1-603.10 of the Code of Virginia shall be repealed upon the Virginia Soil and Water Conservation Board adopting a statewide permit fee schedule pursuant to this act." As of June 2006, no permit fee schedule has been adopted.

Acts 2004, c. 372, cl. 3, provides: "That the provisions of the first enactment clause including the provisions that transfer the responsibility for administering the issuance of national pollutant discharge elimination system permits for the control of stormwater discharges from MS4 and construction activities shall become effective on January 1, 2005, or upon the U.S. Environmental Protection Agency's authorization for delegation of program authority to the Virginia Soil and Water Conservation Board, whichever is the latter." The U.S. Environmental Protection Agency approved the transfer of program authority to the Virginia Soil and Water Conservation Board in a letter dated December 30, 2004.

The section is set out above at the direction of the Virginia Code Commission.

§ 10.1-603.11. Monitoring, reports, investigations, and inspections.

§ 10.1-603.11. **Monitoring, reports, investigations, and inspections.** — A. The permit issuing authority (i) shall provide for periodic inspections of the installation of stormwater management measures (ii) may require monitoring and reports from the person responsible for meeting the permit conditions to ensure compliance with the permit and to determine whether the measures required in the permit provide effective stormwater management, and (iii) conduct such investigations and perform such other actions as are necessary to carry out the provisions of this article. If the permit issuing authority determines that there is a failure to comply with the permit conditions, notice shall be served upon the permittee or person responsible for carrying out the permit conditions by registered or certified mail to the address specified in the permit application, or by delivery at the site of the development activities to the agent or employee supervising such activities. The notice shall specify the measures needed to comply with the permit conditions and shall specify the time within which such measures shall be completed. Upon failure to comply within the time specified, the permit may be revoked by the permit issuing authority or the Board and the permittee or person responsible for carrying out the permit conditions shall be deemed to be in violation of this article and upon conviction shall be subject to the penalties provided by § 10.1-603.14.

B. Notwithstanding subsection A of this section, the following may be applied:

1. Where a county, city, or town administers the local control program and the permit issuing authority are not within the same local government department, the locality may designate one department to inspect, monitor, report, and ensure compliance.

2. Where a permit issuing authority has been established, and such authority is not vested in an employee or officer of local government but in the commissioner of revenue or some other person, the locality shall exercise the responsibilities of the permit issuing authority with respect to monitoring, reports, inspections, and enforcement unless such responsibilities are transferred as provided for in this section. (1989, cc. 467, 499; 2004, c. 372.)

Cross references. — For provisions of Acts 2004, c. 372, cls. 4 through 9, relating to the transfer of authority over stormwater discharge regulation to the Virginia Soil and Water Conservation Board, see the Editor's notes following § 10.1-603.2.

Editor's note. — Acts 2004, c. 372, cl. 3, provides: "That the provisions of the first enactment clause including the provisions that transfer the responsibility for administering the issuance of national pollutant discharge elimination system permits for the control of stormwater discharges from MS4 and construction activities shall become effective on January 1, 2005, or upon the U.S. Environmental Protection Agency's authorization for delegation of program authority to the Virginia Soil and Water Conservation Board, whichever is the latter." The U.S. Environmental Protection Agency approved the transfer of program authority to the Virginia Soil and Water Conservation Board in a letter dated December 30, 2004.

The 2004 amendments. — The 2004 amendment by c. 372 rewrote subsection A; throughout, substituted "permit issuing" for "permit-issuing"; and deleted "and the plan approving authority" following "authority" in subdivision B 1. For effective date, see Editor's note.

§ 10.1-603.12. Department to review local and state agency programs. — A. The Department shall develop and implement a review and evaluation schedule so that the effectiveness of each local government's and state agency's stormwater management program, Municipal Separate Storm Sewer Management Program, and other MS4 permit requirements is evaluated no less than every five years. The review shall include an assessment of the extent to which the program has reduced nonpoint source pollution and mitigated the detrimental effects of localized flooding.

B. If, after such a review and evaluation, a local government is found to have a program that does not comply with the provisions of this article or regulations adopted thereunder, the Board may issue an order requiring that necessary corrective action be taken within a reasonably prescribed time. If the local government has not implemented the corrective action identified by the Board within 30 days following receipt of the notice, or such additional period as is necessary to complete the implementation of the corrective action, then the Board shall take administrative and legal actions to ensure compliance with the provisions of this article. If the program is delegated to the locality by the Board, the Board may revoke such delegation and have the Department administer the program. (1989, cc. 467, 499; 2004, c. 372.)

Cross references. — For provisions of Acts 2004, c. 372, cls. 4 through 9, relating to the transfer of authority over stormwater discharge regulation to the Virginia Soil and Water Conservation Board, see the Editor's notes following § 10.1-603.2.

Editor's note. — Acts 2004, c. 372, cl. 3, provides: "That the provisions of the first enactment clause including the provisions that transfer the responsibility for administering the issuance of national pollutant discharge elimination system permits for the control of stormwater discharges from MS4 and construction activities shall become effective on January 1, 2005, or upon the U.S. Environmental Protection Agency's authorization for delegation of program authority to the Virginia Soil and Water Conservation Board, whichever is the latter." The U.S. Environmental Protection

Agency approved the transfer of program authority to the Virginia Soil and Water Conservation Board in a letter dated December 30, 2004.

The 2004 amendments. — The 2004 amendment by c. 372, in subsection A, in the first sentence, substituted "develop and implement a" for "periodically conduct a comprehensive" and "schedule so that" for "of," inserted the present second sentence, and deleted the former last sentence, which read: "A summary of these reviews and evaluations shall be submitted annually to the General Assembly"; in subsection B, in the first sentence, substituted "adopted" for "promulgated" and "Board" for "Department" and added the second and last sentences; and made a minor stylistic change. For effective date, see Editor's note.

§ **10.1-603.12:1. Right of entry.** — The Department, the permit issuing authority, or any duly authorized agent of the Department or permit issuing authority may, at reasonable times and under reasonable circumstances, enter any establishment or upon any property, public or private, for the purpose of obtaining information or conducting surveys or investigations necessary in the enforcement of the provisions of this article. (2004, c. 372.)

Cross references. — For provisions of Acts 2004, c. 372, cls. 4 through 9, relating to the transfer of authority over stormwater discharge regulation to the Virginia Soil and Water Conservation Board, see the Editor's notes following § 10.1-603.2.

Editor's note. — Acts 2004, c. 372, cl. 3, provides: "That the provisions of the first enactment clause including the provisions that transfer the responsibility for administering the issuance of national pollutant discharge elimination system permits for the control of

stormwater discharges from MS4 and construction activities shall become effective on January 1, 2005, or upon the U.S. Environmental Protection Agency's authorization for delegation of program authority to the Virginia Soil and Water Conservation Board, whichever is the latter." The U.S. Environmental Protection Agency approved the transfer of program authority to the Virginia Soil and Water Conservation Board in a letter dated December 30, 2004.

§ **10.1-603.12:2. Information to be furnished.** — The Board, the Department, or the permit issuing authority may require every permit applicant or permittee to furnish when requested such application materials, plans, specifications, and other pertinent information as may be necessary to determine the effect of his discharge on the quality of state waters, or such other information as may be necessary to accomplish the purposes of this article. Any personal information shall not be disclosed except to an appropriate official of the Board, Department, US EPA, or permit issuing authority or as may be authorized pursuant to the Virginia Freedom of Information Act (§ 2.2-3700 et seq.). However, disclosure of records of the Department, the Board, or the permit issuing authority relating to (i) active federal environmental enforcement actions that are considered confidential under federal law, (ii) enforcement strategies, including proposed sanctions for enforcement actions, and (iii) any secret formulae, secret processes, or secret methods other than effluent data used by any permitee or under that permitee's direction is prohibited. Upon request, such enforcement records shall be disclosed after a proposed sanction resulting from the investigation has been determined by the Department, the Board, or the permit issuing authority. This section shall not be construed to prohibit the disclosure of records related to inspection reports, notices of violation, and documents detailing the nature of any land disturbing activity that may have occurred, or similar documents. (2004, c. 372; 2005, c. 102.)

Cross references. — For provisions of Acts 2004, c. 372, cls. 4 through 9, relating to the transfer of authority over stormwater discharge regulation to the Virginia Soil and Water Conservation Board, see the Editor's notes following § 10.1-603.2.

Editor's note. — Acts 2004, c. 372, cl. 3, provides: "That the provisions of the first enactment clause including the provisions that transfer the responsibility for administering the issuance of national pollutant discharge elimination system permits for the control of stormwater discharges from MS4 and construction activities shall become effective on January 1, 2005, or upon the U.S. Environmental Protection Agency's authorization for delegation of program authority to the Virginia Soil and Water Conservation Board, whichever is the latter." The U.S. Environmental Protection Agency approved the transfer of program authority to the Virginia Soil and Water Conservation Board in a letter dated December 30, 2004.

Acts 2005, c. 102, cl. 2, provides: "That the Governor shall make new appointments for each of the three at-large members of the Board in accordance with the provisions of this act on July 1, 2005. The new appointments of the at-large members of the Board shall go into effect upon the expiration of the current members' terms in January 2006, and the terms shall be staggered as follows: one member for a term of two years; one member for a term of three years; and one member for a term of four years. The Governor shall designate the term to be served by each appointee at the time of appointment and may reappoint the existing at-large members of the Board."

Acts 2005, c. 102, cl. 3, provides: "That the Director of the Department of Conservation and Recreation shall amend the Stormwater Management Regulations by removing the out-of-date Best Management Practices (BMP) nutrient removal efficiency information and adding it into the Virginia Stormwater Management Handbook guidance document where it shall be more effectively updated for public use."

The 2005 amendments. — The 2005 amendment by c. 102 inserted "US EPA" in the second sentence, in the third sentence, deleted "and" preceding "(ii)," inserted "and" and split former clause (ii) into present clauses (ii) and (iii) and inserted "any secret formulae, secret processes, or secret methods other than effluent data used by any permitee or under that permitee's direction" in clause (iii) and inserted "enforcement" in the fourth sentence.

§ 10.1-603.12:3. Private rights not affected. — The fact that any permittee holds or has held a permit issued under this article shall not constitute a defense in any civil action involving private rights. (2004, c. 372.)

Cross references. — For provisions of Acts 2004, c. 372, cls. 4 through 9, relating to the transfer of authority over stormwater discharge regulation to the Virginia Soil and Water Conservation Board, see the Editor's notes following § 10.1-603.2.

Editor's note. — Acts 2004, c. 372, cl. 3, provides: "That the provisions of the first enactment clause including the provisions that transfer the responsibility for administering the issuance of national pollutant discharge elimination system permits for the control of stormwater discharges from MS4 and construction activities shall become effective on January 1, 2005, or upon the U.S. Environmental Protection Agency's authorization for delegation of program authority to the Virginia Soil and Water Conservation Board, whichever is the latter." The U.S. Environmental Protection Agency approved the transfer of program authority to the Virginia Soil and Water Conservation Board in a letter dated December 30, 2004.

§ 10.1-603.12:4. Enforcement by injunction, etc. — It shall be unlawful for any person to fail to comply with any special order or emergency special order that has become final under the provisions of this article. Any person violating or failing, neglecting, or refusing to obey any rule, regulation, ordinance, order, or any permit condition issued by the Board, Department, or permit issuing authority as authorized to do such, or any provisions of this article may be compelled in a proceeding instituted in any appropriate court by the Board, Department, or permit issuing authority to obey same and to comply therewith by injunction, mandamus or other appropriate remedy. (2004, c. 372.)

Cross references. — For provisions of Acts 2004, c. 372, cls. 4 through 9, relating to the transfer of authority over stormwater discharge regulation to the Virginia Soil and Water Conservation Board, see the Editor's notes following § 10.1-603.2.

Editor's note. — Acts 2004, c. 372, cl. 3, provides: "That the provisions of the first enactment clause including the provisions that transfer the responsibility for administering the issuance of national pollutant discharge elimination system permits for the control of stormwater discharges from MS4 and construction activities shall become effective on January 1, 2005, or upon the U.S. Environmental Protection Agency's authorization for delegation of program authority to the Virginia Soil and Water Conservation Board, whichever is the latter." The U.S. Environmental Protection Agency approved the transfer of program authority to the Virginia Soil and Water Conservation Board in a letter dated December 30, 2004.

§ 10.1-603.12:5. Testing validity of regulations; judicial review. —

A. The validity of any regulation adopted by the Board pursuant to this article may be determined through judicial review in accordance with the provisions of the Administrative Process Act (§ 2.2-4000 et seq.).

B. An appeal may be taken from the decision of the court to the Court of Appeals as provided by law. (2004, c. 372.)

Cross references. — For provisions of Acts 2004, c. 372, cls. 4 through 9, relating to the transfer of authority over stormwater discharge regulation to the Virginia Soil and Water Conservation Board, see the Editor's notes following § 10.1-603.2.

Editor's note. — Acts 2004, c. 372, cl. 3, provides: "That the provisions of the first enactment clause including the provisions that transfer the responsibility for administering the issuance of national pollutant discharge elimination system permits for the control of stormwater discharges from MS4 and construction activities shall become effective on January 1, 2005, or upon the U.S. Environmental Protection Agency's authorization for delegation of program authority to the Virginia Soil and Water Conservation Board, whichever is the latter." The U.S. Environmental Protection Agency approved the transfer of program authority to the Virginia Soil and Water Conservation Board in a letter dated December 30, 2004.

§ 10.1-603.12:6. Right to hearing. —

Any permit applicant or permittee under this article aggrieved by any action of the permit issuing authority or Board taken without a formal hearing, or by inaction of the permit issuing authority or Board, may demand in writing a formal hearing by the Board or locality causing such permit applicant's or permittee's grievance, provided a petition requesting such hearing is filed with the Board or the locality within 30 days after notice of such action. (2004, c. 372.)

Cross references. — For provisions of Acts 2004, c. 372, cls. 4 through 9, relating to the transfer of authority over stormwater discharge regulation to the Virginia Soil and Water Conservation Board, see the Editor's notes following § 10.1-603.2.

Editor's note. — Acts 2004, c. 372, cl. 3, provides: "That the provisions of the first enactment clause including the provisions that transfer the responsibility for administering the issuance of national pollutant discharge elimination system permits for the control of stormwater discharges from MS4 and construction activities shall become effective on January 1, 2005, or upon the U.S. Environmental Protection Agency's authorization for delegation of program authority to the Virginia Soil and Water Conservation Board, whichever is the latter." The U.S. Environmental Protection Agency approved the transfer of program authority to the Virginia Soil and Water Conservation Board in a letter dated December 30, 2004.

§ 10.1-603.12:7. Hearings. —

A. The hearings held under this article pertaining to the responsibilities or actions of the Board may be conducted by the Board itself at a regular or special meeting of the Board, or by at least one member of the Board designated by the chairman to conduct such hearings on behalf of the Board at any other time and place authorized by the Board.

B. A verbatim record of the proceedings of such hearings shall be taken and filed with the Board. Depositions may be taken and read as in actions at law.

C. The Board shall have power to issue subpoenas and subpoenas duces tecum, and at the request of any party shall issue such subpoenas. The failure of a witness without legal excuse to appear or to testify or to produce documents shall be acted upon by the Board in the manner prescribed in § 2.2-4022. Witnesses who are subpoenaed shall receive the same fees and reimbursement for mileage as in civil actions.

D. Localities holding hearings under this article shall do so in a manner consistent with this section. (2004, c. 372.)

Cross references. — For provisions of Acts 2004, c. 372, cls. 4 through 9, relating to the transfer of authority over stormwater discharge regulation to the Virginia Soil and Water Conservation Board, see the Editor's notes following § 10.1-603.2.

Editor's note. — Acts 2004, c. 372, cl. 3, provides: "That the provisions of the first enactment clause including the provisions that transfer the responsibility for administering the issuance of national pollutant discharge elimination system permits for the control of stormwater discharges from MS4 and construction activities shall become effective on January 1, 2005, or upon the U.S. Environmental Protection Agency's authorization for delegation of program authority to the Virginia Soil and Water Conservation Board, whichever is the latter." The U.S. Environmental Protection Agency approved the transfer of program authority to the Virginia Soil and Water Conservation Board in a letter dated December 30, 2004.

§ 10.1-603.13. Appeals. — Any permittee or party aggrieved by a permit or enforcement decision of the permit issuing authority or Board, or any person who has participated, in person or by submittal of written comments, in the public comment process related to a final decision of the permit issuing authority or Board under this article, whether such decision is affirmative or negative, is entitled to judicial review thereof in accordance with the provisions of the Administrative Process Act (§ 2.2-4000 et seq.) if such person meets the standard for obtaining judicial review of a case or controversy pursuant to Article III of the United States Constitution. A person shall be deemed to meet such standard if (i) such person has suffered an actual or imminent injury that is an invasion of a legally protected interest and that is concrete and particularized; (ii) such injury is fairly traceable to the decision of the permit issuing authority or the Board and not the result of the independent action of some third party not before the court; and (iii) such injury will likely be redressed by a favorable decision by the court.

The provisions of § 2.2-4030 shall not apply to decisions rendered by localities. (1989, cc. 467, 499; 2004, c. 372.)

Cross references. — For provisions of Acts 2004, c. 372, cls. 4 through 9, relating to the transfer of authority over stormwater discharge regulation to the Virginia Soil and Water Conservation Board, see the Editor's notes following § 10.1-603.2.

Editor's note. — Acts 2004, c. 372, cl. 3, provides: "That the provisions of the first enactment clause including the provisions that transfer the responsibility for administering the issuance of national pollutant discharge elimination system permits for the control of stormwater discharges from MS4 and construction activities shall become effective on January 1, 2005, or upon the U.S. Environmental Protection Agency's authorization for delegation of program authority to the Virginia Soil and Water Conservation Board, whichever is the latter." The U.S. Environmental Protection Agency approved the transfer of program authority to the Virginia Soil and Water Conservation Board in a letter dated December 30, 2004.

The 2004 amendments. — The 2004 amendment by c. 372 rewrote the section. For effective date, see Editor's note.

§ 10.1-603.13:1. Appeal to Court of Appeals. — From the final decision of the circuit court an appeal may be taken to the Court of Appeals as provided in § 17.1-405. (2004, c. 372.)

Cross references. — For provisions of Acts 2004, c. 372, cls. 4 through 9, relating to the transfer of authority over stormwater discharge regulation to the Virginia Soil and Water Conservation Board, see the Editor's notes following § 10.1-603.2.

Editor's note. — Acts 2004, c. 372, cl. 3, provides: "That the provisions of the first enactment clause including the provisions that transfer the responsibility for administering the issuance of national pollutant discharge elimination system permits for the control of stormwater discharges from MS4 and construction activities shall become effective on January 1, 2005, or upon the U.S. Environmental Protection Agency's authorization for delegation of program authority to the Virginia Soil and Water Conservation Board, whichever is the latter." The U.S. Environmental Protection Agency approved the transfer of program authority to the Virginia Soil and Water Conservation Board in a letter dated December 30, 2004.

§ 10.1-603.14. Penalties, injunctions, and other legal actions. — A. Any person who violates any provision of this article, or of any regulations or ordinances adopted hereunder, including those adopted pursuant to the conditions of an MS4 permit or who fails, neglects or refuses to comply with any order of the permit issuing authority, the Department, Board, or court, issued as herein provided, shall be subject to a civil penalty not to exceed $32,500 for each violation within the discretion of the court. Each day of violation of each requirement shall constitute a separate offense. The Board shall adopt a regulation establishing a schedule of civil penalties to be utilized by the permit issuing authority in enforcing the provisions of this article. The Board, Department, or permit issuing authority for the locality wherein the land lies may issue a summons for collection of the civil penalty and the action may be prosecuted in the appropriate circuit court. Any civil penalties assessed by a court as a result of a summons issued by a locality shall be paid into the treasury of the locality wherein the land lies, except where the violator is the locality itself, or its agent. When the penalties are assessed by the court as a result of a summons issued by the Board or Department, or where the violator is the locality itself, or its agent, the court shall direct the penalty to be paid into the state treasury and deposited by the State Treasurer into the Virginia Stormwater Management Fund established pursuant to § 10.1-603.4:1. Such civil penalties paid into the treasury of the locality in which the violation occurred are to be used for the purpose of minimizing, preventing, managing, or mitigating pollution of the waters of the locality and abating environmental pollution therein in such manner as the court may, by order, direct.

B. Any person who willfully or negligently violates any provision of this article, any regulation or order of the Board, order of the permit issuing authority or the Department, ordinance of any locality, any condition of a permit, or any order of a court shall be guilty of a misdemeanor punishable by confinement in jail for not more than 12 months and a fine of not less than $2,500 nor more than $32,500, either or both. Any person who knowingly violates any provision of this article, any regulation or order of the Board, order of the permit issuing authority or the Department, ordinance of any locality, any condition of a permit or any order of a court issued as herein provided, or who knowingly makes any false statement in any form required to be submitted under this article or knowingly renders inaccurate any monitoring device or method required to be maintained under this article, shall be guilty of a felony punishable by a term of imprisonment of not less than one year nor more than three years, or in the discretion of the jury or the court trying the case without a jury, confinement in jail for not more than 12 months and a fine of not less than $5,000 nor more than $50,000 for each violation. Any defendant that is not an individual shall, upon conviction of a violation under this subsection, be sentenced to pay a fine of not less than $10,000. Each day of violation of each requirement shall constitute a separate offense.

C. Any person who knowingly violates any provision of this article, and who knows at that time that he thereby places another person in imminent danger of death or serious bodily harm, shall, upon conviction, be guilty of a felony punishable by a term of imprisonment of not less than two years nor more than 15 years and a fine of not more than $250,000, either or both. A defendant that is not an individual shall, upon conviction of a violation under this subsection, be sentenced to pay a fine not exceeding the greater of $1 million or an amount that is three times the economic benefit realized by the defendant as a result of the offense. The maximum penalty shall be doubled with respect to both fine and imprisonment for any subsequent conviction of the same person under this subsection.

D. Violation of any provision of this article may also include the following sanctions:

1. The Board, Department, or the permit issuing authority may apply to the circuit court in any jurisdiction wherein the land lies to enjoin a violation or a threatened violation of the provisions of this article or of the local ordinance without the necessity of showing that an adequate remedy at law does not exist.

2. With the consent of any person who has violated or failed, neglected or refused to obey any ordinance, any condition of a permit, any regulation or order of the Board, any order of the permit issuing authority or the Department, or any provision of this article, the Board, Department, or permit issuing authority may provide, in an order issued against such person, for the payment of civil charges for violations in specific sums, not to exceed the limit specified in this section. Such civil charges shall be instead of any appropriate civil penalty that could be imposed under this section. Any civil charges collected shall be paid to the locality or state treasury pursuant to subsection A. (1989, cc. 467, 499; 2004, c. 372; 2006, c. 171.)

Cross references. — For provisions of Acts 2004, c. 372, cls. 4 through 9, relating to the transfer of authority over stormwater discharge regulation to the Virginia Soil and Water Conservation Board, see the Editor's notes following § 10.1-603.2.

Editor's note. — Acts 2004, c. 372, cl. 3, provides: "That the provisions of the first enactment clause including the provisions that transfer the responsibility for administering the issuance of national pollutant discharge elimination system permits for the control of stormwater discharges from MS4 and construction activities shall become effective on January 1, 2005, or upon the U.S. Environmental Protection Agency's authorization for delegation of program authority to the Virginia Soil

and Water Conservation Board, whichever is the latter." The U.S. Environmental Protection Agency approved the transfer of program authority to the Virginia Soil and Water Conservation Board in a letter dated December 30, 2004.

The 2004 amendments. — The 2004 amendment by c. 372 rewrote the section. For effective date, see Editor's note.

The 2006 amendments. — The 2006 amendment by c. 171, in subsection A, in the first sentence, inserted "including those adopted pursuant to the conditions of an MS4 permit" and substituted "$32,500" for "$25,000"; and substituted $32,500" for "$25,000" in the first sentence of subsection B.

§ 10.1-603.15. Cooperation with federal and state agencies. — Localities operating their own programs and the Department are authorized to cooperate and enter into agreements with any federal or state agency in connection with permits for land disturbing activities for stormwater management. (1989, cc. 467, 499; 2004, c. 372.)

Cross references. — For provisions of Acts 2004, c. 372, cls. 4 through 9, relating to the

transfer of authority over stormwater discharge regulation to the Virginia Soil and Water Conservation Board, see the Editor's notes following § 10.1-603.2.

Editor's note. — Acts 2004, c. 372, cl. 3, provides: "That the provisions of the first enactment clause including the provisions that transfer the responsibility for administering the issuance of national pollutant discharge elimination system permits for the control of stormwater discharges from MS4 and construction activities shall become effective on January 1, 2005, or upon the U.S. Environmental Protection Agency's authorization for delega-tion of program authority to the Virginia Soil and Water Conservation Board, whichever is the latter." The U.S. Environmental Protection Agency approved the transfer of program authority to the Virginia Soil and Water Conservation Board in a letter dated December 30, 2004.

The 2004 amendments. — The 2004 amendment by c. 372 substituted "permits for land disturbing activities" for "plans." For effective date, see Editor's note.

ARTICLE 1.2.

Flood Prevention and Protection Assistance Fund.

§ 10.1-603.16. Definitions. — As used in this article unless the context requires a different meaning:

"*Authority*" means the Virginia Resources Authority created in Chapter 21 (§ 62.1-197 et seq.) of Title 62.1.

"*Board*" means the Board of Directors of the Virginia Resources Authority.

"*Cost*," as applied to any project financed under the provisions of this article, means the total of all costs incurred by the local government or private entity as reasonable and necessary for carrying out all works and undertakings necessary or incident to the accomplishment of any project. It includes, without limitation, all necessary developmental, planning and feasibility studies, surveys, plans and specifications; hydrologic and hydraulic studies and analyses; architectural, engineering, financial, legal or other special services; mapping; the cost of acquisition of flood-prone land and any buildings and improvements thereon, including the discharge of any obligations of the sellers of such land, buildings or improvements; site preparation and development, including demolition or removal of existing structures; construction and reconstruction; labor; materials, machinery and equipment; the reasonable costs of financing incurred by the local government or private entity in the course of the development of the project; carrying charges incurred before placing the project in service; necessary expenses incurred in connection with placing the project in service; the funding of accounts and reserves that the Authority may require; and the cost of other items that the Authority determines to be reasonable and necessary.

"*Dam owner*" means the owner of the land on which a dam is situated, the holder of an easement permitting the construction of a dam and any person or entity agreeing to maintain a dam.

"*Department*" means the Department of Conservation and Recreation.

"*Director*" means the Director of the Department of Conservation and Recreation.

"*Flood prevention or protection*" means the construction of dams, levees, flood walls, channel improvements or diversions, local flood proofing, evacuation of flood-prone areas or land use controls which reduce or mitigate damage from flooding.

"*Flood prevention or protection studies*" means hydraulic and hydrologic studies of flood plains with historic and predicted floods, the assessment of flood risk and the development of strategies to prevent or mitigate damage from flooding.

"*Fund*" or "*revolving fund*" means the Dam Safety, Flood Prevention and Protection Assistance Fund.

"*Local funds*" means cash provided for project or study implementation that is not derived from federal or state grants or loans.

"*Local government*" means any county, city, town, municipal corporation, authority, district, commission, or political subdivision created by the General Assembly or pursuant to the Constitution or laws of the Commonwealth, or any combination of any two or more of the foregoing.

"*Private entities*" means dam owners, whether individuals, partnerships, corporations, or other nongovernmental entities.

"*Project*" means the development and implementation of activities or measures performed to eliminate, prevent, reduce, or mitigate damages caused by flooding or to identify flood hazards; the design, repair, and safety modifications of a dam or impounding structure, as defined in § 10.1-604, and identified in dam safety reports generated pursuant to § 10.1-607 or 10.1-609; or the mapping and digitization of dam break inundation zones. The term includes, without limitation, the construction, modification or repair of dams, levees, flood walls, channel improvements or diversions; evacuation, relocation, and retrofitting of flood-prone structures; flood warning and response systems; redevelopment, acquisition, and open-space use of flood-prone areas; hydrologic and hydraulic studies of floodplains with historic and predicted floods; remapping of regulated flood hazard areas; the assessment of flood risks; the development of flood hazard mitigation strategies and plans, flood prevention and protection studies, and matching funds for federal funds for these activities. The lands involved with such projects shall be located within the Commonwealth. (1989, cc. 462, 498; 1995, c. 510; 2002, c. 320; 2006, cc. 648, 765.)

The numbers of §§ 10.1-603.16 through 10.1-603.23 were assigned by the Code Commission, the numbers in the 1989 act having been 10.1-603.1 through 10.1-603.8.

Editor's note. — Acts 2006, cc. 648 and 765, cl. 3, provide: "That the Department of Conservation and Recreation shall repeal through an exempt action the Flood Prevention and Protection Assistance Fund Regulations (4 VAC 5-50-10 et seq.)."

Acts 2006, cc. 648 and 765, cl. 4, provide: "That upon the effective date of this act, the Department of Accounts, with the concurrence of the Department of Conservation and Recreation, may transfer the Dam Safety, Flood Prevention and Protection Assistance Fund and its unobligated balance to the Virginia Resources Authority to be administered and managed in accordance with this act."

The 2006 amendments. — The 2006 amendments by cc. 648 and 765 are identical, and inserted the paragraphs defining "Authority," "Board" and "Cost"; inserted "Dam Safety" in the paragraph defining "Fund"; deleted the paragraph defining "Local public body"; and added the paragraphs defining "Local government," "Private entities" and "Project."

§ 10.1-603.17. Dam Safety, Flood Prevention and Protection Assistance Fund established.

— The Dam Safety, Flood Prevention and Protection Assistance Fund is hereby established and set apart as a permanent and nonreverting fund. The Fund shall consist of any moneys appropriated by the General Assembly, funds returned by localities or other public or private sources in the form of interest and repayment of loan principal, deposits pursuant to § 38.2-401.1, all income from the investment of moneys held in the Fund, and any other sums designated for deposit in the Fund from any source public or private, including without limitation any federal grants, and awards or other forms of assistance received by the Commonwealth that are eligible for deposit in the Fund under federal law. Any moneys remaining in the Fund at the end of the biennium including any appropriated funds and all principal interest accrued, interest and payments shall not revert to the general fund. (1989, cc. 462, 498; 2002, c. 320; 2006, cc. 648, 765.)

Cross references. — As to civil penalties and program administration fees to be paid into the Flood Prevention and Protection Assistance Fund, see §§ 10.1-613.2 and 10.1-613.5, respectively.

Editor's note. — Acts 2006, cc. 648 and 765,

cl. 3, provide: "That the Department of Conservation and Recreation shall repeal through an exempt action the Flood Prevention and Protection Assistance Fund Regulations (4 VAC 5-50-10 et seq.)."

Acts 2006, cc. 648 and 765, cl. 4, provide: "That upon the effective date of this act, the Department of Accounts, with the concurrence of the Department of Conservation and Recreation, may transfer the Dam Safety, Flood Prevention and Protection Assistance Fund and its unobligated balance to the Virginia Resources Authority to be administered and managed in accordance with this act."

The 2006 amendments. — The 2006 amendments by cc. 648 and 765 are identical, and added "Dam Safety" at the beginning of the section heading; in the first sentence, inserted "Dam Safety" and added "and set apart as a permanent and nonreverting fund" at the end, and in the second sentence, added the language beginning "deposits pursuant to § 38.2-401.1" and made a related change.

§ 10.1-603.18. Administration of the Fund. — The Authority shall administer and manage the Fund, and establish the interest rates and the repayment terms of such loans as provided in this article, in accordance with a memorandum of agreement with the Director. The Director shall, after consultation with all interested parties, develop a guidance document governing project eligibility and project priority criteria, and the Director, upon approval from the Virginia Soil and Water Conservation Board, shall direct the distribution of loans from the Fund to local governments and private entities and the distribution of grants to local governments. In order to carry out the administration and management of the Fund, the Authority may employ officers, employees, agents, advisers and consultants, including without limitation, attorneys, financial advisors, engineers, and other technical advisors and public accountants, and determine their duties and compensation without the approval of any other agency or instrumentality. The Authority may disburse from the Fund reasonable costs and expenses incurred in the administration and management of the Fund and may establish and collect a reasonable fee for its management services. However, any such fee shall not exceed one-eighth of one percent of any bond par, loan or grant amount. (1989, cc. 462, 498; 1995, c. 510; 2002, c. 320; 2006, cc. 648, 765.)

Editor's note. — Acts 2006, cc. 648 and 765, cl. 3, provide: "That the Department of Conservation and Recreation shall repeal through an exempt action the Flood Prevention and Protection Assistance Fund Regulations (4 VAC 5-50-10 et seq.)."

Acts 2006, cc. 648 and 765, cl. 4, provide: "That upon the effective date of this act, the Department of Accounts, with the concurrence of the Department of Conservation and Recreation, may transfer the Dam Safety, Flood Prevention and Protection Assistance Fund and its unobligated balance to the Virginia Resources Authority to be administered and managed in accordance with this act."

The 2006 amendments. — The 2006 amendments by cc. 648 and 765 are identical, and rewrote the section.

§ 10.1-603.18:1. Deposit of money; expenditures; investments. — All money belonging to the Fund shall be deposited in an account or accounts in banks or trust companies organized under the laws of the Commonwealth or in national banking associations located in Virginia or in savings institutions located in Virginia organized under the laws of the Commonwealth or the United States. The money in these accounts shall be paid by check signed by the Executive Director of the Authority or other officers or employees designated by the Board of Directors of the Authority. All deposits of money shall, if required by the Authority, be secured in a manner determined by the Authority to be prudent, and all banks, trust companies, and savings institutions are authorized to give security for the deposits. Money in the Fund shall not be commingled with other money of the Authority. Money in the Fund not needed for immediate use or disbursement may be invested or reinvested by the Authority in obligations or securities that are considered lawful investments for public funds under the laws of the Commonwealth. (2006, cc. 648, 765.)

Editor's note. — Acts 2006, cc. 648 and 765, cl. 3, provide: "That the Department of Conservation and Recreation shall repeal through an exempt action the Flood Prevention and Protection Assistance Fund Regulations (4 VAC 5-50-10 et seq.)."

Acts 2006, cc. 648 and 765, cl. 4, provide: "That upon the effective date of this act, the Department of Accounts, with the concurrence of the Department of Conservation and Recreation, may transfer the Dam Safety, Flood Prevention and Protection Assistance Fund and its unobligated balance to the Virginia Resources Authority to be administered and managed in accordance with this act."

§ 10.1-603.18:2. Collection of money due Fund. — The Authority is empowered to collect, or to authorize others to collect on its behalf, amounts due to the Fund under any loan to a local government or private entity, including, if appropriate, taking the action required by § 15.2-2659 or 62.1-216.1 to obtain payment of any amounts in default. Proceedings to recover amounts due to the Fund may be instituted by the Authority in the name of the Fund in the appropriate circuit court. (2006, cc. 648, 765.)

Editor's note. — Acts 2006, cc. 648 and 765, cl. 3, provide: "That the Department of Conservation and Recreation shall repeal through an exempt action the Flood Prevention and Protection Assistance Fund Regulations (4 VAC 5-50-10 et seq.)."

Acts 2006, cc. 648 and 765, cl. 4, provide: "That upon the effective date of this act, the Department of Accounts, with the concurrence of the Department of Conservation and Recreation, may transfer the Dam Safety, Flood Prevention and Protection Assistance Fund and its unobligated balance to the Virginia Resources Authority to be administered and managed in accordance with this act."

§ 10.1-603.19. Purposes for which Fund is to be used; Authority to set terms and conditions of loans. — A. The Director is authorized to make grants or loans to any local government for the purpose of assisting the local government in the development and implementation of flood prevention or protection projects, or for flood prevention or protection studies.

B. The Director is authorized to expend from the Fund up to $50,000 annually for cost share with federal agencies in flood protection studies of statewide or regional significance.

C. The Director is also authorized, in order to protect public safety and welfare, to make grants or loans to local governments owning dams and to make loans to private entities for the design, repair and the safety modifications of dams identified in safety reports generated pursuant to § 10.1-607 or 10.1-609, and to make grants for the mapping and digitization of dam break inundation zones.

D. The total amount of expenditures for grants in any fiscal year shall not exceed 50% of the total amount collected in interest or income from the investment of moneys in the Fund from the previous fiscal year as determined at the beginning of the fiscal year.

E. Any grants made from the Fund shall require a 50% project match by the local government applicant. Any loans made from the Fund shall require a minimum of a 10% project match by the applicant.

F. Except as otherwise provided in this article, money in the Fund shall be used solely to make loans or grants to local governments, or loans to private entities to finance or refinance the cost of a project. The local government or private entity to which loans or grants are made, the purposes of the loan or grant, the required match for the specific loan or grant, and the amount of each loan or grant, shall be designated in writing by the Director to the Authority. No loan or grant from the Fund shall exceed the total cost of the project to be financed or the outstanding principal amount of the indebtedness to be refinanced plus reasonable financing expenses. Loans may also be from the Fund, at the Director's discretion, to a local government that has developed a low-interest loan program to provide loans or other incentives to facilitate the correction of dam or impounding structure deficiencies, as required by the Department, provided that the moneys are to be used only for the program and that the dams or impounding structures to be repaired or upgraded are owned by private entities.

G. Except as otherwise provided in this article, the Authority shall determine the interest rate and terms and conditions of any loan from the Fund, which may vary between different loans and between local governments and private entities to finance or refinance the cost of a project. Each loan shall be evidenced by appropriate bonds or notes of the local government or by the appropriate debt instrument for private entities payable to the Fund. Private entities shall duly authorize an appropriate debt instrument and execute same by their authorized legal representatives. The bonds or notes shall have been duly authorized by the local government and executed by its authorized legal representatives. The Authority may require in connection with any loan from the Fund such documents, instruments, certificates, legal opinions, covenants, conditions, and other information as it may deem necessary or convenient to further the purpose of the loan. In addition to any other terms or conditions that the Authority may establish, the Authority may require, as a condition to making any loan from the Fund, that the local government or private entity receiving the loan covenant to perform any of the following:

1. Establish and collect rents, rates, fees, and charges to produce revenue sufficient to pay all or a specified portion of (i) the costs of operation, maintenance, replacement, renewal, and repairs of the project; (ii) any outstanding indebtedness incurred for the purposes of the project, including the principal of, premium, if any, and interest on the loan from the Fund; and (iii) any amounts necessary to create and maintain any required reserve, including any rate stabilization fund deemed necessary or appropriate by the Authority to offset the need, in whole or part, for future increases in rents, rates, fees, or charges;

2. With respect to local governments, levy and collect ad valorem taxes on all property within the jurisdiction of the local government subject to local taxation sufficient to pay the principal of and premium, if any, and interest on the loan from the Fund to the local government;

3. Create and maintain a special fund or funds for the payment of the principal of, premium, if any, and interest on the loan from the Fund and any other amounts becoming due under any agreement entered into in connection with the loan, or for the operation, maintenance, repair, or replacement of the project or any portions thereof or other property of the borrower, and deposit into any fund or funds amounts sufficient to make any payments on the loan as they become due and payable;

4. Create and maintain other special funds as required by the Authority;

5. Perform other acts otherwise permitted by applicable law to secure payment of the principal of, premium, if any, and interest on the loan from the Fund and to provide for the remedies of the Fund in the event of any default by the borrower in payment of the loan, including, without limitation, any of the following:

a. The conveyance of, or the granting of liens on or security interests in, real and personal property, together with all rights, title and interest therein;

b. The procurement of insurance, guarantees, letters of credit and other forms of collateral, security, liquidity arrangements or credit supports for the loan from any source, public or private, and the payment therefor of premiums, fees, or other charges;

c. The combination of one or more projects, or the combination of one or more projects with one or more other undertakings, facilities, utilities, or systems, for the purpose of operations and financing, and the pledging of the revenues from such combined projects, undertakings, facilities, utilities and systems to secure the loan from the Fund borrower made in connection with such combination or any part or parts thereof;

    d. The maintenance, replacement, renewal, and repair of the project; and

    e. The procurement of casualty and liability insurance.

    6. Obtain a review of the accounting and internal controls from the Auditor of Public Accounts or his legally authorized representatives, as applicable. The Authority may request additional reviews at any time during the term of the loan. In addition, anyone receiving a report in accordance with § 10.1-603.23 may request an additional review as set forth in this section; and

    7. Directly offer, pledge, and consent to the Authority to take action pursuant to § 62.1-216.1 to obtain payment of any amounts in default, as applicable.

All local governments or private entities borrowing money from the Fund are authorized to perform any acts, take any action, adopt any proceedings, and make and carry out any contracts that are contemplated by this article. Such contracts need not be identical among all local governments or private entities, but may be structured as determined by the Authority according to the needs of the contracting local governments or private entities and the Fund.

Subject to the rights, if any, of the registered owners of any of the bonds of the Authority, the Authority may consent to and approve any modification in the terms of any loan to any local government. (1989, cc. 462, 498; 1995, c. 510; 2002, c. 320; 2005, c. 80; 2006, cc. 648, 765.)

Editor's note. — Acts 2006, cc. 648 and 765, cl. 3, provide: "That the Department of Conservation and Recreation shall repeal through an exempt action the Flood Prevention and Protection Assistance Fund Regulations (4 VAC 5-50-10 et seq.)."

Acts 2006, cc. 648 and 765, cl. 4, provide: "That upon the effective date of this act, the Department of Accounts, with the concurrence of the Department of Conservation and Recreation, may transfer the Dam Safety, Flood Prevention and Protection Assistance Fund and its unobligated balance to the Virginia Resources Authority to be administered and managed in accordance with this act."

The 2005 amendments. — The 2005 amendment by c. 80 inserted "and to make grants for the mapping and digitization of dam break inundation zones" in subsection C, and made minor stylistic changes.

The 2006 amendments. — The 2006 amendments by cc. 648 and 765 are identical, and rewrote the section.

§ 10.1-603.20. Condition for making loans or grants.

— A. The Director may authorize a loan or grant for flood prevention or protection projects, or for flood prevention or protection studies under the provisions of § 10.1-603.19 only when the following conditions exist:

    1. An application for the loan or grant has been submitted by an applicant in the manner and form specified by the Director, setting forth the amount of the loan or grant requested, and the use to which the loan or grant will be applied. The application shall describe in detail (i) the area to be studied or protected, including the population and the value of property to be protected, historic flooding data and hydrologic studies projecting flood frequency; (ii) the estimated cost-benefit ratio of the project; (iii) the ability of the locality to provide its share of the cost; (iv) the administration of local flood plain management regulations; and (v) other necessary information to establish project or study priority.

    2. The local government agrees and furnishes assurance, satisfactory to the Director, that it will satisfactorily maintain any structure financed, in whole or in part, through the loans or grants provided under this article.

    3. If the requested loan or grant is sought to acquire land, the Director shall require satisfactory evidence prior to acting on the request that the local government will acquire the land if the loan or grant is made.

4. A local government is eligible to receive a grant once every five years, provided that it has a flood mitigation plan approved by the Director and has demonstrated satisfactory evidence of plan implementation. Lacking an approved plan the local government is eligible for a grant once every ten years.

5. [Repealed.]

B. The Director shall develop guidance criteria for making loans and grants for dam safety repair projects. Priority shall be given to making loans for high hazard dams. (1989, cc. 462, 498; 1995, c. 510; 2002, c. 320; 2006, cc. 648, 765.)

Editor's note. — Acts 2006, cc. 648 and 765, in cl. 3 provide: "That the Department of Conservation and Recreation shall repeal through an exempt action the Flood Prevention and Protection Assistance Fund Regulations (4 VAC 5-50-10 et seq.)."

Acts 2006, cc. 648 and 765, in cl. 4 provide: "That upon the effective date of this act, the Department of Accounts, with the concurrence of the Department of Conservation and Recreation, may transfer the Dam Safety, Flood Prevention and Protection Assistance Fund and its unobligated balance to the Virginia Resources Authority to be administered and managed in accordance with this act."

The 2006 amendments. — The 2006 amendments by cc. 648 and 765 are identical, and substituted "an applicant" for "the applicant" in the first sentence of subdivision A 1; substituted "government" for "public body" in subdivisions A 2, present A 3 and twice in present A 4; deleted former subdivision A 3; redesignated former subdivisions A 4 through A 6 as subdivisions A 3 through A 5; deleted former subsections B and C; and added present subsection B.

§§ 10.1-603.21, 10.1-603.22: Repealed by Acts 2006, cc. 648 and 765, cl. 2.

Editor's note. — Acts 2006, cc. 648 and 765, in cl. 3 provide: "That the Department of Conservation and Recreation shall repeal through an exempt action the Flood Prevention and Protection Assistance Fund Regulations (4 VAC 5-50-10 et seq.)."

Acts 2006, cc. 648 and 765, in cl. 4 provide: "That upon the effective date of this act, the Department of Accounts, with the concurrence of the Department of Conservation and Recreation, may transfer the Dam Safety, Flood Prevention and Protection Assistance Fund and its unobligated balance to the Virginia Resources Authority to be administered and managed in accordance with this act."

§ 10.1-603.22:1. Pledge of loans to secure bonds of Authority. — The Authority is empowered at any time and from time to time to pledge, assign, or transfer from the Fund to banks or trust companies designated by the Authority any or all of the assets of the Fund to be held in trust as security for the payment of the principal of, premium, if any, and interest on any or all of the bonds, as defined in § 62.1-199, issued to finance any project. The interests of the Fund in any assets so transferred shall be subordinate to the rights of the trustee under the pledge, assignment, or transfer. To the extent funds are not available from other sources pledged for such purpose, any of the assets or payments of principal and interest received on the assets pledged, assigned, or transferred or held in trust may be applied by the trustee thereof to the payment of the principal of, premium, if any, and interest on such bonds of the Authority secured thereby, and, if such payments are insufficient for such purpose, the trustee is empowered to sell any or all of such assets and apply the net proceeds from the sale to the payment of the principal of, premium, if any, and interest on such bonds of the Authority. Any assets of the Fund pledged, assigned, or transferred in trust as set forth above and any payments of principal, interest, or earnings received thereon shall remain part of the Fund but shall be subject to the pledge, assignment, or transfer to secure the bonds of the Authority and shall be held by the trustee to which they are pledged, assigned, or transferred until no longer required for such purpose by the terms of the pledge, assignment, or transfer. (2006, cc. 648, 765.)

Editor's note. — Acts 2006, cc. 648 and 765, in cl. 3 provide: "That the Department of Conservation and Recreation shall repeal through an exempt action the Flood Prevention and Protection Assistance Fund Regulations (4 VAC 5-50-10 et seq.)."

Acts 2006, cc. 648 and 765, in cl. 4 provide: "That upon the effective date of this act, the Department of Accounts, with the concurrence of the Department of Conservation and Recreation, may transfer the Dam Safety, Flood Prevention and Protection Assistance Fund and its unobligated balance to the Virginia Resources Authority to be administered and managed in accordance with this act."

§ 10.1-603.22:2. Sale of loans. — The Authority is empowered at any time and from time to time to sell, upon such terms and conditions as the Authority shall deem appropriate, any loan, or interest therein, made pursuant to this article. The net proceeds of sale remaining after the payment of the costs and expenses of the sale shall be designated for deposit to, and become part of, the Fund. (2006, cc. 648, 765.)

Editor's note. — Acts 2006, cc. 648 and 765, in cl. 3 provide: "That the Department of Conservation and Recreation shall repeal through an exempt action the Flood Prevention and Protection Assistance Fund Regulations (4 VAC 5-50-10 et seq.)."

Acts 2006, cc. 648 and 765, in cl. 4 provide: "That upon the effective date of this act, the Department of Accounts, with the concurrence of the Department of Conservation and Recreation, may transfer the Dam Safety, Flood Prevention and Protection Assistance Fund and its unobligated balance to the Virginia Resources Authority to be administered and managed in accordance with this act."

§ 10.1-603.22:3. Powers of the Authority. — The Authority is authorized to do any act necessary or convenient to the exercise of the powers granted in this article or reasonably implied thereby. (2006, cc. 648, 765.)

Editor's note. — Acts 2006, cc. 648 and 765, in cl. 3 provide: "That the Department of Conservation and Recreation shall repeal through an exempt action the Flood Prevention and Protection Assistance Fund Regulations (4 VAC 5-50-10 et seq.)."

Acts 2006, cc. 648 and 765, in cl. 4 provide: "That upon the effective date of this act, the Department of Accounts, with the concurrence of the Department of Conservation and Recreation, may transfer the Dam Safety, Flood Prevention and Protection Assistance Fund and its unobligated balance to the Virginia Resources Authority to be administered and managed in accordance with this act."

§ 10.1-603.22:4. Liberal construction of article. — The provisions of this article shall be liberally construed to the end that its beneficial purposes may be effectuated. Insofar as the provisions of this article are inconsistent with the provisions of any other law, general, special or local, the provisions of this article shall be controlling. (2006, cc. 648, 765.)

Editor's note. — Acts 2006, cc. 648 and 765, in cl. 3 provide: "That the Department of Conservation and Recreation shall repeal through an exempt action the Flood Prevention and Protection Assistance Fund Regulations (4 VAC 5-50-10 et seq.)."

Acts 2006, cc. 648 and 765, in cl. 4 provide: "That upon the effective date of this act, the Department of Accounts, with the concurrence of the Department of Conservation and Recreation, may transfer the Dam Safety, Flood Prevention and Protection Assistance Fund and its unobligated balance to the Virginia Resources Authority to be administered and managed in accordance with this act."

§ 10.1-603.23. Record of application for grants or loans and action taken. — A record of each application for a grant or loan and the action taken thereon shall be open to public inspection at the office of the Department. The Authority shall report annually to the General Assembly and the Governor on the Fund and the administration of all grants and loans made from the Fund. (1989, cc. 462, 498; 2006, cc. 648, 765.)

Editor's note. — Acts 2006, cc. 648 and 765, in cl. 3 provide: "That the Department of Conservation and Recreation shall repeal through an exempt action the Flood Prevention and Protection Assistance Fund Regulations (4 VAC 5-50-10 et seq.)."

Acts 2006, cc. 648 and 765, in cl. 4 provide: "That upon the effective date of this act, the Department of Accounts, with the concurrence of the Department of Conservation and Recreation, may transfer the Dam Safety, Flood Prevention and Protection Assistance Fund and its unobligated balance to the Virginia Resources Authority to be administered and managed in accordance with this act."

The 2006 amendments. — The 2006 amendments by cc. 648 and 765 are identical, and in the first sentence, deleted "pursuant to § 10.1-603.19" following "grant or loan" and "and shall be presented to the Governor and members of the legislature prior to budgetary sessions of the General Assembly" following "Department" and added the last sentence.

ARTICLE 2.

Dam Safety Act.

§ **10.1-604. Definitions.** — As used in this article, unless the context requires a different meaning:

"Alteration" means changes to an impounding structure that could alter or affect its structural integrity. Alterations include, but are not limited to, changing the height or otherwise enlarging the dam, increasing normal pool or principal spillway elevation or physical dimensions, changing the elevation or physical dimensions of the emergency spillway, conducting necessary repairs or structural maintenance, or removing the impounding structure.

"Board" means the Soil and Water Conservation Board.

"Construction" means the construction of a new impounding structure.

"Dam break inundation zone" means the area downstream of a dam that would be inundated or otherwise directly affected by the failure of a dam.

"Height" means the structural height of a dam which is defined as the vertical distance from the natural bed of the stream or watercourse measured at the downstream toe of the dam to the top of the dam.

"Impounding structure" means a man-made structure, whether a dam across a watercourse or other structure outside a watercourse, used or to be used to retain or store waters or other materials. The term includes: (i) all dams that are twenty-five feet or greater in height and that create an impoundment capacity of fifteen acre-feet or greater, and (ii) all dams that are six feet or greater in height and that create an impoundment capacity of fifty acre-feet or greater. The term "impounding structure" shall not include: (a) dams licensed by the State Corporation Commission that are subject to a safety inspection program; (b) dams owned or licensed by the United States government; (c) dams operated primarily for agricultural purposes which are less than twenty-five feet in height or which create a maximum impoundment capacity smaller than 100 acre-feet; (d) water or silt retaining dams approved pursuant to § 45.1-222 or § 45.1-225.1; or (e) obstructions in a canal used to raise or lower water.

"Owner" means the owner of the land on which a dam is situated, the holder of an easement permitting the construction of a dam and any person or entity agreeing to maintain a dam.

"Watercourse" means a natural channel having a well-defined bed and banks and in which water normally flows. (1982, c. 583, § 62.1-115.1; 1986, c. 9; 1988, c. 891; 2001, c. 92; 2006, c. 30.)

The 2006 amendments. — The 2006 amendment by c. 30 added the paragraphs defining "Alteration," "Construction," and "Dam break inundation zone"; and in the definition for "Impounding structure," substituted "man-made structure" for "man-made device" in the first sentence and deleted "constructed maintained or" following "(c) dams."

§ **10.1-605. Promulgation of regulations by the Board.** — The Board shall promulgate regulations to ensure that impounding structures in the Commonwealth are properly and safely constructed, maintained and operated. Dam safety regulations promulgated by the State Water Control Board shall remain in full force until amended in accordance with applicable procedures. (1982, c. 583, § 62.1-115.2; 1986, c. 9; 1988, c. 891.)

§ **10.1-605.1. Delegation of powers and duties.** — The Board may delegate to the Director or his designee any of the powers and duties vested in the Board by this article, except the adoption and promulgation of regulations or the issuance of certificates. Delegation shall not remove from the Board authority to enforce the provisions of this article. (2006, c. 30.)

§ **10.1-606. Local advisory committee.** — When requested by the governing body of any affected county or city, the Board shall provide for the creation of a local advisory committee to advise the Board on impoundments within that locality. The advisory committee shall include, but not be limited to, representation of the owner and each affected county or city. Prior to the issuance of any permits under this article, the Board shall advise any existing local advisory committee of any affected jurisdiction for which a permit is being sought, and request comments from the committee on the permit application. No permit shall be issued until at least sixty days after such a local advisory committee has been so advised. (1982, c. 583, § 62.1-115.3; 1984, c. 240; 1988, c. 891.)

§ **10.1-606.1. Authority for localities to map dam break inundation zones.** — A. Any county, city, or town may map dam break inundation zones and is encouraged to incorporate such information into its zoning and subdivision ordinances. Such localities may regulate or limit future development in these areas. However, in no event shall this section be interpreted to supersede or conflict with the authority granted to the Department of Mines, Minerals and Energy for the regulation of mineral extraction activities in the Commonwealth as set out in Title 45.1.

B. The Director may utilize grant funding available from the Dam Safety, Flood Prevention and Protection Assistance Fund and other available sources of funding to assist localities in the development of these maps, provided the localities contribute a local match. The highest priority for awarding funds shall be placed on assisting with the mapping of the highest class of dams.

C. Such maps shall be made available by the locality to the dam owner and the public. All properties identified within the dam break inundation zone shall be incorporated into the dam safety emergency action plan of that dam so as to ensure the proper notification of persons downstream and other affected persons or property owners in the event of a flood hazard or the impending failure of the impounding structure. (2005, c. 80; 2006, cc. 30, 648, 765.)

Editor's note. — Acts 2006, cc. 648 and 765, in cl. 3 provide: "That the Department of Conservation and Recreation shall repeal through an exempt action the Flood Prevention and Protection Assistance Fund Regulations (4 VAC 5-50-10 et seq.)."

Acts 2006, cc. 648 and 765, in cl. 4 provide: "That upon the effective date of this act, the Department of Accounts, with the concurrence of the Department of Conservation and Recreation, may transfer the Dam Safety, Flood Prevention and Protection Assistance Fund and its unobligated balance to the Virginia Resources Authority to be administered and managed in accordance with this act."

The 2006 amendments. — The 2006

amendment by c. 30 inserted "dam break" preceding "inundation zone" in subsections A and C.

The 2006 amendments by cc. 648 and 765 are identical, and inserted "Dam Safety" in the first sentence of subsection B.

§ 10.1-607. Safety inspections. — No one shall maintain a dam which unreasonably threatens the life or property of another. The Board shall cause safety inspections to be made of impounding structures on such schedule as it deems appropriate. The time of the initial inspection and the frequency of reinspection shall depend on such factors as the condition of the structure and its size, type, location and downstream hazard potential. The owners of dams found to have deficiencies which could threaten life or property if not corrected shall take the corrective actions needed to remove such deficiencies within a reasonable time. All safety inspections shall be conducted by or under the supervision of a licensed professional engineer. Each report shall bear the seal and signature of the licensed professional engineer responsible for the inspection.

The Board shall be responsible for the inspection and reinspection of flood control dams where the maintenance and operation of the dam is the responsibility of a soil and water conservation district and where the permit for operation of the impounding structure is held by such a district. (1982, c. 583, § 62.1-115.4; 1986, c. 209; 1988, c. 891; 2000, c. 14.)

§ 10.1-607.1. Criteria for designating a dam as unsafe. — A. Designation of a dam as unsafe shall be based on one or more of the following findings:

1. The dam has serious deficiencies in its design or construction or has a physical condition that if left unaddressed could result in a failure that may result in loss of life or damage to downstream property.

2. The design, construction, operation, or maintenance of the dam is such that its expected performance during flooding conditions threatens the structural integrity of the dam.

B. After completion of the safety inspections pursuant to § 10.1-607, or as otherwise informed of an unsafe condition, the Department shall take actions in accordance with § 10.1-608 or 10.1-609 depending on the degree of hazard and imminence of failure caused by the unsafe condition. (2006, c. 30.)

§ 10.1-608. Unsafe dams presenting imminent danger. — When the Director finds an unsafe dam constituting an imminent danger to life or property, he shall immediately notify the Department of Emergency Management and confer with the owner. The owner of a dam found to constitute an imminent danger to life or property shall take immediate corrective action. If the owner does not take appropriate and timely action to correct the danger found, the Governor shall have the authority to take immediate appropriate action, without the necessity for a hearing, to remove the imminent danger. The Attorney General may bring an action against the owner of the impounding structure for the Commonwealth's expenses in removing the imminent danger. There shall be a lien upon the owner's real estate for the Commonwealth's expenses in removing the imminent danger. The owner may avoid the Commonwealth's costs, and recover any damages, upon proving that the dam was known to be safe at the time such action was taken, and that the owner had provided or offered to immediately provide such proof to the Director before the action complained of was taken. Nothing herein shall in any way limit any authority existing under the Emergency Services and Disaster Law (§ 44-146.13 et seq.). (1982, c. 583, § 62.1-115.5; 1986, c. 9; 1988, c. 891.)

§ 10.1-609. Unsafe dams presenting nonimminent danger. — A. Within a reasonable time after completion of a safety inspection of an impounding structure authorized by § 10.1-607, the Board shall issue a report to the owner of the impounding structure containing its findings and recommendations for correction of any deficiencies which could threaten life or property if not corrected. Owners who have been issued a report containing recommendations for correction of deficiencies shall undertake to implement the recommendations contained in the report according to the schedule of implementation contained in the report. If an owner fails or refuses to commence or diligently implement the recommendations for correction of deficiencies according to the schedule contained in an issued report, the Director shall have the authority to issue an administrative order directing the owner to commence implementation and completion of such recommendations according to the schedule contained in the report with modifications as appropriate. Within thirty days after being served by personal service or by mail with a copy of an order issued pursuant to this section, any owner shall have the right to petition the Board for a hearing. A timely filed petition shall stay the effect of the administrative order.

The hearing shall be conducted before the Board or a designated member thereof pursuant to § 2.2-4019. The Board shall have the authority to affirm, modify, amend or cancel the administrative order. Any owner aggrieved by a decision of the Board after a hearing shall have the right to judicial review of the final Board decision pursuant to the provisions of the Administrative Process Act (§ 2.2-4000 et seq.).

B. The provisions of subsection A of this section notwithstanding, if the Director determines, after the report is issued, that changed circumstances justify reclassifying the deficiencies of an impounding structure as an imminent danger to life or property, the Director may proceed directly under § 10.1-613 for enforcement of his order, and the owner shall have the opportunity to contest the fact based upon which the administrative order was issued.

C. The Director, upon a determination that there is an unsafe condition at an impounding structure, is authorized to cause the lowering or complete draining of such impoundment until the unsafe condition has been corrected at the owner's expense and prior to any authorization to refill.

An owner who fails to comply with the provisions contained in an administrative order of the Department shall be subject to procedures set out in § 10.1-613 and the penalties authorized under §§ 10.1-613.1 and 10.1-613.2.

D. No persons, other than those authorized to maintain an impounding structure, shall interfere with the operation of an impounding structure. (1982, c. 583, § 62.1-115.6; 1986, cc. 9, 615; 1988, c. 891; 1999, c. 110; 2006, c. 30.)

The 2006 amendments. — The 2006 amendment by c. 30, in subsection C, added "at the owner's expense and prior to any authori- zation to refill" in the first paragraph and added the second paragraph.

§ **10.1-609.1. Installation of IFLOWS gauges.** — A soil and water conservation district responsible for the maintenance and operation of a flood control dam shall be permitted to install Integrated Flood Observing and Warning Systems (IFLOWS) gauges and associated equipment, or a device approved by the Department of Emergency Management, while awaiting funds to make structural modifications to correct emergency spillway capacity deficiencies in the dam, identified by the Board in a report issued pursuant to § 10.1-609, when any of the following conditions exist: (i) funds are not available to make such structural modifications to the dam, (ii) the completion of such structural modifications requires the acquisition of additional property or easements by exercise of the power of eminent domain, or (iii) funds for the IFLOWS equipment or an equivalent device have been appropriated by the

General Assembly. Installation of IFLOWS gauges or similar devices shall not affect the regulated status of the dam under the Virginia Dam Safety Act (§ 10.1-604 et seq.). Any IFLOWS gauges and associated equipment shall be installed in a manner approved by the Department of Emergency Management and shall be operated and maintained by the Department of Emergency Management. (1993, c. 709.)

§ **10.1-609.2. Prohibited vegetation.** — Dam owners shall not permit the growth of trees and other woody vegetation and shall remove any such vegetation from the slopes and crest of embankments and the emergency spillway area, and within a distance of 25 feet from the toe of the embankment and abutments of the dam. Owners failing to maintain their dam in accordance with this section shall be subject to enforcement pursuant to § 10.1-613. (2006, c. 30.)

§ **10.1-610. Right of entry.** — The Board and its agents and employees shall have the right to enter any property at reasonable times and under reasonable circumstances to perform such inspections and tests or to take such other actions it deems necessary to fulfill its responsibilities under this article, including the inspection of dams that may be subject to this article, provided that the Board or its agents or employees make a reasonable effort to obtain the consent of the owner of the land prior to entry. If entry is denied, the Board or its designated agents or employees may apply to any magistrate whose territorial jurisdiction encompasses the property to be inspected or entered for a warrant authorizing such investigation, tests or other actions. Such warrant shall issue if the magistrate finds probable cause to believe that there is a dam on such property which is not known to be safe. (1982, c. 583, § 62.1-115.7; 1988, c. 891; 2005, c. 117.)

The **2005 amendments.** — The 2005 amendments by c. 117 rewrote the first sentence and inserted "or its designated agents or employees" in the second sentence.

§ **10.1-610.1. Monitoring progress of work.** — A. During the maintenance, construction, or alteration of any dam or reservoir, the Department shall make periodic inspections for the purpose of securing conformity with the approved plans and specifications. The Department shall require the owner to perform at his expense such work or tests as necessary to obtain information sufficient to enable the Department to determine whether conformity with the approved plans and specifications is being secured.

B. If, after any inspections, investigations, or examinations, or at any time as the work progresses, or at any time prior to issuance of a certificate of approval, it is found by the Director that project modifications or changes are necessary to ensure conformity with the approved plans and specifications, the Director may issue an administrative order to the owner to comply with the plans and specifications. Within 15 calendar days after being served by personal service or by mail with a copy of an order issued pursuant to this section, any owner shall have the right to petition the Board for a hearing. A timely filed petition shall stay the effect of the administrative order. The hearing shall be conducted before the Board or a designated member of the Board pursuant to § 2.2-4019. The Board shall have the authority to affirm, modify, amend, or cancel the administrative order. Any owner aggrieved by a decision of the Board after a hearing shall have the right to judicial review of the final Board decision pursuant to the provisions of the Administrative Process Act (§ 2.2-4000 et seq.).

C. Following the Board hearing, subject to judicial review of the final decision of the Board, if conditions are revealed that will not permit the construction of a safe dam or reservoir, the certificate of approval may be revoked. As part of the revocation, the Board may compel the owner to remove the incomplete structure sufficiently to eliminate any safety hazard to life or property. (2006, c. 30.)

§ **10.1-611. Dam safety coordination.** — The Board shall coordinate all impoundment safety activities in the Commonwealth, which shall include, but not be limited to: (i) the maintenance of an inventory of all impoundment structures, and of all other similar structures which are not regulated under this article to the extent the Board deems necessary; (ii) the maintenance of a repository for record drawings of all such structures to the extent the Board deems necessary; (iii) the maintenance of an inventory of safety inspection reports for each such structure to the extent the Board deems necessary; and (iv) the maintenance of a secondary repository for all dam safety emergency action plans which are primarily filed with the Department of Emergency Management. The Board shall provide technical assistance in the preparation, updating and execution of such plans. It shall establish uniform maintenance-of-records requirements and uniform inspection standards to be applied to all impounding structures in the Commonwealth and to be recommended for all other similar structures. It may inspect or cause to be inspected state-owned or state-licensed dams on a cost reimbursable basis at the request of the state agency owning the state-owned dam or of the licensor of the state-licensed dam. (1982, c. 583, § 62.1-115.8; 1986, c. 9; 1988, c. 891.)

§ **10.1-611.1. Soil and Water Conservation District Dam Maintenance, Repair, and Rehabilitation Fund established; Department to manage; Board to expend moneys; regulations.** — A. There is hereby created in the state treasury a special nonreverting fund to be known as the Soil and Water Conservation District Dam Maintenance, Repair, and Rehabilitation Fund, hereafter referred to as "the Fund." The Fund shall be comprised of moneys appropriated to the Fund by the General Assembly and any other moneys designated for deposit to the Fund from any source, public or private. The Fund shall be established on the books of the Comptroller and the moneys shall be paid into the state treasury and credited to the Fund. Interest earned on moneys in the Fund shall remain in the Fund and be credited to it. Any moneys remaining in the Fund, including interest thereon, at the end of each fiscal year shall not revert to the general fund but shall remain in the Fund. Moneys in the Fund shall be used solely for (i) the maintenance and repair of any dams owned by soil and water conservation districts and (ii) the rehabilitation and major repair of Class I and Class II dams owned by soil and water conservation districts, in order to bring such dams into compliance with regulations promulgated pursuant to Article 2 (§ 10.1-604 et seq.) of Chapter 6 of this title. Expenditures from the Fund made under clause (ii) of this subsection may include, but are not limited to, the following repairs to the infrastructure of a dam: increasing the height of a dam, modifying the spillway, and reducing wave erosion of a dam's inside face. Expenditures and disbursements from the Fund shall be made by the State Treasurer on warrants issued by the Comptroller upon written request signed by the Director of the Department of Conservation and Recreation.

B. The Fund shall be administered and managed by the Department of Conservation and Recreation, subject to the right of the Board, following consultation with the Department of Conservation and Recreation, to direct the distribution of moneys in the Fund to particular soil and water conservation districts.

C. The Board is authorized to promulgate regulations for the proper administration of the Fund. Such regulations may include, but are not limited to, the type and amount of financial assistance, the terms and conditions of the assistance, and project eligibility criteria. (1997, c. 356; 2000, cc. 23, 205.)

§ 10.1-612. Technical Advisory Committee. — The Board shall establish an Impoundment Safety Technical Advisory Committee to provide technical review. The Committee may make recommendations to the Board. (1982, c. 583, § 62.1-115.9; 1988, c. 891.)

§ 10.1-612.1. Temporary stop work order; hearing; injunctive relief. — A. The Director may issue a temporary stop work order on a construction or alteration project if he finds that an owner is constructing or altering a dam without having first obtained the necessary certificate of approval, or if the activities are not in accordance with approved plans and specifications. The order shall include written notice to the owner of the date, time, and location where the owner may appear at a hearing before the Board or a designated member thereof pursuant to § 2.2-4019 to show cause why the temporary order should be vacated. The hearing shall be held within 15 calendar days of the date of the order, unless the owner consents to a longer period.

B. Following the hearing, the Board may affirm or cancel the temporary order and may issue a final order directing that immediate steps be taken to abate or ameliorate any harm or damage arising from the violation. The owner may seek judicial review of the final decision of the Board pursuant to the provisions of the Administrative Process Act (§ 2.2-4000 et seq.).

C. If the violation continues after the Board has issued a final decision and order pursuant to subsection B or a temporary order issued by the Director pursuant to subsection A, the Board may apply for an injunction from the appropriate court. A decision to seek injunctive relief does not preclude other forms of relief, enforcement, or penalties against the owner. (2006, c. 30.)

§ 10.1-613. Enforcement. — Any person or legal entity failing or refusing to comply with an order issued pursuant to this article may be compelled to comply with the order in a proceeding instituted in any appropriate court by the Board. The Board shall bring suit in the name of the Commonwealth in any court of competent jurisdiction to enjoin the unlawful construction, modification, operation, or maintenance of any dam regulated under this article. Such court may require the removal or modification of any such dam by mandatory injunction. If the court orders the removal of the dam, the owner shall be required to bear the expenses of such removal.

Should the Board be required to implement and carry out the action, the Board shall charge the owner for any expenses associated with the action, and if the repayment is not made within 90 days after written demand, the Board may bring an action in the proper court to recover this expense. The Board shall file an action in the court having jurisdiction over any owner or the owner's property for the recovery of such costs. A lien in the amount of such costs shall be automatically created on all property owned by any such owner at or proximate to such dam or reservoir. (1982, c. 583, § 62.1-115.10; 1988, c. 891; 2006, c. 30.)

The 2006 amendments. — The 2006 amendment by c. 30 added the last three sentences in the first paragraph and added the second paragraph.

§ 10.1-613.1. Criminal penalties. — A. It is unlawful for any owner to knowingly:

1. Operate, construct, or alter a dam without an approval as provided in this article;

2. Violate the terms of an approval, order, regulation, or requirement of the Board or Director under this article; or

3. Obstruct, hinder, or prevent the Board or its designated agents or employees from performing duties under this article.

A violation of any provision of this subsection or this article is a Class 3 misdemeanor.

B. Each day that any such violation occurs after notice of the original violation is served upon the violator by the Board or its designated agents or employees by registered mail shall constitute a separate offense. Upon conviction, the violator is subject to a fine not exceeding $500 per day for each day of the offense, not to exceed a total fine of $25,000, with costs imposed at the discretion of the court. In determining the amount of the penalty, the appropriate court shall consider the degree of harm to the public; whether the violation was knowing or willful; the past conduct of the defendant; whether the defendant should have been on notice of the violation; whether the defendant has taken steps to cease, remove, or mitigate the violation; and any other relevant information. (2006, c. 30.)

Cross references. — As to punishment for Class 3 misdemeanors, see § 18.2-11.

§ **10.1-613.2. Civil penalties.** — In addition to or in lieu of any other forfeitures, remedies, or penalties authorized by law or regulations, any owner violating any provision of this article may be assessed a civil penalty of up to $500 per day by the Board not to exceed a maximum of $25,000.

In setting the civil penalty amount, the Board shall consider (i) the nature, duration, and number of previous instances of failure by the owner to comply with requirements of law relating to dam safety and the requirements of Board regulations and orders; (ii) the efforts of the owner to correct deficiencies or other instances of failure to comply with the requirements of law relating to dam safety and the requirements of Board regulations and orders that are the subject of the proposed penalty; (iii) the cost of carrying out actions required to meet the requirements of law and Board regulations and orders; (iv) the hazard classification of the dam; and (v) other factors deemed appropriate by the Board.

All civil penalties will be assessed by written penalty notice from the Board and given by certified mail or personal service. The notice shall state the specific reasons for the penalty, the number of days the Department considers the owner in violation, and the total amount due. Within 30 days after receipt of a copy of the order issued pursuant to this section, any owner subject to the civil penalty provisions shall have the right to petition the Board, in writing, for a hearing. A timely filed petition shall stay the effect of the penalty notice.

The hearing shall be conducted before the Board or a designated member thereof pursuant to § 2.2-4019. The Board shall affirm, modify, amend, or cancel the penalty notice within 10 days following the conclusion of the hearing. Any owner aggrieved by a decision of the Board after a hearing shall have the right to judicial review of the final Board decision pursuant to the provisions of the Administrative Process Act (§ 2.2-4000 et seq.).

If any civil penalty has not been paid within 45 days after the final Board decision or court order has been served on the violator, the Board shall request the Attorney General to institute a civil action in the court of any county in which the violator resides or has his principal place of business to recover the amount of the assessment.

Civil penalties assessed under this section shall be paid into the Flood Prevention and Protection Assistance Fund, established pursuant to § 10.1-603.17, and shall be used for the administration of the dam safety program, including for the repair and maintenance of dams. (2006, c. 30.)

§ 10.1-613.3. No liability of Board, Department, employees, or agents. — An owner may not bring an action against the Commonwealth, the Board, the Department, or agents or employees of the Commonwealth for the recovery of damages caused by the partial or total failure of a dam or reservoir, or by the operation of a dam or reservoir, or by an act or omission in connection with:

1. Approval of the construction, alteration, or maintenance of a dam or reservoir, or approval of flood-operations plans during or after construction;

2. Issuance or enforcement of orders relating to maintenance or operation of the dam or reservoir;

3. Control or regulation of the dam or reservoir;

4. Measures taken to protect against failure of the dam or reservoir during an emergency;

5. Investigations or inspections authorized under this article;

6. Use of design and construction criteria prepared by the Department; or

7. Determination of the hazard classification of the dam. (2006, c. 30.)

§ 10.1-613.4. Liability of owner or operator. — Nothing in this article, and no order, notice, approval, or advice of the Director or Board shall relieve any owner or operator of such a structure from any legal duties, obligations, and liabilities resulting from such ownership or operation. The owner shall be responsible for liability for damage to the property of others or injury to persons, including, but not limited to, loss of life resulting from the operation or failure of a dam. Compliance with this article does not guarantee the safety of a dam or relieve the owner of liability in case of a dam failure. (2006, c. 30.)

§ 10.1-613.5. Program administration fees. — The Board is authorized to establish and collect application fees from any applicant to be deposited into the Flood Prevention and Protection Assistance Fund established pursuant to § 10.1-603.17 for the administration of the dam safety program, administrative review, certifications, and the repair and maintenance of dams. Permit applications shall not be reviewed without a full payment of the required fee. Virginia Soil and Water Conservation Districts shall be exempt from all fees established pursuant to this section. (2006, c. 30.)

ARTICLE 3.

Watershed Improvements Districts.

§ 10.1-614. Establishment within soil and water conservation district authorized. — Whenever it is found that soil and water conservation or water management within a soil and water conservation district or districts will be promoted by the construction of improvements to check erosion, provide drainage, collect sediment or stabilize the runoff of surface water, a small watershed improvement district may be established within such soil and water conservation district or districts in accordance with the provisions of this article. (1956, c. 668, § 21-112.1; 1964, c. 512; 1973, c. 35; 1977, c. 40; 1988, c. 891.)

§ 10.1-615. Petition for establishment; what to set forth. — A. Any twenty-five owners of land lying within the limits of a proposed watershed improvement district, or a majority of such owners if there are fewer than fifty, may file a petition with the directors of the soil and water conservation district or districts in which the proposed watershed improvement district is situated asking that a watershed improvement district be organized to function in the territory described in the petition. The petition shall set forth:

1. The proposed name of the watershed improvement district;

2. That there is need, in the interest of the public health, safety, and welfare, for a watershed improvement district to function in the territory described in the petition;

3. A description of the territory proposed to be organized as a watershed improvement district, which description shall be deemed sufficient if generally accurate;

4. That the territory described in the petition is contiguous and is the same watershed, or is two or more contiguous watersheds;

5. A request that the territory described in the petition be organized as a watershed improvement district;

6. The method for financing the proposed district, whether by means of a tax on all real estate in the proposed district or a service charge on the increase in the fair market value of all real estate in the proposed district caused by the district's project.

B. Land lying within the limits of one watershed improvement district shall not be included in another watershed improvement district. (1956, c. 668, § 21-112.2; 1964, c. 512; 1970, c. 480; 1977, c. 40; 1981, c. 156; 1988, c. 891.)

§ 10.1-616. Notice and hearing on petition; determination of need for district and defining boundaries. — Within thirty days after a petition has been filed with the directors of the soil and water conservation district or districts, they shall cause due notice to be given of a hearing upon the practicability and feasibility of creating the proposed watershed improvement district. All owners of land within the proposed watershed improvement district and all other interested parties shall have the right to attend such a hearing and to be heard. If the directors determine from the hearing that there is need, in the interest of the public health, safety, and welfare, for the organization of the proposed watershed improvement district, they shall record their determination and define the boundaries of the watershed improvement district. The provisions of Article 2 (§ 10.1-502 et seq.) of Chapter 5 of this title shall apply, mutatis mutandis, to such proceedings. (1956, c. 668, § 21-112.3; 1964, c. 512; 1970, c. 480; 1988, c. 891.)

§ 10.1-617. Determination of whether operation of proposed district is feasible; referendum. — If the district directors determine that a need for the proposed watershed improvement district exists and after they define the boundaries of the proposed district, they shall consider the administrative feasibility of operating the proposed watershed improvement district. To assist the district directors in determining such question, a referendum shall be held upon the proposition of the creation of the proposed watershed improvement district. Due notice of the referendum shall be given by the district directors. All owners of land lying within the boundaries of the proposed watershed improvement district shall be eligible to vote in the referendum. The district directors may prescribe necessary regulations governing the conduct of the hearing. (1956, c. 668, § 21-112.4; 1964, c. 512; 1970, c. 480; 1988, c. 891; 1995, c. 654.)

§ 10.1-618. Ballots used in such referendum. — The question shall be submitted by ballots, which shall contain the following question: "Shall a watershed improvement district be created of the lands described below and lying in the county(ies) or city(ies) of .... and ....?

☐ Yes

☐ No"

The ballot shall set forth the boundaries of the proposed district determined by the Board.

The ballot shall also set forth the method or methods of real estate assessment as determined by the district directors. (1956, c. 668, § 21-112.5; 1970, c. 480, § 21-112.4:1; 1977, c. 40; 1988, c. 891.)

§ 10.1-619. Consideration of results of referendum; simple majority vote required. — The results of the referendum shall be considered by the district directors in determining whether the operation of the proposed watershed improvement district is administratively practicable and feasible. The district directors shall not be authorized to determine that operation of the proposed watershed improvement district is administratively practicable and feasible unless a simple majority of the votes cast in the referendum have been cast in favor of the creation of the watershed improvement district. (1956, c. 668, § 21-112.5; 1970, c. 480; 1977, c. 40; 1988, c. 891; 2005, c. 128.)

The **2005 amendments.** — The 2005 amendments by c. 128 substituted "a simple majority" for "at least two thirds" and deleted "which two-thirds vote shall also represent ownership of at least two-thirds of the land in the proposed district" following "referendum" and made a minor punctuation change.

§ 10.1-620. Declaration of organization of district; certification to Board. — If the district directors determine that operation of the proposed watershed improvement district is administratively practicable and feasible, they shall declare the watershed improvement district to be organized and shall record the fact in their official minutes. Following such entry in their official minutes, the district directors shall certify the fact of the organization of the watershed improvement district to the Virginia Soil and Water Conservation Board, and shall furnish a copy of the certification to the clerk of each county or city in which any portion of the watershed improvement district is situated for recordation in the public land records of each such county or city. The watershed improvement district shall thereupon constitute a political subdivision of this Commonwealth. (1956, c. 668, § 21-112.6; 1964, c. 512; 1970, c. 480; 1988, c. 891.)

§ 10.1-621. Establishment of watershed improvement district situated in more than one soil and water conservation district. — If a proposed watershed improvement district is situated in more than one soil and water conservation district, copies of the petition shall be presented to the directors of all the soil and water conservation districts in which the proposed watershed improvement district is situated, and the directors of all affected soil and water conservation districts shall act jointly as a board of directors with respect to all matters concerning the watershed improvement district, including its organization. The watershed improvement district shall be organized in the same manner and shall have the same powers and duties as a watershed improvement district situated entirely in one soil and water conservation district. (1956, c. 668, § 21-112.7; 1964, c. 512; 1970, c. 480; 1988, c. 891.)

§ 10.1-622. Inclusion of additional territory. — Petitions for including additional territory within an existing watershed improvement district may be filed with directors of the soil and water conservation district or districts in which the watershed improvement district is situated, and in such cases the provisions hereof for petitions to organize the watershed improvement district shall be observed to the extent deemed practicable by the district directors. In referenda upon petitions for such inclusion, all owners of land situated in the proposed additional territory shall be eligible to vote. No additional territory shall be included in an existing watershed improvement district unless owners of land representing two-thirds of the acreage proposed to be included vote in favor thereof. (1956, c. 668, § 21-112.8; 1964, c. 512; 1970, c. 480; 1988, c. 891.)

§ 10.1-623. Governing body of district; trustees. — The directors of the soil and water conservation district or districts in which the watershed improvement district is situated shall be the governing body of the watershed improvement district. They may appoint, in consultation with and subject to the approval of the Virginia Soil and Water Conservation Board, three trustees who shall be owners of land within the watershed improvement district. The trustees shall exercise the administrative duties and powers delegated to them by the directors of the soil and water conservation district or districts. The trustees shall hold office at the will of the directors of the soil and water conservation district or districts and the Virginia Soil and Water Conservation Board. The trustees shall designate a chairman and may change such designation. One of the trustees may be selected as treasurer and shall be responsible for the safekeeping of the funds of the watershed improvement district. When a watershed improvement district lies in more than one soil and water conservation district, the directors of all such districts shall act jointly as the governing body of the watershed improvement district. (1956, c. 668, § 21-112.9; 1964, c. 512; 1970, c. 480; 1988, c. 891.)

§ 10.1-624. Officers, agents and employees; surety bonds; annual audit. — The trustees may, with the approval of the directors of the soil and water conservation district or districts, employ such officers, agents, and other employees as they require, and shall determine their qualifications, duties and compensation. The district directors shall provide for the execution of surety bonds for the treasurer and such other trustees, officers, agents, and employees as shall be entrusted with funds or property of the watershed improvement district, and shall publish an annual audit of the accounts of receipts and disbursements of the watershed improvement district. (1956, c. 668, § 21-112.10; 1964, c. 512; 1970, c. 480; 1988, c. 891.)

§ 10.1-625. Status and general powers of district; power to levy tax or service charge; approval of landowners required. — A watershed improvement district shall have all of the powers of the soil and water conservation district or districts in which the watershed improvement district is situated, and in addition shall have the authority to levy and collect a tax or service charge to be used for the purposes for which the watershed improvement district was created. No tax shall be levied nor service charge imposed under this article unless two-thirds of the owners of land, which two-thirds owners shall also represent ownership of at least two-thirds of the land area in such district, voting in a referendum called and held in the manner prescribed in this article, approve the levy of a tax to be expended for the purposes of the watershed improvement district. (1956, c. 668, § 21-112.11; 1964, c. 512; 1981, c. 156; 1988, c. 891; 1995, c. 654.)

§ 10.1-626. Levy of tax or service charge; when district in two or more counties or cities; landbooks certified to treasurers. — A. On or before March 1 of each year, the trustees of the watershed improvement district shall make an estimate of the amount of money they deem necessary to be raised for the year in such district (i) for operating expenses and interest payments and (ii) for amortization of debt, and, after approval by the directors of the soil and water conservation district or districts, and the Virginia Soil and Water Conservation Board, shall establish the tax rate or service charge rate necessary to raise such amount of money. The tax rate or service charge rate to be applied against the amount determined under subsection C or D of this section shall be determined before the date fixed by law for the determination of the general levy by the governing body of the counties or cities in which the district is situated.

B. The trustees of a watershed improvement district which imposes a tax on real estate or a service charge based on the increase in the fair market value of real estate caused by the district's project shall make up a landbook of all properties subject to the watershed improvement district tax or service charge on forms similar to those used by the county or city affected.

A separate landbook shall be made for each county or city if the district is located in more than one county or city. The landbook or landbooks of all properties subject to the district tax or the service charge, along with the tax rate or service charge rate fixed by the governing body of the district for that year, shall be certified to the appropriate county or city treasurer or treasurers, and filed in the clerk's office of such locality or localities, by the governing body of the watershed improvement district on or before the day the county or city landbook is required to be so certified. Such landbook or landbooks shall be subject to the same retention requirements as the county or city landbook.

C. For tax purposes under this article, the assessed valuation of all real estate located in a watershed improvement district shall be the same fair market valuation that appears in the most recent landbook for the county, city, or town wherein the subject property is located. However, in a watershed improvement district which is located in two or more counties or cities and in which there is a disparity of assessed valuations between the counties or cities, the governing body of the watershed improvement district may petition the judge or judges of the circuit courts in which the district is located to appoint one or more persons to assess all of the real estate in the district. The compensation of such person or persons shall be prescribed by the governing body of the district and paid out of the funds of the district.

D. In districts authorized to impose a service charge, the service charge shall be based on the initial increase in fair market value resulting from a project. In order to determine the initial increase in fair market value, the trustees shall subtract the fair market value of each parcel without the project, as shown in the landbook for the year immediately preceding the year in which the project was begun from the fair market value of the parcel following completion of the project. The fair market value of each parcel with the project shall be determined by the district directors in a reasonable manner. The values so determined shall be the values against which the service charge rate is imposed so long as any bonds remain outstanding, and thereafter unless a change is approved by the district directors. If an additional improvement is made while any bonds are outstanding, the district directors may cause a new increase in fair market values to be computed to reflect such improvement. However, while any bonds are outstanding, such newly computed values shall not be used unless the total new increase in fair market values in the district is equal to or greater than the previously determined increase in fair market values. Within thirty days after determining the increase in fair market value for all real estate in the watershed improvement district resulting from the project, the trustees shall mail a notice of such determination to the owner of record of each parcel in the district.

E. The assessments and determinations of increase in fair market value made under the provisions of this section may be used only for the watershed improvement district tax or service charge and shall in no way affect any county or city assessment or levies.

F. Any person, firm, or corporation aggrieved by any determination of increased value made under any provision of this article shall apply in writing to the trustees of the watershed improvement district within sixty days after the mailing of the notice required in subsection D of this section. Such application shall specify the increased value in the opinion of the applicant and the basis for such opinion. The trustees shall rule on all such applications within 120 days after mailing the notice required in subsection D of this section. If any applicant remains aggrieved by the determination of increased value after such a ruling, he may apply to the circuit court of the county or city wherein the land is situated for a correction of such determination of increased value, within the time limits and following the procedures set out in Article 5 (§ 58.1-3980 et seq.) of Chapter 39 of Title 58.1.

G. The provisions of this section shall not be used to change the method of real estate assessment in any watershed improvement district established prior to January 1, 1976. (1981, c. 156, § 21-112.12:1; 1988, c. 891.)

§ 10.1-627. Collection of tax or service charge; proceeds kept in special account; expenditures from such account. — The special tax or service charge levied shall be collected at the same time and in the same manner as county or city taxes with the proceeds therefrom to be kept in a separate account by the county or city treasurer identified by the official name of the watershed improvement district. Expenditures from such account may be made with the approval of the directors of the soil and water conservation district or districts on requisition from the chairman and the treasurer of the board of trustees of the watershed improvement district. (1956, c. 668, § 21-112.13; 1964, c. 512; 1970, c. 480; 1981, c. 156; 1988, c. 891.)

§ 10.1-628. Fiscal powers of governing body; may poll landowners on question of incurring indebtedness or issuing bonds. — The governing body of any watershed improvement district shall have power, subject to the conditions and limitations of this article, to incur indebtedness, borrow funds, and issue bonds of such watershed improvement district. The circuit court of the county or city in which any portion of the watershed improvement district is located, upon the petition of a majority of the members of the governing body of the watershed improvement district, shall order a referendum at any time not less than thirty days from the date of such order, which shall be designated therein, to determine whether the governing body shall incur indebtedness or issue bonds for one or more of the purposes for which the watershed improvement district was created.

The referendum shall be conducted in the manner prescribed by this article for the conduct of other referendums in the watershed improvement districts. (1956, c. 668, §§ 21-112.14, 21-112.15; 1964, c. 512; 1988, c. 891; 1995, c. 654.)

§ 10.1-629. Order authorizing governing body to incur indebtedness or issue bonds. — If the owners of at least two-thirds of the land area in the district vote in the election, and if at least two-thirds of the voters in the election vote in favor of incurring the indebtedness or issuing bonds, the circuit court or courts shall enter an order authorizing the governing body of the watershed improvement district to incur indebtedness or issue bonds for one or more of the purposes for which the district was created. (1956, c. 668, § 21-112.16; 1988, c. 891.)

§ 10.1-630. Type of indebtedness incurred or bonds issued. — The type of indebtedness incurred or bonds issued shall be that adopted by the governing body of the watershed improvement district and approved by the Virginia Soil and Water Conservation Board. (1956, c. 668, § 21-112.17; 1964, c. 512; 1988, c. 891; 1996, cc. 105, 819.)

§ 10.1-631. Annual tax for payment of interest or to amortize indebtedness or bonds. — The governing body of the watershed improvement district shall, if necessary to pay the interest on the indebtedness or bonds or to amortize such indebtedness or bonds, levy an annual tax or service charge in the manner prescribed by § 10.1-626 on all the real estate in the watershed improvement district subject to local taxation, to satisfy such obligations. This tax, irrespective of any approvals required pursuant to § 10.1-614, shall be sufficient to pay interest and to amortize such indebtedness or bonds at the times required. (1956, c. 668, § 21-112.18; 1973, c. 35; 1981, c. 156; 1988, c. 891; 1996, cc. 105, 819.)

§ 10.1-632. Powers granted additional to powers of soil and water conservation district; soil and water conservation district to continue to exercise its powers. — The powers herein granted to watershed improvement districts shall be additional to the powers of the soil and water conservation district or districts in which the watershed improvement district is situated; and the soil and water conservation district or districts shall be authorized, notwithstanding the creation of the watershed improvement district, to continue to exercise their powers within the watershed improvement district. (1956, c. 668, § 21-112.19; 1964, c. 512; 1988, c. 891.)

§ 10.1-633. Power to incur debts and accept gifts, etc.; watershed improvement district to have same powers as soil and water conservation district. — A watershed improvement district shall have power, as set forth in this article, to incur debts and repay them over the period of time and at the rate or rates of interest, not exceeding eight percent, that the lender agrees to. Any watershed improvement district may accept, receive and expend gifts, grants or loans from whatever source received. In addition, they shall have the same powers, to the extent necessary, within the watershed improvement district that the soil and water conservation district or districts in which the same is located exercise or may possess. (1956, c. 668, § 21-112.20; 1964, c. 512; 1977, c. 40; 1988, c. 891.)

§ 10.1-634. Question to be submitted to qualified voters; approval required. — In connection with any referendum held pursuant to the provisions of this article, the directors shall also provide for the submission of the question involved to the qualified voters of the watershed improvement district and any question required to be submitted to referendum hereunder shall only be deemed to be approved, if approved both by vote of the landowners of the district as here above required and by a majority vote of the qualified voters of the district voting in such referendum. (1973, c. 35, § 21-112.20:1; 1988, c. 891.)

§ 10.1-634.1. Conduct of referenda. — A. Except as provided in subsection B, the referenda authorized or required by this article shall be conducted pursuant to regulations prescribed by the Virginia Soil and Water Conservation Board and not as provided for under § 24.2-684.

B. Referenda authorized or required by this article prior to the regulations referred to in subsection A becoming effective shall be conducted by the district directors of the soil and water conservation district in which the watershed improvement district is situated pursuant to the provisions of this article as they were effective on January 1, 1995, and Article 5 (§ 24.2-681 et seq.) of Chapter 6 of Title 24.2. The costs of holding referenda under this subsection shall be paid by the requesting landowners. (1995, c. 654; 1996, c. 983.)

§ 10.1-635. Power of eminent domain. — In addition to any other powers conferred on it by law, any watershed improvement district organized under

240

the provisions of this article shall be authorized to acquire by eminent domain any lands, property rights, franchises, rights-of-way, easements or other property deemed necessary or convenient for the efficient operation of the district. Such proceedings shall be in accordance with and subject to the provisions of the laws of the Commonwealth applicable to the exercise of the power of eminent domain in the name of a public service company and subject to the provisions of Chapter 2 (§ 25.1-200 et seq.) of Title 25.1. (1958, c. 411, § 21-112.21; 1988, c. 891; 2003, c. 940.)

ARTICLE 4.

Conservation, Small Watersheds Flood Control and Area Development Fund.

§ **10.1-636. Definitions.** — As used in this article, unless the context requires a different meaning:

"Board" means the Virginia Soil and Water Conservation Board.

"Facility" means any structures, foundations, appurtenances, spillways, lands, easements and rights-of-way necessary to (i) store additional water for immediate or future use in feasible flood prevention sites; (ii) create the potential to store additional water by strengthening the foundations and appurtenances of structures in feasible flood prevention sites; or (iii) store water in sites not feasible for flood prevention programs, and to properly operate and maintain such stores of water or potential stores of water.

"Fund" or *"revolving fund"* means the Conservation, Small Watersheds Flood Control and Area Development Fund.

"Storing additional water in feasible flood prevention sites" means storage of water for other than flood prevention purposes above the capacity of any given structure to hold water for the purpose of flood prevention in flood prevention sites within a flood prevention project having a favorable benefit-cost ratio where it is economically feasible to provide the capacity to store additional water or the potential for additional water storage capacity. (1970, c. 591, § 21-11.2; 1988, c. 891.)

§ **10.1-637. Fund continued; administrative control.** — The "Conservation, Small Watersheds Flood Control and Area Development Fund," is continued and shall be administered and used as hereinafter provided. The revolving fund shall also consist of any moneys appropriated by the General Assembly.

The administrative control of the fund and the responsibility for the administration of the provisions of this article are hereby vested in the Virginia Soil and Water Conservation Board. The Board is authorized to establish guidelines for the proper administration of the fund and the provisions of this article. (1970, c. 591, §§ 21-11.1, 21-11.4; 1988, c. 891.)

§ **10.1-638. Purposes for which fund to be used.** — A. The Board is authorized, with the concurrence of the State Treasurer, to order the State Comptroller to make loans from the revolving fund to any county, city, town, water authority, utility or service authority or special taxing district, hereafter referred to as the borrower, having the legal capacity and organizational arrangements necessary for obtaining, giving security for, and raising revenues for repaying authorized loans, and for operating and maintaining facilities for which the loan is made. The money loaned shall be used by the borrower for facilities to store additional water in feasible flood prevention sites or to store water in sites not feasible for flood prevention programs. The amount of any loan or the sum of any outstanding loans to any one borrower shall not exceed $500,000 without the written approval of the Governor.

B. To promote the economic growth of the Commonwealth, the Board, after public hearing and with the written approval of the Governor, may invest funds from the revolving fund in facilities to store additional water in feasible flood prevention sites for municipal, industrial, and other beneficial uses where localities fail to do so, or in facilities to create the potential to store additional water in feasible flood prevention sites where impoundment projects are being developed to less than optimum potential, thereby allowing the enlargement of such impoundments as the need arises. Such action may be initiated by a request from the soil and water conservation district or districts encompassing such water storage sites.

C. The Board may draw on the revolving fund to meet maintenance expenses incident to the proper management and operation of facilities resulting from the investments authorized by subsection B above. In addition, the Board may draw on the revolving fund for emergency repairs to the above facilities and facilities constituting the security for loans made by authority of subsection A above. The Board shall not provide funds for emergency repairs to facilities constituting security for loans unless it appears to the Board that funds for repairs are not available from other sources.

D. The Board is authorized to purchase, operate and maintain necessary machinery and other equipment suitable for engineering and other operations incident to soil and water conservation and other purposes of the Board. The Board shall have the custody and control of the machinery and other equipment, and shall provide storage for it, and it shall be available to the districts upon terms the Board prescribes. In addition to other terms the Board may prescribe, it shall have authority to execute rental-purchase contracts with individual districts for the equipment, whereby the title to machinery and other equipment purchased under authority of this law may be transferred to such district when approved by the Board. The Board may, in its discretion, sell the same to any person upon terms and conditions it may deem proper. The proceeds derived from the sale or rental of machinery, provided for in this section and in § 10.1-552, shall be paid into the revolving fund.

E. The Board is authorized to make loans from the revolving fund to any soil and water conservation district for the purchase of necessary machinery and other equipment suitable for engineering and other operations incident to soil and water conservation and other purposes of the district. Terms for loans to districts under this section shall be prescribed by the Board, and payments of interest and principal shall be made to the State Treasurer and credited to the revolving fund. (1970, c. 591, § 21-11.3; 1972, c. 821; 1982, c. 68; 1988, c. 891.)

§ **10.1-639. Conditions for making loan.** — The Board shall authorize the making of a loan under the provisions of § 10.1-638 A only when the following conditions exist:

1. An application for the loan has been submitted by the borrower in the manner and form specified by the Board, setting forth in detail the need for the storage of water, the amount of the loan requested and the use to which the loan shall be applied as well as any efforts made to secure funds from any other source, and such other information required by the Board. The application shall be first submitted to the soil and water conservation district or districts encompassing the watershed wherein the proceeds of the loan would be applied. When the application is approved by the district or districts, the application shall be forwarded to the Board.

2. The borrower agrees and furnishes assurance, satisfactory to the Board, that it will satisfactorily maintain any structure financed in whole or in part through the loans provided by this article.

3. The purpose for which the loan is sought is to acquire land, easements and rights-of-way, or engineering or legal services necessary for a water storage facility or project, or to construct the water storage facility itself.

If the requested loan or any part thereof is for the purpose of acquiring land, easements and rights-of-way, then the loan or part thereof designated for such purpose shall not be granted in the absence of evidence satisfactory to the Board that the borrower requesting the loan will in fact acquire the land, easements or rights-of-way if the loan is granted. (1970, c. 591, § 21-11.5; 1988, c. 891.)

§ 10.1-640. Political subdivisions may borrow from other sources. — Any entity eligible under § 10.1-638 A may borrow funds as provided in this article before, simultaneously, or after borrowing funds from other sources for the same purpose for which funds are borrowed under the provisions of this article. (1970, c. 591, § 21-11.11; 1988, c. 891.)

§ 10.1-641. Powers of Board in aid of the provisions of § 10.1-638. — The Board shall have the following powers to effectuate the provisions of § 10.1-638 B:

1. To expend funds from the revolving fund for field surveys and investigations, notwithstanding the possibility that the Board may subsequently determine that the proposed investment is not feasible.

2. To make and execute contracts and other instruments necessary or convenient to the construction, improvement, operation and maintenance of facilities.

3. To make agreements with and act as agent for the United States, or any of its agencies, or for this Commonwealth or any of its agencies, or any local government in connection with the acquisition, construction, maintenance, operation, or administration of any project in which the Board has invested funds; to accept donations, gifts, and contributions in money, services, materials, or otherwise, from the United States or any of its agencies, or from this Commonwealth or any of its agencies or from any other source; and to use or expend such moneys, services, materials, or other contributions in carrying on its investment function.

4. To obtain options upon and to acquire, by purchase, exchange, lease, gift, grant, bequest, devise, or otherwise, any property, real or personal, or rights or interests therein, and improve any properties acquired. (1970, c. 591, § 21-11.13; 1988, c. 891.)

§ 10.1-642. Record of applications for loans and action taken. — A record of each application for a loan pursuant to § 10.1-639 received by the Board and the action taken thereon shall be open to public inspection at the office of the Board and shall be presented to the Governor and members of the legislature prior to the budgetary sessions of the General Assembly. (1970, c. 591, § 21-11.8; 1988, c. 891.)

§ 10.1-643. Period of loan; interest rate; loan shall constitute a lien. — Any loan made pursuant to the provisions of § 10.1-638 A may be made for any period not to exceed twenty years and shall bear interest at the rate of one percent annually for the first ten years or until such time as water stored under the provisions of this article is used by the borrower for the purpose stated in the application for the loan, if such use occurs within the first ten years. Interest on the loan for the second ten-year period plus the balance of the first ten-year period during which water was used, if any, shall bear interest at a rate set jointly by the Board and the State Treasury Board. Such interest rate shall conform as nearly as possible to the interest on bonds sold for water development or similar purposes within the Commonwealth within the last six months prior to setting such interest rate, taking into consideration any fluctuations of the money market which may have occurred subsequent to the last sale of such bonds within the six-month period. If no such bonds have been sold within the six-month period, the interest rate shall be set to conform as nearly as possible with the rate charged by the commercial money market for such or similar purposes. However, when the attendant facilities, such as but not limited to a filtration plant, pumping station, and pipelines, necessary for the use of the water stored cost the borrower more than $100,000, interest on the loan for the second ten-year period or the ten-year period plus the balance of the first ten-year period during which water was used, if any, shall be at the rate of three percent annually. Any borrower receiving a loan under the provisions of this article shall agree to repay the loan in equal annual installments of principal together with interest at the applicable rate on the unpaid balance of the loan. Payments of interest and principal shall be made to the State Treasurer and credited to the revolving fund, and evidence of debt taken for such loan shall be deposited with the State Treasurer and kept by him. Whenever a loan is made in accordance with the provisions of this article, a lien is hereby created against all of the funds and income of the borrower, as well as upon any real or personal property acquired with loan proceeds. Prepayment of the principal of any such loan, in whole or in part, may be made by the borrower without penalty; however, the borrower shall be liable for interest accrued on the principal at the time of prepayment. (1970, c. 591, § 21-11.6; 1988, c. 891.)

§ **10.1-644. Recovery of money due to fund.** — If a borrower defaults on any payment due the State Treasurer pursuant to § 10.1-643 or on any other obligation incurred pursuant to the provisions of this article, the amounts owed to the fund by the borrower may be recovered by the State Comptroller transferring to the revolving fund the amount of the payment due to the revolving fund from the distribution of state funds to which the defaulting borrower may be entitled pursuant to any state law; or, any money which ought to be paid into the revolving fund may be recoverable with interest by the Commonwealth, in the name of the Board, on motion in the Circuit Court of the City of Richmond. The Attorney General shall institute and prosecute such proceedings after a request for such action has been made by the Board. (1970, c. 591, § 21-11.7; 1988, c. 891.)

§ **10.1-645. Limits on expenditures authorized under § 10.1-638 B; sale of resulting facilities; sale of stored water; renting facilities.** — Expenditures by the Board for any one facility under the provisions of § 10.1-638 B shall not exceed $500,000 without the written approval of the Governor for construction and seeding, acquisition of land, easements, and rights-of-way, engineering costs, appraisal costs, legal services, and other costs related to the facility. The Board is authorized to sell any facility resulting from an expenditure authorized by § 10.1-638 B to any entity to whom a loan could be made pursuant to the provisions of § 10.1-638 A under the terms and conditions prescribed hereinafter. Conveyances of any such facilities shall be executed by the chairman of the Board acting pursuant to a resolution of the Board and shall be approved by the Governor and Attorney General as to form and substance. Upon the transfer of title of such facilities, the purchasing entity shall grant an easement or right-of-way to the appropriate soil and water conservation district to assure the continued operation, inspection and repair of the works of improvement on the land sold, and in all cases, the purchasing entity shall agree to maintain the facility in a satisfactory manner. The Board may contract with an entity eligible to borrow from the revolving fund pursuant to § 10.1-638 A, for the sale of water stored at facilities constructed by expenditures pursuant to § 10.1-638 B. However, it is not the intent of this article to provide a means whereby the Commonwealth shall store and sell water to such entities; therefore, unless extenuating circumstances prevail, such contract shall be entered into with the understanding that such entities shall acquire the rights of the Board in the water storage facility by a future date agreeable to the Board and entity. The Board may lease such facilities to any agency or entity of government, corporation, organization or individual for recreational purposes or any other uses which will not impair the facilities' value for future water supply. Proceeds from the sale of stored water or sale or rental of such facilities shall be placed in the revolving fund. (1970, c. 591, § 21-11.9; 1972, c. 821; 1988, c. 891.)

§ 10.1-646. Purchase price and terms of sales authorized by § 10.1-645. — When an entity, as the term is used in § 10.1-645, agrees to purchase a facility and the rights incident thereto resulting from the storing of additional water in feasible flood prevention sites or the strengthening of foundations and appurtenances of feasible flood prevention sites in which the Board has invested pursuant to § 10.1-638 B, the purchase price shall be the total expenditure from the revolving fund by the Board for such facility plus a surcharge of three percent annually on all funds expended for the facility, other than funds expended pursuant to § 10.1-638 C, from the date of expenditure to the date of purchase by the purchasing entity.

With the approval of the Board, the purchasing entity may finance the purchase price, or any portion thereof, of the facility under the terms and conditions of §§ 10.1-638 A and 10.1-643, and the provisions of §§ 10.1-643 and 10.1-644 shall apply, mutatis mutandis, to such financing. If a purchasing entity finances the purchase of a facility as hereinabove provided, such purchasing entity shall not be precluded from applying for a loan authorized by § 10.1-638 A to the limit imposed by that section to complete any facility purchased to store additional water. (1970, c. 591, § 21-11.10; 1972, c. 821; 1988, c. 891.)

§ 10.1-647. Disposition of facilities financed under article when part of debt remains outstanding. — No facility financed from the revolving fund under the provisions of this article, in whole or in part, shall be sold by an entity when any portion of the debt owed to the revolving fund remains unpaid. However, if the purchaser is an entity having the taxing power, then such sale may be made even though all or a portion of the debt to the revolving fund remains unpaid, if the purchasing entity agrees to assume the obligation to repay the outstanding debt and all interest thereon. If such sale is approved by the Board, then the purchasing entity shall be solely liable for the obligations undertaken by the principal debtor, and the principal debtor shall be released therefrom. (1970, c. 591, § 21-11.12; 1988, c. 891.)

§ 10.1-648. Acquisition of lands, easements, and rights-of-way. — A. The Board, in addition to the provisions of § 10.1-638, may use funds from the revolving fund to pay the cost of the purchase of needed lands, easements, and rights-of-way, or to share the costs thereof with soil and water conservation districts for soil and water conservation and flood control needs when the following conditions have been met:

1. The program of work for the project has been found by the Board to be feasible, practicable and will promote the health, safety, and general welfare of the people of the Commonwealth;

2. The soil and water conservation district or its cosponsors of the project have obtained a minimum of seventy-five percent of the necessary lands, easements, and rights-of-way in the project, or portion of a project (subwatershed) for which funds are requested prior to the use of funds for this purpose;

3. The district and its cosponsors, if any, have submitted a plat to the Board showing the lands, easements and rights-of-way previously acquired, as well as the remaining lands, easements and rights-of-way necessary to the project but not acquired. In addition, the Board may require any other information which it deems necessary. The district and cosponsors shall certify to the Board that funds are unobtainable from any other source to acquire the remaining land, easements, and rights-of-way necessary to the project, in whole or in part;

4. The funds to be used for lands, easements, and rights-of-way shall be granted to the district or cosponsor of the project in whose name the land, easement, or right-of-way shall be recorded.

B. No later than ten years from the purchase of lands and rights-of-way with the funds provided by this section for soil and water conservation and flood control needs, or upon the completion of the watershed project, or a portion of the project (subwatershed) and upon written demand of the owners, their heirs or assigns from whom such land and rights-of-way were acquired, such property shall be reconveyed by the district or cosponsor to the former owners, their heirs or assigns, upon repayment of the original purchase price, without interest, unless such lands and rights-of-way are granted or retained for public purposes as hereinafter provided. After ten years, and no later than twelve years after the purchase date of lands and rights-of-way with the funds provided by this section, unless such lands and rights-of-way are granted or retained for public purposes or reconveyed as provided above, it shall be the duty of the district or cosponsor, to sell the property purchased wholly or partially from the funds provided by this section. The Board shall specify the terms for any such sale. Upon the sale or reconveyance of such property, the district or cosponsor shall remit to the Board a pro rata share of the proceeds of such sale or repayment pursuant to a reconveyance, equal to the percentage of the total cost of the acquisition of such property from any allocation of funds made hereunder and all such remittances shall be deposited to the revolving fund. The district or cosponsor of the project in whose name the acquisition of the land or rights-of-way to be sold is recorded shall retain any easement or right-of-way to assure the continued operation, maintenance, inspection, and repair of the works of improvement constructed on the land to be sold. The district and cosponsor of a project, with the approval of the Board, may grant for public purposes fee title to lands and rights-of-way acquired under the provisions of this section to any political subdivision, including a cosponsor, an agency of the state or federal government, or a regional park authority. (1970, c. 591, § 21-11.14; 1988, c. 891.)

§ **10.1-649. Sale to Board of property and rights-of-way acquired by condemnation.** — For the purpose of § 10.1-638 B the Board is authorized to purchase property and rights-of-way condemned for maintaining, protecting, or providing supplies of water and for water storage purposes under §§ 15.2-1904, 15.2-1907, 15.2-5114, and 21-118 and the condemnor is authorized to sell any such property or rights-of-way to the Board. (1970, c. 591, § 21-11.15; 1988, c. 891; 2003, c. 940.)

ARTICLE 5.

Stream Restoration Assistance Program.

§ **10.1-650. Definitions.** — As used in this article, unless the context clearly requires a different meaning:

"Continual accelerated erosion" means a rapid increase in the erosion rate of stream banks caused by loss of vegetation, diversion of water by constrictions, undermining, and other resultant effects of severe floods.

"*Natural streams*" means nontidal waterways which are part of the natural topography. They usually maintain a continuous or seasonal flow during the year and are characterized as being irregular in cross-section with a meandering course. Constructed channels such as drainage ditches or swales shall not be considered natural streams.

"*Program*" means the Stream Restoration Assistance Program.

"*Stream restoration*" means any combination of structural and vegetative measures which may be taken to restore, stabilize, and protect a natural stream which has been damaged by severe flooding and is consequently subject to continual accelerated erosion or other detrimental effects. The term shall also include measures to return stream flow to its original channel in cases where the stream course has been changed as a result of flooding. (1981, c. 450, § 21-11.23; 1988, c. 891.)

§ **10.1-651. Establishment and administration of Program.** — The Stream Restoration Assistance Program is continued to protect the natural streams of the Commonwealth. The Program shall aid in the stabilization and protection of natural streams which have been severely damaged by naturally occurring flooding events. The Program shall be administered by the Virginia Soil and Water Conservation Board in cooperation with soil and water conservation districts and local governments throughout the Commonwealth. To assist in the development of the Program, the Board shall seek the advisory opinion of the State Water Control Board and the Department of Game and Inland Fisheries. (1981, c. 450, § 21-11.22; 1988, c. 891.)

§ **10.1-652. Program applicability.** — The Stream Restoration Assistance Program shall apply only to natural nontidal streams which have been damaged as a result of naturally occurring flooding events. Streams which have been damaged by land-disturbing activities, vehicular traffic, or other human causes shall not be eligible for assistance under the Program. (1981, c. 450, § 21-11.24; 1988, c. 891.)

§ **10.1-653. Application for assistance.** — Landowners who wish to receive assistance under the Program shall apply to the Virginia Soil and Water Conservation Board. The Board shall provide copies of the applications to the chairmen of the soil and water districts, where applicable, and the local governing bodies having jurisdiction in the area where the damage has occurred. (1981, c. 450, § 21-11.25; 1988, c. 891.)

§ **10.1-654. Damage inspections and reports.** — A. Upon receipt of an application for assistance, the Board shall schedule a field inspection of the affected stream segment to determine the extent of damages. Such field inspections should be scheduled and coordinated so that affected landowners and appropriate conservation districts and local government officials can participate.

B. Following the field inspection, the Board shall prepare an inspection report which includes a recommendation concerning the extent to which the Commonwealth should assist the applicant in restoring the stream.

C. Draft copies of the inspection report shall be submitted to the applicant, persons who attended the field inspection, and chairmen of conservation districts and local governing bodies having jurisdiction in the area where the damage has occurred. These persons shall be given forty-five days to submit written comments and recommendations concerning the report. The final report shall contain copies of all written comments and recommendations received. (1981, c. 450, § 21-11.26; 1988, c. 891.)

§ 10.1-655. Types of assistance. — Upon approval of an application for assistance, the Board may provide technical and financial assistance to the applicant according to the following guidelines:

1. The Board shall maintain a technical staff to recommend stream restoration measures, to estimate costs, and to prepare engineering plans and specifications which may be used to implement such measures. The actual preparation of plans and specifications shall not be undertaken until the applicant certifies that adequate funding is available, and that the plans will be implemented within one year after all necessary permits are obtained.

2. Financial assistance may be provided to applicants to the extent that funds for that purpose are available to the Board. In no case shall such assistance exceed fifty percent of the total cost of construction. Funds shall not be disbursed until the Board has made a final inspection and has determined that all work is adequately completed in accordance with the plans and specifications.

3. To receive financial assistance, applicants must certify that they have explored and exhausted all other possible funding sources. In cases where a national disaster area has been declared, no funding shall be provided under the Program until it is determined to what extent the federal government will participate in stream restoration along the segments under consideration.

When requests for financial assistance exceed available resources, the Board shall set priorities and allocate funds as it deems appropriate to accomplish the maximum benefit. (1981, c. 450, § 21-11.28; 1988, c. 891.)

§ 10.1-656. Board action on assistance requests. — The Board shall consider requests for technical and financial assistance from landowners whose property borders on or contains natural streams which have been damaged by flooding. Upon consideration of the application, inspection report, and any other relevant information, the Board shall determine whether or not assistance shall be provided, and the type and extent of assistance to be provided. In making such determinations, the Board shall consider the potential for continual accelerated erosion of the stream banks in the future and other possible detrimental effects to the stream which may result if no corrective measures are undertaken. In cases where it is determined that there is not likely to be accelerated stream bank erosion or other significant detrimental effects in the future, the assistance request shall not be approved. (1981, c. 450, § 21-11.27; 1988, c. 891.)

§ 10.1-657. Account established. — An account designated as the Stream Restoration Account shall be established to provide grants to landowners who make requests under the Stream Restoration Assistance Programs. The Board may seek money from federal and private sources to establish and maintain the Stream Restoration Fund. (1981, c. 450, § 21-11.29; 1988, c. 891.)

ARTICLE 6.

Comprehensive Flood Control Program.

§ 10.1-658. State interest in flood control. — A. The General Assembly declares that storm events cause recurrent flooding of Virginia's land resources and result in the loss of life, damage to property, unsafe and unsanitary conditions and the disruption of commerce and government services, placing at risk the health, safety and welfare of those citizens living in flood-prone areas of the Commonwealth. Flood waters disregard jurisdictional boundaries, and the public interest requires the management of flood-prone areas in a manner which prevents injuries to persons, damage to property and pollution of state waters.

B. The General Assembly, therefore, supports and encourages those measures which prevent, mitigate and alleviate the effects of stormwater surges and flooding, and declares that the expenditure of public funds and any obligations incurred in the development of flood control and other civil works projects, the benefits of which may accrue to any county, municipality or region in the Commonwealth, are necessary expenses of local and state government. (1989, cc. 468, 497.)

§ **10.1-659. Flood protection programs; coordination.** — The provisions of this chapter shall be coordinated with federal, state and local flood prevention and water quality programs to minimize loss of life, property damage and negative impacts on the environment. This program coordination shall include but not be limited to the following: flood prevention, flood plain management, small watershed protection, dam safety, soil conservation, stormwater management and erosion and sediment control programs of the Department of Conservation and Recreation; the construction activities of the Department of Transportation which result in hydrologic modification of rivers, streams and flood plains; the water quality and other water management programs of the State Water Control Board; forested watershed management programs of the Department of Forestry; the statewide building code and other land use control programs of the Department of Housing and Community Development; local planning assistance programs of the Council on the Environment; the habitat management programs of the Virginia Marine Resources Commission; the hazard mitigation planning and disaster response programs of the Department of Emergency Management; the fish habitat protection programs of the Department of Game and Inland Fisheries; the mineral extraction regulatory program of the Department of Mines, Minerals and Energy; the flood plain restrictions of the Department of Waste Management; the Chesapeake Bay Preservation Area criteria and local government assistance programs of the Chesapeake Bay Local Assistance Board. The Department shall also coordinate and cooperate with localities in rendering assistance to such localities in their efforts to comply with the planning, subdivision of land and zoning provisions of Chapter 22 (§ 15.2-2200 et seq.) of Title 15.2. The Department shall cooperate with other public and private agencies having flood plain management programs, and shall coordinate its responsibilities under this article and any other law. These activities shall constitute the Commonwealth's flood prevention and protection program. (1989, cc. 468, 497.)

CHAPTER 7.

SHORELINE EROSION AND PUBLIC BEACH PRESERVATION.

ARTICLE 1.

Shore Erosion Control.

§ 10.1-700. Definition. — As used in this article, the term "shore erosion" means the process of destruction by the action of water, wind, or ice of the land bordering any body of water including all rivers and the tidal waters of the Commonwealth. (1972, c. 855, § 21-11.17; 1988, c. 891.)

§ 10.1-701. Duties of Department. — The Department shall have the duty to:
1. Coordinate shore erosion control programs of all state agencies and institutions to implement practical solutions to shoreline erosion problems; however, such coordination shall not restrict the statutory authority of the individual agencies having responsibilities relating to shore erosion control;
2. Secure the cooperation and assistance of the United States and any of its agencies to protect waterfront property from destructive shore erosion;
3. Evaluate the effectiveness and practicability of current shore erosion control programs; and
4. Explore all facets of the problems and alternative solutions to determine if other practical and economical methods and practices may be devised to control shore erosion. (1972, c. 855, § 21-11.18; 1980, c. 368; 1988, c. 891.)

§ 10.1-702. Shore Erosion Advisory Service. — The Department is authorized to assist in carrying out the coordination responsibility of shore erosion control programs as herein assigned, and to establish a Shoreline Erosion Advisory Service. (1972, c. 855, § 21-11.19; 1980, c. 368; 1988, c. 891.)

§ 10.1-703. Cooperation and coordination with Virginia Institute of Marine Science. — The Department shall cooperate and coordinate with the Virginia Institute of Marine Science of the College of William and Mary for research, training and technical advice on erosion-related problems. (1980, c. 368, § 21-11.20; 1988, c. 891.)

§ 10.1-704. Use of dredged material for beach nourishment; priority. — The beaches of the Commonwealth shall be given priority consideration as sites for the disposal of that portion of dredged material determined to be suitable for beach nourishment. The Secretary of Natural Resources shall have the responsibility of determining whether the dredged material is suitable for beach nourishment. (1987, cc. 220, 231, § 21-11.16:1; 1988, c. 891.)

ARTICLE 2.

Public Beach Conservation and Development Act.

§ 10.1-705. Definitions. — As used in this article, unless the context requires a different meaning:
"Agency of this Commonwealth" includes the government of this Commonwealth and any subdivision, agency, or instrumentality, corporate or otherwise, of the government of this Commonwealth.

"Board" means the Board of Conservation and Recreation.

"Develop" or *"development"* means the replenishment and restoration of existing public beaches.

"Erosion" means the process of destruction by the action of wind, water, or ice of the land bordering the tidal waters of the Commonwealth.

"Government" or *"governmental"* includes the government of this Commonwealth, the government of the United States, and any subdivision, agency, or instrumentality, corporate or otherwise, of either of them.

"Locality" means a county, city or town.

"Program" means the provisions of the Public Beach Conservation and Development Act.

"Public beach" means a sandy beach located on a tidal shoreline suitable for bathing in a county, city or town and open to indefinite public use.

"Reach" means a shoreline segment wherein there is mutual interaction of the forces of erosion, sediment transport and accretion.

"United States" or *"agencies of the United States"* includes the United States of America, the United States Department of Agriculture, and any other agency or instrumentality, corporate or otherwise, of the United States of America. (1980, c. 428, § 10-217; 1984, c. 750; 1985, c. 448; 1988, c. 891; 2003, cc. 79, 89.)

§ 10.1-706. Duties of the Department. — The Department shall:

1. Promote understanding of the value of public beaches and the causes and effects of erosion;

2. Make available information concerning erosion of public beaches;

3. Encourage research and development of new erosion control techniques and new sources of sand for public beach enhancement. (1980, c. 428, § 10-216; 1984, c. 235; 1988, c. 891.)

§ 10.1-707. Board duties; allocation of funds. — A. The Board shall (i) review the financial needs of localities for implementation of this article; (ii) determine successful applicants; (iii) determine the equitable allocation of funds among participating localities except for allocations provided for in the current general appropriations act; and (iv) oversee local implementation of approved projects.

B. The Department shall provide the Board with staff assistance and shall maintain necessary financial records. (1980, c. 428, § 10-218; 1984, cc. 739, 750; 1985, c. 448; 1986, c. 152; 1988, c. 891; 1989, cc. 656, 660; 2003, cc. 79, 89.)

§ 10.1-708. Relationship of Board and Director; guidelines. — The Board shall be responsible for the allocation of the grant fund established in § 10.1-709. The Board shall submit the names of recipient localities to the Director and the Director shall disburse funds to designated localities. The Board may establish guidelines governing application procedures, allocations or implementation standards. (1980, c. 428, § 10-219; 1984, c. 750; 1988, c. 891.)

§ 10.1-709. Establishment of fund; unexpended money. — A. A special fund to be known as the Public Beach Maintenance and Development Fund shall be established to provide grants to local governments covering up to one-half of the costs of erosion abatement measures designed to conserve, protect, improve, maintain and develop public beaches. No grants to any locality shall exceed 30 percent of the money appropriated to such fund for the biennium unless otherwise provided for in the current general appropriations act. Money appropriated from such fund shall be matched equally by local

funds. Federal funds shall not be used by localities to match money given from the fund. Localities may, however, combine state and local funds to match federal funds for purposes of securing federal grants. Interest earned or moneys received by the Fund shall remain in the Fund and be credited to it. Any money remaining in the Fund at the close of the first fiscal year of a biennium shall not revert to the general fund and shall be reappropriated and allotted.

B. Up to $250,000 per year of the money deposited to the Fund including interest accrued may be used for the Board's administrative and operating expenses including but not limited to expenses of the Board and its members, and expenses related to duties outlined in §§ 10.1-701, 10.1-702, 10.1-703, 10.1-706, and 10.1-707. All such expenditures shall be subject to approval by the Board.

C. Money that remains unobligated by the Board from the fund at the end of the biennium for which it was appropriated shall be retained and shall become a Special Emergency Assistance Fund to be used at the discretion of the Governor for the emergency conservation and development of public beaches damaged or destroyed by an unusually severe storm, hurricane or other natural disaster. (1980, c. 428, § 10-220; 1982, c. 329; 1986, c. 152; 1988, c. 891; 2003, cc. 79, 89.)

§ **10.1-710. Guidelines for allocation of grant funds.** — The Board shall consider the following when selecting localities for program participation and in determining grant allocations:

1. Present and future beach ownership;
2. Erosion caused by public navigational works;
3. Intensity of use;
4. Availability of public beaches in the vicinity;
5. Evidence of a locality's ability and willingness to develop a long-term capacity to combat erosion;
6. Rate of erosion;
7. Actions of a locality which lead to, or may result in, the erosion of beaches; and
8. Such other matters as the Board shall deem sufficient for consideration. (1980, c. 428, § 10-221; 1984, c. 235; 1988, c. 891.)

§ **10.1-711. Local erosion advisory commissions.** — In order to qualify for the program, localities shall establish local erosion advisory commissions which shall determine local erosion problems, review the locality's erosion control projects, suggest strategies for the future, and assess program implementation. (1980, c. 428, § 10-222; 1984, c. 235; 1988, c. 891.)

CHAPTER 8.

HISTORIC LANDMARKS AND MONUMENTS.

§§ **10.1-800 through 10.1-817:** Repealed by Acts 1989, c. 656.

Cross references. — For new chapters relating to historic resources, antiquities, and historic preservation, see Chapters 22 and 24.1 of Title 10.1.

Editor's note. — Repealed Chapter 8 of Title 10.1, relating to historic landmarks and monuments, was enacted as part of Title 10.1 by Acts 1988, c. 891.

Repealed §§ 10.1-812, 10.1-813 and 10.1-814 were amended by Acts 1989, c. 711. Effect has been given in §§ 10.1-2211, 10.1-2212 and 10.1-2213, respectively, to these amendments.

CHAPTER 9.

VIRGINIA ANTIQUITIES ACT.

§§ 10.1-900 through 10.1-906: Repealed by Acts 1989, c. 656.

Cross references. — For present provisions as to the Virginia Antiquities Act, see Chapter 23 of Title 10.1. For new chapters relating to historic resources and historic preservation, see Chapters 22 and 24.1 of Title 10.1.

Editor's note. — Repealed Chapter 9 of Title 10.1, the Virginia Antiquities Act, was enacted as part of Title 10.1 by Acts 1988, c. 891.

CHAPTER 10.

CAVE PROTECTION ACT.

§ 10.1-1000. Definitions. — As used in this chapter, unless the context requires a different meaning:

"Board" means the Cave Board.

"Cave" means any naturally occurring void, cavity, recess, or system of interconnecting passages beneath the surface of the earth or within a cliff or ledge including natural subsurface water and drainage systems, but not including any mine, tunnel, aqueduct, or other man-made excavation, which is large enough to permit a person to enter. The word "cave" includes or is synonymous with cavern, sinkhole, natural pit, grotto, and rock shelter.

"Cave life" means any rare or endangered animal or other life form which normally occurs in, uses, visits, or inhabits any cave or subterranean water system.

"Commercial cave" means any cave utilized by the owner for the purposes of exhibition to the general public as a profit or nonprofit enterprise, wherein a fee is collected for entry.

"Gate" means any structure or device located to limit or prohibit access or entry to any cave.

"Material" means all or any part of any archaeological, paleontological, biological, or historical item including, but not limited to, any petroglyph, pictograph, basketry, human remains, tool, beads, pottery, projectile point, remains of historical mining activity or any other occupation found in any cave.

"Owner" means a person who owns title to land where a cave is located, including a person who owns title to a leasehold estate in such land, and including the Commonwealth and any of its agencies, departments, boards, bureaus, commissions, or authorities, as well as counties, municipalities, and other political subdivisions of the Commonwealth.

"Person" means any individual, partnership, firm, association, trust, or corporation or other legal entity.

"Sinkhole" means a closed topographic depression or basin, generally draining underground, including, but not restricted to, a doline, uvala, blind valley, or sink.

"Speleogen" means an erosional feature of the cave boundary and includes or is synonymous with anastomoses, scallops, rills, flutes, spongework, and pendants.

"Speleothem" means a natural mineral formation or deposit occurring in a cave. This includes or is synonymous with stalagmite, stalactite, helectite, shield, anthodite, gypsum flower and needle, angel's hair, soda straw, drapery, bacon, cave pearl, popcorn (coral), rimstone dam, column, palette, flowstone, et cetera. Speleothems are commonly composed of calcite, epsomite, gypsum, aragonite, celestite, and other similar minerals. (1979, c. 252, § 10-150.12; 1988, c. 891.)

§ **10.1-1001. Cave Board; qualifications; officers.** — A. The Cave Board is continued within the Department of Conservation and Recreation and shall consist of the Director of the Department of Historic Resources, or his designee, serving in an ex officio capacity and eleven citizens of Virginia appointed by the Governor for four-year terms. Appointments shall be made on the basis of activity and knowledge in the conservation, exploration, study and management of caves.

B. The Cave Board shall meet at least three times a year. Six members shall constitute a quorum for the transaction of business. The Board shall annually elect a chairman, vice-chairman and recording secretary and such other officers as the Board deems necessary. (1979, c. 433, §§ 9-152.1, 9-152.2; 1980, c. 745; 1984, c. 750; 1985, c. 448; 1988, c. 891; 1989, c. 656.)

§ **10.1-1002. Powers and duties of Cave Board.** — A. The Cave Board may perform all tasks necessary to carry out the purposes of this chapter, including the following:

1. Accept any gift, money, security or other source of funding and expend such funds to effectuate the purposes of this chapter.

2. Serve as an advisory board to any requesting state agency on matters relating to caves and karst.

3. Conduct and maintain an inventory of publicly owned caves in Virginia.

4. Provide cave management expertise and service to requesting public agencies and cave owners.

5. Maintain a current list of all significant caves in Virginia and report any real and present danger to such caves.

6. Provide cave data for use by state and other governmental agencies.

7. Publish or assist in publishing articles, pamphlets, brochures or books on caves and cave-related concerns.

8. Facilitate data gathering and research efforts on caves.

9. Advise civil defense authorities on the present and future use of Virginia caves in civil defense.

10. Advise on the need for and desirability of a state cave recreation plan.

11. Inform the public about the value of cave resources and the importance of preserving them for the citizens of the Commonwealth.

B. The Cave Board shall have the duty to:

1. Protect the rare, unique and irreplaceable minerals and archaeological resources found in caves.

2. Protect and maintain cave life.

3. Protect the ground water flow which naturally occurs in caves from water pollution.

4. Protect the integrity of caves that have unique characteristics or are exemplary natural community types.

5. Make recommendations to interested state agencies concerning any proposed rule, regulation or administrative policy which directly affects the use and conservation of caves in this Commonwealth.

6. Study any matters of special concern relating to caves and karst. (1979, c. 252, § 10-150.11; 1979, c. 433, §§ 9-152.1, 9-152.3 to 9-152.5; 1980, c. 745; 1984, cc. 734, 750; 1985, c. 448; 1988, c. 891.)

§ 10.1-1003. Permits for excavation and scientific investigation; how obtained; penalties. — A. In addition to the written permission of the owner required by § 10.1-1004 a permit shall be obtained from the Department of Conservation and Recreation prior to excavating or removing any archaeological, paleontological, prehistoric, or historic feature of any cave. The Department shall issue a permit to excavate or remove such a feature if it finds with the concurrence of the Director of the Department of Historic Resources that it is in the best interest of the Commonwealth and that the applicant meets the criteria of this section. The permit shall be issued for a period of two years and may be renewed upon expiration. Such permit shall not be transferable; however, the provisions of this section shall not preclude any person from working under the direct supervision of the permittee.

B. All field investigations, explorations, or recovery operations undertaken under this section shall be carried out under the general supervision of the Department and in a manner to ensure that the maximum amount of historic, scientific, archaeologic, and educational information may be recovered and preserved in addition to the physical recovery of objects.

C. A person applying for a permit pursuant to this section shall:

1. Be a historic, scientific, or educational institution, or a professional or amateur historian, biologist, archaeologist or paleontologist, who is qualified and recognized in these areas of field investigations.

2. Provide a detailed statement to the Department giving the reasons and objectives for excavation or removal and the benefits expected to be obtained from the contemplated work.

3. Provide data and results of any completed excavation, study, or collection at the first of each calendar year.

4. Obtain the prior written permission of the owner if the site of the proposed excavation is on privately owned land.

5. Carry the permit while exercising the privileges granted.

D. Any person who fails to obtain a permit required by subsection A hereof shall be guilty of a Class 1 misdemeanor. Any violation of subsection C hereof shall be punished as a Class 3 misdemeanor, and the permit shall be revoked.

E. The provisions of this section shall not apply to any person in any cave located on his own property. (1979, c. 252, § 10-150.16; 1982, c. 81; 1984, c. 750; 1988, c. 891; 1989, c. 656.)

Cross references. — As to punishment for Class 1 and 3 misdemeanors, see § 18.2-11.

Michie's Jurisprudence. — For related discussion, see 18 M.J. Trespass, § 1.

§ 10.1-1004. Vandalism; penalties. — A. It shall be unlawful for any person, without express, prior, written permission of the owner, to:

1. Break, break off, crack, carve upon, write, burn, or otherwise mark upon, remove, or in any manner destroy, disturb, deface, mar, or harm the surfaces of any cave or any natural material which may be found therein, whether attached or broken, including speleothems, speleogens, and sedimentary deposits. The provisions of this section shall not prohibit minimal disturbance for scientific exploration.

2. Break, force, tamper with, or otherwise disturb a lock, gate, door, or other obstruction designed to control or prevent access to any cave, even though entrance thereto may not be gained.

3. Remove, deface, or tamper with a sign stating that a cave is posted or citing provisions of this chapter.

4. Excavate, remove, destroy, injure, deface, or in any manner disturb any burial grounds, historic or prehistoric resources, archaeological or paleontological site or any part thereof, including relics, inscriptions, saltpeter workings, fossils, bones, remains of historical human activity, or any other such features which may be found in any cave, except those caves owned by the Commonwealth or designated as Commonwealth archaeological sites or zones, and which are subject to the provisions of the Virginia Antiquities Act (§ 10.1-2300 et seq.).

B. Entering or remaining in a cave which has not been posted by the owner shall not by itself constitute a violation of this section.

C. Any violation of this section shall be punished as a Class 1 misdemeanor.

D. The provisions of this section shall not apply to an owner of a cave on his own property. (1979, c. 252, § 10-150.13; 1982, c. 81; 1988, c. 891.)

Cross references. — As to punishment for Class 1 misdemeanors, see § 18.2-11.

§ **10.1-1005. Pollution; penalties.** — A. It shall be unlawful for any person, without express, prior, written permission of the owner, to store, dump, litter, dispose of or otherwise place any refuse, garbage, dead animals, sewage, or toxic substances harmful to cave life or humans, in any cave or sinkhole. It shall also be unlawful to burn within a cave or sinkhole any material which produces any smoke or gas which is harmful to any naturally occurring organism in any cave.

B. Any violation of this section shall be punished as a Class 1 misdemeanor. (1979, c. 252, § 10-150.14; 1982, c. 81; 1988, c. 891.)

Cross references. — As to punishment for Class 1 misdemeanors, see § 18.2-11.

§ **10.1-1006. Disturbance of naturally occurring organisms; scientific collecting permits; penalties.** — A. It shall be unlawful to remove, kill, harm, or otherwise disturb any naturally occurring organisms within any cave, except for safety or health reasons; however, scientific collecting permits may be obtained from the Department.

B. Any violation of this section shall be punished as a Class 3 misdemeanor. (1979, c. 252, § 10-150.15; 1988, c. 891.)

Cross references. — As to punishment for Class 3 misdemeanors, see § 18.2-11.

§ **10.1-1007. Sale of speleothems; penalties.** — It shall be unlawful for any person to sell or offer for sale any speleothems in this Commonwealth, or to export them for sale outside the Commonwealth. Any violation of this section shall be punished as a Class 1 misdemeanor. (1979, c. 252, § 10-150.17; 1982, c. 81; 1988, c. 891.)

Cross references. — As to punishment for Class 1 misdemeanors, see § 18.2-11.

Michie's Jurisprudence. — For related discussion, see 5A M.J. Counties, §§ 72, 77.

§ **10.1-1008. Liability of owners and agents limited; sovereign immunity of Commonwealth not waived.** — Neither the owner of a cave nor his authorized agents acting within the scope of their authority are liable for injuries sustained by any person using the cave for recreational or scientific purposes if no charge has been made for the use of the cave, notwithstanding that an inquiry as to the experience or expertise of the individual seeking consent may have been made.

Nothing in this section shall be construed to constitute a waiver of the sovereign immunity of the Commonwealth or any of its boards, departments, bureaus, or agencies. (1979, c. 252, § 10-150.18; 1988, c. 891.)

CHAPTER 10.1.

VIRGINIA CONSERVATION EASEMENT ACT.

§ 10.1-1009. Definitions. — As used in this chapter, unless the context otherwise requires:

"Conservation easement" means a nonpossessory interest of a holder in real property, whether easement appurtenant or in gross, acquired through gift, purchase, devise, or bequest imposing limitations or affirmative obligations, the purposes of which include retaining or protecting natural or open-space values of real property, assuring its availability for agricultural, forestal, recreational, or open-space use, protecting natural resources, maintaining or enhancing air or water quality, or preserving the historical, architectural or archaeological aspects of real property.

"Holder" means a charitable corporation, charitable association, or charitable trust which has been declared exempt from taxation pursuant to 26 U.S.C.A. § 501 (c) (3) and the primary purposes or powers of which include: (i) retaining or protecting the natural or open-space values of real property; (ii) assuring the availability of real property for agricultural, forestal, recreational, or open-space use; (iii) protecting natural resources; (iv) maintaining or enhancing air or water quality; or (v) preserving the historic, architectural or archaeological aspects of real property.

"Public body" means any entity defined in § 10.1-1700.

"Third party right of enforcement" means a right provided in a conservation easement to enforce any of its terms granted to a governmental body, charitable corporation, charitable association or charitable trust which, although eligible to be a holder, is not a holder. (1988, cc. 720, 891.)

Editor's note. — This chapter was enacted by Acts 1988, c. 720, as §§ 10-158.21 through 10-158.28. Pursuant to Acts 1988, c. 891, cl. 5, these sections have been incorporated into Title 10.1 as §§ 10.1-1009 through 10.1-1016.

Law Review. — For survey article on judi- cial decisions in real estate law from June 1, 2002 through June 1, 2003, see 38 U. Rich. L. Rev. 223 (2003).

Michie's Jurisprudence. — For related discussion, see 6B M.J. Easements, § 2.

CASE NOTES

Legislative intent. — Virginia Conservation Easement Act did not create a new right to burden land by a negative easement in gross for the purpose of land conservation and historic preservation, but facilitated the continued creation of such easements by providing a clear statutory framework under which tax exemp- tions are made available to charitable organizations devoted to those purposes and tax benefits and incentives are provided to the grantors of such easements, contrary to the common law; moreover, the easement at issue was not of a novel character and is consistent with the statutory recognition of negative easements in gross for conservation and historic purposes. United States v. Blackman, 270 Va. 68, 613 S.E.2d 442, 2005 Va. LEXIS 69 (2005).

§ 10.1-1010. Creation, acceptance and duration. — A. A holder may acquire a conservation easement by gift, purchase, devise or bequest.

B. No right or duty in favor of or against a holder and no right in favor of a person having a third-party right of enforcement arises under a conservation easement before its acceptance by the holder and a recordation of the acceptance.

C. A conservation easement shall be perpetual in duration unless the instrument creating it otherwise provides a specific time. For all easements, the holder shall (i) meet the criteria in § 10.1-1009 and (ii) either have had a principal office in the Commonwealth for at least five years, or be a national organization in existence for at least five years which has an office in the Commonwealth and has registered and is in good standing with the State Corporation Commission. Until a holder has met these requirements, the holder may co-hold a conservation easement with another holder that meets the requirements.

D. An interest in real property in existence at the time a conservation easement is created is not impaired by it unless the owner of the interest is a party to the conservation easement or consents to it in writing.

E. No conservation easement shall be valid and enforceable unless the limitations or obligations created thereby conform in all respects to the comprehensive plan at the time the easement is granted for the area in which the real property is located.

F. This chapter does not affect the power of the court to modify or terminate a conservation easement in accordance with the principles of law and equity, or in any way limit the power of eminent domain as possessed by any public body. In any such proceeding the holder of the conservation easement shall be compensated for the value of the easement. (1988, cc. 720, 891; 2000, c. 182; 2003, c. 1014.)

Cross references. — As to loans for conservation or open-space easements, see § 62.1-229.3.

Editor's note. — Acts 2004, c. 364, which amended subsection C by substituting "four years" for "five years," in cl. 2 provided: "That the provisions of this act shall expire on July 1, 2005." The section is set out above without the amendment by Acts 2004, c. 364.

Law Review. — For 2003/2004 survey of environmental law, see 39 U. Rich. L. Rev. 203 (2004).

§ 10.1-1011. Taxation. — A. Where an easement held pursuant to this chapter or the Open-Space Land Act (§ 10.1-1700 et seq.) by its terms is perpetual, neither the interest of the holder of a conservation easement nor a third-party right of enforcement of such an easement shall be subject to state or local taxation nor shall the owner of the fee be taxed for the interest of the holder of the easement.

B. Assessments of the fee interest in land that is subject to a perpetual conservation easement held pursuant to this chapter or the Open-Space Land Act (§ 10.1-1700 et seq.) shall reflect the reduction in the fair market value of the land that results from the inability of the owner of the fee to use such property for uses terminated by the easement. To ensure that the owner of the fee is not taxed on the value of the interest of the holder of the easement, the fair market value of such land (i) shall be based only on uses of the land that are permitted under the terms of the easement and (ii) shall not include any value attributable to the uses or potential uses of the land that have been terminated by the easement.

C. Notwithstanding the provisions of subsection B, land which is (i) subject to a perpetual conservation easement held pursuant to this chapter or the Open-Space Land Act (§ 10.1-1700 et seq.), (ii) devoted to open-space use as defined in § 58.1-3230, and (iii) in any county, city or town which has provided for land use assessment and taxation of any class of land within its jurisdiction pursuant to § 58.1-3231 or § 58.1-3232, shall be assessed and taxed at the use value for open space, if the land otherwise qualifies for such assessment at the time the easement is dedicated. If an easement is in existence at the time the locality enacts land use assessment, the easement shall qualify for such assessment. Once the land with the easement qualifies for land use assessment, it shall continue to qualify so long as the locality has land use assessment. (1988, cc. 720, 891; 1993, c. 390; 1998, c. 487.)

§ **10.1-1012. Notification.** — Whenever any instrument conveying a conservation easement is recorded after July 1, 1988, the party responsible for recording it or his agent shall mail certified copies thereof, together with notice as to the date and place of recordation, to the local jurisdiction in which the real property subject thereto is located, the Attorney General of the Commonwealth, the Virginia Outdoors Foundation and to any public body named in such instrument. Certified copies of the instrument creating such easement, together with information specifying the date and place of its recordation, shall be mailed to the local jurisdiction in which the real property subject thereto is located, the Attorney General of the Commonwealth, the Virginia Outdoors Foundation and to any public body named in such instrument. Whenever any conservation easement is on lands that are part of a historic landmark as certified, either by the United States or the Virginia Historic Landmarks Board, any notice required above shall also be given to the Virginia Historic Landmarks Board. (1988, cc. 720, 891.)

§ **10.1-1013. Standing.** — An action affecting a conservation easement may be brought by:
1. An owner of an interest in real property burdened by the easement;
2. A holder of the easement;
3. A person having an express third-party right of enforcement;
4. The Attorney General of the Commonwealth;
5. The Virginia Outdoors Foundation;
6. The Virginia Historic Landmarks Board;
7. The local government in which the real property is located; or
8. Any other governmental agency or person with standing under other statutes or common law. (1988, cc. 720, 891.)

§ **10.1-1014. Validity.** — A conservation easement is valid even though:
1. It is not appurtenant to an interest in real property;
2. It can be or has been assigned to another holder;
3. It is not of a character that has been recognized traditionally at common law;
4. It imposes a negative burden;
5. It imposes affirmative obligations upon the owner of an interest in the burdened property or upon the holder;
6. The benefit does not touch or concern real property; or
7. There is no privity of estate or of contract.
Except as otherwise provided in this chapter, a conservation easement may be created, conveyed, recorded, assigned, released, modified, terminated, or otherwise altered or affected in the same manner as other easements. (1988, cc. 720, 891.)

§ 10.1-1015. Conveyance to the Commonwealth. — Whenever any holder as defined in this chapter, or the successors or assigns thereof, shall cease to exist, any conservation easement and any right of enforcement held by it shall vest in the Virginia Outdoors Foundation, unless the instrument creating the easement otherwise provides for its transfer to some other holder or public body. In an easement vested in the Virginia Outdoors Foundation by operation of the preceding sentence, the Foundation may retain it or thereafter convey it to any other public body or any holder the Foundation deems most appropriate to hold and enforce such interest in accordance with the purpose of the original conveyance of the easement. (1988, cc. 720, 891.)

§ 10.1-1016. Savings clause. — Nothing herein shall in any way affect the power of a public body under any other statute, including without limitation the Virginia Outdoors Foundation and the Virginia Historic Landmarks Board, to acquire and hold conservation easements or affect the terms of any such easement held by any public body. (1988, cc. 720, 891.)

CHAPTER 10.2.

VIRGINIA LAND CONSERVATION FOUNDATION.

§ 10.1-1017. Foundation created. — There is hereby created the Virginia Land Conservation Foundation, hereinafter referred to as the Foundation, a body politic and corporate to have such powers and duties as hereinafter provided. (1992, c. 426; 1999, cc. 900, 906.)

Law Review. — For an article, "The Rhetoric and Reality of Nature Protection: Toward a New Discourse," see 57 Wash. & Lee L. Rev. 11 (2000).

§ 10.1-1018. Virginia Land Conservation Board of Trustees; membership; terms; vacancies; compensation and expenses. — A. The Foundation shall be governed and administered by a Board of Trustees. The Board shall have a total membership of 19 members that shall consist of 17 citizen members and two ex officio voting members as follows: four citizen members, who may be members of the House of Delegates, to be appointed by the Speaker of the House of Delegates and, if such members are members of the House of Delegates, in accordance with the principles of proportional representation contained in the Rules of the House of Delegates; two citizen members, who may be members of the Senate, to be appointed by the Senate Committee on Rules; 11 nonlegislative citizen members, one from each congressional district, to be appointed by the Governor; and the Secretary of Natural Resources, or his designee, and the Secretary of Agriculture and Forestry, or his designee, to serve ex officio with voting privileges.

Nonlegislative citizen members shall be appointed for four-year terms, except that initial appointments shall be made for terms of one to four years in a manner whereby no more than six members shall have terms that expire in the same year. Legislative members and the ex officio member shall serve terms coincident with their terms of office. Appointments to fill vacancies, other than by expiration of a term, shall be made for the unexpired terms. Vacancies shall be filled in the same manner as the original appointments. All members may be reappointed. However, no Senate member shall serve more than two consecutive four-year terms, no House member shall serve more than four consecutive two-year terms and no nonlegislative citizen member shall serve more than two consecutive four-year terms. The remainder of any term to which a member is appointed to fill a vacancy shall not constitute a term in determining the member's eligibility for reappointment. Nonlegislative citizen members shall have experience or expertise, professional or personal, in one or more of the following areas: natural resource protection and conservation, construction and real estate development, natural habitat protection, environmental resource inventory and identification, forestry management, farming, farmland preservation, fish and wildlife management, historic preservation, and outdoor recreation. At least one of the nonlegislative citizen members shall be a farmer. Members of the Board shall post bond in the penalty of $5,000 with the State Comptroller prior to entering upon the functions of office.

B. The Secretary of Natural Resources shall serve as the chairman of the Board of Trustees. The chairman shall serve until his successor is appointed. The members appointed as provided in subsection A shall elect a vice-chairman annually from among the members of the Board. A majority of the members of the Board serving at any one time shall constitute a quorum for the transaction of business. The board shall meet at the call of the chairman or whenever a majority of the members so request.

C. Trustees of the Foundation shall receive no compensation for their services. All members shall be reimbursed for all reasonable and necessary expenses incurred in the performance of their duties on behalf of the Foundation as provided in §§ 2.2-2813 and 2.2-2825. Funding for the costs of expenses of the members shall be provided by the Department of Conservation and Recreation.

D. The chairman of the Board and any other person designated by the Board to handle the funds of the Foundation shall give bond, with corporate surety, in such penalty as is fixed by the Governor, conditioned upon the faithful discharge of his duties. The premium on the bonds shall be paid from funds available to the Foundation for such purpose.

E. The Board shall seek assistance in developing grant criteria and advice on grant priorities and any other appropriate issues from a task force consisting of the following agency heads or their designees: the Director of the Department of Conservation and Recreation, the Commissioner of Agriculture and Consumer Services, the State Forester, the Director of the Department of Historic Resources, the Director of the Department of Game and Inland Fisheries and the Executive Director of the Virginia Outdoors Foundation. The Board may request any other agency head to serve on or appoint a designee to serve on the task force. (1992, c. 426; 1999, cc. 900, 906; 2000, cc. 21, 294, 494, 1053; 2003, c. 885; 2005, cc. 633, 758; 2006, c. 45.)

Editor's note. — Acts 2005, c. 758, cl. 2, provides: "That this act shall not be construed to affect existing appointments, made by the Senate Committee on Privileges and Elections, for which the terms have not expired. However, any new appointments made after July 1, 2005 shall be made in accordance with the provisions of this act."

The 2005 amendments. — The 2005 amendment by c. 633 deleted former subsection F, which read: "The chairman of the Board shall submit to the Governor and the General Assembly a biennial executive summary of the interim activity and work of the Board no later than the first day of each even-numbered year regular session of the General Assembly. The executive summary shall be submitted as provided in the procedures of the Division of Legislature Automated Systems for the processing of legislative documents and reports and shall be posted on the General Assembly's website."

The 2005 amendment by c. 758, in subsection A, substituted "have a total membership of 18 members that shall consist of" for "consist of 18 members that include" and "Rules" for "Privileges and Elections" in the second sentence.

The 2006 amendments. — The 2006 amendment by c. 45, in the second sentence of subsection A, substituted "19" for "18," "two ex officio voting members" for "one ex officio voting member" and inserted "and the Secretary of Agriculture and Forestry, or his designee."

§ **10.1-1018.1. Reporting.** — The chairman of the Board shall submit to the Governor and the General Assembly, including the Chairmen of the House Committee on Appropriations, the House Committee on Agriculture, Chesapeake and Natural Resources, the Senate Committee on Finance, and the Senate Committee on Agriculture, Conservation and Natural Resources, and to the Director of the Department of Planning and Budget an executive summary and report of the interim activity and work of the Board on or before December 15 of each even-numbered year. The document shall report on the status of the Foundation and its Fund including, but not limited to, (i) implementation of its strategic plan; (ii) land conservation targeting tools developed for the Foundation; (iii) descriptions of projects that received funding; (iv) a description of the geographic distribution of land protected as provided in § 10.1-1021.1; (v) expenditures from, interest earned by, and financial obligations of the Fund; and (vi) progress made toward recognized state and regional land conservation goals. The executive summary and report shall be submitted as provided in the procedures of the Division of Legislative Automated Systems for the processing of legislative documents and reports and shall be posted on the General Assembly's website. (2005, c. 633.)

§ **10.1-1019. Executive secretary; land management.** — A. The Director of the Department of Conservation and Recreation shall serve as executive secretary to the Foundation and shall be responsible for providing technical assistance and performing any administrative duties that the Foundation may direct.

B. The Department of Conservation and Recreation shall administer the Foundation's lands as if such lands were departmental lands, and the regulations established by the Director for the management and protection of departmental lands shall apply to real estate held by the Foundation. The Department's conservation officers commissioned under § 10.1-115 shall have jurisdiction on all of the Foundation's lands and waters. (1992, c. 426; 2000, c. 1053.)

§ **10.1-1020. Virginia Land Conservation Fund; purposes of Foundation.** — A. The Foundation shall establish, administer, manage, including the creation of reserves, and make expenditures and allocations from a special, nonreverting fund in the state treasury to be known as the Virginia Land Conservation Fund, hereinafter referred to as the Fund. The Foundation shall establish and administer the Fund solely for the purposes of:

1. Acquiring fee simple title or other rights, including the purchase of development rights, to interests or privileges in property for the protection or preservation of ecological, cultural or historical resources, lands for recreational purposes, state forest lands, and lands for threatened or endangered species, fish and wildlife habitat, natural areas, agricultural and forestal lands and open space; and

2. Providing grants to state agencies, including the Virginia Outdoors Foundation, and matching grants to other public bodies and holders for

acquiring fee simple title or other rights, including the purchase of development rights, to interests or privileges in real property for the protection or preservation of ecological, cultural or historical resources, lands for recreational purposes, and lands for threatened or endangered species, fish and wildlife habitat, natural areas, agricultural and forestal lands and open space. The Board shall establish criteria for making grants from the Fund, including procedures for determining the amount of each grant and the required match. The criteria shall include provisions for grants to localities for purchase of development rights programs.

Interests in land acquired as provided in subdivision 1 of this subsection may be held by the Foundation or transferred to state agencies or other appropriate holders. Whenever a holder acquires any interest in land other than a fee simple interest as a result of a grant or transfer from the Foundation, such interest shall be held jointly by the holder and a public body. Whenever a holder acquires a fee simple interest in land as a result of a grant or transfer from the Foundation, a public body shall hold an open space easement in such land.

B. The Fund shall consist of general fund moneys and gifts, endowments or grants from the United States government, its agencies and instrumentalities, and funds from any other available sources, public or private. Such moneys, gifts, endowments, grants or funds from other sources may be either restricted or unrestricted. For the purposes of this chapter, *"restricted funds"* shall mean those funds received by the Board to which specific conditions apply; "restricted funds" shall include, but not be limited to, general obligation bond moneys and conditional gifts. *"Unrestricted funds"* shall mean those received by the Foundation to which no specific conditions apply; "unrestricted funds" shall include, but not be limited to, moneys appropriated to the Fund by the General Assembly to which no specific conditions are attached and unconditional gifts.

C. After an allocation for administrative expenses has been made as provided in subsection F, the remaining unrestricted funds in the Fund shall be allocated as follows:

1. Twenty-five percent shall be transferred to the Open-Space Lands Preservation Trust Fund to be used as provided in § 10.1-1801.1; and

2. Seventy-five percent shall be divided equally among the following four uses: (i) natural area protection; (ii) open spaces and parks; (iii) farmlands and forest preservation; and (iv) historic area preservation. Of the amount allocated as provided in this subdivision, at least one third shall be used to secure easements to be held or co-held by a public body.

D. Any moneys remaining in the Fund at the end of a biennium shall remain in the Fund, and shall not revert to the general fund. Interest earned on moneys received by the Fund other than bond proceeds shall remain in the Fund and be credited to it.

E. A portion of the Fund, not to exceed twenty percent of the annual balance of unrestricted funds, may be used to develop properties purchased in fee simple, or through the purchase of development rights, with the assets of the Fund for public use including, but not limited to, development of trails, parking areas, infrastructure, and interpretive projects or to conduct environmental assessments or other preliminary evaluations of properties prior to the acquisition of any property interest.

F. Up to $250,000 per year of the interest generated by the Fund may be used for the Foundation's administrative expenses, including, but not limited to, the expenses of the Board and its members, development of the Foundation's strategic plan, development and maintenance of an inventory of properties as provided in subdivision 1 b of § 10.1-1021, development of a needs assessment for future expenditures as provided in subdivision 1 c of § 10.1-

1021, and fulfillment of reporting requirements. All such expenditures shall be subject to approval by the Board of Trustees.

G. The Comptroller shall maintain the restricted funds and the unrestricted funds in separate accounts.

H. For the purposes of this section, *"public body"* shall have the meaning ascribed to it in § 10.1-1700, and *"holder"* shall have the meaning ascribed to it in § 10.1-1009. (1992, c. 426; 1999, cc. 900, 906; 2000, cc. 494, 1053; 2006, c. 227.)

The 2006 amendments. — The 2006 amendment by c. 227, in subdivisions A 1 and A 2, deleted "to" following "title" and inserted "including the purchase of development rights, to"; and inserted "or through the purchase of development rights" in subsection E.

§ 10.1-1021. Powers of the Foundation. — In order to carry out its purposes, the Foundation shall have the following powers and duties:

1. To prepare a comprehensive plan that recognizes and seeks to implement all of the purposes for which the Foundation is created. In preparing this plan, the Foundation shall:

a. Develop a strategic plan for the expenditure of unrestricted moneys received by the Fund. In developing a strategic plan for expending unrestricted moneys from the Fund, the Board of Trustees shall establish criteria for the expenditure of such moneys. The plan shall take into account the purposes for which restricted funds have been expended or earmarked. Such criteria may include:

(1) The ecological, outdoor recreational, historic, agricultural and forestal value of the property;

(2) An assessment of market values;

(3) Consistency with local comprehensive plans;

(4) Geographical balance of properties and interests in properties to be purchased;

(5) Availability of public and private matching funds to assist in the purchase;

(6) Imminent danger of loss of natural, outdoor, recreational or historic attributes of a significant portion of the land;

(7) Economic value to the locality and region attributable to the purchase; and

(8) Advisory opinions from local governments, state agencies or others;

b. Develop an inventory of those properties in which the Commonwealth holds a legal interest for the purpose set forth in subsection A of § 10.1-1020;

c. Develop a needs assessment for future expenditures from the Fund. In developing the needs assessment, the Board of Trustees shall consider among others the properties identified in the following: (i) Virginia Outdoors Plan, (ii) Virginia Natural Heritage Plan, (iii) Virginia Institute of Marine Science Inventory, (iv) Virginia Joint Venture Board of the North American Waterfowl Management Plan, and (v) Virginia Board of Historic Resources Inventory. In addition, the Board shall consider any information submitted by the Department of Agriculture and Consumer Services on farmland preservation priorities and any information submitted by the Department of Forestry on forest land initiatives and inventories; and

d. Maintain the inventory and needs assessment on an annual basis.

2. To expend directly or allocate the funds received by the Foundation to the appropriate state agencies for the purpose of acquiring those properties or property interests selected by the Board of Trustees. In the case of restricted funds the Board's powers shall be limited by the provisions of § 10.1-1022.

3. To enter into contracts and agreements, as approved by the Attorney General, to accomplish the purposes of the Foundation.

4. To receive and expend gifts, grants and donations from whatever source to further the purposes set forth in subsection B of § 10.1-1020.

5. To sell, exchange or otherwise dispose of or invest as it deems proper the moneys, securities, or other real or personal property or any interest therein given or bequeathed to it, unless such action is restricted by the terms of a gift or bequest. However, the provisions of § 10.1-1704 shall apply to any diversion from open-space use of any land given or bequeathed to the Foundation.

6. To conduct fund-raising events as deemed appropriate by the Board of Trustees.

7. To do any and all lawful acts necessary or appropriate to carry out the purposes for which the Foundation and Fund are established. (1992, c. 426; 1999, cc. 900, 906; 2000, c. 1053; 2005, c. 633.)

The 2005 amendments. — The 2005 amendment by c. 633 renumbered subdivisions 1 a (i) through 1 a (viii) as 1 a 1 through 1 a 8; deleted former subdivision 3 which read: "To submit a report biennially on the status of the Fund to the Governor and the General Assembly including, but not limited to, (i) implementation of its strategic plan, (ii) projects under consideration for acquisition with Fund moneys, and (iii) expenditures from the Fund, including a description of the extent to which such expenditures have achieved a fair geographic distribution of land protected as provided in § 10.1-1021.1" and redesignated former subdivisions 4 through 8 as subdivisions 3 through 7.

§ 10.1-1021.1. Geographic distribution of land protected. — The Foundation shall seek to achieve a fair distribution of land protected throughout the Commonwealth, based upon the following:

1. The importance of conserving land in all regions of the Commonwealth;

2. The importance of protecting specific properties that can benefit all Virginia citizens; and

3. The importance of addressing the particular land conservation needs of areas of the state where Fund moneys are generated. (2000, c. 1053.)

§ 10.1-1022. Expenditure of restricted funds. — The Foundation shall expend restricted funds only in accordance with the applicable restrictions, or allocate such funds to the designated or otherwise appropriate state agency subject to such restrictions. The state agency receiving restricted funds shall expend such funds only in accordance with the applicable restrictions. The Board of Trustees may make such recommendations as are appropriate to the agencies responsible for spending any restricted funds, and the agencies shall consider such recommendations prior to the expenditure of restricted funds received from the Foundation. State agencies and departments receiving funds directly for expenditure for a purpose for which the Foundation is created shall solicit and consider the advice of the Board with respect to the expenditure of such funds prior thereto. This section shall not affect the authority of the Foundation to exercise its discretion with regard to the expenditure or allocation of unrestricted funds received by the Foundation. (1992, c. 426.)

§ 10.1-1022.1. Expenditure of funds for natural area protection. — A. No matching grant shall be made from the Fund to any holder or public body for purchasing an interest in land for the protection of a natural area unless:

1. The holder or public body has demonstrated the necessary commitment and financial capability to manage the property; and

2. The Department has, after reviewing the grant application as provided in subsection B, recommended that the grant be made.

B. Natural area grant applications shall be submitted to the Foundation, which shall forward the application to the Department. The application shall include a budget for the proposed purchase and for the management of the property. The Department shall consider the following in making its recommendation on whether the grant should be made:

1. Whether the project will make a significant contribution to the protection of habitats for rare, threatened, or endangered plant or animal species, rare or state-significant natural communities, other ecological resources, or natural areas of Virginia;

2. Whether the area addresses a protection need identified in the Virginia Natural Heritage Plan;

3. The rarity of the elements targeted for conservation;

4. The size and viability of the site; and

5. Whether the holder or public body has the capability to protect the site from short-term and long-term stresses to the area.

C. Matching grant funds provided pursuant to this section shall be expended by the holder or public body within two years of receiving the funds, except that the Department may grant an extension of up to one year.

D. All property for which a matching grant is made pursuant to this section shall be dedicated as a natural area preserve as provided in § 10.1-213. Any such preserve that was purchased in fee simple by the holder or public body shall be open for public access for a reasonable amount of time each year, except as is necessary to protect sensitive resources or for management purposes, as determined by the holder or public body pursuant to an agreement with the Department. (1999, cc. 900, 906; 2001, cc. 164, 168.)

§ 10.1-1023. Certain expenditures prohibited. — Moneys from the Fund shall not be expended for the acquisition of any property interest through eminent domain. (1992, c. 426.)

§ 10.1-1024. Gifts and bequests to Foundation. — Gifts, devises and bequests of money, securities and other assets accepted by the Foundation, whether personal or real property, shall be deemed to be gifts to the Commonwealth, which shall be exempt from all state and local taxes and shall be regarded as property of the Commonwealth for the purposes of all tax laws. (1992, c. 426; 2000, c. 1053.)

§ 10.1-1025. Forms of accounts and records; audit of same. — The accounts and records of the Foundation showing the receipt and disbursement of funds from whatever source derived shall be in such form as the Auditor of Public Accounts prescribes, provided that such accounts shall correspond as nearly as possible to the accounts and records for such matters maintained by similar enterprises. The accounts and records of the Foundation shall be subject to audit by the Auditor of Public Accounts or his legal representative on an annual basis and the costs of such audit services shall be borne by the Foundation. The Foundation's fiscal year shall be the same as the Commonwealth's. (1992, c. 426.)

§ 10.1-1026. Cooperation of state agencies. — All state officers, agencies, commissions, boards, departments, institutions and foundations shall cooperate with and assist the Foundation in carrying out its purpose and, to that end, may accept any gift or conveyance of real property or interest therein or other property in the name of the Commonwealth from the Foundation. Such property shall be held in possession or used as provided in the terms of the trust, contract or instrumentality by which it was conveyed. (2000, c. 1053.)

SUBTITLE II.

ACTIVITIES ADMINISTERED BY OTHER ENTITIES.

CHAPTER 11.

FOREST RESOURCES AND THE DEPARTMENT OF FORESTRY.

ARTICLE 1.

Department of Forestry.

§ 10.1-1100. Department of Forestry; appointment of the State Forester. — The Department of Forestry, hereinafter referred to in this chapter as the Department, is continued as an agency under the supervision of the Secretary of Commerce and Trade. The Department shall be headed by the State Forester, who shall be appointed by the Governor to serve at his pleasure for a term coincident with his own.

Any vacancy in the office of the State Forester shall be filled by appointment by the Governor pursuant to the provisions of Article V, Section 10 of the Constitution of Virginia.

The State Forester shall be a technically trained forester and shall have both a practical and theoretical knowledge of forestry. (1986, c. 567, § 10-31.1; 1988, c. 891; 1993, c. 699.)

Law Review. — For article addressing significant developments in Virginia law pertaining to air quality, water quality and solid and hazardous waste, between 1990 and 1992, see "Environmental Law," 26 U. Rich. L. Rev. 729 (1992).

Michie's Jurisprudence. — For related discussion, see 18 M.J. Trees and Timber, § 3.

§ 10.1-1101. General powers of Department. — The Department shall have the following general powers, all of which, with the approval of the State Forester, may be exercised by a unit of the Department with respect to matters assigned to that organizational entity:

1. Employ personnel required to carry out the purposes of this chapter;

2. Make and enter into all contracts and agreements necessary or incidental to the performance of its duties and the execution of its powers under this chapter, including, but not limited to contracts with private nonprofit organizations, the United States, other state agencies and governmental subdivisions of the Commonwealth;

3. Accept bequests and gifts of real and personal property as well as endowments, funds, and grants from the United States government and any other source. To these ends, the Department shall have the power to comply with conditions and execute agreements as necessary, convenient or desirable;

4. Promulgate regulations necessary or incidental to the performance of duties or execution of powers conferred under this chapter;

5. Receive, hold in trust and administer any donation made to it for the advancement of forest resources of the Commonwealth;

6. Undertake evaluation and testing of products and technologies relating to replacement of petroleum-based lubricants and hydraulic fluids with lubricants and hydraulic fluids made or derived from vegetables or vegetable oil, and promote the use of such products and technologies found to be beneficial in preserving and enhancing environmental quality; and

7. Do all acts necessary or convenient to carry out the purposes of this chapter. (1986, c. 567, § 10-31.2; 1988, c. 891; 1995, c. 111.)

Editor's note. — Acts 2005, c. 324, cl. 1, provides: "1. That the Virginia State Forest Regulations, 4 VAC 5-40-10 et seq., and the Virginia Reforestation of Timberlands Regulations, 4 VAC 5-60-10 et seq., are hereby transferred from the Department of Conservation and Recreation to the Department of Forestry, effective July 1, 2005, and shall remain in full force and effect until amended, modified, or repealed. The Department of Forestry shall update the terminology and references to the Code of Virginia pursuant to the authority to promulgate regulations provided in subdivision 4 of § 10.1-1101. This update shall be exempt from the provisions of the Administrative Process Act. Any future amendments shall be promulgated in accordance with the provisions of the Administrative Process Act. The Administrative Code numbers shall be changed under that exempt action to conform to the Department of Forestry's regulatory numbering system as assigned by the Virginia Code Commission."

§ **10.1-1102. Board of Forestry.** — The Board of Forestry within the Department of Forestry, referred to in this chapter as the Board, shall be composed of one member from each congressional district appointed by the Governor for a term of four years. Upon notification to the Commonwealth by the United States Department of Justice that there is no objection to Chapter 6 of the 1991 Acts of Assembly, Special Session II, the Governor shall appoint a member to represent the new congressional district. Such member shall serve a term coincident with the terms of the current members. The State Forester shall serve as executive officer of the Board. No member of the Board, except the executive officer, shall be eligible for more than two successive terms; however, persons subsequently appointed to fill vacancies may serve two additional successive terms after the terms of the vacancies they were appointed to fill have expired. All vacancies in the membership of the Board shall be filled by the Governor for the unexpired term.

The Board shall meet at least three times a year for the transaction of business. Special meetings may be held at any time upon the call of the executive officer of the Board, or a majority of the members of the Board.

Members of the Board shall be reimbursed for all reasonable and necessary expenses incurred as a result of their membership on the Board. (Code 1950, § 10-84; 1986, c. 539; 1986, c. 567, § 10-84.1; 1988, c. 891; 1990, c. 127; 1992, c. 145.)

Editor's note. — Chapter 6 of the 1991 Acts of Assembly, Special Session II, referred to in this section, enacted §§ 24.1-17.300 through 24.1-17.314 and repealed §§ 24.1-4.3 and 24.1-5.

§ **10.1-1103. Powers of the Board.** — The Board shall be charged with matters relating to the management of forest resources in the Commonwealth.

The Board shall advise the Governor and the Department on the state of forest resources within the Commonwealth and the management of forest resources. The Board shall encourage persons, agencies, organizations and industries to implement development programs for forest resource management and counsel them in such development. In addition, the Board shall recommend plans for improving the state system of forest protection, management and replacement, and shall prepare an annual report on the progress and conditions of state forest work. (1986, c. 567, § 10-84.2; 1988, c. 891.)

ARTICLE 2.

Duties of the State Forester and General Provisions.

§ 10.1-1104. General powers and duties of State Forester. — The State Forester, under the direction and control of the Governor, shall exercise the powers and perform the duties conferred or imposed upon him by law and shall perform other duties required of him by the Governor or the appropriate citizen boards. (1986, c. 567, § 10-31.3; 1988, c. 891.)

Michie's Jurisprudence. — For related discussion, see 18 M.J. Trees and Timber, § 3.

§ 10.1-1105. Additional powers and duties of State Forester. — The State Forester shall supervise and direct all forest interests and all matters pertaining to forestry within the Commonwealth. He shall have charge of all forest wardens and shall appoint, direct and supervise persons he employs to perform labor in the forest reservations or the nurseries provided for herein, and he is authorized to employ temporary forest wardens to extinguish forest fires in the Commonwealth. He shall take such action as is authorized by law to prevent and extinguish forest fires; develop a program to promote the use of prescribed burning for community protection and ecological, silvicultural, and wildlife management; enforce all laws pertaining to forest and woodlands; prosecute any violation of such laws; develop silvicultural best management practices, including reforestation, prevention of erosion and sedimentation, and maintenance of buffers for water quality, pursuant to Article 12 (§ 10.1-1181.1 et seq.) of this chapter; collect information relative to forest destruction and conditions; direct the protection and improvement of all forest reservations; and, as far as his duties as State Forester will permit, conduct an educational course on forestry at the University of Virginia for credit toward a degree, at farmers' institutes and at similar meetings within the Commonwealth. He shall provide for the protection of state waters from pollution by sediment deposition resulting from silvicultural activities as provided in Article 12 (§ 10.1-1181.1 et seq.) of this chapter. In addition, the State Forester shall cooperate with counties, municipalities, corporations and individuals in preparing plans and providing technical assistance, based on generally accepted scientific forestry principles, for the protection, management and replacement of trees, wood lots and timber tracts and the establishment and preservation of urban forests, under an agreement that the parties obtaining such assistance shall pay the field and traveling expenses of the person employed in preparing such plans. (1986, c. 567, § 10-31.4; 1988, c. 891; 1989, c. 215; 1993, c. 948; 1997, c. 7; 1998, c. 156; 1999, c. 220; 2000, c. 997.)

CASE NOTES

Best management practices do not preempt local ordinances. — A local ordinance may be invalid because it conflicts with a state regulation if the state regulation has the force and effect of law but the best management practices promulgated pursuant to this section are only guidelines for use in forestry activities and do not have the force and effect of law. Dail v. York County, 259 Va. 577, 528 S.E.2d 447, 2000 Va. LEXIS 66 (2000).

§ 10.1-1106. State Forester to control forest reserves and funds; reforesting; preservation of timber, etc. — The care, management and preservation of the forest reserves of the Commonwealth and the forests thereon, and all moneys appropriated in that behalf, or collected therefrom in any way, and all personal and real property acquired to carry out the objects of this chapter, shall be subject to the control of the State Forester.

The State Forester shall observe, ascertain, follow and put into effect the best methods of reforesting cutover and denuded lands, foresting wastelands, preventing the destruction of forests by fire, the administering of forests on forestry principles, the instruction and encouragement of private owners in preserving and growing timber for commercial and manufacturing purposes, and the general conservation of forest tracts around the headwaters and on the watersheds of the watercourses of the Commonwealth. (Code 1950, § 10-32; 1984, c. 750; 1986, c. 567; 1988, c. 891.)

§ 10.1-1107. Purchase of lands and acceptance of gifts for forestry purposes by the State Forester; management; definition of state forests. — A. The State Forester shall have authority to purchase in the name of the Commonwealth lands suitable for state forests. He may accept for state forest purposes gifts, devises and bequests of real and personal property as well as endowments, funds, and grants from any source. Unless otherwise restricted by the terms of the gift, devise or bequest, the State Forester is authorized, in the name of the Commonwealth, to convey or lease any such real property given to it, with the consent and approval of the Governor and the General Assembly and the approval of the instrument as to form by the Attorney General. Mineral and mining rights over and under land donated may be reserved by the donors.

B. The State Forester shall have the power and authority to accept gifts, donations and contributions of land, and to enter into agreements for the acquisition by purchase, lease or otherwise with, the United States, or any agency or agent thereof, of lands for state forests.

C. The State Forester shall have authority to provide for the management, development and utilization of any lands purchased, leased or otherwise acquired, to sell or otherwise dispose of products on or derived from the land, and to enforce regulations governing state forests, the care and maintenance thereof, and the prevention of trespassing thereon, and such other regulations deemed necessary to carry out the provisions of this section. Approval by the Governor or General Assembly shall not be required for the sale or harvesting of timber on state forest lands or other lands over which the Department has supervision and control.

D. In exercising the powers conferred by this section, the State Forester shall not obligate the Commonwealth for any expenditure in excess of any funds either donated or appropriated to the Department for such purpose.

E. One-fourth of the gross proceeds derived from any lands so acquired by the State Forester shall be paid annually by the State Forester to the counties in which such lands are respectively located, and shall become a part of the general funds of such counties.

F. As used in this chapter unless the context requires a different meaning, *"state forest"* means lands acquired for the Commonwealth by purchase, gift or lease pursuant to this section. These lands shall be managed and protected for scientific, recreational and educational purposes. Uses of the state forests shall include, but not be limited to, research, demonstrations, tours, soil and water management and protection, hunting, fishing and other recreational activities.

G. All acquisitions of real property under this section shall be subject to the provisions of § 2.2-1149. The Attorney General shall approve the form of the instruments prior to execution. (Code 1950, § 10-33; 1984, c. 750; 1986, c. 567; 1988, c. 891; 1999, c. 201.)

§ 10.1-1108. Waste and unappropriated lands. — Any waste and unappropriated land, other than ungranted shores of the sea, marsh or meadowlands exempted from grant by the provisions of § 41.1-3, may be set apart permanently for use as state forest land, by a grant and proclamation signed by the Governor upon the receipt from the State Forester of an application requesting that a certain piece, tract or parcel of waste and unappropriated land be so set apart. The State Forester shall submit with the application a copy of a report describing fully the location of the land, its character and suitability for forestry purposes together with a complete metes and bounds description of the boundary of the tract. The Department of General Services shall review the application and recommend either approval or disapproval of the transaction to the Governor. If the Governor determines that the land is more valuable for forestry purposes than for agricultural or any other purposes, he may authorize the preparation of a grant which shall be reviewed for legal sufficiency by the Attorney General for the Governor's signature and the lesser seal of the Commonwealth.

All lands so granted shall be subject to statutes and regulations relating to the regulation, management, protection and administration of state forests. (Code 1950, § 10-34.2; 1950, p. 225; 1984, c. 750; 1986, c. 567; 1988, c. 891; 1995, c. 850.)

§ 10.1-1109. State forests not subject to warrant, survey or patent. — Lands acquired by the Commonwealth for forestry purposes shall not be subject to warrant, survey or patent. (Code 1950, § 10-42; 1988, c. 891.)

§ 10.1-1110. Violation of regulations for supervision of state forests, etc. — Violators of any regulation for the supervision or use of any state forest, park, road, street or highway traversing the same, shall be guilty of a Class 4 misdemeanor. (Code 1950, § 10-43; 1988, c. 891.)

Cross references. — As to punishment for Class 4 misdemeanors, see § 18.2-11.

§ 10.1-1111. Kindling fires on state forests; cutting and removing timber; damaging land or timber. — Any person who kindles fire upon any of the state forests of this Commonwealth, except in accordance with regulations prescribed by the State Forester, or who cuts and removes any timber, or who damages or causes the damage of forestland or timber belonging to the Commonwealth, shall be guilty of a Class 3 misdemeanor for each offense committed. (Code 1950, § 10-44; 1986, c. 539; 1988, c. 891.)

Cross references. — As to punishment for Class 3 misdemeanors, see § 18.2-11.

§ 10.1-1112. Notices relating to forest fires and trespasses. — The State Forester shall distribute notices, printed in large letters on cloth or other suitable material, calling attention to the danger of forest fires, to the forest fire laws, and to trespass laws and their penalties, to forest wardens, and to owners of timberland to be posted by them in conspicuous places. Any person other than a forest warden or the owner of the land on which notices are posted, who tears down, mutilates or defaces any such notice shall be guilty of a Class 4 misdemeanor. (1986, c. 567, § 10-31.5; 1988, c. 891.)

Cross references. — As to punishment for Class 4 misdemeanors, see § 18.2-11.

§ 10.1-1113. Not liable for trespass in performance of duties. — No action for trespass shall lie against the State Forester, or any agent or employee of the State Forester for lawful acts done in performance of his duties. (1986, c. 567, § 10-31.7; 1988, c. 891.)

Michie's Jurisprudence. — For related discussion, see 18 M.J. Trespass, § 1.

§ 10.1-1114. Establishment of nurseries; distribution of seeds and seedlings. — The State Forester may establish and maintain a nursery or nurseries, for the propagation of forest tree seedlings, either upon one or more of the forest reservations of the Commonwealth, or upon such other land as he may and which he is empowered to acquire for that purpose. Seedlings from this nursery may be furnished to the Commonwealth without expense for use upon its state forests or other public grounds or parks. Seeds and seedlings may also be distributed to landowners and citizens of the Commonwealth pursuant to Department regulations. (Code 1950, § 10-36; 1968, c. 40; 1986, c. 567; 1988, c. 891.)

§ 10.1-1115. Sale of trees. — For the purpose of maintaining in perpetuity the production of forest products on state forests, the State Forester may designate and appraise the trees which should be cut under the principles of scientific forest management, and may sell these trees for not less than the appraised value. When the appraised value of the trees to be sold is more than $10,000, the State Forester, before making such sale, shall receive bids therefor, after notice by publication once a week for two weeks in two newspapers of general circulation. The State Forester shall have the right to reject any and all bids and to readvertise for bids. The proceeds arising from the sale of the timber and trees so sold, except as provided in subsection E of § 10.1-1107, shall be paid into the state treasury as provided in § 10.1-1116, and shall be held in the Reforestation Operations Fund for the improvement or protection of state forests or for the purchase of additional lands. (Code 1950, § 10-37; 1970, c. 31; 1986, cc. 539, 567; 1988, c. 891.)

§ 10.1-1116. Reforestation Operations Fund. — All money obtained from the state forests, except as provided in subsection E of § 10.1-1107, shall be paid into the state treasury, to the credit of the Reforestation Operations Fund. The moneys in such fund are to be utilized for state forest protection, management, replacement, and extension, under the direction of the State Forester. (Code 1950, § 10-39; 1986, c. 567; 1988, c. 891.)

§ 10.1-1117. Specialized services or rentals of equipment to landowners, localities and state agencies; fees; disposition of proceeds. — The State Forester may cooperate with landowners, counties, municipalities and state agencies, by making available forestry services consisting of specialized or technical forestry equipment and an operator, or rent to them such specialized equipment. For such services or rentals, a reasonable fee, representing the State Forester's estimate of the cost of such services or rentals, shall be charged.

All moneys paid to the State Forester for such services or rentals shall be deposited in the state treasury to the credit of the Forestry Operations Fund, to be used in the further protection and development of the forest resources of this Commonwealth. Upon presentation of a statement, the landowner, county, municipality or state agency receiving such services or rentals shall pay to the State Forester, within thirty days, the amount of charge shown on the statement. (1964, c. 513, § 10-54.1; 1986, c. 567; 1988, c. 891.)

§ 10.1-1118. Account of receipts and expenditures. — The State Forester shall keep a full and accurate account of the receipts and expenditures of the Department. (Code 1950, § 10-40; 1986, c. 567; 1988, c. 891; 2004, c. 58.)

§ 10.1-1119. Preservation of evidence as to conserving forest supply; reports to General Assembly; publications. — The State Forester shall preserve all evidence taken by him with reference to conserving the forests of the Commonwealth and the methods best adapted to accomplish such object. He shall report his actions, conclusions and recommendations to each session of the General Assembly and from time to time publish for public distribution, in bulletin or other form, such conclusions and recommendations as may be of immediate public interest. (Code 1950, § 10-41; 1984, c. 750; 1986, c. 567; 1988, c. 891.)

§ 10.1-1119.1. State Forests System Fund established. — There is hereby created in the state treasury a special nonreverting fund to be known as the State Forests System Fund, hereafter referred to as "the Fund." The Fund shall be established on the books of the Comptroller. All contributions from income tax refunds and any other source shall be paid into the state treasury and credited to the Fund. Interest earned on moneys in the Fund shall remain in the Fund and be credited to it. Any moneys remaining in the Fund, including interest thereon, at the end of each fiscal year shall not revert to the general fund but shall remain in the Fund. Moneys in the Fund shall be used solely for the purposes of developing and implementing conservation and education initiatives in the state forests system. Expenditures and disbursements from the Fund shall be made by the State Treasurer on warrants issued by the Comptroller upon written request signed by the State Forester. (1999, c. 998.)

ARTICLE 3.

Forest Management of State-Owned Lands Fund.

§ 10.1-1120. Forest Management of State-Owned Lands Fund. — The Forest Management of State-Owned Lands Fund established by the legislature in 1980 is continued. (1980, c. 525, § 10-45.1; 1988, c. 891.)

Cross references. — As to the management, harvesting and sale of timber on lands under control of the Division of Engineering and Buildings, see § 2.2-1158.

§ 10.1-1121. Definitions. — As used in this article unless the context requires a different meaning:
"Fund" means the Forest Management of State-Owned Lands Fund.
"State-owned lands" means forest land owned or managed by the various departments, agencies and institutions of the Commonwealth and designated by the Department in cooperation with the Division of Engineering and Buildings of the Department of General Services as being of sufficient size and value to benefit from a forest management plan. State-owned land shall not include properties held or managed by the Department of Game and Inland Fisheries, the Department of Forestry, or the Department of Conservation and Recreation. (1980, c. 525, § 10-45.2; 1981, c. 219; 1984, c. 750; 1986, c. 567; 1988, c. 891; 1989, c. 656.)

§ 10.1-1122. Management, harvesting, sale of timber on state-owned land. — A. The Department in cooperation with the Division of Engineering and Buildings shall develop a forest management plan for state-owned lands with the assistance of affected state agencies, departments and institutions.

B. Prior to the sale of timber from state-owned lands, the proposed sale shall be first approved by the Department and by the Division of Engineering and Buildings. The Department shall make or arrange for all sales so approved and shall deposit all proceeds to the credit of the Fund, except that when sales are made from timber on land held by special fund agencies or the Department of Military Affairs, or from timber on land which is gift property specified in subsection D of § 2.2-1156, the Department shall deposit in the Fund only so much of the proceeds as are needed to defray the cost of the sale and to implement the forestry management plan on that particular tract of land. The remainder of the proceeds from such a sale shall then be paid over to the special fund agency concerned, the Department of Military Affairs, or the agency or institution holding the gift properties, to be used for the purposes of that agency, department, or institution. (1980, c. 525, § 10-45.3; 1981, c. 219; 1986, c. 567; 1988, c. 891.)

§ 10.1-1123. Use of Fund; management, receipt and expenditure of moneys. — The Fund shall be used to defray the costs of timber sales, to develop forest management plans for state-owned lands pursuant to § 10.1-1124, and to implement those plans. The Department shall have the authority to manage, receive and expend moneys for and from the Fund for these purposes. (1980, c. 525, § 10-45.4; 1981, c. 219; 1986, c. 567; 1988, c. 891.)

ARTICLE 4.

Forest Protection for Cities and Counties.

§ 10.1-1124. Counties and certain cities to pay annual sums for forest protection, etc. — A. Upon presentation to its governing body of an itemized statement duly certified by the State Forester, each county in this Commonwealth, or city which enters into a contract with the State Forester under § 10.1-1125 to provide forest fire prevention, shall repay into the state treasury annually any amounts expended in the preceding year by the State Forester in such county or city for forest protection, forest fire detection, forest fire prevention and forest fire suppression, not to exceed in any one year an amount measured by the acreage, computed upon the basis of five cents per acre of privately owned forests in the county or city, according to the most recent United States Forest Survey. In any additions or deductions of acreage from that given by this survey, any land, other than commercial orchards, sustaining as its principal cover a growth of trees or woody shrubs shall be considered forest land, irrespective of the merchantability of the growth, and cutover land shall be considered as forest land unless it has been cleared or improved for other use. Open land shall be considered as forest land when it bears at least eighty well-distributed seedlings or sprouts of woody species per acre. The amounts so repaid by the counties or cities into the state treasury shall be credited to the Forestry Operations Fund for forest protection, forest fire detection, forest fire prevention and forest fire suppression in the Commonwealth and, with such other funds as may be appropriated by the General Assembly or contributed by the United States or any governmental or private agency for these purposes, shall be used and disbursed by the State Forester for such purposes. In cities this subsection shall be subject to § 10.1-1125.

B. In any case in which the State Forester and the governing body of any county or city cannot agree upon the additions or deductions to privately owned forest acreage in a particular county or city, or to changes in forest acreage from year to year, the question shall be submitted to the judge of the circuit court of the county or city by a summary proceeding, and the decision of the judge certified to the governing body and to the State Forester, respectively, shall be conclusive and final. (Code 1950, § 10-46; 1964, c. 79; 1984, c. 715; 1986, c. 567; 1988, c. 891.)

§ **10.1-1125. Application of Articles 4, 5 and 6 to cities; State Forester authorized to enter into contracts with cities.** — A. In addition to the application of this article and Articles 5 (§ 10.1-1131 et seq.) and 6 (§ 10.1-1135 et seq.) to forestlands lying in counties, such articles shall also apply to forestlands lying within cities. For the purposes of such articles as applied to cities, forest land shall be considered as comprising land which bears at least eighty well-distributed seedlings or sprouts of woody species per acre and which is specifically included in the provisions of the contract with the city.

B. The State Forester is authorized to enter into contracts prepared by the Attorney General with the governing body of any city in which any such forestland is located. The contract shall include provisions for the State Forester to furnish forest fire protection, prevention, detection, and suppression services and to enforce state law applicable to forest fires on forestlands upon any such lands located within a city. The services so provided by the State Forester shall be of the same general type, character, and standard as the same services provided in counties generally. (1964, c. 79, § 10-46.1; 1974, c. 216; 1984, c. 750; 1986, cc. 188, 567; 1988, c. 891.)

§ **10.1-1126. State Forester authorized to enter into agreements with federal agencies.** — The State Forester is authorized to enter into agreements, approved by the Attorney General of Virginia, with agencies of the United States government holding title to forest land in any county, city or town. Any such agreement may include provisions for the State Forester to furnish forest fire protection, prevention, detection, and suppression services together with enforcement of state law applicable to forest fires on forestlands within such county, city or town. Costs of such services provided by the State Forester shall be reimbursed to him as provided in the agreement. The services provided by the State Forester shall be of the same general type, character, and standard as the same services provided in counties, cities and towns generally. (1974, c. 216, § 10-46.2; 1984, c. 750; 1986, cc. 188, 567; 1988, c. 891.)

§ **10.1-1126.1. Silvicultural practices; local government authority limited.** — A. Forestry, when practiced in accordance with accepted silvicultural best management practices as determined by the State Forester pursuant to § 10.1-1105, constitutes a beneficial and desirable use of the Commonwealth's forest resources.

B. Notwithstanding any other provision of law, silvicultural activity, as defined in § 10.1-1181.1, that (i) is conducted in accordance with the silvicultural best management practices developed and enforced by the State Forester pursuant to § 10.1-1105 and (ii) is located on property defined as real estate devoted to forest use under § 58.1-3230 or in a district established pursuant to Chapter 43 (§ 15.2-4300 et seq.) or Chapter 44 (§ 15.2-4400 et seq.) of Title 15.2, shall not be prohibited or unreasonably limited by a local government's use of its police, planning and zoning powers. Local ordinances and regulations shall not require a permit or impose a fee for such silvicultural activity. Local ordinances and regulations pertaining to such silvicultural activity shall be reasonable and necessary to protect the health, safety and welfare of citizens residing in the locality, and shall not be in conflict with the purposes of promoting the growth, continuation and beneficial use of the Commonwealth's privately owned forest resources. Prior to the adoption of any ordinance or regulation pertaining to silvicultural activity, a locality may consult with, and request a determination from, the State Forester as to whether the ordinance or regulation conflicts with the purposes of this section. Nothing in this section shall preclude a locality from requiring a review by the zoning administrator, which shall not exceed ten working days, to determine whether a proposed silvicultural activity complies with applicable local zoning requirements.

C. The provisions of this section shall apply to the harvesting of timber, provided that the area on which such harvesting occurs is reforested artificially or naturally in accordance with the provisions of Chapter 11 (§ 10.1-1100 et seq.) of Title 10.1 or is converted to bona fide agricultural or improved pasture use as described in subsection B of § 10.1-1163.

The provisions of this section shall not apply to land that has been rezoned or converted at the request of the owner or previous owner from an agricultural or rural to a residential, commercial or industrial zone or use.

Nothing in this section shall affect any requirement imposed pursuant to the Chesapeake Bay Preservation Act (§ 10.1-2100 et seq.) or imposed by a locality pursuant to the designation of a scenic highway or Virginia byway in accordance with Article 5 (§ 33.1-62 et seq.) of Chapter 1 of Title 33.1. (1997, c. 7.)

CASE NOTES

Approval by zoning administrator may be required. — This section authorizes a county zoning administrator to review proposed silvicultural activity to determine whether it complies with applicable local zoning requirements and this statutory review process includes a component of evaluation and decision regarding compliance; accordingly, describing the decision a local zoning administrator must make as an "approval" in an ordinance is consistent with authorizing the zoning administrator to make such a determination regarding compliance and does not create a prohibited permit requirement. Dail v. York County, 259 Va. 577, 528 S.E.2d 447, 2000 Va. LEXIS 66 (2000).

Local ordinances affecting silvicultural activity not prohibited. — This section authorizes a county zoning administrator to review proposed silvicultural activity to determine whether it complies with applicable local zoning requirements but there is nothing in this section that suggests that such a compliance review is limited to determining whether the forestry plan complies with zoning ordinances relating to non-silvicultural activities, such as noise abatement ordinances, nor does anything in the statute suggest that a county cannot enact ordinances affecting silvicultural

activity. Dail v. York County, 259 Va. 577, 528 S.E.2d 447, 2000 Va. LEXIS 66 (2000).

Local ordinance restricting clear cutting not prohibited. — A local ordinance providing that clear cutting of trees was not permitted but that the zoning administrator could permit selected thinning based upon best management practices and in accordance with an approved plan was not an absolute prohibition on clear cutting of timber in areas subject to the ordinance but a limitation on clear cutting, which could be altered by the zoning administrator and, therefore, this ordinance did not contravene, and was not preempted by, this section. Dail v. York County, 259 Va. 577, 528 S.E.2d 447, 2000 Va. LEXIS 66 (2000).

Burden not shifted to locality to prove validity of ordinances. — The limitations placed on a locality's general police powers and zoning authority by this section did change the status quo and impose the burden upon localities if they enact requirements that exceed the best management practices promulgated by the state forester to show that the state regulations were inadequate to protect the health, safety and welfare of their citizens and that local regulation was necessary to meet identified shortcomings in the state program. Dail v. York County, 259 Va. 577, 528 S.E.2d 447, 2000 Va. LEXIS 66 (2000).

§ 10.1-1127. County and city levies and appropriations. — The governing bodies of the counties and those cities entering into a contract as provided in § 10.1-1125 are authorized to levy taxes and appropriate money for forest protection, improvement and management. (Code 1950, § 10-47; 1964, c. 79; 1988, c. 891.)

§ 10.1-1127.1. Tree conservation ordinance; civil penalties. — A. The governing body of any county, city or town may adopt a tree conservation ordinance regulating the preservation and removal of heritage, specimen, memorial and street trees, as defined under subsection B of this section, when such preservation and removal are not commercial silvicultural or horticultural activities, including but not limited to planting, managing, or harvesting forest or tree crops. Such ordinance shall consider planned land use by the property owner, may include reasonable fees for the administration and enforcement of the ordinance and may provide for the appointment by the local governing body of an administrator of the ordinance.

B. Any ordinance enacted pursuant to this authority may contain reasonable provisions for the preservation and removal of heritage, specimen, memorial and street trees. For the purpose of this section the following definitions shall apply:

"Arborist" or *"urban forester"* means a person trained in arboriculture, forestry, landscape architecture, horticulture, or related fields and experienced in the conservation and preservation of native and ornamental trees.

"Heritage tree" means any tree that has been individually designated by the local governing body to have notable historic or cultural interest.

"Memorial tree" means any tree that has been individually designated by the local governing body to be a special commemorating memorial.

"Specimen tree" means any tree that has been individually designated by the local governing body to be notable by virtue of its outstanding size and quality for its particular species.

"Street tree" means any tree that has been individually designated by the local governing body and which grows in the street right-of-way or on private property as authorized by the owner and placed or planted there by the local government.

The designation of such trees shall be by an arborist or urban forester and shall be made by ordinance. The individual property owner of such trees shall be notified prior to the hearing on the adoption of such ordinance by certified mail.

C. The provisions of a tree conservation ordinance enacted pursuant to this section shall not apply: (i) to work conducted on federal or state property; (ii) to emergency work to protect life, limb or property; (iii) to routine installation, maintenance and repair of cable and wires used to provide cable television, electric, gas or telephone service; (iv) to activities with minor effects on trees, including but not limited to, home gardening and landscaping of individual homes; and (v) commercial silvicultural or horticultural activities, including but not limited to planting, managing, or harvesting forest or tree crops.

D. In the event that the application of any ordinance regulating the removal of heritage, specimen, memorial or street trees results in any taking of private property for a public purpose or use, the governing body shall compensate by fee or other consideration the property owner for such taking and the ordinance shall so state thereby notifying the owner of his right to seek such fee or other compensation. The provisions of Chapter 2 (§ 25.1-200 et seq.) of Title 25.1 shall apply to the taking of private property for a public purpose pursuant to such local ordinance.

E. Violations of such local ordinance shall be punishable by civil penalties not to exceed $2,500 for each violation.

F. Nothing in this section shall be construed to be in derogation of the authority granted to any county, city or town by the provision of any charter or other provision of law. (1989, c. 678; 2003, c. 940.)

Michie's Jurisprudence. — For related discussion, see 18 M.J. Trees and Timber, § 1.

§ **10.1-1128. Acquisition and administration.** — Each county, city and town acting through its governing body, is authorized to acquire by purchase, gift or bequest tracts of land suitable for the growth of trees and to administer the same, as well as any lands now owned by any such locality and suitable for the growth of trees, as county, city or town forests. (Code 1950, § 10-48; 1988, c. 891.)

§ **10.1-1129. Purchasing real estate outside of boundaries.** — Before any governing body purchases any real estate outside of the county, city or town which it represents pursuant to the provisions of § 10.1-1128, it shall first secure the approval of the governing body of the county, city or town in which the real estate is located. (Code 1950, § 10-49; 1988, c. 891.)

§ **10.1-1130. State Forester to furnish seedlings and technical assistance.** — The State Forester is authorized to supply from any forest tree nursery or nurseries forest tree seedlings and transplants necessary and suitable for reforesting any part or all of any lands acquired or owned and administered by any county, city or town as provided in § 10.1-1128, and to furnish technical assistance and supervision necessary for the proper management and administration of such lands and forests free of cost to counties, cities and towns. The respective counties, cities and towns shall agree to administer such lands in accordance with the practices and principles of scientific forestry as determined by the State Forester or the Board of Forestry. (Code 1950, § 10-50; 1986, c. 567; 1988, c. 891.)

Article 5.

Forestry Services for Landowners.

§ **10.1-1131. Authority of State Forester.** — The State Forester is authorized to designate, upon request of the landowner, forest trees of private forest landowners for sale or removal, by blazing or otherwise, and to measure or estimate the volume of the trees under the terms and conditions hereinafter provided. (Code 1950, § 10-51; 1986, c. 567; 1988, c. 891.)

§ **10.1-1132. Administration by State Forester; services rendered.** — The State Forester shall administer the provisions of this article. The State Forester, or his authorized agent, upon receipt of a request from a forest landowner for technical forestry assistance or service, may (i) designate forest trees for removal for lumber, veneer, poles, piling, pulpwood, cordwood, ties, or other forest products, by blazing, spotting with paint, or otherwise designating in an approved manner; (ii) measure or estimate the commercial volume contained in the trees designated; (iii) furnish the forest landowner with a statement of the volume of the trees so designated and estimated; and (iv) offer general forestry advice concerning the management of the landowner's forest. (Code 1950, § 10-52; 1986, c. 567; 1988, c. 891.)

§ **10.1-1133. Fees for services; free services.** — Upon presentation of a statement for designating, measuring or estimating services specified in § 10.1-1132, the landowner or his agent shall pay to the State Forester within thirty days of receipt of the statement an amount not to exceed five percent of the sale price or fair market value of the stumpage so designated, measured or estimated. However, for the purpose of further encouraging the use of approved scientific forestry principles on the private forestlands of this Commonwealth, and to permit explanation of the application of such principles, the State

Forester may, where he deems it advisable, designate, measure or estimate without charge the trees of a forest landowner on an area not in excess of ten acres. (Code 1950, § 10-53; 1988, c. 891.)

§ 10.1-1134. Disposition of fees. — All moneys paid to the State Forester for services described in this article shall be deposited in the state treasury to the credit of the Forestry Operations Fund, to be used to provide additional similar scientific forestry services to the landowners of this Commonwealth. The State Forester is hereby authorized to utilize any unobligated balances in the fire suppression fund for the purpose of acquiring replacement equipment for forestry management and protection operations. (Code 1950, § 10-54; 1984, c. 715; 1986, c. 567; 1988, c. 891.)

ARTICLE 6.

Forest Wardens and Fires.

§ 10.1-1135. Appointment and compensation of forest wardens; oath; powers. — The State Forester, when he deems it necessary, may request the Governor to commission persons designated by the State Forester to act as forest wardens of the Commonwealth, to enforce the forest laws and, under his direction, to aid in carrying out the purposes of this chapter. Such wardens shall receive compensation as may be provided in accordance with law for the purpose. Before entering upon the duties of their office, forest wardens thus appointed shall take the proper official oath before the clerk of the court of the county or city in which they reside. While holding such office forest wardens shall be conservators of the peace. They also shall have the authority to enforce the provisions of § 62.1-194.2.

The State Forester may designate certain forest wardens to be special forest wardens. Special forest wardens shall have the same authority and power as sheriffs throughout the Commonwealth to enforce the forest laws. (Code 1950, § 10-55; 1964, c. 79; 1970, c. 433; 1986, cc. 188, 567; 1988, cc. 196, 891.)

Cross references. — As to the Line of Duty Act, see § 9.1-400.

Michie's Jurisprudence. — For related discussion, see 8B M.J. Fires, § 14.

§ 10.1-1136. Duties of forest wardens. — The duties of the forest wardens are to (i) enforce all forest and forest fire statutes and regulations of the Commonwealth, (ii) serve as forest fire incident commander and perform other duties as needed in the management and suppression of forest fire incidents as long as the authority granted under this section does not conflict with or diminish the lawful authority, duties, and responsibilities of fire chiefs or other fire service officers in charge, including but not limited to the provisions of Chapter 2 (§ 27-6.1 et seq.) of Title 27, and (iii) protect the forests of the Commonwealth. (Code 1950, § 10-56; 1986, c. 188; 1988, c. 891.)

§ 10.1-1137. Duty in case of fires and payment of costs of suppression. — When any forest warden sees or receives a report of a forest fire, he shall proceed immediately to the scene of the fire and employ such persons and means as in his judgment are expedient and necessary to extinguish the fire, within the limits of the expense he has been authorized to incur in his instructions from the State Forester. He shall keep an itemized account of all expenses incurred and immediately send the account verified by affidavit to the State Forester.

Upon approval by the State Forester the account shall be paid from the Forestry Operations Fund.

No such payment shall be made to any person who has maliciously started the fire or to any person whose negligence caused or contributed to the setting of the fire. (Code 1950, § 10-57; 1964, c. 79; 1986, cc. 188, 567; 1988, c. 891.)

CASE NOTES

Editor's note. — The case below was decided under prior law.

Section 10.1-1139 must be read in conjunction with this section. C & O Ry. v. Crouch, 208 Va. 602, 159 S.E.2d 650, cert. denied, 393 U.S. 845, 89 S. Ct. 128, 21 L. Ed. 2d 115 (1968).

Authority conferred on forest wardens. — The legislature, by the enactment of this section, has conferred upon forest wardens the authority to employ persons to assist in extinguishing forest fires, obviously contemplating a situation where the necessary assistance can be obtained without resort to compulsion. But where the needed assistance cannot be so freely secured, the legislature, by § 10.1-1139, has conferred upon forest wardens the authority to summon persons to help in fighting fires, placing those so summoned under pain of prosecution for their failure or refusal to give aid. C & O Ry. v. Crouch, 208 Va. 602, 159 S.E.2d 650, cert. denied, 393 U.S. 845, 89 S. Ct. 128, 21 L. Ed. 2d 115 (1968).

Liability for injuries sustained by fireman. — One who through negligence starts a fire is not liable, solely because of such negligence, for injuries sustained by a fireman while attempting to suppress the fire, where there are no circumstances to suggest that any negligent act of the defendant caused the fireman to be subjected to risks of injury beyond those inherently involved in fire fighting. Where none but the usual hazards are involved in fighting the fire in question, the fireman assumes the risk thereof. C & O Ry. v. Crouch, 208 Va. 602, 159 S.E.2d 650, cert. denied, 393 U.S. 845, 89 S. Ct. 128, 21 L. Ed. 2d 115 (1968).

§ 10.1-1138. Rewards for information leading to conviction of arsonists or incendiaries.

— The State Forester shall be authorized, whenever it appears to him that forest fires in any part of the Commonwealth are caused by unknown arsonists or incendiaries, to offer a monetary reward for information sufficient to procure conviction in a court of appropriate jurisdiction of the person or persons responsible for such fire. No law-enforcement officer paid in whole or in part from public funds or employee of the Department shall be eligible to receive such reward.

All such reward money shall be paid from funds appropriated for the protection and development of the forest resources of this Commonwealth, and shall not exceed either $10,000 paid in any one fiscal year or $2,000 paid to any one person for information leading to any one conviction. (1966, c. 8, § 10-57.1; 1986, cc. 188, 567; 1988, c. 891.)

§ 10.1-1139. Who may be summoned to aid forest warden.

— Any forest warden to whom written instructions have been issued by the State Forester authorizing him to employ persons to assist in suppressing forest fires, shall have the authority to summon as many able-bodied persons between eighteen and fifty years of age as may, in his discretion, be reasonably necessary to assist in extinguishing any forest fire in any county or city of the Commonwealth which is organized for forest fire control under the direction of the State Forester. Any person summoned by a forest warden to fight a forest fire shall be paid at the rate of pay provided in the Department of Forestry wage scale for fire fighting in effect in the county or city, or part thereof, in which the fire is fought. Wardens shall not summon for such service any person while engaged in maintaining the rights-of-way of railroads for the safe passage of trains, nor any station agent, operator or other person while engaged in duties necessary for the safe operation of trains.

Any person summoned who fails or refuses to assist in fighting the fire, unless the failure is due to physical inability or other valid reason, shall be guilty of a Class 4 misdemeanor. (Code 1950, § 10-59; 1964, c. 79; 1973, c. 401; 1986, c. 188; 1988, c. 891.)

Cross references. — As to punishment for Class 4 misdemeanors, see § 18.2-11.

CASE NOTES

Editor's note. — The case below was decided under prior law.

This section must be read in conjunction with § 10.1-1137. C & O Ry. v. Crouch, 208 Va. 602, 159 S.E.2d 650, cert. denied, 393 U.S. 845, 89 S. Ct. 128, 21 L. Ed. 2d 115 (1968).

Authority conferred on forest wardens. — The legislature, by the enactment of § 10.1-1137, has conferred upon forest wardens the authority to employ persons to assist in extinguishing forest fires, obviously contemplating a situation where the necessary assistance can be obtained without resort to compulsion. But where the needed assistance cannot be so freely secured, the legislature, by this section, has conferred upon forest wardens the authority to summon persons to help in fighting fires, placing those so summoned under pain of prosecution for their failure or refusal to give aid. C & O Ry. v. Crouch, 208 Va. 602, 159 S.E.2d 650, cert. denied, 393 U.S. 845, 89 S. Ct. 128, 21 L. Ed. 2d 115 (1968).

Assistance held voluntary. — The record simply did not support the proposition that the deceased assisted in fighting the fire in question because he was summoned under this section to do so but, rather, because of a prior voluntary arrangement with the forest warden. C & O Ry. v. Crouch, 208 Va. 602, 159 S.E.2d 650, cert. denied, 393 U.S. 845, 89 S. Ct. 128, 21 L. Ed. 2d 115 (1968).

§ 10.1-1140. Liability of warden for trespass. — No action for trespass shall lie against any forest warden on account of lawful acts done in the legal performance of his duties. (Code 1950, § 10-60; 1988, c. 891.)

§ 10.1-1140.1. Defense of forest wardens. — If any commissioned forest warden appointed by the State Forester is brought before any regulatory body, summoned before any grand jury, arrested, indicted or otherwise prosecuted on any criminal charge arising out of any act committed in the discharge of his official duties, the State Forester may employ special counsel approved by the Attorney General to defend the forest warden. Upon a finding that the forest warden did not violate a law or regulation resulting from the act which was subject of the investigation, the State Forester shall pay the special counsel legal fees and expenses subject to the approval of the Attorney General. The payment shall be made from funds appropriated for the administration of the Department of Forestry. (1992, c. 113.)

Michie's Jurisprudence. — For related discussion, see 18 M.J. Trespass, § 1.

§ 10.1-1141. Liability and recovery of cost of fighting forest fires. — The State Forester in the name of the Commonwealth shall collect the costs of fire fighting performed under the direction of a forest warden in accordance with § 10.1-1139 from any person who, negligently or intentionally without using reasonable care and precaution, starts a fire or who negligently or intentionally fails to prevent its escape, which fire burns on any forestland, brushland, grassland or wasteland. Such person shall be liable for the full amount of all expenses incurred by the Commonwealth, for fighting or extinguishing such fire. All expenses collected shall be credited to the Forestry Operations Fund. It shall be the duty of the Commonwealth's attorneys to institute and prosecute proper proceedings under this section, at the instance of the State Forester.

The State Forester may institute an action and recover from either one or both parents of any minor, living with such parents or either of them, the cost of forest fire suppression suffered by reason of the willful or malicious destruction of, or damage to, public or private property by such minor. No more than $750 may be recovered from such parents or either of them as a result of any forest fire incident or occurrence on which such action is based. (Code 1950, §§ 10-58, 10-61; 1964, c. 79; 1986, c. 188; 1988, c. 891.)

§ 10.1-1142. Regulating the burning of woods, brush, etc.; penalties.

— A. It shall be unlawful for any owner or lessee of land to set fire to, or to procure another to set fire to, any woods, brush, logs, leaves, grass, debris, or other inflammable material upon such land unless he previously has taken all reasonable care and precaution, by having cut and piled the same or carefully cleared around the same, to prevent the spread of such fire to lands other than those owned or leased by him. It shall also be unlawful for any employee of any such owner or lessee of land to set fire to or to procure another to set fire to any woods, brush, logs, leaves, grass, debris, or other inflammable material, upon such land unless he has taken similar precautions to prevent the spread of such fire to any other land.

B. Except as provided in subsection C, during the period February 15 through April 30 of each year, even though the precautions required by the foregoing subsection have been taken, it shall be unlawful, in any county or city or portion thereof organized for forest fire control under the direction of the State Forester, for any person to set fire to, or to procure another to set fire to, any brush, leaves, grass, debris or field containing dry grass or other inflammable material capable of spreading fire, located in or within 300 feet of any woodland, brushland, or field containing dry grass or other inflammable material, except between the hours of 4:00 p.m. and 12:00 midnight.

The provisions of this subsection shall not apply to any fires which may be set on federal lands.

C. Subsection B shall not apply to any fire set during the period beginning February 15 through April 30 of each year, if:

1. The fire is set for "prescribed burning" that is conducted in accordance with a "prescription" and managed by a "certified prescribed burn manager" as those terms are defined in § 10.1-1150.1;

2. The burn is conducted in accordance with § 10.1-1150.4;

3. The State Forester has, prior to February 1, approved the prescription for the burn; and

4. The burn is being conducted for one of the following purposes: (i) control of exotic and invasive plant species that cannot be accomplished at other times of the year; (ii) wildlife habitat establishment and maintenance that cannot be accomplished at other times of the year; or (iii) management necessary for natural heritage resources.

The State Forester may on the day of any burn planned to be conducted pursuant to this subsection revoke his approval of the prescription for the burn if hazardous fire conditions exist. The State Forester may revoke the certification of any certified prescribed burn manager who violates any provision of this subsection.

D. Any person who builds a fire in the open air, or uses a fire built by another in the open air, within 150 feet of any woodland, brushland or field containing dry grass or other inflammable material, shall totally extinguish the fire before leaving the area and shall not leave the fire unattended.

E. Any person violating any provisions of this section shall be guilty of a Class 3 misdemeanor for each separate offense. If any forest fire originates as a result of the violation by any person of any provision of this section, such person shall, in addition to the above penalty, be liable to the Commonwealth for the full amount of all expenses incurred by the Commonwealth in suppressing such fire. Such amounts shall be recoverable by action brought by the State Forester in the name of the Commonwealth on behalf of the Commonwealth and credited to the Forestry Operations Fund. (Code 1950, §§ 10-62, 10-63; 1964, c. 79; 1986, c. 188; 1988, c. 891; 1996, cc. 74, 1008; 2001, c. 319; 2006, c. 228.)

Cross references. — As to punishment for Class 3 misdemeanors, see § 18.2-11.

The 2006 amendments. — The 2006 amendment by c. 228, in subsection C, substituted "during the period beginning February 15 through April 30" for "between February 15 and March 1."

Michie's Jurisprudence. — For related discussion, see 2A M.J. Arson, § 2.

CASE NOTES

Specific exemption. — The legislature has specifically exempted from the restriction of this section those fires set on rights-of-way of railway companies by their duly authorized employees. Southern Ry. v. Commonwealth, 205 Va. 114, 135 S.E.2d 160 (1964) (decided under prior law).

§ 10.1-1143. Throwing inflammatory objects from vehicle on highway while in or near certain lands.

— It shall be unlawful for any person to throw, toss or drop from a vehicle moving or standing on a highway any lighted smoking material, lighted match, lighted material of any nature, or any bomb or device liable to set fire to inflammable material on the ground while in or near any forestland, brushland or field containing inflammable vegetation or trash.

Any person violating the provisions of this section shall be guilty of a Class 2 misdemeanor for each separate offense. (1954, c. 35, § 10-64.1; 1986, c. 188; 1988, c. 891.)

Cross references. — As to punishment for Class 2 misdemeanors, see § 18.2-11.

§ 10.1-1144. Failure to clean premises of certain mills.

— Any individual, firm, or corporation responsible for the operation of a saw mill, stave mill, heading mill, or any other mill in, through or near forest or brushland shall clean the premises for at least a distance of fifty yards in all directions from any fires maintained in or about, or in connection with the operation of such mill. The premises shall also be cleaned for a distance of 100 feet in all directions from any sawdust pile, slab pile, or any other inflammable material which accumulates from the operation of such mill, or all matter not essential to the operation of such mill, which is liable to take fire from any sparks emitted from such fires. When any mill is removed or ceases to operate for a period of ten consecutive days, any fire which may be burning in any sawdust pile, slab pile or other debris shall be totally extinguished unless the owner of the land on which such fire is located assumes in writing responsibility for the control of the fire. Any person, firm or corporation violating any of the provisions of this section shall be guilty of a Class 4 misdemeanor. Each day or fraction thereof on which any such mill is operated in violation of the provisions of this section and each day or fraction thereof on which fire is allowed to burn in any sawdust pile, slab pile or other inflammable debris in violation of the provisions of this section, shall be deemed a separate offense.

Whenever it is established that a forest fire originated from a fire maintained in or about any such mill, the individual, firm, or corporation, from whose mill any such fire originated shall immediately become liable for all costs incurred in fighting such fire. (Code 1950, § 10-64; 1986, c. 188; 1988, c. 891.)

Cross references. — As to punishment for Class 4 misdemeanors, see § 18.2-11.

§ 10.1-1145. Failure to properly maintain logging equipment and railroad locomotives. — Logging equipment and railroad locomotives operated in, through, or near forestland, brushland or fields containing dry grass or other inflammable material shall be equipped with appliances and maintained to prevent, as far as may be possible, the escape of fire and sparks from the smokestacks. Any person failing to comply with these requirements shall be guilty of a Class 4 misdemeanor for each offense committed. (Code 1950, § 10-65; 1986, c. 188; 1988, c. 891.)

Cross references. — As to punishment for Class 4 misdemeanors, see § 18.2-11.

§ 10.1-1146: Repealed by Acts 1996, c. 104.

§ 10.1-1147. Removal of inflammable material from lands adjoining right-of-way by railroads. — For the purpose of providing increased protection to forest property from fire originating along railroads, any railroad company shall have the right, subject to the provisions of this section, without liability for trespass to enter upon forest or brushlands for a distance of fifty feet from the railroad right-of-way and to clear from such a strip any inflammable material such as leaves, grass, dead trees, slash and brush, but shall not remove any valuable timber growth or other things of value without consent of and recompense to the owner. Not less than fifteen days prior to clearing such land, the railroad company shall give the owner notice of its intention, together with a transcript of this section, by letter deposited in the United States mail to his last known address. If the owner does not file objections to such clearings with the State Corporation Commission within ten days of the date of such notice he shall be deemed to have given consent. Upon the filing by an owner of such objection showing cause why such clearing should not be done the State Corporation Commission shall review the case and may sustain the objection of the owner or permit the clearing in whole or in part.

The State Corporation Commission may require assistance of the State Forester in furnishing information pertinent to the administration of this section.

The provisions of this section shall not apply to temporary tram roads used for hauling logs and lumber. (Code 1950, § 10-66; 1988, c. 891.)

Michie's Jurisprudence. — For related discussion, see 8B M.J. Fires, § 4.

§ 10.1-1148. Fires caused by violation of provisions of article; liability to Commonwealth. — Individuals and corporations causing fires by violation of any provision of this article shall be liable to the Commonwealth for (i) all damages the Commonwealth sustained by such fire or fires, and (ii) the full amount of all expenses incurred by the Commonwealth, in fighting or extinguishing such fire. (Code 1950, § 10-67; 1964, c. 79; 1988, c. 891.)

§ 10.1-1149. Southeastern Interstate Forest Fire Protection Compact. — Chapter 63 of the 1956 Acts of Assembly authorizing the Governor to execute a compact to promote effective prevention and control of forest fires in the Southeastern region of the United States, is incorporated in this Code by this reference. (1956, c. 63, § 27-5.2; 1988, c. 891.)

§ 10.1-1150. Middle Atlantic Interstate Forest Fire Protection Compact. — Chapter 6 of the 1966 Acts of Assembly authorizing the Governor to execute a compact to promote effective prevention and control of forest fires in the Middle Atlantic region of the United States, is incorporated in this Code by this reference. (1966, c. 6, § 27-5.4; 1988, c. 891.)

Michie's Jurisprudence. — For related discussion, see 8B M.J. Fires, § 14.

ARTICLE 6.1.

Certified Prescribed Burning Manager Program.

§ 10.1-1150.1. Definitions. — As used in this article unless the context requires a different meaning:

"Certified prescribed burn manager" means any person who has successfully completed a certification process established by the State Forester under § 10.1-1150.2.

"Prescribed burning" means the controlled application of fire or wildland fuels in either the natural or modified state, under specified environmental conditions, which allows a fire to be confined to a predetermined area and produces the fire behavior and fire characteristics necessary to attain planned fire treatment and ecological, silvicultural, and wildlife management objectives.

"Prescription" means a written statement defining the objectives to be attained by a prescribed burning and the conditions of temperature, humidity, wind direction and speed, fuel moisture, and soil moisture under which a fire will be allowed to burn. A prescription is generally expressed as an acceptable range of the prescription elements. (1998, c. 156.)

§ 10.1-1150.2. State Forester to establish certification process. — The State Forester shall develop and administer a certification process and training course for any individual who desires to become a certified prescribed burn manager. The training program shall include the following subjects: the legal aspects of prescribed burning, fire behavior, prescribed burning tactics, smoke management, environmental effects, plan preparation, and safety. A final examination on these subjects shall be given to all attendees. The State Forester may charge a reasonable fee to cover the costs of the course and the examination. (1998, c. 156.)

§ 10.1-1150.3. Voluntary certification. — To be certified as a prescribed burn manager, a person shall:

1. Successfully complete all components of the prescribed burn course developed by the State Forester and pass the examination developed for the course;

2. Successfully complete a training course comparable to that developed by the State Forester and pass the examination developed for Virginia's course; or

3. Demonstrate relevant past experience, complete a review course and pass the examination developed for Virginia's course. (1998, c. 156.)

§ 10.1-1150.4. Prescribed burn elements. — Prescribed burning shall be performed in the following manner:

1. A prescription for the prescribed burn shall be prepared by a certified prescribed burn manager prior to the burn. The prescription shall include: (i) the landowner's name, address, and telephone number, and the telephone number of the certified prescribed burn manager who prepared the plan; (ii) a description of the area to be burned, a map of the area to be burned, the objectives of the prescribed burn, and the desired weather conditions or parameters; (iii) a summary of the methods to be used to start, control, and

287

extinguish the prescribed burn; and (iv) a smoke management plan. The smoke management plan shall be based on guidelines presented in the Virginia Department of Forestry publication, "Voluntary Smoke Management Guidelines for Virginia," and the U.S. Forest Service's technical publication, "A Guide to Prescribed Fire in Southern Forests." A copy of the prescription shall be retained at the site throughout the period of the burning;

2. Prescribed burning shall be conducted under the direct supervision of a certified prescribed burn manager, who shall ensure that the prescribed burning is in accordance with the prescription; and

3. The nearest regional office of the Virginia Department of Forestry shall be notified prior to the burn. (1998, c. 156.)

§ 10.1-1150.5. Liability. — A. Any prescribed burning conducted in compliance with the requirements of this article, state air pollution control laws, and any rules adopted by the Virginia Department of Forestry shall be in the public interest and shall not constitute a nuisance.

B. Any landowner or his agent who conducts a prescribed burn in compliance with the requirements of this article, state air pollution control laws, and any rules adopted by the Virginia Department of Forestry shall not be liable for any damage or injury caused by or resulting from smoke.

C. Subsections A and B of this section shall not apply whenever a nuisance or damage results from the negligent or improper conduct of the prescribed burn or when the prescribed burn elements described in § 10.1-1150.4 have not been complied with. (1998, c. 156.)

§ 10.1-1150.6. Revocation of certification. — If the actions of any certified prescribed burn manager or the prescriptions prepared by him violate any provision of this article, state air pollution control laws, or Virginia Department of Forestry rules or threaten public health and safety, his certification may be revoked by the State Forester. (1998, c. 156.)

ARTICLE 7.

Hunting and Trapping in State Forests.

§ 10.1-1151. Necessity for permits. — No person shall hunt or trap in this Commonwealth on any lands which are under the jurisdiction and control of the Department by virtue of purchase, gift, lease or otherwise, and are administered as state forests, without first obtaining, in addition to other licenses and permits required by law, special use permits required by the State Forester pursuant to this article. (Code 1950, § 10-68; 1986, c. 567; 1988, c. 891.)

§ 10.1-1152. State Forester may require permits and fees. — The State Forester is authorized, with the approval of the Board, to require any person who hunts or traps on any of the lands described in § 10.1-1151 to obtain a special use permit or special use permits. Permits to hunt on any such lands shall be issued for a fee, not to exceed $15 annually for each permit, as fixed by the State Forester. Permits to trap on such lands may be issued in combination with the hunting permits, or separately, at a fee not to exceed $15 annually for each such permit, to be fixed by the State Forester. (Code 1950, § 10-69; 1984, c. 715; 1986, cc. 539, 567; 1988, c. 891; 1993, c. 260; 2006, c. 13.)

The 2006 amendments. — The 2006 amendment by c. 13 substituted "$15" for "ten dollars" in the last two sentences.

§ 10.1-1153. Limitations on rights of holders of permits. — Each special use permit shall entitle the holder to hunt and trap, or to trap, in and upon such lands of the state forests as shall be determined by the State Forester and designated on the permit, subject to all other applicable provisions of law or regulations of the Department of Game and Inland Fisheries and to such further conditions and restrictions for safeguarding the state forests as may be imposed by the State Forester and indicated on the permit. In addition to the other provisions of law applicable to hunting and trapping on the lands of the Commonwealth, the State Forester is authorized to impose such restrictions and conditions upon hunting and trapping in the state forests as he deems proper. No such restriction or condition shall be effective for the permit holder unless the restriction or condition is written, printed, stamped or otherwise indicated on the permit. (Code 1950, § 10-70; 1986, c. 567; 1988, c. 891.)

§ 10.1-1154. Issuance of permits and collection of fees; form of permit. — Clerks or other persons authorized to sell hunting and trapping permits of the circuit courts of the counties wherein state forests are located shall issue the special use permits and collect the applicable fees. Each permit shall bear a serial number and shall be in the form prescribed by the State Forester. All necessary special use permits or permit blanks shall be furnished to the clerks or other persons authorized to sell permits by the State Forester. For his services each clerk or other persons shall be entitled to receive twenty-five cents for each permit issued. (Code 1950, § 10-71; 1986, cc. 539, 567; 1988, c. 891.)

§ 10.1-1155. Collections to be paid into state treasury; reports to the Department of Forestry. — Each clerk or other authorized person mentioned in § 10.1-1154 shall pay into the state treasury the gross amount received by him from the sale of special use permits, as follows: (i) for July, August and September, quarterly, not later than October 5; (ii) for October, November and December, quarterly, not later than January 5; (iii) for January, February and March, quarterly, not later than April 5; and (iv) for April, May and June, quarterly, not later than July 5.

At the time of each remittance the clerk or other authorized person shall report to the Department of Forestry on forms prescribed and provided by the State Forester, showing the serial numbers and quantity of permit forms received, sold, and on hand unsold, and the amount of gross collections remitted for the quarter. (Code 1950, § 10-72; 1986, c. 567; 1988, c. 891; 2004, c. 58.)

§ 10.1-1156. Funds credited to Department; disbursements. — All funds paid into the state treasury pursuant to § 10.1-1155, shall be credited to the Department and maintained in the Reforestation Operations Fund to be expended annually, in the following order:

1. One-fourth of the gross revenue so derived shall be paid into the treasuries of the counties wherein state forests are located proportionately according to the revenue derived from the sale of special permits in each respective county, which shall be credited to the general fund of such county;

2. From the balance remaining after providing for such payments to the counties, there shall be paid the costs of preparing and issuing the permits, including the compensation of the clerks or other persons authorized to sell hunting and trapping permits;

3. The remainder may be expended by the State Forester for game and forest management in such state forests. All funds expended by the State Forester in the development, management, and protection of the game

resources in state forests shall be in cooperation with and under the direction of the Department of Game and Inland Fisheries. (Code 1950, § 10-73; 1986, c. 567; 1988, c. 891.)

§ 10.1-1157. Punishment for violations. — Any person who hunts or traps in violation of any provision of this article, or in violation of restrictions and conditions imposed by the State Forester pursuant to the provisions of § 10.1-1153 shall be guilty of a Class 1 misdemeanor and upon conviction shall be punished accordingly. (Code 1950, § 10-74; 1986, cc. 539, 567; 1988, c. 891.)

Cross references. — As to punishment for Class 1 misdemeanors, see § 18.2-11.

ARTICLE 8.

Fire Hazards and Closing of Hunting and Fishing Seasons in Forestlands.

§ 10.1-1158. Prohibition of all open burning where serious fire hazards exist; penalty. — It shall be unlawful when the forestlands, brushlands and fields in this Commonwealth or any part thereof have become so dry as to create a serious fire hazard endangering lives and property, for any persons to do any open burning nearer than 300 feet from any such forestlands, brushlands or fields containing dry grass or other flammable material.

This article shall not be effective until the Governor, upon recommendation of the State Forester, proclaims such a condition to exist in this Commonwealth or any part thereof, and it shall be in effect until the Governor proclaims such condition to have terminated.

It shall be the duty of all authorized law-enforcement officers of the Commonwealth, counties, and municipalities to enforce the provisions of this section.

Any person violating the provisions of this section shall be guilty of a Class 3 misdemeanor for each separate offense. (1986, c. 188, § 27-54.5; 1988, c. 891.)

Cross references. — As to punishment for Class 3 misdemeanors, see § 18.2-11.

§ 10.1-1159. Upon proclamation of Governor certain acts made unlawful where extraordinary fire hazards exist; closing of hunting and fishing seasons. — Upon proclamation of the Governor, it shall be unlawful, when the forestlands, brushlands and fields in the Commonwealth or any part thereof have become so dry as to create an extraordinary fire hazard endangering lives and property, for any person, except the owner, tenant or owner's authorized agent, persons regularly engaged in cutting, processing, or moving forest products, or person on official duty, to enter or travel in any state, county, municipal or private forestlands, brushlands, marshland, fields or idle or abandoned lands in the area so affected except on public highways or well-defined private roads. During such period hunting and fishing seasons shall be closed, except hunting of migratory waterfowl and fishing as hereinafter provided, on all land and water within the Commonwealth or any geographical part thereof affected by proclamation. It shall further be unlawful during such periods for any person to hunt or fish except as hereinafter provided, smoke, burn leaves, grass, brush or debris of any type or to ignite or maintain any open fire nearer than 300 feet from any such forestlands, brushlands or fields containing inflammable vegetation or marshland adjoining such forestlands, brushlands, fields or idle or abandoned lands.

It shall not be unlawful to fish or hunt migratory waterfowl from a boat, or from a blind entirely surrounded by water and reached by a boat, or on nonforested islands at least 300 feet from the mainland shore and reached by a boat, when the boat embarks from and lands at established boat landings, and at no other time touches shore nearer than 300 feet from any forestlands, brushlands, or fields containing inflammable vegetation or marshland adjoining such areas.

It shall be the duty of all authorized law-enforcement officers of the Commonwealth, counties and municipalities to enforce the provisions of this section.

Any person violating the provisions of this section shall be guilty of a Class 2 misdemeanor for each separate offense. (1954, c. 134, § 27-54.1; 1964, c. 65; 1966, c. 302; 1986, c. 188; 1988, c. 891.)

Cross references. — As to punishment for Class 2 misdemeanors, see § 18.2-11.

§ 10.1-1160. Effect of proclamation on hunting season. — When any proclamation is issued pursuant to § 10.1-1158 during any open hunting season (with the exception of any season on migratory birds or waterfowl, the limits of which are prescribed by any agency of the federal government), or when the opening date of any such hunting season occurs while such proclamation is effective, the season, if open, may be extended by the Governor for a period not exceeding the number of legal hunting days during which such proclamation is in effect, beginning on the first legal hunting day after the expiration of the season. If the season is not open, it may open beginning on the first legal hunting day after such proclamation is rescinded and remain open for a period not exceeding the prescribed length of the season. (1954, c. 134, § 27-54.2; 1972, c. 150; 1988, c. 891.)

§ 10.1-1161. Notice of issuance, amendment or rescission of proclamation. — When any proclamation is issued, amended or rescinded the Secretary of the Commonwealth shall promptly give notice thereof through a newspaper or newspapers of general circulation in the area or areas affected. In addition, the Secretary may, in his discretion, give such additional notice as he deems necessary. (Code 1950, § 10-75; 1952, c. 417; 1956, c. 75; 1988, c. 891.)

ARTICLE 9.

Seed Trees.

§ 10.1-1162. Definitions. — As used in this article unless the context requires a different meaning:

"Diameter" means the distance through a tree at the point of average thickness as measured from outside of bark to outside of bark at a point on a trunk ten inches above the general ground level.

"Person" means any landowner, owner of timber, owner of timber rights, sawmill operator, sawmill owner, veneer wood operator, pulpwood contractor, or any person engaged in the business of severing timber from the stump.

"Tree" means any tree of a currently commercially valuable species which is six inches or more in diameter. (Code 1950, § 10-75; 1952, c. 417; 1956, c. 75; 1988, c. 891.)

§ 10.1-1163. Exemptions from article. — A. This article shall not apply to any acre of land on which there are present at the time of final cutting of the timber 400 or more loblolly or white pine seedlings, singly or together, four feet or more in height.

B. This article shall not apply to any person who clears or who procures another to clear his land for bona fide agricultural or improved pasture purposes or for the purpose of subdividing such land for sale for building sites. For the purpose of this article, evidence of intent of bona fide agricultural or improved pasture use shall require, as a minimum and within twelve months from the date of completion of commercial cutting, that the land intended for such use be cleared of all trees, snags, brush, tree tops, and debris by piling and burning or otherwise disposing of same, or by enclosing the area with a well-constructed fence and planting grass seed thereon so as to make a bona fide improved pasture. In the case of clearing for building sites evidence of intent shall be the construction of dwellings or other bona fide structure in progress or completed within two years from the date of completion of commercial cutting.

C. This article shall not apply to land which has been zoned for a more intensive land use than agricultural or forestal use.

D. The provisions of this article shall not apply to any acre or acres of forest land for which a planting, cutting or management plan has been prepared, designed to provide conservation of natural resources, and which plan has been submitted to and approved by the State Forester previous to the cutting of any trees on the acre or acres concerned. If such plan has been submitted to the State Forester by registered or certified mail and he has not approved the plan, or disapproved it with a statement in writing of his reasons therefor, within a period of sixty days from the date of submission, the plan shall be deemed approved and shall be effective for the purposes of this section.

E. The State Forester may grant exemptions from this article to individual landowners who wish to grow hardwoods on their property. The State Forester may place conditions on the exemption as he deems advisable for the conservation of natural resources. (Code 1950, §§ 10-81, 10-82, 10-83; 1950, p. 58; 1952, c. 412; 1956, c. 75; 1960, c. 244; 1988, c. 891; 1996, c. 285; 1997, c. 146.)

§ 10.1-1164. Pine trees to be left uncut for reseeding purposes. — Every landowner who cuts, or any person who cuts or procures another to cut, or any person who owns the timber at the time of cutting and knowingly and willfully allows to be cut, for commercial purposes, timber from ten acres or more of land on which loblolly or white pine, singly or together, occur and constitute twenty-five percent or more of the live trees on each acre or acres, shall reserve and leave uncut and uninjured not less than eight cone-bearing loblolly or white pine trees fourteen inches or larger in diameter on each acre thus cut and upon each acre on which such pine trees occur singly or together, unless there is in effect for such land a planting, cutting or management plan as provided in subsection D of § 10.1-1163. Where eight cone-bearing loblolly or white pine trees fourteen inches or larger in diameter are not present on any particular acre, there shall be left uncut and uninjured for each such pine two cone-bearing pine trees of the largest diameter present less than fourteen inches in diameter. Such pine trees shall be left uncut for the purpose of reseeding the land and shall be healthy, windfirm, and of well-developed crowns, evidencing seed-bearing ability by the presence of cones in the crowns. (Code 1950, § 10-76; 1950, p. 58; 1952, c. 417; 1956, c. 75; 1960, c. 244; 1968, c. 73; 1988, c. 891; 1996, c. 285.)

§ 10.1-1165. When trees left for reseeding purposes may be cut. — Pine trees which are left uncut for purposes of reseeding shall be the property of the landowner but shall not be cut until at least three years have elapsed after the cutting of the timber on such lands. (Code 1950, § 10-77; 1956, c. 75; 1960, c. 244; 1972, c. 163; 1988, c. 891.)

§ 10.1-1166. Posting or publication of notices. — The State Forester shall distribute notices calling attention to the provisions of this article in conspicuous places in all counties and cities where such pine timber grows in appreciable quantities, and may publish notices in newspapers of general circulation in such counties and cities. (Code 1950, § 10-78; 1956, c. 75; 1988, c. 891.)

§ 10.1-1167. Penalty for violation of article. — Any person violating any provision of this article shall be guilty of a misdemeanor and upon conviction shall be fined thirty dollars for each seed tree cut from the land in violation of this article. The total amount of fine for any one acre shall not exceed $240. (Code 1950, § 10-79; 1950, p. 58; 1956, c. 75; 1972, c. 163; 1988, c. 891; 1996, c. 285.)

§ 10.1-1168. Procedure to ensure proper planting after conviction; cash deposit or bond; inspection or planting by State Forester. — When any person is convicted of failing to leave seed trees uncut as required by § 10.1-1164, the judge shall require the person so convicted to immediately post with the court a cash deposit or a bond of a reputable surety company in favor of the State Forester in the amount of thirty dollars for each seed tree cut in violation of this article. The total amount of the cash deposit or bond for any one acre shall not exceed $240.

The judge shall cause the cash deposit or surety bond to be delivered to the State Forester, who shall hold the cash or surety bond in a special account until it is used or released as hereinafter provided. The purpose of the cash or surety bond is to ensure that the general cutover area on which seed trees have been cut in violation of this article shall be planted with tree seedlings of the same species as the trees cut in violation of this article in a manner hereinafter specified.

For each acre on which trees have been cut in violation of this article, a number up to 600, as determined by the State Forester, of tree seedlings shall be planted on the general cutover area on which seed trees were cut in violation. Each seedling shall be planted in a separate hole at least six feet from any other planted seedling. Seedlings shall be planted at least six feet from any sapling or tree which may shade the planted seedling from direct sunlight. If stems of noncommercial species prevent the planting of tree seedlings in the manner herein described on any area in violation, a sufficient number of such stems shall be cut, girdled or poisoned to permit the required number of seedlings to be planted. The seedlings shall be planted during the period of the year when forest tree seedlings are customarily planted in the section of the Commonwealth in which the cutover area is located. After receipt of the tree seedlings from the nursery, care shall be taken to keep the seedling roots in a moist, uninjured condition at all times prior to actual planting, and the seedlings shall be planted in a careful, workmanlike manner. Planted seedlings shall be of the same tree species as the seed trees cut in violation, or if two or more seed tree species are cut in violation, the species of the planted seedlings shall be in proportion to the seed trees cut in violation. The above specified manner of planting and tree species planted shall be observed whether the planting is done by the person found in violation of this article or by the State Forester.

A person convicted of violating this article may plant tree seedlings on the general cutover area of the species and in the manner specified herein within one year following the date of conviction. Upon completion of the planting, the person shall immediately notify the State Forester in writing that the area has been planted. The State Forester or his representative shall then inspect the area and if he finds the planting to be done in accordance with the specifications set forth, he shall notify the person in writing and return the cash deposit or surety bond to the person depositing it.

If, upon inspection, the State Forester finds that the general cutover area or any part thereof has not been planted in the manner and during the period of year specified, or that the area has not been planted previous to one year following the date of conviction, the State Forester shall then plant the area during the next planting season, and do such forest cultural work as he deems necessary by reason of the delayed planting, keeping a careful and accurate account of all costs incurred, including a reasonable administrative cost. Following completion of the planting the State Forester shall prepare a certified statement showing the cost of planting, which shall be paid from the cash deposit, or if a surety bond has been deposited the State Forester shall collect the cost of planting from the bonding company. The State Forester shall then submit to the person making the deposit a certified statement of the cost of planting, together with any cash remaining after paying the cost of planting and forest cultural work.

The State Forester shall not be required to expend for planting and forest cultural operations more than thirty dollars per seed tree cut in violation of this article. (1956, c. 75, § 10-79.1; 1960, c. 269; 1972, c. 163; 1988, c. 891; 1996, c. 285.)

§ **10.1-1169. Liability for failure to carry out planting, cutting or management plan; reforestation of area by State Forester.** — A. Any person failing to carry out, fulfill or complete any term or provision of any planting, cutting, or management plan submitted to and approved by the State Forester as provided in subsection D of § 10.1-1163 shall be liable to the Commonwealth in a civil suit brought by the Attorney General in the name of the Commonwealth in any court of competent jurisdiction for, at least $240 per acre for each acre or part of an acre subject to such plan and legal fees incurred by the Commonwealth. All moneys collected pursuant to this subsection, exclusive of court costs and legal fees incurred by the Commonwealth, shall be delivered to the State Forester, who shall deposit the money in the Forestry Operations Fund in the state treasury until it is used or released as hereinafter provided. Such deposit may only be spent to ensure that the area for which the planting, cutting or management plan was approved by the State Forester shall be reforested in the manner hereinafter specified.

B. During the year following the date of payment of any judgment rendered in favor of the Commonwealth pursuant to subsection A of this section and at the season when forest tree seedlings are customarily planted in the section of the Commonwealth where the planting, cutting or management plan area is located, the State Forester shall plant, or cause to be planted, on the area, as many forest tree seedlings as he deems necessary to reforest the area adequately. The tree species used in reforesting the area may be the same as the pine species cut from the area, or the species may be a mixture suitable for reforesting the area, in the judgment of the State Forester.

C. If, upon inspection, the State Forester finds that the area for which the forest management plan was approved is covered with a growth of woody plants, sprouts, brush and briars of such a density as to retard or preclude the establishment and development of the planted tree seedlings, he may perform or cause to be performed forest cultural measures, such as bulldozing, disking, poisoning by spray, and similar measures, necessary to make the area suitable for the planting, establishment and development of tree seedlings.

D. The State Forester shall keep an accurate account of all costs involved, including reasonable administrative costs, and shall transfer such costs from the Forestry Operations Fund into the Department operating account for protection and development of the forest resources of the Commonwealth. If, after having complied with the reforestation provisions of this section, any money remains in the special account to the credit of any particular case, the unexpended balance shall be paid to the person against whom a judgment was rendered pursuant to the provisions of subsection A.

E. The expenditure by the State Forester for reforestation on any individual area as herein provided shall not exceed the amount of the judgment paid for the reforestation of such area. (1964, c. 235, § 10-83.01; 1972, c. 163; 1986, c. 567; 1988, c. 891; 1996, c. 285.)

ARTICLE 10.

Reforestation of Timberlands.

§ 10.1-1170. Administration of article. — The State Forester shall administer the provisions of this article, including the protection, preservation and perpetuation of forest resources by means of reforestation to allow continuous growth of timber on lands suitable therefor, and is authorized to employ personnel; purchase equipment, materials, and supplies; maintain and transport equipment; and make other expenditures and payments authorized by law, and as directed by the regulations adopted for the administration of this article. In any one fiscal year, the expenditures for salaries of administrative supervisory personnel shall not exceed ten percent of the general fund appropriation and forest products taxes collected and deposited in the Reforestation of Timberlands Fund as provided in § 10.1-1174 for that particular year. (1981, c. 371, § 10-90.31; 1984, c. 750; 1986, c. 567; 1988, c. 891.)

Cross references. — For applicability of article, see § 10.1-1176.

§ 10.1-1171. Exceptions. — A. This article shall not apply to any tract of land in excess of 500 acres under the sole ownership of an individual, corporation, partnership, trust, association, or any other business unit, device, or arrangement.

B. This article shall not apply to any acre or part of an acre on which the landowner is receiving federal financial assistance for growing timber. (1981, c. 371, §§ 10-90.33, 10-90.34, 10-90.35; 1988, c. 891; 1996, c. 733.)

Cross references. — For applicability of article, see § 10.1-1176.

§ 10.1-1172. Reforestation Board; regulations. — The Reforestation Board shall be appointed by the Governor and consist of the following members: three representatives of the pine pulpwood industry, three representatives of the pine lumber industry, one of whom shall be the owner of a sawmill annually producing not more than five million board feet, and three small forest landowners. The State Forester shall be a nonvoting member of the Reforestation Board and shall serve as secretary of the Board.

All members shall be appointed for three-year terms and appointed members may not serve for more than two consecutive terms.

The Reforestation Board shall annually elect a chairman and shall formulate regulations for its organization and procedure.

The Reforestation Board shall meet not less than twice each year, at such location as it may designate, to formulate recommendations to the State Forester concerning regulations and other matters applicable to this article including, but not limited to, types of equipment to be purchased, rental rates for equipment, and reforestation practices. (1981, c. 371, § 10-90.32; 1984, c. 750; 1985, c. 448; 1986, c. 567; 1988, c. 891; 1990, c. 196.)

Cross references. — For applicability of article, see § 10.1-1176.

§ **10.1-1173. Authority of State Forester; reforestation options; lien.** — The State Forester is authorized, upon the request of a landowner, to examine timberland and make recommendations concerning reforestation. He may make available to landowners, with or without charge, use of specialized state-owned equipment and tree seedlings, tree seed, materials, and services of specialized state personnel for the purpose of preparing land for reforestation and reforesting land devoted to growing timber, in accordance with administrative regulations.

Upon the completion of each separate reforestation project in accordance with the recommendations and approval of the State Forester, the State Forester shall determine the total cost of the project including money paid or payable to a contractor for services performed on the project, for labor, and for other costs incurred by the landowner, including a standard rental rate value for use of state-owned equipment and the cost of tree seedlings, tree seed, materials, and specialized state personnel used on the project.

The following incentive to reforesting land may be utilized by the State Forester: whenever a landowner completes a reforestation project in accordance with the recommendations and approval of the State Forester, through the use of his own equipment, material and personnel, or through the employment of a contractor where no state equipment, materials or personnel are used, or are used only in part, the State Forester shall determine the total cost of the project based on current commercial rental rate for machines similar to types used, cost of material, and cost of personnel where the landowner does his own work on the project, or based on the contractor's statement of cost or paid receipts furnished by the landowner where work is done by a contractor together with and at the standard rental value for use of any state-owned specialized equipment, tree seedlings, tree seed, materials, and specialized state personnel used on the project. The State Forester, from funds appropriated for the purposes of this article, may pay to the landowner an amount not to exceed seventy-five percent of the total cost of the project, as above determined, or ninety dollars per acre, whichever is the lesser. (1981, c. 371, § 10-90.36; 1984, c. 750; 1986, c. 567; 1988, c. 891.)

Cross references. — For applicability of article, see § 10.1-1176.

§ **10.1-1174. Reforestation of Timberlands Fund.** — All moneys paid to or collected by the State Forester for rental equipment, tree seedlings, seed and material furnished, and specialized personnel services rendered to a landowner and all moneys collected or received from settlement of liens, including principal, interest and fines, authorized under this article shall be paid into the state treasury. All such moneys shall be credited by the State Comptroller as special revenues to the Reforestation of Timberlands Fund of the Department of Forestry to be expended solely for reforesting privately owned timberlands of the Commonwealth as provided in this article. (1981, c. 371, § 10-90.37; 1984, c. 750; 1986, c. 567; 1988, c. 891.)

Cross references. — For applicability of article, see § 10.1-1176.

§ **10.1-1175. Certain rights of landowner not limited.** — This article shall not limit the right of any landowner to contract with individuals, organizations, and public bodies to provide for the utilization of the land for recreational purposes, or to grant open space easements over the land to public bodies. (1981, c. 371, § 10-90.39; 1988, c. 891.)

Cross references. — For applicability of article, see § 10.1-1176.

§ **10.1-1176. When provisions of article effective.** — This article shall not be effective during any biennium for which the General Assembly fails to appropriate from the state general fund a sum which equals or exceeds the total revenues collected from the forest products tax for the immediately preceding two years; a report of such sum shall be submitted by the State Forester to the Governor on or before November 1 of the last year of the preceding biennium. (1981, c. 371, § 10-90.38; 1988, c. 891; 1998, c. 420.)

ARTICLE 11.

Insect Infestation and Diseases of Forest Trees.

§ **10.1-1177. Authority of Department of Forestry.** — The Department of Forestry is authorized to and responsible for (i) investigating insect infestations and disease infections which affect stands of forest trees, and (ii) devising and demonstrating control measures to interested persons. The State Forester shall administer the provisions of this article. Authority for quarantine procedure now vested in the Department of Agriculture and Consumer Services shall remain in that Department. (1952, c. 657, § 10-90.3; 1986, c. 567; 1988, c. 891.)

§ **10.1-1178. Definitions.** — As used in this article, unless the context requires a different meaning:

"Forest land" means land on which forest trees are found.

"Forest trees" means only those trees which are a part of and constitute a stand of potential, immature, or mature commercial timber trees. The term "forest trees" includes shade trees of any species around houses, along highways and within cities and towns if the trees constitute an insect or disease menace to nearby timber trees or timber stands.

"Infection" means infection by any disease affecting forest trees which is declared by the State Forester to be dangerously injurious to forest trees.

"Infestation" means infestation by means of any insect which is declared by the State Forester to be dangerously injurious to forest trees.

"Person" includes an individual, partnership, corporation, company, society or association. (1952, c. 657, § 10-90.4; 1986, c. 539; 1988, c. 891.)

§ **10.1-1179. State Forester to investigate; notice to landowners.** — Where an insect infestation or disease infection is believed to exist on forest land within this Commonwealth, the State Forester shall investigate the condition. Whenever he finds that an infestation or infection exists he shall give notice in writing by mail or otherwise to each forest landowner within the affected area, advising him of the nature of the infestation or infection and the recommended control measures, and offering him technical advice on methods of carrying out control measures. (1952, c. 657, § 10-90.5; 1988, c. 891.)

§ **10.1-1180. Cooperation with individuals and public agencies.** — The Department of Forestry is authorized to cooperate with persons, counties, state agencies, and United States government agencies, and the appropriate authorities of adjacent states concerning forest tree insect and disease investigation and control, and to accept money, gifts and donations and to disburse the same for the purpose of carrying out the provisions of this article. (1952, c. 657, § 10-90.7; 1986, c. 567; 1988, c. 891.)

§ 10.1-1181. Control of Forest Tree Insects and Diseases Fund. — A special fund in the state treasury known as the Control of Forest Tree Insects and Diseases Fund shall consist of all moneys appropriated thereto by the General Assembly, all revenues collected under the provisions of this article, and any moneys paid into the state treasury or to the State Forester, the Board of Forestry, or the Department of Forestry by the federal government or any agency thereof to be used for the purposes of this article. All such funds are hereby appropriated to the Department of Forestry to be used to carry out the purposes of this article. (1952, c. 657, § 10-90.9; 1986, c. 567; 1988, c. 891.)

ARTICLE 12.

Silvicultural Activities Affecting Water Quality.

§ 10.1-1181.1. Definitions. — As used in this article unless the context requires a different meaning:
"Operator" means any person that operates or has operated or exercises or has exercised control over any silvicultural activity.
"Owner" means any person that (i) owns or leases land on which silvicultural activity occurs or has occurred or (ii) owns timber on land on which silvicultural activity occurs or has occurred.
"Pollution" means such alteration of the physical, chemical or biological properties of any state waters resulting from sediment deposition as will or is likely to create a nuisance or render such waters (i) harmful or detrimental or injurious to the public health, safety or welfare, or to the health of animals, fish or aquatic life; (ii) unsuitable with reasonable treatment for use as present or possible future sources of public water supply; or (iii) unsuitable for recreational, commercial, industrial, agricultural, or other reasonable uses.
"Silvicultural activity" means any forest management activity, including but not limited to the harvesting of timber, the construction of roads and trails for forest management purposes, and the preparation of property for reforestation.
"Special order" means a special order or emergency special order issued under subsection B or C of § 10.1-1181.2. (1993, c. 948; 1998, c. 578.)

§ 10.1-1181.2. Conduct of silvicultural activities; issuance of special orders. — A. If the State Forester believes that an owner or operator has conducted or is conducting or has allowed or is allowing the conduct of any silvicultural activity in a manner that is causing or is likely to cause pollution, he may notify the owner or operator regarding the activity that is causing or likely to cause pollution and recommend (i) corrective measures and (ii) a reasonable time period to prevent, mitigate, or eliminate the pollution. If the owner or operator fails to take action to prevent, mitigate, or eliminate the pollution, the State Forester shall issue a special order pursuant to subsection B or C. Failure of the State Forester to notify an owner or operator of such corrective measures shall not impair the State Forester's authority to issue special orders pursuant to subsection B or C.
B. The State Forester shall have the authority to issue special orders to any owner or operator who has conducted or is conducting, or has allowed or is allowing to be conducted, any silvicultural activity in a manner that is causing

or is likely to cause pollution, to cease immediately all or part of the silvicultural activities on the site, and to implement specified corrective measures within a stated period of time. Such special orders are to be issued only after the owner or operator has been given the opportunity for a hearing with reasonable notice to the owner or operator, or both, of the time, place and purpose thereof, and they shall become effective not less than five days after service as provided in subsection D.

C. If the State Forester finds that any owner or operator is conducting any silvicultural activity in a manner that is causing or is likely to cause an alteration of the physical, chemical or biological properties of any state waters resulting from sediment deposition presenting an imminent and substantial danger to (i) the public health, safety or welfare, or the health of animals, fish or aquatic life; (ii) a public water supply; or (iii) recreational, commercial, industrial, agricultural or other reasonable uses, the State Forester may issue, without advance notice or hearing, an emergency order directing the owner or operator, or both, to cease immediately all or part of the silvicultural activities on the site, and to implement specified corrective measures within a stated period of time. The commencement of proceedings by the State Forester for the issuance of a special order pursuant to subsection B shall not impair the State Forester's authority to issue an emergency special order pursuant to this subsection. The State Forester shall provide an opportunity for a hearing, after reasonable notice as to the time and place thereof to the owner or operator, to affirm, modify, amend or cancel such emergency special order.

D. The owner or operator to whom such special order is directed shall be notified by certified mail, return receipt requested, sent to the last known address of the owner, or operator, or by personal delivery by an agent of the State Forester, and the time limits specified shall be counted from the date of receipt.

E. The State Forester shall not issue a special order to any owner or operator who has incorporated generally acceptable water quality protection techniques in the operation of silvicultural activities, which techniques have failed to prevent pollution, if the State Forester determines that the pollution is the direct result of unusual weather events that could not have been reasonably anticipated.

F. Any hearing required under this section shall be conducted in accordance with § 2.2-4020 unless the parties consent to informal proceedings.

G. The State Forester shall not issue a notice under subsection A or a special order or emergency special order under subsection B or C more than one year after the silvicultural activity has occurred on the property. Any such notice, special order, or emergency special order shall remain in effect until the State Forester determines that corrective measures specified therein have been implemented.

H. Prior to completion but not later than three working days after the commencement of an operation, the operator shall notify the State Forester of the commercial harvesting of timber. For the purpose of this section, commercial harvesting of timber means the harvesting of trees for the primary purpose of transporting to another site for additional manufacturing. The notification may be verbal or written and shall (i) specify the location and the actual or anticipated date of the activity and (ii) be made in a manner prescribed by the State Forester. If an operator fails to comply with the provisions of this subsection, the State Forester may assess a civil penalty of $250 for the initial violation and not more than $1,000 for any subsequent violation within a 24-month period by the operator. Such civil penalties shall be paid into the state treasury and credited to the Virginia Forest Water Quality Fund pursuant to § 10.1-1181.7. (1993, c. 948; 1998, c. 578; 2002, cc. 293, 304, 376; 2003, c. 812; 2004, c. 228.)

Penalties imposed by the Department of Forestry against logging contractors were upheld. — Except for one of the fines assessed, substantial evidence showed that the agency properly followed its statutory mandate in calculating the penalties; moreover, given the clar- ity of the emergency order, there was no basis to question that said decision implied that logging work could resume on a trial basis to see if the corrective actions would "hold up." Campbell v. Dep't of Forestry, 46 Va. App. 91, 616 S.E.2d 33, 2005 Va. App. LEXIS 283 (2005).

§ 10.1-1181.3. Civil penalties. — A.

Any owner or operator who violates, or fails or refuses to obey any special order may be assessed a civil penalty by the State Forester. Such penalty shall not exceed $5,000 for each violation. Each day of a continuing violation may be deemed a separate violation for purposes of assessing penalties. In determining the amount of the penalty, consideration shall be given to the owner's or operator's history of noncompli- ance; the seriousness of the violation, including any irreparable harm to the environment and any hazard to the health or safety of the public; whether the owner or operator was negligent; and the demonstrated good faith of the owner or operator in reporting and remedying the pollution.

B. A civil penalty may be assessed by the State Forester only after the owner or operator has been given an opportunity for a hearing. Any hearing required under this section shall be conducted in accordance with § 2.2-4020, unless the parties consent to informal proceedings. If the owner or operator fails to avail himself of the opportunity for a formal hearing, a civil penalty shall be assessed by the State Forester after the State Forester finds that a violation of a special order has occurred and the amount of the civil penalty warranted, and issues an order requiring that the civil penalty be paid.

C. If a person who is required under this article to pay a civil penalty fails to do so, the State Forester may transmit a true copy of the final order assessing such penalty to the clerk of circuit court of any county or city wherein it is ascertained that the person owing the penalty has any estate; and the clerk to whom such copy is sent shall record it, as a judgment is required by law to be recorded, and shall index the same in the name of the Commonwealth as well as of the person owing the penalty, and thereupon there shall be a lien in favor of the Commonwealth on the property of the owner or operator within such county or city in the amount of the penalty. The State Forester may collect civil penalties that are owed in the same manner as provided by law in respect to judgment of a court of record. All civil penalties shall be paid into the state treasury and deposited by the State Treasurer into the Virginia Forest Water Quality Fund pursuant to § 10.1-1181.7.

D. With the consent of any owner or operator who has violated or failed, neglected or refused to obey any special order of the State Forester issued pursuant to subsection B or C of § 10.1-1181.2, the State Forester may provide, in an order issued by the State Forester against such owner or operator, for the payment of civil charges for violations in specific sums, not to exceed the limit specified in subsection A of this section. Such civil charges shall be in lieu of any civil penalty that could be imposed under subsection A of this section, and shall be placed in the Virginia Forest Water Quality Fund pursuant to § 10.1-1181.7. (1993, c. 948; 2004, c. 228.)

Penalties imposed by the Department of Forestry against logging contractors pur- suant to § 10.1-1181.2 were upheld. — Ex- cept for one of the fines assessed, substantial evidence showed that the agency properly fol- lowed its statutory mandate in calculating the penalties; moreover, given the clarity of the emergency order, there was no basis to question that said decision implied that logging work could resume on a trial basis to see if the

corrective actions would "hold up." Campbell v.
Dep't of Forestry, 46 Va. App. 91, 616 S.E.2d 33,
2005 Va. App. LEXIS 283 (2005).

§ **10.1-1181.4. Final decisions; costs of hearing examiner.** — A. Any final order or decision rendered pursuant to this article shall be reduced to writing and shall contain the explicit findings of fact and conclusions of law upon which the decision is based. Certified copies of the written decision shall be delivered or mailed by certified mail to the parties affected by the decision.

B. If any final agency case decision is rendered following a hearing conducted in accordance with § 2.2-4020 presided over by a hearing officer, the officer shall be paid by the State Forester if the owner or operator is the prevailing party, or by the owner or operator if the State Forester is the prevailing party. The findings of the hearing officer shall specify which party prevailed in the hearing. (1993, c. 948.)

§ **10.1-1181.5. Judicial review.** — Any person aggrieved by a final order or decision under this article shall be entitled to judicial review thereof in accordance with the Administrative Process Act (§ 2.2-4000 et seq.). The commencement of a proceeding for judicial review under this section shall not, unless specifically ordered by the court, operate as a stay of the order or decision of the State Forester. (1993, c. 948.)

CASE NOTES

Applied in Campbell v. Dep't of Forestry, 46
Va. App. 91, 616 S.E.2d 33, 2005 Va. App.
LEXIS 283 (2005).

§ **10.1-1181.6. Enforcement by injunction.** — Any owner or operator violating or failing, neglecting or refusing to obey any special order issued by the State Forester may be compelled in a proceeding instituted in any appropriate circuit court by the State Forester to obey same and to comply therewith by injunction, mandamus or other appropriate remedy, without the necessity of showing that an adequate remedy at law does not exist. (1993, c. 948.)

§ **10.1-1181.7. Virginia Forest Water Quality Fund established; administration and disbursements.** — A. There is hereby established a special, nonreverting fund in the state treasury to be known as the Virginia Forest Water Quality Fund, hereafter referred to as the Fund, to be used for education efforts, promoting the implementation of proper silvicultural activities, research, and monitoring the effectiveness of practices to prevent erosion and sedimentation. The Fund shall be a nonlapsing fund consisting of moneys received and credited to the Fund by the State Treasurer for civil penalties and civil charges assessed pursuant to this article. Interest earned on the Fund shall be credited to the Fund. The Fund shall be established on the books of the State Comptroller. Any money remaining in the Fund at the end of the biennium shall not revert to the general fund but shall remain in the Fund.

B. Disbursement of moneys from the Fund shall be made by the State Comptroller at the written request of the State Forester. Disbursements from the Fund may be made for the purposes set forth in subsection A of this section, including, but not limited to, personnel, administrative, and equipment costs and expenses directly incurred by the Department in connection with such purposes. (1993, c. 948.)

ARTICLE 13.

Foresters.

§ 10.1-1181.8. Definitions. — As used in this article, unless the context requires a different meaning:

"Forester" means any person who is engaged in the science, profession and practice of forestry and who possesses the qualifications required by this article.

"Forestry" means the science, art and practice of creating, managing, using and conserving forests and associated natural resources for human benefit and in a sustainable manner to meet desired goals, needs, and values. (2002, c. 447.)

§ 10.1-1181.9. Requirements for forester title. — In order to use the title of forester in connection with any practice of forestry the person shall hold a baccalaureate or higher degree from a college or university curriculum accredited by the Society of American Foresters and such degree curriculum shall meet the minimum education criterion set forth by the Society in the fields of forest ecology and biology, management of forest resources, and forest resources policy and administration. (2002, c. 447.)

§ 10.1-1181.10. Activities not prohibited. — The provisions of this article shall not prohibit:

1. Any person from performing forestry functions and services so long as he does not represent himself to the public as a forester;

2. An employee or subordinate of a forester from performing forestry functions and services; or

3. The practice of any profession or occupation that is regulated by a regulatory board within the Department of Professional and Occupational Regulation or other state agency. (2002, c. 447.)

§ 10.1-1181.11. Injunctive relief. — The Attorney General or any other person may apply to the circuit court in a jurisdiction where venue is proper for injunctive relief to restrain a person who has violated the provisions of this article. (2002, c. 447.)

§ 10.1-1181.12. Exemption from article. — The provisions of this article shall not apply to any person who supplies the Department of Forestry with information or documentation showing that such person was actively engaged in the practice of forestry for a continuous period of at least ten years prior to July 1, 2002. The Department shall maintain and make available to the public a list of all persons who satisfy the requirements of this section. (2002, c. 447.)

CHAPTER 11.1.

DEPARTMENT OF ENVIRONMENTAL QUALITY.

ARTICLE 1.

General Provisions.

§ 10.1-1182. Definitions. — As used in this chapter, unless the context requires a different meaning:

"Department" means the Department of Environmental Quality.

"Director" means the Director of the Department of Environmental Quality.

"Environment" means the natural, scenic and historic attributes of the Commonwealth.

"Special order" means an administrative order issued to any party that has a stated duration of not more than twelve months and that may include a civil penalty of not more than $10,000. (1992, c. 887; 1996, c. 1005.)

Law Review. — For note on relations between states and Environmental Protection Agency, see 33 Wash. & Lee L. Rev. 590 (1976). For article discussing issues relating to toxic substances litigation, focusing on the Fourth Circuit, see 16 U. Rich. L. Rev. 247 (1982). For article as to common-law principles underlying public interests in tidal water resources, see 23 Wm. & Mary L. Rev. 835 (1982). For survey of Virginia environmental law for the year 1989-1990, see 24 U. Rich. L. Rev. 583 (1990). For article, "State Environmental Programs: A Study in Political Influence and Regulatory Failure," see 31 Wm. & Mary L. Rev. 823 (1990). For article addressing significant developments in Virginia law pertaining to air quality, water quality and solid and hazardous waste, between 1990 and 1992, see "Environmental

Law," 26 U. Rich. L. Rev. 729 (1992).

Research References. — Berz and Spracker, Environmental Law in Real Estate and Business Transactions (Matthew Bender).

Michael B. Gerard, Environmental Law Practice Guide: State and Federal Law (Matthew Bender).

CASE NOTES

Applied in 7-Eleven, Inc. v. Dep't of Envtl. Quality, 42 Va. App. 65, 590 S.E.2d 84, 2003 Va. App. LEXIS 703 (2003).

§ 10.1-1183. Creation of Department of Environmental Quality; statement of policy.

— There is hereby created a Department of Environmental Quality by the consolidation of the programs, functions, staff, facilities, assets and obligations of the following agencies: the State Water Control Board, the Department of Air Pollution Control, the Department of Waste Management, and the Council on the Environment. Wherever in this title and in the Code of Virginia reference is made to the Department of Air Pollution Control, the Department of Waste Management or the Council on the Environment, or any division thereof, it shall mean the Department of Environmental Quality.

It shall be the policy of the Department of Environmental Quality to protect the environment of Virginia in order to promote the health and well-being of the Commonwealth's citizens. The purposes of the Department are:

1. To assist in the effective implementation of the Constitution of Virginia by carrying out state policies aimed at conserving the Commonwealth's natural resources and protecting its atmosphere, land and waters from pollution.

2. To coordinate permit review and issuance procedures to protect all aspects of Virginia's environment.

3. To enhance public participation in the regulatory and permitting processes.

4. To establish and effectively implement a pollution prevention program to reduce the impact of pollutants on Virginia's natural resources.

5. To establish procedures for, and undertake, long-range environmental program planning and policy analysis.

6. To conduct comprehensive evaluations of the Commonwealth's environmental protection programs.

7. To provide increased opportunities for public education programs on environmental issues.

8. To develop uniform administrative systems to ensure coherent environmental policies.

9. To coordinate state reviews with federal agencies on environmental issues, such as environmental impact statements.

10. To promote environmental quality through public hearings and expeditious and comprehensive permitting, inspection, monitoring and enforcement programs, and provide effective service delivery to the regulated community.

11. To advise the Governor and General Assembly, and, on request, assist other officers, employees, and public bodies of the Commonwealth, on matters relating to environmental quality and the effectiveness of actions and programs designed to enhance that quality.

12. To ensure that there is consistency in the enforcement of the laws, regulations and policies as they apply to holders of permits or certificates issued by the Department, whether the owners or operators of such regulated facilities are public sector or private sector entities. (1992, c. 887; 1999, c. 207.)

Law Review. — For comment on nonpoint pollution control in Virginia, see 13 U. Rich. L. Rev. 539 (1979). For article as to common-law principles underlying public interests in tidal water resources, see 23 Wm. & Mary L. Rev. 835 (1982).

The Waste Management Act does not require a local governing body to determine whether a use is in compliance with the act's provisions. Concerned Taxpayers v. County of Brunswick, 249 Va. 320, 455 S.E.2d 712 (1995).

§ 10.1-1184. State Air Pollution Control Board, State Water Control Board, and Virginia Waste Management Board continued. — The State Air Pollution Control Board, State Water Control Board, and Virginia Waste Management Board are continued and shall promote the environmental quality of the Commonwealth. All policies and regulations adopted or promulgated by the State Air Pollution Control Board, State Water Control Board, Virginia Waste Management Board, and the Council on the Environment and in effect on December 31, 1992, shall continue to be in effect until and unless superseded by new policies or regulations. Representatives of the three Boards shall meet jointly at least twice a year to receive public comment and deliberate about environmental issues of concern to the Commonwealth. (1992, c. 887.)

§ 10.1-1185. Appointment of Director; powers and duties of Director. — The Department shall be headed by a Director appointed by the Governor to serve at his pleasure for a term coincident with his own. The Director of the Department of Environmental Quality shall, under the direction and control of the Governor, exercise such power and perform such duties as are conferred or imposed upon him by law and shall perform such other duties as may be required of him by the Governor and the following Boards: the State Air Pollution Control Board, the State Water Control Board, and the Virginia Waste Management Board. The Director or his designee shall serve as executive officer of the aforementioned Boards.

All powers and duties conferred or imposed upon the Executive Director of the Department of Air Pollution Control, the Executive Director of the State Water Control Board, the Administrator of the Council on the Environment, and the Director of the Department of Waste Management are continued and conferred or imposed upon the Director of the Department of Environmental Quality or his designee. Wherever in this title and in the Code of Virginia reference is made to the head of a division, department or agency hereinafter transferred to this Department, it shall mean the Director of the Department of Environmental Quality. (1992, c. 887.)

The Waste Management Act does not require a local governing body to determine whether a use is in compliance with the act's provisions. Concerned Taxpayers v. County of Brunswick, 249 Va. 320, 455 S.E.2d 712 (1995).

§ 10.1-1186. General powers of the Department. — The Department shall have the following general powers, any of which the Director may delegate as appropriate:

1. Employ such personnel as may be required to carry out the duties of the Department;

2. Make and enter into all contracts and agreements necessary or incidental to the performance of its duties and the execution of its powers under this chapter, including, but not limited to, contracts with the United States, other states, other state agencies and governmental subdivisions of the Commonwealth;

3. Accept grants from the United States government and agencies and instrumentalities thereof and any other source. To these ends, the Department shall have the power to comply with such conditions and execute such agreements as may be necessary, convenient, or desirable;

4. Accept and administer services, property, gifts and other funds donated to the Department;

5. Implement all regulations as may be adopted by the State Air Pollution Control Board, the State Water Control Board, and the Virginia Waste Management Board;

6. Administer, under the direction of the Boards, funds appropriated to it for environmental programs and make contracts related thereto;

7. Initiate and supervise programs designed to educate citizens on ecology, pollution and its control, technology and its relationship to environmental problems and their solutions, population and its relation to environmental problems, and other matters concerning environmental quality;

8. Advise and coordinate the responses of state agencies to notices of proceedings by the State Water Control Board to consider certifications of hydropower projects under 33 U.S.C. § 1341;

9. Advise interested agencies of the Commonwealth of pending proceedings when the Department of Environmental Quality intervenes directly on behalf of the Commonwealth in a Federal Energy Regulatory Commission proceeding or when the Department of Game and Inland Fisheries intervenes in a Federal Energy Regulatory Commission proceeding to coordinate the provision of information and testimony for use in the proceedings;

10. Notwithstanding any other provision of law and to the extent consistent with federal requirements, following a proceeding as provided in § 2.2-4019, issue special orders to any person to comply with: (i) the provisions of any law administered by the Boards, the Director or the Department, (ii) any condition of a permit or a certification, (iii) any regulations of the Boards, or (iv) any case decision, as defined in § 2.2-4001, of the Boards or Director. The issuance of a special order shall be considered a case decision as defined in § 2.2-4001. The Director shall not delegate his authority to impose civil penalties in conjunction with issuance of special orders. For purposes of this subdivision, *"Boards"* means the State Air Pollution Control Board, the State Water Control Board, and the Virginia Waste Management Board; and

11. Perform all acts necessary or convenient to carry out the purposes of this chapter. (1992, c. 887; 1996, c. 1005.)

§ **10.1-1186.1. Department to publish toxics inventory.** — The Department of Environmental Quality shall publish in March of each year the information reported by industries pursuant to 42 U.S.C. § 11023 in its document known as the "Virginia Toxic Release Inventory." The report shall be (i) organized by chemical, facility and facility location, and standard industrial classification code, and (ii) distributed to newspapers of general circulation and television and radio stations. The report shall include the information collected for the most recent calendar year for which data is available prior to the March publication date. (1997, c. 155.)

§ **10.1-1186.2. Supplemental environmental projects.** — A. As used in this section, *"supplemental environmental project"* means an environmentally beneficial project undertaken as partial settlement of a civil enforcement action and not otherwise required by law.

B. The State Air Pollution Control Board, the State Water Control Board, the Virginia Waste Management Board, or the Director acting on behalf of one of these boards or under his own authority in issuing any administrative order, or any court of competent jurisdiction as provided for under this Code, may, in its or his discretion and with the consent of the person subject to the order, provide for such person to undertake one or more supplemental environmental projects. The project shall have a reasonable geographic nexus to the violation or, if no such project is available, shall advance at least one of the declared objectives of the environmental law or regulation that is the basis of the enforcement action. Performance of such projects shall be enforceable in the same manner as any other provision of the order.

C. The following categories of projects may qualify as supplemental environmental projects, provided the project otherwise meets the requirements of this section: public health, pollution prevention, pollution reduction, environmental restoration and protection, environmental compliance promotion, and emergency planning and preparedness. In determining the appropriateness and value of a supplemental environmental project, the following factors shall be considered by the enforcement authority: net project costs, benefits to the public or the environment, innovation, impact on minority or low income populations, multimedia impact, and pollution prevention. The costs of those portions of a supplemental environmental project that are funded by state or federal low-interest loans, contracts or grants shall be deducted from the net project cost in evaluating the project. In each case in which a supplemental environmental project is included as part of a settlement, an explanation of the project with any appropriate supporting documentation shall be included as part of the case file.

D. Nothing in this section shall require the disclosure of documents exempt from disclosure pursuant to the Virginia Freedom of Information Act (§ 2.2-3700 et seq.).

E. Any decision whether or not to agree to a supplemental environmental project is within the sole discretion of the applicable board, official or court and shall not be subject to appeal.

F. Nothing in this section shall be interpreted or applied in a manner inconsistent with applicable federal law or any applicable requirement for the Commonwealth to obtain or maintain federal delegation or approval of any regulatory program. (1997, cc. 623, 628.)

The number of this section was assigned by the Code Commission, the number in the 1997 act having been 10.1-1186.1.

Law Review. — For an article reviewing key environmental developments at the federal and state levels during the period from June 1996 to June 1998, see 32 U. Rich. L. Rev. 1217 (1998).

§ 10.1-1186.2:1. Impact of electric generating facilities. — A. The Department and the State Air Pollution Control Board have the authority to consider the cumulative impact of new and proposed electric generating facilities within the Commonwealth on attainment of the national ambient air quality standards.

B. The Department shall enter into a memorandum of agreement with the State Corporation Commission regarding the coordination of reviews of the environmental impacts of proposed electric generating facilities that must obtain certificates from the State Corporation Commission.

C. Prior to the close of the Commission's record on an application for certification of an electric generating facility pursuant to § 56-580, the Department shall provide to the State Corporation Commission a list of all environmental permits and approvals that are required for the proposed electric generating facility and shall specify any environmental issues, identified during the review process, that are not governed by those permits or approvals or are not within the authority of, and not considered by, the Department or other participating governmental entity in issuing such permits or approvals. The Department may recommend to the Commission that the Commission's record remain open pending completion of any required environmental review, approval or permit proceeding. All agencies of the Commonwealth shall provide assistance to the Department, as requested by the Director, in preparing the information required by this subsection. (2002, c. 483.)

Law Review. — For article surveying changes in environmental law in Virginia from June 2001 to June 2002, see 37 U. Rich. L. Rev. 117 (2002). For article on developments in the field of Virginia public utility law from June 2002 through May 2003, see 38 U. Rich. L. Rev. 195 (2003).

§ 10.1-1186.3. Additional powers of Boards; mediation; alternative dispute resolution. — A. The State Air Pollution Control Board, the State Water Control Board and the Virginia Waste Management Board, in their discretion, may employ mediation as defined in § 8.01-581.21, or a dispute resolution proceeding as defined in § 8.01-576.4, in appropriate cases to resolve underlying issues, reach a consensus or compromise on contested issues. An "appropriate case" means any process related to the development of a regulation or the issuance of a permit in which it is apparent that there are significant issues of disagreement among interested persons and for which the Board finds that the use of a mediation or dispute resolution proceeding is in the public interest. The Boards shall consider not using a mediation or dispute resolution proceeding if:

1. A definitive or authoritative resolution of the matter is required for precedential value, and such a proceeding is not likely to be accepted generally as an authoritative precedent;

2. The matter involves or may bear upon significant questions of state policy that require additional procedures before a final resolution may be made, and such a proceeding would not likely serve to develop a recommended policy for the Board;

3. Maintaining established policies is of special importance, so that variations among individual decisions are not increased and such a proceeding would not likely reach consistent results among individual decisions;

4. The matter significantly affects persons or organizations who are not parties to the proceeding;

5. A full public record of the proceeding is important, and a mediation or dispute resolution proceeding cannot provide such a record; and

6. The Board must maintain continuing jurisdiction over the matter with the authority to alter the disposition of the matter in light of changed circumstances, and a mediation or dispute resolution proceeding would interfere with the Board's fulfilling that requirement.

Mediation and alternative dispute resolution as authorized by this section are voluntary procedures which supplement rather than limit other dispute resolution techniques available to the Boards. Mediation or a dispute resolution proceeding may be employed in the issuance of a permit only with the consent and participation of the permit applicant and shall be terminated at the request of the permit applicant.

B. The decision to employ mediation or a dispute resolution proceeding is in a Board's sole discretion and is not subject to judicial review.

C. The outcome of any mediation or dispute resolution proceeding shall not be binding upon a Board, but may be considered by a Board in issuing a permit or promulgating a regulation.

D. Each Board shall adopt rules and regulations, in accordance with the Administrative Process Act, for the implementation of this section. Such rules and regulations shall include: (i) standards and procedures for the conduct of mediation and dispute resolution, including an opportunity for interested persons identified by the Board to participate in the proceeding; (ii) the appointment and function of a neutral, as defined in § 8.01-576.4, to encourage and assist parties to voluntarily compromise or settle contested issues; and (iii) procedures to protect the confidentiality of papers, work product or other materials.

E. The provisions of § 8.01-576.10 concerning the confidentiality of a mediation or dispute resolution proceeding shall govern all such proceedings held pursuant to this section except where a Board uses or relies on information obtained in the course of such proceeding in issuing a permit or promulgating a regulation.

Nothing in this section shall create or alter any right, action or cause of action, or be interpreted or applied in a manner inconsistent with the Administrative Process Act (§ 2.2-4000 et seq.), with applicable federal law or with any applicable requirement for the Commonwealth to obtain or maintain federal delegation or approval of any regulatory program. (1997, cc. 645, 667.)

The number of this section was assigned by the Code Commission, the number in the 1997 act having been 10.1-1186.1.

Law Review. — For an article, "Administrative Procedure," see 31 U. Rich. L. Rev. 907 (1997). For an article reviewing key environmental developments at the federal and state levels during the period from June 1996 to June 1998, see 32 U. Rich. L. Rev. 1217 (1998).

§ 10.1-1186.4. Enforcement powers; federal court. — In addition to the authority of the State Air Pollution Control Board, the State Water Control Board, the Virginia Waste Management Board and the Director to bring actions in the courts of the Commonwealth to enforce any law, regulation, case decision or condition of a permit or certification, the Attorney General is hereby authorized on behalf of such boards or the Director to seek to intervene pursuant to Rule 24 of the Federal Rules of Civil Procedure in any action then pending in a federal court in order to resolve a dispute already being litigated in that court by the United States through the Environmental Protection Agency. (2001, cc. 166, 174.)

Law Review. — For article, "Environmental Law," see 35 U. Rich. L. Rev. 601 (2001).

§ 10.1-1186.5. Creation of the Low Impact Development Assessment Task Force. — A. The Director of the Department shall appoint a Low Impact Development Assessment Task Force. The task force shall operate as an entity within the Department. The task force shall have 10 members appointed by the Director and shall include a representative of the Department of Conservation and Recreation, the Chesapeake Bay Foundation, the Virginia Farm Bureau Federation, the Home Builders Association of Virginia, the Low Impact Development Coalition, the Virginia Association of Counties, the Virginia Municipal League, and three citizen members not affiliated with the organizations designated in this subsection.

B. The task force shall (i) develop a certification process for low impact development techniques in achieving quantifiable pollution prevention or abatement results, (ii) develop such other guidance for local governments and the general public as necessary to promote a more complete understanding of the most effective use of low impact development techniques, (iii) recommend changes to existing statutes and regulations to facilitate the use of low impact development techniques, and (iv) develop a model ordinance for use by local governments.

C. The task force shall submit a preliminary report to the Director by October 1, 2003, and a final report to the Director by October 1, 2004. The Director shall report to the General Assembly on the activities and recommendations of the task force by November 1 of each year in which he receives a report.

D. For purposes of this section, *"low impact development"* means a site-specific system of design and development techniques that can serve as an effective, low-cost alternative to existing stormwater and water quality control methods and that will reduce the creation of storm runoff and pollution and potentially reduce the need to treat or mitigate water pollution. (2003, c. 738; 2005, c. 41.)

Editor's note. — Acts 2003, c. 738, cl. 2, provides: "That the provisions of this act shall be effective until submission of the final report."

Acts 2005, c. 41, cl. 4, provides: "That references to the Chesapeake Bay Local Assistance Department in regulation, local ordinance, guidance, or otherwise shall mean the Department of Conservation and Recreation, and similarly, references to the Executive Director of the Chesapeake Bay Local Assistance Department shall mean the Director of the Department of Conservation and Recreation."

Acts 2005, c. 41, cl. 5, provides: "That the Chesapeake Bay Local Assistance Board shall have the authority to amend, modify, or delete provisions in the Chesapeake Bay Preservation Area Designation and Management Regulations (9-VAC 10-20 et seq.) in order to implement Chapter 372 of the Acts of Assembly of 2004 and the provisions of this act. Those amendments to the regulations necessitated by these acts shall be exempt from Article 2 (§ 2.2-4006 et seq.) of the Administrative Process Act."

The 2005 amendment. — The 2005 amendment by c. 41, in subsection A, substituted "10 members" for "11 members" and deleted "Chesapeake Bay Local Assistance Department" preceding "the Chesapeake Bay Foundation" in the second sentence.

Law Review. — For survey article on judicial decisions in real estate law from June 1, 2002 through June 1, 2003, see 38 U. Rich. L. Rev. 223 (2003).

§ 10.1-1187. Provision of the Code continued. — The conditions, requirements, provisions, contents, powers and duties of any section, article, or chapter of the Code in effect on March 31, 1993, relating to agencies consolidated in this chapter shall apply to the Department of Environmental Quality until superseded by new legislation. (1992, c. 887.)

ARTICLE 1.1.

Virginia Environmental Excellence Program.

§ 10.1-1187.1. Definitions. — *"Board or Boards"* means the State Air Pollution Control Board, the State Water Control Board, and the Virginia Waste Management Board.

"Department" means the Department of Environmental Quality.

"Director" means the Director of the Department of Environmental Quality.

"Environmental Management System" means a comprehensive, cohesive set of documented policies and procedures adopted by a facility or person and used to establish environmental goals, to meet and maintain those goals, to evaluate environmental performance and to achieve measurable or noticeable improvements in environmental performance, through planning, documented management and operational practices, operational changes, self assessments, and management review. The term shall include, but not be limited to, any such system developed in accordance with the International Standards of Operation 14001 standards.

"E2" means an environmental enterprise.

"E3" means an exemplary environmental enterprise.

"E4" means an extraordinary environmental enterprise.

"Facility" means a manufacturing, business, agricultural, or governmental site or installation involving one or more contiguous buildings or structures under common ownership or management.

"Record of sustained compliance" means that the person or facility (i) has no judgment or conviction entered against it, or against any key personnel of the person or facility or any person with an ownership interest in the facility for a criminal violation of environmental protection laws of the United States, the Commonwealth, or any other state in the previous five years; (ii) has been neither the cause of, nor liable for, more than two significant environmental violations in the previous three years; (iii) has no unresolved notices of violations or potential violations of environmental requirements with the Department or one of the Boards; (iv) is in compliance with the terms of any order or decree, executive compliance agreement, or related enforcement measure issued by the Department, one of the Boards, or the U.S. Environmental Protection Agency; and (v) has not demonstrated in any other way an unwillingness or inability to comply with environmental protection requirements. (2005, c. 705.)

§ 10.1-1187.2. Virginia Environmental Excellence Program established. — The Department may establish programs to recognize facilities and persons that have demonstrated a commitment to enhanced environmental performance and to encourage innovations in environmental protection. (2005, c. 705.)

§ 10.1-1187.3. Program categories and criteria. — A. The Director shall establish different categories of participation and the criteria and benefits for each category. Such categories shall include, but not be limited to: (i) E2 facilities, (ii) E3 facilities, and (iii) E4 facilities.

B. In order to participate as an E2 facility, a person or facility shall demonstrate that it (i) is developing an environmental management system or has initiated implementation of an environmental management system, (ii) has a commitment to pollution prevention and a plan to reduce environmental impacts from its operations, and (iii) has a record of sustained compliance with environmental requirements. To apply to become an E2 facility, an applicant shall submit the following information to the Department: (a) a policy statement outlining the applicant's commitment to improving environmental quality, (b) an evaluation of the applicant's environmental impacts, (c) the applicant's objectives and targets for addressing significant environmental impacts, and (d) a description of the applicant's pollution prevention program. A person or facility may participate in this program for up to three years, and may apply to renew its participation at the expiration of each three-year period. Incentives for E2 facilities may include, but are not limited to, the following: public recognition of facility performance and reduced fees.

C. In order to participate as an E3 facility, a person or facility shall demonstrate that it has (i) a fully-implemented environmental management system, (ii) a pollution prevention program with documented results, and (iii) a record of sustained compliance with environmental requirements. To apply to become an E3 facility, an applicant shall submit the following information to the Department: (a) a policy statement outlining the applicant's commitment to improving environmental quality; (b) an evaluation of the applicant's actual and potential environmental impacts; (c) the applicant's objectives and targets for addressing significant environmental impacts; (d) a description of the applicant's pollution prevention program; (e) identification of the applicant's environmental legal requirements; (f) a description of the applicant's environmental management system that identifies roles, responsibilities and authorities, reporting and record-keeping, emergency response procedures, staff training, monitoring, and corrective action processes for noncompliance with the environmental management system; (g) voluntary self-assessments; and (h) procedures for internal and external communications. A person or facility

311

may participate in this program for up to three years, and may apply to renew its participation at the expiration of each three-year period. Incentives for E3 facilities may include, but are not limited to, the following: public recognition of facility performance, reduced fees, reduced inspection priority, a single point-of-contact between the facility and the Department, streamlined environmental reporting, reduced monitoring requirements, prioritized permit and permit amendment review, and the ability to implement alternative compliance measures approved by the appropriate Board in accordance with § 10.1-1187.6.

D. In order to participate as an E4 facility, a person or facility shall meet the criteria for participation as an E3 facility, and shall have (i) implemented and completed at least one full cycle of an environmental management system as verified by an unrelated third-party qualified to audit environmental management systems and (ii) committed to measures for continuous and sustainable environmental progress and community involvement. To apply to become an E4 facility, an applicant shall submit (a) the information required to apply to become an E3 facility, (b) documentation evidencing implementation and completion of at least one full cycle of an environmental management system and evidencing review and verification by an unrelated third party, and (c) documentation that the applicant has committed to measures for continuous and sustainable environmental progress and community involvement. A person or facility may participate in this program for up to three years, and may apply to renew its participation at the expiration of each three-year period. Incentives for E4 facilities may include all of the incentives available to E3 facilities. Any facility or person that has been accepted into the National Performance Track Programs by the U.S. Environmental Protection Agency shall be deemed to be an E4 facility. If acceptance in the Program is revoked or suspended by the U.S. Environmental Protection Agency, participation as an E4 facility shall also be terminated or suspended. (2005, c. 705.)

§ **10.1-1187.4. Procedures for participation.** — A. The Director shall develop guidelines and procedures for implementation of the program, including procedures for submitting applications, guidelines for annual reports from participating persons or facilities, and procedures for reviewing program implementation.

B. Upon review of an application, the Director may approve or deny the person's or facility's participation in the appropriate category within the Virginia Environmental Excellence Program. The denial of a person's or facility's participation in the Virginia Environmental Excellence Program shall not be with prejudice or otherwise prevent reapplication by the person or facility. If a participant fails to maintain a record of sustained compliance, fails to resolve an alleged environmental violation within 180 days, or fails to meet the requirements or criteria for participation in the Virginia Environmental Excellence Program or any category within the program, the Director may revoke or suspend their participation in the program or revoke participation in a higher level and approve its participation in a lower level of the program. The Director shall provide reasonable notice of the reasons for the suspension or revocation and allow the participant to respond prior to making such a decision.

C. The Director's decision to approve, deny, revoke, or suspend a person's or facility's participation in any category of the Virginia Environmental Excellence Program is discretionary, shall not be a case decision as defined in § 2.2-4001, and shall be exempt from judicial review. (2005, c. 705.)

§ **10.1-1187.5. Reporting.** — A. Participants shall submit annual reports in a format and schedule prescribed by the Director, including information on environmental performance relevant to the program.

B. The Department shall submit a report to the Governor and to the members of the House Committee on Agriculture, Chesapeake and Natural Resources and the members of the Senate Committee on Agriculture, Conservation and Natural Resources by December 1 of every even-numbered year, with the last report due on December 1, 2010. The report shall include the information from the participants' reports as well as information on the incentives that have been provided and the innovations that have been developed by the agency and participants. (2005, c. 705.)

§ **10.1-1187.6. Approval of alternate compliance methods.** — A. To the extent consistent with federal law and notwithstanding any other provision of law, the Air Pollution Control Board, the Waste Management Board, and the State Water Control Board may grant alternative compliance methods to the regulations adopted pursuant to their authorities, respectively, under §§ 10.1-1308, 10.1-1402, and 62.1-44.15 for persons or facilities that have been accepted by the Department as meeting the criteria for E3 and E4 facilities under § 10.1-1187.3, including but not limited to changes to monitoring and reporting requirements and schedules, streamlined submission requirements for permit renewals, the ability to make certain operational changes without prior approval, and other changes that would not increase a facility's impact on the environment. Such alternative compliance methods may allow alternative methods for achieving compliance with prescribed regulatory standards, provided that the person or facility requesting the alternative compliance method demonstrates that the method will (i) meet the purpose of the applicable regulatory standard, (ii) promote achievement of those purposes through increased reliability, efficiency, or cost effectiveness, and (iii) afford environmental protection equal to or greater than that provided by the applicable regulatory standard. No alternative compliance method shall be approved that would alter an ambient air quality standard, ground water protection standard, or water quality standard and no alternative compliance method shall be approved that would increase the pollutants released to the environment, increase impacts to state waters, or otherwise result in a loss of wetland acreage.

B. Notwithstanding any other provision of law, an alternate compliance method may be approved under this section after at least 30 days' public notice and opportunity for comment, and a determination that the alternative compliance method meets the requirements of this section.

C. Nothing in this section shall be interpreted or applied in a manner inconsistent with the applicable federal law or other requirement necessary for the Commonwealth to obtain or retain federal delegation or approval of any regulatory program. Before approving an alternate compliance method affecting any such program, each Board may obtain the approval of the federal agency responsible for such delegation or approval. Any one of the Boards may withdraw approval of the alternate compliance method at any time if any conditions under which the alternate compliance method was originally approved change, or if the recipient has failed to comply with any of the alternative compliance method requirements.

D. Upon approval of the alternative compliance method under this section, the alternative compliance method shall be incorporated into the relevant permits as a minor permit modification with no associated fee. The permits shall also contain any such provisions that shall go into effect in the event that the participant fails to fulfill its obligations under the variance, or is removed from the program for reasons specified by the Director under subsection B of § 10.1-1187.4. (2005, c. 705.)

§ **10.1-1187.7. Governor's Environmental Excellence Awards.** — The Governor's Environmental Excellence Awards shall be awarded each year to recognize participants in the Virginia Environmental Excellence Program that have demonstrated extraordinary leadership, innovation, and commitment to implementation of pollution prevention practices and other efforts to reduce environmental impacts and improve Virginia's natural environment. (2005, c. 705.)

ARTICLE 2.

Environmental Impact Reports of State Agencies.

§ 10.1-1188. State agencies to submit environmental impact reports on major projects. — A. All state agencies, boards, authorities and commissions or any branch of the state government shall prepare and submit an environmental impact report to the Department on each major state project.

"Major state project" means the acquisition of an interest in land for any state facility construction, or the construction of any facility or expansion of an existing facility which is hereafter undertaken by any state agency, board, commission, authority or any branch of state government, including state-supported institutions of higher learning, which costs $100,000 or more. For the purposes of this chapter, authority shall not include any industrial development authority created pursuant to the provisions of Chapter 49 (§ 15.2-4900 et seq.) of Title 15.2 or Chapter 643, as amended, of the 1964 Acts of Assembly. Nor shall authority include any housing development or redevelopment authority established pursuant to state law. For the purposes of this chapter, branch of state government shall not include any county, city or town of the Commonwealth.

Such environmental impact report shall include, but not be limited to, the following:

1. The environmental impact of the major state project, including the impact on wildlife habitat;

2. Any adverse environmental effects which cannot be avoided if the major state project is undertaken;

3. Measures proposed to minimize the impact of the major state project;

4. Any alternatives to the proposed construction; and

5. Any irreversible environmental changes which would be involved in the major state project.

For the purposes of subdivision 4 of this subsection, the report shall contain all alternatives considered and the reasons why the alternatives were rejected. If a report does not set forth alternatives, it shall state why alternatives were not considered.

B. For purposes of this chapter, this subsection shall not apply to the review of highway and road construction projects or any part thereof. The Secretaries of Transportation and Natural Resources shall jointly establish procedures for review and comment by state natural and historic resource agencies of highway and road construction projects. Such procedures shall provide for review and comment on appropriate projects and categories of projects to address the environmental impact of the project, any adverse environmental effects which cannot be avoided if the project is undertaken, the measures proposed to minimize the impact of the project, any alternatives to the proposed construction, and any irreversible environmental changes which would be involved in the project. (1973, c. 384, § 10-17.108; 1974, c. 270, § 10.1-1208; 1977, c. 667; 1988, c. 891; 1991, c. 289; 1992, c. 887; 1997, c. 268.)

Cross references. — For requirement that state agencies in preparing their reports and the Council on the Environment in conducting its review consider the impact of projects on prime agricultural land, see § 3.1-18.8.

Law Review. — For an article reviewing key environmental developments at the federal and state levels during the period from June 1996 to

June 1998, see 32 U. Rich. L. Rev. 1217 (1998).　　discussion, see 9A M.J. Health and Sanitation,
Michie's Jurisprudence. — For related　§ 5.

CASE NOTES

Pursuant to former sections 10.1-1208, 10.1-1209 and 10.1-1210, the General Assembly intended to preclude judicial review of the environmental impact report prepared, and conclusions reached. Murray v. Green, 240 Va. 204, 396 S.E.2d 653 (1990).

§ 10.1-1189. Department to review report and make statement to Governor.

— Within sixty days of the receipt of the environmental impact report by the Department, the Department shall review and make a statement to the Governor commenting on the environmental impact of each major state facility. The statement of the Department shall be available to the General Assembly and to the general public at the time of submission by the Department to the Governor. (1973, c. 384, § 10-17.109; 1974, c. 270, § 10.1-1209; 1977, c. 667; 1988, c. 891; 1992, c. 887.)

Cross references. — For requirement that state agencies in preparing their reports and the Council on the Environment in conducting its review consider the impact of projects on prime agricultural land, see § 3.1-18.8.

CASE NOTES

The General Assembly intended to preclude judicial review of the environmental impact report prepared, and conclusions reached, pursuant to this section and former §§ 10.1-1208 and 10.1-1210. Murray v. Green, 240 Va. 204, 396 S.E.2d 653 (1990) (decided under former § 10.1-1209).

§ 10.1-1190. Approval of Governor required for construction of facility.

— The State Comptroller shall not authorize payments of funds from the state treasury for a major state project unless the request is accompanied by the written approval of the Governor after his consideration of the comments of the Department on the environmental impact of the facility. This section shall not apply to funds appropriated by the General Assembly prior to June 1, 1973, or any reappropriation of such funds. (1973, c. 384, § 10-17.110; 1974, c. 270, § 10.1-1210; 1977, c. 667; 1988, c. 891; 1991, c. 289; 1992, c. 887.)

§ 10.1-1191. Development of procedures, etc., for administration of chapter.

— The Department shall, in conjunction with other state agencies, coordinate the development of objectives, criteria and procedures to ensure the orderly preparation and evaluation of environmental impact reports required by this article. These procedures shall provide for submission of impact statements in sufficient time to permit any modification of the major state project which may be necessitated because of environmental impact. (1973, c. 384, § 10-17.111; 1974, c. 270, § 10.1-1211; 1977, c. 667; 1988, c. 891; 1992, c. 887.)

§ 10.1-1192. Cooperation of state agencies.

— All departments, commissions, boards, authorities, agencies, offices and institutions within any branch of the state government shall cooperate with the Department in carrying out the purposes of this article. (1973, c. 384, § 10-17.112; 1974, c. 270, § 10.1-1212; 1977, c. 667; 1988, c. 891; 1992, c. 887.)

ARTICLE 3.

Watershed Planning and Permitting Promotion and Coordination.

§ 10.1-1193. Watershed planning; watershed permitting; promotion and coordination. — A. The Department, with the assistance of the Watershed Planning and Permitting Coordination Task Force, shall undertake such efforts it deems necessary and appropriate to coordinate the watershed-level activities conducted by state and local agencies and authorities and to foster the development of watershed planning by localities. To aid in the coordination and promotion of these activities, the Department shall to the extent practicable in its discretion:

1. Promote and coordinate state and local agencies' and authorities' efforts to undertake watershed planning and watershed permitting;

2. Acquire, maintain and make available informational resources on watershed planning;

3. Promote the continuation of research and dialogue on what is entailed in watershed planning and watershed permitting;

4. Identify sources and methods for providing local officials with technical assistance in watershed planning;

5. Encourage and foster training of local officials in watershed planning;

6. Develop recommendations for needed regulatory and legislative changes to assist local governments in developing and implementing watershed planning;

7. Identify barriers to watershed planning and watershed permitting, including state policies, regulations and procedures, and recommend alternatives to overcome such obstacles; and

8. Develop, foster and coordinate approaches to watershed permitting.

B. The Department shall report annually its watershed planning and permitting activities, findings and recommendations and those of the Task Force to the Governor and the General Assembly.

C. Nothing in this article shall be construed as requiring additional permitting or planning requirements on agricultural or forestal activities. (1995, c. 793.)

§ 10.1-1194. Watershed Planning and Permitting Coordination Task Force created; membership; duties. — A. There is hereby created the Watershed Planning and Permitting Coordination Task Force, which shall be referred to in this article as the Task Force. The Task Force shall be composed of the Directors, or their designees, of the Department of Environmental Quality, the Department of Conservation and Recreation, the Department of Forestry, the Department of Mines, Minerals and Energy, and the Commissioner, or his designee, of the Department of Agriculture and Consumer Services.

B. The Task Force shall meet at least quarterly on such dates and times as the members determine. A majority of the Task Force shall constitute a quorum.

C. The Task Force shall undertake such measures and activities it deems necessary and appropriate to see that the functions of the agencies represented therein, and to the extent practicable of other agencies of the Commonwealth, and the efforts of state and local agencies and authorities in watershed planning and watershed permitting are coordinated and promoted. (1995, c. 793; 2005, c. 41.)

Editor's note. — Acts 2005, c. 41, cl. 4, provides: "That references to the Chesapeake Bay Local Assistance Department in regulation, local ordinance, guidance, or otherwise shall mean the Department of Conservation and Recreation, and similarly, references to the Executive Director of the Chesapeake Bay Local Assistance Department shall mean the Director of the Department of Conservation and Recreation."

Acts 2005, c. 41, cl. 5, provides: "That the Chesapeake Bay Local Assistance Board shall have the authority to amend, modify, or delete provisions in the Chesapeake Bay Preservation Area Designation and Management Regula-tions (9-VAC 10-20 et seq.) in order to implement Chapter 372 of the Acts of Assembly of 2004 and the provisions of this act. Those amendments to the regulations necessitated by these acts shall be exempt from Article 2 (§ 2.2-4006 et seq.) of the Administrative Process Act."

The 2005 amendments. — The 2005 amendment by c. 41 deleted "the Chesapeake Bay Local Assistance Department" following "Minerals and Energy" in the last sentence of subsection A.

§ 10.1-1195. Watershed planning and permitting advisory panels. —
The Task Force may name qualified persons to advisory panels to assist it in carrying out its responsibilities. Panels shall include members representing different areas of interest and expertise in watershed planning and watershed permitting including representatives of local governments, planning district commissions, industry, development interests, education, environmental and public interest groups and the scientific community found in Virginia universities. (1995, c. 793.)

§ 10.1-1196. Guiding definition and principles. — A. The Department,
the Task Force and any advisory panels appointed by the Task Force shall be guided by the following definition of watershed planning: "Watershed planning" is the process of studying the environmental and land use features of a watershed to identify those areas that should be protected and preserved, measures to be utilized to protect such areas, and the character of development in order to avoid and minimize disruption of natural systems. Its focus is not on directing development to particular parcels of land but rather to identify critical resources, and measures to protect those resources, so that development, when it does occur, will not negatively impact water resources. In so doing watershed planning uses and protects ecological processes to lessen the need for structural control methods that require capital costs and maintenance. By including consideration of a watershed and its characteristics, cumulative impacts and interjurisdictional issues are more effectively managed than when solely relying on single-site-permit approaches. Watershed planning can be an important tool for maintaining environmental integrity, economic development and watershed permitting.

B. The Department, the Task Force and any advisory panels appointed by the Task Force shall be guided by the principles contained in the following statement: Stream systems tend to reflect the character of the watershed they drain. Unchecked physical conversion in a watershed accompanying urbanization leads to degraded streams and wetlands. As urbanization continues to spread across the state, natural vegetation, slope and water retention characteristics are replaced by impervious surfaces disrupting the dynamic balance of the natural hydrologic cycle. Poorly planned development can increase peak storm flows and runoff volume, lower water quality and aesthetics, and cause flooding and degradation of downstream communities and ecosystems. (1995, c. 793.)

§ 10.1-1197. Cooperation of state agencies. — All agencies of the Commonwealth shall cooperate with the Department and the Task Force and, upon request, assist the Department and the Task Force in the performance of their efforts in coordinating and promoting watershed planning and watershed permitting. (1995, c. 793.)

ARTICLE 4.

Small Business Environmental Compliance Assistance Fund.

§ 10.1-1197.1. Definitions. — As used in this article, unless the context requires a different meaning:

"Fund" means the Small Business Environmental Compliance Assistance Fund.

"Small business" means a business located in Virginia that (i) employs 100 or fewer people and (ii) is a small business concern as defined in the federal Small Business Act (15 U.S.C. § 631 et seq.) as amended.

"Voluntary pollution prevention measures" means operational or equipment changes that meet the definition of pollution prevention contained in § 10.1-1425.10 and are not otherwise required by law. (1997, cc. 624, 850.)

Cross references. — As to loans from the Fund being exempt from the Administrative Process Act, see § 2.2-4002.

Law Review. — For an article reviewing key environmental developments at the federal and state levels during the period from June 1996 to June 1998, see 32 U. Rich. L. Rev. 1217 (1998).

Research References. — Berz and Spracker, Environmental Law in Real Estate and Business Transactions (Matthew Bender).

§ 10.1-1197.2. Small Business Environmental Compliance Assistance Fund established; administration; collection of money. — A. There is hereby created in the state treasury a special nonreverting fund to be known as the Small Business Environmental Compliance Assistance Fund, hereafter referred to as the "Fund." The Fund shall be comprised of (i) moneys appropriated to the Fund by the General Assembly, (ii) receipts by the Fund from loans made by it, (iii) all income from the investment of moneys held by the Fund, (iv) any moneys transferred from the Virginia Environmental Emergency Response Fund as authorized by § 10.1-2502, and (v) any other moneys designated for deposit to the Fund from any source, public or private. Interest earned on moneys in the Fund shall remain in the Fund and be credited to it. Any moneys remaining in the Fund, including interest thereon, at the end of each fiscal year shall not revert to the general fund but shall remain in the Fund. Moneys in the Fund shall be used solely for the purposes provided in this article. Any moneys appropriated or otherwise credited to the Fund that were received by the Department pursuant to Title V (42 U.S.C. § 7661 et seq.) of the federal Clean Air Act shall be used solely for purposes associated with Title V of the federal Clean Air Act. Expenditures and disbursements from the Fund shall be made by the State Treasurer on warrants issued by the Comptroller upon written request signed by the Director of the Department. The Fund shall be administered and managed by the Department, or any entity operating under a contract or agreement with the Department.

B. The Department, or its designated agent, is empowered to collect moneys due to the Fund. Proceedings to recover moneys due to the Fund may be instituted in the name of the Fund in any appropriate circuit court. (1997, cc. 624, 850.)

§ 10.1-1197.3. Purposes of Fund; loans to small businesses; administrative costs. — A. Moneys in the Fund shall be used to make loans or to guarantee loans to small businesses for the purchase and installation of environmental pollution control and prevention equipment certified by the Department as meeting the following requirements:

1. The air pollution control equipment is needed by the small business to comply with the federal Clean Air Act (42 U.S.C. § 7401 et seq.); or

2. The pollution control equipment will allow the small business to implement voluntary pollution prevention measures.

Moneys in the Fund may also be used to make loans or to guarantee loans to small businesses for the installation of voluntary agricultural best management practices, as defined in § 58.1-339.3.

B. The Department or its designated agent shall determine the terms and conditions of any loan. All loans shall be evidenced by appropriate security as determined by the Department or its designated agent. The Department, or its agent, may require any documents, instruments, certificates, or other information deemed necessary or convenient in connection with any loan from the Fund.

C. A portion of the Fund balance may be used to cover the reasonable and necessary costs of administering the Fund. Unless otherwise authorized by the Governor or his designee, the costs of administering the Fund shall not exceed a base year amount of $65,000 per year, using fiscal year 2000 as the base year, adjusted annually by the Consumer Price Index.

D. The Fund shall not be used to make loans to small businesses for the purchase and installation of equipment needed to comply with an enforcement action by the Department, the State Air Pollution Control Board, the State Water Control Board, or the Virginia Waste Management Board. (1997, cc. 624, 850; 1999, c. 893; 2000, c. 131.)

§ 10.1-1197.4. Annual audit. — The Auditor of Public Accounts shall annually audit the accounts of the Fund when the records of the Department are audited. (1997, cc. 624, 850.)

CHAPTER 11.2.

VOLUNTARY ENVIRONMENTAL ASSESSMENT.

§ 10.1-1198. Voluntary environmental assessment privilege. — A. For purposes of this chapter, unless the context requires a different meaning:

"Environmental assessment" means a voluntary evaluation of activities or facilities or of management systems related to such activities or facilities that is designed to identify noncompliance with environmental laws and regulations, promote compliance with environmental laws and regulations, or identify opportunities for improved efficiency or pollution prevention. An environmental assessment may be conducted by the owner or operator of a facility or an independent contractor at the request of the owner or operator.

"Document" means information collected, generated or developed in the course of, or resulting from, an environmental assessment, including but not limited to field notes, records of observation, findings, opinions, suggestions, conclusions, drafts, memoranda, drawings, photographs, videotape, computer-generated or electronically recorded information, maps, charts, graphs and surveys. "Document" does not mean information generated or developed before the commencement of a voluntary environmental assessment showing non-compliance with environmental laws or regulations or demonstrating a clear, imminent and substantial danger to the public health or environment.

B. No person involved in the preparation of or in possession of a document shall be compelled to disclose such document or information about its contents, or the details of its preparation. Such a document, portion of a document or information is not admissible without the written consent of the owner or operator in an administrative or judicial proceeding and need not be produced as a result of an information request of the Department or other agency of the Commonwealth or political subdivision. This privilege does not extend to a document, portion of a document or information that demonstrates a clear, imminent and substantial danger to the public health or the environment or to a document or a portion of a document required by law or prepared independently of the voluntary environmental assessment process. This privilege does not apply to a document or portion of a document collected, generated or developed in bad faith, nor does it alter, limit, waive or abrogate any other statutory or common law privilege.

C. A person or entity asserting a voluntary environmental assessment privilege has the burden of proving a prima facie case as to the privilege. A party seeking disclosure of a document, portion of a document, or information has the burden of proving the applicability of an exception in subsection B to the voluntary environmental assessment privilege. Upon a showing, based upon independent knowledge, by any party to: (i) an informal fact-finding proceeding held pursuant to § 2.2-4019 at which a hearing officer is present; (ii) a formal hearing pursuant to § 2.2-4020; or (iii) a judicial proceeding that probable cause exists to believe that an exception listed in subsection B to the voluntary environmental assessment privilege is applicable to all or a portion of a document or information, the hearing officer or court may have access to the relevant portion of such document or information for the purposes of an in camera review only to determine whether such exception is applicable. The court or hearing examiner may have access to the relevant portion of a document under such conditions as may be necessary to protect its confidentiality. A moving party who obtains access to the document or information may not divulge any information from the document or other information except as specifically allowed by the hearing examiner or the court. (1995, c. 564.)

The numbers of §§ 10.1-1198 and 10.1-1199 were assigned by the Code Commission, the section numbers in the 1995 act having been 10.1-1193 and 10.1-1194.

Law Review. — For an article reviewing key environmental developments at the federal and state levels during the period from June 1996 to June 1998, see 32 U. Rich. L. Rev. 1217 (1998).

§ 10.1-1199. Immunity against administrative or civil penalties for voluntarily disclosed violation.

— To the extent consistent with requirements imposed by federal law, any person making a voluntary disclosure of information to a state or local regulatory agency regarding a violation of an environmental statute, regulation, permit or administrative order shall be accorded immunity from administrative or civil penalty under such statute, regulation, permit or administrative order. A disclosure is voluntary if (i) it is not otherwise required by law, regulation, permit or administrative order, (ii) it is made promptly after knowledge of the violation is obtained through a voluntary environmental assessment, and (iii) the person making the disclosure corrects the violation in a diligent manner in accordance with a compliance schedule submitted to the appropriate state or local regulatory agencies demonstrating such diligence. Immunity shall not be accorded if it is found that the person making the voluntary disclosure has acted in bad faith. This section does not bar the institution of a civil action claiming compensation for injury to person or property against an owner or operator. (1995, c. 564.)

CHAPTER 12.

ENVIRONMENTAL QUALITY.

§§ 10.1-1200 through 10.1-1212: Repealed by Acts 1992, c. 887.

§§ 10.1-1213 through 10.1-1221: Repealed by Acts 1992, cc. 464 and 887.

Cross references. — For Department of Environmental Quality, see § 10.1-1182 et seq. For present provisions relating to the Virginia Fish Passage Grant and Revolving Loan Fund, see § 29.1-101.2 et seq.

CHAPTER 12.1.

BROWNFIELD RESTORATION AND LAND RENEWAL ACT.

§ 10.1-1230. Definitions. — As used in this chapter:

"Authority" means the Virginia Resources Authority.

"Bona fide prospective purchaser" means a person who acquires ownership, or proposes to acquire ownership, of real property after the release of hazardous substances occurred.

"Brownfield" means real property; the expansion, redevelopment, or reuse of which may be complicated by the presence or potential presence of a hazardous substance, pollutant, or contaminant.

"Cost" as applied to any project financed under the provisions of this chapter, means the reasonable and necessary costs incurred for carrying out all works and undertakings necessary or incident to the accomplishment of any project. It includes, without limitation, all necessary developmental, planning and feasibility studies, surveys, plans and specifications; architectural, engineering, financial, legal or other special services; site assessments, remediation, containment, and demolition or removal of existing structures; the costs of acquisition of land and any buildings and improvements thereon, including the discharge of any obligation of the seller of such land, buildings or improvements; labor; materials, machinery and equipment; the funding of accounts and reserves that the Authority may require; the reasonable costs of financing incurred by the local government in the course of the development of the project; carrying charges incurred prior to completion of the project, and the cost of other items that the Authority determines to be reasonable and necessary.

"Department" means the Department of Environmental Quality.

"Director" means the Director of the Department of Environmental Quality.

"Fund" means the Virginia Brownfields Restoration and Economic Redevelopment Assistance Fund.

"Innocent land owner" means a person who holds any title, security interest or any other interest in a brownfield site and who acquired ownership of the real property after the release of hazardous substances occurred.

"Local government" means any county, city, town, municipal corporation, authority, district, commission, or political subdivision of the Commonwealth created by the General Assembly or otherwise created pursuant to the laws of the Commonwealth or any combination of the foregoing.

"Partnership" means the Virginia Economic Development Partnership.

"Person" means an individual, corporation, partnership, association, governmental body, municipal corporation, public service authority, or any other legal entity.

"Project" means all or any part of the following activities necessary or desirable for the restoration and redevelopment of a brownfield site: (i) environmental or cultural resource site assessments, (ii) monitoring, remediation, cleanup, or containment of property to remove hazardous substances, hazardous wastes, solid wastes or petroleum, (iii) the lawful and necessary removal of human remains, the appropriate treatment of grave sites, and the appropriate and necessary treatment of significant archaeological resources, or the stabilization or restoration of structures listed on or eligible for the Virginia Historic Landmarks Register, (iv) demolition and removal of existing structures, or other site work necessary to make a site or certain real property usable for economic development, and (v) development of a remediation and reuse plan. (2002, c. 378.)

Cross references. — As to loans for remediation of contaminated properties, see § 62.1-229.2.

Law Review. — For article surveying changes in environmental law in Virginia from June 2001 to June 2002, see 37 U. Rich. L. Rev. 117 (2002).

§ 10.1-1231. Brownfield restoration and land renewal policy and programs. — It shall be the policy of the Commonwealth to encourage remediation and restoration of brownfields by removing barriers and providing incentives and assistance whenever possible. The Department of Environmental Quality and the Economic Development Partnership and other appropriate agencies shall establish policies and programs to implement these policies, including a Voluntary Remediation Program, the Brownfields Restoration and Redevelopment Fund, and other measures as may be appropriate. (2002, c. 378.)

§ 10.1-1232. Voluntary Remediation Program. — A. The Virginia Waste Management Board shall promulgate regulations to allow persons who own, operate, have a security interest in or enter into a contract for the purchase of contaminated property to voluntarily remediate releases of hazardous substances, hazardous wastes, solid wastes, or petroleum. The regulations shall apply where remediation has not clearly been mandated by the United States Environmental Protection Agency, the Department or a court pursuant to the Comprehensive Environmental Response, Compensation and Liability Act (42 U.S.C. § 9601 et seq.), the Resource Conservation and Recovery Act (42 U.S.C. § 6901 et seq.), the Virginia Waste Management Act (§ 10.1-1400 et seq.), the State Water Control Law (§ 62.1-44.2 et seq.), or other applicable statutory or common law or where jurisdiction of those statutes has been waived. The regulations shall provide for the following:

1. The establishment of methodologies to determine site-specific risk-based remediation standards, which shall be no more stringent than applicable or appropriate relevant federal standards for soil, groundwater and sediments, taking into consideration scientific information regarding the following: (i)

protection of public health and the environment, (ii) the future industrial, commercial, residential, or other use of the property to be remediated and of surrounding properties, (iii) reasonably available and effective remediation technology and analytical quantitation technology, (iv) the availability of institutional or engineering controls that are protective of human health or the environment, and (v) natural background levels for hazardous constituents;

2. The establishment of procedures that minimize the delay and expense of the remediation, to be followed by a person volunteering to remediate a release and by the Department in processing submissions and overseeing remediation;

3. The issuance of certifications of satisfactory completion of remediation, based on then-present conditions and available information, where voluntary cleanup achieves applicable cleanup standards or where the Department determines that no further action is required;

4. Procedures to waive or expedite issuance of any permits required to initiate and complete a voluntary cleanup consistent with applicable federal law; and

5. Registration fees to be collected from persons conducting voluntary remediation to defray the actual reasonable costs of the voluntary remediation program expended at the site not to exceed the lesser of $5,000 or one percent of the cost of the remediation.

B. Persons conducting voluntary remediations pursuant to an agreement with the Department entered into prior to the promulgation of those regulations may elect to complete the cleanup in accordance with such an agreement or the regulations.

C. Certification of satisfactory completion of remediation shall constitute immunity to an enforcement action under the Virginia Waste Management Act (§ 10.1-1400 et seq.), the State Water Control Law (§ 62.1-44.2 et seq.), Chapter 13 (§ 10.1-1300 et seq.) of this title, or any other applicable law.

D. At the request of a person who owns, operates, holds a security interest in or contracts for the purchase of property from which the contamination to be voluntarily remediated originates, the Department is authorized to seek temporary access to private and public property not owned by such person conducting the voluntary remediation as may be reasonably necessary for such person to conduct the voluntary remediation. Such request shall include a demonstration that the person requesting access has used reasonable effort to obtain access by agreement with the property owner. Such access, if granted, shall be granted for only the minimum amount of time necessary to complete the remediation and shall be exercised in a manner that minimizes the disruption of ongoing activities and compensates for actual damages. The person requesting access shall reimburse the Commonwealth for reasonable, actual and necessary expenses incurred in seeking or obtaining access. Denial of access to the Department by a property owner creates a rebuttable presumption that such owner waives all rights, claims and causes of action against the person volunteering to perform remediation for costs, losses or damages related to the contamination as to claims for costs, losses or damages arising after the date of such denial of access to the Department. A property owner who has denied access to the Department may rebut the presumption by showing that he had good cause for the denial or that the person requesting that the Department obtain access acted in bad faith. (2002, c. 378.)

§ 10.1-1233. Amnesty for voluntary disclosure and restoration of brownfield sites. — The Director may, consistent with programs developed under the federal acts, provide incentives for the voluntary disclosure of brownfield sites and related information regarding potential or known contamination at that site. To the extent consistent with federal law, any person making a voluntary disclosure regarding real or potential contamination at a brownfield site shall not be assessed an administrative or civil penalty under the Virginia Waste Management Act (§ 10.1-1400 et seq.), the State Water Control Law (§ 62.1-44.2 et seq.), the State Air Pollution Control Law (§ 10.1-1300 et seq.), or any other applicable law. A disclosure is voluntary if it is not otherwise required by law, regulation, permit or administrative order and the person making the disclosure adopts a plan to market for redevelopment or otherwise ensure the timely remediation of the site. Immunity shall not be accorded if it is found that the person making the voluntary disclosure has acted in bad faith. (2002, c. 378.)

§ **10.1-1234. Limitations on liability.** — A. The Director may, consistent with programs developed under the federal acts, make a determination to limit the liability of lenders, innocent purchasers or landowners, de minimis contributors or others who have grounds to claim limited responsibility for a containment or cleanup that may be required pursuant to the Virginia Waste Management Act (§ 10.1-1400 et seq.), the State Water Control Law (§ 62.1-44.2 et seq.), the State Air Pollution Control Law (§ 10.1-1300 et seq.), or any other applicable law.

B. A bona fide prospective purchaser shall not be held liable for a containment or cleanup that may be required at a brownfield site pursuant to the Virginia Waste Management Act (§ 10.1-1400 et seq.), the State Water Control Law (§ 62.1-44.2 et seq.), or the State Air Pollution Control Law (§ 10.1-1300 et seq.) if (i) the person did not cause, contribute, or consent to the release or threatened release, (ii) the person is not liable or potentially liable through any direct or indirect familial relationship or any contractual, corporate, or financial relationship or is not the result of a reorganization of a business entity that was potentially liable, (iii) the person exercises appropriate care with respect to hazardous substances found at the facility by taking reasonable steps to stop any continuing release, prevent any threatened future release, and prevent or limit human, environmental, or natural resource exposure to any previously released hazardous substances, and (iv) the person does not impede the performance of any response action. These provisions shall not apply to sites subject to the Resource Conservation and Recovery Act (42 U.S.C. § 6901 et seq.).

C. An innocent land owner who holds title, security interest or any other interest in a brownfield site shall not be held liable for a containment or cleanup that may be required at a brownfield site pursuant to the Virginia Waste Management Act (§ 10.1-1400 et seq.), the State Water Control Law (§ 62.1-44.2 et seq.), or the State Air Pollution Control Law (§ 10.1-1300 et seq.) if (i) the person did not cause, contribute, or consent to the release or threatened release, (ii) the person is not liable or potentially liable through any direct or indirect familial relationship or any contractual, corporate, or financial relationship or is not the result of a reorganization of a business entity that was potentially liable, (iii) the person made all appropriate inquiries into the previous uses of the facility in accordance with generally accepted good commercial and customary standards and practices, including those established by federal law, (iv) the person exercises appropriate care with respect to hazardous substances found at the facility by taking reasonable steps to stop any continuing release, prevent any threatened future release, and prevent or limit human, environmental, or natural resource exposure to any previously released hazardous substances, and (v) the person does not impede the performance of any response action and if either (a) at the time the person acquired the interest, he did not know and had no reason to know that any hazardous substances had been or were likely to have been disposed of on, in, or at the site, or (b) the person is a government entity that acquired the site by escheat or through other involuntary transfer or acquisition. These provisions shall not apply to sites subject to the Resource Conservation and Recovery Act (42 U.S.C. § 6901 et seq.).

D. A person that owns real property that is contiguous to or otherwise similarly situated with respect to, and that is or may be contaminated by a release or threatened release of a hazardous substance from real property that is not owned by that person shall not be considered liable for a containment or cleanup that may be required pursuant to the Virginia Waste Management Act (§ 10.1-1400 et seq.), the State Water Control Law (§ 62.1-44.2 et seq.), or the State Air Pollution Control Law (§ 10.1-1300 et seq.) if the person did not cause, contribute, or consent to the release or threatened release, the person is not liable or potentially liable through any direct or indirect familial relationship or any contractual, corporate, or financial relationship or is not the result of a reorganization of a business entity that was potentially liable, and if such person provides full cooperation, assistance and access to persons that are authorized to conduct response actions at the facility from which there has been a release.

E. The provisions of this section shall not otherwise limit the authority of the Department, the State Water Control Board, the Virginia Waste Management Board, or the State Air Pollution Control Board to require any person responsible for the contamination or pollution to contain or clean up sites where solid or hazardous waste or other substances have been improperly managed. (2002, c. 378.)

OPINIONS OF THE ATTORNEY GENERAL

Purchase of contaminated property at delinquent tax sale. — Purchase of contaminated property by county at a delinquent tax sale may constitute an involuntary transfer or acquisition and thereby qualify the county for protection from liability under subsection C of this section, provided the county meets all conditions set forth in clauses (i) through (v) of that subsection and the site is not subject to the Resource Conservation and Recovery Act. See opinion of Attorney General to Mr. Donald D. Litten, County Attorney for Shenandoah County, 04-061 (9/7/04).

Subsection B of this section would provide liability protection to a third party who purchased contaminated property at a delinquent tax sale with knowledge of the contamination, as a "bona fide prospective purchaser," provided the third party meets the conditions described in clauses (i) through (iv) of that subsection, and the site is not subject to the Resource Conservation and Recovery Act. See opinion of Attorney General to Mr. Donald D. Litten, County Attorney for Shenandoah County, 04-061 (9/7/04).

§ 10.1-1235. Limitation on liability at remediated properties under the jurisdiction of the Comprehensive Environmental Response, Compensation and Liability Act.

— A. Any person not otherwise liable under state law or regulation, who acquires any title, security interest, or any other interest in property located in the Commonwealth listed on the National Priorities List under the jurisdiction of the Comprehensive Environmental Response, Compensation and Liability Act, as amended (42 U.S.C. § 9601 et seq.), after the property has been remediated to the satisfaction of the Administrator of the United States Environmental Protection Agency, shall not be subject to civil enforcement or remediation action under this chapter, Chapter 13 (§ 10.1-1300 et seq.) of this title, the State Water Control Law (§ 62.1-44.2 et seq.), or any other applicable state law, or to private civil suit, related to contamination that was the subject of the satisfactory remediation, existing at or immediately contiguous to the property prior to the person acquiring title, security interest, or any other interest in such property.

B. Any person who acquires any title, security interest, or other interest in property from a person described in subsection A shall not be subject to enforcement or remediation actions or private civil suits to the same extent as the person provided in subsection A.

C. A person who holds title, a security interest, or any other interest in property prior to the property being acquired by a person described in subsection A shall not be relieved of any liability or responsibility by reacquiring title, a security interest, or any other interest in the property.

D. The provisions of this chapter shall not be construed to limit the statutory or regulatory authority of any state agency or to limit the liability or responsibility of any person when the activities of that person alter the remediation referred to in subsection A. The provisions of this section shall not modify the liability, if any, of a person who holds title, a security interest, or any other interest in property prior to satisfactory remediation or the liability of a person who acquires the property after satisfactory remediation for damage caused by contaminants not included in the remediation. (2002, c. 378.)

§ **10.1-1236. Access to abandoned brownfield sites.** — A. Any local government or agency of the Commonwealth may apply to the appropriate circuit court for access to an abandoned brownfield site in order to investigate contamination, to abate any hazard caused by the improper management of substances within the jurisdiction of the Board, or to remediate the site. The petition shall include (i) a demonstration that all reasonable efforts have been made to locate the owner, operator or other responsible party and (ii) a plan approved by the Director and which is consistent with applicable state and federal laws and regulations. The approval or disapproval of a plan shall not be considered a case decision as defined by § 2.2-4001.

B. Any person, local government, or agency of the Commonwealth not otherwise liable under federal or state law or regulation who performs any investigative, abatement or remediation activities pursuant to this section shall not become subject to civil enforcement or remediation action under Chapter 14 (§ 10.1-1400 et seq.) of this title or other applicable state laws or to private civil suits related to contamination not caused by its investigative, abatement or remediation activities.

C. This section shall not in any way limit the authority of the Virginia Waste Management Board, Director, or Department otherwise created by Chapter 14 (§ 10.1-1400 et seq.) of this title. (2002, c. 378.)

§ **10.1-1237. Virginia Brownfields Restoration and Economic Redevelopment Assistance Fund established; uses.** — A. There is hereby created and set apart a special, permanent, perpetual and nonreverting fund to be known as the Virginia Brownfields Restoration and Economic Redevelopment Assistance Fund for the purposes of promoting the restoration and redevelopment of brownfield sites and to address environmental problems or obstacles to reuse so that these sites can be effectively marketed to new economic development prospects. The Fund shall consist of sums appropriated to the Fund by the General Assembly, all receipts by the Fund from loans made by it, all income from the investment of moneys held in the Fund, and any other sums designated for deposit to the Fund from any source, public or private, including any federal grants, awards or other forms of financial assistance received by the Commonwealth.

B. The Authority shall administer and manage the Fund and establish the interest rates and repayment terms of such loans in accordance with a memorandum of agreement with the Partnership. The Partnership shall direct the distribution of loans or grants from the Fund to particular recipients based upon guidelines developed for this purpose. With approval from the Partnership, the Authority may disperse monies from the Fund for the payment of reasonable and necessary costs and expenses incurred in the administration and management of the Fund. The Authority may establish and collect a reasonable fee on outstanding loans for its management services.

C. All money belonging to the Fund shall be deposited in an account or accounts in banks or trust companies organized under the laws of the Commonwealth or in national banking associations located in Virginia or in savings institutions located in Virginia organized under the laws of the Commonwealth or the United States. The money in these accounts shall be paid by check and signed by the Executive Director of the Authority or other officers or employees designated by the Board of Directors of the Authority. All deposits of money shall, if required by the Authority, be secured in a manner determined by the Authority to be prudent, and all banks, trust companies and savings institutions are authorized to give security for the deposits. Money in the Fund shall not be commingled with other money of the Authority. Money in the Fund not needed for immediate use or disbursement may be invested or reinvested by the Authority in obligations or securities that are considered lawful investments for public funds under the laws of the Commonwealth. Expenditures and disbursements from the Fund shall be made by the Authority upon written request signed by the Executive Director of the Virginia Economic Development Partnership.

D. The Authority is empowered to collect, or to authorize others to collect on its behalf, amounts due to the Fund under any loan including, if appropriate, taking the action required by § 15.2-2659 to obtain payment of any amounts in default. Proceedings to recover amounts due to the Fund may be instituted by the Authority in the name of the Fund in the appropriate circuit court.

E. The Partnership may approve grants to local governments for the purposes of promoting the restoration and redevelopment of brownfield sites and to address real environmental problems or obstacles to reuse so that these sites can be effectively marketed to new economic development prospects. The grants may be used to pay the reasonable and necessary costs associated with the restoration and redevelopment of a brownfield site for (i) environmental and cultural resource site assessments, (ii) remediation of a contaminated property to remove hazardous substances, hazardous wastes, or solid wastes, (iii) the necessary removal of human remains, the appropriate treatment of grave sites, and the appropriate and necessary treatment of significant archaeological resources, or the stabilization or restoration of structures listed on or eligible for the Virginia Historic Landmarks Register, (iv) demolition and removal of existing structures, or other site work necessary to make a site or certain real property usable for new economic development, and (v) development of a remediation and reuse plan. The Partnership may establish such terms and conditions as it deems appropriate and shall evaluate each grant request in accordance with the guidelines developed for this purpose. The Authority shall disburse grants from the Fund in accordance with a written request from the Partnership.

F. The Authority may make loans to local governments, public authorities, corporations and partnerships to finance or refinance the cost of any brownfield restoration or remediation project for the purposes of promoting the restoration and redevelopment of brownfield sites and to address real environmental problems or obstacles to reuse so that these sites can be effectively marketed to economic development prospects. The loans shall be used to pay the reasonable and necessary costs related to the restoration and redevelopment of a brownfield site for (i) environmental and cultural resource site assessments, (ii) remediation of a contaminated property to remove hazardous substances, hazardous wastes, or solid wastes, (iii) the necessary removal of human remains, the appropriate treatment of grave sites, and the appropriate and necessary treatment of significant archaeological resources, or the stabilization or restoration of structures listed on or eligible for the Virginia Historic Landmarks Register, (iv) demolition and removal of existing structures, or other site work necessary to make a site or certain real property usable for new economic development, and (v) development of a remediation and reuse plan.

The Partnership shall designate in writing the recipient of each loan, the purposes of the loan, and the amount of each such loan. No loan from the Fund shall exceed the total cost of the project to be financed or the outstanding principal amount of the indebtedness to be refinanced plus reasonable financing expenses.

G. Except as otherwise provided in this chapter, the Authority shall determine the interest rate and terms and conditions of any loan from the Fund, which may vary between local governments. Each loan shall be evidenced by appropriate bonds or notes of the local government payable to the Fund. The bonds or notes shall have been duly authorized by the local government and executed by its authorized legal representatives. The Authority is authorized to require in connection with any loan from the Fund such documents, instruments, certificates, legal opinions and other information as it may deem necessary or convenient. In addition to any other terms or conditions that the Authority may establish, the Authority may require, as a condition to making any loan from the Fund, that the local government receiving the loan covenant perform any of the following:

1. Establish and collect rents, rates, fees, taxes, and charges to produce revenue sufficient to pay all or a specified portion of (i) the costs of the project, (ii) any outstanding indebtedness incurred for the purposes of the project, including the principal of, premium, if any, and interest on the loan from the Fund to the local government, and (iii) any amounts necessary to create and maintain any required reserve.

2. Levy and collect ad valorem taxes on all property within the jurisdiction of the local government subject to local taxation sufficient to pay the principal of and premium, if any, and interest on the loan from the Fund to the local government.

3. Create and maintain a special fund or funds for the payment of the principal of, premium, if any, and interest on the loan from the Fund to the local government and any other amounts becoming due under any agreement entered into in connection with the loan, or the project or any portions thereof or other property of the local government, and deposit into any fund or funds amounts sufficient to make any payments on the loan as they become due and payable.

4. Create and maintain other special funds as required by the Authority.

5. Perform other acts otherwise permitted by applicable law to secure payment of the principal of, premium, if any, and interest on the loan from the Fund to the local government and to provide for the remedies of the Fund in the event of any default by the local government in the payment of the loan, including, without limitation, any of the following:

a. The conveyance of, or the granting of liens on or security interests in, real and personal property, together with all rights, title and interest therein, to the Fund;

b. The procurement of insurance, guarantees, letters of credit and other forms of collateral, security, liquidity arrangements or credit supports for the loan from any source, public or private, and the payment therefor of premiums, fees, or other charges;

c. The combination of one or more projects, or the combination of one or more projects with one or more other undertakings, for the purpose of financing, and the pledging of the revenues from such combined projects and undertakings to secure the loan from the Fund to the local government made in connection with such combination or any part or parts thereof;

d. The maintenance, replacement, renewal, and repair of the project; and

e. The procurement of casualty and liability insurance.

6. Obtain a review of the accounting and the internal controls from the Auditor of Public Accounts or his legally authorized representatives. The

Authority may request additional reviews at any time during the term of the loan.

7. Directly offer, pledge, and consent to the Authority to take action pursuant to § 62.1-216.1 to obtain payment of any amounts in default.

H. All local governments borrowing money from the Fund are authorized to perform any acts, take any action, adopt any proceedings and make and carry out any contracts that are contemplated by this chapter. Such contracts need not be identical among all local governments, but may be structured as determined by the Authority according to the needs of the contracting local governments and the Fund.

I. Subject to the rights, if any, of the registered owners of any of the bonds of the Authority, the Authority may consent to and approve any modification in the terms of any loan to any local government.

J. The Partnership, through its Director, shall have the authority to access and release moneys in the Fund for purposes of this section as long as the disbursement does not exceed the balance of the Fund. If the Partnership, through its Director, requests a disbursement in an amount exceeding the current Fund balance, the disbursement shall require the written approval of the Governor. Disbursements from the Fund may be made for the purposes outlined in this section, including, but not limited to, personnel, administrative and equipment costs and expenses directly incurred by the Partnership or the Authority, or by any other agency or political subdivision acting at the direction of the Partnership.

The Authority is empowered at any time and from time to time to pledge, assign or transfer from the Fund to banks or trust companies designated by the Authority any or all of the assets of the Fund to be held in trust as security for the payment of the principal of, premium, if any, and interest on any or all of the bonds, as defined in § 62.1-199, issued to finance any project. The interests of the Fund in any assets so transferred shall be subordinate to the rights of the trustee under the pledge, assignment or transfer. To the extent funds are not available from other sources pledged for such purpose, any of the assets or payments of principal and interest received on the assets pledged, assigned or transferred or held in trust may be applied by the trustee thereof to the payment of the principal of, premium, if any, and interest on such bonds of the Authority secured thereby, and, if such payments are insufficient for such purpose, the trustee is empowered to sell any or all of such assets and apply the net proceeds from the sale to the payment of the principal of, premium, if any, and interest on such bonds of the Authority. Any assets of the Fund pledged, assigned or transferred in trust as set forth above and any payments of principal, interest or earnings received thereon shall remain part of the Fund but shall be subject to the pledge, assignment or transfer to secure the bonds of the Authority and shall be held by the trustee to which they are pledged, assigned or transferred until no longer required for such purpose by the terms of the pledge, assignment or transfer.

K. The Authority is empowered at any time and from time to time to sell, upon such terms and conditions as the Authority shall deem appropriate, any loan, or interest therein, made pursuant to this chapter. The net proceeds of sale remaining after the payment of the costs and expenses of the sale shall be designated for deposit to, and become part of, the Fund.

L. The Authority may, with the approval of the Partnership, pledge, assign or transfer from the Fund to banks or trust companies designated by the Authority any or all of the assets of the Fund to be held in trust as security for the payment of the principal of, premium, if any, and interest on any or all of the bonds, as defined in § 62.1-199, issued to finance any project. The interests of the Fund in any assets so transferred shall be subordinate to the rights of the trustee under the pledge, assignment or transfer. To the extent funds are not available from other sources pledged for such purpose, any of the assets or payments of principal and interest received on the assets pledged, assigned or transferred or held in trust may be applied by the trustee thereof to the payment of the principal of, premium, if any, and interest on such bonds of the Authority secured thereby, and, if such payments are insufficient for such purpose, the trustee is empowered to sell any or all of such assets and apply the net proceeds from the sale to the payment of the principal of, premium, if any, and interest on such bonds of the Authority. Any assets of the Fund pledged, assigned or transferred in trust as set forth above and any payments of principal, interest or earnings received thereon shall remain part of the Fund but shall be subject to the pledge, assignment or transfer to secure the bonds of the Authority and shall be held by the trustee to which they are pledged, assigned or transferred until no longer required for such purpose by the terms of the pledge, assignment or transfer.

M. The Partnership, in consultation with the Department of Environmental Quality, shall develop guidance governing the use of the Fund and including criteria for project eligibility that considers the extent to which a grant or loan will facilitate the use or reuse of existing infrastructure, the extent to which a grant or loan will meet the needs of a community that has limited ability to draw on other funding sources because of the small size or low income of the community, the potential for redevelopment of the site, the economic and environmental benefits to the surrounding community, and the extent of the perceived or real environmental contamination at the site. The guidelines shall include a requirement for a one-to-one match by the recipient of any grant made by or from the Fund. (2002, c. 378.)

CHAPTER 13.

AIR POLLUTION CONTROL BOARD.

ARTICLE 1.

General Provisions.

§ 10.1-1300. Definitions. — As used in this chapter, unless the context requires a different meaning:

"Advisory Board" means the State Advisory Board on Air Pollution.

"Air pollution" means the presence in the outdoor atmosphere of one or more substances which are or may be harmful or injurious to human health, welfare or safety, to animal or plant life, or to property, or which unreasonably interfere with the enjoyment by the people of life or property.

"Board" means the State Air Pollution Control Board.

"Department" means the Department of Environmental Quality.

"Director" or *"Executive Director"* means the Executive Director of the Department of Environmental Quality.

"Owner" shall have no connotation other than that customarily assigned to the term "person," but shall include bodies politic and corporate, associations, partnerships, personal representatives, trustees and committees, as well as individuals.

"Person" means an individual, corporation, partnership, association, a governmental body, a municipal corporation, or any other legal entity.

"Special order" means a special order issued under § 10.1-1309. (1966, c. 497, § 10-17.10; 1968, c. 311; 1970, c. 469; 1971, Ex. Sess., c. 91; 1972, c. 781; 1985, c. 448; 1988, c. 891; 1990, c. 238; 1991, c. 702; 2004, c. 408.)

Cross references. — As to the creation of the Department of Environmental Quality, effective April 1, 1993, and the consolidation of the Department of Air Pollution Control into that department, see § 10.1-1183. As to the Attorney General's limited authority to institute and conduct criminal prosecutions in the circuit courts of the Commonwealth, see § 2.2-511. As to the environmental laboratory certification program of the Division of Consolidated Laboratory Services, see § 2.2-1105. As to the issuance of general permits under this section being exempt from the Administrative Process Act, see § 2.2-4006.

Law Review. — For article addressing significant developments in Virginia law pertaining to air quality, water quality and solid and hazardous waste, between 1990 and 1992, see "Environmental Law," 26 U. Rich. L. Rev. 729 (1992).

Michie's Jurisprudence. — For related discussion, see 9A M.J. Health and Sanitation, § 1.

CASE NOTES

The broad definition of "owner" in this section includes an owner of a source or potential source of air pollution whether that owner is a natural person, a corporate entity, an association, a personal representative, a trustee or a committee. Citizens for Clean Air v. Commonwealth ex rel. State Air Pollution Control Bd., 13 Va. App. 430, 412 S.E.2d 715 (1991).

Where the term "owner" appears elsewhere than in § 10.1-1318 in the State Air Pollution Control Law, the context clearly indicates that the word is meant to indicate the owner of a source or a potential source of air pollution. Citizens for Clean Air v. Commonwealth ex rel. State Air Pollution Control Bd., 13 Va. App. 430, 412 S.E.2d 715 (1991).

Denial of formal petition for hearing entitles "owner aggrieved" to judicial review. — A final decision on the part of the State Air Pollution Control Board to deny a formal petition for a hearing would, under § 10.1-1318, entitle any "owner aggrieved" by that decision a right to judicial review. Citizens for Clean Air v. Commonwealth ex rel. State Air Pollution Control Bd., 13 Va. App. 430, 412 S.E.2d 715 (1991).

Recourse through the Virginia Administrative Process Act precluded unless party is an owner aggrieved. — The State Air Pollution Control Law contains a specific provision with respect to standing to appeal and, thus, precludes recourse through the Virginia Administrative Process Act, unless the party seeking review is an owner aggrieved by a final decision of the board. Citizens for Clean Air v. Commonwealth ex rel. State Air Pollution Control Bd., 13 Va. App. 430, 412 S.E.2d 715 (1991).

Unincorporated association composed of owners of real property adversely affected by poultry processing facility did not have standing to appeal the State Air Pollution Control Board's denial of the association's petition for a formal hearing regarding issuance of an air permit to the poultry processing facility, because the association was not an "owner" under § 10.1-1318, and the association was not a "party aggrieved" under § 9-6.14:16. Citizens for Clean Air v. Commonwealth ex rel. State Air Pollution Control Bd., 13 Va. App. 430, 412 S.E.2d 715 (1991).

§ 10.1-1301. State Air Pollution Control Board; membership; terms; vacancies. — The State Air Pollution Control Board shall be composed of five members appointed by the Governor for four-year terms. Vacancies other than by expiration of term shall be filled by the Governor by appointment for the unexpired term. (1966, c. 497, § 10-17.11; 1988, c. 891.)

§ 10.1-1302. Qualifications of members of Board. — The members of the Board shall be citizens of the Commonwealth and shall be selected from the Commonwealth at large on the basis of merit without regard to political affiliation. At least a majority of members appointed to the Board shall represent the public interest and not derive any significant portion of their income from persons subject to permits or enforcement orders of the Board. Notwithstanding any other provision of this section relating to Board membership, the qualifications for Board membership shall not be more strict than those which may be required by federal statute or regulations of the United States Environmental Protection Agency. The provisions of this section shall be in addition to the requirements of the State and Local Government Conflict of Interests Act (§ 2.2-3100 et seq.). (1966, c. 497, § 10-17.12; 1979, c. 117; 1987, Sp. Sess., c. 1; 1988, c. 891; 1992, c. 675; 1994, c. 461.)

§ 10.1-1303. Chairman of the Board; Executive Director; cooperation of state agencies. — The Board shall elect its own chairman. The Governor shall appoint an Executive Director who shall serve as executive officer of the Board, but shall not serve as a member thereof. The Board may call upon any state department or agency for technical assistance. All departments and agencies of the Commonwealth shall, upon request, assist the Board in the performance of its duties. (1966, c. 497, § 10-17.14; 1972, c. 781; 1984, c. 444; 1985, c. 397; 1988, c. 891; 1990, c. 238.)

§ **10.1-1304. Meetings of Board; quorum.** — The Board shall meet at least once every three months. Special meetings may be held at any time or place to be determined by the Board upon the call of the chairman or upon written request of any two members. All members shall be notified of the time and place of any meeting at least five days in advance of the meeting. Three members of the Board shall constitute a quorum for the transaction of business. (1966, c. 497, § 10-17.15; 1988, c. 891.)

§ **10.1-1305. Records of proceedings of Board.** — The Board shall keep a complete and accurate record of the proceedings at all its meetings, a copy of which shall be kept on file in the office of the Director and available for public inspection. (1966, c. 497, § 10-17.16; 1977, c. 31; 1988, cc. 26, 891.)

§ **10.1-1306. Inspections, investigations, etc.** — The Board shall make, or cause to be made, such investigations and inspections and do such other things as are reasonably necessary to carry out the provisions of this chapter, within the limits of the appropriations, study grants, funds, or personnel which are available for the purposes of this chapter, including the achievement and maintenance of such levels of air quality as will protect human health, welfare and safety and to the greatest degree practicable prevent injury to plant and animal life and property and which will foster the comfort and convenience of the people of the Commonwealth and their enjoyment of life and property and which will promote the economic and social development of the Commonwealth and facilitate enjoyment of its attractions. (1966, c. 497, § 10-17.17; 1988, c. 891.)

§ **10.1-1307. Further powers and duties of Board.** — A. The Board shall have the power to control and regulate its internal affairs; initiate and supervise research programs to determine the causes, effects, and hazards of air pollution; initiate and supervise statewide programs of air pollution control education; cooperate with and receive money from the federal government or any county or municipal government, and receive money from any other source, whether public or private; develop a comprehensive program for the study, abatement, and control of all sources of air pollution in the Common- wealth; and advise, consult, and cooperate with agencies of the United States and all agencies of the Commonwealth, political subdivisions, private indus- tries, and any other affected groups in furtherance of the purposes of this chapter.

B. The Board may adopt by regulation emissions standards controlling the release into the atmosphere of air pollutants from motor vehicles, only as provided in Article 22 (§ 46.2-1176 et seq.) of Chapter 10 of Title 46.2.

C. After any regulation has been adopted by the Board pursuant to § 10.1-1308, it may in its discretion grant local variances therefrom, if it finds after an investigation and hearing that local conditions warrant. If local variances are permitted, the Board shall issue an order to this effect. Such order shall be subject to revocation or amendment at any time if the Board after a hearing determines that the amendment or revocation is warranted. Variances and amendments to variances shall be adopted only after a public hearing has been conducted pursuant to the public advertisement of the subject, date, time, and place of the hearing at least 30 days prior to the scheduled hearing. The hearing shall be conducted to give the public an opportunity to comment on the variance.

D. After the Board has adopted the regulations provided for in § 10.1-1308, it shall have the power to: (i) initiate and receive complaints as to air pollution; (ii) hold or cause to be held hearings and enter orders diminishing or abating the causes of air pollution and orders to enforce its regulations pursuant to

§ 10.1-1309; and (iii) institute legal proceedings, including suits for injunctions for the enforcement of its orders, regulations, and the abatement and control of air pollution and for the enforcement of penalties.

E. The Board in making regulations and in approving variances, control programs, or permits, and the courts in granting injunctive relief under the provisions of this chapter, shall consider facts and circumstances relevant to the reasonableness of the activity involved and the regulations proposed to control it, including:

1. The character and degree of injury to, or interference with, safety, health, or the reasonable use of property which is caused or threatened to be caused;

2. The social and economic value of the activity involved;

3. The suitability of the activity to the area in which it is located; and

4. The scientific and economic practicality of reducing or eliminating the discharge resulting from such activity.

F. The Board may designate one of its members, the Director, or a staff assistant to conduct the hearings provided for in this chapter. A record of the hearing shall be made and furnished to the Board for its use in arriving at its decision.

G. The Board shall submit an annual report to the Governor and General Assembly on or before October 1 of each year on matters relating to the Commonwealth's air pollution control policies and on the status of the Commonwealth's air quality. (1966, c. 497, §§ 10-17.16, 10-17.18; 1968, c. 311; 1969, Ex. Sess., c. 8; 1970, c. 469; 1972, c. 781; 1973, c. 251; 1977, c. 31; 1980, c. 469; 1984, c. 734; 1988, cc. 26, 891; 1990, c. 231; 2004, c. 650.)

Editor's note. — Acts 2004, c. 650, cl. 3, provides: "That the Division of Legislative Automated Systems shall notify the Governor, the Lieutenant Governor, the Clerk of the House of the Delegates, the Clerk of the Senate, and the Law Librarian of the University of Virginia that the automatic distribution of hard copies of annual and biennial reports pursuant to § 2.2-1127 has been replaced by an on-demand electronic notification and report retrieval system available from the General Assembly's website. The Division shall also notify the members of the General Assembly of the availability of the electronic notification and report retrieval system and the additional option of receiving hardcopies of reports by request."

§ **10.1-1307.01. Further duties of Board; localities particularly affected.** — After June 30, 1994, before promulgating any regulation under consideration, granting any variance to an existing regulation, or issuing any permit for the construction of a new major source or for a major modification to an existing source, if the Board finds that there are localities particularly affected by the regulation, variance or permit, the Board shall:

1. Publish, or require the applicant to publish, a notice in a local paper of general circulation in the localities affected at least thirty days prior to the close of any public comment period. Such notice shall contain a statement of the estimated local impact of the proposed action, which at a minimum shall provide information regarding specific pollutants and the total quantity of each which may be emitted and shall list the type and quantity of any fuels to be used.

2. Mail the notice to the chief elected official and chief administrative officer and the planning district commission for those localities.

Written comments shall be accepted by the Board for at least fifteen days after any hearing on the regulation, variance, or permit, unless the Board votes to shorten the period.

For the purposes of this section, the term *"locality particularly affected"* means any locality which bears any identified disproportionate material air quality impact which would not be experienced by other localities. (1993, c. 944; 1997, c. 612.)

§ 10.1-1307.1. Department continued; appointment of Director. —

A. The Department of Air Pollution Control is continued as an agency within the Secretariat of Natural Resources. The Department shall be headed by a Director appointed by the Governor, subject to confirmation by the General Assembly, to serve at the pleasure of the Governor.

B. In addition to the powers designated elsewhere in this chapter, the Department shall have the power to:

1. Administer the policies and regulations established by the Board pursuant to this chapter;

2. Employ such personnel as may be required to carry out the duties of the Department;

3. Make and enter into all contracts and agreements necessary or incidental to the performance of the Department's duties and the execution of its powers under this chapter, including, but not limited to, contracts with the United States, other states, agencies, and governmental subdivisions of the Commonwealth;

4. Accept grants from the United States government and agencies and instrumentalities thereof and any other source. To these ends, the Department shall have the power to comply with such conditions and execute such agreements as may be necessary, convenient, or desirable; and

5. Perform all acts necessary or convenient to carry out the purposes of this chapter. (1990, c. 238.)

§ 10.1-1307.2. Powers and duties of the Executive Director. — A. The

Executive Director, under the direction and control of the Governor, shall exercise such powers and perform such duties as are conferred or imposed upon him by the law and shall perform such other duties required of him by the Governor and the Board.

B. The Executive Director may be vested with the authority of the Board when it is not in session, subject to such regulations or delegation as may be prescribed by the Board.

In no event shall the Executive Director have the authority to adopt or promulgate any regulation.

C. In addition to the powers designated elsewhere in this chapter, the Director shall have the following general powers:

1. Supervise and manage the Department;

2. Prepare and submit all requests for appropriations and be responsible for all expenditures pursuant to appropriations;

3. Provide investigative and such other services as needed by the Department to enforce applicable laws and regulations;

4. Provide for the administrative functions and services of the Department;

5. Provide such office facilities as will allow the Department to carry out its duties; and

6. Assist the citizens (including corporate citizens) of the Commonwealth by providing guidelines, time tables, suggestions and in general being helpful to applicants seeking state and federal air pollution control permits. (1990, c. 238.)

§ 10.1-1307.3. Executive Director to enforce laws. — The Executive

Director or his duly authorized representative shall have the authority to:

1. Supervise, administer, and enforce the provisions of this chapter and regulations and orders of the Board as are conferred upon him by the Board;

2. Investigate any violations of this chapter and regulations and orders of the Board;

3. Require that air pollution records and reports be made available upon request, and require owners to develop, maintain, and make available such

other records and information as are deemed necessary for the proper enforcement of this chapter and regulations and orders of the Board;

4. Upon presenting appropriate credentials to the owner, operator, or agent in charge:

a. Enter without delay and at reasonable times any business establishment, construction site, or other area, workplace, or environment in this Commonwealth; and

b. Inspect and investigate during regular working hours and at other reasonable times, and within reasonable limits and in a reasonable manner, without prior notice, unless such notice is authorized by the Director or his representative, any such business establishment or place of employment and all pertinent conditions, structures, machines, apparatus, devices, equipment, and materials therein, and question privately any such employer, officer, owner, operator, agent, or employee. If such entry or inspection is refused, prohibited, or otherwise interfered with, the Director shall have the power to seek from a court having equity jurisdiction an order compelling such entry or inspection; and

5. Temporarily suspend the enforcement of any regulation or permit requirement applicable to any part of an electrical generation and transmission system, whether owned or contracted for, when a public electric utility providing power within the Commonwealth so requests and has suffered a force majeure event as defined in subdivision 7 of § 59.1-21.18:2. (1990, c. 238; 1995, c. 184.)

§ **10.1-1308. Regulations.** — A. The Board, after having studied air pollution in the various areas of the Commonwealth, its causes, prevention, control and abatement, shall have the power to promulgate regulations, including emergency regulations, abating, controlling and prohibiting air pollution throughout or in any part of the Commonwealth in accordance with the provisions of the Administrative Process Act (§ 2.2-4000 et seq.), except that a description of provisions of any proposed regulation which are more restrictive than applicable federal requirements, together with the reason why the more restrictive provisions are needed, shall be provided to the standing committee of each house of the General Assembly to which matters relating to the content of the regulation are most properly referable. No such regulation, shall prohibit the burning of leaves from trees by persons on property where they reside if the local governing body of the county, city or town has enacted an otherwise valid ordinance regulating such burning. The regulations shall not promote or encourage any substantial degradation of present air quality in any air basin or region which has an air quality superior to that stipulated in the regulations. Any regulations adopted by the Board to have general effect in part or all of the Commonwealth shall be filed in accordance with the Virginia Register Act (§ 2.2-4100 et seq.).

B. Any regulation that prohibits the selling of any consumer product shall not restrict the continued sale of the product by retailers of any existing inventories in stock at the time the regulation is promulgated.

C. Any regulation requiring the use of stage 1 vapor recovery equipment at gasoline dispensing facilities may be applicable only in areas that have been designated at any time by the U.S. Environmental Protection Agency as nonattainment for the pollutant ozone. For purposes of this section, gasoline dispensing facility means any site where gasoline is dispensed to motor vehicle tanks from storage tanks. (1966, c. 497, §§ 10-17.16, 10-17.18; 1968, c. 311; 1969, Ex. Sess., c. 8; 1970, c. 469; 1972, c. 781; 1973, c. 251; 1980, c. 469; 1984, c. 734; 1988, cc. 26, 891; 1993, c. 456; 1997, c. 55; 2005, c. 66; 2006, c. 71.)

Cross references. — As to alternate compliance methods for persons or facilities meeting the criteria for E3 or E4 facilities under § 10.1-1187.3, see § 10.1-1187.6. As to regulations promulgated by the State Air Pollution Control Board, see 9 VAC 5-10-10 et seq.

The 2005 amendments. — The 2005 amendment by c. 66 substituted language beginning "at a gasoline dispensing facilities ..." and ending "motor vehicle tanks from storage tanks" for "shall require the use of such equipment only in areas that have been designated at any time by the U.S. Environmental Protection Agency as nonattainment areas for the pollutant ozone" in subsection B.

The 2006 amendments. — The 2006 amendment by c. 71 added subsection B and redesignated former subsection B as subsection C.

§ 10.1-1309. Issuance of special orders; civil penalties. — A. The Board shall have the power to issue special orders to:

(i) owners who are permitting or causing air pollution as defined by § 10.1-1300, to cease and desist from such pollution;

(ii) owners who have failed to construct facilities in accordance with or have failed to comply with plans for the control of air pollution submitted by them to and approved by the Board, to construct such facilities in accordance with or otherwise comply with, such approved plans;

(iii) owners who have violated or failed to comply with the terms and provisions of any Board order or directive to comply with such terms and provisions;

(iv) owners who have contravened duly adopted and promulgated air quality standards and policies, to cease such contravention and to comply with air quality standards and policies;

(v) require any owner to comply with the provisions of this chapter and any Board decision; and

(vi) require any person to pay civil penalties of up to $32,500 for each violation, not to exceed $100,000 per order, if (a) the person has been issued at least two written notices of alleged violation by the Department for the same or substantially related violations at the same site, (b) such violations have not been resolved by demonstration that there was no violation, by an order issued by the Board or the Director, or by other means, (c) at least 130 days have passed since the issuance of the first notice of alleged violation, and (d) there is a finding that such violations have occurred after a hearing conducted in accordance with subsection B. The actual amount of any penalty assessed shall be based upon the severity of the violations, the extent of any potential or actual environmental harm, the compliance history of the facility or person, any economic benefit realized from the noncompliance, and the ability of the person to pay the penalty. The Board shall provide the person with the calculation for the proposed penalty prior to any hearing conducted for the issuance of an order that assesses penalties pursuant to this subsection. Penalties shall be paid to the state treasury and deposited by the State Treasurer into the Virginia Environmental Emergency Response Fund (§ 10.1-2500 et seq.). The issuance of a notice of alleged violation by the Department shall not be considered a case decision as defined in § 2.2-4001. Any notice of alleged violation shall include a description of each violation, the specific provision of law violated, and information on the process for obtaining a final decision or fact finding from the Department on whether or not a violation has occurred, and nothing in this section shall preclude an owner from seeking such a determination.

B. Such special orders are to be issued only after a hearing before a hearing officer appointed by the Supreme Court in accordance with § 2.2-4020 with reasonable notice to the affected owners of the time, place and purpose thereof, and they shall become effective not less than five days after service as provided in subsection C below. Should the Board find that any such owner is unreasonably affecting the public health, safety or welfare, or the health of animal or plant life, or property, after a reasonable attempt to give notice, it shall declare a state of emergency and may issue without hearing an emergency special order directing the owner to cease such pollution immediately, and shall within 10 days hold a hearing, after reasonable notice as to the time and place thereof to the owner, to affirm, modify, amend or cancel such emergency special order. If the Board finds that an owner who has been issued a special order or an emergency special order is not complying with the terms thereof, it may proceed in accordance with § 10.1-1316 or 10.1-1320.

C. Any special order issued under the provisions of this section need not be filed with the Secretary of the Commonwealth, but the owner to whom such special order is directed shall be notified by certified mail, return receipt requested, sent to the last known address of such owner, or by personal delivery by an agent of the Board, and the time limits specified shall be counted from the date of receipt.

D. Nothing in this section or in § 10.1-1307 shall limit the Board's authority to proceed against such owner directly under § 10.1-1316 or 10.1-1320 without the prior issuance of an order, special or otherwise. (1971, Ex. Sess., c. 91, § 10-17.18:1; 1973, c. 251; 1988, c. 891; 2005, c. 706.)

Editor's note. — Acts 2005, c. 706, cl. 2, provides: "That the Director of the Department of Environmental Quality shall develop uniform procedures to govern the formal hearings conducted pursuant to this act to ensure they are conducted in accordance with the Administrative Process Act, any policies adopted by the State Water Control Board, the Virginia Waste Management Board, or the State Air Pollution Control Board and to ensure that the facility owners and operators have access to information on how such hearings will be conducted. In addition, the Director of the Department of Environmental Quality shall develop and implement an early dispute resolution process to help identify and resolve disagreements regarding what is required to comply with the regulations promulgated by the State Air Pollution Control Board, the State Water Control Board, the Virginia Waste Management Board and any related guidance. The process shall be available after the issuance of a notice of alleged violation or other notice of deficiency issued by the Department. The early dispute resolution process shall be developed by September 1, 2005, and information on the process shall be provided to the public and to facilities potentially impacted by the provisions of this act."

The 2005 amendments. — The 2005 amendment by c. 706 inserted subdivision A (vi); inserted "before a hearing officer appointed by the Supreme Court in accordance with § 2.2-4020" in subsection B; made related changes; and made minor stylistic changes.

CASE NOTES

"Owner" indicates the owner of a source or a potential source of air pollution. — Where the term "owner" appears elsewhere than in § 10.1-1318 in the State Air Pollution Control Law, the context clearly indicates that the word is meant to indicate the owner of a source or a potential source of air pollution. Citizens for Clean Air v. Commonwealth ex rel. State Air Pollution Control Bd., 13 Va. App. 430, 412 S.E.2d 715 (1991).

§ 10.1-1309.1. Special orders; penalties. — The Board is authorized to issue special orders in compliance with the Administrative Process Act (§ 2.2-4000 et seq.) requiring that an owner file with the Board a plan to abate, control, prevent, remove, or contain any substantial and imminent threat to public health or the environment that is reasonably likely to occur if such source ceases operations. Such plan shall also include a demonstration of financial capability to implement the plan. Financial capability may be demonstrated by the establishment of an escrow account, the creation of a trust fund to be maintained within the Department, submission of a bond, corporate guarantee based on audited financial statements, or such other instruments as the Board may deem appropriate. The Board may require that such plan and instruments be updated as appropriate. The Board shall give due consideration to any plan submitted by the owner in accordance with §§ 10.1-1410, 10.1-1428, and 62.1-44.15:1.1, in determining the necessity for and suitability of any plan submitted under this section.

For the purposes of this section, "ceases operation" means to cease conducting the normal operation of a source which is regulated under this chapter under circumstances where it would be reasonable to expect that such operation will not be resumed by the owner at the source. The term shall not include the sale or transfer of a source in the ordinary course of business or a permit transfer in accordance with Board regulations.

Any person who ceases operations and who knowingly and willfully fails to implement a closure plan or to provide adequate funds for implementation of such plan shall, if such failure results in a significant harm or an imminent and substantial threat of significant harm to human health or the environment, be liable to the Commonwealth and any political subdivision thereof for the costs incurred in abating, controlling, preventing, removing, or containing such harm or threat.

Any person who ceases operations and who knowingly and willfully fails to implement a closure plan or to provide adequate funds for implementation of such plan shall, if such failure results in a significant harm or an imminent and substantial threat of significant harm to human health or the environment, be guilty of a Class 4 felony. (1991, c. 702.)

Cross references. — As to punishment for Class 4 felonies, see § 18.2-10.

§ 10.1-1310. Decision of Board pursuant to hearing.

§ **10.1-1310. Decision of Board pursuant to hearing.** — Any decision by the Board rendered pursuant to hearings under § 10.1-1309 shall be reduced to writing and shall contain the explicit findings of fact and conclusions of law upon which the Board's decision is based. Certified copies of the written decision shall be delivered or mailed by certified mail to the parties affected by it. Failure to comply with the provisions of this section shall render such decision invalid. (1971, Ex. Sess., c. 91, § 10-17.18:2; 1973, c. 251; 1988, c. 891.)

§ **10.1-1310.1. Notification of local government.** — Upon determining that there has been a violation of this chapter or any regulation promulgated under this chapter or order of the Board, and such violation poses an imminent threat to the health, safety or welfare of the public, the Director shall immediately notify the chief administrative officer of any potentially affected local government. Neither the Director, the Commonwealth, nor any employee of the Commonwealth shall be liable for a failure to provide, or a delay in providing, the notification required by this section. (1988, cc. 434, 891; 1990, c. 238.)

Editor's note. — This section was enacted by Acts 1988, c. 434, as § 10-17.18:4. Pursuant to Acts 1988, c. 891, cl. 5, this section has been incorporated into Title 10.1 as § 10.1-1310.1.

§ **10.1-1311. Penalties for noncompliance; judicial review.** — A. The Board is authorized to promulgate regulations providing for the determination of a formula for the basis of the amount of any noncompliance penalty to be assessed by a court pursuant to subsection B hereof, in conformance with the requirements of Section 120 of the federal Clean Air Act, as amended, and any regulations promulgated thereunder. Any regulations promulgated pursuant to this section shall be in accordance with the provisions of the Administrative Process Act (§ 2.2-4000 et seq.).

B. Upon a determination of the amount by the Board, the Board shall petition the circuit court of the county or city wherein the owner subject to such noncompliance assessment resides, regularly or systematically conducts affairs or business activities, or where such owner's property affected by the administrative action is located for an order requiring payment of a noncompliance penalty in a sum the court deems appropriate.

C. Any order issued by a court pursuant to this section may be enforced as a judgment of the court. All sums collected, less the assessment and collection costs, shall be paid into the state treasury and deposited by the State Treasurer into the Virginia Environmental Emergency Response Fund pursuant to Chapter 25 (§ 10.1-2500 et seq.) of this title.

D. Any penalty assessed under this section shall be in addition to permits, fees, orders, payments, sanctions, or other requirements under this chapter, and shall in no way affect any civil or criminal enforcement proceedings brought under other provisions of this chapter. (1979, c. 65, § 10-17.18:3; 1988, c. 891; 1991, c. 718.)

Editor's note. — For Section 120 of the federal Clean Air Act, referred to in subsection A above, see 42 U.S.C.S. § 7420.

§ 10.1-1312. Air pollution control districts. — A. The Board may create, within any area of the Commonwealth, local air pollution control districts comprising a city or county or a part or parts of each, or two or more cities or counties, or any combination or parts thereof. Such local districts may be established by the Board on its own motion or upon request of the governing body or bodies of the area involved.

B. In each district there shall be a local air pollution control committee, the members of which shall be appointed by the Board from lists of recommended nominees submitted by the respective governing bodies of each locality, all or a portion of which are included in the district. The number of members on each committee shall be in the discretion of the Board. When a district includes two or more localities or portions thereof, the Board shall apportion the membership of the committee among the localities, provided that each locality shall have at least one representative on the committee. The members shall not be compensated out of state funds, but may be reimbursed for expenses out of state funds. Localities may provide for the payment of compensation and reimbursement of expenses to the members and may appropriate funds therefore. The portion of such payment to be borne by each locality shall be prescribed by agreement.

C. The local committee is empowered to observe compliance with the regulations of the Board and report instances of noncompliance to the Board, to conduct educational programs relating to air pollution and its effects, to assist the Department in its air monitoring programs, to initiate and make studies relating to air pollution and its effects, and to make recommendations to the Board.

D. The governing body of any locality, wholly or partially included within any such district, may appropriate funds for use by the local committee in air pollution control and studies. (1966, c. 497, § 10-17.19; 1969, Ex. Sess., c. 8; 1972, c. 781; 1988, c. 891.)

§ 10.1-1313. State Advisory Board on Air Pollution. — The Board is authorized to name qualified persons to a State Advisory Board on Air Pollution. (1966, c. 497, § 10-17.20; 1985, c. 448; 1988, c. 891.)

§ 10.1-1314. Owners to furnish plans, specifications and information. — Every owner which the Board has reason to believe is causing, or may be about to cause, an air pollution problem shall on request of the Board furnish such plans, specifications and information as may be required by the Board in the discharge of its duties under this chapter. Any information, except emission data, as to secret processes, formulae or methods of manufacture or production shall not be disclosed in public hearing and shall be kept confidential. If samples are taken for analysis, a duplicate of the analytical report shall be furnished promptly to the person from whom such sample is requested. (1966, c. 497, § 10-17.21; 1968, c. 311; 1975, c. 126; 1988, c. 891.)

§ **10.1-1314.1. Protection of trade secrets.** — Any information, except emissions data, reported to or otherwise obtained by the Director, the Board, or the agents or employees of either which contains or might reveal a trade secret shall be confidential and shall be limited to those persons who need such information for purposes of enforcement of this chapter or the federal Clean Air Act or regulations and orders of the Board. It shall be the duty of each owner to notify the Director or his representatives of the existence of trade secrets when he desires the protection provided herein. (1990, c. 238.)

§ **10.1-1315. Right of entry.** — Whenever it is necessary for the purposes of this chapter, the Board or any member, agent or employee thereof, when duly authorized by the Board, may at reasonable times enter any establishment or upon any property, public or private, to obtain information or conduct surveys or investigations. (1966, c. 497, § 10-17.22; 1988, c. 891.)

§ **10.1-1316. Enforcement and civil penalties.** — A. Any owner violating or failing, neglecting or refusing to obey any provision of this chapter, any Board regulation or order, or any permit condition may be compelled to comply by injunction, mandamus or other appropriate remedy.

B. Without limiting the remedies which may be obtained under subsection A, any owner violating or failing, neglecting or refusing to obey any Board regulation or order, any provision of this chapter, or any permit condition shall be subject, in the discretion of the court, to a civil penalty not to exceed $32,500 for each violation. Each day of violation shall constitute a separate offense. In determining the amount of any civil penalty to be assessed pursuant to this subsection, the court shall consider, in addition to such other factors as it may deem appropriate, the size of the owner's business, the severity of the economic impact of the penalty on the business, and the seriousness of the violation. Such civil penalties shall be paid into the state treasury and deposited by the State Treasurer into the Virginia Environmental Emergency Response Fund pursuant to Chapter 25 (§ 10.1-2500 et seq.) of this title. Such civil penalties may, in the discretion of the court assessing them, be directed to be paid into the treasury of the county, city or town in which the violation occurred, to be used to abate environmental pollution in such manner as the court may, by order, direct, except that where the owner in violation is the county, city or town itself, or its agent, the court shall direct the penalty to be paid into the state treasury and deposited by the State Treasurer into the Virginia Environmental Emergency Response Fund pursuant to Chapter 25 of this title.

C. With the consent of an owner who has violated or failed, neglected or refused to obey any Board regulation or order, or any provision of this chapter, or any permit condition, the Board may provide, in any order issued by the Board against the owner, for the payment of civil charges in specific sums, not to exceed the limit of subsection B. Such civil charges shall be in lieu of any civil penalty which could be imposed under subsection B. Such civil charges shall be paid into the state treasury and deposited by the State Treasurer into the Virginia Environmental Emergency Response Fund pursuant to Chapter 25 of this title.

D. The Board shall develop and provide an opportunity for public comment on guidelines and procedures that contain specific criteria for calculating the appropriate penalty for each violation based upon the severity of the violations, the extent of any potential or actual environmental harm, the compliance history of the facility or person, any economic benefit realized from the noncompliance, and the ability of the person to pay the penalty. (1966, c. 497, § 10-17.23; 1976, c. 622; 1978, c. 475; 1980, c. 378; 1988, c. 891; 1991, c. 718; 1993, c. 13; 2005, c. 706.)

Editor's note. — Acts 2005, c. 706, cl. 2, provides: "That the Director of the Department of Environmental Quality shall develop uniform procedures to govern the formal hearings conducted pursuant to this act to ensure they are conducted in accordance with the Administrative Process Act, any policies adopted by the State Water Control Board, the Virginia Waste Management Board, or the State Air Pollution Control Board and to ensure that the facility owners and operators have access to information on how such hearings will be conducted. In addition, the Director of the Department of Environmental Quality shall develop and implement an early dispute resolution process to help identify and resolve disagreements re-

garding what is required to comply with the regulations promulgated by the State Air Pollution Control Board, the State Water Control Board, the Virginia Waste Management Board and any related guidance. The process shall be available after the issuance of a notice of alleged violation or other notice of deficiency issued by the Department. The early dispute resolution process shall be developed by September 1, 2005, and information on the process shall be provided to the public and to facilities potentially impacted by the provisions of this act."

The 2005 amendments. — The 2005 amendment by c. 706 substituted "$32,500" for "$25,000"; and added subsection D.

§ 10.1-1316.1. Severe ozone nonattainment areas; fees. — A. Except as provided in subsection C, any owner of a stationary source that emits or has the potential to emit 25 tons or more per year of volatile organic compounds or 25 tons or more of nitrogen oxides and is located in an area designated by the U.S. Environmental Protection Agency as a severe ozone nonattainment area shall pay a fee to the Department for deposit in the Vehicle Emissions Inspection Program Fund, established pursuant to § 46.2-1182.2 to be used for air quality evaluation and improvements, if the area fails to attain the ambient air quality standard for ozone by the applicable attainment date established pursuant to 42 U.S.C. §§ 7502 and 7511 of the Clean Air Act. Such fees shall be assessed for emissions in each calendar year beginning in the year after the attainment date and for each calendar year thereafter as set forth in this section and shall continue until the area is redesignated as an attainment area for the ozone standard.

B. The fee shall be determined in accordance with the following:

1. The fee shall equal $5,000, adjusted in accordance with subdivision B 3, per ton of volatile organic compounds or nitrogen oxides emitted by the stationary source during the previous calendar year in excess of 80 percent of the baseline amount, computed under subdivision B 2.

2. For purposes of this section, the baseline amount shall be the lower of (i) the amount of actual volatile organic compounds or nitrogen oxide emissions or (ii) the amount of volatile organic compounds or nitrogen oxide emissions allowed under the permit applicable to the stationary source during the attainment year, or, if no such permit has been issued for the attainment year, the amount of volatile organic compounds or nitrogen oxide emissions allowed under the applicable implementation plan during the attainment year. The Department may calculate the baseline amount over a period of more than one calendar year, provided such determination is consistent with federal requirements.

3. The fee amount under subdivision B 1 shall be adjusted each year beginning in 1991 by the percentage, if any, by which the Consumer Price Index for the most recent calendar year ending before the beginning of such

year exceeds the Consumer Price Index for the calendar year 1989. The Consumer Price Index for any calendar year is the average of the Consumer Price Index for all urban consumers published by the U.S. Department of Labor as of the close of the 12-month period ending on August 31 of each calendar year. The revision of the Consumer Price Index that is most consistent with the Consumer Price Index for the calendar year 1989 shall be used.

C. Notwithstanding any provision of this section, no owner shall be required to pay any fee under subsection A with respect to emissions during any year that is treated as an extension year under 42 U.S.C. § 7511 (a) (5) of the Clean Air Act and no owner shall be required to pay any fee under subsection A if such fees would not otherwise be imposed pursuant to 42 U.S.C. § 7511d.

D. Payment is due by August 31 of each year. The Department shall issue annual notices of the fees to owners on or before August 1 of each year. Each notice shall include a summary of the data on which the fee is based. The Board may establish additional procedures for the assessment and collection of such fees. The failure to pay within 90 days from the receipt of the notice shall be grounds to institute a collection action against the owner of the stationary source.

E. Fees collected pursuant to this section shall not supplant or reduce the general fund appropriation to the Department.

F. These fees shall be used to pay expenses related to air quality monitoring and evaluation in the Commonwealth and measures to improve air quality in areas designated by the U.S. Environmental Protection Agency as severe nonattainment areas. The fees that may be generated may be used for matching grants. (2004, c. 408.)

§ **10.1-1317. Judicial review of regulations of Board.** — The validity of any regulation may be determined through judicial review in accordance with the provisions of the Administrative Process Act (§ 2.2-4000 et seq.). (1971, Ex. Sess., c. 91, § 10-17.23:1; 1986, c. 615; 1988, c. 891.)

§ **10.1-1318. Appeal from decision of Board.** — A. Any owner aggrieved by a final decision of the Board under § 10.1-1309, § 10.1-1322 or subsection D of § 10.1-1307 is entitled to judicial review thereof in accordance with the provisions of the Administrative Process Act (§ 2.2-4000 et seq.).

B. Any person who has participated, in person or by submittal of written comments, in the public comment process related to a final decision of the Board under § 10.1-1322 and who has exhausted all available administrative remedies for review of the Board's decision, shall be entitled to judicial review of the Board's decision in accordance with the provisions of the Administrative Process Act (§ 2.2-4000 et seq.) if such person meets the standard for obtaining judicial review of a case or controversy pursuant to Article III of the United States Constitution. A person shall be deemed to meet such standard if (i) such person has suffered an actual or imminent injury which is an invasion of a legally protected interest and which is concrete and particularized; (ii) such injury is fairly traceable to the decision of the Board and not the result of the independent action of some third party not before the court; and (iii) such injury will likely be redressed by a favorable decision by the court. (1971, Ex. Sess., c. 91, § 10-17.23:2; 1986, c. 615; 1988, c. 891; 1993, c. 997; 1996, c. 1032.)

Editor's note. — Acts 1996, c. 1032, cl. 3 provides: "[t]hat the second enactment of this act shall not be effective unless and until a final and unappealable decision of a court of competent jurisdiction has declared that subsection B of § 10.1-1318 as it is currently effective does not meet the requirements for state program approval under Title V of the federal Clean Air Act or regulations promulgated thereunder with respect to standing to seek judicial review of state permitting decisions."

Acts 1996, c. 1032, cl. 5, as added by Acts 1997, c. 520, cl. 1, provides: "That the 'final and unappealable decision of a court of competent jurisdiction' referred to in enactment clauses 3 and 4 was rendered by the United States Supreme Court in the case of Commonwealth vs. Browner on January 21, 1997."

Law Review. — For an article reviewing key environmental developments at the federal and state levels during the period from June 1996 to June 1998, see 32 U. Rich. L. Rev. 1217 (1998).

CASE NOTES

Denial of formal petition for hearing entitles "owner aggrieved" to judicial review. — A final decision on the part of the State Air Pollution Control Board to deny a formal petition for a hearing would, under this section, entitle any "owner aggrieved" by that decision a right to judicial review. Citizens for Clean Air v. Commonwealth ex rel. State Air Pollution Control Bd., 13 Va. App. 430, 412 S.E.2d 715 (1991).

Where the term "owner" appears elsewhere than in this section in the State Air Pollution Control Law, the context clearly indicates that the word is meant to indicate the owner of a source or a potential source of air pollution. Citizens for Clean Air v. Commonwealth ex rel. State Air Pollution Control Bd.,

13 Va. App. 430, 412 S.E.2d 715 (1991).

Unincorporated association composed of owners of real property adversely affected by poultry processing facility did not have standing to appeal the State Air Pollution Control Board's denial of the association's petition for a formal hearing regarding issuance of an air permit to the poultry processing facility, because the association was not an "owner" under § 10.1-1318, and the association was not a "party aggrieved" under § 9-6.14:16. Citizens for Clean Air v. Commonwealth ex rel. State Air Pollution Control Bd., 13 Va. App. 430, 412 S.E.2d 715 (1991).

Applied in Virginia v. United States, 926 F. Supp. 537 (E.D. Va. 1995).

§ 10.1-1319. Appeal to Court of Appeals. — The Commonwealth or any party aggrieved by any final decision of the judge shall have, regardless of the amount involved, the right to appeal to the Court of Appeals. The procedure shall be the same as that provided by law concerning appeals and supersedeas. (1966, c. 497, § 10-17.28; 1984, c. 703; 1988, c. 891.)

§ 10.1-1320. Penalties; chapter not to affect right to relief or to maintain action. — Any owner knowingly violating any provision of this chapter, Board regulation or order, or any permit condition shall upon conviction be guilty of a misdemeanor and shall be subject to a fine of not more than $10,000 for each violation within the discretion of the court. Each day of violation shall constitute a separate offense.

Nothing in this chapter shall be construed to abridge, limit, impair, create, enlarge or otherwise affect substantively or procedurally the right of any person to damages or other relief on account of injury to persons or property. (1966, c. 497, § 10-17.29; 1972, c. 781; 1973, c. 251; 1988, c. 891; 1993, c. 13; 1995, c. 135.)

§ 10.1-1320.1. Duty of attorney for the Commonwealth. — It shall be the duty of every attorney for the Commonwealth to whom the Director or his authorized representative has reported any violation of this chapter or any regulation or order of the Board, to cause proceedings to be prosecuted without delay for the fines and penalties in such cases. (1990, c. 238.)

§ 10.1-1321. Local ordinances. — A. Existing local ordinances adopted prior to July 1, 1972, shall continue in force; however, in the event of a conflict between a Board regulation and a local ordinance adopted prior to July 1, 1972, the Board regulation shall govern, except when the conflicting local ordinance is more stringent.

B. The governing body of any locality proposing to adopt an ordinance, or an amendment to an existing ordinance, relating to air pollution after June 30, 1972, shall first obtain the approval of the Board as to the provisions of the ordinance or amendment. No ordinance or amendment, except an ordinance or amendment pertaining solely to open burning, shall be approved by the Board which regulates any emission source that is required to register with the Board or to obtain a permit pursuant to this chapter and the Board's regulations. (1966, c. 497, § 10-17.30; 1972, c. 781; 1988, c. 891; 1994, c. 358.)

Law Review. — For comment, "Waste to Energy: Environmental and Local Government Concerns," see 19 U. Rich. L. Rev. 373 (1985).

§ 10.1-1321.1. When application for permit considered complete. —

A. No application for a permit for a new or major modified stationary air pollution source shall be considered complete unless the applicant has provided the Director with notification from the governing body of the county, city, or town in which the source is to be located that the location and operation of the source are consistent with all ordinances adopted pursuant to Chapter 22 (§ 15.2-2200 et seq.) of Title 15.2.

B. The governing body shall inform in writing the applicant and the Department of the source's compliance or noncompliance not more than forty-five days from receipt by the chief executive officer, or his agent, of a request from the applicant.

C. Should the governing body fail to provide written notification as specified in subsection B of this section, the requirement for such notification as specified in subsection A of this section is waived.

D. The provisions of this section shall apply only to applications received after July 1, 1990. (1990, c. 235; 1993, c. 739.)

§ 10.1-1322. Permits. —

A. Pursuant to regulations adopted by the Board, permits may be issued, amended, revoked or terminated and reissued by the Department and may be enforced under the provisions of this chapter in the same manner as regulations and orders. Failure to comply with any condition of a permit shall be considered a violation of this chapter and investigations and enforcement actions may be pursued in the same manner as is done with regulations and orders of the Board under the provisions of this chapter.

B. The Board by regulation may prescribe and provide for the payment and collection of annual permit program fees for air pollution sources. Annual permit program fees shall not be collected until (i) the federal Environmental Protection Agency approves the Board's operating permit program established pursuant to Title V of the federal Clean Air Act or (ii) the Governor determines that such fees are needed earlier to maintain primacy over the program. The annual fees shall be based on the actual emissions (as calculated or estimated) of each regulated pollutant, as defined in § 502 of the federal Clean Air Act, in tons per year, not to exceed 4,000 tons per year of each pollutant for each source. The annual permit program fees shall not exceed a base year amount of $25 per ton using 1990 as the base year, and shall be adjusted annually by the Consumer Price Index as described in § 502 of the federal Clean Air Act. Permit program fees for air pollution sources who receive state operating permits in lieu of Title V operating permits shall be paid in the first year and thereafter shall be paid biennially. The fees shall approximate the direct and indirect costs of administering and enforcing the permit program, and of administering the small business stationary source technical and environmental compliance assistance program as required by the federal Clean Air Act. The Board shall also collect permit application fee amounts not to exceed $30,000 from applicants for a permit for a new major stationary source. The permit application fee amount paid shall be credited towards the amount of annual fees owed pursuant to this section during the first two years of the source's operation. The fees shall be exempt from statewide indirect costs charged and collected by the Department of Accounts.

C. When adopting regulations for permit program fees for air pollution sources, the Board shall take into account the permit fees charged in neighboring states and the importance of not placing existing or prospective industry in the Commonwealth at a competitive disadvantage.

D. On or before January 1 of every even-numbered year, the Department shall make an evaluation of the implementation of the permit fee program and provide this evaluation in writing to the Senate Committee on Agriculture, Conservation and Natural Resources, the Senate Committee on Finance, the House Committee on Appropriations, the House Committee on Agriculture, Chesapeake and Natural Resources, and the House Committee on Finance. This evaluation shall include a report on the total fees collected, the amount of general funds allocated to the Department, the Department's use of the fees and the general funds, the number of permit applications received, the number of permits issued, the progress in eliminating permit backlogs, and the timeliness of permit processing.

E. To the extent allowed by federal law and regulations, priority for utilization of permit fees shall be given to cover the costs of processing permit applications in order to more efficiently issue permits.

F. Fees collected pursuant to this section shall not supplant or reduce in any way the general fund appropriation to the Department.

G. The permit fees shall apply to permit programs in existence on July 1, 1992, any additional permit programs that may be required by the federal government and administered by the Board, or any new permit program required by the Code of Virginia.

H. The permit program fee regulations promulgated pursuant to this section shall not become effective until July 1, 1993.

I. [Expired.] (1978, c. 818, § 10-17.30:1; 1988, c. 891; 1992, c. 488; 1993, c. 711; 1994, c. 227; 1995, c. 158; 2004, cc. 249, 324; 2005, c. 633.)

Editor's note. — For § 502 of the federal Clean Air Act, referred to in subsection B above, see 42 U.S.C.S. § 7661a.

Acts 2004, cc. 249 and 324, cls. 3 to 7, provide:

"3. That the regulations adopted by the State Air Pollution Control Board, the Virginia Waste Management Board, and the State Water Control Board to initially implement the provisions of this act shall be exempt from Article 2 (§ 2.2-4006 et seq.) of Chapter 40 of Title 2.2 of the Code of Virginia and shall become effective upon filing with the Registrar of Regulations. Thereafter, any amendments to the fee schedule shall not be exempted from Article 2 (§ 2.2-4006 et seq.).

"4. That it is the General Assembly's intent that the Department of Environmental Quality (DEQ) shall evaluate and implement measures to improve the long-term effectiveness and efficiency of its programs in ensuring the Commonwealth's air quality, water quality and land resources are protected and to ensure the maximum value from the funding provided for the Commonwealth's environmental programs. To assist DEQ in accomplishing such goals, a management efficiency peer review shall be conducted of the Virginia Pollutant Discharge Elimination System permit programs and the air permit program implemented by the agency. The review shall evaluate (i) operational changes that would improve the efficiency and

effectiveness of the agency's operations, (ii) ways to reduce the costs of compliance, and (iii) the adequacy and appropriateness of staffing levels to meet state and federal requirements. The review shall be led by a consulting firm with expertise and previous experience in conducting similar reviews of state agencies and private firms and shall include a peer review team appointed by the Director of DEQ, consisting of individuals familiar with the permit program including, but not limited to, persons nominated by the Virginia Association of Counties, the Virginia Chemistry Council, the Virginia Manufacturers Association, the Virginia Municipal League, the Hampton Roads Planning District Commission, and the Virginia Association of Municipal Wastewater Agencies. All individuals serving on the peer review team shall have previous training and experience in preparing applications for permits issued under the Virginia Pollutant Discharge Elimination System Permit program or the air permitting program. The consulting firm shall be selected by agreement between the Director of DEQ and the peer review team members from the previously mentioned organizations and in accordance with the Virginia Procurement Act. The review shall be completed and a written report containing findings and recommendations for the implementation of any practices, procedures or other steps necessary to increase the efficiency of DEQ shall be forwarded to the members of the peer review team by September 15, 2006. The report shall include information, to the extent available, on whether or not the recommendations would change the level of environmental protection, the estimated savings to DEQ and the regulated community, and any barriers to implementation. The report and DEQ's responses and plans for implementation of such recommendations shall be forwarded to the Chairmen of the House Committee on Agriculture, Chesapeake and Natural Resources, the House Committee on Appropriations, the Senate Committee on Agriculture, Conservation and Natural Resources, and the Senate Committee on Finance by October 15, 2006.

"5. That a review of DEQ's solid waste permitting and inspection programs shall be conducted in order to ensure that those programs provide maximum efficiency consistent with protection of the environment and public health. The review shall be conducted by DEQ with the active participation of persons qualified by training and experience in the management and operation of solid waste facilities, who shall be recommended by the Virginia Waste Industries Association, the Solid Waste Association of North America and the Southwest Virginia Solid Waste Management Association. The review shall be completed and a written report containing findings and recommendations for the implementation of any practices, procedures or other steps necessary to increase the efficiency of DEQ shall be forwarded to the members of the peer review team by September 15, 2006. The report shall include information, to the extent available, on whether or not the recommendations would change the level of environmental protection, the estimated savings to DEQ and the regulated community, and any barriers to implementation. The report and DEQ's responses and plans for implementation of such recommendations shall be forwarded to the Chairmen of the House Committee on Agriculture, Chesapeake and Natural Resources, the House Committee on Appropriations, the Senate Committee on Agriculture, Conservation and Natural Resources, and the Senate Committee on Finance by October 15, 2006.

"6. That in order to accomplish the intent of the General Assembly, DEQ shall:

"a. Implement a streamlined permit application to be used for renewals of previously granted environmental permits where there has been no significant change in the permitted activity or applicable statutory or regulatory requirements during the previous permit term. Such streamlined permit renewal application shall be designed, to the extent not prohibited by federal law or regulation, to avoid the submission and duplication of information that has previously been submitted by the applicant and achieve maximum efficiency and economy for both the permittee and DEQ, and DEQ shall work with the peer review team to develop these applications with the goal of minimizing the amount of duplicate, costly work on the part of the permit renewal applicants and DEQ;

"b. Expeditiously implement electronic permitting, filing and reporting procedures so as to improve access to information, reduce the costs of compliance, and reduce costs to DEQ;

"c. Explore ways to reduce compliance costs to the permittee and reduce DEQ's oversight costs for ensuring compliance. The options to be explored shall include, but not be limited to, increased utilization of certified evaluations (i.e., by professional engineers) as a method of ensuring compliance while reducing the need for physical inspections; and

"d. Encourage efficient and effective environmental performance by deeming a facility's demonstration of a proven environmental management system, such as ISO 14001, along with a commitment to pollution prevention, annual progress reporting, and a record of sustained compliance as meeting the criteria for acceptance into DEQ's programs for environmental excellence.

"7. That if general fund revenues in excess of $500,000 per year over the Governor's submitted budget for natural resources for the 2004-2006 biennium are appropriated by the 2004 Appropriation Act and are allocated for implementation of the water permit programs, the water permit fees set forth in or established pursuant to this act shall be reduced by a pro rata basis." No appropriation over and above was made; therefore there will be no fee reduction.

The 2005 amendments. — The 2005 amendment by c. 633, in subsection D, inserted "or before" preceding "January 1," deleted "1993, and December 1" preceding "of every even-numbered year," "thereafter" preceding "the Department shall make" and made minor stylistic changes.

Law Review. — For 1994 survey of environmental law in Virginia, see 28 U. Rich. L. Rev. 1041 (1994). For 2003/2004 survey of environmental law, see 39 U. Rich. L. Rev. 203 (2004).

§ 10.1-1322.1. Air Pollution Permit Program Fund established; use of moneys. — A. Notwithstanding the provisions of § 2.2-1802, all moneys collected pursuant to §§ 10.1-1322 and 10.1-1322.2 shall be paid into the state treasury and credited to a special nonreverting fund known as the Air Pollution Permit Program Fund, which is hereby established.

B. Any moneys remaining in the Fund shall not revert to the general fund but shall remain in the Fund. Interest earned on such moneys shall remain in the Fund and be credited to it.

C. The Department of Air Pollution Control is authorized and empowered to release moneys from the Fund, on warrants issued by the State Comptroller, for the purposes of carrying out the provisions of this chapter under the direction of the Executive Director.

D. An accounting of moneys received by and distributed from the permit fund shall be kept by the Comptroller and furnished upon request to the Governor or the General Assembly. (1992, c. 488.)

§ **10.1-1322.2. Preliminary program permit fees.** — A. Prior to the adoption and implementation of a permit fee schedule as authorized under subsection B of § 10.1-1322, the owners of sources of air pollution which are registered by the Department in accordance with the regulations of the Board are assessed preliminary program permit fees on an annual basis in accordance with subsection C of this section. These fees shall be deposited in the Air Pollution Permit Program Fund established by § 10.1-1322.1. The Department shall issue annual notices of the fees to owners of registered sources on or before August 1 of each fiscal year. Each notice of a fee shall include a summary of the data on which the fee is based. Fees shall be payable thirty days after receipt of notice. Failure to make timely payment within ninety days shall be grounds to institute a collection action against the owner of the registered source by the Attorney General.

B. The provisions of this section shall be applicable to all owners in cases where the aggregate of all pollutants emitted (as calculated or estimated) by all sources owned or controlled by the same owner, or by any entity controlling, controlled by, or under common control with such owner, are greater than 500 tons per year. Any individual stationary source with actual emissions (as calculated or estimated) of less than 100 tons per year shall not be subject to a fee under subsection C of this section. Determination of the tons per year of air pollution shall be based on all actual pollutants emitted during the prior calendar year.

C. The Department shall assess preliminary program permit fees uniformly, based on the aggregate of all pollutants emitted (as calculated or estimated) during the calendar year immediately preceding the fiscal year, in an amount calculated to produce revenue totaling $3.1 million. In no instance shall a preliminary fee assessed in any calendar year exceed $100,000 per source. The establishment of a fee schedule under this subsection shall be exempt from the provisions of Article 2 (§ 2.2-4006 et seq.) of Chapter 40 of Title 2.2.

D. Notices of preliminary program permit fees shall not be issued for any fiscal year in which the fees for the operating permit program are in effect in accordance with regulations adopted pursuant to subsection B of § 10.1-1322. Should a permit program fee become due and payable during a fiscal year when the owner has paid a preliminary program permit fee, the permit program fee shall be reduced in an amount equal to the pro rata share of the preliminary program permit fee for the months remaining in the fiscal year. The pro rata share is determined by dividing the fee into twelve equal parts and multiplying that sum by the number of months remaining in the fiscal year.

E. Utilization of the fees collected pursuant to this section shall be limited to the agency's direct and indirect costs of processing permits in order to more efficiently issue permits and to prepare for and begin implementation of the federal Clean Air Act requirements. The fees shall be exempt from statewide indirect costs charged and collected by the Department of Accounts.

F. Fees collected pursuant to this section shall not supplant or reduce in any way the general fund appropriation to the Department. (1992, c. 488.)

Cross references. — As to exemptions, generally, to the Administrative Process Act, see § 2.2-4002.

§ 10.1-1322.3. Emissions trading programs; emissions credits; Board to promulgate regulations.

— In accordance with § 10.1-1308, the Board may promulgate regulations to provide for emissions trading programs to achieve and maintain the National Ambient Air Quality Standards established by the United States Environmental Protection Agency, under the federal Clean Air Act. The regulations shall create an air emissions banking and trading program for the Commonwealth, to the extent not prohibited by federal law, that results in net air emission reductions, creates an economic incentive for reducing air emissions, and allows for continued economic growth through a program of banking and trading credits or allowances. The regulations applicable to the electric power industry shall foster competition in the electric power industry, encourage construction of clean, new generating facilities, provide without charge new source set-asides of five percent for the first five plan years and two percent per year thereafter, and provide an initial allocation period of five years. In promulgating such regulations the Board shall consider, but not be limited to, the inclusion of provisions concerning (i) the definition and use of emissions reduction credits or allowances from mobile and stationary sources, (ii) the role of offsets in emissions trading, (iii) interstate or regional emissions trading, (iv) the mechanisms needed to facilitate emissions trading and banking, and (v) the role of emissions allocations in emissions trading. No regulations shall prohibit the direct trading of air emissions credits or allowances between private industries, provided such trades do not adversely impact air quality in Virginia. (1994, c. 204; 1999, c. 1022; 2001, c. 580; 2004, c. 334.)

Editor's note. — Acts 2004, c. 334, cl. 2, provides: "Nothing in this act, however, shall be construed to interfere with, apply to, or affect the auction of Virginia's allocation of nitrogen oxide pollution credits set aside for new sources of electric power generation and other facilities for the years 2004 and 2005 as authorized by Chapter 1042 of the Acts of Assembly of 2003."

Law Review. — For 2000 survey of Virginia environmental law, see 34 U. Rich. L. Rev. 799 (2000).

§ 10.1-1322.4. Permit modifications for alternative fuels or raw materials.

— Unless required by the federal government, no additional permit or permit modifications shall be required by the Board, for the use, by any source, of an alternative fuel or raw material, if the owner demonstrates to the Board that as a result of trial burns at their facility or other facilities or other sufficient data that the emissions resulting from the use of the alternative fuel or raw material supply are decreased. (1994, c. 717.)

The number of this section was assigned by the Virginia Code Commission, the number in the 1994 act having been 10.1-1322.3.

ARTICLE 2.

Small Business Technical and Environmental Compliance Assistance Program.

§ 10.1-1323. Small business stationary source technical and environmental compliance assistance program.

— A. There is hereby created within the Department a small business stationary source technical and environmental compliance assistance program to facilitate compliance by small business stationary sources with the provisions of the federal Clean Air Act. The program shall be administered by the Department.

B. Except as provided in subsections C and D of this section, any stationary source is eligible for the program that:

1. Is owned or operated by a person that employs 100 or fewer individuals;

2. Is a small business concern as defined in the federal Small Business Act;

3. Is not a major stationary source;

4. Does not emit fifty tons or more per year of any regulated pollutant; and

5. Emits less than seventy-five tons per year of all regulated pollutants.

C. Upon petition by a source owner, the Board may, after notice and opportunity for public comment, include as a small business stationary source for purposes of this section any stationary source which does not meet the criteria of subdivision B 3, B 4 or B 5 of this section but which does not emit more than 100 tons per year of all regulated pollutants.

D. The Board, in consultation with the Administrator of the United States Environmental Protection Agency and the Administrator of the United States Small Business Administration and after providing notice and opportunity for public hearing, may exclude as a small business stationary source for purposes of this article any category or subcategory of sources that the Board determines to have sufficient technical and financial capabilities to meet the requirements of the federal Clean Air Act without the application of this section. (1992, c. 303.)

§ **10.1-1324. Office of Small Business Ombudsman created.** — An Office of Small Business Ombudsman is hereby created within the Department. The Office shall be headed by an ombudsman appointed by the Executive Director. The Small Business Ombudsman shall provide direct oversight of the small business stationary source technical and environmental compliance assistance program. (1992, c. 303.)

§ **10.1-1325. Small Business Environmental Compliance Advisory Panel created; membership; terms; compensation and expenses.** — The Small Business Environmental Compliance Advisory Panel (the Panel) is hereby established as an advisory panel in the executive branch of state government. It shall be composed of seven members appointed for four years or until their successors have been appointed. Vacancies occurring other than by expiration of a term shall be filled for the unexpired term. Vacancies shall be filled in the same manner as the original appointments. Appointments shall be made in compliance with the Clean Air Act pursuant to 42 U.S.C. § 7661f, as amended, as follows:

1. Two members, who are not owners, or representatives of owners, of small business stationary sources, appointed by the Governor to represent the general public;

2. Two members appointed by the House of Delegates who are owners, or who represent owners, of small business stationary sources (one member each by the Speaker of the House of Delegates and Minority Leader of the House of Delegates);

3. Two members appointed by the Senate who are owners, or who represent owners, of small business stationary sources (one member each by the Majority and Minority Leaders of the Senate); and

4. One member appointed by the Executive Director.

Members of Panel shall receive no compensation for their service, but shall be entitled to reimbursement for all reasonable and necessary expenses incurred in the performance of their duties as provided in §§ 2.2-2813 and 2.2-2825. The costs of expenses of the members shall be paid from such funds as may be available under Subchapter V (42 U.S.C. § 7661 et seq.) of the Clean Air Act, as amended. (1992, c. 303; 2004, c. 1000.)

§ **10.1-1326. Duties of the Advisory Board.** — The Small Business Environmental Compliance Advisory Board shall:

1. Render advisory opinions concerning the effectiveness of the Small Business Stationary Source Technical and Environmental Compliance Assistance Program, difficulties encountered, and degree and severity of enforcement;

2. Make periodic reports to the General Assembly and the Administrator of the U.S. Environmental Protection Agency concerning the compliance of the State Small Business Stationary Source Technical and Environmental Compliance Assistance Program with the requirements of the federal Paperwork Reduction Act, the federal Regulatory Flexibility Act, and the federal Equal Access to Justice Act;

3. Review information for small business stationary sources to ensure that such information is understandable by the layperson; and

4. Develop and disseminate reports and advisory opinions through the Office of Small Business Ombudsman. (1992, c. 303.)

ARTICLE 3.

Air Emissions Control.

§ **10.1-1327. Definitions.** — As used in this article, unless the context requires a different meaning:

"Electric generating facility" means a facility with one or more electric generating units.

"Electric generating unit" means (i) a unit that is serving a generator with nameplate capacity of more than 25 megawatts (MW) of electricity producing electricity for sale; or (ii) a cogeneration unit serving a generator with a nameplate capacity of more than 25 MW and supplying in any calendar year more than one-third of the unit's potential electric output capacity or 219,000 MWh, whichever is greater, to any utility power distribution system for sale. For subsections A and B of § 10.1-1328, the term shall only include those units that combust any fossil fuel, and are covered by the Clean Air Interstate Rule (CAIR). For subsections C and D of § 10.1-1328, the term shall include only those units that are fueled by coal.

"Mercury" means mercury and mercury compounds in either a gaseous or particulate form.

"Ozone season" means the period May 1 through September 30 of a year. (2006, cc. 867, 920.)

Editor's note. — Acts 2006, cc. 867 and 920, in cl. 2, provide: "That the Department of Environmental Quality shall conduct a detailed assessment of mercury deposition in Virginia in order to determine whether particular circumstances exist that justify, from a health and cost and benefit perspective, requiring additional steps to be taken to control mercury emissions within Virginia. The assessment shall also include (i) an evaluation of the state of mercury control technology for coal-fired boilers, including the technical and economic feasibility of such technology and (ii) an assessment of the mercury reductions and benefits expected to be achieved by the implementation of the CAIR and CAMR regulations. The Department shall complete its preliminary assessment as soon as practicable, but not later than October 15, 2007, and shall report the final findings and recommendations made as a result of the assessment to the Chairmen of the House Committee on Agriculture, Chesapeake and Natural Resources and the Senate Committee on Agriculture, Conservation and Natural Resources as soon as practicable, but no later than October 15, 2008."

§ **10.1-1328. Emissions rates and limitations.** — A. To ensure that the Commonwealth meets the emissions budgets established by the federal Environmental Protection Agency (EPA) in its CAIR, the Board shall promulgate regulations that provide:

1. Beginning on January 1, 2009, and each year continuing through January 1, 2014, all electric generating units within the Commonwealth shall collectively be allocated allowances of 36,074 tons of nitrogen oxide (NOx) annually, and 15,994 tons of NOx during an ozone season;

2. Beginning on January 1, 2010, and each year continuing through January 1, 2014, all electric generating units within the Commonwealth shall collectively be allocated allowances of 63,478 tons of sulfur dioxide (SO_2) annually, unless a different allocation is established by the Administrator of the EPA;

3. Beginning on January 1, 2015, all electric generating units within the Commonwealth shall collectively be allocated allowances of 44,435 tons of SO_2 annually, 30,062 tons of NOx annually, and 13,328 tons of NOx during an ozone season, unless a different allocation is established for SO_2 by the Administrator of the EPA;

4. The rules shall include a 5% set-aside of NOx allowances during the first five years of the program and 2% thereafter for new sources, including renewables and energy efficiency projects; and

5. The regulation shall provide for participation in the EPA-administered cap and trade system for NOx and SO_2 to the fullest extent permitted by federal law except that the Board may prohibit electric generating facilities located within a nonattainment area in the Commonwealth from meeting their NOx and SO_2 compliance obligations through the purchase of allowances from in-state or out-of-state facilities.

B. To further protect Virginia's environment regarding control of NOx emissions from electric generating units, the owner of one or more electric generating units that are located within the Commonwealth and whose combined emissions of NOx from such units exceeded 40,000 tons in 2004 shall achieve an amount of early reductions in NOx emissions during the 2007 or 2008 annual control periods equal to the total number of allowances in the Virginia compliance supplement pool established by the EPA in the CAIR. The reductions achieved under this provision will be fully eligible for early reduction credits and allowance allocations provided from the compliance supplement pool under the early reduction credit provisions of the CAIR rule. The regulations shall include provisions for the distribution of the allowances from the Virginia compliance supplement pool established by the EPA for early reduction credits, and the state shall award the owner of electric generating units subject to this subsection NOx allowances in accordance therewith. The requirement to achieve early reductions of NOx under this subsection shall not restrict the ability to bank or sell the allowances provided to the owner under the early reduction credit provisions of the CAIR rule submitted to the EPA in the federal CAIR annual NOx trading program or restrict the ability of the use of such allowances to demonstrate compliance with the CAIR.

C. To ensure compliance with the EPA requirements regarding control of mercury emissions from electric generating units, the Board shall adopt and submit to the EPA the model Clean Air Mercury Rule (CAMR) promulgated by the EPA, including full participation by Virginia electric generating units in the EPA's national mercury trading program. This model rule shall include a set-aside of mercury allowances for new sources not to exceed 5% of the total state budget for each control period during the first five years of the program and 2% thereafter.

D. To further protect Virginia's environment regarding control of mercury emissions from electric generating units, the Board shall adopt a separate state-specific rule that shall not be submitted to the EPA. This state-specific rule shall apply to the owner of one or more electric generating units that are located within the Commonwealth and whose combined emissions of mercury from such units exceeded 200 pounds in 1999. This state-specific rule shall differ from the model CAMR only in the following respects:

1. For the owner of one or more electric generating units that are located

within the Commonwealth and whose combined emissions of mercury from such units exceeded 900 pounds in 1999, the state-specific rule shall allocate a separate set of state-only mercury allowances equal to the CAMR allocation, and such owner shall be permitted to demonstrate compliance with the state-specific rule by showing that total mercury emissions from all of its electric generating units located within the Commonwealth do not exceed the total mercury allowances allocated to those units in the aggregate, and the compliance date for Phase 2 emission limits shall be January 1, 2015.

2. The owner of one or more electric generating units that are located within the Commonwealth and whose combined emissions of mercury from those units in 1999 were less than 900 pounds and whose combined capacity within the Commonwealth is greater than or equal to 600 MW, shall be permitted to satisfy its compliance obligations under the state-specific rule through the surrender of CAMR allowances that meet the following requirements: the allowances to be used are allocated to a facility under the control of the same owner or operator or under common control by the same parent corporation; the allowances used are generated and capable of being lawfully traded under the CAMR; and the surplus allowances are generated through the installation of emission controls at a facility located a straight line distance from the border of the Commonwealth of less than or equal to 200 km.

3. The owners subject to the state-specific rule shall not be permitted to purchase allowances to demonstrate compliance with the regulations the Board adopts to implement this subsection. This prohibition does not include the transfer of credits authorized by subdivision 2.

4. Nothing in the state-specific mercury rule shall be construed to prohibit the banking, use, or selling of allowances under the CAMR, and compliance with the CAMR and the state-specific mercury rule shall be determined separately and in accordance with the terms of each rule.

E. The Board shall adopt regulations governing mercury emissions that meet, but do not exceed, the requirements and implementation timetables for (i) any coke oven batteries for which the EPA has promulgated standards under § 112(d) of the Clean Air Act, and (ii) facilities subject to review under § 112(k) of the Clean Air Act and that receive scrap metal from persons subject to § 46.2-635 of the Code of Virginia.

F. To further protect Virginia's environment, the Board shall prohibit any electric generating facility located within a nonattainment area from meeting its mercury compliance obligations through the purchase of allowances from another facility, except that such facilities shall be able to demonstrate compliance with allowances allocated to another facility that is under the control of the same owner or operator or under common control by the same parent corporation and is located within 200 km of Virginia's border. (2006, cc. 867, 920.)

CHAPTER 14.

VIRGINIA WASTE MANAGEMENT ACT.

ARTICLE 1.

General Provisions.

§ 10.1-1400. Definitions. — As used in this chapter unless the context requires a different meaning:

"Applicant" means any and all persons seeking or holding a permit required under this chapter.

"Board" means the Virginia Waste Management Board.

"Composting" means the manipulation of the natural aerobic process of decomposition of organic materials to increase the rate of decomposition.

"Department" means the Department of Environmental Quality.

"Director" means the Director of the Department of Environmental Quality.

"Disclosure statement" means a sworn statement or affirmation, in such form as may be required by the Director, which includes:

1. The full name, business address, and social security number of all key personnel;

2. The full name and business address of any entity, other than a natural person, that collects, transports, treats, stores, or disposes of solid waste or hazardous waste in which any key personnel holds an equity interest of five percent or more;

3. A description of the business experience of all key personnel listed in the disclosure statement;

4. A listing of all permits or licenses required for the collection, transportation, treatment, storage or disposal of solid waste or hazardous waste issued to or held by any key personnel within the past 10 years;

5. A listing and explanation of any notices of violation, prosecutions, administrative orders (whether by consent or otherwise), license or permit suspensions or revocations, or enforcement actions of any sort by any state, federal or local authority, within the past 10 years, which are pending or have concluded with a finding of violation or entry of a consent agreement, regarding an allegation of civil or criminal violation of any law, regulation or requirement relating to the collection, transportation, treatment, storage or

disposal of solid waste or hazardous waste by any key personnel, and an itemized list of all convictions within 10 years of key personnel of any of the following crimes punishable as felonies under the laws of the Commonwealth or the equivalent thereof under the laws of any other jurisdiction: murder; kidnapping; gambling; robbery; bribery; extortion; criminal usury; arson; burglary; theft and related crimes; forgery and fraudulent practices; fraud in the offering, sale, or purchase of securities; alteration of motor vehicle identification numbers; unlawful manufacture, purchase, use or transfer of firearms; unlawful possession or use of destructive devices or explosives; violation of the Drug Control Act, Chapter 34 (§ 54.1-3400 et seq.) of Title 54.1; racketeering; or violation of antitrust laws;

6. A listing of all agencies outside the Commonwealth which have regulatory responsibility over the applicant or have issued any environmental permit or license to the applicant within the past 10 years, in connection with the applicant's collection, transportation, treatment, storage, or disposal of solid waste or hazardous waste;

7. Any other information about the applicant and the key personnel that the Director may require that reasonably relates to the qualifications and ability of the key personnel or the applicant to lawfully and competently operate a solid waste management facility in Virginia; and

8. The full name and business address of any member of the local governing body or planning commission in which the solid waste management facility is located or proposed to be located, who holds an equity interest in the facility.

"Disposal" means the discharge, deposit, injection, dumping, spilling, leaking or placing of any solid waste into or on any land or water so that such solid waste or any constituent thereof may enter the environment or be emitted into the air or discharged into any waters, including ground waters.

"Equity" includes both legal and equitable interests.

"Federal acts" means any act of Congress providing for waste management and regulations promulgated thereunder.

"Hazardous material" means a substance or material in a form or quantity which may pose an unreasonable risk to health, safety or property when transported, and which the Secretary of Transportation of the United States has so designated by regulation or order.

"Hazardous substance" means a substance listed under United States Public Law 96-510, entitled the Comprehensive Environmental Response Compensation and Liability Act.

"Hazardous waste" means a solid waste or combination of solid waste which, because of its quantity, concentration or physical, chemical or infectious characteristics, may:

1. Cause or significantly contribute to an increase in mortality or an increase in serious irreversible or incapacitating illness; or

2. Pose a substantial present or potential hazard to human health or the environment when improperly treated, stored, transported, disposed of, or otherwise managed.

"Hazardous waste generation" means the act or process of producing hazardous waste.

"Household hazardous waste" means any waste material derived from households (including single and multiple residences, hotels, motels, bunkhouses, ranger stations, crew quarters, campgrounds, picnic grounds and day-use recreation areas) which, except for the fact that it is derived from a household, would be classified as a hazardous waste, including but not limited to, nickel, cadmium, mercuric oxide, manganese, zinc-carbon or lead batteries; solvent-based paint, paint thinner, paint strippers, or other paint solvents; any product containing trichloroethylene, toxic art supplies, used motor oil and unusable gasoline or kerosene, fluorescent or high intensity light bulbs,

ammunition, fireworks, banned pesticides, or restricted-use pesticides as defined in § 3.1-249.27. All empty household product containers and any household products in legal distribution, storage or use shall not be considered household hazardous waste.

"Key personnel" means the applicant itself and any person employed by the applicant in a managerial capacity, or empowered to make discretionary decisions, with respect to the solid waste or hazardous waste operations of the applicant in Virginia, but shall not include employees exclusively engaged in the physical or mechanical collection, transportation, treatment, storage, or disposal of solid or hazardous waste and such other employees as the Director may designate by regulation. If the applicant has not previously conducted solid waste or hazardous waste operations in Virginia, the term also includes any officer, director, partner of the applicant, or any holder of five percent or more of the equity or debt of the applicant. If any holder of five percent or more of the equity or debt of the applicant or of any key personnel is not a natural person, the term includes all key personnel of that entity, provided that where such entity is a chartered lending institution or a reporting company under the Federal Securities Exchange Act of 1934, the term does not include key personnel of such entity. Provided further that the term means the chief executive officer of any agency of the United States or of any agency or political subdivision of the Commonwealth, and all key personnel of any person, other than a natural person, that operates a landfill or other facility for the disposal, treatment or storage of nonhazardous solid waste under contract with or for one of those governmental entities.

"Manifest" means the form used for identifying the quantity, composition, origin, routing and destination of hazardous waste during its transportation from the point of generation to the point of disposal, treatment or storage of such hazardous waste.

"Mixed radioactive waste" means radioactive waste that contains a substance which renders the mixture a hazardous waste.

"Open dump" means a site on which any solid waste is placed, discharged, deposited, injected, dumped or spilled so as to create a nuisance or present a threat of a release of harmful substances into the environment or present a hazard to human health.

"Person" includes an individual, corporation, partnership, association, a governmental body, a municipal corporation or any other legal entity.

"Radioactive waste" or *"nuclear waste"* includes:

1. *"Low-level radioactive waste"* material that:

a. Is not high-level radioactive waste, spent nuclear fuel, transuranic waste, or by-product material as defined in section 11e (2) of the Atomic Energy Act of 1954 (42 U.S.C. § 2014 (e) (2)); and

b. The Nuclear Regulatory Commission, consistent with existing law, classifies as low-level radioactive waste; or

2. *"High-level radioactive waste"* which means:

a. The highly radioactive material resulting from the reprocessing of spent nuclear fuel, including liquid waste produced directly in reprocessing and any solid material derived from such liquid waste that contains fission products in sufficient concentrations; and

b. Other highly radioactive material that the Nuclear Regulatory Commission, consistent with existing law, determines by rule requires permanent isolation.

"Recycling residue" means the (i) nonmetallic substances, including but not limited to plastic, rubber, and insulation, which remain after a shredder has separated for purposes of recycling the ferrous and nonferrous metal from a motor vehicle, appliance, or other discarded metallic item and (ii) organic waste remaining after removal of metals, glass, plastics and paper which are

to be recycled as part of a resource recovery process for municipal solid waste resulting in the production of a refuse derived fuel.

"Resource conservation" means reduction of the amounts of solid waste that are generated, reduction of overall resource consumption and utilization of recovered resources.

"Resource recovery" means the recovery of material or energy from solid waste.

"Resource recovery system" means a solid waste management system which provides for collection, separation, recycling and recovery of solid wastes, including disposal of nonrecoverable waste residues.

"Sanitary landfill" means a disposal facility for solid waste so located, designed and operated that it does not pose a substantial present or potential hazard to human health or the environment, including pollution of air, land, surface water or ground water.

"Sludge" means any solid, semisolid or liquid wastes with similar characteristics and effects generated from a public, municipal, commercial or industrial wastewater treatment plant, water supply treatment plant, air pollution control facility or any other waste producing facility.

"Solid waste" means any garbage, refuse, sludge and other discarded material, including solid, liquid, semisolid or contained gaseous material, resulting from industrial, commercial, mining and agricultural operations, or community activities but does not include (i) solid or dissolved material in domestic sewage, (ii) solid or dissolved material in irrigation return flows or in industrial discharges which are sources subject to a permit from the State Water Control Board, or (iii) source, special nuclear, or by-product material as defined by the Federal Atomic Energy Act of 1954, as amended.

"Solid waste management facility" means a site used for planned treating, long term storage, or disposing of solid waste. A facility may consist of several treatment, storage, or disposal units.

"Transport" or *"transportation"* means any movement of property and any packing, loading, unloading or storage incidental thereto.

"Treatment" means any method, technique or process, including incineration or neutralization, designed to change the physical, chemical or biological character or composition of any waste to neutralize it or to render it less hazardous or nonhazardous, safer for transport, amenable to recovery or storage or reduced in volume.

"Vegetative waste" means decomposable materials generated by yard and lawn care or land-clearing activities and includes, but is not limited to, leaves, grass trimmings, and woody wastes such as shrub and tree prunings, bark, limbs, roots, and stumps.

"Waste" means any solid, hazardous or radioactive waste as defined in this section.

"Waste management" means the collection, source separation, storage, transportation, transfer, processing, treatment and disposal of waste or resource recovery.

"Yard waste" means decomposable waste materials generated by yard and lawn care and includes leaves, grass trimmings, brush, wood chips, and shrub and tree trimmings. Yard waste shall not include roots or stumps that exceed six inches in diameter. (1986, c. 492, §§ 10-264, 10-268; 1987, c. 120; 1988, cc. 117, 891; 1990, cc. 499, 781, 919; 1993, cc. 214, 215, 496; 1996, c. 236; 1997, c. 294; 2001, c. 569; 2003, c. 620.)

Cross references. — As to the Attorney General's limited authority to institute and conduct criminal prosecutions in the circuit courts of the Commonwealth, see § 2.2-511. As to the environmental laboratory certification program of the Division of Consolidated Laboratory Services, see § 2.2-1105. As to classification and punishment for felonies in the Commonwealth of Virginia generally, see § 18.2-9 et seq.

Editor's note. — For the federal Comprehensive Environmental Response Compensation and Liability Act, P.L. 96-510, referred to
in the definition of "hazardous substance"
above, see generally 42 U.S.C.S. § 9601 et seq.

Law Review. — For article discussing issues
relating to toxic substances litigation, focusing
on the Fourth Circuit, see 16 U. Rich. L. Rev.
247 (1982). For article, "Environmental Liens
and Title Insurance," see 23 U. Rich. L. Rev. 305
(1989). For article addressing significant developments in Virginia law pertaining to air quality, water quality and solid and hazardous
waste, between 1990 and 1992, see "Environ-

mental Law," 26 U. Rich. L. Rev. 729 (1992). For
an article reviewing key environmental developments at the federal and state levels during
the period from June 1996 to June 1998, see 32
U. Rich. L. Rev. 1217 (1998). For article, "Environmental Law," see 35 U. Rich. L. Rev. 601
(2001).

Research References. — Cooke and Davis,
The Law of Hazardous Waste: Management,
Cleanup, Liability, and Litigation (Matthew
Bender).

Michie's Jurisprudence. — For related
discussion, see 9A M.J. Health and Sanitation,
§ 5.

CASE NOTES

**The reception of woody waste from off-
site sources constituted the disposal of
"solid waste"** as defined in this section.
Ticonderoga Farms, Inc. v. County of Loudoun,
242 Va. 170, 409 S.E.2d 446 (1991).

**Company's composting activities consti-
tuted disposal of solid waste rather than
recycling.** — Where no one could state with
assurance how long it would take stumps to
decompose into useful compost, they would lie

on the surface of the land as solid waste discarded by developers, and at some future time,
the stumps and other waste could become an
"effective substitute for a commercial product,"
that expectation was too remote to exempt the
composting activities from solid waste regulation in the meantime. These activities were not
exempt from regulation as "recycling."
Ticonderoga Farms, Inc. v. County of Loudoun,
242 Va. 170, 409 S.E.2d 446 (1991).

§ 10.1-1401. Virginia Waste Management Board continued. — A. The
Virginia Waste Management Board is continued and shall consist of seven
Virginia residents appointed by the Governor. Notwithstanding any other
provision of this section relating to Board membership, the qualifications for
Board membership shall not be more strict than those which may be required
by federal statute or regulations of the United States Environmental Protec-
tion Agency. Upon initial appointment, three members shall be appointed for
four-year terms, two for three-year terms, and two for two-year terms.
Thereafter, all members shall be appointed for terms of four years each.
Vacancies occurring other than by expiration of a term shall be filled by the
Governor for the unexpired portion of the term.

B. The Board shall adopt rules and procedures for the conduct of its
business.

C. The Board shall elect a chairman from among its members.

D. A quorum shall consist of four members. The decision of a majority of
those present and voting shall constitute a decision of the Board; however, a
vote of the majority of the Board membership is required to constitute a final
decision on certification of site approval. Meetings may be held at any time or
place determined by the Board or upon call of the chairman or upon written
request of any two members. All members shall be notified of the time and
place of any meeting at least five days in advance of the meeting. (1986, c. 492,
§ 10-265; 1988, c. 891; 1994, c. 461.)

§ 10.1-1402. Powers and duties of the Board. — The Board shall carry
out the purposes and provisions of this chapter and compatible provisions of
federal acts and is authorized to:

1. Supervise and control waste management activities in the Commonwealth.

2. Consult, advise and coordinate with the Governor, the Secretary, the
General Assembly, and other state and federal agencies for the purpose of
implementing this chapter and the federal acts.

3. Provide technical assistance and advice concerning all aspects of waste management.

4. Develop and keep current state waste management plans and provide technical assistance, advice and other aid for the development and implementation of local and regional waste management plans.

5. Promote the development of resource conservation and resource recovery systems and provide technical assistance and advice on resource conservation, resource recovery and resource recovery systems.

6. Collect data necessary to conduct the state waste programs, including data on the identification of and amounts of waste generated, transported, stored, treated or disposed, and resource recovery.

7. Require any person who generates, collects, transports, stores or provides treatment or disposal of a hazardous waste to maintain records, manifests and reporting systems required pursuant to federal statute or regulation.

8. Designate, in accordance with criteria and listings identified under federal statute or regulation, classes, types or lists of waste that it deems to be hazardous.

9. Consult and coordinate with the heads of appropriate state and federal agencies, independent regulatory agencies and other governmental instrumentalities for the purpose of achieving maximum effectiveness and enforcement of this chapter while imposing the least burden of duplicative requirements on those persons subject to the provisions of this chapter.

10. Apply for federal funds and transmit such funds to appropriate persons.

11. Promulgate and enforce regulations, and provide for reasonable variances and exemptions necessary to carry out its powers and duties and the intent of this chapter and the federal acts, except that a description of provisions of any proposed regulation which are more restrictive than applicable federal requirements, together with the reason why the more restrictive provisions are needed, shall be provided to the standing committee of each house of the General Assembly to which matters relating to the content of the regulation are most properly referable.

12. Subject to the approval of the Governor, acquire by purchase, exercise of the right of eminent domain as provided in Chapter 2 (§ 25.1-200 et seq.) of Title 25.1, grant, gift, devise or otherwise, the fee simple title to any lands, selected in the discretion of the Board as constituting necessary and appropriate sites to be used for the management of hazardous waste as defined in this chapter, including lands adjacent to the site as the Board may deem necessary or suitable for restricted areas. In all instances the Board shall dedicate lands so acquired in perpetuity to such purposes. In its selection of a site pursuant to this subdivision, the Board shall consider the appropriateness of any state-owned property for a disposal site in accordance with the criteria for selection of a hazardous waste management site.

13. Assume responsibility for the perpetual custody and maintenance of any hazardous waste management facilities.

14. Collect, from any person operating or using a hazardous waste management facility, fees sufficient to finance such perpetual custody and maintenance due to that facility as may be necessary. All fees received by the Board pursuant to this subdivision shall be used exclusively to satisfy the responsibilities assumed by the Board for the perpetual custody and maintenance of hazardous waste management facilities.

15a. Collect, from any person operating or proposing to operate a hazardous waste treatment, storage or disposal facility or any person transporting hazardous waste, permit fees sufficient to defray only costs related to the issuance of permits as required in this chapter in accordance with Board regulations, but such fees shall not exceed costs necessary to implement this subdivision. All fees received by the Board pursuant to this subdivision shall be used exclusively for the hazardous waste management program set forth herein.

15b. Collect fees from large quantity generators of hazardous wastes.

16. Collect, from any person operating or proposing to operate a sanitary landfill or other facility for the disposal, treatment or storage of nonhazardous solid waste: (i) permit application fees sufficient to defray only costs related to the issuance, reissuance, amendment or modification of permits as required in this chapter in accordance with Board regulations, but such fees shall not exceed costs necessary to issue, reissue, amend or modify such permits and (ii) annual fees established pursuant to § 10.1-1402.1:1. All such fees received by the Board shall be used exclusively for the solid waste management program set forth herein. The Board shall establish a schedule of fees by regulation as provided in §§ 10.1-1402.1, 10.1-1402.2 and 10.1-1402.3.

17. Issue, deny, amend and revoke certification of site suitability for hazardous waste facilities in accordance with this chapter.

18. Make separate orders and regulations it deems necessary to meet any emergency to protect public health, natural resources and the environment from the release or imminent threat of release of waste.

19. Take actions to contain or clean up sites or to issue orders to require cleanup of sites where solid or hazardous waste, or other substances within the jurisdiction of the Board, have been improperly managed and to institute legal proceedings to recover the costs of the containment or clean-up activities from the responsible parties.

20. Collect, hold, manage and disburse funds received for violations of solid and hazardous waste laws and regulations or court orders pertaining thereto pursuant to subdivision 19 of this section for the purpose of responding to solid or hazardous waste incidents and clean-up of sites that have been improperly managed, including sites eligible for a joint federal and state remedial project under the federal Comprehensive Environmental Response, Compensation, and Liability Act of 1980, Public Law 96-510, as amended by the Superfund Amendments and Reauthorization Act of 1986, Public Law 99-499, and for investigations to identify parties responsible for such mismanagement.

21. Abate hazards and nuisances dangerous to public health, safety or the environment, both emergency and otherwise, created by the improper disposal, treatment, storage, transportation or management of substances within the jurisdiction of the Board.

22. Notwithstanding any other provision of law to the contrary, regulate the management of mixed radioactive waste.

23. **(Expires July 1, 2012)** Adopt regulations concerning the criteria and standards for removal of mercury switches by vehicle demolishers. (1986, cc. 492, 566, § 10-266; 1987, c. 122; 1988, cc. 117, 891; 1990, cc. 499, 919; 1991, c. 718; 1992, c. 853; 1993, c. 456; 2003, c. 940; 2004, cc. 249, 324; 2006, cc. 16, 163.)

Cross references. — As to alternate compliance methods for persons or facilities meeting the criteria for E3 or E4 facilities under § 10.1-1187.3, see § 10.1-1187.6.

Editor's note. — For federal Comprehensive Environmental Response, Compensation, and Liability Act of 1980, P.L. 96-510, as amended by the Superfund Amendments and Reauthorization Act of 1986, P.L. 99-499, referred to in subdivision 20 above, see generally 42 U.S.C.S. § 9601 et seq.

Acts 2004, cc. 249 and 324, cls. 3 to 7, provide:

"3. That the regulations adopted by the State Air Pollution Control Board, the Virginia Waste Management Board, and the State Water Control Board to initially implement the provisions of this act shall be exempt from Article 2 (§ 2.2-4006 et seq.) of Chapter 40 of Title 2.2 of the Code of Virginia and shall become effective upon filing with the Registrar of Regulations. Thereafter, any amendments to the fee schedule shall not be exempted from Article 2 (§ 2.2-4006 et seq.).

"4. That it is the General Assembly's intent that the Department of Environmental Quality (DEQ) shall evaluate and implement measures to improve the long-term effectiveness and efficiency of its programs in ensuring the Commonwealth's air quality, water quality and land resources are protected and to ensure the maximum value from the funding provided for the Commonwealth's environmental programs. To assist DEQ in accomplishing such goals, a management efficiency peer review shall be conducted of the Virginia Pollutant Discharge Elimination System permit programs and the air permit program implemented by the agency. The review shall evaluate (i) operational changes that would improve the efficiency and effectiveness of the agency's operations, (ii) ways to reduce the costs of compliance, and (iii) the adequacy and appropriateness of staffing levels to meet state and federal requirements. The review shall be led by a consulting firm with expertise and previous experience in conducting similar reviews of state agencies and private firms and shall include a peer review team appointed by the Director of DEQ, consisting of individuals familiar with the permit program including, but not limited to, persons nominated by the Virginia Association of Counties, the Virginia Chemistry Council, the Virginia Manufacturers Association, the Virginia Municipal League, the Hampton Roads Planning District Commission, and the Virginia Association of Municipal Wastewater Agencies. All individuals serving on the peer review team shall have previous training and experience in preparing applications for permits issued under the Virginia Pollutant Discharge Elimination System Permit program or the air permitting program. The consulting firm shall be selected by agreement between the Director of DEQ and the peer review team members from the previously mentioned organizations and in accordance with the Virginia Procurement Act. The review shall be completed and a written report containing findings and recommendations for the implementation of any practices, procedures or other steps necessary to increase the efficiency of DEQ shall be forwarded to the members of the peer review team by September 15, 2006. The report shall include information, to the extent available, on whether or not the recommendations would change the level of environmental protection, the estimated savings to DEQ and the regulated community, and any barriers to implementation. The report and DEQ's responses and plans for implementation of such recommendations shall be forwarded to the Chairmen of the House Committee on Agriculture, Chesapeake and Natural Resources, the House Committee on Appropriations, the Senate Committee on Agriculture, Conservation and Natural Resources, and the Senate Committee on Finance by October 15, 2006.

"5. That a review of DEQ's solid waste permitting and inspection programs shall be conducted in order to ensure that those programs provide maximum efficiency consistent with protection of the environment and public health. The review shall be conducted by DEQ with the active participation of persons qualified by training and experience in the management and operation of solid waste facilities, who shall be recommended by the Virginia Waste Industries Association, the Solid Waste Association of North America and the Southwest Virginia Solid Waste Management Association. The review shall be completed and a written report containing findings and recommendations for the implementation of any practices, procedures or other steps necessary to increase the efficiency of DEQ shall be forwarded to the members of the peer review team by September 15, 2006. The report shall include information, to the extent available, on whether or not the recommendations would change the level of environmental protection, the estimated savings to DEQ and the regulated community, and any barriers to implementation. The report and DEQ's responses and plans for implementation of such recommendations shall be forwarded to the Chairmen of the House Committee on Agriculture, Chesapeake and Natural Resources, the House Committee on Appropriations, the Senate Committee on Agriculture, Conservation and Natural Resources, and the Senate Committee on Finance by October 15, 2006.

"6. That in order to accomplish the intent of the General Assembly, DEQ shall:

"a. Implement a streamlined permit application to be used for renewals of previously granted environmental permits where there has been no significant change in the permitted activity or applicable statutory or regulatory requirements during the previous permit term. Such streamlined permit renewal application shall be designed, to the extent not prohibited by federal law or regulation, to avoid the submission and duplication of information that has previously been submitted by the applicant and achieve maximum efficiency and economy for both the permittee and DEQ, and DEQ shall work with the peer review team to develop these applications with the goal of minimizing the amount of duplicate, costly work on the part of the permit renewal applicants and DEQ;

"b. Expeditiously implement electronic permitting, filing and reporting procedures so as to improve access to information, reduce the costs of compliance, and reduce costs to DEQ;

"c. Explore ways to reduce compliance costs to the permittee and reduce DEQ's oversight costs for ensuring compliance. The options to be explored shall include, but not be limited to, increased utilization of certified evaluations (i.e., by professional engineers) as a method of ensuring compliance while reducing the need for physical inspections; and

"d. Encourage efficient and effective environmental performance by deeming a facility's demonstration of a proven environmental management system, such as ISO 14001, along with a commitment to pollution prevention, annual progress reporting, and a record of sustained compliance as meeting the criteria for acceptance into DEQ's programs for environmental excellence.

"7. That if general fund revenues in excess of $500,000 per year over the Governor's submitted budget for natural resources for the 2004-2006 biennium are appropriated by the 2004 Appropriation Act and are allocated for implementation of the water permit programs, the water permit fees set forth in or established pursuant to this act shall be reduced by a pro rata basis." No appropriation over and above was made; therefore there will be no fee reduction.

Acts 2006, cc. 16 and 163, in cl. 2 provide: "That prior to January 1, 2007, the Virginia Waste Management Board shall consult with the Commissioner of the Department of Motor Vehicles and industry representatives and issue guidelines or regulations concerning the criteria and standards for removal of mercury switches by vehicle demolishers. Removal of mercury switches shall not be required in cases where it is unreasonable, impractical, or the vehicle has been damaged in such a way as to prevent removal. The Virginia Waste Management Board shall consult with vehicle manufacturers to develop guidelines or regulations for storage, shipping, recycling, or disposal of mercury switches removed from vehicles. Manufacturers shall participate individually or as a group in providing for postremoval handling of mercury switches. Adoption of such regulations shall be exempt from the provisions of the Administrative Process Act (§ 2.2-4000 et seq. of the Code of Virginia)."

Acts 2006, cc. 16 and 163, which added subdivision 23, in cl. 3 provide: "That the provisions of this act shall expire on July 1, 2012."

The 2006 amendments. — The 2006 amendments by cc. 16 and 163, which expire July 1, 2012, are identical, and added subdivision 23.

Law Review. — For 2003/2004 survey of environmental law, see 39 U. Rich. L. Rev. 203 (2004).

§ 10.1-1402.01. Further duties of Board; localities particularly affected. — After June 30, 1994, before promulgating any regulation under consideration or granting any variance to an existing regulation, or issuing any treatment, storage, or disposal permit, except for an emergency permit, if the Board finds that there are localities particularly affected by the regulation, variance or permit, the Board shall:

1. Publish, or require the applicant to publish, a notice in a local paper of general circulation in the localities affected at least thirty days prior to the close of any public comment period. Such notice shall contain a statement of the estimated local impact of the proposed action, which at a minimum shall include information on the location and type of waste treated, stored or disposed.

2. Mail the notice to the chief elected official and chief administrative officer and planning district commission for those localities.

Written comments shall be accepted by the Board for at least fifteen days after any hearing on the regulation, variance, or permit, unless the Board votes to shorten the period.

For the purposes of this section, the term *"locality particularly affected"* means any locality which bears any identified disproportionate material environmental impact which would not be experienced by other localities. For the purposes of this section, the transportation of waste shall not constitute a material environmental impact. (1993, c. 944.)

§ 10.1-1402.1. Permit fee regulations. — Regulations promulgated by the Board which establish a permit fee assessment and collection system pursuant to subdivisions 15a, 15b and 16 of § 10.1-1402 shall be governed by the following:

1. Permit fees charged an applicant shall reflect the average time and complexity of processing a permit in each of the various categories of permits and permit actions. No fees shall be charged for minor modifications or minor amendments to such permits. For purposes of this subdivision, *"minor permit modifications"* or *"minor amendments"* means specific types of changes, defined by the Board, that are made to keep the permit current with routine changes

to the facility or its operation and that do not require extensive review. A minor permit modification or amendment does not substantially alter permit conditions, increase the size of the operation, or reduce the capacity of the facility to protect human health or the environment.

2. When promulgating regulations establishing permit fees, the Board shall take into account the permit fees charged in neighboring states and the importance of not placing existing or prospective industries in the Commonwealth at a competitive disadvantage.

3. On January 1, 1993, and January 1 of every even-numbered year thereafter, the Board shall evaluate the implementation of the permit fee program and provide this evaluation in writing to the Senate Committees on Agriculture, Conservation and Natural Resources, and Finance; and the House Committees on Appropriations, Agriculture, Chesapeake and Natural Resources, and Finance. This evaluation shall include a report on the total fees collected, the amount of general funds allocated to the Department, the Department's use of the fees and the general funds, the number of permit applications received, the number of permits issued, the progress in eliminating permit backlogs, and the timeliness of permit processing.

4. Fees collected pursuant to subdivisions 15a, 15b or 16 of § 10.1-1402 shall not supplant or reduce in any way the general fund appropriation to the Board.

5. These permit fees shall be collected in order to recover a portion of the agency's costs associated with (i) the processing of an application to issue, reissue, amend or modify permits, which the Board has authority to issue for the purpose of more efficiently and expeditiously processing and maintaining permits and (ii) the inspections necessary to assure the compliance of large quantity generators of hazardous waste. The fees shall be exempt from statewide indirect costs charged and collected by the Department of Accounts. (1992, c. 853; 2002, c. 822; 2004, cc. 249, 324.)

Editor's note. — Acts 2002, c. 822, cl. 3, as amended by Acts 2004, cc. 249 and 324, cls. 2, provide: "That the provisions of § 10.1-1402.1 shall expire on July 1, 2004." The section is set out above without the amendments made by Acts 2002, c. 822.

Acts 2004, cc. 249 and 324, cls. 3 to 7, provide: "3. That the regulations adopted by the State Air Pollution Control Board, the Virginia Waste Management Board, and the State Water Control Board to initially implement the provisions of this act shall be exempt from Article 2 (§ 2.2-4006 et seq.) of Chapter 40 of Title 2.2 of the Code of Virginia and shall become effective upon filing with the Registrar of Regulations. Thereafter, any amendments to the fee schedule shall not be exempted from Article 2 (§ 2.2-4006 et seq.).

"4. That it is the General Assembly's intent that the Department of Environmental Quality (DEQ) shall evaluate and implement measures to improve the long-term effectiveness and efficiency of its programs in ensuring the Commonwealth's air quality, water quality and land resources are protected and to ensure the maximum value from the funding provided for the Commonwealth's environmental programs. To assist DEQ in accomplishing such goals, a management efficiency peer review shall be conducted of the Virginia Pollutant Discharge Elimination System permit programs and the air permit program implemented by the agency. The review shall evaluate (i) operational changes that would improve the efficiency and effectiveness of the agency's operations, (ii) ways to reduce the costs of compliance, and (iii) the adequacy and appropriateness of staffing levels to meet state and federal requirements. The review shall be led by a consulting firm with expertise and previous experience in conducting similar reviews of state agencies and private firms and shall include a peer review team appointed by the Director of DEQ, consisting of individuals familiar with the permit program including, but not limited to, persons nominated by the Virginia Association of Counties, the Virginia Chemistry Council, the Virginia Manufacturers Association, the Virginia Municipal League, the Hampton Roads Planning District Commission, and the Virginia Association of Municipal Wastewater Agencies. All individuals serving on the peer review team shall have previous training and experience in preparing applications for permits issued under the Virginia Pollutant Discharge Elimination System Permit program or the air permitting program. The consulting firm shall be selected by agreement between the Director of DEQ and the peer review team members from the previously mentioned organizations and in accordance with the Virginia Procurement Act. The review shall be completed and a written report containing findings and recommendations for the implementation of any practices, procedures or other steps necessary to increase the efficiency of DEQ shall be forwarded to the members of the peer review team by September 15, 2006. The report shall include information, to the extent available, on whether or not the recommendations would change the level of environmental protection, the estimated savings to DEQ and the regulated community, and any barriers to implementation. The report and DEQ's responses and plans for implementation of such recommendations shall be forwarded to the Chairmen of the House Committee on Agriculture, Chesapeake and Natural Resources, the House Committee on Appropriations, the Senate Committee on Agriculture, Conservation and Natural Resources, and the Senate Committee on Finance by October 15, 2006.

"5. That a review of DEQ's solid waste permitting and inspection programs shall be conducted in order to ensure that those programs provide maximum efficiency consistent with protection of the environment and public health. The review shall be conducted by DEQ with the active participation of persons qualified by training and experience in the management and operation of solid waste facilities, who shall be recommended by the Virginia Waste Industries Association, the Solid Waste Association of North America and the Southwest Virginia Solid Waste Management Association. The review shall be completed and a written report containing findings and recommendations for the implementation of any practices, procedures or other steps necessary to increase the efficiency of DEQ shall be forwarded to the members of the peer review team by September 15, 2006. The report shall include information, to the extent available, on whether or not the recommendations would change the level of environmental protection, the estimated savings to DEQ and the regulated community, and any barriers to implementation. The report and DEQ's responses and plans for implementation of such recommendations shall be forwarded to the Chairmen of the House Committee on Agriculture, Chesapeake and Natural Resources, the House Committee on Appropriations, the Senate Committee on Agriculture, Conservation and Natural Resources, and the Senate Committee on Finance by October 15, 2006.

"6. That in order to accomplish the intent of the General Assembly, DEQ shall:

"a. Implement a streamlined permit application to be used for renewals of previously granted environmental permits where there has been no significant change in the permitted activity or applicable statutory or regulatory requirements during the previous permit term. Such streamlined permit renewal application shall be designed, to the extent not prohibited by federal law or regulation, to avoid the submission and duplication of information that has previously been submitted by the applicant and achieve maximum efficiency and economy for both the permittee and DEQ, and DEQ shall work with the peer review team to develop these applications with the goal of minimizing the amount of duplicate, costly work on the part of the permit renewal applicants and DEQ;

"b. Expeditiously implement electronic permitting, filing and reporting procedures so as to improve access to information, reduce the costs of compliance, and reduce costs to DEQ;

"c. Explore ways to reduce compliance costs to the permittee and reduce DEQ's oversight costs for ensuring compliance. The options to be explored shall include, but not be limited to, increased utilization of certified evaluations (i.e., by professional engineers) as a method of ensuring compliance while reducing the need for physical inspections; and

"d. Encourage efficient and effective environmental performance by deeming a facility's demonstration of a proven environmental management system, such as ISO 14001, along with a commitment to pollution prevention, annual progress reporting, and a record of sustained compliance as meeting the criteria for acceptance into DEQ's programs for environmental excellence.

"7. That if general fund revenues in excess of $500,000 per year over the Governor's submitted budget for natural resources for the 2004-2006 biennium are appropriated by the 2004 Appropriation Act and are allocated for implementation of the water permit programs, the water permit fees set forth in or established pursuant to this act shall be reduced by a pro rata basis." No appropriation over and above was made; therefore there will be no fee reduction.

Law Review. — For article surveying changes in environmental law in Virginia from June 2001 to June 2002, see 37 U. Rich. L. Rev. 117 (2002).

§ 10.1-1402.1:1. Annual fees for nonhazardous solid waste management facilities. — A. In addition to the permit fees assessed and collected pursuant to § 10.1-1402.1, the Board shall collect an annual fee from any person operating a sanitary landfill or other facility permitted under this chapter for the disposal, storage, or treatment of nonhazardous solid waste. The fees shall be exempt from statewide indirect cost charged and assessed by

the Department of Accounts. Annual fees shall reflect the time and complexity of inspecting and monitoring the different categories of facilities. Any annual fee that is based on volume shall be calculated using the tonnage reported by each facility pursuant to § 10.1-1413.1 for the preceding year. The annual fee shall be assessed as follows:

1. Noncaptive industrial landfills $8,000
2. Construction and demolition debris landfills $4,000
3. Sanitary landfills shall be assessed a fee based on their annual tonnage as follows:

Annual Tonnage	Base Fee	Fee per ton over base fee
Up to 10,000	$ 1,000	
10,001 to 100,000	$ 1,000	$.09
100,001 to 250,000	$10,000	$.09
250,001 to 500,000	$23,500	$.075
500,001 to 1,000,000	$42,250	$.06
1,000,001 to 1,500,000	$72,250	$.05
Over 1,500,000	$97,250	$.04

4. Incinerators and energy recovery facilities shall be assessed a fee based upon their annual tonnage as follows:

Annual Tonnage	Fee
10,000 or less	$2,000
10,001 to 50,000	$3,000
50,001 to 100,000	$4,000
100,001 or more	$5,000

5. Other types of facilities shall be assessed an annual fee as follows:

Composting	$500
Regulated medical waste	$1,000
Materials recovery	$2,000
Transfer station	$2,000
Facilities in post-closure care	$500

B. The Board shall by regulation prescribe the manner and schedule for remitting fees imposed by this section and may allow for the quarterly payment of any such fees. The payment of any annual fee amounts owed shall be deferred until January 1, 2005, if the person subject to those fees submits a written request to the Department prior to October 1, 2004. The selection of this deferred payment option shall not reduce the amount owed.

C. The regulation shall include provisions allowing the Director to waive or reduce fees assessed during a state of emergency or for waste resulting from emergency response actions.

D. The Board may promulgate regulations establishing a schedule of reduced permit fees for facilities that have established a record of compliance with the terms and requirements of their permits and shall establish criteria, by regulation, to provide for reductions in the annual fee amount assessed for facilities based upon acceptance into the Department's programs to recognize excellent environmental performance.

E. The operator of a facility owned by a private entity and subject to any fee imposed pursuant to this section shall collect such fee as a surcharge on any fee schedule established pursuant to law, ordinance, resolution or contract for solid waste processing or disposal operations at the facility. (2004, cc. 249, 324.)

Editor's note. — Acts 2004, cc. 249 and 324, cls. 3 to 7, provide:

"3. That the regulations adopted by the State Air Pollution Control Board, the Virginia Waste Management Board, and the State Wa-ter Control Board to initially implement the provisions of this act shall be exempt from Article 2 (§ 2.2-4006 et seq.) of Chapter 40 of Title 2.2 of the Code of Virginia and shall become effective upon filing with the Registrar of Regulations. Thereafter, any amendments to the fee schedule shall not be exempted from Article 2 (§ 2.2-4006 et seq.).

"4. That it is the General Assembly's intent that the Department of Environmental Quality (DEQ) shall evaluate and implement measures to improve the long-term effectiveness and efficiency of its programs in ensuring the Commonwealth's air quality, water quality and land resources are protected and to ensure the maximum value from the funding provided for the Commonwealth's environmental programs. To assist DEQ in accomplishing such goals, a management efficiency peer review shall be conducted of the Virginia Pollutant Discharge Elimination System permit programs and the air permit program implemented by the agency. The review shall evaluate (i) operational changes that would improve the efficiency and effectiveness of the agency's operations, (ii) ways to reduce the costs of compliance, and (iii) the adequacy and appropriateness of staffing levels to meet state and federal requirements. The review shall be led by a consulting firm with expertise and previous experience in conducting similar reviews of state agencies and private firms and shall include a peer review team appointed by the Director of DEQ, consisting of individuals familiar with the permit program including, but not limited to, persons nominated by the Virginia Association of Counties, the Virginia Chemistry Council, the Virginia Manufacturers Association, the Virginia Municipal League, the Hampton Roads Planning District Commission, and the Virginia Association of Municipal Wastewater Agencies. All individuals serving on the peer review team shall have previous training and experience in preparing applications for permits issued under the Virginia Pollutant Discharge Elimination System Permit program or the air permitting program. The consulting firm shall be selected by agreement between the Director of DEQ and the peer review team members from the previously mentioned organizations and in accordance with the Virginia Procurement Act. The review shall be completed and a written report containing findings and recommendations for the implementation of any practices, procedures or other steps necessary to increase the efficiency of DEQ shall be forwarded to the members of the peer review team by September 15, 2006. The report shall include information, to the extent available, on whether or not the recommendations would change the level of environmental protection, the estimated savings to DEQ and the regulated community, and any barriers to implementation. The report and DEQ's responses and plans for implementation of such recommendations shall be forwarded to the Chairmen of the House Committee on Agriculture, Chesapeake and Natural Resources, the House Committee on Appropriations, the

Senate Committee on Agriculture, Conservation and Natural Resources, and the Senate Committee on Finance by October 15, 2006.

"5. That a review of DEQ's solid waste permitting and inspection programs shall be conducted in order to ensure that those programs provide maximum efficiency consistent with protection of the environment and public health. The review shall be conducted by DEQ with the active participation of persons qualified by training and experience in the management and operation of solid waste facilities, who shall be recommended by the Virginia Waste Industries Association, the Solid Waste Association of North America and the Southwest Virginia Solid Waste Management Association. The review shall be completed and a written report containing findings and recommendations for the implementation of any practices, procedures or other steps necessary to increase the efficiency of DEQ shall be forwarded to the members of the peer review team by September 15, 2006. The report shall include information, to the extent available, on whether or not the recommendations would change the level of environmental protection, the estimated savings to DEQ and the regulated community, and any barriers to implementation. The report and DEQ's responses and plans for implementation of such recommendations shall be forwarded to the Chairmen of the House Committee on Agriculture, Chesapeake and Natural Resources, the House Committee on Appropriations, the Senate Committee on Agriculture, Conservation and Natural Resources, and the Senate Committee on Finance by October 15, 2006.

"6. That in order to accomplish the intent of the General Assembly, DEQ shall:

"a. Implement a streamlined permit application to be used for renewals of previously granted environmental permits where there has been no significant change in the permitted activity or applicable statutory or regulatory requirements during the previous permit term. Such streamlined permit renewal application shall be designed, to the extent not prohibited by federal law or regulation, to avoid the submission and duplication of information that has previously been submitted by the applicant and achieve maximum efficiency and economy for both the permittee and DEQ, and DEQ shall work with the peer review team to develop these applications with the goal of minimizing the amount of duplicate, costly work on the part of the permit renewal applicants and DEQ;

"b. Expeditiously implement electronic permitting, filing and reporting procedures so as to improve access to information, reduce the costs of compliance, and reduce costs to DEQ;

"c. Explore ways to reduce compliance costs to the permittee and reduce DEQ's oversight costs for ensuring compliance. The options to be explored shall include, but not be limited to, increased utilization of certified evaluations (i.e., by professional engineers) as a method of ensuring compliance while reducing the need for physical inspections; and

"d. Encourage efficient and effective environmental performance by deeming a facility's demonstration of a proven environmental management system, such as ISO 14001, along with a commitment to pollution prevention, annual progress reporting, and a record of sustained compliance as meeting the criteria for acceptance into DEQ's programs for environmental excellence.

"7. That if general fund revenues in excess of $500,000 per year over the Governor's submitted budget for natural resources for the 2004-2006 biennium are appropriated by the 2004 Appropriation Act and are allocated for implementation of the water permit programs, the water permit fees set forth in or established pursuant to this act shall be reduced by a pro rata basis." No appropriation over and above was made; therefore there will be no fee reduction.

§ 10.1-1402.2. Permit Program Fund established; use of moneys. —
A. There is hereby established a special, nonreverting fund in the state treasury to be known as the Virginia Waste Management Board Permit Program Fund, hereafter referred to as the Fund. Notwithstanding the provisions of § 2.2-1802, all moneys collected pursuant to subdivision 16 of § 10.1-1402 shall be paid into the state treasury to the credit of the Fund.

B. Any moneys remaining in the Fund shall not revert to the general fund but shall remain in the Fund. Interest earned on such moneys shall remain in the Fund and be credited to it.

C. The Board is authorized and empowered to release moneys from the Fund, on warrants issued by the State Comptroller, for the purposes of recovering portions of the costs of processing applications under subdivision 16 of § 10.1-1402 under the direction of the Director.

D. An accounting of moneys received by and distributed from the Fund shall be kept by the State Comptroller and furnished upon request to the Governor or the General Assembly. (1992, c. 853.)

§ 10.1-1402.3. Conformance with federal requirements. — Notwithstanding the provisions of this article, any fee system developed by the Board may be modified by regulation promulgated by the Board, as may be necessary to conform with the requirements of federal acts and any regulations promulgated thereunder. Any modification imposed under this section shall be submitted to the members of the Senate Committees on Agriculture, Conservation and Natural Resources, and Finance; and the House Committees on Appropriations, Conservation and Natural Resources, and Finance. (1992, c. 853.)

§ 10.1-1403. Advisory committees. — The Governor shall appoint such advisory committees as he may deem necessary to aid in the development of an effective waste management program. (1986, c. 492, § 10-267; 1988, c. 891.)

§ 10.1-1404. Department continued; general powers. — A. The Department of Waste Management is continued. The Department shall be headed by a Director, who shall be appointed by the Governor to serve at his pleasure for a term coincident with his own or until a successor shall be appointed and qualified.

B. In addition to the powers designated elsewhere in this chapter, the Department shall have the power to:

1. Administer the policies and regulations established by the Board pursuant to this chapter;

2. Employ such personnel as may be required to carry out the purposes of this chapter;

369

3. Make and enter into all contracts and agreements necessary or incidental to the performance of its duties and the execution of its powers under this chapter, including, but not limited to, contracts with the United States, other state agencies and governmental subdivisions of the Commonwealth; and

4. Provide upon request and without charge, technical assistance to local governing bodies regarding stockpiling of tires pursuant to its authority in this chapter to promote resource conservation and resource recovery systems. The governing body of any county, city or town may adopt an ordinance regulating the stockpiling of tires, including but not limited to, the location of such stockpiles and the number of tires to be deposited at the site. (1986, c. 492, § 10-268; 1988, c. 891.)

Cross references. — As to the creation of the Department of Environmental Quality, effective April 1, 1993, and the consolidation of the Department of Waste Management into that department, see § 10.1-1183.

§ 10.1-1405. Powers and duties of Director. — A. The Director, under the direction and control of the Secretary of Natural Resources, shall exercise such powers and perform such duties as are conferred or imposed upon him by law and shall perform any other duties required of him by the Governor or the Board.

B. In addition to the other responsibilities set forth herein, the Director shall carry out management and supervisory responsibilities in accordance with the regulations and policies of the Board. In no event shall the Director have the authority to promulgate any final regulation.

The Director shall be vested with all the authority of the Board when it is not in session, subject to such regulations as may be prescribed by the Board.

C. The Director shall serve as the liaison with the United States Department of Energy on matters concerning the siting of high-level radioactive waste repositories, pursuant to the terms of the Nuclear Waste Policy Act of 1982.

D. The Director shall obtain a criminal records check pursuant to § 19.2-389 of key personnel listed in the disclosure statement when the Director determines, in his sole discretion, that such a records check will serve the purposes of this chapter. (1986, c. 492, § 10-269; 1988, c. 891; 1990, c. 919.)

§ 10.1-1406. Exemptions from liability; expedited settlements. — A. No person shall be liable under the provisions of subdivision 19 of § 10.1-1402 for cleanup or to reimburse the Virginia Environmental Emergency Response Fund if he can establish by a preponderance of the evidence that the violation and the damages resulting therefrom were caused solely by:

1. An act of God;

2. An act of war;

3. An act or omission of a third party other than an employee or agent of the defendant, or other than one whose act or omission occurs in connection with a contractual relationship, existing directly or indirectly, with the defendant (except where the sole contractual arrangement arises from a published tariff and acceptance for carriage by a common carrier by rail), if the defendant establishes by a preponderance of the evidence that (i) he exercised due care with respect to the hazardous waste or hazardous substance concerned, taking into consideration the characteristics of such hazardous waste or hazardous substance, in light of all relevant facts and circumstances and (ii) he took precautions against foreseeable acts or omissions of any such third party and the consequences that could foreseeably result from such acts or omissions; or

4. Any combination of subdivisions 1 through 3 of this section. For purposes of this section, the term "contractual arrangement" shall have the meaning ascribed to it in 42 U.S.C. § 9601(35).

B. The Board may, consistent with programs developed under the federal acts, expedite a determination to limit the liability of innocent landowners, de minimis contributors or others who have grounds to claim limited responsibility for a containment or cleanup which may be required pursuant to this chapter. (1986, c. 566, § 10-270; 1988, cc. 627, 891; 1990, cc. 472, 919; 1991, c. 718; 1999, c. 798.)

Law Review. — For 2000 survey of Virginia environmental law, see 34 U. Rich. L. Rev. 799 (2000).

§ **10.1-1406.1. Access to abandoned waste sites.** — A. For the purposes of this section, *"abandoned waste site"* means a waste site for which (i) there has not been adequate remediation or closure as required by Chapter 14 (§ 10.1-1400 et seq.) of this title, (ii) adequate financial assurances as required by § 10.1-1410 or § 10.1-1428 are not provided, and (iii) the owner, operator, or other person responsible for the cost of cleanup or remediation under state or federal law or regulation cannot be located.

B. Any local government or agency of the Commonwealth may apply to the appropriate circuit court for access to an abandoned waste site in order to investigate contamination, to abate any hazard caused by the improper management of substances within the jurisdiction of the Board, or to remediate the site. The petition shall include (i) a demonstration that all reasonable efforts have been made to locate the owner, operator or other responsible party and (ii) a plan approved by the Director and which is consistent with applicable state and federal laws and regulations. The approval or disapproval of a plan shall not be considered a case decision as defined by § 2.2-4001.

C. Any person, local government, or agency of the Commonwealth not otherwise liable under federal or state law or regulation who performs any investigative, abatement or remediation activities pursuant to this section shall not become subject to civil enforcement or remediation action under this chapter or other applicable state laws or to private civil suits related to contamination not caused by its investigative, abatement or remediation activities.

D. This section shall not in any way limit the authority of the Board, Director, or Department otherwise created by Chapter 14 of this title. (1996, c. 547.)

§ **10.1-1406.2. Conditional exemption for coal and mineral mining overburden or solid waste.** — The provisions of this chapter shall not apply to coal or mineral mining overburden returned to the mine site or solid wastes from the extraction, beneficiation, and processing of coal or minerals that are managed in accordance with requirements promulgated by the Department of Mines, Minerals and Energy. (1999, cc. 584, 613, 947.)

Law Review. — For 2000 survey of Virginia environmental law, see 34 U. Rich. L. Rev. 799 (2000).

§ **10.1-1407:** Repealed by Acts 1988, cc. 696, 891.

§ **10.1-1407.1. Notification of local government of violation.** — Upon determining that there has been a violation of a regulation promulgated under this chapter and such violation poses an imminent threat to the health, safety or welfare of the public, the Director shall immediately notify the chief administrative officer of any potentially affected local government. Neither the Director, the Commonwealth, nor any employee of the Commonwealth shall be liable for a failure to provide, or a delay in providing, the notification required by this section. (1988, cc. 434, 891.)

ARTICLE 2.

Solid Waste Management.

§ 10.1-1408: Repealed by Acts 1988, cc. 696, 891.

§ 10.1-1408.1. Permit required; open dumps prohibited. — A. No person shall operate any sanitary landfill or other facility for the disposal, treatment or storage of nonhazardous solid waste without a permit from the Director.

B. No application for (i) a new solid waste management facility permit or (ii) application for a permit amendment or variance allowing a category 2 landfill, as defined in this section, to expand or increase in capacity shall be complete unless it contains the following:

1. Certification from the governing body of the county, city or town in which the facility is to be located that the location and operation of the facility are consistent with all applicable ordinances. The governing body shall inform the applicant and the Department of the facility's compliance or noncompliance not more than 120 days from receipt of a request from the applicant. No such certification shall be required for the application for the renewal of a permit or transfer of a permit as authorized by regulations of the Board;

2. A disclosure statement, except that the Director, upon request and in his sole discretion, and when in his judgment other information is sufficient and available, may waive the requirement for a disclosure statement for a captive industrial landfill when such a statement would not serve the purposes of this chapter;

3. If the applicant proposes to locate the facility on property not governed by any county, city or town zoning ordinance, certification from the governing body that it has held a public hearing, in accordance with the applicable provisions of § 15.2-2204, to receive public comment on the proposed facility. Such certification shall be provided to the applicant and the Department within 120 days from receipt of a request from the applicant;

4. If the applicant proposes to operate a new sanitary landfill or transfer station, a statement, including a description of the steps taken by the applicant to seek the comments of the residents of the area where the sanitary landfill or transfer station is proposed to be located, regarding the siting and operation of the proposed sanitary landfill or transfer station. The public comment steps shall be taken prior to filing with the Department the notice of intent to apply for a permit for the sanitary landfill or transfer station as required by the Department's solid waste management regulations. The public comment steps shall include publication of a public notice once a week for two consecutive weeks in a newspaper of general circulation serving the locality where the sanitary landfill or transfer station is proposed to be located and holding at least one public meeting within the locality to identify issues of concern, to facilitate communication and to establish a dialogue between the applicant and persons who may be affected by the issuance of a permit for the sanitary landfill or transfer station. The public notice shall include a statement of the applicant's intent to apply for a permit to operate the proposed sanitary landfill or transfer station, the proposed sanitary landfill or transfer station site location, the date, time and location of the public meeting the applicant will hold and the name, address and telephone number of a person employed by the

372

applicant, who can be contacted by interested persons to answer questions or receive comments on the siting and operation of the proposed sanitary landfill or transfer station. The first publication of the public notice shall be at least fourteen days prior to the public meeting date.

The provisions of this subdivision shall not apply to applicants for a permit to operate a new captive industrial landfill or a new construction-demolition-debris landfill;

5. If the applicant is a local government or public authority that proposes to operate a new municipal sanitary landfill or transfer station, a statement, including a description of the steps taken by the applicant to seek the comments of the residents of the area where the sanitary landfill or transfer station is proposed to be located, regarding the siting and operation of the proposed sanitary landfill or transfer station. The public comment steps shall be taken prior to filing with the Department the notice of intent to apply for a permit for the sanitary landfill or transfer station as required by the Department's solid waste management regulations. The public comment steps shall include the formation of a citizens' advisory group to assist the locality or public authority with the selection of a proposed site for the sanitary landfill or transfer station, publication of a public notice once a week for two consecutive weeks in a newspaper of general circulation serving the locality where the sanitary landfill or transfer station is proposed to be located, and holding at least one public meeting within the locality to identify issues of concern, to facilitate communication and to establish a dialogue between the applicant and persons who may be affected by the issuance of a permit for the sanitary landfill or transfer station. The public notice shall include a statement of the applicant's intent to apply for a permit to operate the proposed sanitary landfill or transfer station, the proposed sanitary landfill or transfer station site location, the date, time and location of the public meeting the applicant will hold and the name, address and telephone number of a person employed by the applicant, who can be contacted by interested persons to answer questions or receive comments on the siting and operation of the proposed sanitary landfill or transfer station. The first publication of the public notice shall be at least fourteen days prior to the public meeting date. For local governments that have zoning ordinances, such public comment steps as required under §§ 15.2-2204 and 15.2-2285 shall satisfy the public comment requirements for public hearings and public notice as required under this section. Any applicant which is a local government or public authority that proposes to operate a new transfer station on land where a municipal sanitary landfill is already located shall be exempt from the public comment requirements for public hearing and public notice otherwise required under this section;

6. If the application is for a new municipal solid waste landfill or for an expansion of an existing municipal solid waste landfill, a statement, signed by the applicant, guaranteeing that sufficient disposal capacity will be available in the facility to enable localities within the Commonwealth to comply with solid waste management plans developed pursuant to § 10.1-1411, and certifying that such localities will be allowed to contract for and to reserve disposal capacity in the facility. This provision shall not apply to permit applications from one or more political subdivisions for new landfills or expanded landfills that will only accept municipal solid waste generated within those political subdivisions' jurisdiction or municipal solid waste generated within other political subdivisions pursuant to an interjurisdictional agreement;

7. If the application is for a new municipal solid waste landfill or for an expansion of an existing municipal solid waste landfill, certification from the governing body of the locality in which the facility would be located that a host agreement has been reached between the applicant and the governing body unless the governing body or a public service authority of which the governing

body is a member would be the owner and operator of the landfill. The agreement shall, at a minimum, have provisions covering (i) the amount of financial compensation the applicant will provide the host locality, (ii) daily travel routes and traffic volumes, (iii) the daily disposal limit, and (iv) the anticipated service area of the facility. The host agreement shall contain a provision that the applicant will pay the full cost of at least one full-time employee of the locality whose responsibility it will be to monitor and inspect waste transportation and disposal practices in the locality. The host agreement shall also provide that the applicant shall, when requested by the host locality, split air and water samples so that the host locality may independently test the sample, with all associated costs paid for by the applicant. All such sampling results shall be provided to the Department. For purposes of this subdivision, "host agreement" means any lease, contract, agreement or land use permit entered into or issued by the locality in which the landfill is situated which includes terms or conditions governing the operation of the landfill;

8. If the application is for a locality-owned and locality-operated new municipal solid waste landfill or for an expansion of an existing such municipal solid waste landfill, information on the anticipated (i) daily travel routes and traffic volumes, (ii) daily disposal limit, and (iii) service area of the facility; and

9. If the application is for a new solid waste management facility permit or for modification of a permit to allow an existing solid waste management facility to expand or increase its capacity, the application shall include certification from the governing body for the locality in which the facility is or will be located that: (i) the proposed new facility or the expansion or increase in capacity of the existing facility is consistent with the applicable local or regional solid waste management plan developed and approved pursuant to § 10.1-1411; or (ii) the local government or solid waste management planning unit has initiated the process to revise the solid waste management plan to include the new or expanded facility. Inclusion of such certification shall be sufficient to allow processing of the permit application, up to but not including publication of the draft permit or permit amendment for public comment, but shall not bind the Director in making the determination required by subdivision D 1.

C. Notwithstanding any other provision of law:

1. Every holder of a permit issued under this article who has not earlier filed a disclosure statement shall, prior to July 1, 1991, file a disclosure statement with the Director.

2. Every applicant for a permit under this article shall file a disclosure statement with the Director, together with the permit application or prior to September 1, 1990, whichever comes later. No permit application shall be deemed incomplete for lack of a disclosure statement prior to September 1, 1990.

3. Every applicant shall update its disclosure statement quarterly to indicate any change of condition that renders any portion of the disclosure statement materially incomplete or inaccurate.

4. The Director, upon request and in his sole discretion, and when in his judgment other information is sufficient and available, may waive the requirements of this subsection for a captive industrial waste landfill when such requirements would not serve the purposes of this chapter.

D. 1. Except as provided in subdivision D 2, no permit for a new solid waste management facility nor any amendment to a permit allowing facility expansion or an increase in capacity shall be issued until the Director has determined, after an investigation and analysis of the potential human health, environmental, transportation infrastructure, and transportation safety impacts and needs and an evaluation of comments by the host local government, other local governments and interested persons, that (i) the proposed facility, expansion, or increase protects present and future human health and safety and the environment; (ii) there is a need for the additional capacity; (iii) sufficient infrastructure will exist to safely handle the waste flow; (iv) the increase is consistent with locality-imposed or state-imposed daily disposal limits; (v) the public interest will be served by the proposed facility's operation or the expansion or increase in capacity of a facility; and (vi) the proposed solid waste management facility, facility expansion, or additional capacity is consistent with regional and local solid waste management plans developed pursuant to § 10.1-1411. The Department shall hold a public hearing within the said county, city or town prior to the issuance of any such permit for the management of nonhazardous solid waste. Subdivision D 2, in lieu of this subdivision, shall apply to nonhazardous industrial solid waste management facilities owned or operated by the generator of the waste managed at the facility, and that accept only waste generated by the facility owner or operator. The Board shall have the authority to promulgate regulations to implement this subdivision.

2. No new permit for a nonhazardous industrial solid waste management facility that is owned or operated by the generator of the waste managed at the facility, and that accepts only waste generated by the facility owner or operator, shall be issued until the Director has determined, after investigation and evaluation of comments by the local government, that the proposed facility poses no substantial present or potential danger to human health or the environment. The Department shall hold a public hearing within the county, city or town where the facility is to be located prior to the issuance of any such permit for the management of nonhazardous industrial solid waste.

E. The permit shall contain such conditions or requirements as are necessary to comply with the requirements of this Code and the regulations of the Board and to protect present and future human health and the environment.

The Director may include in any permit such recordkeeping, testing and reporting requirements as are necessary to ensure that the local governing body of the county, city or town where the waste management facility is located is kept timely informed regarding the general nature and quantity of waste being disposed of at the facility. Such recordkeeping, testing and reporting requirements shall require disclosure of proprietary information only as is necessary to carry out the purposes of this chapter. At least once every ten years, the Director shall review and issue written findings on the environmental compliance history of each permittee, material changes, if any, in key personnel, and technical limitations, standards, or regulations on which the original permit was based. The time period for review of each category of permits shall be established by Board regulation. If, upon such review, the Director finds that repeated material or substantial violations of the permittee or material changes in the permittee's key personnel would make continued operation of the facility not in the best interests of human health or the environment, the Director shall amend or revoke the permit, in accordance herewith. Whenever such review is undertaken, the Director may amend the permit to include additional limitations, standards, or conditions when the technical limitations, standards, or regulations on which the original permit was based have been changed by statute or amended by regulation or when any of the conditions in subsection B of § 10.1-1409 exist. The Director may deny, revoke, or suspend any permit for any of the grounds listed under subsection A of § 10.1-1409.

F. There shall exist no right to operate a landfill or other facility for the disposal, treatment or storage of nonhazardous solid waste or hazardous waste within the Commonwealth. Permits for solid waste management facilities shall not be transferable except as authorized in regulations promulgated by the Board. The issuance of a permit shall not convey or establish any property rights or any exclusive privilege, nor shall it authorize any injury to private property or any invasion of personal rights or any infringement of federal, state, or local law or regulation.

G. No person shall dispose of solid waste in open dumps.

H. No person shall own, operate or allow to be operated on his property an open dump.

I. No person shall allow waste to be disposed of on his property without a permit. Any person who removes trees, brush, or other vegetation from land used for agricultural or forestal purposes shall not be required to obtain a permit if such material is deposited or placed on the same or other property of the same landowner from which such materials were cleared. The Board shall by regulation provide for other reasonable exemptions from permitting requirements for the disposal of trees, brush and other vegetation when such materials are removed for agricultural or forestal purposes.

When promulgating any regulation pursuant to this section, the Board shall consider the character of the land affected, the density of population, and the volume of waste to be disposed, as well as other relevant factors.

J. No permit shall be required pursuant to this section for recycling or for temporary storage incidental to recycling. As used in this subsection, "recycling" means any process whereby material which would otherwise be solid waste is used or reused, or prepared for use or reuse, as an ingredient in an industrial process to make a product, or as an effective substitute for a commercial product.

K. The Board shall provide for reasonable exemptions from the permitting requirements, both procedural and substantive, in order to encourage the development of yard waste composting facilities. To accomplish this, the Board is authorized to exempt such facilities from regulations governing the treatment of waste and to establish an expedited approval process. Agricultural operations receiving only yard waste for composting shall be exempt from permitting requirements provided that (i) the composting area is located not less than 300 feet from a property boundary, is located not less than 1,000 feet from an occupied dwelling not located on the same property as the composting area, and is not located within an area designated as a flood plain as defined in § 10.1-600; (ii) the agricultural operation has at least one acre of ground suitable to receive yard waste for each 150 cubic yards of finished compost generated; (iii) the total time for the composting process and storage of material that is being composted or has been composted shall not exceed eighteen months prior to its field application or sale as a horticultural or agricultural product; and (iv) the owner or operator of the agricultural operation notifies the Director in writing of his intent to operate a yard waste composting facility and the amount of land available for the receipt of yard waste. In addition to the requirements set forth in clauses (i) through (iv) of the preceding sentence, the owner and operator of any agricultural operation that receives more than 6,000 cubic yards of yard waste generated from property not within the control of the owner or the operator in any twelve-month period shall be exempt from permitting requirements provided (i) the owner and operator submit to the Director an annual report describing the volume and types of yard waste received by such operation for composting and (ii) the operator shall certify that the yard waste composting facility complies with local ordinances. The Director shall establish a procedure for the filing of the notices, annual reports and certificates required by this subsection and shall prescribe the forms for the annual reports and certificates. Nothing contained in this article shall prohibit the sale of composted yard waste for horticultural or agricultural use, provided that any composted yard waste sold as a commercial fertilizer with claims of specific nutrient values, promoting plant growth, or of conditioning soil shall be sold in accordance with the Virginia

Fertilizer Act (§ 3.1-106.1 et seq.). As used in this subsection, "agricultural operation" shall have the same meaning ascribed to it in subsection B of § 3.1-22.29.

The operation of a composting facility as provided in this subsection shall not relieve the owner or operator of such a facility from liability for any violation of this chapter.

L. The Board shall provide for reasonable exemptions from the permitting requirements, both procedural and substantive, in order to encourage the development of facilities for the decomposition of vegetative waste. To accomplish this, the Board shall approve an expedited approval process. As used in this subsection, the decomposition of vegetative waste means a natural aerobic or anaerobic process, active or passive, which results in the decay and chemical breakdown of the vegetative waste. Nothing in this subsection shall be construed to prohibit a city or county from exercising its existing authority to regulate such facilities by requiring, among other things, permits and proof of financial security.

M. In receiving and processing applications for permits required by this section, the Director shall assign top priority to applications which (i) agree to accept nonhazardous recycling residues and (ii) pledge to charge tipping fees for disposal of nonhazardous recycling residues which do not exceed those charged for nonhazardous municipal solid waste. Applications meeting these requirements shall be acted upon no later than six months after they are deemed complete.

N. Every solid waste management facility shall be operated in compliance with the regulations promulgated by the Board pursuant to this chapter. To the extent consistent with federal law, those facilities which were permitted prior to March 15, 1993, and upon which solid waste has been disposed of prior to October 9, 1993, may continue to receive solid waste until they have reached their vertical design capacity, provided that the facility is in compliance with the requirements for liners and leachate control in effect at the time of permit issuance, and further provided that on or before October 9, 1993, the owner or operator of the solid waste management facility submits to the Director:

1. An acknowledgement that the owner or operator is familiar with state and federal law and regulations pertaining to solid waste management facilities operating after October 9, 1993, including postclosure care, corrective action and financial responsibility requirements;

2. A statement signed by a registered professional engineer that he has reviewed the regulations established by the Department for solid waste management facilities, including the open dump criteria contained therein; that he has inspected the facility and examined the monitoring data compiled for the facility in accordance with applicable regulations; and that, on the basis of his inspection and review, he has concluded that: (i) the facility is not an open dump, (ii) the facility does not pose a substantial present or potential hazard to human health and the environment, and (iii) the leachate or residues from the facility do not pose a threat of contamination or pollution of the air, surface water or ground water in a manner constituting an open dump or resulting in a substantial present or potential hazard to human health or the environment; and

3. A statement signed by the owner or operator (i) that the facility complies with applicable financial assurance regulations and (ii) estimating when the facility will reach its vertical design capacity.

The facility may not be enlarged prematurely to avoid compliance with state or federal regulations when such enlargement is not consistent with past operating practices, the permit or modified operating practices to ensure good management.

Facilities which are authorized by this subsection to accept waste for disposal beyond the waste boundaries existing on October 9, 1993, shall be as follows:

Category 1: Nonhazardous industrial waste facilities that are located on property owned or controlled by the generator of the waste disposed of in the facility;

Category 2: Nonhazardous industrial waste facilities other than those that are located on property owned or controlled by the generator of the waste disposed of in the facility, provided that the facility accepts only industrial waste streams which the facility has lawfully accepted prior to July 1, 1995, or other nonhazardous industrial waste as approved by the Department on a case-by-case basis; and

Category 3: Facilities that accept only construction-demolition-debris waste as defined in the Board's regulations.

The Director may prohibit or restrict the disposal of waste in facilities described in this subsection which contains hazardous constituents as defined in applicable regulations which, in the opinion of the Director, would pose a substantial risk to health or the environment. Facilities described in category 3 may expand laterally beyond the waste disposal boundaries existing on October 9, 1993, provided that there is first installed, in such expanded areas, liners and leachate control systems meeting the applicable performance requirements of the Board's regulations, or a demonstration is made to the satisfaction of the Director that such facilities satisfy the applicable variance criteria in the Board's regulations.

Owners or operators of facilities which are authorized under this subsection to accept waste for disposal beyond the waste boundaries existing on October 9, 1993, shall ensure that such expanded disposal areas maintain setback distances applicable to such facilities under the Board's current regulations and local ordinances. Prior to the expansion of any facility described in category 2 or 3, the owner or operator shall provide the Director with written notice of the proposed expansion at least sixty days prior to commencement of construction. The notice shall include recent groundwater monitoring data sufficient to determine that the facility does not pose a threat of contamination of groundwater in a manner constituting an open dump or creating a substantial present or potential hazard to human health or the environment. The Director shall evaluate the data included with the notification and may advise the owner or operator of any additional requirements that may be necessary to ensure compliance with applicable laws and prevent a substantial present or potential hazard to health or the environment.

Facilities, or portions thereof, which have reached their vertical design capacity shall be closed in compliance with regulations promulgated by the Board.

Nothing in this subsection shall alter any requirement for groundwater monitoring, financial responsibility, operator certification, closure, postclosure care, operation, maintenance or corrective action imposed under state or federal law or regulation, or impair the powers of the Director pursuant to § 10.1-1409.

O. Portions of a permitted solid waste management facility used solely for the storage of household hazardous waste may store household hazardous waste for a period not to exceed one year, provided that such wastes are properly contained and are segregated to prevent mixing of incompatible wastes.

P. Any permit for a new municipal solid waste landfill, and any permit amendment authorizing expansion of an existing municipal solid waste landfill, shall incorporate conditions to require that capacity in the landfill will be available to localities within the Commonwealth that choose to contract for and reserve such capacity for disposal of such localities' solid waste in accordance with solid waste management plans developed by such localities pursuant to § 10.1-1411. This provision shall not apply to permit applications from one or more political subdivisions for new landfills or expanded landfills that will only accept municipal solid waste generated within the political subdivision or subdivisions' jurisdiction or municipal solid waste generated within other political subdivisions pursuant to an interjurisdictional agreement.

Q. No owner or operator of a municipal solid waste management facility shall accept wastes for incineration or disposal from a vehicle operating with four or more axles unless the transporter of the waste provides certification, in a form prescribed by the Board, that the waste is free of substances not authorized for acceptance at the facility.

R. No application for coverage under a permit-by-rule or for modification of coverage under a permit-by-rule shall be complete unless it contains certification from the governing body of the locality in which the facility is to be located that the facility is consistent with the solid waste management plan developed and approved in accordance with § 10.1-1411. (1988, cc. 696, 891; 1989, c. 623; 1990, cc. 360, 781, 919; 1992, c. 286; 1993, cc. 214, 469, 476, 496; 1994, c. 614; 1995, c. 442; 1996, c. 236; 1997, c. 875; 1999, cc. 580, 584, 611, 613, 947; 2000, cc. 420, 422; 2006, c. 62.)

Cross references. — As to restrictions on the operation of landfills, see § 10.1-1413.2.

Editor's note. — Acts 1988, c. 304 provides that the governing body of any county having a population of not less than 35,300 nor more than 35,600 may by ordinance regulate the depositing of debris in landfills in that county. Any such ordinance may include regulation of the tracking of mud upon highways within one-half mile of any such landfill by vehicles using the landfill.

Acts 1999, c. 611, cl. 2, and cc. 580, 584, 611, 613, and 947, cl. 3, provides: "That the amendments made by this act to § 10.1-1408.1 shall not apply to any notice of intent or application for, or the processing and issuance of, any permit or permit amendment for a solid waste management facility for which such notice of intent or application was submitted to the Department on or before November 13, 1998."

At the direction of the Virginia Code Commission, the language included in Acts 1999, cc. 580, 611, effecting subdivision D 1, cl. (iv), which read "the increase is consistent with requirements of 10.1-1408.3" was not set out.

Acts 2006, c. 478, which expires July 1, 2006, in cl. 1 provides: "§ 1. That no application for a Virginia Pollutant Discharge Elimination System permit authorizing direct or indirect discharge of stormwater runoff from a new municipal solid waste landfill into a local watershed

protection district established and designated as such by city ordinance prior to January 1, 2006, shall be considered complete unless it contains certification from the local governing body of the city in which the discharge is to take place, that the discharge is consistent with the city's ordinance establishing and designating the local watershed protection district. This section shall apply to applications for new or modified individual Virginia Pollutant Discharge Elimination System permits and for new or modified coverage under general Virginia Pollutant Discharge Elimination System permits. Nothing in this section shall apply to any municipal solid waste landfill in operation on or before January 1, 2006."

The 2006 amendments. — The 2006 amendment by c. 62 added subdivision B 9 and made related changes; inserted "proposed solid waste management facility, facility expansion, or" in clause (vi) of subdivision D 1; and added subsection R.

Law Review. — For note, "Federal and State Remedies to Clean Up Hazardous Waste Sites," see 20 U. Rich. L. Rev. 379 (1986). As to legislation on solid and hazardous waste, see 22 U. Rich. L. Rev. 587 (1988). For survey on environmental law in Virginia for 1989, see 23 U. Rich. L. Rev. 625 (1989). For 1995 survey of environmental law, see 29 U. Rich. L. Rev. 1053 (1995). For 2000 survey of Virginia environmental law, see 34 U. Rich. L. Rev. 799 (2000).

CASE NOTES

Constitutionality. — This statute's imposition of certification requirements on transporters of solid waste is unconstitutional under the dormant commerce clause in that it disproportionately burdens transporters carrying waste from outside of Virginia. Waste Mgmt. Hold-

ings, Inc. v. Gilmore, 252 F.3d 316, 2001 U.S. App. LEXIS 11573 (4th Cir. 2001), cert. denied, 535 U.S. 904, 122 S. Ct. 1203, 152 L. Ed. 2d 142 (2002).

Purpose of certification requirement. — No reasonable juror could find that the provisions of this statute requiring certain transporters of solid waste to provide certifications that the waste is free of substances not authorized for acceptance at the facility had a purpose other than to reduce the flow of municipal solid waste generated outside of Virginia into Virginia for disposal. Waste Mgmt. Holdings, Inc. v. Gilmore, 252 F.3d 316, 2001 U.S. App. LEXIS 11573 (4th Cir. 2001), cert. denied, 535 U.S. 904, 122 S. Ct. 1203, 152 L. Ed. 2d 142 (2002).

The Waste Management Act does not require a local governing body to determine whether a use is in compliance with the act's provisions. Concerned Taxpayers v. County of Brunswick, 249 Va. 320, 455 S.E.2d 712 (1995).

Land used for offices and monitoring wells not subject to permit requirements. — The use of land for offices and monitoring wells does not constitute the treatment, storage or disposal of solid waste, and since land used for those purposes does not become part of a solid waste management facility, the requirements of subdivision B 1 of this section do not apply. Aegis Waste Solutions, Inc. v. Concerned Taxpayers of Brunswick County, 261 Va. 395, 544 S.E.2d 660, 2001 Va. LEXIS 46 (2001).

Requirements for subsection D determination. — The director's determination must appear on the face of the agency record. Subsection D does not mandate that the director's determination be reduced to writing. Thus, it may be preserved as part of the Department of Environmental Quality record in a recorded or written format. Browning-Ferris Indus. of S. Atl., Inc. v. Residents Involved in Saving the Env't, Inc., 254 Va. 278, 492 S.E.2d 431 (1997).

The director's determination in subsection D must be made with a degree of particularity that demonstrates a substantive consideration of the statutory factors. A conclusional recitation of the statutory language or a statement that the director complied with the statute is insufficient to satisfy this statutory mandate. The analysis which the director employs in considering the statutory factors is a matter submitted to his discretion and expertise under the statutory scheme. Browning-Ferris Indus. of S. Atl., Inc. v. Residents Involved in Saving the Env't, Inc., 254 Va. 278, 492 S.E.2d 431 (1997).

Upholding DEQ's decision to issue permit. — The DEQ's decision to issue a permit was made in compliance with this section as the decision was made with a degree of particularity that demonstrated a substantive consideration of the statutory factors and expressed the DEQ's determination that the proposed facility posed no substantial present or potential danger to human health or the

environment. Residents Involved in Saving Env't, Inc. v. Commonwealth ex rel. Dep't of Waste Mgt., No. 3103-99-2, 2000 Va. App. LEXIS 547 (Ct. of Appeals July 25, 2000).

Failure to make explicit determination pursuant to subsection D. — Director's failure to make an explicit determination pursuant to subsection D was not harmless error under former § 9-6.14:17 (iii) [now § 2.2-4027]. That provision subjects the failure to comply with required procedures to a harmless error analysis. Here, however, the statutory compliance issue involved a substantive provision which was a prerequisite to the issuance of a permit. Thus, the director's action was not subject to harmless error review. Browning-Ferris Indus. of S. Atl., Inc. v. Residents Involved in Saving the Env't, Inc., 254 Va. 278, 492 S.E.2d 431 (1997).

Finding that facility posed no threat to human health or environment required. — The Director failed to comply with this section in issuing the permit to the company. The record showed that the Director and the Department's staff reviewed the permit application, drafted a permit, held a public hearing and received comments. However, before issuing the permit neither the Director nor the staff made a finding that the facility posed no threat to human health or the environment. Thus the issuance of the permit alone was insufficient to satisfy the statutory mandate of this section. Residents Involved in Saving Env't, Inc. v. Commonwealth, Dep't of Envtl. Quality, 22 Va. App. 532, 471 S.E.2d 796 (1996).

Failure to notify department not waiver of right to object. — County could not be deemed to have waived its right to object to the issuance of a permit for a landfill by failing to notify the Department of Waste Management within 30 days of any objections because no zoning ordinance existed at the time of required certification. Notestein v. Board of Supvrs., 240 Va. 146, 393 S.E.2d 205 (1990).

Company's composting activities constituted disposal of solid waste rather than recycling. — Where no one could state with assurance how long it would take stumps to decompose into useful compost, they would lie on the surface of the land as solid waste discarded by developers, and at some future time, the stumps and other waste could become an "effective substitute for a commercial product," that expectation was too remote to exempt the composting activities from solid waste regulation in the meantime. These activities were not exempt from regulation as "recycling." Ticonderoga Farms, Inc. v. County of Loudoun, 242 Va. 170, 409 S.E.2d 446 (1991).

Applied in Campbell v. Dep't of Forestry, 46 Va. App. 91, 616 S.E.2d 33, 2005 Va. App. LEXIS 283 (2005).

CIRCUIT COURT OPINIONS

Failure to make explicit determination pursuant to subsection D. — Where the Virginia Water Control Board issues permits which are compliant with applicable provisions of state and federal law, including water quality standards, considering § 62.1-44.15, the statute that authorizes the Board to issue such permits, there was no requirement that the Board or its Director make explicit findings that the proposed discharge caused or contributed to water control violations and that the proposed discharge was compatible with existing uses by wildlife and recreation, before issuing a water sewage discharge permit.

Crutchfield v. State Water Control Bd., 64 Va. Cir. 211, 2004 Va. Cir. LEXIS 202 (Richmond 2004).

Certifications. — Because subsection N of this section did not address "separate units" or "closed areas," the County was authorized to use a disputed area of a landfill in accordance with its solid waste certification; the Department of Environmental Quality was given the opportunity to review the County's prioritization rank. Rockbridge County v. Burnley, 68 Va. Cir. 403, 2005 Va. Cir. LEXIS 251 (Rockbridge County Aug. 17, 2005).

§ 10.1-1408.2. Certification and on-site presence of facility operator.

— A. On and after January 1, 1993, no person shall be employed as a waste management facility operator, nor shall any person represent himself as a waste management facility operator, unless such person has been licensed by the Board for Waste Management Facility Operators.

B. On and after January 1, 1993, all solid waste management facilities shall operate under the direct supervision of a waste management facility operator licensed by the Board for Waste Management Facility Operators. (1991, cc. 551, 737; 1997, c. 885.)

Editor's note. — Acts 1995, c. 737, cl. 3, provides that "the provisions of this act shall take effect July 1, 1996, or after the Director of DEQ certifies that the activities contemplated under 10.1-1408.2, as amended by this act, will not result in higher certification fees for waste management facility operators, whichever occurs later." On May 26, 1996, the Director of DEQ certified that the fees would increase. Therefore, the changes made by c. 737 for 1995 will not take effect.

§ 10.1-1408.3. Caps on levels of disposal.

— A. The amount of municipal solid waste received at any landfill authorized to accept such waste shall not exceed an average of 2,000 tons per day, or the documented average actual amount of municipal solid waste received by such landfill on a daily basis during 1998, as reported to the Department of Environmental Quality pursuant to § 10.1-1413.1, whichever is greater, unless the landfill has received approval from the Board pursuant to subsection B for a larger tonnage allotment. The "average actual amount" shall be calculated by dividing the documented 1998 volume reported pursuant to § 10.1-1413.1 by the number of days the landfill received solid waste in 1998. Municipal solid waste removed from a landfill without adequate liner and leachate collection systems and transferred to a landfill with adequate liner and leachate collection systems shall not be included in the calculation of the allowable average daily tonnage pursuant to this section. However, the removal and transfer shall be conducted pursuant to an arrangement entered into prior to January 1, 1999, to which the locality where the waste will be redeposited is a party. For purposes of determining compliance with this section, daily averages shall be calculated based on disposal over a seven-day period.

B. In considering requests for increased tonnage allotments, the Board shall consider those factors set forth in subsection D of § 10.1-1408.1 and other factors it deems appropriate to protect the health, safety and welfare of the people of Virginia and Virginia's environmental and natural resources. No request for an increased tonnage allotment shall be approved by the Board until a public hearing on the proposed increase has been held in the locality where the landfill requesting the increase is located.

C. For any landfill in operation for less than two consecutive years as of December 31, 1998, the documented average actual amount of municipal solid waste received at the landfill on a daily basis shall be based on any consecutive ninety-day period during 1998 but shall not exceed 2,400 tons per day.

D. The provisions of this section shall not be construed as allowing activities related to waste disposal that exceed those that may be found in state or local permits, regulations, ordinances, agreements, contracts or other instruments related to particular facilities or localities. (1999, cc. 580, 611.)

Law Review. — For 2000 survey of Virginia environmental law, see 34 U. Rich. L. Rev. 799 (2000).

CASE NOTES

Constitutionality. — This section, which imposes caps on the amount of waste that landfills may accept, is not a neutral statute with only incidental effects on interstate commerce, but is, rather, a protectionist measure intended to saddle those outside the state with the burden of slowing the flow of waste into Virginia landfills; due to its protectionist nature, this section is subject to the virtual per se rule of invalidity under the Commerce Clause. Hence, the court would grant preliminary injunction against enforcement, pending resolution on the merits. Waste Mgt. Holdings, Inc. v. Gilmore, 64 F. Supp. 2d 523 (E.D. Va. 1999).

This statute's imposition of a cap on the amount of solid waste a landfill may accept in a day is unconstitutional under the dormant commerce clause in that it disproportionately burdens transporters of waste from out of state without regard to the standards imposed by the states of origin regarding the materials that may be disposed of as solid waste. Waste Mgmt. Holdings, Inc. v. Gilmore, 252 F.3d 316, 2001 U.S. App. LEXIS 11573 (4th Cir. 2001), cert. denied, 535 U.S. 904, 122 S. Ct. 1203, 152 L. Ed. 2d 142 (2002).

Purpose. — No reasonable juror could find that the provisions of this statute capping the amount of solid waste a landfill could accept per day had a purpose other than to reduce the flow of municipal solid waste generated outside of Virginia into Virginia for disposal. Waste Mgmt. Holdings, Inc. v. Gilmore, 252 F.3d 316, 2001 U.S. App. LEXIS 11573 (4th Cir. 2001), cert. denied, 535 U.S. 904, 122 S. Ct. 1203, 152 L. Ed. 2d 142 (2002).

Daily caps unconstitutional under commerce clause. — This section, which caps the amount of waste landfills may receive in a single day, must be examined under strict scrutiny because it discriminates facially against out-of-state interests, and because the state plainly can not demonstrate that no adequate, nondiscriminatory alternatives exist that would protect local interests just as well as this section, the statute unconstitutionally interferes with interstate commerce in violation of the commerce clause. Waste Mgt. Holdings v. Gilmore, 87 F. Supp. 2d 536, 2000 U.S. Dist. LEXIS 1056 (E.D. Va. 2000), aff'd, in part vacated, in part, 252 F.3d 316 (4th Cir. 2001).

§ 10.1-1408.4. Landfill siting review. — A. Before granting a permit which approves site suitability for a new municipal solid waste landfill, the Director shall determine, in writing, that the site on which the landfill is to be constructed is suitable for the construction and operation of such a landfill. In making his determination, the Director shall consider and address, in addition to such others as he deems appropriate, the following factors:

1. Based on a written, site-specific report prepared by the Virginia Department of Transportation, the adequacy of transportation facilities that will be available to serve the landfill, including the impact of the landfill on local traffic volume, road congestion, and highway safety;

2. The potential impact of the proposed landfill on parks and recreational areas, public water supplies, marine resources, wetlands, historic sites, fish and wildlife, water quality, and tourism; and

3. The geologic suitability of the proposed site, including proximity to areas of seismic activity and karst topography.

The applicant shall provide such information on these factors as the Director may request.

B. In addition to such other types of locations as may be determined by the Board, no new municipal solid waste landfill shall be constructed:

1. In a 100-year flood plain;

2. In any tidal wetland or nontidal wetland contiguous to any surface water body, except in accordance with § 10.1-1408.5;

3. Within three miles upgradient of any existing surface or groundwater public water supply intake or reservoir. However, a new municipal solid waste landfill may be constructed within a closer distance but no closer than one mile from any existing surface or groundwater public water supply intake or reservoir if: (i) the proposed landfill would meet all of the other requirements of this chapter and subtitle D of the federal Resource Conservation and Recovery Act, including alternative liner systems approved in accordance with that Act; (ii) the permit requires that groundwater protection standards be established and approved by the Director prior to the receipt of waste; (iii) the permit requires installation of at least two synthetic liners under the waste disposal areas and requires leachate collection systems to be installed above and below the uppermost liner; (iv) the permit requires all groundwater monitoring wells located within the facility's boundary and between the landfill and any water supply intake to be sampled quarterly and the results reported to the Department within 15 days of the owner or operator receiving the laboratory analysis; and (v) the proposed landfill meets any other conditions deemed necessary by the Director, in consultation with the Commissioner of Health, to protect against groundwater and surface water contamination. In the Counties of Mecklenburg and Halifax, a new municipal solid waste landfill may be exempt from the provisions of this subdivision and may be constructed within a shorter distance from an existing surface or groundwater public water supply intake or reservoir if the Director determines that such distance would not be detrimental to human health and the environment;

4. In any area vulnerable to flooding resulting from dam failures;

5. Over a sinkhole or less than 100 feet above a solution cavern associated with karst topography;

6. In any park or recreational area, wildlife management area or area designated by any federal or state agency as the critical habitat of any endangered species; or

7. Over an active fault.

C. There shall be no additional exemptions granted from this section unless (i) the proponent has submitted to the Department an assessment of the potential impact to public water supplies, the need for the exemption, and the alternatives considered and (ii) the Department has made the information available for public review for at least 60 days prior to the first day of the next Regular Session of the General Assembly. (1999, cc. 584, 613, 947; 2001, c. 767; 2003, c. 834; 2005, c. 920.)

The number of this section was assigned by the Virginia Code Commission, the number in the 1999 act having been 10.1-1408.3.

The 2005 amendments. — The 2005 amendment by c. 920 added the exception at the end of subdivision B 2; divided the former provisions of subdivision B 3 into the present first and third sentences thereof, inserted the present second sentence and "exempt from the provisions of this subdivision and may be" in the third sentence, and made a related change; and added subsection C.

Law Review. — For 2000 survey of Virginia environmental law, see 34 U. Rich. L. Rev. 799 (2000).

§ **10.1-1408.5. Special provisions regarding wetlands.** — A. The Director shall not issue any solid waste permit for a new municipal solid waste landfill or the expansion of a municipal solid waste landfill that would be sited in a wetland, provided that this subsection shall not apply to subsection B or the (i) expansion of an existing municipal solid waste landfill located in a city with a population between 41,000 and 52,500 when the owner or operator of the landfill is an authority created pursuant to § 15.2-5102 that has applied for a permit under § 404 of the federal Clean Water Act prior to January 1, 1989, and the owner or operator has received a permit under § 404 of the federal Clean Water Act and § 62.1-44.15:5 of this Code, or (ii) construction of a new municipal solid waste landfill in any county with a population between 29,200 and 30,000, according to the 1990 United States Census, and provided that the municipal solid waste landfills covered under clauses (i) and (ii) have complied with all other applicable federal and state environmental laws and regulations. It is expressly understood that while the provisions of this section provide an exemption to the general siting prohibition contained herein; it is not the intent in so doing to express an opinion on whether or not the project should receive the necessary environmental and regulatory permits to proceed. For the purposes of this section, the term "expansion of a municipal solid waste landfill" shall include the siting and construction of new cells or the expansion of existing cells at the same location.

B. The Director may issue a solid waste permit for the expansion of a municipal solid waste landfill located in a wetland only if the following conditions are met: (i) the proposed landfill site is at least 100 feet from any surface water body and at least one mile from any tidal wetland; (ii) the Director determines, based upon the existing condition of the wetland system, including, but not limited to, sedimentation, toxicity, acidification, nitrification, vegetation, and proximity to existing permitted waste disposal areas, roads or other structures, that the construction or restoration of a wetland system in another location in accordance with a Virginia Water Protection Permit approved by the State Water Control Board would provide higher quality wetlands; and (iii) the permit requires a minimum two-to-one wetlands mitigation ratio. This subsection shall not apply to the exemptions provided in clauses (i) and (ii) of subsection A.

C. Ground water monitoring shall be conducted at least quarterly by the owner or operator of any existing solid waste management landfill, accepting municipal solid waste, that was constructed on a wetland, has a potential hydrologic connection to such a wetland in the event of an escape of liquids from the facility, or is within a mile of such a wetland, unless the Director determines that less frequent monitoring is necessary. This provision shall not limit the authority of the Board or the Director to require that monitoring be conducted more frequently than quarterly. If the landfill is one that accepts only ash, ground water monitoring shall be conducted semiannually, unless more frequent monitoring is required by the Board or the Director. All results shall be reported to the Department.

D. This section shall not apply to landfills which impact less than two acres of nontidal wetlands.

E. For purposes of this section, *"wetland"* means any tidal wetland or nontidal wetland contiguous to any tidal wetland or surface water body.

F. There shall be no additional exemptions granted from this section unless (i) the proponent has submitted to the Department an assessment of the potential impact to wetlands, the need for the exemption, and the alternatives considered and (ii) the Department has made the information available for public review for at least 60 days prior to the first day of the next Regular Session of the General Assembly. (1999, c. 876; 2001, c. 767; 2005, c. 920.)

The number of this section was assigned by the Virginia Code Commission, the number in the 1999 act having been 10.1-1408.3.

Editor's note. — For § 404 of the Clean Water Act, referred to in subsection A above, see 33 U.S.C.S. § 1344.

The 2005 amendments. — The 2005 amendment by c. 920 inserted "subsection B or" in the introductory clause of the first sentence of subsection A and added the last sentence thereof; redesignated former subsections B through D as present subsections C through E; added present subsections B and F; deleted "of Environmental Quality" at the end of subsec-

tion C; and substituted "two" for "1.25" in subsection D.

Law Review. — For 2000 survey of Virginia environmental law, see 34 U. Rich. L. Rev. 799 (2000).

§ 10.1-1409. Revocation or amendment of permits. — A. Any permit issued by the Director pursuant to this article may be revoked, amended or suspended on any of the following grounds or on such other grounds as may be provided by the regulations of the Board:

1. The permit holder has violated any regulation or order of the Board, any condition of a permit, any provision of this chapter, or any order of a court, where such violation results in a release of harmful substances into the environment or poses a threat of release of harmful substances into the environment or presents a hazard to human health, or the violation is representative of a pattern of serious or repeated violations which, in the opinion of the Director, demonstrate the permittee's disregard for or inability to comply with applicable laws, regulations or requirements;

2. The sanitary landfill or other facility used for disposal, storage or treatment of solid waste is maintained or operated in such a manner as to pose a substantial present or potential hazard to human health or the environment;

3. The sanitary landfill, or other facility used for the disposal, storage or treatment of solid waste, because of its location, construction or lack of protective construction or measures to prevent pollution, poses a substantial present or potential hazard to human health or the environment;

4. Leachate or residues from the sanitary landfill or other facility used for the disposal, storage or treatment of solid waste pose a substantial threat of contamination or pollution of the air, surface waters or ground water;

5. The person to whom the permit was issued abandons or ceases to operate the facility, or sells, leases or transfers the facility without properly transferring the permit in accordance with the regulations of the Board;

6. As a result of changes in key personnel, the Director finds that the requirements necessary for issuance of a permit are no longer satisfied;

7. The applicant has knowingly or willfully misrepresented or failed to disclose a material fact in applying for a permit or in his disclosure statement, or in any other report or certification required under this law or under the regulations of the Board, or has knowingly or willfully failed to notify the Director of any material change to the information in its disclosure statement; or

8. Any key personnel has been convicted of any of the following crimes punishable as felonies under the laws of the Commonwealth or the equivalent thereof under the laws of any other jurisdiction: murder; kidnapping; gambling; robbery; bribery; extortion; criminal usury; arson; burglary; theft and related crimes; forgery and fraudulent practices; fraud in the offering, sale, or purchase of securities; alteration of motor vehicle identification numbers; unlawful manufacture, purchase, use or transfer of firearms; unlawful possession or use of destructive devices or explosives; violation of the Drug Control Act, Chapter 34 (§ 54.1-3400 et seq.) of Title 54.1; racketeering; violation of antitrust laws; or has been adjudged by an administrative agency or a court of competent jurisdiction to have violated the environmental protection laws of the United States, the Commonwealth or any other state and the Director determines that such conviction or adjudication is sufficiently probative of the applicant's inability or unwillingness to operate the facility in a lawful manner, as to warrant denial, revocation, amendment or suspension of the permit.

In making such determination, the Director shall consider:

(a) The nature and details of the acts attributed to key personnel;

(b) The degree of culpability of the applicant, if any;

(c) The applicant's policy or history of discipline of key personnel for such activities;

(d) Whether the applicant has substantially complied with all rules, regulations, permits, orders and statutes applicable to the applicant's activities in Virginia;

(e) Whether the applicant has implemented formal management controls to minimize and prevent the occurrence of such violations; and

(f) Mitigation based upon demonstration of good behavior by the applicant including, without limitation, prompt payment of damages, cooperation with investigations, termination of employment or other relationship with key personnel or other persons responsible for the violations or other demonstrations of good behavior by the applicant that the Director finds relevant to its decision.

B. The Director may amend or attach conditions to a permit when:

1. There is a significant change in the manner and scope of operation which may require new or additional permit conditions or safeguards to protect the public health and environment;

2. There is found to be a possibility of pollution causing significant adverse effects on the air, land, surface water or ground water;

3. Investigation has shown the need for additional equipment, construction, procedures and testing to ensure the protection of the public health and the environment from significant adverse effects; or

4. The amendment is necessary to meet changes in applicable regulatory requirements.

C. If the Director finds that solid wastes are no longer being stored, treated or disposed at a facility in accordance with Board regulations, he may revoke the permit issued for such facility. As a condition to granting or continuing in effect a permit, he may also require the permittee to provide perpetual care and surveillance of the facility.

D. If the Director summarily suspends a permit pursuant to subdivision 18 of § 10.1-1402, the Director shall hold a conference pursuant to § 2.2-4019 within forty-eight hours to consider whether to continue the suspension pending a hearing to amend or revoke the permit, or to issue any other appropriate order. Notice of the hearing shall be delivered at the conference or sent at the time the permit is suspended. Any person whose permit is suspended by the Director shall cease activity for which the permit was issued until the permit is reinstated by the Director or by a court. (1986, c. 492, § 10-272; 1988, cc. 569, 891; 1990, c. 919.)

§ 10.1-1410. Financial responsibility for abandoned facilities; penalties.

— A. The Board shall promulgate regulations which ensure that if a facility for the disposal, transfer, or treatment of solid waste is abandoned, the costs associated with protecting the public health and safety from the consequences of such abandonment may be recovered from the person abandoning the facility. A facility that receives solid waste from a ship, barge or other vessel and is regulated under § 10.1-1454.1 shall be considered a transfer facility for the purposes of this subsection.

B. The regulations may include provisions for bonding, the creation of a trust fund to be maintained within the Department, self-insurance, other forms of commercial insurance, or such other mechanism as the Department may deem appropriate. Regulations governing the amount thereof shall take into consideration the potential for contamination and injury by the solid waste, the cost of disposal of the solid waste and the cost of restoring the facility to a safe condition. Any bonding requirements shall include a provision authorizing the use of personal bonds or other similar surety deemed sufficient to provide the protections specified in subsection A upon a finding by the Director that commercial insurance or surety bond cannot be obtained in the voluntary market due to circumstances beyond the control of the permit holder. Any commercial insurance or surety obtained in the voluntary market shall be written by an insurer licensed pursuant to Chapter 10 (§ 38.2-1000 et seq.) of Title 38.2.

C. No state governmental agency shall be required to comply with such regulations.

D. Forfeiture of any financial obligation imposed pursuant to this section shall not relieve any holder of a permit issued pursuant to the provisions of this article of any other legal obligations for the consequences of abandonment of any facility.

E. Any funds forfeited prior to July 1, 1995, pursuant to this section and the regulations of the Board shall be paid over to the county, city or town in which the abandoned facility is located. The county, city or town in which the facility is located shall expend forfeited funds as necessary to restore and maintain the facility in a safe condition.

F. Any funds forfeited on or after July 1, 1995, pursuant to this section and the regulations of the Board shall be paid over to the Director. The Director shall then expend forfeited funds as necessary solely to restore and maintain the facility in a safe condition. Nothing in this section shall require the Director to expend funds from any other source to carry out the activities contemplated under this subsection.

G. Any person who knowingly and willfully abandons a solid waste management facility without proper closure or without providing adequate financial assurance instruments for such closure shall, if such failure to close results in a significant harm or an imminent and substantial threat of significant harm to human health or the environment, be liable to the Commonwealth and any political subdivision for the costs incurred in abating, controlling, preventing, removing, or containing such harm or threat.

Any person who knowingly and willfully abandons a solid waste management facility without proper closure or without providing adequate financial assurance instruments for such closure shall, if such failure to close results in a significant harm or an imminent and substantial threat of significant harm to human health or the environment, be guilty of a Class 4 felony. (1986, c. 492, § 10-273; 1987, cc. 258, 291; 1988, c. 891; 1991, c. 702; 1993, c. 837; 1995, c. 739; 2000, cc. 137, 138.)

Cross references. — As to punishment for Class 4 felonies, see § 18.2-10.

Law Review. — For 2000 survey of Virginia environmental law, see 34 U. Rich. L. Rev. 799 (2000).

§ 10.1-1410.1. Sanitary landfill final closure plans; notification requirements.

— When any owner or operator of a sanitary landfill submits by certified mail a final closure plan in accordance with the requirements of this chapter and the regulations adopted thereunder, the Department shall within ninety days of its receipt of such plan, notify by certified mail the owner or operator of the Department's decision to approve or disapprove the final closure plan. The ninety-day period shall begin on the day the Department receives the plan by certified mail. (1988, cc. 332, 891.)

§ 10.1-1410.2. Landfill postclosure monitoring, maintenance and plans.

— A. The owner and operator of any solid waste landfill permitted under this chapter shall be responsible for ensuring that such landfill is properly closed in accordance with the Board's regulations and that the landfill is maintained and monitored after closure so as to protect human health and the environment. Maintenance and monitoring of solid waste landfills after closure shall be in accordance with the Board's regulations. At all times during the operational life of a solid waste landfill, the owner and operator shall provide to the Director satisfactory evidence of financial assurance consistent with all federal and state laws and regulations to ensure that the landfill will be:

1. Closed in accordance with the Board's regulations and the closure plan approved for the landfill; and

2. Monitored and maintained after closure, for such period of time as provided in the Board's regulations or for such additional period as the Director shall determine is necessary, in accordance with a postclosure plan approved by the Director.

B. Not less than 180 days prior to the completion of the postclosure monitoring and maintenance period as prescribed by the Board's regulations or by the Director, the owner or operator shall submit to the Director a certificate, signed by a professional engineer licensed in the Commonwealth, that postclosure monitoring and maintenance have been completed in accordance with the postclosure plan. The certificate shall be accompanied by an evaluation, prepared by a professional engineer licensed in the Commonwealth and signed by the owner or operator, assessing and evaluating the landfill's potential for harm to human health and the environment in the event that postclosure monitoring and maintenance are discontinued. If the Director determines that continued postclosure monitoring or maintenance is necessary to prevent harm to human health or the environment, he shall extend the postclosure period for such additional time as the Director deems necessary to protect human health and the environment and shall direct the owner or operator to submit a revised postclosure plan and to continue postclosure monitoring and maintenance in accordance therewith. Requirements for financial assurance as set forth in subsection A shall apply throughout such extended postclosure period. (1999, cc. 584, 613, 947.)

Law Review. — For 2000 survey of Virginia environmental law, see 34 U. Rich. L. Rev. 799 (2000).

§ 10.1-1410.3. Operating burn pits at closed landfills. — The Department shall develop policies and procedures to allow for the infrequent burning of vegetative waste at permitted landfills that have ceased accepting waste but have not been released from postclosure care requirements. The policies and procedures developed shall include measures to ensure protection of public health and the environment, including (i) limits to the amount of vegetative waste that may be burned, (ii) the types of materials that may be burned, (iii) the frequency of the burning, (iv) the length of time the burning occurs, and (v) an evaluation of other alternatives for managing the vegetative waste. Nothing in this section shall be construed to prohibit a city or locality from exercising its authority to regulate such facilities by requiring among other things, permits or approvals. (2006, c. 19.)

§ 10.1-1411. Regional and local solid waste management plans. — A. The Board is authorized to promulgate regulations specifying requirements for local and regional solid waste management plans.

To implement regional plans, the Governor may designate regional boundaries. The governing bodies of the counties, cities and towns within any region so designated shall be responsible for the development and implementation of a comprehensive regional solid waste management plan in cooperation with any planning district commission or commissions in the region. Where a county, city or town is not part of a regional plan, it shall develop and implement a local solid waste management plan in accordance with the Board's regulations. For purposes of this section, each region or locality so designated shall constitute a solid waste planning unit.

B. The Board's regulations shall include all aspects of solid waste management including waste reduction, recycling and reuse, storage, treatment, and disposal and shall require that consideration be given to the handling of all types of nonhazardous solid waste generated in the region or locality. In promulgating such regulations, the Board shall consider urban concentrations, geographic conditions, markets, transportation conditions, and other appropriate factors and shall provide for reasonable variances and exemptions thereto, as well as variances or exemptions from the minimum recycling rates specified herein when market conditions beyond the control of a county, city, town, or region make such mandatory rates unreasonable.

C. The Board's regulations shall permit the following credits, provided that the aggregate of all such credits permitted shall not exceed five percentage points of the annual municipal solid waste recycling rate achieved for each solid waste planning unit:

1. A credit of one ton for each ton of recycling residue generated in Virginia and deposited in a landfill permitted under subsection M of § 10.1-1408.1;

2. A credit of two percentage points of the minimum recycling rate mandated for the solid waste planning unit for a source reduction program that is implemented with the solid waste planning unit. The existence and operation of such a program shall be certified by the solid waste planning unit;

3. A credit of one ton for each ton of any solid waste material that is reused; and

4. A credit of one ton for each ton of any nonmunicipal solid waste material that is recycled.

D. Each solid waste planning unit shall maintain a minimum recycling rate for municipal solid waste generated within the solid waste planning unit pursuant to the following schedule:

1. Except as provided in subdivision 2, each solid waste planning unit shall maintain a minimum 25% recycling rate; or

2. Each solid waste planning unit shall maintain a minimum 15% recycling rate if it has (i) a population density rate of less than 100 persons per square mile according to the most recent United States Census, or (ii) a not seasonally adjusted civilian unemployment rate for the immediately preceding calendar year that is at least 50% greater than the state average as reported by the Virginia Employment Commission for such year.

After July 1, 2007, no permit for a new sanitary landfill, incinerator, or waste-to-energy facility, or for an expansion, increase in capacity, or increase in the intake rate of an existing sanitary landfill, incinerator, or waste-to-energy facility shall be issued until the solid waste planning unit within which the facility is located has a solid waste management plan approved by the Board in accordance with the regulations, except as provided in this subsection. Failure to attain a mandated municipal solid waste recycling rate shall not be the sole cause for the denial of any permit or permit amendment, except as provided herein for sanitary landfills, incinerators, or waste-to-energy facilities, provided that all components of the solid waste management plan for the planning unit are in compliance with the regulations. The provisions of this subsection shall not be applicable to permits or permit amendments required for the operation or regulatory compliance of any existing facility, regardless of type, nor shall it be cause for the delay of any technical or administrative review of pending amendments thereto.

If a county levies a consumer utility tax and the ordinance provides that revenues derived from such source, to the extent necessary, be used for solid waste disposal, the county may charge a town or its residents, establishments and institutions an amount not to exceed their pro rata cost, based upon population for such solid waste management if the town levies a consumer utility tax. This shall not prohibit a county from charging for disposal of industrial or commercial waste on a county-wide basis, including that originating within the corporate limits of towns. (1986, c. 492, § 10-274; 1987, c. 249; 1988, c. 891; 1989, c. 440; 1990, cc. 574, 781; 1991, c. 237; 1995, c. 216; 1997, c. 495; 2006, cc. 7, 40.)

The 2006 amendments. — The 2006 amendments by cc. 7 and 40 are nearly identical, and inserted the present subsection and subdivision designations; added the last sentence in subsection A; deleted the last two sentences of subsection B, which read: "The regulations shall permit a credit of one ton for each one ton of recycling residue generated in Virginia and deposited in a landfill permitted under subsection L of § 10.1-1408.1. The total annual credits shall not exceed one fifth of the twenty-five percent requirement"; added sub-

section C; and in subsection D, rewrote the first paragraph, added subdivisions D 1 and D 2, and rewrote the next-to-last paragraph.

Subsection D is set out in the form above at the direction of the Virginia Code Commission.

Law Review. — For survey on environmental law in Virginia for 1989, see 23 U. Rich. L. Rev. 625 (1989). For an article reviewing key environmental developments at the federal and state levels during the period from June 1996 to June 1998, see 32 U. Rich. L. Rev. 1217 (1998).

§ 10.1-1412. Contracts by counties, cities and towns. — Any county, city or town may enter into contracts for the supply of solid waste to resource recovery facilities. (1986, c. 492, § 10-275; 1988, c. 891.)

§ 10.1-1413. State aid to localities for solid waste disposal. — A. To assist localities in the collection, transportation, disposal and management of solid waste in accordance with federal and state laws, regulations and procedures, each county, city and town may receive for each fiscal year from the general fund of the state treasury sums appropriated for such purposes. The Director shall distribute such grants on a quarterly basis, in advance, in accordance with Board regulations, to those counties, cities and towns which submit applications therefor.

B. Any county, city or town applying for and receiving such funds shall utilize the funds only for the collection, transportation, disposal or management of solid waste. The Director shall cause the use and expenditure of such funds to be audited and all funds not used for the specific purposes stated herein shall be refunded to the general fund.

C. All funds granted under the provisions of this section shall be conditioned upon and subject to the satisfactory compliance by the county, city or town with applicable federal and state legislation and regulations. The Director may conduct periodic inspections to ensure satisfactory compliance. (1986, c. 492, § 10-276; 1988, c. 891.)

§ 10.1-1413.1. Waste information and assessment program. — A. The Department shall report by June 30 of each year the amount of solid waste, by weight or volume, disposed of in the Commonwealth during the preceding calendar year. The report shall identify solid waste by the following categories: (i) municipal solid waste; (ii) construction and demolition debris; (iii) incinerator ash; (iv) sludge other than sludge that is land applied in accordance with § 62.1-44.19:3; and (v) tires. For each such category the report shall include an estimate of the amount that was generated outside of the Commonwealth and the jurisdictions where such waste originated, if known. The report shall also estimate the amount of solid waste managed or disposed of by each of the following methods: (i) recycling; (ii) composting; (iii) landfilling; and (iv) incineration.

B. All permitted facilities that treat, store or dispose of solid waste shall provide the Department not more than annually, upon request, with such information in their possession as is reasonably necessary to prepare the report required by this section. At the option of the facility owner, the data collected may include an accounting of the facility's economic benefits to the locality where the facility is located including the value of disposal and recycling facilities provided to the locality at no cost or reduced cost, direct employment associated with the facility, and other economic benefits resulting from the facility during the preceding calendar year. No facility shall be required pursuant to this section to provide information that is a trade secret as defined in § 59.1-336.

C. This section shall not apply to captive waste management facilities. (1997, c. 512.)

ARTICLE 2.1.

Virginia Landfill Clean-up and Closure Fund.

§ 10.1-1413.2. Requirements for landfill closure. — The Department shall prioritize the closure of landfills that are owned by local governments or political subdivisions, or that are located in the locality and have been abandoned in violation of this chapter, and are not equipped with liner and leachate control systems meeting the requirements of the Board's regulations. The prioritization shall be based on the greatest threat to human health and the environment. The Department shall establish a schedule, after public notice and a period for public comment, based upon that prioritization requiring municipal solid waste landfills to cease accepting solid waste in, and to prepare financial closure plans for, disposal areas permitted before October 9, 1993. No municipal solid waste landfill may continue accepting waste after 2020 in any disposal area not equipped with a liner system approved by the Department pursuant to a permit issued after October 9, 1993. Notwithstanding the provisions of subsection N of § 10.1-1408.1, failure by a landfill owner or operator to comply with the schedule established by the Department shall be a violation of this chapter. The provisions of this subsection shall not apply to municipal solid waste landfills utilizing double synthetic liner systems permitted between December 21, 1988, and October 9, 1993, that are part of a post-mining land use plan approved under Chapter 19 (§ 45.1-226 et seq.) of Title 45.1. (1999, cc. 584, 613, 947; 2000, c. 308; 2002, cc. 492, 518; 2004, c. 872.)

Law Review. — For 2000 survey of Virginia environmental law, see 34 U. Rich. L. Rev. 799 (2000).

ARTICLE 3.

Litter Control and Recycling.

§ 10.1-1414. Definitions. — As used in this article, unless the context requires a different meaning:

"Advisory Board" means the Litter Control and Recycling Fund Advisory Board;

"Disposable package" or *"container"* means all packages or containers intended or used to contain solids, liquids or materials and so designated;

"Fund" means the Litter Control and Recycling Fund;

"Litter" means all waste material disposable packages or containers but not including the wastes of the primary processes of mining, logging, sawmilling, farming, or manufacturing;

"Litter bag" means a bag, sack, or durable material which is large enough to serve as a receptacle for litter inside a vehicle or watercraft which is similar in size and capacity to a state approved litter bag;

"Litter receptacle" means containers acceptable to the Department for the depositing of litter;

"Person" means any natural person, corporation, association, firm, receiver, guardian, trustee, executor, administrator, fiduciary, representative or group of individuals or entities of any kind;

"Public place" means any area that is used or held out for use by the public, whether owned or operated by public or private interests;

"Recycling" means the process of separating a given waste material from the waste stream and processing it so that it may be used again as a raw material for a product which may or may not be similar to the original product;

"Sold within the Commonwealth" or *"sales of the business within the Commonwealth"* means all sales of retailers engaged in business within the Commonwealth and in the case of manufacturers and wholesalers, sales of products for use and consumption within the Commonwealth;

"Vehicle" includes every device capable of being moved upon a public highway and in, upon, or by which any person or property may be transported upon a public highway, except devices moved by human power or used exclusively upon stationary rails or tracks; and

"Watercraft" means any boat, ship, vessel, barge, or other floating craft. (1987, c. 234, § 10-277.1; 1988, c. 891; 1995, c. 417.)

§ 10.1-1415. Litter Control Program. — The Department shall support local, regional and statewide programs to control, prevent and eliminate litter from the Commonwealth and to encourage the recycling of discarded materials to the maximum practical extent. Every department of state government and all governmental units and agencies of the Commonwealth shall cooperate with the Department in the administration and enforcement of this article.

This article is intended to add to and coordinate existing litter control removal and recycling efforts, and not to terminate existing efforts nor, except as specifically stated, to repeal or affect any state law governing or prohibiting litter or the control and disposition of waste. (1987, c. 234, § 10-277; 1988, c. 891; 1989, c. 284; 1995, c. 417.)

§ 10.1-1415.1. Labeling of plastic container products required; penalty. — A. It shall be unlawful for any person to sell, expose for sale, or distribute any plastic bottle or rigid plastic container unless the container is labeled indicating the plastic resin used to produce the container. Such label shall appear on or near the bottom of the container, be clearly visible, and consist of a number placed within three triangulated arrows and letters placed below the triangle of arrows. The triangulated arrows shall be equilateral, formed by three arrows with the apex of each point of the triangle at the midpoint of each arrow, rounded with a short radius. The pointer (arrowhead) of each arrow shall be at the midpoint of each side of the triangle with a short gap separating the pointer from the base of the adjacent arrow. The triangle, formed by three arrows curved at their midpoints, shall depict a clockwise path around the code number. The numbers and letters shall be as follows:

1. For polyethylene terepthalate, the letters "PETE" and the number 1.
2. For high density polyethylene, the letters "HDPE" and the number 2.
3. For vinyl, the letter "V" and the number 3.
4. For low density polyethylene, the letters "LDPE" and the number 4.
5. For polypropylene, the letters "PP" and the number 5.
6. For polystyrene, the letters "PS" and the number 6.
7. For any other plastic resin, the letters "OTHER" and the number 7.

B. As used in subsection A of this section:

"Container," unless otherwise specified, refers to "rigid plastic container" or "plastic bottle" as those terms are defined below.

"Plastic bottle" means a plastic container intended for single use that has a neck that is smaller than the container, accepts a screw-type, snap cap or other closure and has a capacity of sixteen fluid ounces or more but less than five gallons.

"Rigid plastic container" means any formed or molded container, other than a bottle, intended for single use, composed predominantly of plastic resin, and having a relatively inflexible finite shape or form with a capacity of eight ounces or more but less than five gallons.

C. Any person convicted of a violation of the provisions of subsection A of this section shall be punished by a fine of not more than fifty dollars. Each day of violation shall constitute a separate offense. (1990, c. 519.)

§ 10.1-1415.2. Plastic holding device prohibited. — A. On and after January 1, 1993, it shall be unlawful to sell or offer for sale beverage containers connected to each other, using rings or other devices constructed of plastic which is not degradable or recyclable.

B. For the purpose of this section:

"Beverage container" means the individual bottle, can, jar, or other sealed receptacle, in which a beverage is sold, and which is constructed of metal, glass, or plastic, or other material, or any combination of these materials. "Beverage container" does not include cups or other similar open or loosely sealed containers.

"Degradable" means decomposition by photodegradation or biodegradation within a reasonable period of time upon exposure to natural elements. (1991, c. 209.)

Michie's Jurisprudence. — For related discussion, see 9A M.J. Health and Sanitation, § 5.

§ 10.1-1416. Collection and survey of litter. — Collections and surveys of the kinds of litter that are discarded in violation of the laws of the Commonwealth shall be conducted as the need is determined by the Department, after receipt of the recommendations of the Advisory Board, or as directed by the General Assembly. The survey shall include litter found throughout the Commonwealth, including standard metropolitan statistical areas and rural and recreational areas. To the fullest extent possible, in standard metropolitan statistical areas the Department of Transportation shall make use of local litter and trash collection services through arrangements with local governing bodies and appropriate agencies, in the discharge of the duties imposed by this section. The Department of Transportation shall report to the Governor, the General Assembly and the Department as to the amount of litter collected pursuant to this section and shall include in its report an analysis of litter types, their weights and volumes, and, where practicable, the recyclability of the types of products, packages, wrappings and containers which compose the principal amounts of the litter collected. The products whose packages, wrappings and containers constitute the litter shall include, but not be limited to the following categories:

1. Food for human or pet consumption;
2. Groceries;
3. Cigarettes and tobacco products;
4. Soft drinks and carbonated waters;
5. Beer and other malt beverages;

6. Wine;
7. Newspapers and magazines;
8. Paper products and household paper;
9. Glass containers;
10. Metal containers;
11. Plastic or fiber containers made of synthetic material;
12. Cleaning agents and toiletries;
13. Nondrug drugstore sundry products;
14. Distilled spirits; and
15. Motor vehicle parts. (1987, c. 234, § 10-277.3; 1988, c. 891; 1995, c. 417.)

§ **10.1-1417. Enforcement of article.** — The Department shall have the authority to contract with other state and local governmental agencies having law-enforcement powers for services and personnel reasonably necessary to carry out the provisions of this article. In addition, all law-enforcement officers in the Commonwealth and those employees of the Department of Game and Inland Fisheries vested with police powers shall enforce the provisions of this article and regulations adopted hereunder, and are hereby empowered to arrest without warrant, persons violating any provision of this article or any regulations adopted hereunder. The foregoing enforcement officers may serve and execute all warrants and other process issued by the courts in enforcing the provisions of this article and regulations adopted hereunder. (1987, c. 234, § 10-277.4; 1988, c. 891.)

§ **10.1-1418. Penalty for violation of article.** — Every person convicted of a violation of this article for which no penalty is specifically provided shall be punished by a fine of not more than fifty dollars for each such violation. (1987, c. 234, § 10-277.5; 1988, c. 891.)

§ **10.1-1418.1. Improper disposal of solid waste; civil penalties.** — A. It shall be the duty of all persons to dispose of their solid waste in a legal manner.

B. Any owner of real estate in this Commonwealth, including the Commonwealth or any political subdivision thereof, upon whose property a person improperly disposes of solid waste without the landowner's permission, shall be entitled to bring a civil action for such improper disposal of solid waste. When litter is improperly disposed upon land owned by the Commonwealth, any resident of the Commonwealth shall have standing to bring a civil action for such improper disposal of solid waste. When litter is improperly disposed of upon land owned by any political subdivision of this Commonwealth, any resident of that political subdivision shall have standing to bring a civil action for such improper disposal of solid waste. When any person improperly disposes of solid waste upon land within the jurisdiction of any political subdivision, that political subdivision shall have standing to bring a civil action for such improper disposal of solid waste.

C. In any civil action brought pursuant to the provisions of this section, when the plaintiff establishes by a preponderance of the evidence that (i) the solid waste or any portion thereof had been in possession of the defendant prior to being improperly disposed of on any of the properties referred to in subsection A of this section and (ii) no permission had been given to the defendant to place the solid waste on such property, there shall be a rebuttable presumption that the defendant improperly disposed of the solid waste. When the solid waste has been ejected from a motor vehicle, the owner or operator of such motor vehicle shall in any civil action be presumed to be the person ejecting such matter. However, such presumption shall be rebuttable by competent evidence. This presumption shall not be applicable to a motor vehicle rental or leasing company that owns the vehicle.

D. Whenever a court finds that a person has improperly disposed of solid waste pursuant to the provisions of this section, the court shall assess a civil penalty of up to $5,000 against such defendant. All civil penalties assessed pursuant to this section shall be paid into the state treasury and deposited by the State Treasurer into the Virginia Environmental Emergency Response Fund pursuant to Chapter 25 (§ 10.1-2500 et seq.) of this title, except as provided in subsection E.

E. Any civil penalty assessed pursuant to this section in a civil action brought by a political subdivision shall be paid into the treasury of the political subdivision, except where the violator of this section is the political subdivision or its agent.

F. A court may award any person or political subdivision bringing suit pursuant to this section the cost of suit and reasonable attorney's fees. (1990, c. 430; 1991, c. 718; 1992, c. 27; 1997, c. 353.)

CIRCUIT COURT OPINIONS

Applicability. — While a permit may be required to move or alter a septic system, this section does not provide a private remedy. Since Virginia had no betterment statute providing a remedy for misplaced improvements, the owner had no right to maintain any portion of his septic system on his neighbor's lot, and it was not unlawful, nor did it give rise to any right of action by the owner so long as the truncation acts occurred wholly on the neighbor's lot; however, the portion of the owner's allegations intimating that the neighbor trespassed onto his property to effect the capping of the line was a viable claim. Clark v. Scheulen, 65 Va. Cir. 415, 2004 Va. Cir. LEXIS 269 (Warren County 2004).

§ 10.1-1418.2. Improper disposal of tires; exemption; penalty. —

A. For the purposes of this section:

"Convenience center" means a collection point for the temporary storage of waste tires provided for individuals who choose to transport waste tires generated on their own premises to an established centralized point, rather than directly to a disposal facility. To be classified as a convenience center, the collection point shall not receive waste tires from collection vehicles that have collected waste from more than one real property owner. A convenience center shall have a system of regularly scheduled collections and may be covered or uncovered.

"Speculatively accumulated waste tires" means any waste tires that are accumulated before being used, reused, or reclaimed or in anticipation of potential use, reuse, or reclamation. Waste tires are not being accumulated speculatively when at least 75 percent of the waste tires accumulated are being removed from the site annually.

B. It shall be unlawful for any person to store, dispose of, speculatively accumulate or otherwise place more than 100 waste tires on public or private property, without first having obtained a permit as required by § 10.1-1408.1 or in a manner inconsistent with any local ordinance. No person shall allow others to store, dispose of, speculatively accumulate or otherwise place on his property more than 100 waste tires, without first having obtained a permit as required by § 10.1-1408.1.

C. Any person who knowingly violates any provision of this section shall be guilty of a Class 1 misdemeanor. However, any person who knowingly violates any provision of this section and such violation involves 500 or more waste tires shall be guilty of a Class 6 felony.

D. Salvage yards licensed by the Department of Motor Vehicles shall be exempt from this section, provided that they are holding fewer than 300 waste tires and that the waste tires do not pose a hazard or a nuisance or present a threat to human health and the environment.

E. As used in this section, the terms *"store"* and *"otherwise place"* shall not be construed as meaning the holding of fewer than 500 tires for bona fide uses related to the growing, harvesting or processing of agricultural or forest products.

F. The provisions of this section shall not apply to the (i) storage of less than 1,500 waste tires in a container at a convenience center or at a salvage yard licensed by the Department of Motor Vehicles, as long as the tires are not being speculatively accumulated, or (ii) storage of tires for recycling or for processing to use in manufacturing a new product, as long as the tires are not being speculatively accumulated.

G. The provisions of this section shall not apply to the storage of tires for recycling or for processing to use in manufacturing a new product, as long as the tires are not being speculatively accumulated.

H. Nothing in this section shall limit enforcement of the prohibitions against littering and the improper disposal of solid waste contained elsewhere in this chapter. (1994, c. 556; 1997, c. 353; 2003, c. 101.)

Cross references. — As to punishment for Class 6 felonies, see § 18.2-10. As to punishment for Class 1 misdemeanors, see § 18.2-11.

Law Review. — For 2003/2004 survey of environmental law, see 39 U. Rich. L. Rev. 203 (2004).

CASE NOTES

Sufficiency of the evidence. — Because defendant conceded at trial to storing more than 500 waste tires without a permit and continued to place additional waste tires on the property in violation of a consent order, the evidence was sufficient to convict defendant of violating § 10.1-1418.2. Lawless v. Commonwealth, — Va. App. —, — S.E.2d —, 2005 Va. App. LEXIS 523 (Dec. 20, 2005).

§ 10.1-1418.3. Liability for large waste tire pile fires; exclusions. —

A. For the purposes of this section:

"Tire pile" means an unpermitted accumulation of more than 100 waste tires.

B. For any tire pile that (i) is included in the survey of waste tire piles completed by the Department in 1993 or (ii) contains tires that were placed on property with the consent of the property owner, any person who owns or is legally responsible for such a tire pile that burns or is burned and any person who owns or is legally responsible for the property where the tire pile is located shall be responsible for the damage caused by the fire and by any waste or chemical constituents released into the environment to any person who sustains damage from the fire or from any released wastes or chemical constituents. It shall not be necessary for the claimant to show that the damage was caused by negligence on the part of such owners, legally responsible persons or other person who set or caused to be set the fire that burns the tires. Damages include, but are not limited to, the cost for any repair, replacement, remediation, or other appropriate action required as a result of the fire. This liability shall be in addition to, and not in lieu of, any other liability authorized by statute or regulation. Without limiting what constitutes consent, acceptance of compensation for the placement of tires on one's property shall be deemed to be consent.

C. Any person who sets or causes to be set the fire that burns the tire pile shall be responsible for the damage caused by the fire and by any waste or chemical constituents released into the environment to any person who sustains damage from the fire or from any released wastes or chemical constituents. It shall not be necessary for the claimant to show that the damage was caused by negligence on the part of such owners, legally responsible persons or other persons who set or caused to be set the fire that burns the tires. Damages shall include, but are not limited to, the cost for any repair, replacement, remediation, or other appropriate action required as a result of the fire. This liability shall be in addition to, and not in lieu of, any liability authorized by statute or regulation.

D. Any person who transfers waste tires for disposition and has taken all reasonable steps to ensure proper disposition of the waste tires shall not be held liable under the standard set forth in this section. Documentation that a person has taken all reasonable steps to ensure proper disposition of the waste tires may include, but is not limited to, utilization of the Waste Tire Certification developed by the Department and any equivalent manifest or tracking system. (1996, c. 734; 2003, c. 101.)

§ **10.1-1418.4. Removal of waste tire piles; cost recovery; right of entry.** — Notwithstanding any other provision, upon the failure of any owner or operator to remove or remediate a waste tire pile in accordance with an order issued pursuant to this chapter or § 10.1-1186, the Director may enter the property and remove the waste tires. The Director is authorized to recover from the owner of the site or the operator of the tire pile the actual and reasonable costs incurred to complete such removal or remediation. If a request for reimbursement is not paid within 30 days of the receipt of a written demand for reimbursement, the Director may refer the demand for reimbursement to the Attorney General for collection or may secure a lien in accordance with § 10.1-1418.5. (2003, c. 101.)

Editor's note. — Acts 2003, c. 101, cl. 3, provides: "That the revenue generated by this act shall be used solely for the removal and recycling of tires from waste tire piles. The Department of Environmental Quality shall report by December 1 of each year to the Chairmen of the Senate Committee on Agriculture, Conservation and Natural Resources and the House Committee on Agriculture, Chesapeake and Natural Resources on the use of these funds and the progress in cleaning up tire piles."

§ **10.1-1418.5. Lien for waste tire pile removal.** — A. The Commonwealth shall have a lien, if perfected as hereinafter provided, on land subject to removal action under § 10.1-1418.4 for the amount of the actual and reasonable costs incurred to complete such removal action.

B. The Director shall perfect the lien given under the provisions of this section by filing, within six months after completion of the removal, in the clerk's office of the court of the county or city in which the land or any part of the land is situated, a statement consisting of (i) the name of the owner of record of the property sought to be charged, (ii) an itemized account of moneys expended for the removal work, and (iii) a brief description of the property to which the lien attaches.

C. It shall be the duty of the clerk of the court in whose office the statement described in subsection B is filed to record the statement in the deed books of the office and to index the statement in the general index of deeds in the name of the Commonwealth as well as the owner of the property, and shall show the type of such lien. From the time of such recording and indexing, all persons shall be deemed to have notice thereof.

D. Liens acquired under this section shall have priority as a lien second only to the lien of real estate taxes imposed upon the land.

E. Any party having an interest in the real property against which a lien has been filed may, within 60 days of such filing, petition the court of equity having jurisdiction wherein the property or some portion of the property is located to hold a hearing to review the amount of the lien. After reasonable notice to the Director, the court shall hold a hearing to determine whether such costs were reasonable. If the court determines that such charges were excessive, it shall determine the proper amount and order that the lien and the record be amended to show the new amount.

F. Liens acquired under this article shall be satisfied to the extent of the value of the consideration received at the time of transfer of ownership. Any unsatisfied portion shall remain as a lien on the property and shall be satisfied in accordance with this section. The proceeds from any lien shall be deposited in the Waste Tire Trust Fund established pursuant to § 10.1-1422.3. If an owner fails to satisfy a lien as provided herein, the Director may proceed to enforce the lien by a bill filed in the court of equity having jurisdiction wherein the property or some portion of the property is located. (2003, c. 101.)

Editor's note. — Acts 2003, c. 101, cl. 3, provides: "That the revenue generated by this act shall be used solely for the removal and recycling of tires from waste tire piles. The Department of Environmental Quality shall report by December 1 of each year to the Chairmen of the Senate Committee on Agriculture, Conservation and Natural Resources and the House Committee on Agriculture, Chesapeake and Natural Resources on the use of these funds and the progress in cleaning up tire piles."

§ 10.1-1419. Litter receptacles; placement; penalty for violations. — A. The Board shall promulgate regulations establishing reasonable guidelines for the owners or persons in control of any property which is held out to the public as a place for assemblage, the transaction of business, recreation or as a public way who may be required to place and maintain receptacles acceptable to the Board.

In formulating such regulations the Board shall consider, among other public places, the public highways of the Commonwealth, all parks, campgrounds, trailer parks, drive-in restaurants, construction sites, gasoline service stations, shopping centers, retail store parking lots, parking lots of major industrial and business firms, marinas, boat launching areas, boat moorage and fueling stations, public and private piers and beaches and bathing areas. The number of such receptacles required to be placed as specified herein shall be determined by the Board and related to the need for such receptacles. Such litter receptacles shall be maintained in a manner to prevent overflow or spillage.

B. A person owning or operating any establishment or public place in which litter receptacles of a design acceptable to the Board are required by this section shall procure and place such receptacles at his own expense on the premises in accordance with Board regulations.

C. Any person who fails to place and maintain such litter receptacles on the premises in the number and manner required by Board regulation, or who violates the provisions of this section or regulations adopted hereunder shall be subject to a fine of twenty-five dollars for each day of violation. (1987, c. 234, § 10-277.6; 1988, c. 891.)

§ 10.1-1420. Litter bag. — The Department may design and produce a litter bag bearing the state anti-litter symbol and a statement of the penalties prescribed for littering. Such litter bags may be distributed by the Department of Motor Vehicles at no charge to the owner of every licensed vehicle in the Commonwealth at the time and place of the issuance of a license or renewal thereof. The Department may make the litter bags available to the owners of watercraft in the Commonwealth and may also provide the litter bags at no charge to tourists and visitors at points of entry into the Commonwealth and at visitor centers to the operators of incoming vehicles and watercraft. (1987, c. 234, § 10-277.7; 1988, c. 891.)

§ 10.1-1421. Responsibility for removal of litter from receptacles. — The responsibility for the removal of litter from litter receptacles placed at parks, beaches, campgrounds, trailer parks, and other public places shall remain upon those state and local agencies now performing litter removal services. The removal of litter from litter receptacles placed on private property used by the public shall remain the duty of the owner or operator of such private property. (1987, c. 234, § 10-277.8; 1988, c. 891.)

§ **10.1-1422. Further duties of Department.** — In addition to the foregoing duties the Department shall:

1. Serve as the coordinating agency between the various industry and business organizations seeking to aid in the recycling and anti-litter effort;

2. Recommend to local governing bodies that they adopt ordinances similar to the provisions of this article;

3. Cooperate with all local governments to accomplish coordination of local recycling and anti-litter efforts;

4. Encourage all voluntary local recycling and anti-litter campaigns seeking to focus the attention of the public on the programs of the Commonwealth to control and remove litter and encourage recycling;

5. Investigate the availability of, and apply for, funds available from any private or public source to be used in the program provided for in this article;

6. Allocate funds annually for the study of available research and development in recycling and litter control, removal, and disposal, as well as study methods for implementation in the Commonwealth of such research and development. In addition, such funds may be used for the development of public educational programs concerning the litter problem and recycling. Grants shall be made available for these purposes to those persons deemed appropriate and qualified by the Board or the Department;

7. Investigate the methods and success of other techniques in recycling and the control of litter, and develop, encourage and coordinate programs in the Commonwealth to utilize successful techniques in recycling and the control and elimination of litter; and

8. Expend, after receiving the recommendations of the Advisory Board, at least 90% of the funds deposited annually into the Fund pursuant to contracts with localities. The Department may enter into contracts with planning district commissions for the receipt and expenditure of funds attributable to localities which designate in writing to the Department a planning district commission as the agency to receive and expend funds hereunder. (1987, c. 234, § 10-277.9; 1988, c. 891; 1995, c. 417; 2006, c. 6.)

The 2006 amendments. — The 2006 amendment by c. 6 substituted "90%" for "seventy-five percent" in the first sentence of subdivision 8.

§ **10.1-1422.01. Litter Control and Recycling Fund established; use of moneys; purpose of Fund.** — A. All moneys collected from the taxes imposed under §§ 58.1-1700 through 58.1-1710 and by the taxes increased by Chapter 616 of the 1977 Acts of Assembly, shall be paid into the treasury and credited to a special nonreverting fund known as the Litter Control and Recycling Fund, which is hereby established. The Fund shall be established on the books of the Comptroller. Any moneys remaining in the Fund shall not revert to the general fund but shall remain in the Fund. Interest earned on such moneys shall remain in the Fund and be credited to it. The Director is authorized to release money from the Fund on warrants issued by the Comptroller after receiving and considering the recommendations of the Advisory Board for the purposes enumerated in subsection B of this section.

B. Moneys from the Fund shall be expended, according to the allocation formula established in subsection C of this section, for the following purposes:

1. Local litter prevention and recycling grants to localities that meet the criteria established in § 10.1-1422.04;

2. Litter prevention and recycling grants to localities and nonprofit entities meeting the criteria established in § 10.1-1422.05; and

3. Payment to (i) the Department to process the grants authorized by this article and (ii) the actual administrative costs of the Advisory Board. The Director shall assign one person in the Department to serve as a contact for persons interested in the Fund.

C. All moneys deposited into the Fund shall be expended pursuant to the following allocation formula:

1. Ninety percent for grants made to localities pursuant to subdivision B 1 of this section;

2. Five percent for litter prevention and recycling grants made pursuant to subdivision B 2 of this section; and

3. Up to a maximum of 5% for the actual administrative expenditures authorized pursuant to subdivision B 3 of this section. (1995, c. 417; 2006, c. 6.)

Editor's note. — Acts 1995, c. 417, cl. 2, provides: "That the provisions of §§ 10.1-1422.02 and 10.1-1422.03 of the Code of Virginia shall become effective on July 1, 1995, and the other provisions of the first enactment shall become effective on July 1, 1996."

The 2006 amendments. — The 2006 amendment by c. 6, in subdivision B 2, deleted "Statewide and regional" preceding "Litter" and substituted "grants to localities and nonprofit entities" for "educational program grants to persons"; in subdivision B 3, inserted "actual" in clause (ii); and in subsection C, substituted "Ninety" for "Seventy-five" at the beginning of subdivision C 1, substituted "Five percent for litter prevention and recycling" for "Twenty percent for statewide and regional educational program" in subdivision C 2, and substituted "Up to a maximum of 5% for the actual administrative" for "Five percent for the administrative" in subdivision C 3.

§ 10.1-1422.02. Litter Control and Recycling Fund Advisory Board established; duties and responsibilities.

— There is hereby created the Litter Control and Recycling Fund Advisory Board. The Advisory Board shall:

1. Review applications received by the Department for grants from the Fund and make recommendations to the Director for the award of all grants authorized pursuant to § 10.1-1422.01;

2. Promote the control, prevention and elimination of litter from the Commonwealth and encourage the recycling of discarded materials to the maximum practical extent; and

3. Advise the Director on such other litter control and recycling matters as may be requested by the Director or any other state agency. (1995, c. 417.)

Editor's note. — Acts 1995, c. 417, cl. 2, provides: "That the provisions of §§ 10.1-1422.02 and 10.1-1422.03 of the Code of Virginia shall become effective on July 1, 1995, and the other provisions of the first enactment shall become effective on July 1, 1996."

§ 10.1-1422.03. Membership, meetings, and staffing.

— A. The Advisory Board shall consist of five persons appointed by the Governor. Three members shall represent persons paying the taxes which are deposited into the Fund and shall include one member appointed from nominations submitted by recognized industry associations representing retailers; one member appointed from nominations submitted by recognized industry associations representing soft drink distributors; and one member appointed from nominations submitted by recognized industry associations representing beer distributors. One member shall be a local litter or recycling coordinator. One member shall be from the general public.

B. The initial terms of the members of the Advisory Board shall expire July 1, 1999, and five members shall be appointed or reappointed effective July 1,

1999, for terms as follows: one member shall be appointed for a term of one year; one member shall be appointed for a term of two years; one member shall be appointed for a term of three years; and two members shall be appointed for terms of four years unless found to violate subsection E of this section. Thereafter, all appointments shall be for terms of four years except for appointments to fill vacancies, which shall be for the unexpired term. They shall not receive a per diem, compensation for their service, or travel expenses.

C. The Advisory Board shall elect a chairman and vice-chairman annually from among its members. The Advisory Board shall meet at least twice annually on such dates and at such times as they determine. Three members of the Advisory Board shall constitute a quorum.

D. Staff support and actual associated administrative expenses of the Advisory Board shall be provided by the Department from funds allocated from the Fund.

E. Any member who is absent from three consecutive meetings of the Advisory Board, as certified by the Chairman of the Advisory Board to the Secretary of the Commonwealth, shall be dismissed as a member of the Advisory Board. The replacement of any dismissed member shall be appointed pursuant to subsection A of this section and meet the same membership criteria as the member who has been dismissed. (1995, c. 417; 1998, c. 86; 2006, c. 6.)

Editor's note. — Acts 1995, c. 417, cl. 2, provides: "That the provisions of §§ 10.1-1422.02 and 10.1-1422.03 of the Code of Virginia shall become effective on July 1, 1995, and the other provisions of the first enactment shall become effective on July 1, 1996."

The 2006 amendments. — The 2006 amendment by c. 6 inserted "actual" following "Staff support and" in subsection D.

OPINIONS OF THE ATTORNEY GENERAL

Compensation of members. — Members of the Litter Control and Recycling Fund Advisory Board are not entitled to compensation or reimbursement of expenses under § 2.2-2813.

See opinion of Attorney General to The Honorable Stephen H. Martin, Member, Senate of Virginia, 03-032 (9/11/03).

§ 10.1-1422.04. Local litter prevention and recycling grants; eligibility and funding process.

— The Director shall award local litter prevention and recycling grants to localities that apply for such grants and meet the eligibility requirements established in the Department's Guidelines for Litter Prevention and Recycling Grants (DEQ-LPR-2) which were in effect on January 1, 1995, and as may be amended by the Advisory Board after notice and opportunity to be heard by persons interested in grants awarded pursuant to this section. Grants awarded by the Director shall total the amount of Litter Control and Recycling Funds available annually as provided in subdivision B 1 of § 10.1-1422.01. (1995, c. 417.)

Editor's note. — Acts 1995, c. 417, cl. 2, provides: "That the provisions of §§ 10.1-1422.02 and 10.1-1422.03 of the Code of Virginia shall become effective on July 1, 1995, and the other provisions of the first enactment shall become effective on July 1, 1996."

§ 10.1-1422.05. Litter control and recycling grants.

— The Director, after receiving the recommendations of the Advisory Board, shall award litter prevention and recycling grants to localities that meet the requirements established in § 10.1-1422.04, and to any nonprofit entity composed of representatives of localities who meet the criteria established in § 10.1-1422.04. These grants shall be awarded for the public purpose of developing and implementing local, regional, and statewide litter control and recycling programs for which the grants provided for in § 10.1-1422.04 are found by the Director to be inadequate. Grants awarded by the Director pursuant to this section shall total the amount of litter control and recycling funds available annually as provided in subdivision B 2 of § 10.1-1422.01. (1995, c. 417; 2006, c. 6.)

Editor's note. — Acts 1995, c. 417, cl. 2, provides: "That the provisions of §§ 10.1-1422.02 and 10.1-1422.03 of the Code of Virginia shall become effective on July 1, 1995, and the other provisions of the first enactment shall become effective on July 1, 1996."

The 2006 amendments. — The 2006 amendment by c. 6 deleted "Statewide and regional" before "Litter" in the section catchline, rewrote the first sentence and added the second sentence.

§ **10.1-1422.1. Disposal of waste tires.** — The Department shall develop and implement a plan for the management and transportation of all waste tires in the Commonwealth. (1989, c. 630; 1993, c. 211.)

Editor's note. — Acts 1989, c. 630, cl. 2 provided that this section would expire on December 31, 1994. However, Acts 1993, c. 211, cl. 2 amends Acts 1989, c. 630, cl. 2, by deleting the expiration date; therefore, this section will not expire on December 31, 1994.

Law Review. — For survey on environmental law in Virginia for 1989, see 23 U. Rich. L. Rev. 625 (1989). For survey on taxation in Virginia for 1989, see 23 U. Rich. L. Rev. 839 (1989).

§ **10.1-1422.2. Recycling residues; testing.** — The Department shall develop and implement a plan for the testing of recycling residues generated in the Commonwealth to determine whether they are nonhazardous. The costs of conducting such tests shall be borne by the person wishing to dispose of such residues. (1990, c. 781.)

§ **10.1-1422.3. Waste Tire Trust Fund established; use of moneys; purpose of Fund.** — A. All moneys collected pursuant to § 58.1-642, minus the necessary expenses of the Department of Taxation for the administration of this tire recycling fee as certified by the Tax Commissioner, shall be paid into the treasury and credited to a special nonreverting fund known as the Waste Tire Trust Fund, which is hereby established. Any moneys remaining in the Fund shall not revert to the general fund but shall remain in the Fund. Interest earned on such moneys shall remain in the Fund and be credited to it. The Department of Waste Management is authorized and empowered to release moneys from the Fund, on warrants issued by the State Comptroller, for the purposes enumerated in this section, or any regulations adopted thereunder.

B. Moneys from the Fund shall be expended to:

1. Pay the costs of implementing the waste tire plan authorized by § 10.1-1422.1, as well as the costs of any programs created by the Department pursuant to such a plan;

2. Provide partial reimbursement to persons for the costs of using waste tires or chips or similar materials; and

3. Pay the costs to remove waste tire piles from property pursuant to § 10.1-1418.4, to the extent funds are available from the increased revenues generated by the increased tire recycling fee collected beginning July 1, 2003, and ending July 1, 2006, in accordance with § 58.1-641.

C. Reimbursements under § 10.1-1422.4 shall not be made until regulations establishing reimbursement procedures have become effective. (1993, c. 211; 2003, c. 101.)

Law Review. — For 2003/2004 survey of environmental law, see 39 U. Rich. L. Rev. 203 (2004).

§ 10.1-1422.4. Partial reimbursement for waste tires; eligibility; promulgation of regulations.

— A. The intent of the partial reimbursement of costs under this section is to promote the use of waste tires by enhancing markets for waste tires or chips or similar materials.

B. Any person who (i) purchases waste tires generated in Virginia and who uses the tires or chips or similar materials for resource recovery or other appropriate uses as established by regulation may apply for partial reimbursement of the cost of purchasing the tires or chips or similar materials or (ii) uses but does not purchase waste tires or chips or similar materials for resource recovery or other appropriate uses as established by regulation may apply for a reimbursement of part of the cost of such use.

C. To be eligible for the reimbursement (i) the waste tires or chips or similar materials shall be generated in Virginia, and (ii) the user of the waste tires shall be the end user of the waste tires or chips or similar materials. The end user does not have to be located in Virginia.

D. Reimbursements from the Waste Tire Trust Fund shall be made at least quarterly.

E. The Board shall promulgate regulations necessary to carry out the provisions of this section. The regulations shall include, but not be limited to:

1. Defining the types of uses eligible for partial reimbursement;

2. Establishing procedures for applying for and processing of reimbursements; and

3. Establishing the amount of reimbursement.

F. For the purposes of this section *"end user"* means (i) for resource recovery, the person who utilizes the heat content or other forms of energy from the incineration or pyrolysis of waste tires, chips or similar materials and (ii) for other eligible uses of waste tires, the last person who uses the tires, chips, or similar materials to make a product with economic value. If the waste tire is processed by more than one person in becoming a product, the end user is the last person to use the tire as a tire, as tire chips, or as similar material. A person who produces tire chips or similar materials and gives or sells them to another person to use is not an end user. (1993, c. 211; 1997, c. 627.)

§ 10.1-1422.5: Repealed by Acts 2001, c. 569.

Cross references. — For present provisions as to used motor oil, see § 10.1-1422.6.

§ 10.1-1422.6. Used motor oil, oil filters, and antifreeze; signs; establishment of statewide program.

— A. The Department shall establish a statewide used motor oil, oil filters, and antifreeze management program. The program shall encourage the environmentally sound management of motor oil, oil filters, and antifreeze by (i) educating consumers on the environmental benefits of proper management, (ii) publicizing options for proper disposal, and (iii) promoting a management infrastructure that allows for the convenient recycling of these materials by the public. The Department may contract with a qualified public or private entity to implement this program.

B. The Department shall maintain a statewide list of sites that accept used (i) motor oil, (ii) oil filters, and (iii) antifreeze from the public. The list shall be updated at least annually. The Department shall create, maintain, and promote an Internet Web site where consumers may receive information describing the location of collection sites in their locality to properly dispose of used motor oil, oil filters, and antifreeze.

C. The Department shall establish an ongoing outreach program to existing and potential collection sites that provides a point of contact for questions and disseminates information on (i) the way to establish a collection site, (ii) technical issues associated with being a collection site, and (iii) the benefits of continued participation in the program.

D. Any person who sells motor oil, oil filters, or antifreeze at the retail level and who does not accept the return of used motor oil, oil filters, or antifreeze shall post a sign that encourages the environmentally sound management of these products and provides a Web site address where additional information on the locations of used motor oil, oil filters and antifreeze collection sites are available. This sign shall be provided by the Department or its designee to all establishments selling motor oil, oil filters, or antifreeze. In determining the size and manner in which such signs may be affixed or displayed at the retail establishment, the Department shall give consideration to the space available in such retail establishments.

E. Any person who violates any provision of subsection D shall be subject to a fine of twenty-five dollars. (2001, c. 569.)

Law Review. — For article, "Environmental Law," see 35 U. Rich. L. Rev. 601 (2001).

§ 10.1-1423. Notice to public required. — Pertinent portions of this article shall be posted along the public highways of the Commonwealth, at public highway entrances to the Commonwealth, in all campgrounds and trailer parks, at all entrances to state parks, forest lands and recreational areas, at all public beaches, and at other public places in the Commonwealth where persons are likely to be informed of the existence and content of this article and the penalties for violating its provisions. (1987, c. 234, § 10-277.11; 1988, c. 891.)

§ 10.1-1424. Allowing escape of load material; penalty. — No vehicle shall be driven or moved on any highway unless the vehicle is constructed or loaded to prevent any of its load from dropping, sifting, leaking or otherwise escaping therefrom. However, sand or any substance for increasing traction during times of snow and ice may be dropped for the purpose of securing traction, or water or other substances may be sprinkled on a roadway in cleaning or maintaining the roadway by the Commonwealth or local government agency having that responsibility. Any person operating a vehicle from which any glass or objects have fallen or escaped which could constitute an obstruction or damage a vehicle or otherwise endanger travel upon a public highway shall immediately cause the highway to be cleaned of all glass or objects and shall pay any costs therefor. Violation of this section shall constitute a Class 1 misdemeanor. (1986, c. 757, § 10-211; 1987, c. 234, § 10-277.12; 1988, c. 891.)

Cross references. — As to punishment for Class 1 misdemeanors, see § 18.2-11.

§ 10.1-1424.1. Material containing fully halogenated chloro-fluoro-carbons prohibited; penalty. — A. On and after January 1, 1992, it shall be unlawful for any distributor or manufacturer knowingly to sell or offer for sale, for purposes of resale, any packaging materials that contain fully halogenated chloro-fluorocarbons as a blowing or expansion agent.

B. Any person convicted of a violation of the provisions of this section shall be guilty of a Class 3 misdemeanor. (1991, c. 101.)

Cross references. — As to punishment for Class 3 misdemeanors, see § 18.2-11.

§ 10.1-1424.2. Products containing trichloroethylene prohibited; penalty. — As of January 1, 2004, it shall be unlawful for any person to knowingly sell or distribute for retail sale in the Commonwealth any product containing trichloroethylene if such product is manufactured for or commonly used as an adhesive for residential hardwood floor installation.

As of January 1, 2006, it shall be unlawful for any person to knowingly sell or distribute for retail sale in the Commonwealth any product manufactured on or after January 1, 2004, for any household or residential purpose if such product contains trichloroethylene. Any person convicted of a violation of this section shall be guilty of a Class 3 misdemeanor. (2003, c. 620.)

Cross references. — As to punishment for Class 3 misdemeanors, see § 18.2-11.

§ 10.1-1425. Preemption of certain local ordinances. — The provisions of this article shall supersede and preempt any local ordinance which attempts to regulate the size or type of any container or package containing food or beverage or which requires a deposit on a disposable container or package. (1987, c. 234, § 10-277.14; 1988, c. 891.)

ARTICLE 3.1.

Lead Acid Batteries.

§ 10.1-1425.1. Lead acid batteries; land disposal prohibited; penalty. — A. It shall be unlawful for any person to place a used lead acid battery in mixed municipal solid waste or to discard or otherwise dispose of a lead acid battery except by delivery to a battery retailer or wholesaler, or to a secondary lead smelter, or to a collection or recycling facility authorized under the laws of this Commonwealth or by the United States Environmental Protection Agency. As used in this article, the term *"lead acid battery"* shall mean any wet cell battery.

B. It shall be unlawful for any battery retailer to dispose of a used lead acid battery except by delivery to (i) the agent of a battery wholesaler or a secondary lead smelter, (ii) a battery manufacturer for delivery to a secondary lead smelter, or (iii) a collection or recycling facility authorized under the laws of this Commonwealth or by the United States Environmental Protection Agency.

C. Any person found guilty of a violation of this section shall be punished by a fine of not more than fifty dollars. Each battery improperly disposed of shall constitute a separate violation. (1990, c. 520.)

§ 10.1-1425.2. Collection of lead acid batteries for recycling. — Any person selling lead acid batteries at retail or offering lead acid batteries for retail sale in the Commonwealth shall:

1. Accept from customers, at the point of transfer, used lead acid batteries of the type and in a quantity at least equal to the number of new batteries purchased, if offered by customers; and

2. Post written notice which shall be at least 8 ½ inches by 11 inches in size and which shall include the universal recycling symbol and the following

language: (i) "It is illegal to discard a motor vehicle battery or other lead acid battery," (ii) "Recycle your used batteries," and (iii) "State law requires us to accept used motor vehicle batteries or other lead acid batteries for recycling, in exchange for new batteries purchased." (1990, c. 520.)

§ **10.1-1425.3. Inspection of battery retailers; penalty.** — The Department shall produce, print, and distribute the notices required by § 10.1-1425.2 to all places in the Commonwealth where lead acid batteries are offered for sale at retail. In performing its duties under this section, the Department may inspect any place, building, or premise subject to the provisions of § 10.1-1425.2. Authorized employees of the Department may issue warnings to persons who fail to comply with the provisions of this article. Any person found guilty of failing to post the notice required under § 10.1-1425.2 after receiving a warning to do so pursuant to this section shall be punished by a fine of not more than fifty dollars. (1990, c. 520.)

§ **10.1-1425.4. Lead acid battery wholesalers; penalty.** — A. It shall be unlawful for any person selling new lead acid batteries at wholesale to not accept from customers at the point of transfer, used lead acid batteries of the type and in a quantity at least equal to the number of new batteries purchased, if offered by customers. A person accepting batteries in transfer from a battery retailer shall be allowed a period not to exceed ninety days to remove batteries from the retail point of collection.

B. Any person found guilty of a violation of this section shall be punished by a fine of not more than fifty dollars. Each battery unlawfully refused by a wholesaler or not removed from the retail point of collection within ninety days shall constitute a separate violation. (1990, c. 520.)

§ **10.1-1425.5. Construction of article.** — The provisions of this article shall not be construed to prohibit any person who does not sell new lead acid batteries from collecting and recycling such batteries. (1990, c. 520.)

ARTICLE 3.2.

Recycling Duties of State Agencies and State Universities.

§ **10.1-1425.6. Recycling programs of state agencies.** — A. It shall be the duty of each state university and state agency of the Commonwealth, including the General Assembly, to establish programs for the use of recycled materials and for the collection, to the extent feasible, of all recyclable materials used or generated by such entities, including, at a minimum, used motor oil, glass, aluminum, office paper and corrugated paper. Such programs shall be in accordance with the programs and plans developed by the Department of Waste Management, which shall serve as the lead agency for the Commonwealth's recycling efforts. The Department shall develop such programs and plans by July 1, 1991.

B. In fulfilling its duties under this section, each agency of the Commonwealth shall implement procedures for (i) the collection and storage of recyclable materials generated by such agency, (ii) the disposal of such materials to buyers, and (iii) the reduction of waste materials generated by such agency. (1990, c. 616.)

The number for this article, and the numbers for the sections contained therein, §§ 10.1-1425.6 through 10.1-1425.9, were assigned by the Virginia Code Commis-sion, the numbers in the 1990 act having been Article 3.1, and 10.1-1425.1 through 10.1-1425.5, respectively.

Cross references. — As to this section and

the implementation by state agencies of purchase programs for recycled goods under the Virginia Public Procurement Act, see § 2.2-4323.

§ **10.1-1425.7. Duty of the Department of Business Assistance.** — The Department of Business Assistance shall assist the Department by encouraging and promoting the establishment of appropriate recycling industries in the Commonwealth. (1990, c. 616; 1996, cc. 589, 599.)

Cross references. — As to this section and the implementation by state agencies of purchase programs for recycled goods under the Virginia Public Procurement Act, see § 2.2-4323.

§ **10.1-1425.8. Department of Transportation; authority and duty.** — The Department of Transportation is authorized to conduct recycling research projects, including the establishment of demonstration projects which use recycled products in highway construction and maintenance. Such projects may include by way of example and not by limitation the use of ground rubber from used tires or glass for road surfacing, resurfacing and sub-base materials, as well as the use of plastic or mixed plastic materials for ground or guard rail posts, right-of-way fence posts and sign supports.

The Department of Transportation shall periodically review and revise its bid procedures and specifications to encourage the use of products and materials with recycled content in its construction and maintenance programs.

The Commonwealth Transportation Commissioner may continue to provide for the collection of used motor oil and motor vehicle antifreeze from the general public at maintenance facilities in the County of Bath. The Commonwealth Transportation Commissioner may designate the source of funding for the collection and disposal of these materials. (1990, c. 616; 1993, c. 801; 1994, c. 419; 1995, c. 109; 1996, c. 290.)

Cross references. — As to this section and the implementation by state agencies of purchase programs for recycled goods under the Virginia Public Procurement Act, see § 2.2-4323.

§ **10.1-1425.9. Duties of the Department of Education.** — With the assistance of the Department of Waste Management, the Department of Education shall develop by July 1, 1992, guidelines for public schools regarding (i) the use of recycled materials, (ii) the collection of recyclable materials, and (iii) the reduction of solid waste generated in such school's offices, classrooms and cafeterias. (1990, c. 616.)

ARTICLE 3.3.

Pollution Prevention Program.

§ **10.1-1425.10. Definition.** — As used in this article, unless the context requires a different meaning:

"Pollution prevention" means eliminating or reducing the use, generation or release at the source of environmental waste. Methods of pollution prevention include, but are not limited to, equipment or technology modifications; process or procedure modifications; reformulation or redesign of products; substitution of raw materials; improvements in housekeeping, maintenance, training, or inventory control; and closed-loop recycling, onsite process-related recycling, reuse or extended use of any material utilizing equipment or methods which are an integral part of a production process. The term shall not include any practice which alters the physical, chemical, or biological characteristics or the

407

volume of an environmental waste through a process or activity which itself is not integral to and necessary for the production of a product or the providing of a service, and shall not include treatment, increased pollution control, off-site or nonprocess-related recycling, or incineration.

"Toxic or hazardous substance" means (i) all of the chemicals identified on the Toxic Chemical List established pursuant to § 313 of the Emergency Planning and Community Right-to-Know Act, 42 U.S.C. § 11001 et seq. (P.L. 99-499), and (ii) all of the chemicals listed pursuant to §§ 101 (14) and 102 of the Comprehensive Environmental Response, Compensation and Liability Act, 42 U.S.C. § 9601 et seq. (P.L. 92-500). (1993, c. 459; 1994, c. 169.)

Editor's note. — For §§ 104(14) and 102 of the Comprehensive Environmental Response, Compensation and Liability Act, referred to above, see 42 U.S.C.S. §§ 9601(14) and 9602.

§ 10.1-1425.11. Establishment of pollution prevention policy. — It shall be the policy of the Commonwealth (i) that the Commonwealth should encourage pollution prevention activities by removing barriers and providing incentives and assistance, and (ii) that the generation of environmental waste should be reduced or eliminated at the source, whenever feasible; environmental waste that is generated should be reused whenever feasible; environmental waste that cannot be reduced or reused should be recycled whenever feasible; environmental waste that cannot be reduced, reused, or recycled should be treated in an environmentally safe manner; and disposal should be employed only as a last resort and should be conducted in an environmentally safe manner. It shall also be the policy of the Commonwealth to minimize the transfer of environmental wastes from one environmental medium to another. (1993, c. 459.)

§ 10.1-1425.12. Pollution prevention assistance program. — The Department shall establish a voluntary pollution prevention assistance program designed to assist all persons in promoting pollution prevention measures in the Commonwealth. The program shall emphasize assistance to local governments and businesses that have inadequate technical and financial resources to obtain information and to assess and implement pollution prevention measures. The program may include, but shall not be limited to:

1. Establishment of a pollution prevention clearinghouse for all available information concerning waste reduction, waste minimization, source reduction, economic and energy savings, and pollution prevention;

2. Assistance in transferring information concerning pollution prevention technologies through workshops, conferences and handbooks;

3. Cooperation with university programs to develop pollution prevention curricula and training;

4. Technical assistance to generators of toxic or hazardous substances, including onsite consultation to identify alternative methods that may be applied to prevent pollution; and

5. Researching and recommending incentive programs for innovative pollution prevention programs.

To be eligible for onsite technical assistance, a generator of toxic or hazardous substances must agree to allow information regarding the results of such assistance to be shared with the public, provided that the identity of the generator shall be made available only with its consent and trade-secret information shall remain protected. (1993, c. 459; 1994, c. 169.)

§ 10.1-1425.13. Pollution prevention advisory panels. — The Director is authorized to name qualified persons to pollution prevention advisory panels to assist the Department in administering the pollution prevention assistance

program. Panels shall include members representing different areas of inter-est in and potential support for pollution prevention, including industry, education, environmental and public interest groups, state government and local government. (1993, c. 459.)

§ 10.1-1425.14. Pilot projects. — The Department may sponsor pilot projects to develop and demonstrate innovative technologies and methods for pollution prevention. The results of all such projects shall be available for use by the public, but trade secret information shall remain protected. (1993, c. 459.)

§ 10.1-1425.15. Waste exchange. — The Department may establish an industrial environmental waste material exchange that provides for the exchange, between interested persons, of information concerning (i) particular quantities of industrial environmental waste available for recovery; (ii) per-sons interested in acquiring certain types of industrial environmental waste for purposes of recovery; and (iii) methods for the treatment and recovery of industrial environmental waste. The industrial environmental waste materi-als exchange may be operated under one or more reciprocity agreements providing for the exchange of the information for similar information from a program operated in another state. The Department may contract for a private person or public entity to establish or operate the industrial environmental waste materials exchange. The Department may prescribe rules concerning the establishment and operation of the industrial environmental waste mate-rials exchange, including the setting of subscription fees to offset the cost of participating in the exchange. (1993, c. 459.)

§ 10.1-1425.16. Trade secret protection. — All trade secrets obtained pursuant to this article by the Department or its agents shall be held as confidential. (1993, c. 459.)

§ 10.1-1425.17. Evaluation report. — The Department shall submit an annual report to the Governor and the appropriate committees of the General Assembly. The report shall include an evaluation of its pollution prevention activities. The report shall be submitted by December 1 of each year, beginning in 1994. The report shall include, to the extent available, information regard-ing progress in expanding pollution prevention activities in the Common-wealth. (1993, c. 459.)

§ 10.1-1425.18. Pollution prevention grants. — The Department may make grants to identify pollution prevention opportunities and to study or determine the feasibility of applying specific technologies and methods to prevent pollution. Persons who use, generate or release environmental waste may receive grants under this section. (1993, c. 459.)

§ 10.1-1425.19. Inspections and enforcement actions by the Depart-ment. — A. The Department shall seek to ensure, where appropriate, that any inspections conducted pursuant to Chapters 13 (§ 10.1-1300 et seq.) and 14 (§ 10.1-1400 et seq.) of this title and Chapter 3.1 (§ 62.1-44.2 et seq.) of Title 62.1 (i) are multimedia in approach; (ii) are performed by teams of inspectors authorized to represent the air, water and solid waste programs within the Department; and (iii) minimize duplication of inspections, reporting requirements, and enforcement efforts.

B. The Department may allow any person found to be violating any law or standard for which the Department has enforcement jurisdiction to develop a plan to reduce the use or generation of toxic or hazardous substances through pollution prevention incentives or initiatives and, to the maximum extent possible, implement the plan as part of coming into compliance with the violated law or standard. This shall in no way affect the Commonwealth's ability and responsibility to seek penalties in enforcement activities. (1994, c. 169.)

ARTICLE 3.4.

Reduction of Heavy Metals in Packaging Act.

§ 10.1-1425.20. Findings and intent. — A. The General Assembly finds that:

1. The management of solid waste can pose a wide range of hazards to public health and safety and to the environment;

2. Packaging comprises a significant percentage of the overall waste stream;

3. The presence of heavy metals in packaging is a concern because of the potential presence of heavy metals in residue from manufacturers' recycling processes, in emissions or ash when packaging is incinerated, or in leachate when packaging is landfilled; and

4. Lead, mercury, cadmium, and hexavalent chromium, on the basis of scientific and medical evidence, are of particular concern.

B. It is the intent of the General Assembly to:

1. Reduce the toxicity of packaging;

2. Eliminate the addition of heavy metals to packaging; and

3. Achieve reductions in toxicity without impeding or discouraging the expanded use of recovered material in the production of products, packaging, and its components. (1994, c. 944.)

The numbers of §§ 10.1-1425.20 through 10.1-1425.25 were assigned by the Code Commission, the numbers in the 1994 act having been 10.1-1425.19 through 10.1-1425.24.

§ 10.1-1425.21. Definitions. — As used in this article, unless the context requires a different meaning:

"Distributor" means any person who takes title to products or packaging purchased for resale.

"Intentional introduction" means the act of deliberately using a regulated heavy metal in the formulation of a package or packaging component where its continued presence in the final package or packaging component is to provide a specific characteristic or quality. The use of a regulated heavy metal as a processing agent or intermediate to impart certain chemical or physical changes during manufacturing, whereupon the incidental retention of a residue of the metal in the final package or packaging component is neither desired nor deliberate is not considered to be "intentional introduction" where the final package or packaging component is in compliance with subsection C of § 10.1-1425.22.

"Manufacturer" means any person that produces products, packages, packaging, or components of products or packaging.

"Package" means any container which provides a means of marketing, protecting, or handling a product, including a unit package, intermediate package, or a shipping container, as defined in the American Society for Testing and Materials (ASTM) specification D996. The term includes, but is not limited to, unsealed receptacles such as carrying cases, crates, cups, pails, rigid foil and other trays, wrapping and wrapping film, bags, and tubs.

"Packaging component" means any individual assembled part of a package, including, but not limited to, interior and exterior blocking, bracing, cushion-

ing, weatherproofing, exterior strapping, coatings, closures, inks, and labels. Tin-plated steel that meets ASTM specification A-623 shall be considered as a single package component. Electro-galvanized coated steel that meets ASTM specification A-525, and hot-dipped coated galvanized steel that meets ASTM specification A-879 shall be treated in the same manner as tin-plated steel. (1994, c. 944; 1995, c. 115.)

§ **10.1-1425.22. Schedule for removal of incidental amounts of heavy metals.** — A. On and after July 1, 1995, no manufacturer or distributor shall offer for sale, sell, or offer for promotional purposes in the Commonwealth a package or packaging component which includes, in the package itself or in any packaging component, inks, dyes, pigments, adhesives, stabilizers, or any other additives containing lead, cadmium, mercury, or hexavalent chromium which has been intentionally introduced as an element during manufacturing or distribution, and which exceeds a concentration level established by this article. This prohibition shall not apply to the incidental presence of any of these elements in a package or packaging component.

B. On and after July 1, 1995, no manufacturer or distributor shall offer for sale, sell, or offer for promotional purposes in the Commonwealth a product in a package which includes, in the package itself or in any of the packaging components, inks, dyes, pigments, adhesives, stabilizers, or any other additives containing lead, cadmium, mercury, or hexavalent chromium which has been intentionally introduced as an element during manufacturing or distribution, and which exceeds a concentration level established by this article. This prohibition shall not apply to the incidental presence of any of these elements in a package or packaging component.

C. The sum of the concentration levels of lead, cadmium, mercury, and hexavalent chromium present in a package or packaging component shall not exceed the following:

1. Six hundred parts per million by weight on and after July 1, 1995;
2. Two hundred fifty parts per million by weight on and after July 1, 1996; and
3. One hundred parts per million by weight on and after July 1, 1997.

D. Concentration levels of lead, cadmium, mercury, and hexavalent chromium shall be determined using ASTM test methods, as revised, or U.S. Environmental Protection Agency Test Methods for Evaluating Solid Waste, S-W 846, as revised. (1994, c. 944.)

§ **10.1-1425.23. Exemptions.** — The following packaging and packaging components shall be exempt from the requirements of this Act:

1. Packaging or packaging components with a code indicating a date of manufacture prior to July 1, 1995;
2. Packages or packaging components to which lead, cadmium, mercury or hexavalent chromium has been added in the manufacturing, forming, printing or distribution process in order to comply with health or safety requirements of federal law, provided that (i) the manufacturer of a package or packaging component must petition the Board for any exemption for a particular package or packaging component; (ii) the Board may grant an exemption for up to two years if warranted by the circumstances; and (iii) such an exemption may, upon reapplication for exemption and meeting the criterion of this subdivision, be renewed at two-year intervals;
3. Packages and packaging components to which lead, cadmium, mercury or hexavalent chromium has been added in the manufacturing, forming, printing or distribution process for which there is no feasible alternative, provided that (i) the manufacturer of a package or packaging component must petition the Board for any exemption for a particular package or packaging component; (ii)

411

the Board may grant an exemption for up to two years if warranted by the circumstances; and (iii) such an exemption may, upon reapplication for exemption and meeting the criterion of this subdivision, be renewed at two-year intervals. For purposes of this subdivision, a use for which there is no feasible alternative is one in which the regulated substance is essential to the protection, safe handling, or function of the package's contents;

4. Packages and packaging components that would not exceed the maximum contaminant levels established but for the addition of recovered or recycled materials; and

5. Packages and packaging components used to contain alcoholic beverages, as defined in § 4.1-100, bottled prior to July 1, 1992. (1994, c. 944; 1995, c. 115.)

§ 10.1-1425.24. Certificate of compliance. — A. On and after July 1, 1995, each manufacturer or distributor of packaging or packaging components shall make available to purchasers, the Department, and the public, upon request, certificates of compliance which state that the manufacturer's or distributor's packaging or packaging components comply with, or are exempt from, the requirements of this article.

B. If the manufacturer or distributor of the package or packaging component reformulates or creates a new package or packaging component that results in an increase in the level of heavy metals higher than the original certificate of compliance, the manufacturer or distributor shall provide an amended or new certificate of compliance for the reformulated package or packaging component. (1994, c. 944.)

§ 10.1-1425.25. Promulgation of regulations. — The Board may promulgate regulations if regulations are necessary to implement and manage the provisions of this article. The Director is authorized to name qualified persons to an advisory panel of affected interests and the public to assist the Department in implementing the provisions of this article. (1994, c. 944.)

ARTICLE 3.5.

Cathode Ray Tubes Recycling.

§ 10.1-1425.26. Cathode ray tube special waste recycling program. — A. As used in this section *"cathode ray tube"* means an intact glass tube used to provide the visual display in televisions, computer monitors, oscilloscopes and similar scientific equipment, but does not include the other components of an electronic product containing a cathode ray tube even if the product and the cathode ray tube are disassembled.

B. The Board shall promulgate regulations to encourage cathode ray tube and electronics recycling.

C. Any locality may, by ordinance, prohibit the disposal of cathode ray tubes in any privately operated landfill within its jurisdiction, provided the locality has implemented a recycling program that is capable of handling all cathode ray tubes generated within its jurisdiction. However, no such ordinance shall contain any provision that penalizes anyone other than the initial generator of such cathode ray tubes. (2003, c. 743.)

Law Review. — For 2003/2004 survey of environmental law, see 39 U. Rich. L. Rev. 203 (2004).

ARTICLE 4.

Hazardous Waste Management.

§ 10.1-1426. Permits required; waiver of requirements; reports; conditional permits. — A. No person shall transport, store, provide treatment for, or dispose of a hazardous waste without a permit from the Director.

B. Any person generating, transporting, storing, providing treatment for, or disposing of a hazardous waste shall report to the Director, by such date as the Board specifies by regulation, the following: (i) his name and address, (ii) the name and nature of the hazardous waste, and (iii) the fact that he is generating, transporting, storing, providing treatment for or disposing of a hazardous waste. A person who is an exempt small quantity generator of hazardous wastes, as defined by the administrator of the Environmental Protection Agency, shall be exempt from the requirements of this subsection.

C. Any permit shall contain the conditions or requirements required by the Board's regulations and the federal acts.

D. Upon the issuance of an emergency permit for the storage of hazardous waste, the Director shall notify the chief administrative officer of the local government for the jurisdiction in which the permit has been issued.

E. The Director may deny an application under this article on any grounds for which a permit may be amended, suspended or revoked listed under subsection A of § 10.1-1427.

F. Any locality or state agency may collect hazardous waste from exempt small quantity generators for shipment to a permitted treatment or disposal facility if done in accordance with (i) a permit to store, treat, or dispose of hazardous waste issued pursuant to this chapter or (ii) a permit to transport hazardous waste, and the wastes collected are stored for no more than 10 days prior to shipment to a permitted treatment or disposal facility. If household hazardous waste is collected and managed with hazardous wastes collected from exempt small quantity generators, all waste shall be managed in accordance with the provisions of this subsection. (1986, cc. 492, 563, § 10-279; 1988, c. 891; 1992, c. 463; 2004, c. 442.)

Law Review. — For note, "Federal and State Remedies to Clean Up Hazardous Waste Sites," see 20 U. Rich. L. Rev. 379 (1986). For 2003/2004 survey of environmental law, see 39 U. Rich. L. Rev. 203 (2004).

§ 10.1-1427. Revocation, suspension or amendment of permits. — A. Any permit issued by the Director pursuant to this article may be revoked, amended or suspended on any of the following grounds or on such other grounds as may be provided by the regulations of the Board:

1. The permit holder has violated any regulation or order of the Board, any condition of a permit, any provision of this chapter, or any order of a court, where such violation (i) results in a release of harmful substances into the environment, (ii) poses a threat of release of harmful substances into the environment, (iii) presents a hazard to human health, or (iv) is representative of a pattern of serious or repeated violations which, in the opinion of the Director, demonstrates the permittee's disregard for or inability to comply with applicable laws, regulations or requirements;

2. The person to whom the permit was issued abandons, sells, leases or ceases to operate the facility permitted;

3. The facilities used in the transportation, storage, treatment or disposal of hazardous waste are operated, located, constructed or maintained in such a manner as to pose a substantial present or potential hazard to human health or the environment, including pollution of air, land, surface water or ground water;

4. Such protective construction or equipment as is found to be reasonable, technologically feasible and necessary to prevent substantial present or potential hazard to human health and welfare or the environment has not been installed at a facility used for the storage, treatment or disposal of a hazardous waste; or

5. Any key personnel have been convicted of any of the following crimes punishable as felonies under the laws of the Commonwealth or the equivalent thereof under the laws of any other jurisdiction: murder; kidnapping; gambling; robbery; bribery; extortion; criminal usury; arson; burglary; theft and related crimes; forgery and fraudulent practices; fraud in the offering, sale, or purchase of securities; alteration of motor vehicle identification numbers; unlawful manufacture, purchase, use or transfer of firearms; unlawful possession or use of destructive devices or explosives; violation of the Drug Control Act (§ 54.1-3400 et seq.); racketeering; violation of antitrust laws; or has been adjudged by an administrative agency or a court of competent jurisdiction to have violated the environmental protection laws of the United States, the Commonwealth, or any other state and the Director determines that such conviction or adjudication is sufficiently probative of the applicant's inability or unwillingness to operate the facility in a lawful manner, as to warrant denial, revocation, amendment or suspension of the permit.

In making such determination, the Director shall consider:

a. The nature and details of the acts attributed to key personnel;

b. The degree of culpability of the applicant, if any;

c. The applicant's policy or history of discipline of key personnel for such activities;

d. Whether the applicant has substantially complied with all rules, regulations, permits, orders and statutes applicable to the applicant's activities in Virginia;

e. Whether the applicant has implemented formal management control to minimize and prevent the occurrence of such violations; and

f. Mitigation based upon demonstration of good behavior by the applicant including, without limitation, prompt payment of damages, cooperation with investigations, termination of employment or other relationship with key personnel or other persons responsible for the violations or other demonstrations of good behavior by the applicant that the Director finds relevant to his decision.

B. The Director may amend or attach conditions to a permit when:

1. There is a significant change in the manner and scope of operation which may require new or additional permit conditions or safeguards to protect the public health and environment;

2. There is found to be a possibility of pollution causing significant adverse effects on the air, land, surface water or ground water;

3. Investigation has shown the need for additional equipment, construction, procedures and testing to ensure the protection of the public health and the environment from significant adverse effects; or

4. The amendment is necessary to meet changes in applicable regulatory requirements.

C. If the Director finds that hazardous wastes are no longer being stored, treated or disposed of at a facility in accordance with Board regulations, the Director may revoke the permit issued for such facility or, as a condition to granting or continuing in effect a permit, may require the person to whom the permit was issued to provide perpetual care and surveillance of the facility. (1986, c. 492, § 10-280; 1988, c. 891; 1992, c. 463.)

§ 10.1-1428. Financial responsibility for abandoned facilities; penalties. — A. The Board shall promulgate regulations which ensure that, if a facility in which hazardous waste is stored, treated, or disposed is closed or abandoned, the costs associated with protecting the public health and safety from the consequences of such abandonment may be recovered from the person abandoning the facility.

B. Such regulations may include bonding requirements, the creation of a trust fund to be maintained within the Department, self-insurance, other forms of commercial insurance, or other mechanisms that the Department deems appropriate. Regulations governing the amount thereof shall take into consideration the potential for contamination and injury by the hazardous waste, the cost of disposal of the hazardous waste and the cost of restoring the facility to a safe condition.

C. No state agency shall be required to comply with such regulations.

D. Forfeiture of any financial obligation imposed pursuant to this section shall not relieve any holder of a permit issued pursuant to this article of any other legal obligations for the consequences of abandonment of any facility.

E. Any funds forfeited pursuant to this section and the regulations of the Board shall be paid over to the Director, who shall then expend the forfeited funds as necessary to restore and maintain the facility in a safe condition. Nothing in this section shall require the Director to expend funds from any other source to carry out the activities contemplated under this section.

F. Any person who knowingly and willfully abandons a hazardous waste management facility without proper closure or without providing adequate financial assurance instruments for such closure shall, if such failure to close results in a significant harm or an imminent and substantial threat of significant harm to human health or the environment, be liable to the Commonwealth and any political subdivision for the costs incurred in abating, controlling, preventing, removing, or containing such harm or threat.

Any person who knowingly and willfully abandons a hazardous waste management facility without proper closure or without providing adequate financial assurance instruments for such closure shall, if such failure to close results in a significant harm or an imminent and substantial threat of significant harm to human health or the environment, be guilty of a Class 4 felony. (1986, c. 492, § 10-281; 1988, c. 891; 1991, c. 702; 2005, c. 180.)

Cross references. — As to punishment for Class 4 felonies, see § 18.2-10.

The 2005 amendments. — The 2005 amendment by c. 180, in subsection E, substituted "over to the Director, who shall then" for "to the county, city or town in which the abandoned facility is located. The county, city or town in which the facility is located shall" in the former first and second sentences to make the first sentence, and added the last sentence.

§ 10.1-1429. Notice of release of hazardous substance. — Any person responsible for the release of a hazardous substance from a fixed facility which poses an immediate or imminent threat to public health and who is required by law to notify the National Response Center shall notify the chief administrative officer or his designee of the local government of the jurisdiction in which the release occurs and shall also notify the Department. (1986, c. 492, § 10-282; 1988, c. 891.)

Law Review. — For an article reviewing key environmental developments at the federal and state levels during the period from June 1996 to June 1998, see 32 U. Rich. L. Rev. 1217 (1998).

ARTICLE 4.1.

Voluntary Remediation.

§§ **10.1-1429.1 through 10.1-1429.3:** Repealed by Acts 2002, c. 378, cl. 2, effective July 1, 2002.

Cross references. — For the Brownfield Restoration and Land Renewal Act, see now § 10.1-1230 et seq.

Editor's note. — Acts 2002, c. 378, cl. 3, provides: "That regulations promulgated by the Virginia Waste Management Board pursuant to § 10.1-1429.1 shall remain in effect until amended or repealed."

Acts 2002, c. 378, cl. 4, provides: "That any certificates of satisfactory completion issued by the Virginia Waste Management Board pursuant to § 10.1-1429.1 shall remain in effect unless rescinded by the Board."

ARTICLE 4.2.

Remediated Property Fresh Start Program.

§ 10.1-1429.4: Repealed by Acts 2002, c. 378, cl. 2, effective July 1, 2002.

Cross references. — For the Brownfield Restoration and Land Renewal Act, see now § 10.1-1230 et seq.

ARTICLE 5.

Radioactive Waste.

§ 10.1-1430. Authority of Governor to enter into agreements with federal government; effect on federal licenses. — The Governor is authorized to enter into agreements with the federal government providing for discontinuance of the federal government's responsibilities with respect to low-level radioactive waste and the assumption thereof by the Commonwealth. (1986, c. 492, § 10-283; 1988, c. 891.)

§ 10.1-1431. Authority of Board to enter into agreements with federal government, other states or interstate agencies; training programs for personnel. — A. The Board, with the prior approval of the Governor, is authorized to enter into agreements with the federal government, other states or interstate agencies, whereby the Commonwealth will perform, on a cooperative basis with the federal government, other states or interstate agencies, inspections or other functions relating to control of low-level radioactive waste.

B. The Board may institute programs to train personnel to carry out the provisions of this article and, with the prior approval of the Governor, may make such personnel available for participation in any program of the federal government, other states or interstate agencies in furtherance of this chapter. (1986, c. 492, § 10-284; 1988, c. 891.)

§ 10.1-1432. Further powers of Board. — The Board shall have the power, subject to the approval of the Governor:

1. To acquire by purchase, exercise the right of eminent domain as provided in Chapter 2 (§ 25.1-200 et seq.) of Title 25.1 grant, gift, devise or otherwise, the fee simple title to or any acceptable lesser interest in any lands, selected in the discretion of the Board as constituting necessary, desirable or acceptable sites for low-level radioactive waste management, including lands adjacent to a project site as in the discretion of the Board may be necessary or suitable for restricted areas. In all instances lands that are to be designated as radioactive waste material sites shall be acquired in fee simple absolute and dedicated in perpetuity to such purpose;

2. To convey or lease, for such term as in the discretion of the Board may be in the public interest, any lands so acquired, either for a fair and reasonable

consideration or solely or partly as an inducement to the establishment or location in the Commonwealth of any scientific or technological facility, project, satellite project or nuclear storage area; but subject to such restraints as may be deemed proper to bring about a reversion of title or termination of any lease if the grantee or lessee ceases to use the premises or facilities in the conduct of business or activities consistent with the purposes of this article. However, radioactive waste material sites may be leased but may not otherwise be disposed of except to another department, agency or institution of the Commonwealth or to the United States;

3. To assume responsibility for perpetual custody and maintenance of radioactive waste held for custodial purposes at any publicly or privately operated facility located within the Commonwealth if the parties operating such facilities abandon their responsibility and whenever the federal government or any of its agencies has not assumed the responsibility. In such event, the Board may collect fees from private or public parties holding radioactive waste for perpetual custodial purposes in order to finance such perpetual custody and maintenance as the Board may undertake. The fees shall be sufficient in each individual case to defray the estimated cost of the Board's custodial management activities for that individual case. All such fees, when received by the Board, shall be credited to a special fund of the Department, shall be used exclusively for maintenance costs or for otherwise satisfying custodial and maintenance obligations; and

4. To enter into an agreement with the federal government or any of its authorized agencies to assume perpetual maintenance of lands donated, leased, or purchased from the federal government or any of its authorized agencies and used as custodial sites for radioactive waste. (1986, c. 492, § 10-285; 1988, c. 891; 2003, c. 940.)

ARTICLE 6.

Siting of Hazardous Waste Facilities.

§ 10.1-1433. Definitions. — As used in this article, unless the context requires a different meaning:

"Applicant" means the person applying for a certification of site suitability or submitting a notice of intent to apply therefor.

"Application" means an application to the Board for a certification of site suitability.

"Certification of site suitability" or *"certification"* means the certification issued by the Board pursuant to this chapter.

"Criteria" means the criteria adopted by the Board, pursuant to § 10.1-1436.

"Fund" means the Technical Assistance Fund created pursuant to § 10.1-1448.

"Hazardous waste facility" or *"facility"* means any facility, including land and structures, appurtenances, improvements and equipment for the treatment, storage or disposal of hazardous wastes, which accepts hazardous waste for storage, treatment or disposal. For the purposes of this article, it does not include: (i) facilities which are owned and operated by and exclusively for the on-site treatment, storage or disposal of wastes generated by the owner or operator; (ii) facilities for the treatment, storage or disposal of hazardous wastes used principally as fuels in an on-site production process; (iii) facilities used exclusively for the pretreatment of wastes discharged directly to a publicly owned sewage treatment works.

"Hazardous waste management facility permit" means the permit for a hazardous waste management facility issued by the Director or the U.S. Environmental Protection Agency.

417

"Host community" means any county, city or town within whose jurisdictional boundaries construction of a hazardous waste facility is proposed.

"On-site" means facilities that are located on the same or geographically contiguous property which may be divided by public or private right-of-way, and the entrance and exit between the contiguous properties is at a cross-roads intersection so that the access is by crossing, as opposed to going along, the right-of-way. On-site also means noncontiguous properties owned by the same person but connected by a right-of-way which the owner controls and to which the public does not have access.

"Operator" means a person who is responsible for the overall operation of a facility.

"Owner" means a person who owns a facility or a part of a facility.

"Storage" means the containment or holding of hazardous wastes pending treatment, recycling, reuse, recovery or disposal.

"Treatment" means any method, technique or process, including incineration or neutralization, designed to change the physical, chemical or biological character or composition of any hazardous waste to neutralize it or to render it less hazardous or nonhazardous, safer for transport, amenable to recovery or storage or reduced in volume. (1986, c. 492, § 10-288; 1988, c. 891.)

§ 10.1-1434. Additional powers and duties of the Board. — A. In addition to its other powers and duties, with regard to hazardous waste the Board shall have the power and duty to:

1. Require that hazardous waste is treated, stored and disposed of properly;

2. Provide information to the public regarding the proper methods of hazardous waste disposal;

3. Establish procedures, where feasible, to eliminate or reduce the disproportionate burden which may be placed on a community in which is located a hazardous waste treatment, storage or disposal facility, by any means appropriate, including mitigation or compensation;

4. Require that the Department compiles, maintains, and makes available to the public, information on the use and availability of conflict resolution techniques so that controversies and conflicts over the local impacts of hazardous waste facility siting decisions may be resolved by negotiation, mediation or similar techniques;

5. Encourage, whenever possible, alternatives to land burial of hazardous wastes, which will reduce, separate, neutralize, recycle, exchange or destroy hazardous wastes; and

6. Regulate hazardous waste treatment, storage and disposal facilities and require that the costs of long-term post-closure care and maintenance of these facilities is born by their owners and operators.

B. In addition to its other powers and duties, with regard to certification of hazardous waste facility sites the Board shall have the power and duty to:

1. Subject to the approval of the Governor, request the use of the resources and services of any state department or agency for technical assistance in the performance of the Board's duties;

2. Hold public meetings or hearings on any matter related to the siting of hazardous waste facilities;

3. Coordinate the preparation of and to adopt criteria for the siting of hazardous waste facilities;

4. Grant or deny certification of site approval for construction of hazardous waste facilities;

5. Promulgate regulations and procedures for approval of hazardous waste facility sites;

6. Adopt a schedule of fees to charge applicants and to collect fees for the cost of processing applications and site certifications; and

7. Perform any acts authorized by this chapter under, through or by means of its own officers, agents and employees, or by contract with any person. (1986, c. 492, §§ 10-287, 10-290; 1988, c. 891.)

Law Review. — For note, "Federal and State Remedies to Clean Up Hazardous Waste Sites," see 20 U. Rich. L. Rev. 379 (1986).

§ 10.1-1435. Certification of site approval required; "construction" defined; remedies.
— A. No person shall construct or commence construction of a hazardous waste facility without first obtaining a certification of site approval by the Board in the manner prescribed herein. For the purpose of this section, *"construct"* and *"construction"* mean (i) with respect to new facilities, the significant alteration of a site to install permanent equipment or structures or the installation of permanent equipment or structures; (ii) with respect to existing facilities, the alteration or expansion of existing structures or facilities to initially accommodate hazardous waste, any expansion of more than fifty percent of the area or capacity of an existing hazardous waste facility, or any change in design or process of a hazardous waste facility that will, in the opinion of the Board, result in a substantially different type of facility. Construction does not include preliminary engineering or site surveys, environmental studies, site acquisition, acquisition of an option to purchase or activities normally incident thereto.

B. Upon receiving a written request from the owner or operator of the facility, the Board may allow, without going through the procedures of this article, any changes in the facilities which are designed to:

1. Prevent a threat to human health or the environment because of an emergency situation;

2. Comply with federal or state laws and regulations; or

3. Demonstrably result in safer or environmentally more acceptable processes.

C. Any person violating this section may be enjoined by the circuit court of the jurisdiction wherein the facility is located or the proposed facility is to be located. Such an action may be instituted by the Board, the Attorney General, or the political subdivision in which the violation occurs. In any such action, it shall not be necessary for the plaintiff to plead or prove irreparable harm or lack of an adequate remedy at law. No person shall be required to post any injunction bond or other security under this section. No action may be brought under this section after a certification of site approval has been issued by the Board, notwithstanding the pendency of any appeals or other challenges to the Board's action. In any action under this section, the court may award reasonable costs of litigation, including attorney and expert witness fees, to any party if the party substantially prevails on the merits of the case and if in the determination of the court the party against whom the costs are awarded has acted unreasonably. (1986, c. 492, § 10-291; 1988, c. 891.)

§ 10.1-1436. Site approval criteria.
— A. The Board shall promulgate criteria for approval of hazardous waste facility sites. The criteria shall be designed to prevent or minimize the location, construction, or operation of a hazardous waste facility from resulting in (i) any significant adverse impact on the environment and natural resources, and (ii) any significant adverse risks to public health, safety or welfare. The criteria shall also be designed to eliminate or reduce to the extent practicable any significant adverse impacts on the quality of life in the host community and the ability of its inhabitants to maintain quiet enjoyment of their property. The criteria shall ensure that previously approved local comprehensive plans are considered in the certification of hazardous waste facility sites.

B. To avoid, to the maximum extent feasible, duplication with existing agencies and their areas of responsibility, the criteria shall reference, and the Board shall list in the draft and final certifications required hereunder, the agency approvals required and areas of responsibility concerning a site and its operation. The Board shall not review or make findings concerning the adequacy of those agency approvals and areas of responsibility.

C. The Board shall make reasonable efforts to reduce or eliminate duplication between the criteria and other applicable regulations and requirements.

D. The criteria may be amended or modified by the Board at any time. (1986, c. 492, § 10-292; 1988, c. 891.)

§ 10.1-1437. Notice of intent to file application for certification of site approval.

— A. Any person may submit to the Board a notice of intent to file an application for a certification of site approval. The notice shall be in such form as the Board may prescribe by regulation. Knowingly falsifying information, or knowingly withholding any material information, shall void the notice and shall constitute a felony punishable by confinement in the penitentiary for one year or, in the discretion of the jury or the court trying the case without a jury, confinement in jail for not more than twelve months, a fine of not more than $10,000, or both.

Any state agency filing a notice of intent shall include therein a statement explaining why the Commonwealth desires to build a hazardous waste facility and how the public interest would be served thereby.

B. Within forty-five days of receipt of such a notice, the Board shall determine whether it is complete. The Board shall reject any incomplete notice, advise the applicant of the information required to complete it, and allow reasonable time to correct any deficiencies.

C. Upon receipt of the notice, the Board, at the applicant's expense, shall:

1. Deliver or cause to be delivered a copy of the notice of intent together with a copy of this article to the governing body of each host community and to each person owning property immediately adjoining the site of the proposed facility; and

2. Have an informative description of the notice published in a newspaper of general circulation in each host community once each week for four successive weeks. The description shall include the name and address of the applicant, a description of the proposed facility and its location, the places and times where the notice of intent may be examined, the address and telephone number of the Board or other state agency from which information may be obtained, and the date, time and location of the initial public briefing meeting on the notice. (1986, c. 492, § 10-293; 1988, c. 891.)

§ 10.1-1438. Powers of governing body of host community; technical assistance.

— A. The governing body of a host community shall have the power to:

1. Hire and pay consultants and other experts on behalf of the host community in matters pertaining to the siting of the facility;

2. Receive and disburse moneys from the fund, and any other moneys as may be available; and

3. Enter into a contract, which may be assignable at the parties' option, binding upon the governing body of the host community and enforceable against it and future governing bodies of the host community in any court of competent jurisdiction, with an applicant by signing a siting agreement pursuant to § 10.1-1442.

B. The Board shall make available to the governing body from the fund a reasonable sum of money to be determined by the Board. This shall be used by the governing body to hire consultants to provide it with technical assistance and information necessary to aid the governing body in its review of the siting proposal, negotiations with the applicant and the development of a siting agreement.

Unused moneys from the fund shall be returned to the Board. The governing body shall provide the Board with a certified accounting statement of any moneys expended from the fund.

C. The governing body of the host community may appoint a local advisory committee to facilitate communication and the exchange of information among the local government, the community, the applicant and the Board.

D. Notwithstanding the foregoing provisions of this article, the governing body of a host community may notify the Board, within fifteen days after the briefing meeting pursuant to § 10.1-1439, that it has elected to waive further participation under the provisions of this article. After receiving notification from the host community, the Board may issue certification of site approval without further participation by the host community under the provisions of this section and § 10.1-1442. Nothing shall prevent a host community from submitting comments on the application or participating in any public hearing or meeting held pursuant to this chapter, nor shall the host community be precluded from enforcing its regulations and ordinances as provided by subsection G of § 10.1-1446. (1986, c. 492, § 10-294; 1988, c. 891.)

§ **10.1-1439. Briefing meetings.** — A. Not more than seventy-five nor less than sixty days after the delivery of the notice of intent to the host community, the Board shall conduct a briefing meeting in or in reasonable proximity to the host community. A quorum of the Board shall be present. Notice of the date, time, place and purpose of the briefing session shall be prepared by the Board and shall accompany the notice of intent delivered pursuant to subdivision 1 of subsection C of § 10.1-1437 and shall be included in the notice published pursuant to subdivision 2 of subsection C of § 10.1-1437.

At least one representative of the applicant shall be present at the briefing meeting.

The Board shall adopt procedures for the conduct of briefing meetings. The briefing meeting shall provide information on the proposed site and facility and comments, suggestions and questions thereon shall be received.

B. The Board may conduct additional briefing meetings at any time in or near a host community, provided that at least fifteen days in advance of a meeting, notice of the date, time, place and purpose of the meeting is delivered in writing to the applicant, each member of the governing body and to all owners of property adjoining the proposed site.

C. A stenographic or electronic record shall be made of all briefing meetings. The record shall be available for inspection during normal business hours. (1986, c. 492, § 10-295; 1988, c. 891.)

§ **10.1-1440. Impact analysis.** — A. The applicant shall submit to the Board a draft impact analysis for the proposed facility within ninety days after the initial briefing meeting. At the applicant's expense, copies of the draft impact analysis shall be furnished as follows: five to the host community, and one to each person owning property adjoining the site of the proposed facility. At least one copy shall be made available at a convenient location in the host community for public inspection and copying during normal business hours.

B. The draft impact analysis shall include a detailed assessment of the project's suitability with respect to the criteria and other information the Board may require by regulation.

C. The Board, at the applicant's expense, shall cause notice of the filing of the draft impact analysis to be made in the manner provided in § 10.1-1447 within ten days of receipt. The notice shall include (i) a general description of the analysis, (ii) a list of recipients, (iii) a description of the places and times that the analysis will be available for inspection, (iv) a description of the Board's procedures for receiving comments on the analysis, and (v) the addresses and telephone numbers for obtaining information from the Board.

D. The Board shall allow forty-five days after publication of notice for comment on the draft impact analysis. No sooner than thirty and no more than forty days after publication of notice of the draft impact analysis, the Board shall conduct a public meeting on the draft impact analysis in or near the host community. The meeting shall be for the purpose of explaining, answering questions and receiving comments on the draft impact analysis. A representative of the governing body and a representative of the applicant shall be present at the meeting.

E. Within ten days after the close of the comment period, the Board shall forward to the applicant a copy of all comments received on the draft impact analysis, together with its own comments.

F. The applicant shall prepare and submit a final impact analysis to the Board after receiving the comments. The final impact analysis shall reflect the comments as they pertain to each of the items listed in subsection B of this section. Upon request, a copy of the final impact analysis shall be provided by the applicant to each of the persons who received the draft impact analysis.

G. This section shall not apply when the host community has elected to waive participation under subsection D of § 10.1-1438. (1986, c. 492, § 10-296; 1988, c. 891.)

§ **10.1-1441. Application for certification of site approval.** — A. At any time within six months after submission of the final impact analysis, the applicant may submit to the Board an application for certification of site approval. The application shall contain:

1. Conceptual engineering designs for the proposed facility;

2. A detailed description of the facility's suitability to meet the criteria promulgated by the Board, including any design and operation measures that will be necessary or otherwise undertaken to meet the criteria; and

3. A siting agreement, if one has been executed pursuant to subsection C of § 10.1-1442, or, if none has been executed, a statement to that effect.

B. The application shall be accompanied by whatever fee the Board, by regulation, prescribes pursuant to § 10.1-1434.

C. The Board shall review the application for completeness and notify the applicant within fifteen days of receipt that the application is incomplete or complete.

If the application is incomplete, the Board shall advise the applicant of the information necessary to make the application complete. The Board shall take no further action until the application is complete.

If the application is complete, the Board shall direct the applicant to furnish copies of the application to the following: five to the host community, one to the Director, and one to each person owning property adjoining the proposed site. At least one copy of the application shall be made available by the applicant for inspection and copying at a convenient place in a host community during normal business hours.

D. The Board shall cause notice of the application to be made in the manner provided in § 10.1-1447 and shall notify each governing body that upon publication of the notice the governing body shall conclude all negotiations with the applicant within thirty days of publication of the notice. The applicant and the governing body may, by agreement, extend the time for negotiation to a fixed date and shall forthwith notify the Board of this date. The Board may also extend the time to a fixed date for good cause shown.

If the host community has waived participation under the provisions of subsection D of § 10.1-1438, the Board shall, at the time that notice of the application is made, request that the governing body submit, within thirty days of receiving notice, a report meeting the requirements of subdivision 2 of subsection E of this section.

E. At the end of the period specified in subsection D of this section, a governing body shall submit to the Board and to the applicant a report containing:

1. A complete siting agreement, if any, or in case of failure to reach full agreement, a description of points of agreement and unresolved points; and

2. Any conditions or restrictions on the construction, operation or design of the facility that are required by local ordinance.

F. If the report is not submitted within the time required, the Board may proceed as specified in subsection A of § 10.1-1443.

G. The applicant may submit comments on the report of the governing body at any time prior to the issuance of the draft certification of site approval.

H. Notwithstanding any other provision of this chapter, if the host community has notified the Board, pursuant to subsection D of § 10.1-1438, that it has elected to waive further participation hereunder, the Board shall so notify the applicant within fifteen days of receipt of notice from the host community, and shall advise the applicant of the time for submitting its application for certification of site approval. The applicant shall submit its application within the time prescribed by the Board, which time shall not be less than ninety days unless the applicant agrees to a shorter time. (1986, c. 492, § 10-297; 1988, c. 891.)

Cross references. — As to records which are excluded from the provisions of the Virginia Freedom of Information Act, see § 2.2-3705.1 et seq.

§ **10.1-1442. Negotiations; siting agreement.** — A. The governing body or its designated representatives and the applicant, after submission of notice of intent to file an application for certification of site approval, may meet to discuss any matters pertaining to the site and the facility, including negotiations of a siting agreement. The time and place of any meeting shall be set by agreement, but at least forty-eight hours' notice shall be given to members of the governing body and the applicant.

B. The siting agreement may include any terms and conditions, including mitigation of adverse impacts and financial compensation to the host community, concerning the facility.

C. The siting agreement shall be executed by the signatures of (i) the chief executive officer of the host community, who has been so directed by a majority vote of the local governing body, and (ii) the applicant or authorized agent.

D. The Board shall assist in facilitating negotiations between the local governing body and the applicant.

E. No injunction, stay, prohibition, mandamus or other order or writ shall lie against the conduct of negotiations or discussions concerning a siting agreement or against the agreement itself, except as they may be conducted in violation of the provisions of this chapter or any other state or federal law. (1986, c. 492, § 10-298; 1988, c. 891.)

§ **10.1-1443. Draft certification of site approval.** — A. Within thirty days after receipt of the governing body's report or as otherwise provided in subsection F of § 10.1-1441, the Board shall issue or deny a draft certification of site approval.

When application is made pursuant to subsection H of § 10.1-1441, the Board shall issue or deny draft certification of site approval within ninety days after receipt of the completed application.

B. The Board may deny the application for certification of site approval if it finds that the applicant has failed or refused to negotiate in good faith with the governing body for the purpose of attempting to develop a siting agreement.

C. The draft certification of site approval shall specify the terms, conditions and requirements that the Board deems necessary to protect health, safety, welfare, the environment and natural resources.

D. Copies of the draft certification of site approval, together with notice of the date, time and place of public hearing required under § 10.1-1444, shall be delivered by the Board to the governing body of each host community, and to persons owning property adjoining the site for the proposed facility. At least one copy of the draft certification shall be available at a convenient location in the host community for inspection and copying during normal business hours. (1986, c. 492, § 10-299; 1988, c. 891.)

§ 10.1-1444. Public hearing on draft certification of site approval. —

A. The Board shall conduct a public hearing on the draft certification not less than fifteen nor more than thirty days after the first publication of notice. A quorum of the Board shall be present. The hearing shall be conducted in the host community.

B. Notice of the hearing shall be made at the applicant's expense and in the manner provided in § 10.1-1447. It shall include:

1. A brief description of the terms and conditions of the draft certification;

2. Information describing the date, time, place and purpose of the hearing;

3. The name, address and telephone number of an official designated by the Board from whom interested persons may obtain access to documents and information concerning the proposed facility and the draft application;

4. A brief description of the rules and procedures to be followed at the hearing and the time for receiving comments; and

5. The name, address and telephone number of an official designated by the Board to receive written comments on the draft certification.

C. The Board shall designate a person to act as hearing officer for the receipt of comments and testimony at the public hearing. The hearing officer shall conduct the hearing in an expeditious and orderly fashion, according to such rules and procedures as the Board shall prescribe.

D. A transcript of the hearing shall be made and shall be incorporated into the hearing record.

E. Within fifteen days after the close of the hearing, the hearing officer shall deliver a copy of the hearing record to each member of the Board. The hearing officer may prepare a summary to accompany the record, and this summary shall become part of the record. (1986, c. 492, § 10-300; 1988, c. 891.)

§ 10.1-1445. Final decision on certification of site approval. —

A. Within forty-five days after the close of the public hearing, the Board shall meet within or near the host community and shall vote to issue or deny the certification of site approval. The Board may include in the certification any terms and conditions which it deems necessary and appropriate to protect and prevent injury or adverse risk to health, safety, welfare, the environment and natural resources. At least seven days' notice of the date, time, place and purpose of the meeting shall be made in the manner provided in § 10.1-1447. No testimony or evidence will be received at the meeting.

B. The Board shall grant the certification of site approval if it finds:

1. That the terms and conditions thereof will protect and prevent injury or unacceptable adverse risk to health, safety, welfare, the environment and natural resources;

2. That the facility will comply and be consistent with the criteria promulgated by the Board; and

3. That the applicant has made reasonable and appropriate efforts to reach a siting agreement with the host community including, though not limited to, efforts to mitigate or compensate the host community and its residents for any adverse economic effects of the facility. This requirement shall not apply when the host community has waived participation pursuant to subsection D of § 10.1-1438.

C. The Board's decision to grant or deny certification shall be based on the hearing record and shall be accompanied by the written findings of fact and conclusions upon which the decision was based. The Board shall provide the applicant and the governing body of the host community with copies of the decision, together with the findings and conclusions, by certified mail.

D. The grant or denial of certification shall constitute final action by the Board. (1986, c. 492, § 10-301; 1988, c. 891.)

§ **10.1-1446. Effect of certification.** — A. Grant of certification of site approval shall supersede any local ordinance or regulation that is inconsistent with the terms of the certification. Nothing in this chapter shall affect the authority of the host community to enforce its regulations and ordinances to the extent that they are not inconsistent with the terms and conditions of the certification of site approval. Grant of certification shall not preclude or excuse the applicant from the requirement to obtain approval or permits under this chapter or other state or federal laws. The certification shall continue in effect until it is amended, revoked or suspended.

B. The certification may be amended for cause under procedures and regulations prescribed by the Board.

C. The certification shall be terminated or suspended (i) at the request of the owner of the facility; (ii) upon a finding by the Board that conditions of the certification have been violated in a manner that poses a substantial risk to health, safety or the environment; (iii) upon termination of the hazardous waste facility permit by the Director or the EPA Administrator; or (iv) upon a finding by the Board that the applicant has knowingly falsified or failed to provide material information required in the notice of intent and application.

D. The facility owner shall promptly notify the Board of any changes in the ownership of the facility or of any significant changes in capacity or design of the facility.

E. Nothing in the certification shall constitute a defense to liability in any civil action involving private rights.

F. The Commonwealth may not acquire any site for a facility by eminent domain prior to the time certification of site approval is obtained. However, any agency or representative of the Commonwealth may enter upon a proposed site pursuant to the provisions of § 25.1-203.

G. The governing body of the host community shall have the authority to enforce local regulations and ordinances to the extent provided by subsection A of this section and the terms of the siting agreement. The local governing body may be authorized by the Board to enforce specified provisions of the certification. (1986, c. 492, § 10-302; 1988, c. 891; 2003, c. 940.)

§ **10.1-1447. Public participation; notice.** — A. Public participation in the development, revision and implementation of regulations and programs under this chapter shall be provided for, encouraged and assisted by the Board.

B. Whenever notice is required to be made under the terms of this chapter, unless the context expressly and exclusively provides otherwise, it shall be disseminated as follows:

1. By publication once each week for two successive weeks in a newspaper of general circulation within the area to be affected by the subject of the notice;

2. By broadcast over one or more radio stations within the area to be affected by the subject of the notice;

3. By mailing to each person who has asked to receive notice; and
4. By such additional means as the Board deems appropriate.

C. Every notice shall provide a description of the subject for which notice is made and shall include the name and telephone number of a person from whom additional information may be obtained. (1986, c. 492, § 10-303; 1988, c. 891.)

§ 10.1-1448. Technical Assistance Fund. — A special fund, to be known as the Technical Assistance Fund, is created in the Office of the State Treasurer. The Fund shall consist of appropriations made to the Fund by the General Assembly. The Board shall make moneys from the Fund available to any host community for the purposes set out in subsection C of § 10.1-1438. (1986, c. 492, § 10-304; 1988, c. 891.)

§ 10.1-1449. Siting Dedicated Revenue Fund. — There is hereby established in the state treasury a special dedicated revenue fund to be designated as the "Siting Dedicated Revenue Fund," which shall consist of fees and other payments made by applicants to process applications for site certification as provided in § 10.1-1434, and other moneys appropriated thereto, gifts, grants, and the interest accruing thereon. (1986, c. 602, § 10-304.1; 1988, c. 891.)

ARTICLE 7.

Transportation of Hazardous Materials.

§ 10.1-1450. Waste Management Board to promulgate regulations regarding hazardous materials. — The Board shall promulgate regulations designating the manner and method by which hazardous materials shall be loaded, unloaded, packed, identified, marked, placarded, stored and transported. Such regulations shall be no more restrictive than any applicable federal laws or regulations. (1986, c. 492, § 10-305; 1988, c. 891; 1992, c. 208; 1997, c. 260.)

Cross references. — For present provisions relating to granting of variances for commercial drivers transporting hazardous wastes, see § 46.2-341.9:1.

Michie's Jurisprudence. — For related discussion, see 2B M.J. Aviation, § 1; 3B M.J. Carriers, § 96.

§ 10.1-1451. Enforcement of article and regulations. — The Department of State Police and all other law-enforcement officers of the Commonwealth who have satisfactorily completed the course in Hazardous Materials Compliance and Enforcement as prescribed by the U.S. Department of Transportation, Research and Special Programs Administration, Office of Hazardous Materials Transportation, in federal safety regulations and safety inspection procedures pertaining to the transportation of hazardous materials, shall enforce the provisions of this article, and any rule or regulation promulgated hereunder. Those law-enforcement officers certified to enforce the provisions of this article and any regulation promulgated hereunder, shall annually receive in-service training in current federal safety regulations and safety inspection procedures pertaining to the transportation of hazardous materials. (1986, c. 492, § 10-306; 1988, cc. 14, 891.)

§ 10.1-1452. Article not to preclude exercise of certain regulatory powers. — The provisions of this article shall not preclude the exercise of the statutory and regulatory powers of any agency, department or political subdivision of the Commonwealth having statutory authority to regulate hazardous materials on specified highways or portions thereof. (1986, c. 492, § 10-307; 1988, c. 891.)

§ 10.1-1453. Exceptions. — This article shall not apply to regular military or naval forces of the United States, the duly authorized militia of any state or territory thereof, police or fire departments, or sheriff's offices and regional jails of this Commonwealth, provided the same are acting within their official capacity and in the performance of their duties, or to the transportation of hazardous radioactive materials in accordance with § 44-146.30. (1986, c. 492, § 10-308; 1988, c. 891; 1995, c. 112.)

§ 10.1-1454. Transportation under United States regulations. — Any person transporting hazardous materials in accordance with regulations promulgated under the laws of the United States, shall be deemed to have complied with the provisions of this article, except when such transportation is excluded from regulation under the laws or regulations of the United States. (1986, c. 492, § 10-309; 1988, c. 891.)

Law Review. — For 2003/2004 survey of environmental law, see 39 U. Rich. L. Rev. 203 (2004).

Michie's Jurisprudence. — For related discussion, see 2B M.J. Aviation, § 1.

ARTICLE 7.1.

Transportation of Solid and Medical Wastes on State Waters.

§ 10.1-1454.1. Regulation of wastes transported by water. — A. The Board shall develop regulations governing the commercial transport, loading and off-loading of nonhazardous solid waste (except scrap metal, dredged material, recyclable construction demolition debris being transported directly to a processing facility for recycling or reuse, and source-separated recyclables), municipal and industrial sludge, and regulated medical waste by ship, barge or other vessel upon the navigable waters of the Commonwealth as are necessary to protect the health, safety, and welfare of the citizens of the Commonwealth and to protect the Commonwealth's environment and natural resources from pollution, impairment or destruction. Included in the regulations shall be provisions governing (i) the issuance of permits by rule to facilities receiving nonhazardous solid waste (except scrap metal, dredged material, recyclable construction demolition debris being transported directly to a processing facility for recycling or reuse, and source-separated recyclables), municipal and industrial sludge, and regulated medical waste from a ship, barge or other vessel transporting such wastes upon the navigable waters of the Commonwealth and (ii) to the extent allowable under federal law and regulation, the commercial transport of nonhazardous solid wastes (except scrap metal, dredged material, recyclable construction demolition debris being transported directly to a processing facility for recycling or reuse, and source-separated recyclables), municipal and industrial sludge, and regulated medical waste upon the navigable waters of the Commonwealth and the loading and off-loading of ships, barges and other vessels transporting such waste.
B. 1. Included in the regulations shall be requirements, to the extent allowable under federal law, that: (a) containers holding wastes be watertight and be designed, constructed, secured and maintained so as to prevent the escape of wastes, liquids and odors and to prevent the loss or spillage of wastes in the event of an accident; (b) containers be tested at least two times a year and be accompanied by a certification from the container owner that such

testing has shown that the containers are watertight; (c) each container be listed on a manifest designed to assure that the waste being transported in each container is suitable for the destination facility; and (d) containers be secured to the barges to prevent accidents during transportation, loading and unloading.

2. For the purposes of this section and the regulations promulgated hereunder, a container shall satisfy clauses (a) and (b) of subdivision B 1, if it meets the following requirements:

a. Each container shall be certified for special service by a Delegated Approval Authority approved by the U.S. Coast Guard in accordance with 49 CFR Parts 450 through 453 as having met the requirements for the approval of prototype containers described in §§ 1.5 and 1.17.2 of the Rules for Certification of Cargo Containers, 1998, American Bureau of Shipping, including a special container prototype test as follows: a minimum internal head of three inches of water shall be applied to all sides, seams, bottom and top of the container for at least 15 minutes of each side, seam, bottom and top, during which the container shall remain free from the escape of water.

b. Each container shall be certified by the Delegated Approval Authority as having passed the following test when the container is placed in service and at least once every six months thereafter while it remains in service:

(1) Each container shall have a minimum internal head of 24 inches of water applied to the container in an upright position for at least 15 minutes during which the container shall remain free from the escape of water. All wastewater and contaminated water resulting from this test procedure shall be disposed of in compliance with the applicable regulations of the State Water Control Board.

(2) Each container shall be visually inspected for damage on all sides, plus the top and bottom, and shall have no visible holes, gaps, or structural damage affecting its integrity or performance.

c. Following each unloading of solid waste from a container, each container shall be visually inspected, as practical, at the solid waste management facility immediately upon unloading for damage on all sides, plus top and bottom, and shall have no visible holes, gaps, or structural damage affecting its integrity or performance.

3. It shall be a violation of this chapter if during transportation, holding, or storage operations, or in the event of an accident, there is an: (i) entry of liquids into a container; (ii) escape, loss, or spillage of wastes or liquids from a container; or (iii) escape of odors from a container.

C. A facility utilized to receive nonhazardous solid waste (except scrap metal, dredged material, recyclable construction demolition debris being transported directly to a processing facility for recycling or reuse, and source-separated recyclables), municipal and industrial sludge, or regulated medical waste from a ship, barge or other vessel regulated pursuant to subsection A, arriving at the facility upon the navigable waters of the Commonwealth, is a solid waste management facility and is subject to the requirements of this chapter. On and after the effective date of the regulations promulgated under subsection A, no new or existing facilities shall receive any wastes regulated under subsection A from a ship, barge or other vessel without a permit issued in accordance with the Board's regulations.

D. 1. The Board shall, by regulation, establish a fee schedule, payable by the owner or operator of any ship, barge or other vessel carrying, loading or off-loading waste regulated under this article on the navigable waters of the Commonwealth, for the purpose of funding the administrative and enforcement costs of this article associated with such operations including, but not limited to, the inspection and monitoring of such ships, barges or other vessels to ensure compliance with this article, and for funding activities authorized by this section to abate pollution caused by barging of waste, to improve water quality, or for other waste-related purposes.

2. The owner or operator of a facility permitted to receive wastes regulated under this article from a ship, barge or other vessel shall be assessed a permit fee in accordance with the criteria set forth in § 10.1-1402.1. However, such fees shall also include an additional amount to cover the Department's costs for facility inspections that it shall conduct on at least a quarterly basis.

3. The fees collected pursuant to this article shall be deposited into a separate account within the Virginia Waste Management Board Permit Program Fund (§ 10.1-1402.2) and shall be treated as are other moneys in that fund except that they shall only be used for the purposes of this article, and for funding purposes authorized by this article to abate pollution caused by barging of waste, to improve water quality, or for other waste-related purposes.

E. The Board shall promulgate regulations requiring owners and operators of ships, barges and other vessels transporting wastes regulated under this article to demonstrate financial responsibility sufficient to comply with the requirements of this article as a condition of operation. Regulations governing the amount of any financial responsibility required shall take into consideration: (i) the risk of potential damage or injury to state waters and the impairment of beneficial uses that may result from spillage or leakage from the ship, barge or vessel; (ii) the potential costs of containment and cleanup; and (iii) the nature and degree of injury or interference with general health, welfare and property that may result.

F. The owner or operator of a ship, barge or other vessel from which there is spillage or loss to state waters of wastes subject to regulations under this article shall immediately report such spillage or loss in accordance with the regulations of the Board and shall immediately take all such actions as may be necessary to contain and remove such wastes from state waters.

G. No person shall transport wastes regulated under this article on the navigable waters of the Commonwealth by ship, barge or other vessel unless such ship, barge or vessel and the containers carried thereon are designed, constructed, loaded, operated and maintained so as to prevent the escape of liquids, waste and odors and to prevent the loss or spillage of waste in the event of an accident. A violation of this subsection shall be a Class 1 misdemeanor. For the purposes of this subsection, the term "odors" means any emissions that cause an odor objectionable to individuals of ordinary sensibility.

H. The Director may grant variances for the commercial transport, loading, and off-loading of solid waste on waters of the Commonwealth from the requirements of this section provided: (i) travel on state waters is minimized; (ii) the solid waste is easily identifiable, is not hazardous, and is containerized so as to prevent the escape of liquids, waste, and odors; (iii) the containers are secured to the vessel to prevent spillage; (iv) the amount of solid waste transported does not exceed 300 tons annually; and (v) the activity will not occur when weather conditions pose a risk of the vessel losing its load. (1998, cc. 705, 717; 1999, c. 608; 2003, c. 830; 2005, cc. 130, 232; 2006, c. 477.)

Cross references. — As to punishment for Class 1 misdemeanors, see § 18.2-11.

The 2005 amendments. — The 2005 amendments by cc. 130 and 232 are identical, and added subsection G.

The 2006 amendments. — The 2006 amendment by c. 477 inserted the subdivision B 1 designation and deleted "Also" at the beginnning of subdivision B 1; inserted subdivisions B 2 and B 3; and redesignated former subsections B through G as subsections C through H.

Law Review. — For 2000 survey of Virginia environmental law, see 34 U. Rich. L. Rev. 799 (2000).

CASE NOTES

Constitutionality. — Because the stacking provisions in this section as it read prior to its amendment in 2003, which required that containerized waste be stacked no more than two high, would have a lopsided effect on the importation of out-of-state waste and would essentially preclude the use of barges in Virginia to transport such waste, they were subject to strict scrutiny and the virtual per se rule of invalidity under the Commerce Clause. Hence, the court would grant preliminary injunction against enforcement, pending resolution on the merits. Waste Mgt. Holdings, Inc. v. Gilmore, 64 F. Supp. 2d 523 (E.D. Va. 1999).

Stacking provision unconstitutional under commerce clause. — No reasonable juror could find the provisions of this section as it read prior to its amendment in 2003, banning the stacking of containers holding solid waste more than two high, had a purpose other than to reduce the flow of municipal solid waste generated outside of Virginia into Virginia for disposal. Waste Mgmt. Holdings, Inc. v. Gilmore, 252 F.3d 316, 2001 U.S. App. LEXIS 11573 (4th Cir. 2001), cert. denied, 535 U.S. 904, 122 S. Ct. 1203, 152 L. Ed. 2d 142 (2002).

Savings clause does not bar challenge to statute. — The saving clauses stating that these provisions would be implemented only to the extent allowed by federal law did not prevent a plaintiff from challenging the stacking provision in this section as it read prior to amendment in 2003, because the language of this clause was repugnant to the straightforward, limiting language of the statutory provisions. Waste Mgmt. Holdings, Inc. v. Gilmore, 252 F.3d 316, 2001 U.S. App. LEXIS 11573 (4th Cir. 2001), cert. denied, 535 U.S. 904, 122 S. Ct. 1203, 152 L. Ed. 2d 142 (2002).

Negative impact on interstate commerce established. — Parties asserting that the ban on stacking solid waste containers more than two containers high, in this section as it read prior to amendment in 2003, violated the Commerce Clause were only required to show how the ban, if enforced, would negatively impact interstate commerce to a greater degree than intrastate commerce, and this they had done. Waste Mgmt. Holdings, Inc. v. Gilmore, 252 F.3d 316, 2001 U.S. App. LEXIS 11573 (4th Cir. 2001), cert. denied, 535 U.S. 904, 122 S. Ct. 1203, 152 L. Ed. 2d 142 (2002).

CIRCUIT COURT OPINIONS

Per ton fee upheld. — Trial court upheld the administrative regulation adopted by the Virginia Waste Management Board of a one dollar per ton of waste fee off-loaded at facilities that receive solid and medical waste transported on state waters, as evidence in the record supported imposition of that fee. James River Ass'n v. Commonwealth ex rel. Waste Mgmt. Bd., 67 Va. Cir. 44, 2005 Va. Cir. LEXIS 148 (Richmond Feb. 4, 2005).

Standing water test invalidated. — Evidence in the record did not support the Virginia Waste Management Board's adoption of the regulation that prescribed a 24-inch standing water test to determine whether containers handling certain types of waste were watertight; by definition, that test did not determine whether a container, which was nine-feet high, was watertight, and a court was authorized to invalidate agency action where such action was neither supported by the record nor justified by statutory authority, as was true of the 24-inch standing water test. James River Ass'n v. Commonwealth ex rel. Waste Mgmt. Bd., 67 Va. Cir. 44, 2005 Va. Cir. LEXIS 148 (Richmond Feb. 4, 2005).

§ **10.1-1454.2:** Repealed by Acts 2003, c. 830.

ARTICLE 7.2.

Transportation of Municipal Solid and Medical Waste by Truck.

§ **10.1-1454.3. Regulation of road transportation of waste.** — A. The Board, in consultation with the appropriate agencies, shall develop regulations governing the commercial transport of nonhazardous municipal solid waste, except scrap metal and source-separated recyclables, and regulated medical waste by truck as are necessary to protect the health, safety, and welfare of the citizens of the Commonwealth, and to protect the Commonwealth's environment and natural resources from pollution, impairment, or destruction. Included in the regulations, to the extent allowable under federal law and regulation, shall be provisions:

1. Governing the transport of wastes by truck and the design and construction of the containers and trailers transporting waste by truck so that they will be designed, constructed and maintained so as to, as much as is reasonably practicable, prevent the escape of wastes and liquids and to prevent the loss or spillage of wastes to the extent possible in the event of an accident; and

2. Requiring owners of trucks transporting wastes regulated under this article to demonstrate financial responsibility sufficient to comply with the requirements of this article as a condition of operation. Regulations governing the amount of any financial responsibility required shall take into consideration (i) the risk of potential damage or injury that may result from spillage or leakage; (ii) the potential costs of containment and cleanup; and (iii) the nature and degree of injury or interference with general health, welfare and property that may result.

B. The owner or operator of a truck from which there is spillage or loss of wastes subject to regulations under this article shall immediately report such spillage or loss in accordance with the regulations of the Board and shall immediately take all such actions as may be necessary to contain and remove such wastes.

C. No person shall transport by truck wastes regulated under this article unless the containers carried thereon are designed, constructed, loaded, operated and maintained in accordance with the regulations developed pursuant to subsection A. A violation of this subsection shall be a Class 1 misdemeanor.

D. For the purposes of this section, the term *"truck"* means any tractor truck semitrailer combination with four or more axles. (1999, cc. 584, 613, 947.)

The number of this section was assigned by the Virginia Code Commission, the number in the 1999 act having been 10.1-1454.2.

Cross references. — As to punishment for Class 1 misdemeanors, see § 18.2-11.

Law Review. — For 2000 survey of Virginia environmental law, see 34 U. Rich. L. Rev. 799 (2000).

CASE NOTES

Constitutionality. — This statute's imposition of certain requirements on large trucks carrying solid waste is unconstitutional under the dormant commerce clause in that it disproportionately burdens trucks carrying waste from outside of Virginia. Waste Mgmt. Holdings, Inc. v. Gilmore, 252 F.3d 316, 2001 U.S. App. LEXIS 11573 (4th Cir. 2001), cert. denied, 535 U.S. 904, 122 S. Ct. 1203, 152 L. Ed. 2d 142 (2002).

No reasonable juror could find that the provisions of this statute imposing certain requirements on large trucks used to carry solid waste had a purpose other than to reduce the flow of municipal solid waste generated outside of Virginia into Virginia for disposal. Waste Mgmt. Holdings, Inc. v. Gilmore, 252 F.3d 316, 2001 U.S. App. LEXIS 11573 (4th Cir. 2001), cert. denied, 535 U.S. 904, 122 S. Ct. 1203, 152 L. Ed. 2d 142 (2002).

Savings clause does not bar challenge to statute. — The saving clauses stating that this provision will be implemented only to the extent allowed by federal law does not prevent a plaintiff from challenging the four-or-more-axle provision because the language of this clause is repugnant to the straightforward, limiting language of the statutory provisions. Waste Mgmt. Holdings, Inc. v. Gilmore, 252 F.3d 316, 2001 U.S. App. LEXIS 11573 (4th Cir. 2001), cert. denied, 535 U.S. 904, 122 S. Ct. 1203, 152 L. Ed. 2d 142 (2002).

ARTICLE 8.

Penalties, Enforcement and Judicial Review.

§ 10.1-1455. Penalties and enforcement. — A. Any person who violates any provision of this chapter, any condition of a permit or certification, or any regulation or order of the Board shall, upon such finding by an appropriate circuit court, be assessed a civil penalty of not more than $32,500 for each day

431

of such violation. All civil penalties under this section shall be recovered in a civil action brought by the Attorney General in the name of the Commonwealth. Such civil penalties shall be paid into the state treasury and deposited by the State Treasurer into the Virginia Environmental Emergency Response Fund pursuant to Chapter 25 (§ 10.1-2500 et seq.) of this title.

B. In addition to the penalties provided above, any person who knowingly transports any hazardous waste to an unpermitted facility; who knowingly transports, treats, stores, or disposes of hazardous waste without a permit or in violation of a permit; or who knowingly makes any false statement or representation in any application, disclosure statement, label, manifest, record, report, permit, or other document filed, maintained, or used for purposes of hazardous waste program compliance shall be guilty of a felony punishable by a term of imprisonment of not less than one year nor more than five years and a fine of not more than $32,500 for each violation, either or both. The provisions of this subsection shall be deemed to constitute a lesser included offense of the violation set forth under subsection I.

Each day of violation of each requirement shall constitute a separate offense.

C. The Board is authorized to issue orders to require any person to comply with the provisions of any law administered by the Board, the Director or the Department, any condition of a permit or certification, or any regulations promulgated by the Board or to comply with any case decision, as defined in § 2.2-4001, of the Board or Director. Any such order shall be issued only after a hearing in accordance with § 2.2-4020 with at least 30 days' notice to the affected person of the time, place and purpose thereof. Such order shall become effective not less than 15 days after mailing a copy thereof by certified mail to the last known address of such person. The provisions of this section shall not affect the authority of the Board to issue separate orders and regulations to meet any emergency as provided in § 10.1-1402.

D. Any person willfully violating or refusing, failing or neglecting to comply with any regulation or order of the Board or the Director, any condition of a permit or certification or any provision of this chapter shall be guilty of a Class 1 misdemeanor unless a different penalty is specified.

Any person violating or failing, neglecting, or refusing to obey any lawful regulation or order of the Board or the Director, any condition of a permit or certification or any provision of this chapter may be compelled in a proceeding instituted in an appropriate court by the Board or the Director to obey such regulation, permit, certification, order or provision of this chapter and to comply therewith by injunction, mandamus, or other appropriate remedy.

E. Without limiting the remedies which may be obtained in this section, any person violating or failing, neglecting or refusing to obey any injunction, mandamus or other remedy obtained pursuant to this section shall be subject, in the discretion of the court, to a civil penalty not to exceed $32,500 for each violation. Such civil penalties shall be paid into the state treasury and deposited by the State Treasurer into the Virginia Environmental Emergency Response Fund pursuant to Chapter 25 of this title. Each day of violation of each requirement shall constitute a separate offense. Such civil penalties may, in the discretion of the court assessing them, be directed to be paid into the treasury of the county, city or town in which the violation occurred, to be used to abate environmental pollution in such manner as the court may, by order, direct, except that where the owner in violation is the county, city or town itself, or its agent, the court shall direct the penalty to be paid into the state treasury and deposited by the State Treasurer into the Virginia Environmental Emergency Response Fund pursuant to Chapter 25 of this title.

F. With the consent of any person who has violated or failed, neglected or refused to obey any regulation or order of the Board or the Director, any condition of a permit or any provision of this chapter, the Board may provide, in an order issued by the Board against such person, for the payment of civil charges for past violations in specific sums, not to exceed the limits specified in this section. Such civil charges shall be instead of any appropriate civil penalty which could be imposed under this section. Such civil charges shall be paid into the state treasury and deposited by the State Treasurer into the Virginia Environmental Emergency Response Fund pursuant to Chapter 25 of this title.

G. In addition to all other available remedies, the Board may issue administrative orders for the violation of (i) any law or regulation administered by the Board; (ii) any condition of a permit or certificate issued pursuant to this chapter; or (iii) any case decision or order of the Board. Issuance of an administrative order shall be a case decision as defined in § 2.2-4001 and shall be issued only after a hearing before a hearing officer appointed by the Supreme Court in accordance with § 2.2-4020. Orders issued pursuant to this subsection may include civil penalties of up to $32,500 per violation not to exceed $100,000 per order, and may compel the taking of corrective actions or the cessation of any activity upon which the order is based. The Board may assess penalties under this subsection if (a) the person has been issued at least two written notices of alleged violation by the Department for the same or substantially related violations at the same site, (b) such violations have not been resolved by demonstration that there was no violation, by an order issued by the Board or the Director, or by other means, (c) at least 130 days have passed since the issuance of the first notice of alleged violation, and (d) there is a finding that such violations have occurred after a hearing conducted in accordance with this subsection. The actual amount of any penalty assessed shall be based upon the severity of the violations, the extent of any potential or actual environmental harm, the compliance history of the facility or person, any economic benefit realized from the noncompliance, and the ability of the person to pay the penalty. The Board shall provide the person with the calculation for the proposed penalty prior to any hearing conducted for the issuance of an order that assesses penalties pursuant to this subsection. Penalties shall be paid to the state treasury and deposited by the State Treasurer into the Virginia Environmental Emergency Response Fund (§ 10.1-2500 et seq.). The issuance of a notice of alleged violation by the Department shall not be considered a case decision as defined in § 2.2-4001. Any notice of alleged violation shall include a description of each violation, the specific provision of law violated, and information on the process for obtaining a final decision or fact finding from the Department on whether or not a violation has occurred, and nothing in this section shall preclude an owner from seeking such a determination. Orders issued pursuant to this subsection shall become effective five days after having been delivered to the affected persons or mailed by certified mail to the last known address of such persons. Should the Board find that any person is adversely affecting the public health, safety or welfare, or the environment, the Board shall, after a reasonable attempt to give notice, issue, without a hearing, an emergency administrative order directing the person to cease the activity immediately and undertake any needed corrective action, and shall within 10 days hold a hearing, after reasonable notice as to the time and place thereof to the person, to affirm, modify, amend or cancel the emergency administrative order. If the Board finds that a person who has been issued an administrative order or an emergency administrative order is not complying with the order's terms, the Board may utilize the enforcement and penalty provisions of this article to secure compliance.

H. In addition to all other available remedies, the Department and generators of recycling residues shall have standing to seek enforcement by injunction of conditions which are specified by applicants in order to receive the priority treatment of their permit applications pursuant to § 10.1-1408.1.

I. Any person who knowingly transports, treats, stores, disposes of, or exports any hazardous waste in violation of this chapter or in violation of the regulations promulgated by the Board and who knows at the time that he thereby places another person in imminent danger of death or serious bodily injury, shall, upon conviction, be guilty of a felony punishable by a term of imprisonment of not less than two years nor more than 15 years and a fine of not more than $250,000, either or both. A defendant that is not an individual shall, upon conviction of violating this section, be subject to a fine not exceeding the greater of $1 million or an amount that is three times the economic benefit realized by the defendant as a result of the offense. The maximum penalty shall be doubled with respect to both fine and imprisonment for any subsequent conviction of the same person.

J. Criminal prosecutions under this chapter shall be commenced within three years after discovery of the offense, notwithstanding the provisions of any other statute.

K. The Board shall be entitled to an award of reasonable attorneys' fees and costs in any action brought by the Board under this section in which it substantially prevails on the merits of the case, unless special circumstances would make an award unjust.

L. The Board shall develop and provide an opportunity for public comment on guidelines and procedures that contain specific criteria for calculating the appropriate penalty for each violation based upon the severity of the violations, the extent of any potential or actual environmental harm, the compliance history of the facility or person, any economic benefit realized from the noncompliance, and the ability of the person to pay the penalty. (1986, c. 492, § 10-310; 1988, c. 891; 1990, cc. 12, 781, 912, 919; 1991, c. 718; 1993, c. 23; 1998, c. 837; 1999, c. 876; 2005, cc. 133, 706.)

Cross references. — As to punishment for Class 1 misdemeanors, see § 18.2-11. As to the definition of "racketeering activity" and the Virginia Racketeer Influenced and Corrupt Organization Act, see § 18.2-513 et seq.

Editor's note. — Acts 1993, c. 23, which amended this section, in cl. 2 provides: "The provisions of this act are declaratory of existing law."

Acts 2005, c. 706, cl. 2, provides: "That the Director of the Department of Environmental Quality shall develop uniform procedures to govern the formal hearings conducted pursuant to this act to ensure they are conducted in accordance with the Administrative Process Act, any policies adopted by the State Water Control Board, the Virginia Waste Management Board, or the State Air Pollution Control Board and to ensure that the facility owners and operators have access to information on how such hearings will be conducted. In addition, the Director of the Department of Environmental Quality shall develop and implement an early dispute resolution process to help identify and resolve disagreements re-

garding what is required to comply with the regulations promulgated by the State Air Pollution Control Board, the State Water Control Board, the Virginia Waste Management Board and any related guidance. The process shall be available after the issuance of a notice of alleged violation or other notice of deficiency issued by the Department. The early dispute resolution process shall be developed by September 1, 2005, and information on the process shall be provided to the public and to facilities potentially impacted by the provisions of this act."

The 2005 amendments. — The 2005 amendment by c. 133 substituted "$32,500" for "$25,000" in subsections A, B, and E; inserted "in accordance with § 2.2-4020" in the second sentence in subsection C and made minor stylistic changes.

The 2005 amendment by c. 706 substituted "$32,500" for "$25,000" in subsections A, B, and E; inserted "in accordance with § 2.2-4020" in the second sentence of subsection C; rewrote subsection G; and added subsection L and made minor stylistic changes.

§ 10.1-1456. Right of entry to inspect, etc.; warrants. — Upon presentation of appropriate credentials and upon consent of the owner or custodian, the Director or his designee shall have the right to enter at any reasonable time onto any property to inspect, investigate, evaluate, conduct tests or take

samples for testing as he reasonably deems necessary in order to determine whether the provisions of any law administered by the Board, Director or Department, any regulations of the Board, any order of the Board or Director or any conditions in a permit, license or certificate issued by the Board or Director are being complied with. If the Director or his designee is denied entry, he may apply to an appropriate circuit court for an inspection warrant authorizing such investigation, evaluation, inspection, testing or taking of samples for testing as provided in Chapter 24 (§ 19.2-393 et seq.) of Title 19.2. (1986, c. 492, § 10-311; 1988, c. 891.)

§ 10.1-1457. Judicial review. — A. Except as provided in subsection B, any person aggrieved by a final decision of the Board or Director under this chapter shall be entitled to judicial review thereof in accordance with the Administrative Process Act (§ 2.2-4000 et seq.).

B. Any person who has participated, in person or by the submittal of written comments, in the public comment process related to a final decision of the Board or Director under § 10.1-1408.1 or § 10.1-1426 and who has exhausted all available administrative remedies for review of the Board's or Director's decision, shall be entitled to judicial review thereof in accordance with the Administrative Process Act (§ 2.2-4000 et seq.) if such person meets the standard for obtaining judicial review of a case or controversy pursuant to Article III of the United States Constitution. A person shall be deemed to meet such standard if (i) such person has suffered an actual or imminent injury which is an invasion of a legally protected interest and which is concrete and particularized; (ii) such injury is fairly traceable to the decision of the Board and not the result of the independent action of some third party not before the court; and (iii) such injury will likely be redressed by a favorable decision by the court. (1986, c. 492, § 10-312; 1988, c. 891; 1996, c. 1032.)

Editor's note. — Acts 1996, c. 1032, cl. 3 provides: "[t]hat the second enactment of this act shall not be effective unless and until a final and unappealable decision of a court of competent jurisdiction has declared that subsection B of § 10.1-1318 as it is currently effective does not meet the requirements for state program approval under Title V of the federal Clean Air Act or regulations promulgated thereunder with respect to standing to seek judicial review of state permitting decisions."

Acts 1996, c. 1032, cl. 5, as added by Acts 1997, c. 520, cl. 1, provides: "That the 'final and unappealable decision of a court of competent jurisdiction' referred to in enactment clauses 3 and 4 was rendered by the United States Supreme Court in the case of Commonwealth vs. Browner on January 21, 1997."

CASE NOTES

Standing to challenge permit. — A church and a corporation of residents were "aggrieved persons" and had standing to challange the issuance of a landfill permit where he church, a legal entity owning property adjacent to the landfill, alleged that its water well and cemetery would be affected by the landfill operations and the residents corporation's members, many of whom were adjacent landowners, alleged injury to their water supplies and property values as a result of the operation of the landfill. Residents Involved in Saving Env't, Inc. v. Commonwealth ex rel. Dep't of Waste Mgt., No. 3103-99-2, 2000 Va. App. LEXIS 547 (Ct. of Appeals July 25, 2000).

While the trial court erred in holding that the plain language of § 62.1-44.29 did not confer representational standing on two citizen groups in their challenge against the issuance of a water protection permit to a developer, and they did not have standing to sue in their own right, said holding failed to address whether the citizens alleged sufficient injury to confer standing on a member of either of their groups in a personal and individual manner; thus, the matter was remanded for a determination as to whether the citizens alleged sufficient facts to grant them representational standing. Chesapeake Bay Found., Inc. v. Commonwealth ex rel. State Water Control Bd., 46 Va. App. 104, 616 S.E.2d 39, 2005 Va. App. LEXIS 286 (2005).

Standing to challenge agency decision. — River association did not have standing to challenge, in its representative capacity, Virginia Waste Management Board's decision to charge a fee to transport waste on Virginia's waters because the plain language of Virginia's Administrative Process Act, § 2.2-4000, et seq., clearly provided that standing to seek judicial review of a decision of the board was not conferred on persons in a representative capacity; however, the association stated sufficient facts to show that it was a "person aggrieved" under § 10.1-1457; thus it did have standing to appeal the Board's decision. James River Ass'n v. Commonwealth ex rel. Waste Mgmt. Bd., 63 Va. Cir. 602, 2004 Va. Cir. LEXIS 88 (Richmond 2004).

CHAPTER 15.

SOUTHEAST INTERSTATE LOW-LEVEL RADIOACTIVE WASTE MANAGEMENT COMPACT.

§ 10.1-1500. Compact entered into and enacted into law. — The Commonwealth of Virginia hereby enters into and enacts into law the Southeast Interstate Low-Level Radioactive Waste Management Compact to become a party to the compact with the parties and upon the conditions named therein, which compact shall be in the form which follows and which as initially enacted in this section is as agreed to September 10, 1982.

ARTICLE I. POLICY AND PURPOSE

There is hereby created the Southeast Interstate Low-Level Radioactive Waste Management Compact. The party states recognize and declare that each state is responsible for providing for the availability of capacity either within or outside the state for disposal of low-level radioactive waste generated within its borders, except for waste generated as a result of defense activities of the federal government or federal research and development activities. They also recognize that the management of low-level radioactive waste is handled most efficiently on a regional basis. The party states further recognize that the Congress of the United States, by enacting the Low-Level Radioactive Waste Policy Act (P.L. 96-573), has provided for and encouraged the development of low-level radioactive waste compacts as a tool for disposal of such wastes. The party states recognize that the safe and efficient management of low-level radioactive waste generated within the region requires that sufficient capacity to dispose of such waste be properly provided.

It is the policy of the party states to: enter into a regional low-level radioactive waste management compact for the purpose of providing the instrument and framework for a cooperative effort, provide sufficient facilities for the proper management of low-level radioactive waste generated in the region, promote the health and safety of the region, limit the number of facilities required to effectively and efficiently manage low-level radioactive waste generated in the region, encourage the reduction of the amounts of low-level waste generated in the region, distribute the costs, benefits and obligations of successful low-level radioactive waste management equitably among the party states, and ensure the ecological management of low-level radioactive wastes.

Implicit in the Congressional consent to this compact is the expectation by the Congress and the party states that the appropriate federal agencies will actively assist the Compact Commission and the individual party states to this compact by:

1. Expeditious enforcement of federal rules, regulations and laws; and

2. Imposing sanctions against those found to be in violation of federal rules, regulations and laws; and

3. Timely inspections of their licensees to determine their capability to adhere to such rules, regulations and laws; and

4. Timely provision of technical assistance to this compact in carrying out their obligations under the Low-Level Radioactive Waste Policy Act as amended.

ARTICLE II. DEFINITIONS

As used in this compact, unless the context clearly requires a different construction:

a. *"Commission"* or *"Compact Commission"* means the Southeast Interstate Low-Level Radioactive Waste Management Commission.

b. *"Facility"* means a parcel of land, together with the structures, equipment and improvements thereon or appurtenant thereto, which is used or is being developed for the treatment, storage or disposal of low-level radioactive waste.

c. *"Generator"* means any person who produces or possesses low-level radioactive waste in the course of or as an incident to manufacturing, power generation, processing, medical diagnosis and treatment, research, or other industrial or commercial activity. This does not include persons who provide a service to generators by arranging for the collection, transportation, storage or disposal of wastes with respect to such waste generated outside the region.

d. *"High-level waste"* means irradiated reactor fuel, liquid wastes from reprocessing irradiated reactor fuel and solids into which such liquid wastes have been converted, and other high-level radioactive waste as defined by the U.S. Nuclear Regulatory Commission.

e. *"Host state"* means any state in which a regional facility is situated or is being developed.

f. *"Low-level radioactive waste"* or *"waste"* means radioactive waste not classified as high-level radioactive waste, transuranic waste, spent nuclear fuel or by-product material as defined in section 11 e. (2) of the Atomic Energy Act of 1954, or as may be further defined by federal law or regulation.

g. *"Party state"* means any state which is a signatory party to this compact.

h. *"Person"* means any individual, corporation, business enterprise or other legal entity (either public or private).

i. *"Region"* means the collective party states.

j. *"Regional facility"* means (1) a facility as defined in this article which has been designated, authorized, accepted or approved by the Commission to receive waste or (2) the disposal facility in Barnwell County, South Carolina, owned by the State of South Carolina and as licensed for the burial of low-level radioactive waste on July 1, 1982, but in no event shall this disposal facility serve as a regional facility beyond December 31, 1992.

k. *"State"* means a state of the United States, the District of Columbia, the Commonwealth of Puerto Rico, the Virgin Islands or any other territorial possession of the United States.

l. *"Transuranic wastes"* means waste material containing transuranic elements with contamination levels as determined by the regulations of (1) the U.S. Nuclear Regulatory Commission or (2) any host state, if it is an agreement under section 274 of the Atomic Energy Act of 1954.

m. *"Waste management"* means the storage, treatment or disposal of waste.

437

ARTICLE III. RIGHTS AND OBLIGATIONS

The rights granted to the party states by this compact are additional to the rights enjoyed by sovereign states, and nothing in this compact shall be construed to infringe upon, limit or abridge those rights.

a. Subject to any license issued by the U.S. Nuclear Regulatory Commission or a host state each party state shall have the right to have all wastes generated within its borders stored, treated, or disposed of, as applicable at regional facilities, and additionally shall have the right of access to facilities made available to the region through agreements entered into by the Commission pursuant to Article IV e. 9. The right of access by a generator within a party state to any regional facility is limited by its adherence to applicable state and federal law and regulation.

b. If no operating regional facility is located within the borders of a party state and the waste generated within its borders must therefore be stored, treated, or disposed of at a regional facility in another party state, the party state without such facilities may be required by the host state or states to establish a mechanism which provides compensation for access to the regional facility according to terms and conditions established by the host state(s) and approved by a two-thirds vote of the Commission.

c. Each party state shall establish the capability to regulate, license and ensure the maintenance and extended care of any facility within its borders. Host states are responsible for the availability, the subsequent post closure observation and maintenance, and the extended institutional control of their regional facilities, in accordance with the provisions of Article V, section b.

d. Each party state shall establish the capability to enforce any applicable federal or state laws and regulations pertaining to the packaging and transportation of waste generated within or passing through its borders.

e. Each party state shall provide to the Commission on an annual basis, any data and information necessary to the implementation of the Commission's responsibilities. Each party state shall establish the capability to obtain any data and information necessary to meet its obligation herein defined.

f. Each party state shall, to the extent authorized by federal law, require generators within its borders to use the best available waste management technologies and practices to minimize the volumes of wastes requiring disposal.

ARTICLE IV. THE COMMISSION

a. There is hereby created the Southeast Interstate Low-Level Radioactive Waste Management Commission ("the Commission" or "Compact Commission"). The Commission shall consist of two voting members from each party state to be appointed according to the laws of each state. The appointing authorities of each state must notify the Commission in writing of the identity of its members and any alternates. An alternate may act on behalf of the member only in the member's absence.

b. Each Commission member shall be entitled to one vote. No action of the Commission shall be binding unless a majority of the total membership cast their vote in the affirmative, or unless a greater than majority vote is specifically required by any other provision of this compact.

c. The Commission shall elect from among its members a presiding officer. The Commission shall adopt and publish, in convenient form, by-laws which are consistent with this compact.

d. The Commission shall meet at least once a year and shall also meet upon the call of the presiding officer, by petition of a majority of the party states, or upon the call of a host state. All meetings of the Commission shall be open to the public.

e. The Commission has the following duties and powers:

1. To receive and approve the application of a non-party state to become an eligible state in accordance with Article VII b.; and

2. To receive and approve the application of an eligible state to become a party state in accordance with Article VII c.; and

3. To submit an annual report and other communications to the governors and to the presiding officer of each body of the legislature of the party states regarding the activities of the Commission; and

4. To develop and use procedures for determining, consistent with considerations for public health and safety, the type and number of regional facilities which are presently necessary and which are projected to be necessary to manage waste generated within the region; and

5. To provide the party states with reference guidelines for establishing the criteria and procedures for evaluating alternative locations for emergency or permanent regional facilities; and

6. To develop and adopt within one year after the Commission is constituted as provided for in Article VII, section d., procedures and criteria for identifying a party state as a host state for a regional facility as determined pursuant to the requirements of this article. In accordance with these procedures and criteria, the Commission shall identify a host state for the development of a second regional disposal facility within three years after the Commission is constituted as provided for in Article VII, section d. and shall seek to ensure that such facility is licensed and ready to operate as soon as required but in no event later than 1991.

In developing criteria, the Commission must consider the following: the health, safety, and welfare of the citizens of the party states; the existence of regional facilities within each party state; the minimization of waste transportation; the volumes and types of wastes generated within each party state; and the environmental, economic and ecological impacts on the air, land, and water resources of the party states.

The Commission shall conduct such hearings; require such reports, studies, evidence and testimony; and do what is required by its approved procedures in order to identify a party state as a host state for a needed facility; and

7. In accordance with the procedures and criteria developed pursuant to section e. 6. of this article, to designate, by a two-thirds vote, a host state for the establishment of a needed regional facility. The Commission shall not exercise this authority unless the party states have failed to voluntarily pursue the development of such facility. The Commission shall have the authority to revoke the membership of a party state that willfully creates barriers to the siting of a needed regional facility; and

8. To require of and obtain from party states, eligible states seeking to become party states, and non-party states seeking to become eligible states, data and information necessary to the implementation of Commission responsibilities; and

9. Notwithstanding any other provision of this compact, to enter into agreements with any person, state, or similar regional body or group of states for the importation of waste into the region and for the right of access to facilities outside the region for waste generated within the region. Such authorization to import requires a two-thirds majority vote of the Commission, including an affirmative vote of both representatives of the host state in which any affected regional facility is located. This shall be done only after an assessment of the affected facilities' capability to handle such wastes; and

10. To act or appear on behalf of any party state or states, only upon written request of both members of the Commission for such state or states, as an intervenor or party in interest before Congress, state legislatures, any court of law, or federal, state or local agency, board or commission which has jurisdiction over the management of wastes.

The authority to act, intervene or otherwise appear shall be exercised by the Commission only after approval by a majority vote of the Commission.

11. To revoke the membership of a party state in accordance with Article VII f.

f. The Commission may establish such advisory committees as it deems necessary for the purpose of advising the Commission on any and all matters pertaining to the management of low-level radioactive waste.

g. The Commission may appoint or contract for and compensate such limited staff necessary to carry out its duties and functions. The staff shall serve at the Commission's pleasure irrespective of the civil service, personnel or other merit laws of any of the party states or the federal government and shall be compensated from funds of the Commission. In selecting any staff, the Commission shall assure that the staff has adequate experience and formal training to carry out such functions as may be assigned to it by the Commission. If the Commission has a headquarters it shall be in a party state.

h. Funding for the Commission shall be provided as follows:

1. Each eligible state, upon becoming a party state, shall pay $25,000 to the Commission which shall be used for costs of the Commission's services.

2. Each state hosting a regional disposal facility shall annually levy special fees or surcharges on all users of such facility, based upon the volume of wastes disposed of at such facilities, the total of which:

(a) Shall be sufficient to cover the annual budget of the Commission; and

(b) Shall represent the financial commitments of all party states to the Commission; and

(c) Shall be paid to the Commission, provided, however, that each host state collecting such fees or surcharges may retain a portion of the collection sufficient to cover its administrative costs of collection, and that the remainder be sufficient only to cover the approved annual budgets of the Commission.

3. The Commission shall set and approve its first annual budget as soon as practicable after its initial meeting. Host states for disposal facilities shall begin imposition of the special fees and surcharges provided for in this section as soon as practicable after becoming party states, and shall remit to the Commission funds resulting from collection of such special fees and surcharges within sixty days of their receipt.

i. The Commission shall keep accurate accounts of all receipts and disbursements and independent certified public accountant shall annually audit all receipts and disbursements of Commission funds, and submit an audit report to the Commission. Such audit report shall be made a part of the annual report of the Commission required by Article IV e. 3.

j. The Commission may accept for any of its purposes and functions any and all donations, grants of money, equipment, supplies, materials and services (conditional or otherwise) from any state or the United States or any subdivision or agency thereof, or interstate agency, or from any institution, person, firm or corporation, and may receive, utilize and dispose of the same. The nature, amount and condition, if any, attendant upon any donation or grant accepted pursuant to this paragraph together with the identity of the donor, grantor or lender, shall be detailed in the annual report of the Commission.

k. The Commission shall not be responsible for any costs associated with (1) the creation of any facility, (2) the operation of any facility, (3) the stabilization and closure of any facility, (4) the post-closure observation, and maintenance of any facility, or (5) the extended institutional control, after post-closure observation and maintenance of any facility.

l. As of January 1, 1986, the management of wastes at regional facilities is restricted to wastes generated within the region, and to wastes generated within non-party states when authorized by the Commission pursuant to the provisions of this Compact. After January 1, 1986, the Commission may prohibit the exportation of waste from the region for the purposes of management.

m. 1. The Commission herein established is a legal entity separate and distinct from the party states, capable of acting in its own behalf, and shall be so liable for its actions. Liabilities of the Commission shall not be deemed liabilities of the party states. Members of the Commission shall not be personally liable for action taken by them in their official capacity.

Except as specifically provided in this compact, nothing in this compact shall be construed to alter the incidence of liability of any kind for any act, omission, course of conduct, or on account of any causal or other relationships. Generators, transporters of wastes, owners and operators of sites shall be liable for their acts, omissions, conduct, or relationships in accordance with all laws relating thereto.

ARTICLE V. DEVELOPMENT AND OPERATION OF FACILITIES

a. Any party state which becomes a host state in which a regional facility is operated, shall not be designated by the Compact Commission as a host state for an additional regional facility until each party state has fulfilled its obligation, as determined by the Commission, to have a regional facility operated within its borders.

b. A host state desiring to close a regional facility located within its borders may do so only after notifying the Commission in writing of its intention to do so and the reasons therefore. Such notification shall be given to the Commission at least four years prior to the intended date of closure. Notwithstanding the four year notice requirement herein provided, a host state is not prevented from closing its facility or establishing conditions of use and operations as necessary for the protection of the health and safety of its citizens. A host state may terminate or limit access to its regional facility if it determines Congress has materially altered the conditions of this compact.

c. Each party state designated as a host state for a regional facility shall take appropriate steps to ensure that an application for a license to construct and operate a facility of the designated type is filed with and issued by the appropriate authority.

d. No party state shall have any form of arbitrary prohibition on the treatment, storage or disposal of low-level radioactive waste within its border.

e. No party state shall be required to operate a regional facility for longer than a twenty-year period or to dispose of more than 32,000,000 cubic feet of low-level radioactive waste, whichever first occurs.

ARTICLE VI. OTHER LAWS AND REGULATIONS

a. Nothing in this compact shall be construed to:

1. Abrogate or limit the applicability of any act of Congress or diminish or otherwise impair the jurisdiction of any federal agency expressly conferred thereon by the Congress;

2. Abrogate or limit the regulatory responsibility and authority of the U.S. Nuclear Regulatory Commission or of an agreement state under section 274 of the Atomic Energy Act of 1954 in which a regional facility is located;

3. Make inapplicable to any person or circumstance any other law of a party state which is not inconsistent with this compact;

4. Make unlawful the continued development and operation of any facility already licensed for development or operation on the date this compact becomes effective, except that any such facility shall comply with Article III, Article IV and Article V and shall be subject to any action lawfully taken pursuant thereto;

5. Prohibit any storage or treatment of waste by the generator on its own premises;

6. Affect any judicial or administrative proceeding pending on the effective date of this compact;

7. Alter the relations between, and the respective internal responsibilities of, the government of a party state and its subdivisions;

8. Affect the generation, treatment, storage or disposal of waste generated by the atomic energy defense activities of the Secretary of the U.S. Department of Energy or federal research and development activities as defined in P.L. 96-573;

9. Affect the rights and powers of any party state and its political subdivisions to regulate and license any facility within its borders or to affect the rights and powers of any party state and its political subdivisions to tax or impose fees on the waste managed at any facility within its borders.

b. No party state shall pass any law or adopt any regulation which is inconsistent with this compact. To do so may jeopardize the membership status of the party state.

c. Upon formation of the compact, no law or regulation of a party state or of any subdivision or instrumentality thereof may be applied so as to restrict or make more inconvenient access to any regional facility by the generators of another party state than for the generators of the state where the facility is situated.

d. Restrictions of waste management of regional facilities pursuant to Article IV l. shall be enforceable as a matter of state law.

ARTICLE VII. ELIGIBLE PARTIES, WITHDRAWAL, REVOCATION, ENTRY INTO FORCE, TERMINATION

a. This compact shall have as initially eligible parties the States of Alabama, Florida, Georgia, Mississippi, North Carolina, South Carolina, Tennessee and Virginia.

b. Any state not expressly declared eligible to become a party state to this compact in section a. of this article may petition the Commission, once constituted, to be declared eligible. The Commission may establish such conditions as it deems necessary and appropriate to be met by a state wishing to become eligible to become a party state to this compact pursuant to the provisions of this section. Upon satisfactorily meeting such conditions and upon the affirmative vote of two-thirds of the Commission, including the affirmative vote of both representatives of a host state in which any affected regional facility is located, the petitioning state shall be eligible to become a party state to this compact and may become a party state in the same manner as those states declared eligible in section a. of this article.

c. Each state eligible to become a party state shall be declared a party state upon enactment of this compact into law by the state and upon payment of the fees required by Article IV, h. 1. The Commission shall be the sole judge of the qualifications of the party states and of its members and of their compliance with the conditions and requirements of this compact and the laws of the party states relating to the enactment of this compact.

d. 1. The first three states eligible to become party states to this compact which enact this compact into law and appropriate the fees required by Article IV, h. 1. shall immediately, upon the appointment of their Commission members, constitute themselves as the Southeast Low-Level Radioactive Waste Management Commission, shall cause legislation to be introduced in the Congress which grants the consent of the Congress to this compact, and shall do those things necessary to organize the Commission and implement the provisions of this compact.

2. All succeeding states eligible to become party states to this compact shall be declared party states pursuant to the provisions of section c. of this article.

3. The consent of the Congress shall be required for full implementation of this compact. The provisions of Article V, d. shall not become effective until the effective date of the import ban authorized by Article IV, l. as approved by Congress. The Congress may by law withdraw its consent only every five years.

e. No state which holds membership in any other regional compact for the management of low-level radioactive waste may be considered by the Compact Commission for eligible state status or party state status.

f. Any party state which fails to comply with the provisions of this compact or to fulfill the obligations incurred by becoming a party state to this compact may be subject to sanctions by the Commission, including suspension of its rights under this compact and revocation of its status as a party state. Any sanction shall be imposed only on the affirmative vote of at least two-thirds of the Commission members. Revocation of party state status may take effect on the date of the meeting at which the Commission approves the resolution imposing such sanction, but in no event shall revocation take effect later than 90 days from the date of such meeting. Rights and obligations incurred by being declared a party state to this compact shall continue until the effective date of the sanction imposed or as provided in the resolution of the Commission imposing the sanction.

The Commission shall, as soon as practicable after the meeting at which a resolution revoking status as a party state is approved, provide written notice of the action along with a copy of the resolution to the governors, the presidents of the senates, and the speakers of the house of representatives of the party states, as well as chairmen of the appropriate committees of the Congress.

g. Subject to provisions of Article VII, h., any party state may withdraw from this compact by enacting a law repealing the compact, provided that if a regional facility is located within such state, such regional facility shall remain available to the region for four years after the date the Commission receives verification in writing from the governor of such party state of the rescission of the compact. The Commission, upon receipt of the notification, shall as soon as practicable provide copies of such notification to the governors, the presidents of the senates, and the speakers of the house of representatives of the party states as well as the chairman of the appropriate committees of the Congress.

h. The right of a party state to withdraw pursuant to Article VII, g. shall terminate thirty days following the commencement of operation of the second host state disposal facility. Thereafter a party state may withdraw only with the unanimous approval of the Commission and with the consent of Congress. For purposes of this subsection, the low-level radioactive waste disposal facility located in Barnwell County, South Carolina shall be considered the first host state disposal facility.

i. This compact may be terminated only by the affirmative action of the Congress or by the rescission of all laws enacting the compact in each party state.

ARTICLE VIII. PENALTIES

a. Each party state, consistently with its own law, shall prescribe and enforce penalties against any person not an official of another state for violation of any provision of this compact.

b. Each party state acknowledges that the receipt by a host state of waste packaged or transported in violation of applicable laws and regulations can result in imposition of sanctions by the host state which may include suspension or revocation of the violator's right of access to the facility in the host state.

ARTICLE IX. SEVERABILITY AND CONSTRUCTION

The provisions of this compact shall be severable and if any phrase, clause, sentence or provision of this compact is declared by a court of competent jurisdiction to be contrary to the Constitution of any participating state or of the United States or the applicability thereof to any government, agency, person or circumstance is held invalid, the validity of the remainder of this compact and the applicability thereof to any other government, agency, person or circumstances shall not be affected thereby. If any provision of this compact shall be held contrary to the constitution of any state participating therein, the compact shall remain in full force and effect as to the state affected as to all severable matters. The provisions of this compact shall be liberally construed to give effect to the purposes thereof. (1983, c. 213, § 32.1-238.6:1; 1988, cc. 390, 891.)

Compact cross references. — As to provisions of other member states, see:

Alabama: Code of Ala. § 22-32-1 et seq.

Florida: Fla. Stat. § 404.30.

Georgia: O.C.G.A. §§ 12-8-120 — 12-8-123.

Mississippi: Miss. Code Ann. §§ 57-47-1 — 57-47-9.

Tennessee: Tenn. Code Ann. § 68-202-701 et seq.

Editor's note. — As enacted, Article IV above contains a subdivision m. 1., but no m. 2.

Law Review. — For note, "The Role of Localities in the Transportation and Disposal of Nuclear Wastes," see 18 U. Rich. L. Rev. 655 (1984).

DECISIONS FROM COMPACT MEMBER STATES

Delay in establishing a low-level radioactive waste disposal facility as prescribed by the Compact Commission exposes a member state to severe sanctions from its compact partners. Richmond County v. North Carolina Low-Level Radioactive Waste Mgt. Auth., 335 N.C. 77, 436 S.E.2d 113 (1993). Final decision pending in Alabama v. North Carolina, 540 U.S. 1014, 124 S. Ct. 597, 157 L. Ed. 2d 427 (2003).

§ 10.1-1501. Commissioners and alternates. — The Governor shall appoint two Commissioners and two alternates pursuant to Article IV, paragraph a. of the Compact, subject to confirmation by the General Assembly, to serve at his pleasure. The appointees shall be individuals qualified and experienced in the field of low-level radioactive waste generation, treatment, storage, transportation and disposal. (1982, c. 518, § 32.1-238.7; 1988, c. 891.)

§ 10.1-1502. Expenses of Commissioners and alternates. — The Commissioners and alternates shall be reimbursed out of moneys appropriated for such purposes all sums which they necessarily expend in the discharge of their duties as members of the Southeast Interstate Low-Level Radioactive Waste Commission. (1982, c. 518, § 32.1-238.8; 1988, c. 891.)

§ 10.1-1503. Cooperation of state and local agencies. — All agencies, departments and officers of the Commonwealth and its political subdivisions are hereby authorized and directed to cooperate with the Commission in the furtherance of activities pursuant to the Compact. (1982, c. 518, § 32.1-238.9; 1988, c. 891.)

§ 10.1-1504. Board to enforce Compact; penalty. — The Virginia Waste Management Board is authorized to enforce the provisions of this chapter. Any person not an official of another party state to the Compact who violates any provision of this chapter shall be subject to a civil penalty of not more than $25,000 per day for each violation. (1991, c. 83.)

CHAPTER 16.

VIRGINIA RECREATIONAL FACILITIES AUTHORITY ACT.

§ 10.1-1600. Definitions. — As used in this chapter, unless the context requires a different meaning:

"*Authority*" means the Virginia Recreational Facilities Authority.

"*Board*" means the board of directors of the Authority.

"*Bonds*" means notes, bonds, certificates and other evidences of indebtedness or obligations of the Authority.

"*Federal agency*" means the United States of America, the President of the United States of America, and any department, corporation, agency, or instrumentality created, designated, or established by the United States of America.

"*Project*" means the construction, improvement, furnishing, maintenance, acquisition or operation of any facility that will further the purposes of the Authority, together with all property, rights, easements and interests which may be acquired by the Authority. (1986, c. 360, § 10-158.2; 1988, c. 891.)

§ 10.1-1601. Authority created. — In order to (i) provide a high quality recreational attraction in the western part of the Commonwealth; (ii) expand the historical knowledge of adults and children; (iii) promote tourism and economic development in the Commonwealth; (iv) set aside and conserve scenic and natural areas along the Roanoke River and preserve open-space lands; and (v) enhance and expand research and educational programs, there is created a political subdivision of the Commonwealth to be known as "The Virginia Recreational Facilities Authority." The Authority's exercise of the powers conferred by this chapter shall be deemed to be the performance of an essential governmental function. (1986, c. 360, § 10-158.3; 1988, c. 891.)

§ 10.1-1602. Board of directors. — The Authority shall be governed by a board of directors consisting of 19 members who shall be appointed as follows: two members of the Senate to be appointed by the Senate Committee on Rules; four members of the House of Delegates to be appointed by the Speaker of the House of Delegates in accordance with the principles of proportional representation contained in the Rules of the House of Delegates; and 13 nonlegislative citizen members to be appointed by the Governor, upon consideration of the recommendation of the River Foundation, if any, and subject to confirmation by the General Assembly. Nonlegislative citizen members of the Authority shall be citizens of the Commonwealth.

Legislative members shall serve terms coincident with their terms of office. After the initial staggering of terms, nonlegislative citizen members shall be appointed for a term of five years. Vacancies in the membership of the Board shall be filled for the unexpired portion of the term in the same manner as original appointments are made. All members may be reappointed.

Immediately after appointment, the directors shall enter upon the performance of their duties. The Board shall annually elect a chairman and vice-chairman from its members, and shall also elect annually a secretary, who may or may not be a member of the Board. The Board may also elect other subordinate officers who may or may not be members of the Board, as it deems proper. Seven directors shall constitute a quorum for the transaction of the business of the Authority, and no vacancy in the membership of the Board shall impair the right of a quorum to exercise all the rights and perform all the duties of the Authority. The Board may employ an executive director to direct the day-to-day activities of the Authority and carry out the powers and duties delegated to him. The executive director shall serve at the pleasure of the Board. The executive director and employees of the Authority shall be compensated in the manner provided by the Board and shall not be subject to the provisions of the Virginia Personnel Act (§ 2.2-2900 et seq.).

Legislative members of the Authority shall receive such compensation as provided in § 30-19.12, and nonlegislative citizen members shall receive such compensation for the performance of their duties as provided in § 2.2-2813. All members shall be reimbursed for all reasonable and necessary expenses incurred in the performance of their duties as provided in §§ 2.2-2813 and 2.2-2825. Funding for the costs of compensation and expenses of the members shall be provided by the Virginia Recreational Facilities Authority. (1986, c. 360, § 10-158.4; 1988, c. 891; 1989, c. 226; 1990, c. 210; 2005, c. 768; 2006, c. 22.)

The 2005 amendments. — The 2005 amendment by c. 768 rewrote the first and second paragraphs, substituted "Ten" for "Seven" at the beginning of the fourth sentence of the third paragraph and added the last paragraph.

The 2006 amendments. — The 2006 amendment by c. 22 substituted "Seven" for "Ten" at the beginning of the fourth sentence of the third paragraph.

§ **10.1-1603. Powers of Authority.** — The Authority is granted all powers necessary or convenient for carrying out its statutory purposes, including the following rights and powers:

1. To acquire by gift, devise, purchase, or otherwise, absolutely or in trust, and to hold, use, lease as lessee and unless otherwise restricted by the terms of the gift or devise, to lease as lessor, convey, sell or otherwise dispose of any property, real or personal, or any estate or interest therein including water rights. However, the Authority shall have no power to encumber its real property or create any estate or interest therein other than encumbrances on structures not extending to the real property upon which such structures are constructed.

2. To make and enter into any contracts and agreements with any appropriate person or federal agency. Such contracts include but are not limited to (i) agreements with the Commonwealth, or any agency thereof, to lease property owned or controlled by the Commonwealth, for the purpose of construction, improvement, maintenance, or operation of any project or activity that will further the purposes described in this chapter; and (ii) agreements with any person to sublease property owned or controlled by the Common-

wealth or to issue licenses for the purpose of construction, improvement, maintenance, or operation of any project or activity that will further the purposes described in this chapter.

3. To plan, develop, carry out, construct, improve, rehabilitate, repair, furnish, maintain, and operate projects.

4. To promulgate regulations concerning the use of properties under its control to protect such property and the public thereon.

5. To fix, alter, charge, and collect rates, rentals, and other charges for the use of projects of, or for the sale of products of or for the services rendered by the Authority. Such charges shall be used to pay the expenses of the Authority, the planning, development, construction, improvement, rehabilitation, repair, furnishing, maintenance, and operation of its projects and properties, the costs of accomplishing its purposes set forth in § 10.1-1601, and the principal of and interest on its obligations, and to fulfill the terms and provisions of any agreements made with the purchasers or holders of any such obligations. Such fees, rents and charges shall not be subject to supervision or regulation by any commission, board, or agency of the Commonwealth or any political subdivision thereof.

6. To borrow money, make and issue bonds including bonds that the Authority may determine to issue for the purposes set forth in § 10.1-1601 or of refunding bonds previously issued by the Authority. The Authority shall have the right to secure the payment of all bonds, or any part thereof, by pledge or deed of trust of all or any of its revenues, rentals, and receipts or of any project or property, tangible or intangible, or any interest therein. However, the Authority shall have no power to encumber its real property or create any estate or interest therein other than encumbrances on structures not extending to the real property upon which such structures are located. The bonds may be secured by a pledge of any grant or contribution from a person or federal agency. The Authority shall have the power to make agreements with the purchasers or holders of the bonds or with others in connection with the bonds, whether issued or to be issued, as it deems advisable, and in general to provide for the security for the bonds and the rights of the bond holders.

7. To employ consultants, attorneys, architects, engineers, accountants, financial experts, investment bankers, superintendents, managers and such other employees and agents as may be necessary, and to fix their compensation to be payable from funds made available to the Authority.

8. To receive and accept from any federal agency, foundation, or person, grants, loans, gifts or contributions of money, property, or other things of value, to be held, used and applied only for the purposes for which the grant or contribution is made or to be expended in accomplishing the objectives of the Authority.

9. To develop, undertake and provide programs, alone or in conjunction with any person or federal agency, for scientific research, continuing education, and in-service training, provided that credit towards a degree, certificate or diploma shall be granted only if the education is provided in conjunction with an institution of higher education authorized to operate in the Commonwealth; and to foster the utilization of scientific research information, discoveries and data.

10. To pledge or otherwise encumber all or any of the revenues or receipts of the Authority as security for all or any of the obligations of the Authority.

11. To do all acts and things necessary or convenient to carry out the powers granted by this chapter or any other acts. (1986, c. 360, § 10-158.5; 1988, c. 891; 1991, c. 706.)

§ **10.1-1604. Form, terms, and execution of bonds.** — A. The bonds of each issue shall be dated, shall bear interest at rates fixed by the Authority, shall mature at a time not exceeding forty years from their date, as determined by the Authority, and may be made redeemable before maturity, at the option of the Authority, at a price and under terms and conditions fixed by the Authority prior to the issuance of the bonds. The Authority shall determine the form of bonds and manner of execution of the bonds and shall fix the denomination of the bonds and the place of payment of principal and interest, which may be at any bank or trust company.

B. The bonds shall be signed by the chairman or vice-chairman of the Authority, or if authorized by the Authority, shall bear his facsimile signature, and the official seal of the Authority, or, if authorized by the Authority, a facsimile signature thereof shall be impressed or imprinted thereon and attested by the secretary or any assistant secretary of the Authority, or, if authorized by the Authority, with the facsimile signature of such secretary or assistant secretary. Any coupons attached to bonds issued by the Authority shall bear the signature or facsimile signature of the chairman or vice-chairman of the Authority. If any officer whose signature or facsimile signature appears on any bonds or coupons ceases to be an officer before the delivery of the bonds, the signature or facsimile shall nevertheless be valid for all purposes. Any bonds may bear the facsimile signature of, or may be signed by, persons who are the proper officers to sign the bonds at the actual time of the execution of such bonds although at the date of the bonds such persons may not have been officers. (1986, c. 360, § 10-158.6; 1988, c. 891.)

§ **10.1-1605. Issuance and sale of bonds.** — The bonds may be issued in coupon or in registered form, or both, as the Authority may determine, and provision may be made for the registration of any coupon bonds as to principal alone and also as to both principal and interest, for the reconversion into coupon bonds of any bonds registered as to both principal and interest, and for the interchange of registered and coupon bonds. The Authority may sell such bonds in the manner, either at public or private sale, and for the price, that it determines will best effect the purposes of this chapter. Bonds may be issued under the provisions of this chapter without obtaining the consent of any commission, board or agency of the Commonwealth or of any political subdivision, and without any other proceedings or conditions other than those which are specifically required by this chapter. (1986, c. 360, § 10-158.6; 1988, c. 891.)

§ **10.1-1606. Use of bond proceeds.** — The proceeds of the bonds of each issue shall be used solely for the purposes of the Authority provided in the resolution authorizing the issuance of the bonds or in the trust agreement authorized in this chapter. (1986, c. 360, § 10-158.6; 1988, c. 891.)

§ **10.1-1607. Interim receipts or temporary bonds.** — The Authority is authorized to issue interim receipts or temporary bonds as provided in § 15.2-2616 and to execute and deliver new bonds in place of bonds mutilated, lost or destroyed, as provided in § 15.2-2621. (1986, c. 360, § 10-158.6; 1988, c. 891.)

§ **10.1-1608. Faith and credit of Commonwealth or political subdivision not pledged.** — No obligation of the Authority shall constitute a debt, or pledge of the faith and credit, of the Commonwealth or of any political subdivision, but shall be payable solely from the revenue and other funds of the Authority which have been pledged. All such obligations shall contain on the face a statement to the effect that the Commonwealth, political subdivisions, and the Authority shall not be obligated to pay the obligation or the interest except from revenues and other funds of the Authority which have been pledged, and that neither the faith and credit nor the taxing power of the Commonwealth or of any political subdivision is pledged to the payment of the principal of or the interest on such obligations. (1986, c. 360, § 10-158.6; 1988, c. 891.)

§ **10.1-1609. Expenses of the Authority.** — All expenses incurred in carrying out the provisions of this chapter shall be payable solely from funds provided under the provisions of this chapter and no liability shall be incurred by the Authority beyond the extent to which moneys are provided under the provisions of this chapter. (1986, c. 306, § 10-158.6; 1988, c. 891.)

§ **10.1-1610. Trust agreement securing bonds.** — In the discretion of the Authority any bonds issued under the provisions of this chapter may be secured by a trust agreement between the Authority and a corporate trustee, which may be any trust company or bank having the powers of a trust company. The trust agreement or the resolution providing for the issuance of bonds may pledge or assign the revenues to be received and provide for the mortgage of any project or property or any part thereof. However, the Authority shall have no power to encumber its real property or create any estate or interest therein other than encumbrances on structures not extending to the real property upon which such structures are located. The trust agreement or resolution may contain reasonable, proper and lawful provisions for protecting and enforcing the rights and remedies of the bondholders. The trust agreement or resolution may include covenants setting forth the duties of the Authority in relation to the acquisition of property and the planning, development, acquisition, construction, rehabilitation, establishment, improvement, extension, enlargement, maintenance, repair, operation and insurance of the project in connection with which such bonds have been authorized, the rates and fees to be charged, the custody, safeguarding and application of all moneys, and conditions or limitations with respect to the issuance of additional bonds. It shall be lawful for any bank or trust company incorporated under the laws of the Commonwealth which may act as depository of the proceeds of bonds or of revenue, to furnish such indemnifying bonds or to pledge such securities as may be required by the Authority. The trust agreement may set forth the rights of action by bondholders and other provisions the Authority deems reasonable and proper for the security of the bondholders. All expenses incurred in carrying out the provisions of the trust agreement or resolution may be treated as a part of the operation of the project. (1986, c. 360, § 10-158.7; 1988, c. 891; 1991, c. 706.)

§ **10.1-1611. Moneys received deemed trust funds.** — All moneys received pursuant to the authority of this chapter, whether as proceeds from the sale of bonds or as revenues, shall be deemed to be trust funds to be held and applied solely as provided in this chapter. The resolution authorizing the bonds of any issue or the trust agreement securing such bonds shall provide that any officer with whom, or any bank or trust company with which, such moneys are deposited shall act as a trustee of such moneys and shall hold and apply the moneys for the purposes hereof, subject to such regulations as this chapter and the resolution or trust agreement may provide. (1986, c. 360, § 10-158.8; 1988, c. 891.)

§ **10.1-1612. Proceedings by bondholder or trustee to enforce rights.** — Any holder of bonds issued under the provisions of this chapter or any of the applicable coupons, and the trustee under any trust agreement, except to the extent the rights herein given may be restricted by the trust agreement or the resolution authorizing the issuance of such bonds, may protect and enforce rights under the laws of the Commonwealth or under the trust agreement or resolution, and may enforce all duties required by this chapter or by the trust agreement or resolution to be performed by the Authority or by any officer thereof, including the fixing, charging, and collecting of rates, rentals, and other charges. (1986, c. 360, § 10-158.9; 1988, c. 891.)

§ 10.1-1613. Bonds made securities for investment and deposit. — Bonds issued by the Authority under the provisions of this chapter are hereby made securities in which all public officers and public bodies of the Commonwealth and its political subdivisions, all insurance companies, trust companies, banking associations, investment companies, executors, administrators, trustees, and other fiduciaries may properly and legally invest funds, including capital in their control or belonging to them. Such bonds are hereby made securities which may properly and legally be deposited with and received by any state or municipal officer or any agency or political subdivision of the Commonwealth for any purpose authorized by law. (1986, c. 360, § 10-158.10; 1988, c. 891.)

§ 10.1-1614. Revenue refunding bonds; bonds for refunding and for cost of additional projects. — The Authority is authorized to provide for the issuance of revenue refunding bonds of the Authority for the purpose of refunding any bonds then outstanding which have been issued under the provisions of this chapter, including the payment of any redemption premium and any interest accrued or to accrue to the date of redemption of such bonds, and, if deemed advisable by the Authority, for the additional purpose of constructing improvements, extensions, or enlargements of the projects in connection with which the bonds to be refunded have been issued. The Authority is further authorized to provide by resolution for the issuance of its revenue bonds for the combined purpose of (i) refunding any bonds then outstanding which have been issued under the provisions of this chapter, including the payment of any redemption premium and any interest accrued or to accrue to the date of redemption of such bonds, and (ii) paying all or any part of the cost of any additional project or any portion thereof. The issuance of such bonds, the maturities and other details, the rights of the holders, and the rights, duties and obligations of the Authority shall be governed by the provisions of this chapter. (1986, c. 360, § 10-158.11; 1988, c. 891.)

§ 10.1-1615. Grants or loans of public or private funds. — The Authority is authorized to accept, receive, receipt for, disburse, and expend federal and state moneys and other moneys, public or private, made available by grant, loan or otherwise, to accomplish any of the purposes of this chapter. All federal moneys accepted under this section shall be accepted and expended by the Authority upon terms and conditions prescribed by the United States and consistent with state law. All state moneys accepted under this section shall be accepted and expended by the Authority upon terms and conditions prescribed by the Commonwealth. (1986, c. 360, § 10-158.12; 1988, c. 891.)

§ 10.1-1616. Exemption from taxes or assessments. — The exercise of the powers granted by this chapter is for the benefit of the people of the Commonwealth, for the increase of their commerce and prosperity, and for the improvement of their health and living conditions. Since the operation and maintenance of projects by the Authority and the undertaking of activities in furtherance of the purpose of the Authority will constitute the performance of essential governmental functions, the Authority shall not be required to pay any taxes or assessments upon any project or any property acquired or used by the Authority under the provisions of this chapter or upon the income therefrom, including sales and use taxes on tangible personal property used in the operations of the Authority. Any bonds issued under the provisions of this chapter, their transfer and the income which may result, including any profit made on the sale, shall be free from state and local taxation. The exemption hereby granted shall not be construed to extend to persons conducting business on the premises of a facility for which local or state taxes would otherwise be required. (1986, c. 360, § 10-158.13; 1988, c. 891.)

§ **10.1-1617. Moneys of Authority.** — All moneys of the Authority, from whatever source derived, shall be paid to the treasurer of the Authority. Such moneys shall be deposited by the treasurer in one or more banks or trust companies, in one or more special accounts. All banks and trust companies are authorized to give security for such deposits, if required by the Authority. The moneys in the accounts shall be paid out on the warrant or other order of the treasurer of the Authority or any person authorized by the Authority to execute such warrants or orders. The Auditor of Public Accounts of the Commonwealth, and his legally authorized representatives, shall examine the accounts and books of the Authority. (1986, c. 360, § 10-158.15; 1988, c. 891.)

§ **10.1-1618. Title to property.** — The Authority may acquire title to property in its own name or in the name of the Commonwealth for and on behalf of the Authority. In the event the Authority ceases to operate its projects and to promote the purposes stated in § 10.1-1601 or is dissolved, the title to real property held by the Authority shall transfer to the Commonwealth and be administered by the Department of Conservation and Recreation; provided however, in the event that an environmental audit of any real property or interest therein, or portion of such property, to be transferred pursuant to this section discloses any environmental liability or violation of law or regulation, present or contingent, the Governor may reject the transfer of any portion of such property which he determines to be environmentally defective. (1986, c. 360, § 10-158.16; 1988, c. 891; 1991, c. 706.)

§ **10.1-1619. Violation of regulations.** — Violation of any regulation adopted pursuant to § 10.1-1603 which would have been a violation of law or ordinance if committed on a public street or highway shall be tried and punished as if it had been committed on a public street or highway. Any other violation of such regulations shall be punishable as a Class 1 misdemeanor. (1986, c. 360, § 10-158.17; 1988, c. 891.)

Cross references. — As to punishment for Class 1 misdemeanors, see § 18.2-11.

§ **10.1-1620. Appointment of special conservators of the peace.** — The chairman of the Authority or his designee may apply to the circuit court of any county or city for the appointment of one or more special conservators of the peace under procedures specified by § 19.2-13. (1986, c. 360, § 10-158.18; 1988, c. 891.)

§ **10.1-1621. Conveyance or lease of park to Authority.** — The Commonwealth or any county, municipality, or other public body is authorized to convey or lease to the Authority, with or without consideration, any property to use for projects that will further the purposes described in this chapter. (1986, c. 360, § 10-158.19; 1988, c. 891.)

§ 10.1-1622. Recordation of conveyances of real estate to Authority.
— No deed purporting to convey real estate to the Authority shall be recorded unless accepted by a person authorized to act on behalf of the Authority, which acceptance shall appear on the face of the deed. (1986, c. 360, § 10-158.20; 1988, c. 891.)

CHAPTER 17.

OPEN-SPACE LAND ACT.

§ 10.1-1700. Definitions.
— As used in this article, unless the context requires a different meaning:

"Open-space easement" means a nonpossessory interest of a public body in real property, whether easement appurtenant or in gross, acquired through gift, purchase, devise, or bequest imposing limitations or affirmative obligations, the purposes of which include retaining or protecting natural or open-space values of real property, assuring its availability for agricultural, forestal, recreational, or open-space use, protecting natural resources, maintaining or enhancing air or water quality, or preserving the historical, architectural or archaeological aspects of real property.

"Open-space land" means any land which is provided or preserved for (i) park or recreational purposes, (ii) conservation of land or other natural resources, (iii) historic or scenic purposes, (iv) assisting in the shaping of the character, direction, and timing of community development, or (v) wetlands as defined in § 28.2-1300.

"Public body" means any state agency having authority to acquire land for a public use, or any county or municipality, any park authority, any public recreational facilities authority, any soil and water conservation district, any community development authority formed pursuant to Article 6 (§ 15.2-5152 et seq.) of Chapter 51 of Title 15.2, or the Virginia Recreational Facilities Authority. (1966, c. 461, § 10-156; 1974, c. 348; 1986, c. 360; 1988, c. 891; 1997, c. 130; 2000, cc. 181, 724, 747.)

Cross references. — As to power of service districts to acquire, by purchase, gift, etc., title or interests of not less than five years' duration in real property that will provide a means for the preservation or provision of open-space land, as provided for in § 10.1-1700 et seq., see subdivision 11 of § 15.2-2403. As to the authority of community development authorities to dedicate land pursuant to this Act, see § 15.2-5158.

Law Review. — For article surveying developments in real estate and land use law in Virginia from June 1, 2001 through June 1, 2002, see 37 U. Rich. L. Rev. 271 (2002).

Construction with other law. — Virginia Conservation Easement Act did not create a new right to burden land by a negative easement in gross for the purpose of land conservation and historic preservation, but facilitated the continued creation of such easements by providing a clear statutory framework under which tax exemptions are made available to charitable organizations devoted to those purposes and tax benefits and incentives are provided to the grantors of such easements, contrary to the common law; moreover, the easement at issue was not of a novel character and is consistent with the statutory recognition of negative easements in gross for conservation and historic purposes. United States v. Blackman, 270 Va. 68, 613 S.E.2d 442, 2005 Va. LEXIS 69 (2005).

§ 10.1-1701. Authority of public bodies to acquire or designate property for use as open-space land.

— To carry out the purposes of this chapter, any public body may (i) acquire by purchase, gift, devise, bequest, grant or otherwise title to or any interests or rights of not less than five years' duration in real property that will provide a means for the preservation or provision of open-space land and (ii) designate any real property in which it has an interest of not less than five years' duration to be retained and used for the preservation and provision of open-space land. Any such interest may also be perpetual.

The use of the real property for open-space land shall conform to the official comprehensive plan for the area in which the property is located. No property or interest therein shall be acquired by eminent domain by any public body for the purposes of this chapter; however, this provision shall not limit the power of eminent domain as it was possessed by any public body prior to the passage of this chapter. (1966, c. 461, § 10-152; 1974, c. 259; 1981, c. 64; 1988, c. 891.)

§ 10.1-1702. Further powers of public bodies.

— A. A public body shall have the powers necessary or convenient to carry out the purposes and provisions of this chapter, including the following powers:

1. To borrow funds and make expenditures;

2. To advance or accept advances of public funds;

3. To apply for and accept and utilize grants and any other assistance from the federal government and any other public or private sources, to give such security as may be required and to enter into and carry out contracts or agreements in connection with the assistance, and to include in any contract for assistance from the federal government such conditions imposed pursuant to federal laws as the public body may deem reasonable and appropriate and which are not inconsistent with the purposes of this chapter;

4. To make and execute contracts and other instruments;

5. In connection with the real property acquired and designated for the purposes of this chapter, to provide or to arrange or contract for the provision, construction, maintenance, operation, or repair by any person or agency, public or private, of services, privileges, works, streets, roads, public utilities or other facilities or structures that may be necessary to the provision, preservation, maintenance and management of the property as open-space land;

6. To insure or provide for the insurance of any real or personal property or operations of the public body against any risks or hazards, including the power to pay premiums on the insurance;

7. To demolish or dispose of any structures or facilities which may be detrimental to or inconsistent with the use of real property as open-space land; and

8. To exercise its functions and powers under this chapter jointly or cooperatively with public bodies of one or more states, if they are so authorized by state law, and with one or more public bodies of this Commonwealth, and to enter into agreements for joint or cooperative action.

B. For the purposes of this chapter, the Commonwealth or a county, city or town may:

1. Appropriate funds;

2. Issue and sell its general obligation bonds in the manner and within the limitations prescribed by the applicable laws of the Commonwealth;

3. Exercise its powers under this chapter through a board or commission, or through such office or officers as its governing body by resolution determines or as the Governor determines in the case of the Commonwealth; and

4. Levy taxes and assessments. (1966, c. 461, § 10-154; 1988, c. 891.)

§ 10.1-1703. Acquisition of title subject to reservation of farming or timber rights; acquisition of easements, etc.; property to be made available for farming and timber uses.

— Any public body is authorized to acquire (i) unrestricted fee simple title to tracts; (ii) fee simple title to such land subject to reservation of rights to use such lands for farming or to reservation of timber rights thereon; or (iii) easements in gross or such other interests in real estate of not less than five years' duration as are designed to maintain the character of such land as open-space land. Any such interest may also be perpetual. Whenever practicable in the judgment of the public body, real property acquired pursuant to this chapter shall be made available for agricultural and timbering uses which are compatible with the purposes of this chapter. (1966, c. 461, § 10-158; 1974, c. 259; 1981, c. 64; 1988, c. 891.)

CASE NOTES

Construction with other law. — Virginia Conservation Easement Act did not create a new right to burden land by a negative easement in gross for the purpose of land conservation and historic preservation, but facilitated the continued creation of such easements by providing a clear statutory framework under which tax exemptions are made available to charitable organizations devoted to those purposes and tax benefits and incentives are provided to the grantors of such easements, contrary to the common law; moreover, the easement at issue was not of a novel character and is consistent with the statutory recognition of negative easements in gross for conservation and historic purposes. United States v. Blackman, 270 Va. 68, 613 S.E.2d 442, 2005 Va. LEXIS 69 (2005).

§ 10.1-1704. Diversion of property from open-space land use; conveyance or lease of open-space land.

— A. No open-space land, the title to or interest or right in which has been acquired under this chapter and which has been designated as open-space land under the authority of this chapter, shall be converted or diverted from open-space land use unless (i) the conversion or diversion is determined by the public body to be (a) essential to the orderly development and growth of the locality and (b) in accordance with the official comprehensive plan for the locality in effect at the time of conversion or diversion and (ii) there is substituted other real property which is (a) of at least equal fair market value, (b) of greater value as permanent open-space land than the land converted or diverted and (c) of as nearly as feasible equivalent usefulness and location for use as permanent open-space land as is the land converted or diverted. The public body shall assure that the property substituted will be subject to the provisions of this chapter.

B. A public body may convey or lease any real property it has acquired and which has been designated for the purposes of this chapter. The conveyance or lease shall be subject to contractual arrangements that will preserve the property as open-space land, unless the property is to be converted or diverted from open-space land use in accordance with the provisions of subsection A of this section. (1966, c. 461, § 10-153; 1988, c. 891; 1997, c. 338.)

§ 10.1-1705. Chapter controlling over other laws; powers supplemental.

— Insofar as the provisions of this chapter are inconsistent with the provisions of any other law, the provisions of this chapter shall be controlling.

The powers conferred by this chapter shall be in addition and supplemental to the powers conferred by any other law. (1966, c. 461, § 10-157; 1988, c. 891.)

CHAPTER 18.

VIRGINIA OUTDOORS FOUNDATION.

§ 10.1-1800. Establishment and administration of Foundation; appointment, terms, chairman, quorum, etc., of board of trustees. — The Virginia Outdoors Foundation is established to promote the preservation of open-space lands and to encourage private gifts of money, securities, land or other property to preserve the natural, scenic, historic, scientific, open-space and recreational areas of the Commonwealth. The Virginia Outdoors Foundation is a body politic and shall be governed and administered by a board of trustees composed of seven trustees from the Commonwealth at large to be appointed by the Governor for four-year terms. Appointments shall be made to achieve a broad geographical representation of members. Vacancies shall be filled for the unexpired term. No trustee-at-large shall be eligible to serve more than two consecutive four-year terms. All trustees-at-large shall post bond in the penalty of $5,000 with the State Comptroller prior to entering upon the functions of office.

The Governor shall appoint a chairman of the board from among the seven trustees-at-large. A majority of the members of the board serving at any one time shall constitute a quorum for the transaction of business. (1966, c. 525, §§ 10-159 to 10-162; 1970, c. 757; 1988, c. 891; 1991, c. 190; 2000, cc. 21, 294; 2003, cc. 78, 90.)

CASE NOTES

Applied in United States v. Blackman, 270 Va. 68, 613 S.E.2d 442, 2005 Va. LEXIS 69 (2005).

§ 10.1-1801. Powers of Foundation. — The Virginia Outdoors Foundation shall have the following general powers:

1. To have succession until dissolved by the General Assembly, in which event title to the properties of the Foundation, both real and personal, shall, insofar as consistent with existing contractual obligations and subject to all other legally enforceable claims or demands by or against the Foundation, pass to and become vested in the Commonwealth;

2. To sue and be sued in contractual matters in its own name;

3. To promulgate regulations as it deems necessary for the administration of its functions in accordance with the Administrative Process Act (§ 2.2-4000 et seq.);

4. To accept, hold, and administer gifts and bequests of money, securities, or other property, absolutely or in trust, for the purposes for which the Founda-

tion is created. Unless otherwise restricted by the terms of the gift or bequest, the Foundation is authorized to sell, exchange, or otherwise dispose of and to invest or reinvest in such investments as it may determine the moneys, securities, or other property given or bequeathed to it. The principal of such funds, together with the income therefrom and all other revenues, shall be placed in such depositories as the Foundation shall determine and shall constitute a special fund and be subject to expenditure by the Foundation without further appropriation. The Foundation shall not engage in any business except in the furtherance of its objectives;

5. To acquire by gift, devise, purchase, or otherwise, absolutely or in trust, and to hold and, unless otherwise restricted by the terms of the gift or devise, to encumber, convey, or otherwise dispose of, any real property, or any estate or interest therein, as may be necessary and proper in carrying into effect the purposes of the Foundation;

6. To enter into contracts generally and to execute all instruments necessary or appropriate to carry out its purposes;

7. To appoint and prescribe the duties of such officers, agents, and employees as may be necessary to carry out its functions, and to fix and pay such compensation to them for their services as the Foundation may determine; and

8. To perform any lawful acts necessary or appropriate to carry out the purposes of the Foundation. (1966, c. 525, § 10-163; 1988, c. 891.)

Cross references. — As to fee for open-space preservation, see § 58.1-817.

§ 10.1-1801.1. Open-Space Lands Preservation Trust Fund. — A. The Foundation shall establish, administer, manage, including the creation of reserves, and make expenditures and allocations from a special nonreverting fund in the state treasury to be known as the Open-Space Lands Preservation Trust Fund, hereinafter referred to as the Fund. The Foundation shall establish and administer the Fund solely for the purpose of providing grants in accordance with this section to localities acquiring open-space easements or persons conveying conservation or open-space easements on agricultural, forestal, or other open-space land pursuant to the Open-Space Land Act (§ 10.1-1700 et seq.) and, if applicable, the Virginia Conservation Easement Act (§ 10.1-1009 et seq.).

B. The Fund shall consist of general fund moneys, gifts, endowments or grants from the United States government, its agencies and instrumentalities, and funds from any other available sources, public or private.

C. Any moneys remaining in the Fund at the end of a biennium shall remain in the Fund, and shall not revert to the general fund. Interest earned on moneys received by the Fund shall remain in the Fund and be credited to it.

D. The purpose of grants made from the Fund shall be to aid localities acquiring open-space easements or persons conveying conservation or open-space easements with the costs associated with the conveyance of the easements, which may include legal costs, appraisal costs or all or part of the value of the easement. In cases where a grant is used to purchase all or part of the value of an easement, moneys from the Fund may also be used by the Foundation to pay for an appraisal, provided that the appraisal is the only appraisal paid for by the Foundation in the acquisition of a particular easement. To be eligible for a grant award, the conservation or open-space easement shall provide that:

1. The easement is perpetual in duration;

2. The easement is conveyed to the Foundation and a local coholder; and

3. If the local coholder ceases to exist, the easement shall vest solely in the Foundation. If a local coholder of an easement for which a grant has been

awarded under this section ceases to exist, the Foundation shall within two years convey the interest in the easement that was held by the local coholder to another qualified local coholder. If no qualified local coholder is willing to accept the easement, the Foundation shall diligently continue to seek a qualified local coholder.

For the purposes of this section, *"local coholder"* means the governing body of the locality in which the easement is located; a holder as defined in § 10.1-1009; a public recreational facilities authority; other local entity authorized by statute to hold open-space or preservation easements, or a soil and water conservation district, if authorized to hold an easement under the Open-Space Land Act (§ 10.1-1700 et seq.). The Board of Historic Resources may be a local coholder if the easement is on land that abuts land on which a designated historic landmark, building, structure, district, object or site is located.

E. The Foundation shall establish guidelines for submittal and evaluation of grant applications. In evaluating grant applications, the Foundation may give priority to applications that:

1. Request a grant to pay only legal and appraisal fees for a conservation or open-space easement that is being donated by the landowner;

2. Request a grant to pay costs associated with conveying a conservation or open-space easement on a family-owned or family-operated farm; or

3. Demonstrate the applicant's financial need for a grant.

F. No open-space land for which a grant has been awarded under this section shall be converted or diverted from open-space land use unless:

1. Such conversion or diversion is in compliance with subsection A of § 10.1-1704; and

2. The easement on the land substituted for land subject to an easement with respect to which a grant has been made under this section meets the eligibility requirements of this section.

G. Up to $100,000 per year of any interest generated by the Fund may be used for the Foundation's administrative expenses. (1997, c. 338; 1999, c. 927; 2000, c. 181; 2003, cc. 78, 90.)

§ 10.1-1801.2: Repealed by Acts 2003, cc. 78 and 90, cl. 2.

§ 10.1-1802. Annual report. — The Foundation shall submit an annual report to the Governor and General Assembly on or before November 1 of each year. The report shall contain, at a minimum, the annual financial statements of the Foundation for the year ending the preceding June 30. (1966, c. 525, § 10-164; 1984, c. 734; 1985, c. 146; 1988, c. 891; 2004, c. 650.)

Editor's note. — Acts 2004, c. 650, cl. 3, provides: "That the Division of Legislative Automated Systems shall notify the Governor, the Lieutenant Governor, the Clerk of the House of the Delegates, the Clerk of the Senate, and the Law Librarian of the University of Virginia that the automatic distribution of hard copies of annual and biennial reports pursuant to § 2.2-1127 has been replaced by an on-demand electronic notification and report retrieval system available from the General Assembly's website. The Division shall also notify the members of the General Assembly of the availability of the electronic notification and report retrieval system and the additional option of receiving hardcopies of reports by request."

§ 10.1-1803. Gifts, devises and bequests. — Gifts, devises or bequests, whether personal or real property, and the income therefrom, accepted by the Foundation, shall be deemed to be gifts to the Commonwealth, which shall be exempt from all state and local taxes, and shall be regarded as the property of the Commonwealth for the purposes of all tax laws. (1966, c. 525, § 10-165; 1988, c. 891.)

§ **10.1-1804. Cooperation of state agencies, etc.** — All state officers, agencies, commissions, departments, and institutions are directed to cooperate with and assist the Virginia Outdoors Foundation in carrying out its purpose, and to that end may accept any gift or conveyance of land or other property in the name of the Commonwealth from the Foundation. Such property shall be held in possession or used as provided in the terms of the trust, contract, or instrument by which it is conveyed. (1966, c. 525, § 10-166; 1988, c. 891.)

CHAPTER 19.

VIRGINIA BEACH EROSION COUNCIL.

§§ 10.1-1900, 10.1-1901: Repealed by Acts 1989, c. 659.

Editor's note. — Acts 1989, c. 659, cl. 2 provides that as of July 1, 1989, the City of Virginia Beach shall be deemed successor in interest of all rights, titles and interest in and to any real or tangible personal property vested in the Virginia Beach Erosion Council.

CHAPTER 20.

VIRGINIA MUSEUM OF NATURAL HISTORY.

§ **10.1-2000. Museum created; essential governmental function.** — There is hereby created an institution of the Commonwealth of Virginia to be known as "The Virginia Museum of Natural History," hereinafter referred to as the "Museum." The Museum is hereby declared to be a public body and instrumentality for the purpose of preserving and protecting Virginia's natural history. The exercise by the Museum of the powers conferred by this chapter shall be deemed an essential governmental function. (1988, cc. 707, 891.)

§ **10.1-2001. Purposes.** — The purposes of the Virginia Museum of Natural History are:
1. To investigate, preserve and exhibit the various elements of natural history found in Virginia and other parts of the United States and the world;
2. To foster an understanding and appreciation of how man and the earth have evolved;
3. To encourage and promote research in the varied natural heritage of Virginia and other parts of the world;
4. To encourage individuals and scholars to study our natural history and to apply this understanding of the past to the challenge of the future;
5. To establish a state museum of natural history in Virginia where specimens of natural history, especially those of Virginia origin, can be properly housed, cared for, cataloged and studied and to ensure a permanent repository of our natural heritage; and

6. To coordinate an efficient network in Virginia where researchers and the public can readily use the natural history material of the Museum, its branches, Virginia's institutions of higher education and other museums. These purposes are hereby declared to be a matter of legislative determination. (1988, cc. 707, 891.)

§ 10.1-2002. Board of trustees; appointment of members. — The Museum shall be governed by a board of trustees consisting of twenty-five members appointed by the Governor. Two of the members appointed to the Board shall be members of the Virginia Academy of Science. The appointments shall be subject to confirmation by the General Assembly if in session and, if not, then at its next succeeding session. The Board of Trustees shall be referred to as the "Board." (1988, cc. 707, 891.)

§ 10.1-2003. Terms of members; vacancies. — The members of the Board shall be appointed for terms of five years each, except that the initial appointments to the Board shall be for such terms of less than five years as may be necessary to stagger the expiration of terms so that the terms of not more than seven members expire in any one year. Members of the Board may be suspended or removed by the Governor at his pleasure and the unexpired term of any member shall lapse upon his failure for any reason to attend four consecutive regular meetings of the Board. The initial appointments of members for terms of less than five years shall be deemed appointments to fill vacancies. No person shall be eligible to serve for or during more than two successive terms; however, any person appointed to fill a vacancy may be eligible for two additional successive terms after the term of the vacancy for which he was appointed has expired. The members of the Board shall receive no salaries. (1988, cc. 707, 891; 2001, c. 163.)

§ 10.1-2004. Annual meeting; Officers of Board; executive committee. — The Board shall designate one regular meeting to be held annually each fiscal year. At each regular annual meeting, the Board shall select a chairman and a vice-chairman from its membership, and appoint an executive committee to consist of not less than three nor more than five of its membership, including the chairman and vice-chairman for the transaction of business in the recess of the Board. (1988, cc. 707, 891; 2001, c. 163.)

§ 10.1-2005. Oath of members. — Before entering upon the discharge of his duties, each member of the Board shall take the usual oath of office. (1988, cc. 707, 891.)

§ 10.1-2006. Bonds of members. — Each member of the Board shall give bond, with corporate surety, in such penalty as is fixed by the Governor, conditioned upon the faithful discharge of his duties. The premium on the bonds shall be paid from funds available to the Museum. (1988, cc. 707, 891.)

§ 10.1-2007. Meetings of Board. — The Board shall establish a regular meeting schedule and may meet at such other times as it deems appropriate or upon call of the chairman, when in his opinion a meeting is expedient or necessary. (1988, cc. 707, 891; 2001, c. 163.)

§ 10.1-2008. Quorum of Board. — A simple majority of the members of the Board then serving shall constitute a quorum. In absence of a quorum, and provided that the chairman or vice-chairman and at least two other members of the Board are present, a meeting may proceed to receive information, but not take any action upon, items listed on the meeting agenda distributed in advance to the full membership. (1988, cc. 707, 891; 2001, c. 163.)

§ 10.1-2009. Powers and duties of Board. — A. The Board is hereby authorized:

1. To manage, control, maintain and operate the Museum and to provide for the erection, care and preservation of all property belonging to the Museum;

2. To appoint the Director of the Museum, and prescribe his duties and salary and to employ such deputies and assistants as may be required;

3. To prescribe rules and regulations for the operation of the Museum, including, but not limited to, the kinds and types of research, instruction and exhibits, and the making of plans for expansion of the Museum;

4. To employ planning consultants and architects in relation to expansion of the Museum;

5. To acquire by purchase, gift, loan or otherwise land necessary for establishment and expansion of the Museum, and exhibits and displays;

6. To enter into agreements with institutions of higher education in Virginia to work cooperatively on research projects of mutual interest and benefit;

7. To establish a foundation to assist in fund raising efforts to supplement the state funds provided to the Museum;

8. To enter into contracts for construction of physical facilities;

9. To enter into contracts approved by the Attorney General to further the purposes of the Museum;

10. To adopt a seal, flag or other emblems; and

11. To charge for admission to the Museum, if deemed appropriate.

B. With prior annual written approval of the Governor, the Board of Trustees of the Virginia Museum of Natural History may supplement the salary of the Director of the Museum from nonstate funds. In approving a supplement, the Governor may be guided by criteria that provide a reasonable limit on the total additional income of the Director. The criteria may include, but need not be limited to, a consideration of the salaries paid to similar officials at comparable museums of other states. The Board shall report approved supplements to the Department of Human Resource Management for retention in its records. (1988, cc. 707, 891; 2004, c. 870.)

§ 10.1-2010. Agents and employees. — The Director may engage or authorize the engagement of agents and employees necessary to the operation and maintenance of the Museum, subject to the approval of the Board. (1988, cc. 707, 891.)

§ 10.1-2011. Acceptance of gifts; expenditures; certain powers of educational institutions to apply. — A. The Board is authorized to receive and administer grants from agencies of the United States government, and gifts, bequests and devises of property, and to expend or authorize the expenditure of funds derived from such sources and funds appropriated by the General Assembly to the Museum.

B. Notwithstanding any law to the contrary, the Museum shall be deemed to be an institution of higher education within the meaning of §§ 23-3.1 and 23-9.2. (1988, cc. 707, 891; 2004, c. 870.)

§ 10.1-2012. Annual report. — The Board of Trustees shall submit an annual report to the Governor and General Assembly on or before November 1 of each year. Such report shall contain, at a minimum, the annual financial statements of the Museum for the year ending the preceding June 30. (1988, cc. 707, 891; 2004, c. 650.)

Editor's note. — Acts 2004, c. 650, cl. 3, provides: "That the Division of Legislative Automated Systems shall notify the Governor, the Lieutenant Governor, the Clerk of the House of the Delegates, the Clerk of the Senate, and the Law Librarian of the University of Virginia that the automatic distribution of hard copies of annual and biennial reports pursuant to § 2.2-1127 has been replaced by an on-demand electronic notification and report retrieval system available from the General Assembly's website. The Division shall also notify the members of the General Assembly of the availability of the electronic notification and report retrieval system and the additional option of receiving hardcopies of reports by request."

CHAPTER 21.

CHESAPEAKE BAY PRESERVATION ACT.

ARTICLE 1.

General Provisions.

§ 10.1-2100. Cooperative state-local program. — A. Healthy state and local economies and a healthy Chesapeake Bay are integrally related; balanced economic development and water quality protection are not mutually exclusive. The protection of the public interest in the Chesapeake Bay, its tributaries, and other state waters and the promotion of the general welfare of the people of the Commonwealth require that: (i) the counties, cities, and towns of Tidewater Virginia incorporate general water quality protection measures into their comprehensive plans, zoning ordinances, and subdivision ordinances; (ii) the counties, cities, and towns of Tidewater Virginia establish programs, in accordance with criteria established by the Commonwealth, that define and protect certain lands, hereinafter called Chesapeake Bay Preservation Areas, which if improperly developed may result in substantial damage to the water quality of the Chesapeake Bay and its tributaries; (iii) the Commonwealth make its resources available to local governing bodies by providing financial and technical assistance, policy guidance, and oversight when requested or otherwise required to carry out and enforce the provisions of this chapter; and (iv) all agencies of the Commonwealth exercise their delegated authority in a manner consistent with water quality protection provisions of local comprehensive plans, zoning ordinances, and subdivision ordinances when it has been determined that they comply with the provisions of this chapter.

B. Local governments have the initiative for planning and for implementing the provisions of this chapter, and the Commonwealth shall act primarily in a supportive role by providing oversight for local governmental programs, by establishing criteria as required by this chapter, and by providing those resources necessary to carry out and enforce the provisions of this chapter. (1988, cc. 608, 891.)

Cross references. — As to establishment of stormwater management programs by localities, see § 10.1-603.3.

Law Review. — For article, "Legal Issues Affecting Local Governments in Implementing the Chesapeake Bay Preservation Act," see 24 U. Rich. L. Rev. 1 (1989). For article, "Response to Legal Issues Affecting Local Governments in Implementing the Chesapeake Bay Preservation Act," see 24 U. Rich. L. Rev. 385 (1990). For note, "The Chesapeake Bay Preservation Act: The Problem With State Land Regulation of Interstate Resources," see 31 Wm. & Mary L. Rev. 735 (1990). For article, "Federal Minimums: Insufficient to Save the Bay," see 29 U. Rich. L. Rev. 635 (1995). For an article reviewing key environmental developments at the federal and state levels during the period from June 1996 to June 1998, see 32 U. Rich. L. Rev. 1217 (1998).

CIRCUIT COURT OPINIONS

Chesapeake Bay Preservation Act is not a "no growth" act. — Zoning board of appeals erred in interpreting the Chesapeake Bay Preservation Act as a "no growth" statute, and thereby limiting the ability of property owners' to develop their property. Chappell v. Bd. of Zoning Appeals for Fairfax, 65 Va. Cir. 142, 2004 Va. Cir. LEXIS 139 (Fairfax County 2004).

City's designation of streams and property reversed as ultra vires. — City's designation of streams as perennial and property surrounding the streams as Resource Protection Areas under the Chesapeake Bay Preservation Act (Act), § 10.1-2100 et seq., was reversed as ultra vires; the regulations implementing the Act prior to 2002 defined a tributary stream as a stream identified as perennial on the United States Geological Survey map, which the streams at issue were not, and there was no indication that the city had developed or used a scientifically valid system of in-field indicators of perennial flow, as required under 9 VAC § 10-20-80 (D), or that such system had been adopted into the local program and applied consistently, as required by the amended regulation. Pony Farm Assocs., L.L.C. v. City of Richmond, 62 Va. Cir. 386, 2003 Va. Cir. LEXIS 282 (Richmond 2003).

OPINIONS OF THE ATTORNEY GENERAL

Constitutionality of amendments of regulations. — Amendments by the Chesapeake Bay Local Assistance Board to its Chesapeake Bay Preservation Area Designation and Management Regulations do not violate the Equal Protection Clause of the Constitution of the United States. See opinion of Attorney General to W. Leslie Kilduff, Jr., County Attorney for Northumberland County, 02-052 (10/30/02).

§ **10.1-2101. Definitions.** — For the purposes of this chapter, the following words shall have the meanings respectively ascribed to them:

"Board" means Chesapeake Bay Local Assistance Board.

"Chesapeake Bay Preservation Area" means an area delineated by a local government in accordance with criteria established pursuant to § 10.1-2107.

"Criteria" means criteria developed by the Board pursuant to § 10.1-2107 of this chapter for the purpose of determining the ecological and geographic extent of Chesapeake Bay Preservation Areas and for use by local governments in permitting, denying, or modifying requests to rezone, subdivide, or to use and develop land in Chesapeake Bay Preservation Areas.

"Department" means the Department of Conservation and Recreation.

"Director" means the Director of the Department of Conservation and Recreation.

"Person" means any corporation, association, or partnership, one or more individuals, or any unit of government or agency thereof.

"Secretary" means the Secretary of Natural Resources.

"State waters" means all waters, on the surface or under the ground, wholly or partially within or bordering the Commonwealth or within its jurisdiction.

"Tidewater Virginia" means the following jurisdictions:

The Counties of Accomack, Arlington, Caroline, Charles City, Chesterfield, Essex, Fairfax, Gloucester, Hanover, Henrico, Isle of Wight, James City, King George, King and Queen, King William, Lancaster, Mathews, Middlesex, New Kent, Northampton, Northumberland, Prince George, Prince William, Richmond, Spotsylvania, Stafford, Surry, Westmoreland, and York, and the Cities of Alexandria, Chesapeake, Colonial Heights, Fairfax, Falls Church, Fredericksburg, Hampton, Hopewell, Newport News, Norfolk, Petersburg, Poquoson, Portsmouth, Richmond, Suffolk, Virginia Beach, and Williamsburg. (1988, cc. 608, 891; 2005, c. 41.)

Editor's note. — Acts 2005, c. 41, cl. 3, provides: "That the regulations of the Chesapeake Bay Local Assistance Board and any attendant forms, guidance documents, legal opinions, or other legal documents produced by or for the Board shall remain in full force and effect until amended, modified, or repealed."

Acts 2005, c. 41, cl. 4, provides: "That references to the Chesapeake Bay Local Assistance Department in regulation, local ordinance, guidance, or otherwise shall mean the Department of Conservation and Recreation, and similarly, references to the Executive Director of the Chesapeake Bay Local Assistance Department shall mean the Director of the Depart-ment of Conservation and Recreation."

Acts 2005, c. 41, cl. 5, provides: "That the Chesapeake Bay Local Assistance Board shall have the authority to amend, modify, or delete provisions in the Chesapeake Bay Preservation Area Designation and Management Regulations (9-VAC 10-20 et seq.) in order to implement Chapter 372 of the Acts of Assembly of 2004 and the provisions of this act. Those amendments to the regulations necessitated by these acts shall be exempt from Article 2 (§ 2.2-4006 et seq.) of the Administrative Process Act."

The 2005 amendments. — The 2005 amendment by c. 41, rewrote the definitions following "Department" and "Director."

§ 10.1-2102. Chesapeake Bay Local Assistance Board established. —

A. There is hereby established the Chesapeake Bay Local Assistance Board. The Board shall consist of nine Tidewater Virginia residents appointed by the Governor, subject to confirmation by the General Assembly. The Board shall consist of at least one individual from each Planning District in which there is located one or more Tidewater Virginia localities. Members of the Board shall be representative of, but not limited to, citizens with an interest in and experience with local government, business, the use and development of land, agriculture, forestry and the protection of water quality. Upon initial appointment, three members shall be appointed for four-year terms, three for three-year terms, and three for two-year terms. Thereafter, all members shall be appointed for terms of four years each. Vacancies occurring other than by expiration of a term shall be filled by the Governor in the same manner as the original appointment for the unexpired portion of the term.

B. The Board shall adopt rules and procedures for the conduct of its business.

C. The Board shall elect a chairman from among its members.

D. A quorum shall consist of five members. The decision of a majority of those members present and voting shall constitute a decision of the Board; however, a favorable vote of the majority of the Board membership is required to adopt criteria pursuant to § 10.1-2107 of this chapter or for any action taken by the Board under subdivision 8 of § 10.1-2103. If at a meeting of the Board action will be taken under subdivision 8 of § 10.1-2103 with respect to the comprehensive plan, zoning or subdivision ordinance of a county, city or town, written notice of such meeting shall be given to the governing body of the locality at least ten days in advance of the meeting.

E. The Board shall meet at least four times a year, and other meetings may be held at any time or place determined by the Board or upon call of the chairman or upon written request to the chairman of any two members. All members shall be duly notified of the time and place of any regular or other meeting at least ten days in advance of such meetings.

F. The Board shall keep a complete and accurate record of its proceedings. A copy of the record shall be available for public inspection and copying. (1988, cc. 608, 891.)

§ **10.1-2103. Powers and duties of the Board.** — The Board is responsible for carrying out the purposes and provisions of this chapter and is authorized to:

1. Provide land use and development and water quality protection information and assistance to the various levels of local, regional and state government within the Commonwealth.

2. Consult, advise, and coordinate with the Governor, the Secretary, the General Assembly, other state agencies, regional agencies, local governments and federal agencies for the purpose of implementing this chapter.

3. Provide financial and technical assistance and advice to local governments and to regional and state agencies concerning aspects of land use and development and water quality protection pursuant to this chapter.

4. Promulgate regulations pursuant to the Administrative Process Act (§ 2.2-4000 et seq.).

5. Develop, promulgate and keep current the criteria required by § 10.1-2107.

6. Provide technical assistance and advice or other aid for the development, adoption and implementation of local comprehensive plans, zoning ordinances, subdivision ordinances, and other land use and development and water quality protection measures utilizing criteria established by the Board to carry out the provisions of this chapter.

7. Develop procedures for use by local governments to designate Chesapeake Bay Preservation Areas in accordance with the criteria developed pursuant to § 10.1-2107.

8. Ensure that local government comprehensive plans, zoning ordinances and subdivision ordinances are in accordance with the provisions of this chapter. Determination of compliance shall be in accordance with the provisions of the Administrative Process Act (§ 2.2-4000 et seq.).

9. Make application for federal funds that may become available under federal acts and to transmit such funds when applicable to any appropriate person.

10. Take administrative and legal actions to ensure compliance by counties, cities and towns with the provisions of this chapter including the proper enforcement and implementation of, and continual compliance with, this chapter.

11. Perform such other duties and responsibilities related to the use and development of land and the protection of water quality as the Secretary may assign.

12. Enter into contracts necessary and convenient to carry out the provisions of this chapter. (1988, cc. 608, 891; 1997, c. 266.)

Law Review. — For article, "Legal Issues Affecting Local Governments in Implementing the Chesapeake Bay Preservation Act," see 24 U. Rich. L. Rev. 1 (1989).

OPINIONS OF THE ATTORNEY GENERAL

Intervention by Chesapeake Bay Local Assistance Board. — The Chesapeake Bay Local Assistance Board has authority to "intervene" on its own or on behalf of a person who believes a local governing body is disregarding its zoning ordinances or misinterpreting certain criteria designed to protect the quality of state waters, and the Board is also authorized to institute or take administrative and legal actions to ensure compliance with the Chesapeake Bay Preservation Act. See opinion of Attorney General to Mr. Michael D. Clower, Executive Director, Chesapeake Bay Local Assistance Department, 00-087 (11/26/01).

No authority to issue cease and desist order or to seek injunction. — Neither the Executive Director of the Chesapeake Bay Local Assistance Department [now the Director of the Department of Conservation and Recreation] nor the Chesapeake Bay Local Assistance Board have the authority to issue a cease and desist order to a locality that is violating the Chesapeake Bay Preservation Act or to request the Attorney General to seek an injunction against a locality that violates a cease and desist order. See opinion of Attorney General to Mr. Michael D. Clower, Executive Director, Chesapeake Bay Local Assistance Department, 00-087 (11/26/01).

§ 10.1-2104. Exclusive authority of Board to institute legal actions.

— The Board shall have the exclusive authority to institute or intervene in legal and administrative actions to ensure compliance by local governing bodies with this chapter and with any criteria or regulations adopted hereunder. (1988, cc. 608, 891; 1997, c. 266.)

OPINIONS OF THE ATTORNEY GENERAL

Intervention by Chesapeake Bay Local Assistance Board. — The Chesapeake Bay Local Assistance Board has authority to "intervene" on its own or on behalf of a person who believes a local governing body is disregarding its zoning ordinances or misinterpreting certain criteria designed to protect the quality of state waters, and the Board is also authorized to institute or take administrative and legal actions to ensure compliance with the Chesapeake Bay Preservation Act. See opinion of Attorney General to Mr. Michael D. Clower, Executive Director, Chesapeake Bay Local Assistance Department, 00-087 (11/26/01).

No authority to issue cease and desist order or to seek injunction. — Neither the Executive Director of the Chesapeake Bay Local Assistance Department [now the Director of the Department of Conservation and Recreation] nor the Chesapeake Bay Local Assistance Board have the authority to issue a cease and desist order to a locality that is violating the Chesapeake Bay Preservation Act or to request the Attorney General to seek an injunction against a locality that violates a cease and desist order. See opinion of Attorney General to Mr. Michael D. Clower, Executive Director, Chesapeake Bay Local Assistance Department, 00-087 (11/26/01).

§ 10.1-2105: Repealed by Acts 2005, c. 41, c. 2.

Editor's note. — Acts 2005, c. 41, cl. 3, provides: "That the regulations of the Chesapeake Bay Local Assistance Board and any attendant forms, guidance documents, legal opinions, or other legal documents produced by or for the Board shall remain in full force and effect until amended, modified, or repealed."

Acts 2005, c. 41, cl. 4, provides: "That references to the Chesapeake Bay Local Assistance Department in regulation, local ordinance, guidance, or otherwise shall mean the Department of Conservation and Recreation, and similarly, references to the Executive Director of the Chesapeake Bay Local Assistance Department shall mean the Director of the Department of Conservation and Recreation."

§ 10.1-2106. Powers and duties of Director.

— A. In addition to the other responsibilities set forth herein, the Director shall carry out management and supervisory responsibilities in accordance with the regulations and policies of the Board. In no event shall the Director have the authority to promulgate any final regulations.

B. The Director shall be vested with all the authority of the Board, including the authority granted by § 10.1-2104, when it is not in session, subject to such regulations as may be prescribed by the Board. (1988, cc. 608, 891; 1997, c. 266; 2005, c. 41.)

Editor's note. — Acts 2005, c. 41, cl. 3, provides: "That the regulations of the Chesapeake Bay Local Assistance Board and any attendant forms, guidance documents, legal opinions, or other legal documents produced by or for the Board shall remain in full force and effect until amended, modified, or repealed."

Acts 2005, c. 41, cl. 4, provides: "That references to the Chesapeake Bay Local Assistance Department in regulation, local ordinance, guidance, or otherwise shall mean the Department of Conservation and Recreation, and similarly, references to the Executive Director of the Chesapeake Bay Local Assistance Department shall mean the Director of the Department of Conservation and Recreation."

Acts 2005, c. 41, cl. 5, provides: "That the Chesapeake Bay Local Assistance Board shall have the authority to amend, modify, or delete provisions in the Chesapeake Bay Preservation Area Designation and Management Regulations (9-VAC 10-20 et seq.) in order to implement Chapter 372 of the Acts of Assembly of 2004 and the provisions of this act. Those amendments to the regulations necessitated by these acts shall be exempt from Article 2 (§ 2.2-4006 et seq.) of the Administrative Process Act."

The 2005 amendments. — The 2005 amendment by c. 41 deleted former subsection A, which read: "The Director under the direction and control of the Secretary, shall exercise such powers and perform such duties as are conferred or imposed upon him by law and shall perform any other duties required of him by the Governor or the Board."; and redesignated former subsections B and C as present subsections A and B.

OPINIONS OF THE ATTORNEY GENERAL

No authority to issue cease and desist order or to seek injunction. — Neither the Executive Director of the Chesapeake Bay Local Assistance Department [now the Director of the Department of Conservation and Recreation] nor the Chesapeake Bay Local Assistance Board have the authority to issue a cease and desist order to a locality that is violating the Chesapeake Bay Preservation Act or to request the Attorney General to seek an injunction against a locality that violates a cease and desist order. See opinion of Attorney General to Mr. Michael D. Clower, Executive Director, Chesapeake Bay Local Assistance Department, 00-087 (11/26/01).

§ **10.1-2107. Board to develop criteria.** — A. In order to implement the provisions of this chapter and to assist counties, cities and towns in regulating the use and development of land and in protecting the quality of state waters, the Board shall promulgate regulations which establish criteria for use by local governments to determine the ecological and geographic extent of Chesapeake Bay Preservation Areas. The Board shall also promulgate regulations which establish criteria for use by local governments in granting, denying, or modifying requests to rezone, subdivide, or to use and develop land in these areas.

B. In developing and amending the criteria, the Board shall consider all factors relevant to the protection of water quality from significant degradation as a result of the use and development of land. The criteria shall incorporate measures such as performance standards, best management practices, and various planning and zoning concepts to protect the quality of state waters while allowing use and development of land consistent with the provisions of this chapter. The criteria adopted by the Board, operating in conjunction with other state water quality programs, shall encourage and promote: (i) protection of existing high quality state waters and restoration of all other state waters to a condition or quality that will permit all reasonable public uses and will support the propagation and growth of all aquatic life, including game fish, which might reasonably be expected to inhabit them; (ii) safeguarding the clean waters of the Commonwealth from pollution; (iii) prevention of any increase in pollution; (iv) reduction of existing pollution; and (v) promotion of water resource conservation in order to provide for the health, safety and welfare of the present and future citizens of the Commonwealth.

C. Prior to the development or amendment of criteria, the Board shall give due consideration to, among other things, the economic and social costs and benefits which can reasonably be expected to obtain as a result of the adoption or amendment of the criteria.

D. In developing such criteria the Board may consult with and obtain the comments of any federal, state, regional, or local agency that has jurisdiction by law or special expertise with respect to the use and development of land or the protection of water. The Board shall give due consideration to the comments submitted by such federal, state, regional, or local agencies.

E. Criteria shall be adopted by July 1, 1989. (1988, cc. 608, 891.)

§ **10.1-2108. Local government authority.** — Counties, cities, and towns are authorized to exercise their police and zoning powers to protect the quality of state waters consistent with the provisions of this chapter. (1988, cc. 608, 891.)

Law Review. — For article, "Legal Issues Affecting Local Governments in Implementing the Chesapeake Bay Preservation Act," see 24 U. Rich. L. Rev. 1 (1989).

§ **10.1-2109. Local governments to designate Chesapeake Bay Preservation Areas; incorporate into local plans and ordinances; impose civil penalties.** — A. Counties, cities and towns in Tidewater Virginia shall use the criteria developed by the Board to determine the extent of the Chesapeake Bay Preservation Area within their jurisdictions. Designation of Chesapeake Bay Preservation Areas shall be accomplished by every county, city and town in Tidewater Virginia not later than twelve months after adoption of criteria by the Board.

B. Counties, cities, and towns in Tidewater Virginia shall incorporate protection of the quality of state waters into each locality's comprehensive plan consistent with the provisions of this chapter.

C. All counties, cities and towns in Tidewater Virginia shall have zoning ordinances which incorporate measures to protect the quality of state waters in the Chesapeake Bay Preservation Areas consistent with the provisions of this chapter. Zoning in Chesapeake Bay Preservation Areas shall comply with all criteria set forth in or established pursuant to § 10.1-2107.

D. Counties, cities and towns in Tidewater Virginia shall incorporate protection of the quality of state waters in Chesapeake Bay Preservation Areas into their subdivision ordinances consistent with the provisions of this chapter. Counties, cities and towns in Tidewater Virginia shall ensure that all subdivisions developed pursuant to their subdivision ordinances comply with all criteria developed by the Board.

E. In addition to any other remedies which may be obtained under any local ordinance enacted to protect the quality of state waters in Chesapeake Bay Preservation Areas, counties, cities and towns in Tidewater Virginia may incorporate the following penalties into their zoning, subdivision or other ordinances:

1. Any person who: (i) violates any provision of any such ordinance or (ii) violates or fails, neglects, or refuses to obey any local governmental body's or official's final notice, order, rule, regulation, or variance or permit condition authorized under such ordinance shall, upon such finding by an appropriate circuit court, be assessed a civil penalty not to exceed $5,000 for each day of violation. Such civil penalties may, at the discretion of the court assessing them, be directed to be paid into the treasury of the county, city or town in which the violation occurred for the purpose of abating environmental damage to or restoring Chesapeake Bay Preservation Areas therein, in such a manner as the court may direct by order, except that where the violator is the county, city or town itself or its agent, the court shall direct the penalty to be paid into the state treasury.

2. With the consent of any person who: (i) violates any provision of any local ordinance related to the protection of water quality in Chesapeake Bay Preservation Areas or (ii) violates or fails, neglects, or refuses to obey any local governmental body's or official's notice, order, rule, regulation, or variance or permit condition authorized under such ordinance, the local government may provide for the issuance of an order against such person for the one-time payment of civil charges for each violation in specific sums, not to exceed $10,000 for each violation. Such civil charges shall be paid into the treasury of

the county, city or town in which the violation occurred for the purpose of abating environmental damage to or restoring Chesapeake Bay Preservation Areas therein, except that where the violator is the county, city or town itself or its agent, the civil charges shall be paid into the state treasury. Civil charges shall be in lieu of any appropriate civil penalty that could be imposed under subdivision 1 of this subsection. Civil charges may be in addition to the cost of any restoration required or ordered by the local governmental body or official. (1988, cc. 608, 891; 1998, cc. 700, 714.)

Law Review. — For article, "Legal Issues Affecting Local Governments in Implementing the Chesapeake Bay Preservation Act," see 24 U. Rich. L. Rev. 1 (1989). For an article reviewing key environmental developments at the federal and state levels during the period from June 1996 to June 1998, see 32 U. Rich. L. Rev. 1217 (1998).

CIRCUIT COURT OPINIONS

City's designation of streams and property reversed as ultra vires. — City's designation of streams as perennial and property surrounding the streams as as Resource Protection Areas under the city's Chesapeake Bay Preservation Act, ordinance was improper and was reversed as ultra vires; the regulations implementing the Act prior to 2002 defined a tributary stream as a stream identified as perennial on the United States Geological Survey map, which the streams at issue were not, and there was no indication that the city had developed or used a scientifically valid system of in-field indicators of perennial flow, as required under 9 VAC § 10-20-80 (D), or that such system had been adopted into the local program and applied consistently, as required by the amended regulation. Pony Farm Assocs., L.L.C. v. City of Richmond, 62 Va. Cir. 386, 2003 Va. Cir. LEXIS 282 (Richmond 2003).

OPINIONS OF THE ATTORNEY GENERAL

Intervention by Chesapeake Bay Local Assistance Board. — The Chesapeake Bay Local Assistance Board has authority to "intervene" on its own or on behalf of a person who believes a local governing body is disregarding its zoning ordinances or misinterpreting certain criteria designed to protect the quality of state waters, and the Board is also authorized to institute or take administrative and legal actions to ensure compliance with the Chesapeake Bay Preservation Act. See opinion of Attorney General to Mr. Michael D. Clower, Executive Director, Chesapeake Bay Local Assistance Department, 00-087 (11/26/01).

§ 10.1-2110. Local governments outside of Tidewater Virginia may adopt provisions. — Any local government, although not a part of Tidewater Virginia may employ the criteria developed pursuant to § 10.1-2107 and may incorporate protection of the quality of state waters into their comprehensive plans, zoning ordinances and subdivision ordinances consistent with the provisions of this chapter. (1988, cc. 608, 891.)

§ 10.1-2111. Local government requirements for water quality protection. — Local governments shall employ the criteria promulgated by the Board to ensure that the use and development of land in Chesapeake Bay Preservation Areas shall be accomplished in a manner that protects the quality of state waters consistent with the provisions of this chapter. (1988, cc. 608, 891.)

OPINIONS OF THE ATTORNEY GENERAL

Intervention by Chesapeake Bay Local Assistance Board. — The Chesapeake Bay Local Assistance Board has authority to "intervene" on its own or on behalf of a person who believes a local governing body is disregarding its zoning ordinances or misinterpreting certain criteria designed to protect the quality of state waters, and the Board is also authorized to institute or take administrative and legal actions to ensure compliance with the Chesa-

peake Bay Preservation Act. See opinion of
Attorney General to Mr. Michael D. Clower,
Executive Director, Chesapeake Bay Local As-
sistance Department, 00-087 (11/26/01).

§ 10.1-2112. Advisory state review of local government decisions. —
In addition to any other review requirements of this chapter, the Board shall,
upon request by any county, city or town, review any application for the use or
development of land in that county, city or town for consistency with the
provisions of this chapter. Any such review shall be completed and a report
submitted to such county, city or town within ninety days of such request.
(1988, cc. 608, 891.)

§ 10.1-2113. Effect on other governmental authority. — The authori-
ties granted herein are supplemental to other state, regional and local
governmental authority. No authority granted to a local government by this
chapter shall affect in any way the authority of the State Water Control Board
to regulate industrial or sewage discharges under Articles 3 (§ 62.1-44.16 et
seq.) and 4 (§ 62.1-44.18 et seq.) of the State Water Control Law (§ 62.1-44.2
et seq.). No authority granted to a local government by this chapter shall limit
in any way any other planning, zoning, or subdivision authority of that local
government. (1988, cc. 608, 891.)

§ 10.1-2114. State agency consistency. — All agencies of the Common-
wealth shall exercise their authorities under the Constitution and laws of
Virginia in a manner consistent with the provisions of comprehensive plans,
zoning ordinances and subdivision ordinances that comply with §§ 10.1-2109
and 10.1-2110. (1988, cc. 608, 891.)

Law Review. — For article, "Legal Issues
Affecting Local Governments in Implementing
the Chesapeake Bay Preservation Act," see 24
U. Rich. L. Rev. 1 (1989).

§ 10.1-2115. Vested rights protected. — The provisions of this chapter
shall not affect vested rights of any landowner under existing law. (1988, cc.
608, 891.)

ARTICLE 2.

Chesapeake Bay Advisory Committee.

§ 10.1-2116: Repealed by Acts 2004, c. 1000.

Cross references. — For current provisions
as to the Chesapeake Bay Restoration Fund
Advisory Committee, see § 30-256.

CHAPTER 21.1.

VIRGINIA WATER QUALITY IMPROVEMENT ACT OF 1997.

469

ARTICLE 1.

General Provisions.

§ 10.1-2117. Definitions. — As used in this chapter, unless the context requires a different meaning:

"Biological nutrient removal technology" means technology that will typically achieve at least an 8 mg/L total nitrogen concentration or at least a 1 mg/L total phosphorus concentration in effluent discharges.

"Chesapeake Bay Agreement" means the Chesapeake Bay Agreement of 2000 and any amendments thereto.

"Eligible nonsignificant discharger" means any publicly owned treatment works that is not a significant discharger but due to expansion or new construction is subject to a technology-based standard under § 62.1-44.19:15 or 62.1-44.19:16.

"Fund" means the Virginia Water Quality Improvement Fund established by Article 4 (§ 10.1-2128 et seq.) of this chapter.

"Individual" means any corporation, foundation, association or partnership or one or more natural persons.

"Institutions of higher education" means any educational institution meeting the requirements of § 60.2-220.

"Local government" means any county, city, town, municipal corporation, authority, district, commission or political subdivision of the Commonwealth.

"Nonpoint source pollution" means pollution of state waters washed from the land surface in a diffuse manner and not resulting from a discernible, defined or discrete conveyance.

"Nutrient removal technology" means state-of-the-art nutrient removal technology, biological nutrient removal technology, or other nutrient removal technology.

"Point source pollution" means pollution of state waters resulting from any discernible, defined or discrete conveyances.

"Publicly owned treatment works" means a publicly owned sewage collection system consisting of pipelines or conduits, pumping stations and force mains, and all other construction, devices, and appliances appurtenant thereto, or any equipment, plant, treatment works, structure, machinery, apparatus, interest in land, or any combination of these, not including an onsite sewage disposal

470

system, that is used, operated, acquired, or constructed for the storage, collection, treatment, neutralization, stabilization, reduction, recycling, reclamation, separation, or disposal of wastewater, or for the final disposal of residues resulting from the treatment of sewage, including but not limited to: treatment or disposal plants; outfall sewers, interceptor sewers, and collector sewers; pumping and ventilating stations, facilities, and works; and other real or personal property and appurtenances incident to their development, use, or operation.

"Reasonable sewer costs" means the amount expended per household for sewer service in relation to the median household income of the service area as determined by guidelines developed and approved by the State Water Control Board for use with the Virginia Water Facilities Revolving Fund established pursuant to Chapter 22 (§ 62.1-224 et seq.) of Title 62.1.

"Significant discharger" means (i) a publicly owned treatment works discharging to the Chesapeake Bay watershed with a design capacity of 0.5 million gallons per day or greater, (ii) a publicly owned treatment works discharging to the Chesapeake Bay watershed east of the fall line with a design capacity of 0.1 million gallons per day or greater, (iii) a planned or newly expanding publicly owned treatment works discharging to the Chesapeake Bay watershed, which is expected to be in operation by 2010 with a permitted design of 0.5 million gallons per day or greater, or (iv) a planned or newly expanding publicly owned treatment works discharging to the Chesapeake Bay watershed east of the fall line with a design capacity of 0.1 million gallons per day or greater, which is expected to be in operation by 2010.

"State-of-the-art nutrient removal technology" means technology that will achieve at least a 3 mg/L total nitrogen concentration or at least a 0.3 mg/L total phosphorus concentration in effluent discharges.

"State waters" means all waters on the surface or under the ground, wholly or partially within or bordering the Commonwealth or within its jurisdictions.

"Tributary strategy plans" means plans that are developed by the Secretary of Natural Resources pursuant to the provisions of the Chesapeake Bay Agreement for the tidal tributaries of the Chesapeake Bay and the tidal creeks and embayments of the western side of the Eastern Shore of Virginia. This term shall include any amendments to the tributary strategy plans initially developed by the Secretary of Natural Resources pursuant to the Chesapeake Bay Agreement.

"Water Quality Improvement Grants" means grants available from the Fund for projects of local governments, institutions of higher education, and individuals (i) to achieve nutrient reduction goals in tributary strategy plans or applicable regulatory requirements or (ii) to achieve other water quality restoration, protection or enhancement benefits. (1997, cc. 21, 625, 626; 1999, c. 257; 2005, cc. 704, 707, 709; 2006, c. 236.)

Editor's note. — Acts 2005, cc. 704, 707, and 709, cl. 2, provides: "That the Chairmen of the House Committee on Appropriations, the House Committee on Agriculture, Chesapeake and Natural Resources, the House Committee on Finance, the Senate Committee on Agriculture, Conservation and Natural Resources and the Senate Committee on Finance, in consultation with the Secretary of Natural Resources and the Secretary of Agriculture and Forestry shall by November 30, 2005, develop recommendations for a permanent source of funding that will sufficiently and predictably generate the necessary revenue to fund the tributary strategy plans to remove the Chesapeake Bay

and its tidal tributaries from the Clean Water Act section 303(d) list of impaired waters and to remove those waters located outside the Chesapeake Bay watershed from the impaired waters list."

The 2005 amendments. — The 2005 amendments by cc. 704, 707, and 709 are identical, and inserted the definitions for "Chesapeake Bay Agreement," "Publicly owned treatment works," "Significant discharger," "State-of-the-art nutrient removal technology," and "Tributary strategy plans"; and in the definition of "Water Quality Improvement Grants," inserted "strategy" preceding "plans," and deleted "developed pursuant to §§ 2.2-218 through 2.2-220" at the end of clause (i).

The 2006 amendments. — The 2006 amendment by c. 236 inserted the definitions of "Biological nutrient removal technology," "Eligible nonsignificant discharger" and "Nutrient removal technology" and inserted "or applicable regulatory requirements" in the definition of "Water Quality Improvement Grants."

Law Review. — For an article reviewing key environmental developments at the federal and state levels during the period from June 1996 to June 1998, see 32 U. Rich. L. Rev. 1217 (1998).

Michie's Jurisprudence. — For related discussion, see 20 M.J. Waters and Watercourses, §§ 3, 19.

§ 10.1-2118. Cooperative program established. — It shall be the policy of the Commonwealth, and it is the purpose of this chapter, to restore and improve the quality of state waters and to protect them from impairment and destruction for the benefit of current and future citizens of the Commonwealth. The General Assembly further determines and finds that the quality of state waters is subject to potential pollution and degradation, including excess nutrients, from both point and nonpoint source pollution and that the purposes of the State Water Control Law (§ 62.1-44.2 et seq.) and all other laws related to the restoration, protection and improvement of the quality of state waters will be enhanced by the implementation of the provisions of this chapter. The General Assembly further determines and finds that the restoration, protection and improvement of the quality of state waters is a shared responsibility among state and local governments and individuals and to that end this chapter establishes cooperative programs related to nutrient reduction and other point and nonpoint sources of pollution. (1997, cc. 21, 625, 626.)

§ 10.1-2119. Effect of chapter on other governmental authority. — The authorities and powers granted by the provisions of this chapter are supplemental to other state and local governmental authority and do not limit in any way other water quality restoration, protection and enhancement authority of any agency or local government of the Commonwealth. All counties, cities and towns are authorized to exercise their police and zoning powers to protect the quality of state waters from nonpoint source pollution as provided in this Code. (1997, cc. 21, 625, 626.)

ARTICLE 2.

Cooperative Point Source Pollution Program.

§ 10.1-2120. Definitions. — As used in this article, unless the context requires a different meaning:

"Department" means the Department of Environmental Quality.

"Director" means the Director of the Department of Environmental Quality. (1997, cc. 21, 625, 626.)

§ 10.1-2121. Cooperative point source pollution program. — In order to restore, protect and improve the quality of the bays, lakes, rivers, streams, creeks, and other state waters, and to achieve the pollution reduction goals, including those related to nutrient reduction, established in commitments made by the Commonwealth to water quality restoration, protection and improvement, including but not limited to the Chesapeake Bay Agreement, as amended, the Department shall assist local governments and individuals in the control of point source pollution, including nutrient reductions, through technical and financial assistance made available through grants provided from the Fund. In providing this technical and financial assistance the Department shall give initial priority to local government capital construction projects designed to achieve nutrient reduction goals, as provided in § 10.1-

2131, consistent with those established in the Chesapeake Bay Agreement, as amended, and thereafter to efforts consistent with other commitments made by the Commonwealth. In pursuing implementation of this cooperative program, it is the intent of the Commonwealth to annually seek and provide funding necessary to meet its commitments under any fully executed grant agreement pursuant to the provisions of §§ 10.1-2130 and 10.1-2131. (1997, cc. 21, 625, 626.)

§ 10.1-2122. Additional powers and duties of the Director. — In furtherance of the purposes of this article, the Director is authorized to utilize the Fund for the purpose of providing Water Quality Improvement Grants as prescribed in Article 4 (§ 10.1-2128 et seq.) of this chapter. (1997, cc. 21, 625, 626.)

ARTICLE 3.

Cooperative Nonpoint Source Pollution Program.

§ 10.1-2123. Definitions. — As used in this article, unless the context requires a different meaning:
"Board" means the Board of Conservation and Recreation.
"Department" means the Department of Conservation and Recreation.
"Director" means the Director of the Department of Conservation and Recreation. (1997, cc. 21, 625, 626.)

§ 10.1-2124. Cooperative nonpoint source pollution program. — A. The state has the responsibility under Article XI of the Constitution of Virginia to protect the bays, lakes, rivers, streams, creeks, and other state waters of the Commonwealth from pollution and impairment. Commercial and residential development of land as well as agricultural and other land uses may cause the impairment of state waters through nonpoint source pollution. In the exercise of their authority to control land use and development, it is the responsibility of counties, cities, and towns to consider the protection of all bays, lakes, rivers, streams, creeks, and other state waters from nonpoint source pollution. The exercise of environmental stewardship by individuals is necessary to protect state waters from nonpoint source pollution. To promote achievement of the directives of Article XI of the Constitution of Virginia and to implement the cooperative programs established by this chapter, the state shall assist local governments, soil and water conservation districts and individuals in restoring, protecting and improving water quality through grants provided from the Fund.
B. In order to restore, protect, and improve the quality of all bays, lakes, rivers, streams, creeks, and other state waters, and to achieve the pollution reduction goals, including nutrient reduction goals, established in commitments made by the Commonwealth to water quality restoration, protection, and enhancement, including but not limited to the Chesapeake Bay Agreement, as amended, the Department shall assist local governments, soil and water conservation districts, and individuals in the control of nonpoint source pollution, including nutrient reduction, through technical and financial assistance made available through grants provided from the Fund as provided in § 10.1-2132.
C. In order to engage stakeholders within each of the Commonwealth's 14 major river basins to develop comprehensive strategic plans to mitigate and prevent local nonpoint source water pollution, the Department may establish the Watershed Coordination Program, hereinafter referred to as "the Program." The Program shall continue the work of watershed roundtables,

support citizen stewardship activities, and be coordinated with the agencies of the Secretariat of Natural Resources, the Department of Forestry, and the Department of Agriculture and Consumer Services. The Program shall be funded with private funds; however, the Department may assist with the initial costs associated with the development of the Program to the extent that funding is available. The Department may assist in fund-raising efforts to supplement the Fund and provide assistance to the fund-raising efforts of the watershed roundtables. The Program shall strive to provide appropriate incentives for achievements to include public recognition and awards. (1997, cc. 21, 625, 626; 2004, c. 413.)

§ 10.1-2125. Powers and duties of the Board. — The Board, in meeting its responsibilities under the cooperative program established by this article, after consultation with other appropriate agencies, is authorized and has the duty to:

1. Encourage and promote nonpoint source pollution control and prevention, including nutrient control and prevention, for the: (i) protection of public drinking water supplies; (ii) promotion of water resource conservation; (iii) protection of existing high quality state waters and restoration of all other state waters to a condition or quality that will permit all reasonable beneficial uses and will support the propagation and growth of all aquatic life, including finfish and shellfish, which might reasonably be expected to inhabit them; (iv) protection of all state waters from nonpoint source pollution; (v) prevention of any increase in nonpoint source pollution; (vi) reduction of existing nonpoint source pollution; (vii) attainment and maintenance of water quality standards established under subdivisions (3a) and (3b) of § 62.1-44.15; and (viii) attainment of commitments made by the Commonwealth to water quality restoration, protection and enhancement including the goals of the Chesapeake Bay Agreement, as amended, all in order to provide for the health, safety and welfare of the present and future citizens of the Commonwealth.

2. Provide technical assistance and advice to local governments and individuals concerning aspects of water quality restoration, protection and improvement relevant to nonpoint source pollution.

3. Apply for, and accept, federal funds and funds from any other source, public or private, that may become available and to transmit such funds to the Fund for the purpose of providing Water Quality Improvement Grants as prescribed in Article 4 (§ 10.1-2128 et seq.) of this chapter.

4. Enter into contracts necessary and convenient to carry out the provisions of this article.

5. Seek the assistance of other state agencies and entities including but not limited to the Department of Forestry and the Virginia Soil and Water Conservation Board as appropriate in carrying out its responsibilities under this chapter. (1997, cc. 21, 625, 626; 2005, c. 41.)

Editor's note. — Acts 2005, c. 41, cl. 4, provides: "That references to the Chesapeake Bay Local Assistance Department in regulation, local ordinance, guidance, or otherwise shall mean the Department of Conservation and Recreation, and similarly, references to the Executive Director of the Chesapeake Bay Local Assistance Department shall mean the Director of the Department of Conservation and Recreation."

Acts 2005, c. 41, cl. 5, provides: "That the Chesapeake Bay Local Assistance Board shall have the authority to amend, modify, or delete provisions in the Chesapeake Bay Preservation Area Designation and Management Regulations (9-VAC 10-20 et seq.) in order to implement Chapter 372 of the Acts of Assembly of 2004 and the provisions of this act. Those amendments to the regulations necessitated by these acts shall be exempt from Article 2 (§ 2.2-4006 et seq.) of the Administrative Process Act."

The 2005 amendments. — The 2005 amendment by c. 41 deleted "the Chesapeake Bay Local Assistance Department" preceding "the Department of Forestry" in subdivision 5.

§ 10.1-2126. Additional powers and duties of Director. — A. In furtherance of the purposes of this article, the Director is authorized to utilize the Fund for the purpose of providing Water Quality Improvement Grants as prescribed in Article 4 (§ 10.1-2128 et seq.) of this chapter.

B. The Director shall be vested with the authority of the Board when the Board is not in session, subject to such limitations as may be prescribed by the Board. In no event shall the Director have the authority to promulgate any final regulation pursuant to the provisions of this chapter. (1997, cc. 21, 625, 626.)

§ 10.1-2127. Nonpoint source pollution water quality assessment. — A. The Department, in conjunction with other state agencies, shall evaluate and report on the impacts of nonpoint source pollution on water quality and water quality improvement to the Governor and the General Assembly. This evaluation shall be incorporated into the § 305(b) water quality report of the Clean Water Act developed pursuant to § 62.1-44.19:5. The evaluation shall at a minimum include considerations of water quality standards, fishing bans, shellfish contamination, aquatic life monitoring, sediment sampling, fish tissue sampling and human health standards. The report shall be produced in accordance with the schedule required by federal law, but shall incorporate at least the preceding five years of data. Data older than five years shall be incorporated when scientifically appropriate for trend analysis. The report shall, at a minimum, include an assessment of the geographic regions where water quality is demonstrated to be impaired or degraded as the result of nonpoint source pollution and an evaluation of the basis or cause for such impairment or degradation.

B. The Department and a county, city or town or any combination of counties, cities and towns comprising all or part of any geographic region identified pursuant to subsection A as contributing to the impairment or degradation of state waters may develop a cooperative program to address identified nonpoint source pollution impairment or degradation, including excess nutrients. The program may include, in addition to other elements, a delineation of state and local government responsibilities and duties and may provide for the implementation of initiatives to address the causes of nonpoint source pollution, including those related to excess nutrients. These initiatives may include the modification, if necessary, of local government land use control ordinances. All state agencies shall cooperate and provide assistance in developing and implementing such programs.

C. The Department and a county, city or town or any combination of counties, cities and towns comprising all or part of any geographic region not identified pursuant to subsection A as contributing to the impairment or degradation of state waters may develop a cooperative program to prevent nonpoint source pollution impairment or degradation. The program may include, in addition to other elements, a delineation of state and local government responsibilities and duties and may provide for the implementation of initiatives to address the nonpoint source pollution causes, including the modification, if necessary, of local government land use control ordinances. All state agencies shall cooperate and provide assistance in developing and implementing such programs.

D. The Department shall, on or before January 1 of each year, report to the Governor and the General Assembly on whether cooperative nonpoint source pollution programs, including nutrient reduction programs, developed pursuant to this section are being effectively implemented to meet the objectives of this article. (1997, cc. 21, 625, 626; 2003, c. 741.)

Editor's note. — For § 305(b) of the Clean Water Act, referred to in subsection A above, see 33 U.S.C.S. § 1315(b).

ARTICLE 4.

Virginia Water Quality Improvement Fund.

§ 10.1-2128. Virginia Water Quality Improvement Fund established; purposes. — A. There is hereby established in the state treasury a special permanent, nonreverting fund, to be known as the "Virginia Water Quality Improvement Fund." The Fund shall be established on the books of the Comptroller. The Fund shall consist of sums appropriated to it by the General Assembly which shall include, unless otherwise provided in the general appropriation act, 10 percent of the annual general fund revenue collections that are in excess of the official estimates in the general appropriation act and 10 percent of any unreserved general fund balance at the close of each fiscal year whose reappropriation is not required in the general appropriation act. The Fund shall also consist of such other sums as may be made available to it from any other source, public or private, and shall include any penalties or damages collected under this article, federal grants solicited and received for the specific purposes of the Fund, and all interest and income from investment of the Fund. Any sums remaining in the Fund, including interest thereon, at the end of each fiscal year shall not revert to the general fund but shall remain in the Fund. All moneys designated for the Fund shall be paid into the state treasury and credited to the Fund. Moneys in the Fund shall be used solely for Water Quality Improvement Grants. Expenditures and disbursements from the Fund shall be made by the State Treasurer on warrants issued by the Comptroller upon the written request of the Director of the Department of Environmental Quality or the Director of the Department of Conservation and Recreation as provided in this chapter.

B. The purpose of the Fund is to provide Water Quality Improvement Grants to local governments, soil and water conservation districts, institutions of higher education and individuals for point and nonpoint source pollution prevention, reduction and control programs and efforts undertaken in accordance with the provisions of this chapter. The Fund shall not be used for agency operating expenses or for purposes of replacing or otherwise reducing any general, nongeneral, or special funds allocated or appropriated to any state agency; however, nothing in this section shall be construed to prevent the award of a Water Quality Improvement Grant to a local government in connection with point or nonpoint pollution prevention, reduction and control programs or efforts undertaken on land owned by the Commonwealth and leased to the local government. In keeping with the purpose for which the Fund is created, it shall be the policy of the General Assembly to provide annually its share of financial support to qualifying applicants for grants in order to fulfill the Commonwealth's responsibilities under Article XI of the Constitution of Virginia.

C. For the fiscal year beginning July 1, 2005, $50 million shall be appropriated from the general fund and deposited into the Fund. This appropriation and any amounts appropriated to the Fund in subsequent years in addition to any amounts deposited to the Fund pursuant to the provisions of subsection A of § 10.1-2128 shall be used solely to finance the costs of design and installation of nutrient removal technology at publicly owned treatment works designated as significant dischargers or eligible nonsignificant dischargers for compliance with the effluent limitations for total nitrogen and total phosphorus as required by the tributary strategy plans or applicable regulatory requirements.

At such time as grant agreements specified in § 10.1-2130 have been signed by every significant discharger and eligible nonsignificant discharger and available funds are sufficient to implement the provisions of such grant agreements, the House Committee on Agriculture, Chesapeake and Natural Resources, the House Committee on Appropriations, the Senate Committee on Agriculture, Conservation and Natural Resources, and the Senate Committee on Finance shall review the financial assistance provided under this section and determine (i) whether such deposits should continue to be made, (ii) the size of the deposit to be made, (iii) the programs and activities that should be financed by such deposits in the future, and (iv) whether the provisions of this section should be extended. (1997, cc. 21, 625, 626; 1999, c. 257; 2001, c. 264; 2005, cc. 704, 707, 709; 2006, c. 236.)

Editor's note. — Acts 2005, cc. 704, 707, and 709, cl. 2, provides: "That the Chairmen of the House Committee on Appropriations, the House Committee on Agriculture, Chesapeake and Natural Resources, the House Committee on Finance, the Senate Committee on Agriculture, Conservation and Natural Resources and the Senate Committee on Finance, in consultation with the Secretary of Natural Resources and the Secretary of Agriculture and Forestry shall by November 30, 2005, develop recommendations for a permanent source of funding that will sufficiently and predictably generate the necessary revenue to fund the tributary strategy plans to remove the Chesapeake Bay and its tidal tributaries from the Clean Water Act section 303(d) list of impaired waters and to remove those waters located outside the Chesapeake Bay watershed from the impaired waters list."

The 2005 amendments. — The 2005 amendments by cc. 704, 707 and 709 are identical, and added the last sentence in subsection B, added subsection C, and made minor stylistic changes.

The 2006 amendments. — The 2006 amendment by c. 236, in subsection C, in the second sentence of the first paragraph, deleted "biological nutrient removal facilities or other" following "installation of" and inserted "or eligible nonsignificant dischargers," and in the second paragraph, inserted "and eligible nonsignificant discharger."

§ 10.1-2129. Agency coordination; conditions of grants. — A. If, in any fiscal year beginning on or after July 1, 2005, there are appropriations to the Fund in addition to those made pursuant to subsection A of § 10.1-2128, the Secretary of Natural Resources shall distribute those moneys in the Fund provided from the 10 percent of the annual general fund revenue collections that are in excess of the official estimates in the general appropriation act, and the 10 percent of any unreserved general fund balance at the close of each fiscal year whose reappropriation is not required in the general appropriation act, as follows:

1. Seventy percent of the moneys shall be distributed to the Department of Conservation and Recreation and shall be administered by it for the sole purpose of implementing projects or best management practices that reduce nitrogen and phosphorus nonpoint source pollution, with a priority given to agricultural best management practices. In no single year shall more than 60 percent of the moneys be used for projects or practices exclusively within the Chesapeake Bay watershed; and

2. Thirty percent of the moneys shall be distributed to the Department of Environmental Quality, which shall use such moneys for making grants for the sole purpose of designing and installing nutrient removal technologies for publicly owned treatment works designated as significant dischargers or eligible nonsignificant dischargers. The moneys shall also be available for grants when the design and installation of nutrient removal technology utilizes the Public-Private Education Facilities and Infrastructure Act (§ 56-575.1 et seq.).

3. Except as otherwise provided in the Appropriation Act, in any fiscal year when moneys are not appropriated to the Fund in addition to those specified in subsection A of § 10.1-2128, or when moneys appropriated to the Fund in

addition to those specified in subsection A of § 10.1-2128 are less than 40 percent of those specified in subsection A of § 10.1-2128, the Secretary of Natural Resources, in consultation with the Secretary of Agriculture and Forestry, the State Forester, the Commissioner of Agriculture and Consumer Services, and the Directors of the Departments of Environmental Quality and Conservation and Recreation, and with the advice and guidance of the Board of Conservation and Recreation, the Virginia Soil and Water Conservation Board, the State Water Control Board, and the Chesapeake Bay Local Assistance Board, and following a public comment period of at least 30 days and a public hearing, shall allocate those moneys deposited in the Fund between point and nonpoint sources, both of which shall receive moneys in each such year.

B. 1. Except as may otherwise be specified in the general appropriation act, the Secretary of Natural Resources, in consultation with the Secretary of Agriculture and Forestry, the State Forester, the Commissioner of Agriculture and Consumer Services, and the Directors of the Departments of Environmental Quality and Conservation and Recreation, and with the advice and guidance of the Board of Conservation and Recreation, the Virginia Soil and Water Conservation Board, the State Water Control Board, and the Chesapeake Bay Local Assistance Board, shall develop written guidelines that (i) specify eligibility requirements; (ii) govern the application for and the distribution and conditions of Water Quality Improvement Grants; and (iii) list criteria for prioritizing funding requests.

2. In developing the guidelines the Secretary shall evaluate and consider, in addition to such other factors as may be appropriate to most effectively restore, protect and improve the quality of state waters: (i) specific practices and programs proposed in any tributary strategy plan, and the associated effectiveness and cost per pound of nutrients removed; (ii) water quality impairment or degradation caused by different types of nutrients released in different locations from different sources; and (iii) environmental benchmarks and indicators for achieving improved water quality. The process for development of guidelines pursuant to this subsection shall, at a minimum, include (a) use of an advisory committee composed of interested parties; (b) a 60-day public comment period on draft guidelines; (c) written responses to all comments received; and (d) notice of the availability of draft guidelines and final guidelines to all who request such notice.

3. In addition to those the Secretary deems advisable to most effectively restore, protect and improve the quality of state waters, the criteria for prioritizing funding requests shall include: (i) the pounds of total nitrogen and the pounds of total phosphorus reduced by the project; (ii) whether the location of the water quality restoration, protection or improvement project or program is within a watershed or subwatershed with documented water nutrient loading problems or adopted nutrient reduction goals; (iii) documented water quality impairment; and (iv) the availability of other funding mechanisms. Notwithstanding the provisions of subsection E of § 10.1-2131, the Director of the Department of Environmental Quality may approve a local government point source grant application request for any single project that exceeds the authorized grant amount outlined in subsection E of § 10.1-2131. Whenever a local government applies for a grant that exceeds the authorized grant amount outlined in this chapter or when there is no stated limitation on the amount of the grant for which an application is made, the Directors and the Secretary shall consider the comparative revenue capacity, revenue efforts and fiscal stress as reported by the Commission on Local Government. The development or implementation of cooperative programs developed pursuant to subsection B of § 10.1-2127 shall be given a high priority in the distribution of Virginia Water Quality Improvement Grants from the moneys allocated to nonpoint source pollution. (1997, cc. 21, 625, 626; 1999, c. 509; 2005, cc. 41, 704, 707, 709; 2006, c. 236.)

Editor's note. — Acts 2005, c. 41, cl. 4, provides: "That references to the Chesapeake Bay Local Assistance Department in regulation, local ordinance, guidance, or otherwise shall mean the Department of Conservation and Recreation, and similarly, references to the Executive Director of the Chesapeake Bay Local Assistance Department shall mean the Director of the Department of Conservation and Recreation."

Acts 2005, c. 41, cl. 5, provides: "That the Chesapeake Bay Local Assistance Board shall have the authority to amend, modify, or delete provisions in the Chesapeake Bay Preservation Area Designation and Management Regulations (9-VAC 10-20 et seq.) in order to implement Chapter 372 of the Acts of Assembly of 2004 and the provisions of this act. Those amendments to the regulations necessitated by these acts shall be exempt from Article 2 (§ 2.2-4006 et seq.) of the Administrative Process Act."

Acts 2005, cc. 704, 707, and 709, cl. 2, are identical, and provide: "That the Chairmen of the House Committee on Appropriations, the House Committee on Agriculture, Chesapeake and Natural Resources, the House Committee on Finance, the Senate Committee on Agriculture, Conservation and Natural Resources and the Senate Committee on Finance, in consultation with the Secretary of Natural Resources and the Secretary of Agriculture and Forestry shall by November 30, 2005, develop recommendations for a permanent source of funding that will sufficiently and predictably generate the necessary revenue to fund the tributary strategy plans to remove the Chesapeake Bay and its tidal tributaries from the Clean Water Act section 303(d) list of impaired waters and to remove those waters located outside the Chesapeake Bay watershed from the impaired waters list."

The 2005 amendments. — The 2005 amendment by c. 41 deleted "Chesapeake Bay Local Assistance Department" in subsections A and B.

The 2005 amendments by cc. 704, 707, and 709, are identical, and rewrote subsection A; redesignated former subsection B as subdivisions B 1 through B 3; in subdivision B 1, inserted "Secretary of Agriculture and Forestry, the" preceding "State Forester," "the Commissioner of Agriculture and Consumer Services" preceding "and the Directors," and deleted "and of the Chesapeake Bay Local Assistance Department" preceding "and with the advice and guidance"; in subdivision B 2, inserted "strategy" preceding "plan," deleted "required by §§ 2.2-218 through 2.2-220" preceding "and the associated," substituted "(a), (b), (c), and (d)" for the second set of clauses "(i), (ii), (iii), and (iv)"; rewrote subdivision B 3; and made minor stylistic changes.

The 2006 amendments. — The 2006 amendment by c. 236, in subdivision A 2, deleted "state of the art" preceding "nutrient removal" in the first and second sentences and inserted "or eligible nonsignificant dischargers" at the end of the first sentence.

§ 10.1-2130. General provisions related to grants from the Fund. —

All Water Quality Improvement Grants shall be governed by a legally binding and enforceable grant agreement between the recipient and the granting agency. In addition to provisions providing for payment of the total amount of the grant, the agreement shall, at a minimum, also contain provisions that govern design and installation and require proper long-term operation, monitoring and maintenance of funded projects, including design and performance criteria, as well as contractual or stipulated penalties in an amount sufficient to ensure compliance with the agreement, which may include repayment with interest, for any breach of the agreement, including failure to properly operate, monitor or maintain. Grant agreements shall be made available for public review and comment for a period of no less than thirty days but no more than sixty days prior to execution. The granting agency shall cause notice of a proposed grant agreement to be given to all applicants for Water Quality Improvement Grants whose applications are then pending and to any person requesting such notice. (1997, cc. 21, 625, 626; 1999, c. 509.)

§ 10.1-2131. Point source pollution funding; conditions for approval. —

A. The Department of Environmental Quality shall be the lead state agency for determining the appropriateness of any grant related to point source pollution to be made from the Fund to restore, protect or improve state water quality.

B. The Director of the Department of Environmental Quality shall, subject to available funds and in coordination with the Director of the Department of Conservation and Recreation, direct the State Treasurer to make Water

Quality Improvement Grants in accordance with the guidelines established pursuant to § 10.1-2129. The Director of the Department of Environmental Quality shall enter into grant agreements with all facilities designated as significant dischargers or eligible nonsignificant dischargers that apply for grants; however, all such grant agreements shall contain provisions that payments thereunder are subject to the availability of funds.

C. Notwithstanding the priority provisions of § 10.1-2129, the Director of the Department of Environmental Quality shall not authorize the distribution of grants from the Fund for purposes other than financing the cost of design and installation of nutrient removal technology at publicly owned treatment works until such time as all tributary strategy plans are developed and implemented unless he finds that there exists in the Fund sufficient funds for substantial and continuing progress in implementation of the tributary strategy plans. In addition to the provisions of § 10.1-2130, all grant agreements related to nutrients shall include: (i) numerical technology-based effluent concentration limitations on nutrient discharges to state waters based upon the technology installed by the facility; (ii) enforceable provisions related to the maintenance of the numerical concentrations that will allow for exceedences of 0.8 mg/L for total nitrogen or no more than 10 percent, whichever is greater, for exceedences of 0.1 mg/L for total phosphorus or no more than 10%, and for exceedences caused by extraordinary conditions; and (iii) recognition of the authority of the Commonwealth to make the Virginia Water Facilities Revolving Fund (§ 62.1-224 et seq.) available to local governments to fund their share of the cost of designing and installing nutrient removal technology based on financial need and subject to availability of revolving loan funds, priority ranking and revolving loan distribution criteria. If, pursuant to § 10.1-1187.6, the State Water Control Board approves an alternative compliance method to technology-based concentration limitations in Virginia Pollutant Discharge Elimination System permits, the concentration limitations of the grant agreement shall be suspended subject to the terms of such approval. The cost of the design and installation of nutrient removal technology at publicly owned treatment works meeting the nutrient reduction goal in an applicable tributary strategy plan or an applicable regulatory requirement and incurred prior to the execution of a grant agreement is eligible for reimbursement from the Fund provided the grant is made pursuant to an executed agreement consistent with the provisions of this chapter.

Subsequent to the implementation of the tributary strategy plans, the Director may authorize disbursements from the Fund for any water quality restoration, protection and improvements related to point source pollution that are clearly demonstrated as likely to achieve measurable and specific water quality improvements, including, but not limited to, cost effective technologies to reduce nutrient loads. Notwithstanding the previous provisions of this subsection, the Director may, at any time, authorize grants, including grants to institutions of higher education, for technical assistance related to nutrient reduction.

D. The grant percentage provided for financing the costs of the design and installation of nutrient removal technology at publicly owned treatment works shall be based upon the financial need of the community as determined by comparing the annual sewer charges expended within the service area to the reasonable sewer cost established for the community.

E. Grants shall be awarded in the following manner:

1. In communities for which the ratio of annual sewer charges to reasonable sewer cost is less than 0.30, the Director of the Department of Environmental Quality shall authorize grants in the amount of 35 percent of the costs of the design and installation of nutrient removal technology;

2. In communities for which the ratio of annual sewer charges to reasonable sewer cost is equal to or greater than 0.30 and less than 0.50, the Director shall

authorize grants in the amount of 45 percent of the costs of the design and installation of nutrient removal technology;

3. In communities for which the ratio of annual sewer charges to reasonable sewer cost is equal to or greater than 0.50 and less than 0.80, the Director shall authorize grants in the amount of 60 percent of the costs of design and installation of nutrient removal technology; and

4. In communities for which the ratio of annual sewer charges to reasonable sewer cost is equal to or greater than 0.80, the Director shall authorize grants in the amount of 75 percent of the costs of the design and installation of nutrient removal technology. (1997, cc. 21, 625, 626; 1999, cc. 257, 509; 2005, cc. 704, 707, 709; 2006, c. 236.)

Editor's note. — Acts 2005, cc. 704, 707, and 709, cl. 2 provide: "That the Chairmen of the House Committee on Appropriations, the House Committee on Agriculture, Chesapeake and Natural Resources, the House Committee on Finance, the Senate Committee on Agriculture, Conservation and Natural Resources and the Senate Committee on Finance, in consultation with the Secretary of Natural Resources and the Secretary of Agriculture and Forestry shall by November 30, 2005, develop recommendations for a permanent source of funding that will sufficiently and predictably generate the necessary revenue to fund the tributary strategy plans to remove the Chesapeake Bay and its tidal tributaries from the Clean Water Act section 303(d) list of impaired waters and to remove those waters located outside the Chesapeake Bay watershed from the impaired waters list."

The 2005 amendments. — The 2005 amendments by cc. 704, 707, and 709 are identical, and rewrote subsection B; in subsection C, deleted "at least fifty percent of" preceding "the cost of design," "required by §§ 2.2-218

through 2.2-220" preceding "are developed and implemented," and "At least fifty percent of" at the beginning of the third sentence; substituted "tributary strategy plan" for "tributary plans" throughout; added subsections D and E; and made minor stylistic changes.

The 2006 amendments. — The 2006 amendment by c. 236 inserted "or eligible non-significant dischargers" in the second sentence of subsection B; deleted "biological nutrient removal facilities or other" preceding "nutrient removal technology" throughout subsections C and E; in subsection C, in clause (i), substituted "technology-based effluent concentration limitations" for "concentrations" and "based upon the technology installed by the facility" for "designed to achieve the nutrient reduction goals of the applicable tributary strategy plan," in clause (ii), inserted "0.8 mg/L for total nitrogen or" and "whichever is greater, for exceedences of 0.1 mg/L for total phosphorus or no more than 10%," inserted the third sentence, and in fourth sentence, inserted "or an applicable regulatory requirement"; and deleted "biological nutrient removal facilities and other" in subsection D.

§ 10.1-2132. Nonpoint source pollution funding; conditions for approval. — A. The Department of Conservation and Recreation shall be the lead state agency for determining the appropriateness of any grant related to nonpoint source pollution to be made from the Fund to restore, protect and improve the quality of state waters.

B. The Director of the Department of Conservation and Recreation shall, subject to available funds and in coordination with the Director of the Department of Environmental Quality, direct the State Treasurer to make Water Quality Improvement Grants in accordance with the guidelines established pursuant to § 10.1-2129. The Director shall manage the allocation of grants from the Fund to ensure the full funding of executed grant agreements.

C. Grant funding may be made available to local governments, soil and water conservation districts, institutions of higher education and individuals who propose specific initiatives that are clearly demonstrated as likely to achieve reductions in nonpoint source pollution, including, but not limited to, excess nutrients and suspended solids, to improve the quality of state waters. Such projects may include, but are in no way limited to, the acquisition of conservation easements related to the protection of water quality and stream buffers; conservation planning and design assistance to develop nutrient management plans for agricultural operations; instructional education directly associated with the implementation or maintenance of a specific non-point source pollution reduction initiative; implementation of cost-effective nutrient reduction practices; and reimbursement to local governments for tax credits and other kinds of authorized local tax relief that provides incentives for water quality improvement. The Director shall give priority consideration to the distribution of grants from the Fund for the purposes of implementing tributary strategy plans, with a priority given to agricultural practices. In no single year shall more than 60 percent of the moneys be used for projects or practices exclusively within the Chesapeake Bay watershed. (1997, cc. 21, 625, 626; 1999, cc. 257, 509, 549; 2005, cc. 704, 707, 709.)

Editor's note. — Acts 2005, cc. 704, 707, and 709, cl. 2 provide: "That the Chairmen of the House Committee on Appropriations, the House Committee on Agriculture, Chesapeake and Natural Resources, the House Committee on Finance, the Senate Committee on Agriculture, Conservation and Natural Resources and the Senate Committee on Finance, in consultation with the Secretary of Natural Resources and the Secretary of Agriculture and Forestry shall by November 30, 2005, develop recommendations for a permanent source of funding that will sufficiently and predictably generate the necessary revenue to fund the tributary strategy plans to remove the Chesapeake Bay and its tidal tributaries from the Clean Water Act section 303(d) list of impaired waters and to remove those waters located outside the Chesapeake Bay watershed from the impaired waters list."

The 2005 amendments. — The 2005 amendments by cc. 704, 707, and 709 are identical, and rewrote the last sentence in subsection C.

§ **10.1-2133. Annual report by State Comptroller.** — The State Comptroller shall, by January 1 of each year, certify to the chairmen of the House Committee on Appropriations and the Senate Committee on Finance, the total amount of annual general fund revenue collections in excess of the official estimate in the general appropriation act, the total amount of the unreserved general fund balance whose reappropriation is not required in the general appropriation act at the close of the previous fiscal year and the total amount of funds that are to be directed to the credit of the Virginia Water Quality Improvement Fund under this article unless otherwise provided in the general appropriation act. (1997, cc. 21, 625, 626.)

§ **10.1-2134. Annual report by Directors of the Departments of Environmental Quality and Conservation and Recreation.** — The Directors of the Departments of Environmental Quality and Conservation and Recreation shall, by January 1 of each year, report to the Governor and the General Assembly the amounts and recipients of grants made from the Virginia Water Quality Improvement Fund and the specific and measurable pollution reduction achievements to state waters anticipated as a result of each grant award, together with the amounts of continued funding required for the coming fiscal year under all fully executed grant agreements. (1997, cc. 21, 625, 626.)

CHAPTER 21.2.

FOUNDATION FOR VIRGINIA'S NATURAL RESOURCES.

(For contingent expiration date — see note)

§ 10.1-2135. (For contingent expiration — see note) Foundation for Virginia's Natural Resources created.

— There is hereby created the Foundation for Virginia's Natural Resources, hereinafter referred to as the Foundation, a body politic to assist in developing and to encourage the nonregulatory conservation programs within the agencies of the Secretariats of Natural Resources and Agriculture and Forestry; to foster collaboration and partnerships among businesses, communities, and the Commonwealth's environmental enhancement programs; and to have such powers and duties as hereinafter provided. (2005, c. 351.)

Contingent expiration. — Acts 2005, c. 351, cl. 2, provides: "That the provisions of this act shall expire should no funds from any source be received in the Foundation for Virginia's Natural Resources Trust Fund by July 1, 2007."

§ 10.1-2136. (For contingent expiration — see note) Foundation for Virginia's Natural Resources Board of Trustees; membership; terms; expenses.

— A. The Foundation shall be governed and administered by a Board of Trustees. The Board shall consist of 13 citizen members from the Commonwealth to be appointed by the Governor, and the Secretaries of Natural Resources and Agriculture and Forestry, or their designees, to serve ex officio with voting privileges. Appointments shall be made so that each of the 13 major river basins, pursuant to § 10.1-2137, is represented insuring there is adequate representation from the agriculture and forestry industries. Citizen members shall be appointed for four-year terms, except that initial appointments shall be made for terms of one to four years in a manner whereby no more than four members shall have terms that expire in the same year. The ex officio members shall serve a term coincident with their terms of office. Appointments to fill vacancies, other than by expiration of a term, shall be made for the unexpired terms. Vacancies shall be filled in the same manner as the original appointments. All members may be reappointed. However, no citizen member shall serve more than two consecutive four-year terms. The remainder of any term to which a member is appointed to fill a vacancy shall not constitute a term in determining the member's eligibility for reappointment.

B. The Governor shall appoint a chairman of the Board of Trustees. The members shall elect a vice-chairman annually from among the members of the Board. A majority of the members of the Board serving at any one time shall constitute a quorum for the transaction of business. The Board shall meet at least four times a year and at the call of the chairman or whenever a majority of the members so request.

C. The Board shall seek assistance in developing grant criteria and advice on grant priorities and any other appropriate issues from a task force consisting of the following agency heads or their designees: the Director of the Department of Conservation and Recreation, the Commissioner of Agriculture and Consumer Services, the State Forester, the Director of the Department of Historic Resources, the Director of the Department of Game and Inland Fisheries, and the Director of the Department of Environmental Quality, and the Director of the Virginia Museum of Natural History. The Board may request any other agency head, agency employee, or environmental steward to serve on the task force.

D. The chairman of the Board shall submit to the Governor and the General Assembly a biennial executive summary of the interim activity and work of the Board no later than the first day of each even-numbered year regular session of the General Assembly. The executive summary shall be submitted as provided in the procedures of the Division of Legislative Automated Systems for the processing of legislative documents and reports and shall be posted on the General Assembly's website.

E. Members shall receive no compensation for their services, but shall be reimbursed out of the Fund for all reasonable and necessary expenses incurred in the performance of their duties as provided in §§ 2.2-2813 and 2.2-2825. (2005, c. 351.)

Contingent expiration. — See Editor's note under § 10.1-2135.

§ 10.1-2137. (For contingent expiration — see note) Major river basins. — For the purposes of this chapter, the 13 major river basins shall include the: Shenandoah, Potomac, Rappahannock, York, Blackwater/Chowan, Lower James, Piedmont James, Upper James, Roanoke, New, Upper Tennessee/Holston, Big Sandy Rivers, and the Eastern Shore. (2005, c. 351.)

Contingent expiration. — See Editor's note under § 10.1-2135.

§ 10.1-2138. (For contingent expiration — see note) Powers and duties of Foundation. — A. The Foundation for Virginia's Natural Resources shall promote environmental education, pollution prevention, and citizen monitoring by fostering and supporting collaborative efforts among businesses, citizens, communities, local governments, and state agencies.

B. The Foundation shall develop goals and guidelines for submittal and evaluation of grant applications for funds from the Foundation for Virginia's Natural Resources Trust Fund that are consistent with the goals set out in subsection A and that may include, but not be limited to, cooperative programs with, or project grants to, localities, state agencies, the federal government, soil and water conservation districts, or any not-for-profit agency, institution, organization, or entity, public or private, whose purpose is to provide environmental education, pollution prevention, or citizen monitoring.

C. The Foundation shall have the following general powers:

1. To sue and be sued in contractual matters in its own name;

2. To accept, hold, and administer gifts and bequests of money, securities, or other property from any source, absolutely or in trust, for the purposes for which the Foundation is created. Unless otherwise restricted by the terms of the gift or bequest, the Foundation is authorized to sell, exchange, or otherwise dispose of and to invest or reinvest in such investments as it may determine the moneys, securities, or other property given or bequeathed to it. The principal of such funds, together with the income therefrom and all other revenues, shall be placed in such depositories as the Foundation shall determine and shall constitute a special fund and be subject to expenditure by the Foundation without further appropriation. The Foundation shall not engage in any business except in the furtherance of its objectives;

3. To enter into contracts generally and to execute all instruments necessary or appropriate to carry out its purposes;

4. To appoint and prescribe the duties of such officers, agents, and employees as may be necessary to carry out its functions, and to fix and pay such compensation to them for their services as the Foundation may determine;

5. To conduct fundraising events and activities as deemed appropriate by the Board; and

6. To perform any lawful acts necessary or appropriate to carry out the purposes of the Foundation. (2005, c. 351.)

Contingent expiration. — See Editor's note under § 10.1-2135.

§ 10.1-2139. (For contingent expiration — see note) Foundation for Virginia's Natural Resources Trust Fund. — A. The Foundation for Virginia's Natural Resources shall establish, administer, manage, including the creation of reserves, and make expenditures and allocations from a special nonreverting fund in the state treasury to be known as the Virginia's Natural Resources Trust Fund, hereinafter referred to as "the Fund." The Foundation shall establish and administer the Fund solely for the purpose of carrying out the provisions of this chapter.

B. The Fund shall consist of gifts, endowments, or grants from the United States government, its agencies and instrumentalities, and funds from any other available sources, public or private.

C. Any moneys remaining in the Fund, including interest thereon, at the end of each fiscal year shall not revert to the general fund but shall remain in the Fund. Moneys in the Fund shall be used solely for the purposes of carrying out the provisions of this chapter, including encouraging and supporting education and outreach strategies for environmental education, pollution prevention, or citizen monitoring. Expenditures and disbursements from the Fund shall be made by the State Treasurer on warrants issued by the Comptroller upon written request signed by a duly authorized member of the Board of Trustees. (2005, c. 351.)

Contingent expiration. — See Editor's note under § 10.1-2135.

SUBTITLE III.

ACTIVITIES ADMINISTERED BY THE DEPARTMENT OF HISTORIC RESOURCES.

CHAPTER 22.

HISTORIC RESOURCES.

ARTICLE 1.

Department of Historic Resources.

§ **10.1-2200. Definitions.** — As used in this subtitle unless the context requires a different meaning:

"*Board*" means the Board of Historic Resources.

"*Department*" means the Department of Historic Resources.

"*Director*" means the Director of the Department of Historic Resources. (1989, c. 656.)

§ **10.1-2201. Department created; appointment of Director; Director to serve as State Historic Preservation Officer.** — There is hereby created a Department of Historic Resources. The Department shall be headed by a Director.

The Director shall be appointed by the Governor to serve at his pleasure for a term coincident with his own. The Director shall be subject to confirmation by the General Assembly if it is in session when the appointment is made, and if not then in session, at the next succeeding session.

The Director shall also serve as the State Historic Preservation Officer for the purposes of carrying out the National Historic Preservation Act of 1966 (P.L. 89-665), as amended. (1989, c. 656.)

Editor's note. — For the National Historic Preservation Act of 1966, P.L. 89-665, see 16 U.S.C.S. § 470 et seq.

§ **10.1-2202. Powers and duties of the Director.** — In addition to the powers and duties conferred upon the Director elsewhere and in order to encourage, stimulate, and support the identification, evaluation, protection, preservation, and rehabilitation of the Commonwealth's significant historic, architectural, archaeological, and cultural resources; in order to establish and maintain a permanent record of those resources; and in order to foster a greater appreciation of these resources among the citizens of the Commonwealth, the Director shall have the following powers and duties which may be delegated by the Director:

1. To employ such personnel as may be required to carry out those duties conferred by law;

2. To make and enter into all contracts and agreements necessary or incidental to the performance of his duties and the execution of his powers, including but not limited to contracts with private nonprofit organizations, the United States, other state agencies and political subdivisions of the Commonwealth;

3. To apply for and accept bequests, grants and gifts of real and personal property as well as endowments, funds, and grants from the United States government, its agencies and instrumentalities, and any other source. The Director shall have the authority to comply with such conditions and execute such agreements as may be necessary, convenient or desirable;

4. To perform acts necessary or convenient to carry out the duties conferred by law;

5. To promulgate regulations, in accordance with the Virginia Administrative Process Act (§ 2.2-4000 et seq.) and not inconsistent with the National Historic Preservation Act (P.L. 89-665) and its attendant regulations, as are necessary to carry out all responsibilities incumbent upon the State Historic Preservation Officer, including at a minimum criteria and procedures for submitting nominations of properties to the National Park Service for inclusion in the National Register of Historic Places or for designation as National Historic Landmarks;

6. To conduct a broad survey and to maintain an inventory of buildings, structures, districts, objects, and sites of historic, architectural, archaeological, or cultural interest which constitute the tangible remains of the Commonwealth's cultural, political, economic, military, or social history;

7. To publish lists of properties, including buildings, structures, districts, objects, and sites, designated as landmarks by the Board, to inspect designated properties from time to time, and periodically publish a complete register of designated properties setting forth appropriate information concerning those properties;

8. With the consent of the landowners, to provide appropriately designed markers for designated buildings, structures, districts, objects and sites;

9. To acquire and to administer designated landmarks, or easements or interests therein;

10. To aid and to encourage counties, cities and towns to establish historic zoning districts for designated landmarks and to adopt regulations for the preservation of historical, architectural, archaeological, or cultural values;

11. To provide technical advice and assistance to individuals, groups and governments conducting historic preservation programs and regularly to seek advice from the same on the effectiveness of Department programs;

12. To prepare and place, in cooperation with the Department of Transportation, highway historical markers approved by the Board of Historic Resources on or along the highway or street closest to the location which is intended to be identified by the marker;

13. To develop a procedure for the certification of historic districts and structures within the historic districts for federal income tax purposes;

14. To aid and to encourage counties, cities, and towns in the establishment of educational programs and materials for school use on the importance of Virginia's historic, architectural, archaeological, and cultural resources;

15. To conduct a program of archaeological research with the assistance of the State Archaeologist which includes excavation of significant sites, acquisition and maintenance of artifact collections for the purposes of study and display, and dissemination of data and information derived from the study of sites and collections;

16. To manage and administer the Historic Resources Fund as provided in § 10.1-2202.1; and

17. **(For contingent expiration — see Editor's note)** To manage and administer the Virginia Historic Preservation and Museum Assistance Grant Program and Fund as provided in §§ 10.1-2208.1 and 10.1-2208.2. (1989, c. 656; 1992, cc. 256, 801; 1995, c. 21; 2005, c. 85; 2006, c. 32.)

Editor's note. — For the National Historic Preservation Act of 1966, P.L. 89-665, see 16 U.S.C.S. § 470 et seq.

Acts 2005, c. 85, which added subdivision 17, in cl. 2 provides: "That should no funds from any source be received in the fund by July 1, 2007, the provisions of this act shall expire."

Acts 2006, c. 32, cl. 2, provides: "That the provisions of this act are declaratory of existing law."

The 2005 amendments. — The 2005 amendment by c. 85 added subdivision 17 and made related changes. For contingent expiration, see Editor's note.

The 2006 amendments. — The 2006 amendment by c. 32 inserted "including buildings, structures, districts, objects, and sites" following "list of properties" in subdivision 7; deleted "and sites" following "landmarks" in subdivision 9; and inserted "or cultural" and made a related change in subdivision 10.

OPINIONS OF THE ATTORNEY GENERAL

Matter delegated to Department of Historic Resources. — The Attorney General declined to render an opinion regarding whether a building located in a historic district and fitting the definition of a "ruin" may be removed, as the Department of Historic Resources was the appropriate agency to make such a determination. See opinion of Attorney General to The Honorable Johnny S. Joannou, Member, House of Delegates, 01-052 (6/29/01).

§ 10.1-2202.1. Historic Resources Fund established; administration; purpose.

— A. There is hereby established a special, nonreverting fund in the state treasury to be known as the Historic Resources Fund, hereafter referred to as the Fund. The Fund shall be administered and managed by the Director and used for the general purposes of education, financing of museum operating and capital expenses, performing research, and conducting special historic preservation projects as identified by the Department and the donors. The Fund shall consist of appropriations from the General Assembly designated for the Fund, any gifts and bequests, cash and noncash, and all proceeds from the sale of Department publications and educational or promotional material, income from contracted services, and grants. Initial funding shall be made by a transfer of existing donations and special funds consistent with the intent of this new fund.

B. The Fund shall be established on the books of the State Comptroller. Any moneys remaining in the Fund shall not revert to the general fund but shall remain in the Fund. Interest earned on such moneys shall remain in the Fund and be credited to it. Any income earned from gifts, bequests, securities, and other property shall be deposited to the credit of the Fund. (1995, c. 21.)

§ 10.1-2202.2. Preservation Easement Fund established; uses.

— A. There is hereby created in the state treasury a special nonreverting fund to be known as the Preservation Easement Fund, hereafter referred to as "the Fund." The Fund shall be established on the books of the Comptroller. The Fund shall consist of general funds appropriated by the General Assembly and funds received as gifts, endowments, or grants from the United States Government, its agencies and instrumentalities, and funds from any other available sources, public or private. All such funds shall be paid into the state treasury and credited to the Fund. Interest earned on moneys in the Fund shall remain in the Fund and be credited to it. Any moneys remaining in the Fund, including interest thereon, at the end of each fiscal year shall not revert to the general fund but shall remain in the Fund.

Moneys in the Fund shall be used solely for the purposes of: (i) supporting and promoting a broad-based easement program and (ii) providing grants in accordance with this section to persons who convey a perpetual easement to the Board pursuant to the Open-Space Land Act (§ 10.1-1700 et seq.) and, if applicable, the Virginia Conservation Easement Act (§ 10.1-1009 et seq.) for the purposes of preserving real property which is important for its historical, architectural or archaeological aspects. Expenditures and disbursements from the Fund shall be made by the State Treasurer on warrants issued by the Comptroller upon written request signed by the Director.

B. The Director shall establish, administer, manage, and make expenditures and allocations from the Fund.

C. Grants from the Fund may be made to persons conveying a perpetual easement to the Board to pay some or all of the costs associated with such conveyance, which may include the cost of registering the property with the Virginia Landmarks Register and the National Register of Historic Places, and legal, survey, appraisal and other costs.

D. The Director shall establish guidelines for the submittal and evaluation of grant applications and for the award of grants from the Fund. The guidelines shall authorize the Director to give priority to applications that demonstrate the applicant's financial need for a grant. (1998, c. 479.)

§ 10.1-2202.3. Stewardship of state-owned historic properties. —
A. In order to consider the broad public interest and protect the financial investment in state-owned historic assets, the Department shall develop, on a biennial basis, a report on the stewardship of state-owned properties. The report shall include, but not be limited to, a priority list of the Commonwealth's most significant state-owned properties that are eligible for but not designated on the Virginia Landmarks Register pursuant to § 10.1-2206.1. The report shall also provide a priority list of significant state-owned properties, designated on or eligible for the Virginia Landmarks Register, which are threatened with the loss of historic integrity or functionality. In developing the report, the Department shall, in addition to significance and threat, take into account other public interest considerations associated with landmark designation and the provision of proper care and maintenance of property. These considerations shall include: (i) potential financial consequences to the Commonwealth associated with failure to care for and maintain property, (ii) significant public educational potential, (iii) significant tourism opportunities, and (iv) community values and comments. The report shall be forwarded to all affected state agencies, including institutions of higher learning, the Governor, the Secretary of Administration, the Secretary of Natural Resources, the Secretary of Finance, and the General Assembly. All agencies of the Commonwealth shall assist and support the development of the report by providing information and access to property as may be requested.

B. Each agency that owns property included in the report required by subsection A shall initiate consultation with the Department within 60 days of receipt of the report and make a good faith effort to reach a consensus decision on designation of an unlisted property and on the feasibility, advisability, and general manner of addressing property needs in the case of a threatened historic property.

C. The Department shall prepare a biennial status report summarizing actions, decisions taken, and the condition of properties previously identified as priorities. The status report, which may be combined with the report required pursuant to subsection A, shall be forwarded to all affected state agencies, including institutions of higher learning, as well as to the Governor, the Secretary of Administration, the Secretary of Natural Resources, the Secretary of Finance, and the General Assembly.

D. The reports required in subsections A and C shall be completed and distributed as required no later than May 1 of each odd-numbered year, so that information contained therein is available to the agencies, the Secretary of Finance, the Secretary of Administration, and the Governor, as well as the General Assembly, during budget preparation. (2006, c. 747.)

§ 10.1-2203. Board of Historic Resources membership; appointment; terms. — A. The Virginia Historic Landmarks Board within the executive branch of state government is continued as the Board of Historic Resources and shall consist of seven members. The members of the Board shall initially be appointed for terms of office as follows: two for a one-year term, two for a two-year term, two for a three-year term, and one for a four-year term. Appointments thereafter shall be made for four-year terms, except appointments to fill vacancies occurring other than by expiration of term, which shall be filled for the unexpired term.

B. In making appointments to the Board, the Governor shall consult with agencies and organizations in Virginia that have as their principal interest the study of Virginia's history and the preservation of Virginia's historic, architectural, archaeological, and cultural resources. The Governor shall also consult appropriate agencies and organizations that represent business and property interests that may be affected by actions of the Board. (1966, c. 632, § 10-136; 1968, c. 612; 1976, c. 484; 1984, c. 750; 1986, c. 608; 1988, c. 891, § 10.1-800; 1989, c. 656; 1992, c. 801.)

§ 10.1-2204. Duties of Board of Historic Resources. — A. The Board of Historic Resources shall:

1. Designate historic landmarks, including buildings, structures, districts, objects and sites which constitute the principal historical, architectural, archaeological, and cultural resources which are of local, statewide or national significance and withdraw designation either upon a determination by the Board that the property has failed to retain those characteristics for which it was designated or upon presentation of new or additional information proving to the satisfaction of the Board that the designation had been based on error of fact;

2. Establish and endorse appropriate historic preservation practices for the care and management of designated landmarks;

3. Approve the proposed text and authorize the manufacture of highway historical markers;

4. Acquire by purchase or gift designated landmarks, or easements or interests therein;

5. Review the programs and services of the Department of Historic Resources, including annual plans and make recommendations to the Director and the Governor concerning the effectiveness of those programs and services;

6. In cooperation with the Department, and through public lectures, writings, and other educational activities, promote awareness of the importance of historic resources and the benefits of their preservation and use; and

7. Apply for gifts, grants and bequests for deposit in the Historic Resources Fund to promote the missions of the Board and the Department.

B. For the purposes of this chapter, designation by the Board of Historic Resources shall mean an act of official recognition designed (i) to educate the public to the significance of the designated resource and (ii) to encourage local governments and property owners to take the designated property's historic, architectural, archaeological, and cultural significance into account in their planning, the local government comprehensive plan, and their decision making. Such designation, itself, shall not regulate the action of local governments or property owners with regard to the designated property. (1966, c. 632, § 10-138; 1984, c. 750, § 10-259; 1986, c. 608; 1988, c. 891, § 10.1-801; 1989, c. 656; 1992, c. 801; 1995, c. 21; 2006, c. 32.)

Editor's note. — Acts 1992, c. 801, cl. 3 provides: "That the Department of Historic Resources shall conduct an evaluation of the Board of Historic Resources' designation of any historic district designated after January 1, 1989, which has not been listed in the National

Register of Historic Places. In conducting its evaluation, the Department of Historic Resources shall consult with the boards of supervisors of the counties or their representatives, and with the owners of the property located within the designated historic districts. The evaluation shall include:

"1. An examination of the documentary information that led to the designation and of any new or additional documentary information presented to the Department, in order to determine whether either or both of the designations or the boundaries of the historic districts were based on any error of fact and whether these findings provide grounds for recommending that the designations be amended or withdrawn;

"2. An examination of (i) all land uses permitted by existing zoning within designated areas, (ii) possible land uses pursuant to any zoning changes currently contemplated by the counties or indicated by their current master plans, and (iii) all development proposals made known to the Department of Historic Resources by the counties or by the property owners;

"3. An identification of those development proposals that may be necessity or choice be dependent upon federal funding or licensure, and thus subject to the consultation process required by Section 106 of the National Historic Preservation Act and, to the extent practicable, an identification of probable outcomes of that consultation process and of possible strategies for successful resolution of any disagreements;

"4. Any analysis of the Virginia Department of Transportation's continuing ability to meet existing transportation needs, as well as those needs created by anticipated development, in the historic districts;

"5. An identification of any smaller areas within the designated historic districts that the Department of Historic Resources believes should be high priority areas for preservation and an identification of strategies for accomplishing that preservation in a manner that is fair to current property owners; and

"6. An analysis of whether either or both of the designations by the Board of Historic Resources of the battlefields as historic districts, or the determinations of eligibility for the National Register of Historic Places made by the National Park Service pursuant to the National Historic Preservation Act, should be amended or withdrawn as the development identified in item 2 is carried out."

Acts 2006, c. 32, cl. 2, provides: "That the provisions of this act are declaratory of existing law."

The 2006 amendments. — The 2006 amendment by c. 32, in subdivision A 1, inserted "including" and substituted "archaeological, and cultural resources" for "and archaeological sites"; and deleted "and sites" following "designated landmarks" in subdivision A 4.

CASE NOTES

The Historic Landmarks Commission (now Board) is not vested with the power of eminent domain. Virginia Historic Landmarks Comm'n v. Board of Supvrs., 217 Va. 468, 230 S.E.2d 449 (1976) (decided under former § 10.1-801).

For case involving the effect of the des- ignation of an area as an historical district on property rights and public notice and hearing, see Virginia Historic Landmarks Comm'n v. Board of Supvrs., 217 Va. 468, 230 S.E.2d 449 (1976) (decided under former § 10.1-801).

§ 10.1-2205. Board shall promulgate regulations; penalty. — The Board shall promulgate regulations necessary to carry out its powers and duties, including at a minimum criteria and procedures for the designation of historic landmarks, including buildings, structures, districts, objects, and sites. Such regulations shall be not inconsistent with the National Historic Preservation Act (P.L. 89-665) and its attendant regulations. The regulations of the Board shall be promulgated in accordance with the Virginia Administrative Process Act (§ 2.2-4000 et seq.).

Any person who violates any regulation adopted pursuant to this section shall be subject to a civil penalty not to exceed $500. Any civil penalty collected pursuant to this section shall be deposited into the state treasury. (1989, c. 656; 1992, cc. 180, 801; 2006, c. 32.)

Editor's note. — Acts 1989, c. 656 provides in cl. 3 that the Governor may transfer any employees to support the changes in organiza- tion or responsibility resulting from or required by the act.

Acts 2006, c. 32, cl. 2, provides: "That the

provisions of this act are declaratory of existing law."

The 2006 amendments. — The 2006 amendment by c. 32 substituted "including buildings, structures, districts, objects, and sites" for "and historic districts" in the first sentence of the first paragraph.

§ **10.1-2206:** Repealed by Acts 1992, c. 801.

Cross references. — For present provisions, see § 10.1-2206.1.

§ **10.1-2206.1. Procedure for designating a historic district, building, structure, or site as a historic landmark; National Register of Historic Places, National Historic Landmarks; historic district defined.** — A. In any county, city, or town where the Board proposes to designate a historic district, building, structure, object, or site as a historic landmark, or where the Director proposes to nominate property to the National Park Service for inclusion in the National Register of Historic Places or for designation as a National Historic Landmark, the Department shall give written notice of the proposal to the governing body and to the owner, owners, or the owner's agent, of property proposed to be so designated or nominated, and to the owners, or their agents, of all abutting property and property immediately across the street or road from the property.

B. Prior to the designation or nomination of a historic district, the Department shall hold a public hearing at the seat of government of the county, city, or town in which the proposed historic district is located or within the proposed historic district. The public hearing shall be for the purpose of supplying additional information to the Board and to the Director. The time and place of such hearing shall be determined in consultation with a duly authorized representative of the local governing body, and shall be scheduled at a time and place that will reasonably allow for the attendance of the affected property owners. The Department shall publish notice of the public hearing once a week for two successive weeks in a newspaper published or having general circulation in the county, city, or town. Such notice shall specify the time and place of the public hearing at which persons affected may appear and present their views, not less than six days nor more than twenty-one days after the second publication of the notice in such newspaper. In addition to publishing the notice, the Department shall give written notice of the public hearing at least five days before such hearing to the owner, owners, or the owner's agent, of each parcel of real property to be included in the proposed historic district, and to the owners, or their agents, of all abutting property and property immediately across the street or road from the included property. Notice required to be given to owners by this subsection may be given concurrently with the notice required to be given to the owners by subsection A. The Department shall make and maintain an appropriate record of all public hearings held pursuant to this section.

C. Any written notice required to be given by the Department to any person shall be deemed to comply with the requirements of this section if sent by first class mail to the last known address of such person as shown on the current real estate tax assessment books, provided that a representative of the Department shall make an affidavit that such mailings have been made.

D. The local governing body and property owners shall have thirty days from the date of the notice required by subsection A, or, in the case of a historic district, thirty days from the date of the public hearing required by subsection B to provide comments and recommendations, if any, to the Board and to the Director.

E. For the purposes of this chapter, a historic district means a geographically definable area which contains a significant concentration of historic buildings, structures or sites having a common historical, architectural, archaeological, or cultural heritage, and which may contain local tax parcels having separate owners. Contributing properties within a registered district are historic landmarks by definition.

F. All regulations promulgated by the Director pursuant to § 10.1-2202 and all regulations promulgated by the Board pursuant to § 10.1-2205 shall be consistent with the provisions of this section. (1992, c. 801; 2006, c. 32.)

Editor's note. — Acts 2006, c. 32, cl. 2, provides: "That the provisions of this act are declaratory of existing law."

The 2006 amendments. — The 2006 amendment by c. 32, in the section catchline, inserted "as a historic landmark"; in subsection A, deleted "landmark" preceding "building, structure, object, or site" and inserted "as a historic landmark," inserted "so" following "property proposed to be" and deleted "as a historic landmark building, structure, object, or site or to be included in a historic district" following "designated or nominated"; and in subsection E, inserted "archaeological" following "architectural," substituted "may contain" for "contains" and added the last sentence.

CASE NOTES

For case involving the effect of the designation of an area as an historical district on property rights and public notice and hearing, see Virginia Historic Landmarks Comm'n v. Board of Supvrs., 217 Va. 468, 230 S.E.2d 449 (1976) (decided under former §§ 10.1-803 and 10.1-2206).

§ 10.1-2206.2. Consent of owners required for certain designations by the Board. — A. Before the Board shall designate any building, structure, district, object, or site as a historic landmark in accordance with § 10.1-2204, the owners of such property proposed for designation shall be given the opportunity to concur in or object to such designation by the Board. If a majority of the owners of the property within such area proposed for designation object to such designation, the Board shall take no formal action to designate the property as historic until such objection is withdrawn.

B. For the purposes of this section, majority of owners of the property shall mean a majority of the number of property owners of or within the proposed property or district.

C. Nothing contained herein shall be deemed or construed to affect any local government charter or ordinance regarding historic districts or historic preservation. (1992, c. 801; 2006, c. 32.)

Editor's note. — Acts 2006, c. 32, cl. 2, provides: "That the provisions of this act are declaratory of existing law."

The 2006 amendments. — The 2006 amendment by c. 32, in subsection A, deleted "historic district, landmark" preceding "building, structure" and inserted "district, object" thereafter, and inserted "as a historic landmark" preceding "in accordance with § 10.1-2204."

§ 10.1-2207. Property to reflect change in market value. — Where the Commonwealth has obtained from a landowner an easement or other partial interest in property which places restrictions on the use or development of that property so as to preserve those features which led to the designation of that property as an historic landmark, the easement or other partial interest shall be recorded in the clerk's office of the county or city where deeds are admitted to record. Assessments for local taxation of the property shall reflect any resulting change in the market value of the property, as prescribed by § 58.1-3205. The Director shall notify the official having the taxing power to make assessments of properties for purposes of taxation within the locality of the restrictions that have been placed on the property. (1966, c. 632, §§ 10-138, 10-139; 1984, cc. 675, 750; 1986, c. 608; 1988, c. 891, § 10.1-808; 1989, c. 656.)

§ 10.1-2208. Supervision of expenditure of appropriations made to nonstate agencies. — The Director shall oversee the expenditure of state appropriations made available to nonstate agencies, whether private or municipal, for purposes related to the historical collections, historic landmarks, and historic sites of Virginia, to assure that such purposes are consistent with the statewide plan for historic preservation as established by the Director. The Director shall establish and require adherence to sound professional standards of historical, architectural and archaeological research in the planning, preservation, restoration, interpretation and display of such collections, landmarks, and sites. (1972, c. 119, § 10-138.1; 1984, c. 750; 1988, c. 891, § 10.1-809; 1989, c. 656.)

§ 10.1-2208.1. (Contingent expiration — see note) Virginia Historic Preservation and Museum Assistance Grant Program. — A. The Virginia Historic Preservation and Museum Assistance Grant Program is hereby established within the Department to provide grants to implement and encourage the preservation and interpretation of historic properties for the economic, educational, and cultural benefit of Virginia citizens and communities.

B. The Department shall adopt procedures to administer the Virginia Historic Preservation and Museum Assistance Grant Program and Fund to carry out the purposes of the Program consistent with state procurement and accounting requirements. The procedures shall include: (i) application procedures; (ii) procedures for adequate public notice of available assistance; (iii) provisions and guidelines for the review of plans and specifications and the inspection of projects during construction or implementation; (iv) selection criteria that the Department shall consider in approving grant applications; (v) provisions and certifications to ensure that state funds are spent and accounted for appropriately and in accordance with state procurement requirements; and (vi) procedures for consulting with and reporting to the Board in the oversight of the Program and for consulting with other state agencies and preservation organizations as appropriate in developing and implementing the Program. (2005, c. 85.)

Contingent expiration. — Acts 2005, c. 85, which enacted this section, in cl. 2 provides: "That should no funds from any source be received in the fund by July 1, 2007, the provisions of this act shall expire."

§ 10.1-2208.2. (Contingent expiration — see note) Virginia Historic Preservation and Museum Assistance Grant Fund; established. — There is hereby created in the state treasury a special nonreverting fund to be known as the Virginia Historic Preservation and Museum Assistance Grant Fund, hereafter referred to as "the Fund." The Fund shall be established on the books of the Comptroller. All funds as may be appropriated and such gifts, donations, grants, bequests, and other funds as may be received shall be paid into the state treasury and credited to the Fund. Interest earned on moneys in the Fund shall remain in the Fund and be credited to it. Any moneys remaining in the Fund, including interest thereon, at the end of each fiscal year shall not revert to the general fund but shall remain in the Fund. Moneys in the Fund shall be used solely for the purposes of making grants to nonprofit organizations, localities, business entities, and individuals for the purpose of: (i) acquiring, rehabilitating, restoring, or interpreting historic properties; (ii) financing costs directly related to a rehabilitation or restoration project, which may include the costs of studies, surveys, plans and specifications, and architectural, engineering or other special services; or (iii) funding historic preservation education and promotion, including the research, survey, and evaluation of historic properties and the preparation of historic preservation planning documents and educational materials. Expenditures and disbursements from the Fund shall be made by the State Treasurer on warrants issued by the Comptroller upon written request signed by the Director. (2005, c. 85.)

Contingent expiration. — Acts 2005, c. 85, which enacted this section, in cl. 2 provides: "That should no funds from any source be received in the fund by July 1, 2007, the provisions of this act shall expire."

§ 10.1-2209. Erection of markers, requirements, etc., without certificate of approval forbidden.

— It shall be unlawful to post or erect any historical marker, monument, sign or notice, on public property or upon any public street, road or highway in the Commonwealth bearing any legend, inscription or notice which purports to record any historic event, incident or fact, or to maintain any such historical marker, monument, notice, or sign posted or erected after June 17, 1930, unless a written certificate has been issued by the Board or an appropriate predecessor agency attesting to the validity and correct record of the historic event, incident or fact set forth in the marker. (Code 1950, § 42-66; 1950, p. 47; 1964, c. 152; 1970, c. 606, § 10-145.2; 1976, c. 88; 1984, c. 750, § 10-261; 1986, c. 608; 1988, c. 891, § 10.1-810; 1989, c. 656.)

§ 10.1-2210. Erection of markers by local governing bodies.

— A. The governing body of any county, city or town may, at its own expense, have erected a historical marker commemorating any person, event or place upon any public street, road or highway within its boundaries, provided that the person, event or place to be commemorated is identified with or representative of a local aspect of history. The governing body, or its duly authorized agent, shall first determine, on the basis of documented research, that the text of the marker appears to be true and correct. The local markers shall differ in style and appearance from state historical markers, and shall display, on the face of the markers, prominent notice of the governing body, or its agent, which approved the text of the marker. Design, appearance and size and height specifications for local markers shall be reviewed and approved by the Board.

B. If the person, event or place to be commemorated is prominently identified with, or best representative of a major aspect of state or national history, then the text of the marker shall be approved as provided in § 10.1-2209. (1970, c. 606, § 10-145.6; 1976, c. 88; 1988, c. 891, § 10.1-811; 1989, c. 656.)

§ 10.1-2211. Disbursement of funds appropriated for caring for Confederate cemeteries and graves.

— A. At the direction of the Director, the Comptroller of the Commonwealth is instructed and empowered to draw annual warrants upon the State Treasurer from any sums that may be provided in the general appropriation act, in favor of the treasurers of the Confederate memorial associations and chapters of the United Daughters of the Confederacy set forth in subsection B of this section. Such sums shall be expended by the associations and organizations for the routine maintenance of their respective Confederate cemeteries and graves and for the graves of Confederate soldiers and sailors not otherwise cared for in other cemeteries, and in erecting and caring for markers, memorials, and monuments to the memory of such soldiers and sailors. All such associations and organizations, through their proper officers, are required after July 1 of each year to submit to the Director a certified statement that the funds appropriated to the association or organization in the preceding fiscal year were or will be expended for the routine maintenance of cemeteries specified in this section and the graves of Confederate soldiers and sailors and in erecting and caring for markers, memorials and monuments to the memory of such soldiers and sailors. An association or organization failing to comply with any of the requirements of this section shall be prohibited from receiving moneys allocated under this section for all subsequent fiscal years until the association or organization fully complies with the requirements.

B. Allocation of appropriations made pursuant to this section shall be based on the number of graves, monuments and markers as set forth opposite the association's or organization's name, or as documented by each association or organization multiplied by the rate of $5 or the average actual cost of routine maintenance, whichever is greater, for each grave, monument or marker in the care of a Confederate memorial association or chapter of the United Daughters of the Confederacy. For the purposes of this section the "average actual cost of care" shall be determined by the Department in a biennial survey of at least four properly maintained cemeteries, each located in a different geographical region of the Commonwealth.

IN THE COUNTIES OF: NUMBER:

Accomack
    Robert E. Lee Chapter, U.D.C., Belle Haven 10
Albemarle
    Albemarle Chapter, U.D.C 50
    Mountain Plain Cemetery, Crozet 15
    Mt. Zion United Methodist Church, Esmont 10
    Scottsville Chapter, U.D.C 40
    Westerly Chapel Cemetery, Free Union 15
Amelia
    Grub Hill Church 10
Appomattox
    Appomattox Chapter, U.D.C 50
Augusta
    Augusta Stone Presbyterian Church Cemetery 40
    Salem Lutheran Church Cemetery 37
    Trinity Lutheran Church Cemetery 13
Botetourt
    Fairview Cemetery Association, Inc 20
    Glade Creek Cemetery Corporation 10
Buchanan
    Ratliff 30
Carroll
    Floyd Webb Cemetery 16
    Robinson Cemetery 10
    Worrell Cemetery 10
Charles City County
    Salem Church Cemetery 35
Chesterfield
    Ettrick Cemetery 47
Craig
    Archibald A. Caldwell Cemetery 4
Culpeper
    Culpeper Chapter, U.D.C 10
Dinwiddie
    Dinwiddie Confederate Memorial Association 15
Fairfax
    Fairfax Chapter, U.D.C 15
    Robert E. Lee Chapter No. 56 36
Fauquier
    Black Horse Chapter, U.D.C 10
    Marshall Cemetery 10

Piedmont Chapter, U.D.C 10
Upperville Methodist Church Cemetery 10
Floyd
   Floyd County Confederate Memorial Association 20
   Southward Cemetery 10
Giles
   McComas Chapter, U.D.C 15
Goochland
   Goochland Chapter, U.D.C 15
Grayson
   A. B. Cox Cemetery 10
   Atkins Memorial Cemetery 10
   Bethel Church Cemetery 10
   Bridlecreek Cemetery 10
   Camet B. Cox Cemetery 10
   Comer's Rock Cemetery 10
   Cox's Chapel 10
   Fellowship Baptist Cemetery 10
   Fries Ridge Cemetery 10
   Forest Cemetery 10
   Fox Creek Cemetery 10
   Funk Cemetery 10
   Gold Hill Cemetery 10
   Grubbs Chapel Cemetery 10
   Hale Cemetery 15
   Hines Branch Cemetery 10
   Independence Cemetery 10
   Jerusalem Methodist Episcopal Church Cemetery 10
   Lebanon Cemetery 10
   Liberty Hill Cemetery 15
   Long Branch Cemetery 10
   New Hope Cemetery 10
   Oak Grove Cemetery 10
   Potato Creek Cemetery 10
   Pugh Cemetery 10
   Rhudy Cemetery 10
   Round Meadows Cemetery 10
   Rugby Cemetery 10
   Saddle Creek Cemetery 10
   Sawyers Family Cemetery 10
   Spring Valley Cemetery 10
   Whitetop Cemetery 10
Greene
   Gentry Methodist Church Cemetery 10
Halifax
   Grace Churchyard, Inc., Seaton 3
   Halifax Chapter, U.D.C 20
   St. John's Episcopal Church 31
Hanover
   Hanover Chapter, U.D.C 20
Henrico
   Emmanual Episcopal Church at Brook Hill 86
Isle of Wight
   Isle of Wight Chapter, U.D.C 20
Lee
   Light Horse Harry Lee Chapter, U.D.C 100
   Ely Cemetery 30

Loudoun
  Ebenezer Cemetery 15
  Lakeview Cemetery, Hamilton 15
  Lee Chapter No. 179 10
  Leesburg Union Cemetery 15
  Sharon Cemetery, Middleburg 20
Louisa
  Oakland Cemetery 70
Lunenburg
  Sons of the Confederate Veterans Old Free State Camp #1746 141
Madison
  Madison Chapter, U.D.C 10
Mecklenburg
  Boydton Chapter, U.D.C 10
  Armistead-Goode Chapter, U.D.C 10
Montgomery
  Doctor Harvey Black Chapter, U.D.C 10
  White Cemetery, Inc 10
Nelson
  Nelson County Confederate Memorial Association 10
Nottoway
  Confederate Memorial Board 15
Orange
  Maplewood Cemetery, Gordonsville 696
  Preddys Creek Cemetery 10
  13th Virginia Regiment Chapter, U.D.C 30
Patrick
  Confederate Memorial Association 40
Pittsylvania
  Rawley Martin Chapter, U.D.C 30
Powhatan
  Huguenot Springs Cemetery 130
Prince Edward
  Farmville Chapter, U.D.C 50
Prince George
  City Point Chapter, U.D.C., for use at Old Town Cemetery 20
Pulaski
  Pulaski Chapter, U.D.C 10
Roanoke
  Southern Cross Chapter, U.D.C 10
  Old Tombstone Cemetery 20
Rockbridge
  New Monmouth Presbyterian Church 80
  New Providence Presbyterian Church 98
Rockingham
  Cedar Grove Cemetery 68
  Cooks Creek Presbyterian Church Cemetery 39
  Singers Glen Cemetery 19
  St. Johns Lutheran Cemetery 10
Scott
  Prospect Community Cemetery 20
  McKenney-Carter Cemetery Association 20
  Confederate Memorial Branch, Wolfe Cemetery Association, Yuma 15
  Estill Memorial Cemetery Association 35
  Lawson Confederate Memorial Cemetery 10
  Mount Pleasant Cemetery 20

Salling Memorial, Slant 20
Rollins Cemetery 10
Daugherty Cemetery 20
Nickelsville Baptist Church Cemetery 20
Shenandoah
New Market Confederate Memorial Association 40
Stover Camp Chapter, U.D.C 10
Mt. Jackson-Old Soldier Cemetery 100
Smyth
Aspenvale Cemetery 10
Blue Springs Cemetery, Sugar Grove 10
Centenary Cemetery 10
Chatham Hill Cemetery 10
Greenwood Cemetery 10
Holston Chapter, U.D.C 20
Keesling Cemetery, Rural Retreat 10
Middle Fork Cemetery 10
Morgan Cemetery, Sugar Grove 10
Mt. Carmel Cemetery 20
Mountain View Cemetery, Chilhowie 10
Mt. Zion Cemetery 10
Pleasant Hill Cemetery, Groseclose 12
Ridgedale Cemetery, Rich Valley 10
Riverside Cemetery in Rich Valley 10
Round Hill Cemetery 20
Slemp Cemetery, Sugar Grove 10
St. James Cemetery, Chilhowie 10
South Fork Baptist Cemetery 10
Steffey Cemetery, Groseclose 10
Wassum Cemetery, Atkins 10
Zion Methodist Cemetery, Rich Valley 14
Riverside Cemetery on South Fork 10
Royal Oak Cemetery 10
St. Clairs Bottom Cemetery, Chilhowie 10
Sulphur Springs Cemetery 10
Southampton
Southampton Chapter, U.D.C 40
Spotsylvania
Ladies Confederate Memorial Association 300
Surry
General William Mahone Chapter, U.D.C 40
Tazewell
Maplewood Cemetery 20
Hankins Cemetery 20
Warren
Warren Rifles Chapter, U.D.C 25
Washington
Anna Stonewall Jackson Chapter, U.D.C 20
Emory and Henry Cemetery 203
Greendale Cemetery 20
Warren Cemetery 20
Wise
Big Stone Gap Chapter, U.D.C 20
Wythe
Asbury Cemetery, Rural Retreat 10
Fairview Cemetery, Rural Retreat 10

Galilee Christian Church Cemetery 10
Grubbs Cemetery 10
Kemberling Cemetery 10
Marvin Cemetery 30
Mt. Ephraim Cemetery 10
Mount Mitchell Cemetery 10
Mountain View Cemetery 46
Murphysville Cemetery 10
St. John's Cemetery 10
St. Mary's Cemetery 10
St. Paul's Cemetery 14
St. Peter's Lutheran Church Cemetery 12
Speedwell Methodist Cemetery 10
Wythe-Gray Chapter, U.D.C 20
Zion Cemetery 10
York
Bethel Memorial Association 20
IN THE CITIES OF:
Alexandria
Old Dominion Rifles Confederate Memorial Association 160
Bristol
Bristol Confederate Memorial Association 60
Charlottesville
Effort Baptist Church 10
Clifton Forge
Julia Jackson Chapter, U.D.C 15
Chesapeake
Norfolk County Grays Chapter 2535, U.D.C 8
Covington
Alleghany Chapter, U.D.C 30
Danville
Eliza Johns Chapter, U.D.C 201
Fredericksburg
Fredericksburg Confederate Memorial Association 200
Hampton
Hampton Chapter, U.D.C 60
Harrisonburg
Turner Ashby Chapter, U.D.C 60
Woodbine Cemetery 140
Lexington
Rockbridge Chapter, U.D.C 126
Lynchburg
Lynchburg Confederate Memorial Association 30
Manassas
Ladies Confederate Memorial Association of Manassas 15
Martinsville
Mildred Lee Chapter, U.D.C 10
Newport News
Bethel Chapter, U.D.C 50
Norfolk
Hope Maury Chapter, U.D.C 10
Pickett-Buchanan Chapter, U.D.C 20
Petersburg
Petersburg Chapter, U.D.C., for Prince George County 15
Ladies Memorial Association of Petersburg 140
Portsmouth
Ladies Confederate Memorial Association 15

Radford
  New River Gray's Chapter, U.D.C 15
  Radford Chapter, U.D.C 15
Richmond
  Centennial Chapter, U.D.C 20
  Elliott Grays Chapter, U.D.C 15
  Janet Randolph Chapter, U.D.C 15
  Lee Chapter, U.D.C 20
  Sons of Confederate Veterans — Virginia Division 2294
  Richmond-Stonewall Jackson Chapter, U.D.C 110
Roanoke
  Roanoke Chapter, U.D.C 40
  William Watts Chapter, U.D.C 40
Salem
  Southern Cross Chapter, U.D.C 271
Staunton
  Confederate Section, Thornrose Cemetery 600
Vinton
  Major Wm. F. Graves Chapter, U.D.C 40
Williamsburg
  Williamsburg Chapter, U.D.C 125
Winchester
  Stonewall Confederate Memorial Association 2112

C. In addition to funds that may be provided pursuant to subsection B of this section, any of the Confederate memorial associations and chapters of the United Daughters of the Confederacy set forth in subsection B may apply to the Director for grants to perform extraordinary maintenance, renovation, repair or reconstruction of any of their respective Confederate cemeteries and graves and for the graves of Confederate soldiers and sailors. These grants shall be made from any appropriation made available by the General Assembly for such purpose. In making such grants, the Director shall give full consideration to the assistance available from the United States Department of Veterans Affairs, or other agencies, except in those instances where such assistance is deemed by the Director to be detrimental to the historical, artistic or architectural significance of the site.

D. Local matching funds shall not be required for grants made pursuant to this section. (Code 1950, § 2.1-206.1; 1977, c. 242; 1978, c. 726; 1979, cc. 19, 151; 1980, c. 672; 1981, c. 537, § 10.145.11; 1984, cc. 412, 750; 1985, cc. 263, 267; 1986, cc. 120, 385; 1988, cc. 310, 891, § 10.1-812; 1989, cc. 656, 711; 1992, c. 640; 1994, c. 78; 1995, c. 176; 1997, cc. 72, 255, 270, 811; 1998, c. 233; 1999, c. 473; 2000, c. 114; 2001, cc. 267, 279, 284; 2002, cc. 181, 188, 225; 2003, c. 585; 2006, cc. 489, 630.)

Cross references. — As to the availability of state funds to nonstate agencies, see § 2.2-1505.

Editor's note. — Acts 1997, c. 811, c. 2, provides: "That the provision of this act relating to the Sons of the Confederate Veterans, Oakwood Committee, shall become effective on July 1, 1998, and only if funding to implement that provision in an amount consistent with provisions of subsection B of § 10.1-2211 is provided in the general appropriation act for each fiscal year of the biennium ending June 30, 2000." It appears the appropriation was not made.

Acts 1997, c. 811, cl. 3, provides: "That notwithstanding any other provision of this act or any provision of subsection C of § 10.1-2211, the Sons of the Confederate Veterans, Oakwood Committee, shall be eligible, beginning July 1, 1997, for a one time grant that is subject to the approval of the Director and not to exceed $ 30,000, for purposes consistent with those of subsection C of § 10.1-2211. Notwithstanding the provisions of subsection C of § 10.1-2211 relating to the funding source for grants, the grant may be made from available appropriated funds."

The 2006 amendments. — The 2006 amendment by c. 489 substituted "Sons of Confederate Veterans — Virginia Division" for

"Oakwood Confederate Cemetery Trust, Inc." in the Richmond listings in subsection B.

The 2006 amendment by c. 630 substituted "2112" for "180" in the listing for "Stonewall Confederate Memorial Association" in subsection B.

§ 10.1-2211.1. Disbursement of funds appropriated for caring for Revolutionary War cemeteries and graves. — A. At the direction of the Director, the Comptroller of the Commonwealth is instructed and empowered to draw annual warrants upon the State Treasurer from any sums that may be provided in the general appropriation act, in favor of the treasurers of Revolutionary War memorial associations caring for cemeteries as set forth in subsection B. Such sums shall be expended by the associations for the routine maintenance of their respective Revolutionary War cemeteries and graves and for the graves of Revolutionary War soldiers and sailors not otherwise cared for in other cemeteries, and in erecting and caring for markers, memorials, and monuments to the memory of such soldiers and sailors. All such associations, through their proper officers, are required after July 1 of each year to submit to the Director a certified statement that the funds appropriated to the association or organization in the preceding fiscal year were or will be expended for the routine maintenance of cemeteries specified in this section and the graves of Revolutionary War soldiers and sailors and in erecting and caring for markers, memorials and monuments to the memory of such soldiers and sailors. A cemetery association failing to comply with any of the requirements of this section shall be prohibited from receiving moneys allocated under this section for all subsequent fiscal years until the association fully complies with the requirements.

B. Allocation of appropriations made pursuant to this section shall be based on the number of graves, monuments and markers as set forth opposite the cemetery name, or as documented by each association multiplied by the rate of five dollars or the average actual cost of routine maintenance, whichever is greater, for each grave, monument or marker in the care of a cemetery association. For the purposes of this section the "average actual cost of care" shall be determined by the Department in a biennial survey of at least four properly maintained cemeteries, each located in a different geographical region of the Commonwealth.

IN THE COUNTIES OF: NUMBER:

Amherst
    St. Matthews Episcopal Church 3
Augusta
    Bethel Presbyterian Church 33
    Glebe Burying Ground 11
    Mossy Creek Cemetery 6
    Augusta Stone Presbyterian Church 44
    Hebron Presbyterian Church 6
    Old Providence Presbyterian Church 20
    Rocky Spring Presbyterian Church 4
    St. John's Reformed Lutheran Church 4
    St. Peter's Lutheran Church 3
    Tinkling Springs Presbyterian Church 13
    Trinity Lutheran Church 8
Botetourt
    Fincastle Presbyterian Church 28
Campbell
    Callaway-Steptoe Cemetery 4
    Cobbs Hall Farm 3
    Concord Presbyterian Church 4
    Family Cemetery at Avoca 3

Mount Airy Family Cemetery 3
Haden Family Cemetery on Phillips Farm 3
Hat Creek Presbyterian Church 3
Clarke
  Old Chapel Churchyard 3
Culpeper
  Culpeper Cemetery 3
  Masonic Cemetery 3
Dinwiddie
  Sweden Plantation 3
Floyd
  Pine Creek Cemetery 4
Franklin
  Tanyard-Benard-Hill Cemetery 3
Greenesville
  Robinson Family Cemetery 3
Halifax
  Terry Family Cemetery 5
Hanover
  Spring Grove Cemetery 5
Henry
  Leatherwood Plantation 5
Loudoun
  Ketoctin Cemetery 7
Louisa
  Little River Baptist Church 3
Nelson
  Cub Creek Road Cemetery 10
Page
  Printz Family Cemetery 3
Pittsylvania
  Buckler Family Cemetery 3
Roanoke
  Walton Family Cemetery 3
Rockingham
  Dayton Cemetery 3
  Old Peaked Mountain Church 30
Russell
  Soloman Litton Hollow Cemetery 4
Shenandoah
  St. Mary's Lutheran Church 7
Tazewell
  Thompson Family Cemetery 4
Washington
  Green Spring Church 6
  Sinking Spring Cemetery 9
Wythe
  St. John's Lutheran Church 5
  St. Paul's Lutheran Church 4
IN THE CITIES OF:
Alexandria
  Christ Church Cemetery 8
  Old Presbyterian Meeting House 43
Fairfax
  Fairfax City Cemetery 3
  Pohick Church Cemetery 3
  Washington Family Tomb 3

Fredericksburg
    Fredericksburg Cemetery 5
    Masonic Cemetery 6
    St. George's Episcopal Church 3
Lexington
    Stonewall Jackson Memorial Cemetery 19
    Washington and Lee University 3
Lynchburg
    Old City Cemetery 3
Newport News
    Warwick Burial Ground 3
Norfolk
    St. Paul's Cemetery 3
Portsmouth
    Cedar Grove 4
    Trinity Episcopal Church 5
Richmond
    Hollywood Cemetery 4
    Shockoe Hill Cemetery 8
    St. John's Episcopal Church 4
Rockbridge
    Falling Spring Presbyterian Church 6
    High Bridge Presbyterian Church 3
    New Providence Presbyterian Church 15
    Timber Ridge Cemetery 9
Staunton
    Trinity Episcopal Church 17
Williamsburg
    Bruton Parish Church 4
Winchester
    Mount Hebron Cemetery 31
    Old Opequon Presbyterian Church 10

C. In addition to funds that may be provided pursuant to subsection B, any of the associations set forth in subsection B may apply to the Director for grants to perform extraordinary maintenance, renovation, repair or reconstruction of any of their respective Revolutionary War cemeteries and graves and for the graves of Revolutionary War soldiers and sailors. These grants shall be made from any appropriation made available by the General Assembly for such purpose. In making such grants, the Director shall give full consideration to the assistance available from the United States Department of Veterans Affairs, or other agencies, except in those instances where such assistance is deemed by the Director to be detrimental to the historical, artistic or architectural significance of the site.

D. Local matching funds shall not be required for grants made pursuant to this section. (2002, c. 256.)

§ 10.1-2212. Listing of certain historical societies receiving appropriations. — A. At the direction of the Director, the Comptroller of the Commonwealth is instructed and empowered to draw annual warrants upon the State Treasurer, as provided in the general appropriations act, in favor of the treasurers of certain historical societies, museums, foundations, and associations for use in caring for and maintaining collections, exhibits, sites, and facilities owned by such historical organizations, specified as follows:

1. Virginia Historical Society. For aid in maintaining Battle Abbey at Richmond.

2. Confederate Museum at Richmond. For the care of Confederate collections and maintenance of the Virginia Room.

3. Valentine Museum at Richmond. For providing exhibits to the public schools of Virginia.

4. Woodrow Wilson Birthplace Foundation, Incorporated. To aid in restoring and maintaining the Woodrow Wilson home at Staunton.

5. Robert E. Lee Memorial Association, Incorporated. To aid in further development of "Stratford" in Westmoreland County.

6. Poe Foundation, Incorporated. To aid in maintaining the Poe Shrine at Richmond.

7. Patrick Henry Memorial Foundation at Brookneal. To aid in maintaining home.

8. Hanover County Branch, Association for the Preservation of Virginia Antiquities. To aid in maintaining the Patrick Henry home at "Scotchtown" in Hanover County.

9. Historic Lexington Foundation. To aid in restoration and maintenance of the Stonewall Jackson home at Lexington.

10. "Oatlands," Incorporated. To aid in maintaining "Oatlands" in Loudoun County.

11. Montgomery County Branch, Association for the Preservation of Virginia Antiquities. To aid in maintaining Smithfield Plantation House.

12. The Last Capitol of the Confederacy. For the preservation of the Last Capitol of the Confederacy in Danville.

13. Association for the Preservation of Virginia Antiquities. For assistance in maintaining certain historic landmarks throughout the Commonwealth.

14. The Corporation for Jefferson's "Poplar Forest." To aid in restoring, maintaining, and operating "Poplar Forest," Thomas Jefferson's Bedford County home.

15. Belle Grove, Incorporated. To aid in providing educational programs for Virginia students.

16. George Washington's Fredericksburg Foundation. To aid in the restoration and perpetuation of "Ferry Farm," George Washington's boyhood home.

17. Montpelier National Trust for Historic Preservation. To aid in restoring, maintaining, and operating Montpelier, the lifelong home of President James Madison, in Orange County.

18. Eastern Shore of Virginia Historical Society. To aid in restoring, maintaining and operating Kerr Place in Accomack County.

19. New Town Improvement and Civic Club, Inc. To aid in restoring, maintaining and operating Little England Chapel, a landmark to Hampton's first generation of freedmen, in the City of Hampton.

20. Woodlawn Plantation. To aid in the preservation and maintenance of Woodlawn Plantation.

21. Friends of Historic Huntley. To support the research and preservation of Historic Huntley Mansion.

22. Menokin Foundation, Incorporated. To aid in further development of Menokin, home of Francis Lightfoot Lee.

23. Historic Gordonsville, Inc., the owner of the Gordonsville Exchange Hotel. To aid in maintaining the Gordonsville Exchange Hotel and in providing educational programs for Virginia's students.

B. Organizations receiving state funds as provided for in this section shall certify to the satisfaction of the Department that matching funds from local or private sources are available in an amount at least equal to the amount of the request in cash or in kind contributions which are deemed acceptable to the Department.

C. Requests for funding of historical societies or like organizations as set forth in subsection A shall be considered by the Governor and the General Assembly only in even-numbered years. (1981, c. 537, § 10-145.12; 1984, cc. 2, 528, 563, 750; 1987, c. 481; 1988, c. 891, § 10.1-813; 1989, cc. 656, 711; 1990, c. 817; 1993, c. 264; 1994, cc. 162, 495; 1995, c. 28; 1996, cc. 227, 420; 1998, c. 172; 2000, cc. 7, 18.)

Cross references. — As to the availability of state funds to nonstate agencies, see § 2.2-1505.

§ 10.1-2213. Procedure for appropriation of state funds for historic preservation. — A. No state funds, other than for the maintenance and operation of those facilities specified in § 10.1-2211 or 10.1-2212 and for the purchase of property for preservation of historical resources by the Virginia Land Conservation Foundation as provided in Chapter 10.2 (§ 10.1-1017 et seq.) of this title, shall be appropriated or expended for or to historical societies, museums, foundations, associations, or local governments as set forth in the general appropriations act for the maintenance of collections and exhibits or for the maintenance, operation, and interpretation of sites and facilities owned by historical organizations unless:

1. A request and completed application for state aid is filed by the organization with the Department, on forms prescribed by the Department, on or before July 1 prior to each regular session of the General Assembly in an even-numbered year. Requests shall be considered by the Governor and the General Assembly only in even-numbered years. The Department shall review each application made by an organization for state aid prior to consideration by the General Assembly. The Department shall provide a timely review of any amendments proposed by members of the General Assembly to the chairmen of the House Appropriations and Senate Finance Committees. The review shall examine the merits of each request, including data showing the percentage of nonstate funds raised by the organization for the proposed project. The review and analysis provided by the Department shall be strictly advisory. The Department shall forward to the Department of Planning and Budget any application that is not for the maintenance of collections and exhibits or for the maintenance, operation, and interpretation of sites and facilities owned by historical organizations. Such applications shall be governed by the procedures identified in § 2.2-1505.

2. Such organization shall certify to the satisfaction of the Department that matching funds from local or private sources are available in an amount at least equal to the amount of the request in cash or in kind contributions which are deemed acceptable to the Department. These matching funds must be concurrent with the project for which the state grant is requested. Contributions received and spent prior to the state grant shall not be considered in satisfying the requirements of this subdivision.

3. Such organization shall provide documentation of its tax exempt status under § 501(c)(3) of the United States Internal Revenue Code.

4. Such organization shall certify that the applicant has read and acknowledged all information and requirements regarding how the grants will be administered and how funds will be disbursed.

5. Such organization shall state in its application the purpose of the grant. The grant recipient must justify and request in writing approval by the Department for changes in the scope of the project prior to implementing those changes. If grant funds are used for something other than the purpose for which they were requested without prior review and approval by the Department, then all state funds must be returned.

6. Such organization shall submit documentation on match funding and approved expenditures shall be submitted with all requests for disbursement.

7. Such organization shall provide progress reports as prescribed by the Department. At a minimum such reports shall be submitted with reimbursement requests and a final report at the conclusion of the project.

8. Such organization receiving the state grant shall comply with applicable state procurement requirements pursuant to the Virginia Public Procurement Act (§ 2.2-4300 et seq.).

9. In the case of new construction or ground disturbing activities funded by grants, the organization shall afford the Department an opportunity to review the potential impact on any historic resources. Such review shall be provided by the Department within 15 days of receipt of completed information.

10. For all grants for capital projects, whether for new construction, rehabilitation, or restoration, funds shall be disbursed only as reimbursement for approved activities.

For the purposes of this section, no grant shall be approved for private institutions of higher education or religious organizations.

B. In addition to the requirements of subsection A of this section, no state funds other than for those facilities specified in § 10.1-2211 or 10.1-2212 shall be appropriated or expended for the renovation or reconstruction of any historic site as set forth in § 2.2-1505 unless:

1. The property is designated as a historic landmark by the Board and is located on the register prepared by the Department pursuant to § 10.1-2202 or has been declared eligible by the Board for such designation but has not actually been placed on the register of buildings and sites provided for in § 10.1-2202;

2. The society, museum, foundation, or association owning such property enters into an agreement with the Department that the property will be open to the public for at least 100 days per year for no less than five years following completion, renovation, or reconstruction;

3. The organization submits the plans and specifications of the project to the Department for review and approval to ensure that the project meets generally accepted standards for historic preservation; and

4. The organization owning the property grants to the Commonwealth a perpetual easement placing restrictions on the use or development of the property satisfactory to the Board, if the organization has received $50,000 or more within a four-year period pursuant to this section. The easement shall be for the purpose of preserving those features of the property which led to its designation as a historic landmark.

Nothing contained in this subsection shall prohibit any organization from charging a reasonable admission fee during the five-year period required in subdivision 2 herein if the fee is comparable to fees charged at similar facilities in the area.

C. The Department shall be responsible for the administration of this section and §§ 10.1-2211 and 10.1-2212 and the disbursement of all funds appropriated thereto.

State funds appropriated for the operation of historical societies, museums, foundations and associations shall be expended for historical facilities, reenactments, meetings, conferences, tours, seminars, or other general operating expenses as may be specified in the general appropriations act. Funds appropriated for these purposes shall be distributed annually to the treasurers of any such organizations. The appropriations act shall clearly designate that all such funds are to be used for the operating expenses of such organization. (1981, c. 537, § 10-145.13; 1987, c. 481; 1988, c. 891, § 10.1-814; 1989, cc. 656, 711; 1992, cc. 138, 426; 1999, cc. 900, 906; 2005, c. 86.)

Cross references. — As to the availability of state funds to nonstate agencies, see § 2.2-1505.

Editor's note. — For § 501(c)(3) of the Internal Revenue Code, see 26 U.S.C.S. § 501(c)(3).

The 2005 amendments. — The 2005 amendment by c. 86, in subsection A, substituted "operation, and interpretation" for "and operation" in the introductory language and subdivision 1, inserted "and completed application" and substituted "July 1 prior to" for "the opening day of" in subdivision 1, and added subdivisions 4 through 10; and made minor stylistic changes.

§ 10.1-2213.1. Matching grants for contributions to a material restoration of a Presidential home. — A. As used in this section, unless the context requires a different meaning:

"Charitable contribution" means a cash contribution from an individual, estate, corporation, partnership, trust, foundation, fund, association or any other entity or organization provided that (i) the contribution is allowable as a deduction for federal tax purposes or (ii) would have been allowable as a deduction for federal tax purposes had the entity or organization been subject to federal taxes.

"Eligible restoration expenses" means expenses incurred in the material restoration of a historic presidential home and, except in the case of demolition necessary to accomplish the restoration plan, added to the property's capital account.

"Foundation" means an entity that is exempt from federal taxation under § 501(c)(3) of the Internal Revenue Code of 1986, as may be amended, that is primarily responsible for the material restoration of a historic presidential home.

"Historic presidential home" means any home of a President of the United States located in Orange County, Virginia that is individually designated as a National Historic Landmark by the United States Secretary of the Interior.

"Material restoration" means restoration work (i) that restores a historic presidential home to within the period of significance stated in the National Historic Landmark individual designation of such home by the United States Secretary of the Interior, (ii) that is consistent with "The Secretary of the Interior's Standards for Restoration," and (iii) the cost of which amounts to at least 50 percent of the assessed value of such home for local real estate tax purposes for the year prior to the initial expenditure of any eligible restoration expenses, unless such home is an owner-occupied building, in which case the cost shall amount to at least 25 percent of the assessed value of such home for local real estate tax purposes for the year prior to the initial expenditure of any eligible restoration expenses.

B. The Commonwealth shall provide matching grants for charitable contributions received on or after July 1, 2003, by the Foundation that are actually spent or expended by the Foundation in the material restoration of a historic presidential home. The amount of the matching grant to be paid by the Commonwealth shall equal $0.20 for each $1 of charitable contribution that is actually spent or expended by the Foundation in the material restoration of a historic presidential home.

C. In January of each calendar year the Foundation shall submit to the Director the total amount of charitable contributions it received that were actually spent or expended in the immediately preceding calendar year for the material restoration of a historic presidential home. As a condition of receiving a matching grant, the Foundation shall at the same time submit to the Director such other information requested by the Director that is reasonably necessary to verify such charitable contributions and the actual use of such contributions.

The Director shall, as soon as practicable after receiving such submission and verifying such charitable contributions and their actual expenditure for the material restoration of a historic presidential home, make a written certification to the Comptroller of the amount of the grant to be paid to the Foundation. The amount of the grant for each calendar year shall be paid to the Foundation in six equal annual installments on March 15 of each year beginning with the year of the Director's certification for the relevant calendar year.

D. In no case shall the total amount of grants paid under this section exceed 20 percent of the estimated eligible restoration expenses of the historic presidential home. The Director is authorized to suspend the processing of charitable contribution submissions made by the Foundation if the Director reasonably believes that (i) such maximum amount may be exceeded or (ii) the material restoration will not be performed or such restoration work has been indefinitely suspended. (2005, c. 470.)

Editor's note. — For § 501(c)(3) of the Internal Revenue Code, see 26 U.S.C.S. § 501(c)(3).

Acts 2005, c. 470, cl. 2, provides: "That the Director of the Department of Historic Resources shall develop and publish guidelines for purposes of implementing the provisions of this act. The guidelines shall include, but shall not be limited to, processes and procedures for identifying and establishing requirements for charitable contributions that are actually spent or expended for the material restoration of a historic presidential home located in Orange County, Virginia. Such guidelines shall be exempt from the Administrative Process Act (§ 2.2-4000 et seq.) of the Code of Virginia."

§ 10.1-2214. Underwater historic property; penalty. — A. *"Underwater historic property"* means any submerged shipwreck, vessel, cargo, tackle or underwater archaeological specimen, including any object found at underwater refuse sites or submerged sites of former habitation, that has remained unclaimed on the state-owned subaqueous bottom and has historic value as determined by the Department.

B. Underwater historic property shall be preserved and protected and shall be the exclusive property of the Commonwealth. Preservation and protection of such property shall be the responsibility of all state agencies including but not limited to the Department, the Virginia Institute of Marine Science, and the Virginia Marine Resources Commission. Insofar as may be practicable, such property shall be preserved, protected and displayed for the public benefit within the county or city within which it is found, or within a museum operated by a state agency.

C. It shall be unlawful for any person, firm or corporation to conduct any type of recovery operations involving the removal, destruction or disturbance of any underwater historic property without first applying for and receiving a permit from the Virginia Marine Resources Commission to conduct such operations pursuant to § 28.2-1203. If the Virginia Marine Resources Commission, with the concurrence of the Department and in consultation with the Virginia Institute of Marine Science and other concerned state agencies, finds that granting the permit is in the best interest of the Commonwealth, it shall grant the applicant a permit. The permit shall provide that all objects recovered shall be the exclusive property of the Commonwealth. The permit shall provide the applicant with a fair share of the objects recovered, or in the discretion of the Department, a reasonable percentage of the cash value of the objects recovered to be paid by the Department. Title to all objects recovered shall be retained by the Commonwealth unless or until they are released to the applicant by the Department. All recovery operations undertaken pursuant to a permit issued under this section shall be carried out under the general supervision of the Department and in accordance with § 28.2-1203 and in such a manner that the maximum amount of historical, scientific, archaeological and educational information may be recovered and preserved in addition to the physical recovery of items. The Virginia Marine Resources Commission shall not grant a permit to conduct operations at substantially the same location described and covered by a permit previously granted if recovery operations are being actively pursued, unless the holder of the previously granted permit concurs in the grant of another permit.

D. The Department may seek a permit pursuant to this section and § 28.2-1203 to preserve and protect or recover any underwater historic property.

E. Any person violating the provisions of this section shall be guilty of a Class 1 misdemeanor and, in addition, shall forfeit to the Commonwealth any objects recovered. (1984, c. 750, § 10-262; 1988, c. 891, § 10.1-817; 1989, c. 656.)

Cross references. — As to punishment for Class 1 misdemeanors, see § 18.2-11.

ARTICLE 2.

Virginia War Memorial.

§§ 10.1-2215, 10.1-2216: Repealed by Acts 1992, c. 592.

Cross references. — For present provisions relating to the Virginia War Memorial Foundation, see § 2.2-2705 et seq.

CHAPTER 23.

VIRGINIA ANTIQUITIES ACT.

§ 10.1-2300. Definitions. — As used in this chapter, unless the context requires a different meaning:

"Field investigation" means the study of the traces of human culture at any site by means of surveying, sampling, excavating, or removing surface or subsurface material, or going on a site with that intent.

"Object of antiquity" means any relic, artifact, remain, including human skeletal remains, specimen, or other archaeological article that may be found on, in or below the surface of the earth which has historic, scientific, archaeologic or educational value.

"Person" means any natural individual, partnership, association, corporation or other legal entity.

"Site" means a geographical area on dry land that contains any evidence of human activity which is or may be the source of important historic, scientific, archaeologic or educational data or objects.

"State archaeological site" means an area designated by the Department in which it is reasonable to expect to find objects of antiquity.

"State archaeological zone" means an interrelated grouping of state archaeological sites.

"State archaeologist" means the individual designated pursuant to § 10.1-2301.

"State-controlled land" means any land owned by the Commonwealth or under the primary administrative jurisdiction of any state agency. State agency shall not mean any county, city or town, or any board or authority organized under state law to perform local or regional functions. Such land includes but is not limited to state parks, state wildlife areas, state recreation areas, highway rights-of-way and state-owned easements. (1977, c. 424, § 10-150.3; 1984, c. 750; 1988, c. 891, § 10.1-900; 1989, c. 656; 2005, c. 457.)

The 2005 amendments. — The 2005
amendment by c. 457 inserted the definition of
"State archaeologist."

§ 10.1-2301. Duties of Director. — The Director shall:

1. Coordinate all archaeological research on state-controlled land and in state archaeological sites and zones;

2. Coordinate a survey of significant archaeological sites located on state-controlled land, and upon request, survey and officially recognize significant archaeological sites on privately owned property;

3. Identify, evaluate, preserve and protect sites and objects of antiquity which have historic, scientific, archaeologic or educational value and are located on state-controlled land or on state archaeological sites or zones;

4. Protect archaeological sites and objects located on state-controlled land or on state archaeological sites or zones from neglect, desecration, damage and destruction;

5. Ensure that archaeological sites and objects located on state-controlled land or on state archaeological sites or zones are identified, evaluated and properly explored so that adequate records may be made;

6. Encourage private owners of designated state archaeological sites to cooperate with the Commonwealth to preserve the site;

7. Encourage a statewide archaeological education program to inform the general public of the importance of its irreplaceable archaeological heritage; and

8. Designate the State Archaeologist to (i) assist the Director by coordinating, overseeing, or otherwise carrying out the provisions of this chapter and (ii) perform such other duties as required by the Director. The State Archaeologist shall be a technically trained archaeologist and shall have both a practical and theoretical knowledge of archaeology. (1977, c. 424, §§ 10-150.2, 10-150.8; 1984, c. 750; 1988, c. 891, § 10.1-901; 1989, c. 656; 2005, c. 457.)

The 2005 amendments. — The 2005
amendment by c. 457 added subdivision 8 and
made a related change.

§ 10.1-2302. Permit required to conduct field investigations; ownership of objects of antiquity; penalty. — A. It shall be unlawful for any person to conduct any type of field investigation, exploration or recovery operation involving the removal, destruction or disturbance of any object of antiquity on state-controlled land, or on a state archaeological site or zone without first receiving a permit from the Director.

B. The Director may issue a permit to conduct field investigations if the Director finds that it is in the best interest of the Commonwealth, and the applicant is a historic, scientific, or educational institution, professional archaeologist or amateur, who is qualified and recognized in the area of field investigations or archaeology.

C. The permit shall require that all objects of antiquity that are recovered from state-controlled land shall be the exclusive property of the Commonwealth. Title to some or all objects of antiquity which are discovered or removed from a state archaeological site not located on state-controlled land may be retained by the owner of such land. All objects of antiquity that are discovered or recovered on or from state-controlled land shall be retained by the Commonwealth, unless they are released to the applicant by the Director.

D. All field investigations, explorations, or recovery operations undertaken pursuant to a permit issued under this section shall be carried out under the general supervision of the Director and in a manner to ensure that the maximum amount of historic, scientific, archaeologic and educational information may be recovered and preserved in addition to the physical recovery of objects.

E. If the field investigation described in the application is likely to interfere with the activity of any state agency, no permit shall be issued unless the applicant has secured the written approval of such agency.

F. Any person who violates the provisions of this section shall be guilty of a Class 1 misdemeanor. (1977, c. 424, § 10-150.5; 1984, c. 750; 1988, c. 891, § 10.1-903; 1989, c. 656.)

Cross references. — As to punishment for
Class 1 misdemeanors, see § 18.2-11.

§ 10.1-2303. Control of archaeological sites; authority of Director to contract. — A. The Commonwealth of Virginia reserves to itself, through the Director, the exclusive right and privilege of field investigation on sites that are on state-controlled land. The Director shall first obtain all permits of other state agencies required by law. The Director is authorized to permit others to conduct such investigations.

B. All objects of antiquity derived from or found on state-controlled land shall remain the property of the Commonwealth. (1977, c. 424, §§ 10-150.4, 10-150.6; 1984, c. 750; 1988, c. 891, § 10.1-904; 1989, c. 656.)

§ 10.1-2304. Designating archaeological sites and zones. — The Director may designate state archaeological sites and state archaeological zones on private property or on property owned by any county, city or town, or board or authority organized to perform local or regional functions in the Commonwealth provided that the Director secures the express prior written consent of the owner of the property involved. No state archaeological site or zone located on private property may be established within the boundaries of any county, city or town which has established a local archaeological commission or similar entity designated to preserve, protect and identify local sites and objects of antiquity without the consent of the local governing body. Field investigations may not be conducted on a designated site without a permit issued by the Director pursuant to § 10.1-2302. (1977, c. 424, § 10-150.7; 1984, c. 750; 1988, c. 891, § 10.1-905; 1989, c. 656.)

§ 10.1-2305. Permit required for the archaeological excavation of human remains. — A. It shall be unlawful for any person to conduct any type of archaeological field investigation involving the removal of human skeletal remains or associated artifacts from any unmarked human burial regardless of age of an archaeological site and regardless of ownership without first receiving a permit from the Director.

B. Where unmarked burials are not part of a legally chartered cemetery, archaeological excavation of such burials pursuant to a permit from the Director shall be exempt from the requirements of §§ 57-38.1 and 57-39. However, such exemption shall not apply in the case of human burials within formally chartered cemeteries that have been abandoned.

C. The Department shall be considered an interested party in court proceedings considering the abandonment of legally constituted cemeteries or family graveyards with historic significance. A permit from the Director is required if archaeological investigations are undertaken as a part of a court-approved removal of a cemetery.

D. The Board shall promulgate regulations implementing this section that provide for appropriate public notice prior to issuance of a permit, provide for appropriate treatment of excavated remains, the scientific quality of the research conducted on the remains, and the appropriate disposition of the remains upon completion of the research. The Department may carry out such excavations and research without a permit, provided that it has complied with the substantive requirements of the regulations promulgated pursuant to this section.

E. Any interested party may appeal the Director's decision to issue a permit or to act directly to excavate human remains to the local circuit court. Such appeal must be filed within fourteen days of the Director's decision. (1989, c. 656.)

§ 10.1-2306. Violations; penalty. — It shall be unlawful to intentionally deface, damage, destroy, displace, disturb or remove any object of antiquity on any designated state archaeological site or state-controlled land.

Any person who violates this section shall be guilty of a Class 1 misdemeanor. (1977, c. 424, § 10-150.10; 1988, c. 891, § 10.1-906; 1989, c. 656.)

Cross references. — As to punishment for Class 1 misdemeanors, see § 18.2-11.

CHAPTER 24.

Virginia Historic Preservation Foundation.

§§ 10.1-2400 through 10.1-2404: Repealed by Acts 1999, c. 558, effective January 1, 2003.

Editor's note. — Acts 1999, c. 558, cl. 4, provides: "That Chapter 24 (§§ 10.1-2400 through 10.1-2404) of Title 10.1 of the Code of Virginia is repealed effective January 1, 2003, if the assets of the Virginia Historic Trust Fund have not been reconveyed to the Virginia His- toric Preservation Foundation under subsection C of § 2 of the second enactment of this act." The Virginia Code Commission has indicated that this contingency was met. Chapter 24 is repealed effective January 1, 2003.

CHAPTER 24.1.

Historic Preservation Trust Fund.

§ 10.1-2404.1. Establishment of Historic Preservation Trust Fund. — The Board of Trustees of the Virginia Historic Preservation Foundation and the Director of the Department of Historic Resources are authorized on behalf of the Commonwealth to enter into a trust agreement with the Association for the Preservation of Virginia Antiquities, whereby the Association for the Preservation of Virginia Antiquities shall be trustee and the Commonwealth shall be beneficiary. The Board of Trustees of the Virginia Historic Preservation Foundation is authorized to create a trust fund, to be known as the Historic Preservation Trust Fund, known hereafter as the "Trust Fund," by transferring all of the assets of the Virginia Historic Preservation Revolving Fund to the Association for the Preservation of Virginia Antiquities, as Trustee of the Trust Fund, including its cash, notes, mortgages, other securities, real estate and all its other assets, to be administered as follows:

1. The Trustee shall serve without compensation;

2. The Trust Fund shall be administered and managed by the Property Committee of the Association for the Preservation of Virginia Antiquities;

3. The Director of the Department of Historic Resources, or his designee, shall serve as a voting member of the Property Committee of the Association for the Preservation of Virginia Antiquities on all questions concerning properties to be acquired and sold by the Trust Fund;

4. The Trust Fund shall be used for the sole purpose of preserving properties listed or eligible for listing on the Virginia Landmarks Register through the acquisition of such properties, or interests therein, the donation of a perpetual preservation easement on such properties to the Board of Historic Resources, and the subsequent resale of properties, or interests therein, thus protected to appropriate individuals, corporations, partnerships, associations or other legal entities, or the resale or transfer to appropriate public agencies, when, in the discretion of the Trustee, such action is the best feasible means of protecting such properties from an identifiable threat of destruction or from the loss of those qualities for which they were designated or eligible to be designated as landmarks by the Board of Historic Resources; and

5. The Trust Fund shall be operated as a revolving fund and all proceeds from the resale of properties, and any income which may accrue on the trust properties, shall be returned to and deposited in the Trust Fund.

The terms, conditions and form of the trust agreement shall be reviewed and approved by the Governor and the Attorney General. (1999, c. 558.)

The number of this section was assigned by the Virginia Code Commission, the 1999 act having assigned no number.

§ **10.1-2404.2. Operations of fund; termination.** — A. The Trust Fund shall consist of the property received pursuant to § 10.1-2404.1 and any gifts, grants, or appropriations made to the Trust Fund. Gifts and bequests of money, securities, and other property to the Trust Fund, and the income therefrom, shall be deemed to be gifts to the Commonwealth and therefore exempt from all state and local taxes. Any income earned from gifts, bequests, rent, securities, and other property of the Trust Fund shall be the property of the Trust Fund. Any gifts received by the Virginia Historic Preservation Foundation while the Association for the Preservation of Virginia Antiquities is administering the Trust Fund, as well as any income which may accrue thereon, shall be deposited in the Trust Fund within ninety days of receipt.

B. By November 1 of each year, the Association for the Preservation of Virginia Antiquities shall submit a copy of its audited financial statement to the Director of the Department of Historic Resources and to the Attorney General.

C. Prior to January 1, 2003, the Board of Trustees of the Virginia Historic Preservation Foundation is authorized to review the operation of the Trust Fund. If it finds that such operation is not fulfilling the requirements of the trust agreement, it may recommend to the Governor that the trust agreement with the Association for the Preservation of Virginia Antiquities be terminated. If the Governor finds that such termination is in the best interest of the Commonwealth, he may direct the Association for the Preservation of Virginia Antiquities to reconvey all the assets of the Trust Fund to the Virginia Historic Preservation Foundation.

D. On and after January 1, 2003, if the Fund has not been reconveyed to the Virginia Historic Preservation Foundation, (i) the Foundation shall cease to exist and its minutes and any remaining assets shall become the property of the Department of Historic Resources and (ii) the Attorney General shall have the authority to take legal action on behalf of the Commonwealth to enforce the terms of the trust agreement established under § 10.1-2404.1. (1999, c. 558.)

The number of this section was assigned
by the Virginia Code Commission, the 1999 act
having assigned no number.

CHAPTER 25.

VIRGINIA ENVIRONMENTAL EMERGENCY RESPONSE FUND.

§ 10.1-2500. Virginia Environmental Emergency Response Fund established. — A. There is hereby established the Virginia Environmental Emergency Response Fund, hereafter referred to as the Fund, to be used (i) for the purpose of emergency response to environmental pollution incidents and for the development and implementation of corrective actions for pollution incidents, other than pollution incidents addressed through the Virginia Underground Petroleum Storage Tank Fund, as described in § 62.1-44.34:11 of the State Water Control Law, (ii) to conduct assessments of potential sources of toxic contamination in accordance with the policy developed pursuant to § 62.1-44.19:10, and (iii) to assist small businesses for the purposes described in § 10.1-1197.3.

B. The Fund shall be a nonlapsing revolving fund consisting of grants, general funds, and other such moneys as appropriated by the General Assembly, and moneys received by the State Treasurer for:

1. Noncompliance penalties assessed pursuant to § 10.1-1311, civil penalties assessed pursuant to subsection B of § 10.1-1316 and civil charges assessed pursuant to subsection C of § 10.1-1316.

2. Civil penalties assessed pursuant to subsection C of § 10.1-1418.1, civil penalties assessed pursuant to subsections A and E of § 10.1-1455 and civil charges assessed pursuant to subsection F of § 10.1-1455.

3. Civil charges assessed pursuant to subdivision 8d of § 62.1-44.15 and civil penalties assessed pursuant to subsection (a) of § 62.1-44.32, excluding assessments made for violations of Article 9 (§ 62.1-44.34:8 et seq.) or 10 (§ 62.1-44.34:10 et seq.), Chapter 3.1 of Title 62.1, or a regulation, administrative or judicial order, or term or condition of approval relating to or issued under those articles.

4. Civil penalties and civil charges assessed pursuant to § 62.1-270.

5. Civil penalties assessed pursuant to subsection A of § 62.1-252 and civil charges assessed pursuant to subsection B of § 62.1-252.

6. Civil penalties assessed in conjunction with special orders by the Director pursuant to § 10.1-1186 and by the Waste Management Board pursuant to subsection G of § 10.1-1455. (1991, c. 718; 1992, c. 812; 1997, cc. 624, 850; 1998, c. 837; 2000, cc. 17, 1043.)

Law Review. — For an article reviewing key environmental developments at the federal and state levels during the period from June 1996 to June 1998, see 32 U. Rich. L. Rev. 1217 (1998).

§ 10.1-2501. Administration of the Fund. — All moneys received by the State Treasurer for the civil penalties and civil charges referred to in § 10.1-2500, and all reimbursements received under § 10.1-2502 shall be and hereby are credited to the Fund. Interest earned on the Fund shall be credited to the Fund. The Fund shall be established on the books of the State Comptroller. Any moneys remaining in the Fund at the end of the biennium shall not revert to the general fund but shall remain in the Fund. (1991, c. 718; 1992, c. 887.)

§ **10.1-2502. Disbursements from the Fund; transfer of funds to the Small Business Environmental Compliance Assistance Fund.** — The disbursement of moneys from the Fund shall be made by the State Comptroller at the written request of the Director of the Department of Environmental Quality. The Director shall have the authority to access the Fund for up to $100,000 per occurrence as long as the disbursement does not exceed the balance for the agency account. If the Director requests a disbursement in excess of $100,000 or an amount exceeding the remaining agency balance, the disbursement shall require the written approval of the Governor. The Department of Environmental Quality shall develop guidelines which, after approval by the Governor, determine how the Fund can be used for the purposes described herein.

Disbursements from the Fund may be made for the purposes outlined in § 10.1-2500, including, but not limited to, personnel, administrative, and equipment costs and expenses directly incurred by the above-mentioned agencies or by any other agency or political subdivision, acting at the direction of one of the above-mentioned agencies, in and for preventing or alleviating damage, loss, hardship, or suffering caused by environmental pollution incidents.

The agency shall promptly seek reimbursement from any person causing or contributing to an environmental pollution incident for all sums disbursed from the Fund for the protection, relief and recovery from loss or damage caused by such person. In the event a request for reimbursement is not paid within sixty days of receipt of a written demand, the claim shall be referred to the Attorney General for collection. The agency shall be allowed to recover all legal and court costs and other expenses incident to such actions for collection.

In any year in which the Fund balance exceeds two million dollars, the Director may transfer such excess amount to the Small Business Environmental Compliance Assistance Fund established pursuant to § 10.1-1197.2. (1991, c. 718; 1992, c. 887; 1997, cc. 624, 850.)

CHAPTER 26.

Invasive Species Council.

§§ **10.1-2600 through 10.1-2609:** Expired.

Editor's note. — This chapter expired by the terms of Acts 2003, c. 433, cl. 2, on July 1, 2006.